ASIAN ECONOMIC INTEGRATION REPORT 2021

MAKING DIGITAL PLATFORMS WORK FOR ASIA AND THE PACIFIC

FEBRUARY 2021

ASIAN DEVELOPMENT BANK

6 ADB Avenue, Mandaluyong City, 1550 Metro Manila, Philippines
Tel +63 2 8632 4444; Fax +63 2 8636 2444
www.adb.org

ISBN 978-92-9262-715-7 (print); 978-92-9262-716-4 (electronic); 978-92-9262-717-1 (ebook)
Publication Stock No. TCS210048-2
DOI: http://dx.doi.org/10.22617/TCS210048-2

Corrigenda to ADB publications may be found at http://www.adb.org/publications/corrigenda.

Notes:
In this publication, "$" refers to United States dollars, unless otherwise stated.
All masthead photos are from ADB.

ADB recognizes "China" as the People's Republic of China; "Hong Kong" as Hong Kong, China; "Korea" as the Republic of Korea; and "Vietnam" as Viet Nam.

Cover design by Erickson Mercado.

CONTENTS

TABLES, FIGURES, AND BOXES

TABLES

FIGURES

BOXES

FOREWORD

The coronavirus disease (COVID-19) pandemic disrupted both supply and demand sides of an interconnected world economy during 2020. Asia and the Pacific was not immune. Lockdowns and travel and trade restrictions affected nearly all aspects of cross-border economic activity. Trade was hit hard as demand fell. Global supply chains were forced to adapt. Foreign direct investment slowed. Financial vulnerabilities were heightened. Overseas migration and worker remittances were severely disrupted. And tourism, important to many of the region's economies, was particularly hard hit.

The *Asian Economic Integration Report (AEIR) 2021* examines the initial impact on trade, investment, finance, and people's mobility across the region as the pandemic struck. The report looks at how regional economies individually or collectively respond to the crisis by, for example, leveraging rapid technological progress, digitalization, and increasing services trade to reconnect and recover. Although the pandemic is not over yet, the Asia and Pacific region has demonstrated a great deal of resilience, due in part to authorities' swift policy responses and regional cooperation efforts. And it suggests how better managing globalization and regional integration could help seize the potential opportunities as economies gradually recover in a post-COVID-19 environment.

The report also uses ADB's Asia-Pacific Regional Cooperation and Integration Index (ARCII) to help explain the state of regional cooperation and integration in Asia, across subregions, and in comparison to other regions in the world. Reflecting the growing importance of the digital economy and environmental sustainability for the region's cooperation efforts, this year's ARCII adds two new dimensions to the index: (i) technology and digital connectivity, and (ii) environmental cooperation and regional public goods. It also analyzes how a country's geographic position influences its level of regional integration.

This year's AEIR theme chapter is on digital platforms and how they can accelerate digital transformation across the region. Digital platforms continue to transform the way we work, socialize, and create economic value. While digital transformation shows great speed and adaptability during the pandemic, new risks and challenges such as digital divide and cybersecurity issues come to light. This underscores the importance and urgency for policies and regulations that can manage the disruptions and maximize gains from the digital economy. These range from widening access to promoting digital inclusion, e-health, and online learning, to ensuring data privacy and security, fighting cybercrime, and preventing cyberattacks, among others. While coordination among national agencies is critical, regional cooperation needs will only grow in importance on critical issues such as data transfer, taxation, and the financing needed to boost support for sustainable and inclusive digital development.

Yasuyuki Sawada
Chief Economist and Director General
Economic Research and Regional Cooperation Department
Asian Development Bank

ACKNOWLEDGMENTS

The Asian Economic Integration Report (AEIR) 2021 was prepared by the Regional Cooperation and Integration Division (ERCI) of ADB's Economic Research and Regional Cooperation Department (ERCD), under the overall supervision of ERCI Director Cyn-Young Park. Jong Woo Kang coordinated overall production assisted by Mara Claire Tayag. ERCI consultants under Technical Assistance 9657: Asian Economic Integration: Building Knowledge for Policy Dialogue, 2018–2021 (Subproject 1) contributed data compilation, research, and analysis.

Contributing authors include James Villafuerte and Rogelio Mercado Jr., with data support from Mara Claire Tayag and Pilar Dayag (Managing Globalization and Regional Integration Post-COVID-19); Jong Woo Kang, Marife Lou Bacate, Dorothea Ramizo, and Joshua Anthony Gapay (Trade and the Global Value Chains: The Challenging Trade Environment and Changing Global Value Chain Landscape); Jong Woo Kang, Rolando Avendaño, and Clemence Fatima Cruz (Cross-Border Investment: Riding the Pandemic Tide in Cross-Border Investments); Peter Rosenkranz, Rogelio Mercado Jr., Ana Kristel Lapid, and Dominique Hannah Sy (Financial Integration: Heightened Financial Vulnerabilities amid the Pandemic); Kijin Kim, Matthias Helble, Ma. Concepcion Latoja, and Won Hee Cho, with data support from Pilar Dayag and Sol Francesca Cortes (Movement of People: People Mobility Hampered by the Pandemic and Virus Containment Measures); and Rolando Avendaño, Clarisa Joy Flaminiano, Lovely Ann Tolin, and Bahodir Ganiev (Asia-Pacific Regional Cooperation and Integration Index: Regional Integration Moving Ahead as Measured by Integration Index). The chapter "Updates on Subregional Cooperation Initiatives" was consolidated by Paulo Rodelio Halili based on contributions by regional departments of ADB: Saad Abdullah Paracha, Xinglan Hu, and Ronaldo Oblepias (Central Asia Regional Economic Cooperation subsection); Greater Mekong Subregion (GMS) Secretariat (GMS subsection); East Asia Department's Regional Cooperation and Integration team (East Asia subsection); Ronald Antonio Butiong, Dongxiang Li, Aileen Pangilinan, Jesusito Tranquilino, and Leticia de Leon (South Asia Subregional Economic Cooperation subsection); and Cara Tinio, Rommel Rabanal, Inez Mikkelsen-Lopez, and Ki-Fung Lam (Pacific subsection).

James Villafuerte coordinated and contributed to the production of the theme chapter, "Making Digital Platforms Work for Asia and the Pacific, " with Josef Yap as the economic editor. Background papers were provided by Thomas Abell, Ma. Diyina Arbo, Jose Ramon Albert, Rolando Avendaño, Michael Bainbridge, Lora Kryz Baje, Eduardo Banzon, Connie Bayudan-Dacuycuy, Johannes Benjamin Bernabe, Sylwyn Calizo Jr., Kimberly Diet, Jessmond Elvina, Yueling Huang, Ryan Jacildo, Shanti Jagannathan, Yunkai Li, Philip Libre, Badri Narayanan, Aniceto Orbeta Jr., Francis Mark Quimba, Maureen Ane Rosellon, Peter Rosenkranz, Raymond Francis Sarmiento, Ramonette Serafica, Lars Serzo, Aiko Kikkawa Takenaka, James Villafuerte, Trevor Weltman, and Philip Christian Zuniga. Arjan Paulo Salvanera constructed and managed the internal digital platform databases, with support from Eva Marie Aragones, and provided data assistance to authors. Mara Claire Tayag provided the overall research support, along with Paulo Rodelio Halili, and Marilyn Parra, with assistance from Joshua Anthony Gapay. The theme chapter benefited from comments and suggestions provided by the participants of the following workshops and events: "The Emergence of the Platform Economy: Challenges and Opportunities in Developing Asia" held on 5-6 December 2019 in ADB headquarters, Manila; "Virtual Conference on Making Digital Platforms Work for Asia" held on 25–26 June 2020, ADB headquarters, Manila; "AEIR 2021 Theme Chapter Internal Workshop on Making Digital Platforms Work for Asia and the Pacific" held on 24 August 2020, Manila; and "Workshop: Asian Economic Integration Report 2021" held on 9 September 2020, Manila.

Guy Sacerdoti and James Unwin edited the report. Joseph Manglicmot typeset and produced the layout, Erickson Mercado created the cover design and assisted in typesetting. Tuesday Soriano proofread the report. Paulo Rodelio Halili, Aleli Rosario, and Carol Ongchangco helped in proofreading. Support for AEIR 2021 printing and publishing was provided by the Printing Services Unit of ADB's Office of Administrative Services and by the Publishing and Dissemination Unit of the Department of Communications. Carol Ongchangco, Pia Asuncion Tenchavez, Maria Criselda Aherrera, and Marilyn Parra provided administrative and secretarial support, and helped organize the AEIR workshops, launch events, and other AEIR-related seminars and briefings. Ami Takagawa, with support from Lean Alfred Santos, of the Department of Communications coordinated the dissemination of AEIR 2021.

DEFINITIONS

The economies covered in the *Asian Economic Integration Report 2021* (AEIR 2021) are grouped by major analytic or geographic group.

- Asia refers to the 49 Asia and Pacific members of the Asian Development Bank (ADB), which includes Japan and Oceania (Australia and New Zealand) in addition to the 46 developing Asian economies.

- Subregional economic groupings are listed below:

  - Central Asia comprises Armenia, Azerbaijan, Georgia, Kazakhstan, the Kyrgyz Republic, Tajikistan, Turkmenistan, and Uzbekistan.
  - East Asia comprises the People's Republic of China; Hong Kong, China; Japan; the Republic of Korea; Mongolia; and Taipei,China.
  - South Asia comprises Afghanistan, Bangladesh, Bhutan, India, Maldives, Nepal, Pakistan, and Sri Lanka.
  - Southeast Asia comprises Brunei Darussalam, Cambodia, Indonesia, the Lao People's Democratic Republic, Malaysia, Myanmar, the Philippines, Singapore, Thailand, Timor-Leste, and Viet Nam.
  - The Pacific comprises the Cook Islands, the Federated States of Micronesia, Fiji, Kiribati, the Marshall Islands, Nauru, Niue, Papua New Guinea, Palau, Samoa, Solomon Islands, Tonga, Tuvalu, and Vanuatu.
  - Oceania includes Australia and New Zealand.

Unless otherwise specified, the symbol "$" and the word "dollar" refer to US dollars, and percent changes are year-on-year.

ABBREVIATIONS

ABEC	Almaty-Bishkek Economic Corridor
ADB	Asian Development Bank
AEIR	Asian Economic Integration Report
AMRO	ASEAN+3 Macroeconomic Research Office
APTA	Asia-Pacific Trade Agreement
ARCII	Asia-Pacific Regional Cooperation and Integration Index
ASEAN	Association of Southeast Asian Nations (Brunei Darussalam, Cambodia, Indonesia, the Lao People's Democratic Republic, Malaysia, Myanmar, the Philippines, Singapore, Thailand, and Viet Nam)
ASEAN+3	ASEAN plus Japan, the People's Republic of China, and the Republic of Korea
BIS	Bank for International Settlements
BIT	bilateral investment treaty
BOP	balance of payments
CAREC	Central Asia Regional Economic Cooperation
CITA	CAREC Integrated Trade Agenda
COVID-19	coronavirus disease
CMIM	Chiang Mai Initiative Multilateralization
CPIS	Coordinated Portfolio Investment Survey
CPMM	CAREC corridor performance measurement and monitoring
CPTPP	Comprehensive and Progressive Agreement for Trans-Pacific Partnership
CTC	change of tariff classification
CWRD	Central and West Asia Department
DVA	domestic value added
EARD	East Asia Department
ECD	economic corridor development
EU	European Union (Austria, Belgium, Bulgaria, Croatia, Cyprus, Czechia, Denmark, Estonia, Finland, France, Germany, Greece, Hungary, Ireland, Italy, Latvia, Lithuania, Luxembourg, Malta, the Netherlands, Poland, Portugal, Romania, Slovakia, Slovenia, Spain, Sweden, and the United Kingdom)
EUA	euro area (Austria, Belgium, Cyprus, Estonia, Finland, France, Germany, Greece, Ireland, Italy, Latvia, Lithuania, Luxembourg, Malta, the Netherlands, Portugal, Slovakia, Slovenia, and Spain)
FDI	foreign direct investment
FSI	financial stress index
FVA	foreign value added
FTA	free trade agreement
GATT	General Agreement on Tariffs and Trade
GDP	gross domestic product
GFC	global financial crisis
GMRA	Greater Mekong Railway Association
GMS	Greater Mekong Subregion
GVC	global value chain

HPV	human papillomavirus
IATA	International Air Transport Association
ICT	information and communication technology
IIA	international investment agreement
IIP	international investment position
ILO	International Labour Organization
IMAR	Inner Mongolia Autonomous Region
IMF	International Monetary Fund
ISD	investor–state dispute
IT	information technology
KNOMAD	Global Knowledge Partnership on Migration and Development
Lao PDR	Lao People's Democratic Republic
M&A	merger and acquisition
MSMEs	micro, small, and medium-sized enterprises
MW	megawatt
NPL	nonperforming loan
OECD	Organisation for Economic Co-operation and Development
PARD	Pacific Department
PCV	pneumococcal conjugate
PRC	People's Republic of China
RCEP	Regional Cooperation Economic Partnership
RCI	regional cooperation and integration
RDV	returned domestic value-added
RIF	regional investment framework
RKSI	Regional Knowledge Sharing Initiative
ROW	rest of the world
RVA	regional value chain
SARD	South Asia Department
SASEC	South Asia Subregional Economic Cooperation
SASEC OP	SASEC Operational Plan
SMEs	small and medium-sized enterprises
SEZ	special economic zone
SPS	sanitary and phytosanitary
TA	technical assistance
TAD	temporary admission document
UK	United Kingdom
UN	United Nations
UNWTO	United Nations World Tourism Organization
US	United States
VII	Vaccine Independence Initiative
VIX	volatility index
WTO	World Trade Organization

HIGHLIGHTS

Managing Globalization and Regional Integration Post-COVID-19

- **The coronavirus disease (COVID-19) pandemic has weighed heavily on health and economic systems worldwide; it severely disrupted Asia's cross-border trade and economic activities, and exposed vulnerabilities of global supply chains.**[a] Yet, Asia immensely benefited from open trade and investment, with the region's export-driven growth strategy and attractiveness to foreign direct investment (FDI) lifting millions out of poverty over half a century. The ongoing pandemic also highlights the benefits of rapid technological progress, digitalization, and increasing services trade in connecting the global economy even closer and providing new forms of global linkages. Intensifying these structural changes can be the basis of robust, resilient, and sustainable economic recovery. More so, the crisis creates an opportunity for greater global and regional cooperation to (i) contain and suppress COVID-19; (ii) strengthen global supply chains for essential commodities (including food, medical supplies, and vaccines); and (iii) make the world safer from natural hazards and pandemics by investing in projects with high social impact and economic returns.

The Challenging Trade Environment and Changing Global Value Chain Landscape

- **Asia's trade growth was hit hard by the pandemic amid contracting global demand; nevertheless, recent high frequency data indicate a tempered yet gradual recovery.** Having peaked in 2017, Asia's trade growth began to slow down in the second half of 2018. This came in the wake of rising trade tensions between the United States (US) and the People's Republic of China (PRC) along with continued moderation in global economic growth. Asia's merchandise trade volume already contracted 0.5% in 2019 after growing by 4.1% in 2018—a deeper slump than the 0.1% global trade contraction in 2019 (from 2.9% growth in 2018). By May 2020, Asia's trade in volume had contracted by 10.1% year-on-year (y-o-y). Nevertheless, high frequency indicators—such as global shipping and packaging indexes and port calls—and recent monthly trade data suggest Asia's trade growth could recover faster than anticipated. However, the persistent pandemic and risk of a double-dip recession could weigh on a sustained recovery. The region's intraregional trade share remained stable at 57.5% in 2019, above the 56.5% average over 2012–2018. This remains higher than North America (40.9%) and lower than the European Union (EU) (63.2%).

- **Asia has relatively strong regional value chain linkages—as measured by the regional value chain to global value chain intensity ratio.** After peaking in 2011–2013, global value chain expansion has been stagnating in recent years. The reshoring of supply chain networks to domestic economies, while only partial, could significantly reduce international trade compared with the status quo. By reshoring production networks, a country usually intends to decrease reliance on intermediate goods imports and outsourcing of production and process them locally instead.

[a] Asia refers to the 49 Asia and Pacific members of the Asian Development Bank (ADB), which includes Japan and Oceania (Australia and New Zealand) in addition to the 46 developing member economies.

Based on simulations using ADB's Multi-Regional Input–Output Tables—which can trace spillover impacts across trade supply chains—global trade is estimated to contract by 13%–22% when 10%–20% of overseas supply chains are reshored. The pandemic likely prompting an impetus to reengineer or diversify the existing supply chains, strengthening regional trade integration could help regional economies navigate the shifting global trade landscape to sustain trade growth. Against this backdrop, the region needs to embrace stronger trade liberalization and facilitation efforts, which includes pursuing trade agreements, in particular regional and mega trade deals.

Riding the Pandemic Tide in Cross-Border Investments

- **Inward FDI to Asia slid by 7.7% in 2019 compared with 2018—at $510.5 billion, while global FDI increased by 3.0%; investment flows both globally and to the region will likely fall further in 2020.** The drop in Asia's inward FDI in 2019 resulted mainly from weakening global demand for electronics and automotive products, as well as persistent trade tensions between the US and the PRC. Yet in 2019, Asia's intraregional FDI share remained stable at 51.7%. An expected decline in reinvested earnings during the pandemic—accounting for about half of 2019 global FDI—will likely reduce FDI inflows in 2020. Asian economies were among the hardest hit globally in reduced FDI inflows during the first quarter of 2020. Greenfield investments and mergers and acquisitions (M&As) in the region declined by 35.2% and 27.8% y-o-y, respectively (compared with global contractions of 27.0% and 49.2%). Globally, as well as regionally, investments in coal, oil, and gas plunged significantly in the first quarter of 2020, as did investments in hotels and tourism. This was followed by real estate, leisure, entertainment, and transportation. Nevertheless, recent firm-level activity in M&As in the region shows signs of recovery during the second quarter, as countries started to reopen and ease some pandemic-related restrictions.

- **Asia's outward investment rose 4.3% in 2019—at $531.4 billion, it accounted for 40.5% of global outward investments; outward investment dropped in the first quarter of 2020.** Japan was the top source of global FDI in 2019, investing in the US, Australia, and Thailand, among others. Other top regional sources of global FDI were the PRC; Hong Kong, China; the Republic of Korea; and Singapore. Asia's outward investment was not immune to the pandemic impact. Firm-level data show Asia's outward greenfield investment and M&As declined y-o-y by 27.0% and 64.3%, respectively, in the first quarter of 2020. The PRC's investment in cross-border projects in transportation and warehousing, chemicals, and electronic components declined, as did Japan's M&A in pharmaceuticals. Nevertheless, Asia's outward FDI showed signs of a rebound in the second quarter of 2020, in particular for M&As. Globally, some countries have tightened FDI screening measures to safeguard key sectors from possible predatory takeovers amid the pandemic. While some were also intended to protect national security and public interest, FDI regulatory restrictions could hinder global FDI flows. While policy makers should be cognizant about potential investor–state disputes over policy measures taken in response to exceptional circumstances such as the pandemic, bilateral investment treaties could open more windows for new FDI inflows.

Heightened Financial Vulnerabilities amid the Pandemic

- **COVID-19-induced economic slowdowns in the first quarter of 2020 led to a shift in investor risk appetite and increased financial volatility; this resulted in a flight to safety and tightened liquidity conditions for emerging market economies.** COVID-19 unraveled global financial markets in the first quarter of 2020, testing Asia's financial resilience. As liquidity conditions tightened and financial market stress emerged, by mid-March 2020 regional equity prices plunged by around 30% in several markets from their January values. Several of the region's currencies also weakened, while portfolio equity flows reversed—leaving an outflow of $57 billion—in the first quarter of 2020. However, swift policy responses by authorities across the region (and globally) helped ease liquidity conditions and restored investor sentiment by June 2020. Nevertheless, the risks of tighter liquidity and waning investor risk appetite remained large in the latter half of 2020 amid the rising numbers of infections globally.

- **Asia's cross-border asset holdings and liabilities increased in 2019, following a slight dip in 2018; the region's investors continued to hold considerably more assets and liabilities outside the region than within Asia.** Faced with common global uncertainties and concurrent policy responses, the contribution of global shocks to variations in Asia's asset price returns rose sharply and remained larger than the share of regional shocks. Nevertheless, the extent to which external (both global and regional) shocks explain the variations of the local asset returns were relatively small compared with the 2008–2009 global financial crisis. As of the end of 2019, Asia's investors continued to hold considerably more non-regional assets and liabilities than regional ones, with two-thirds held in economies outside the region. This highlights the region's elevated financial market exposure to external growth prospects, investment sentiments, and liquidity conditions. Moreover, almost half of Asia's international asset holdings are denominated in US dollar, and 25% of its external liabilities are in US dollar. Focusing on debt stocks, the share of US dollar denomination is higher at 63% of the region's international assets and 50% of its liabilities. This reflects the dominance of the US dollar in the international financial system and the region's reliance on the US dollar for its cross-border trade and financial transactions.

- **The pandemic has revealed several looming financial risks that policy makers in the region should guard against to safeguard regional financial stability.** Although early financial market jitters were quickly quelled through swift and aggressive policy interventions, globally as well as regionally, the region's policy makers need to remain vigilant and monitor potential economic and financial risks. Policy responses, led by aggressive fiscal support during the pandemic—although necessary and appropriate—could accelerate debt accumulation across economies. This could possibly lead to a deterioration of debt quality post-pandemic. Risks associated with credit growth and debt accumulation by households and nonfinancial institutions could also threaten regional banking stability and undermine economic recovery. Furthermore, the pandemic exposed the Asian banking sector's structural vulnerability given the liquidity mismatches associated with increased international activity and a reliance on US dollar funding by non-US banks. These looming risks call for strengthening regional financial cooperation to safeguard the region's financial stability and resilience. While it is important to broaden and deepen local currency capital markets, the region needs to pursue further reforms and intensify efforts to strengthen financial safety nets.

People Mobility Hampered by the Pandemic and Virus Containment Measures

- **The health and socioeconomic impact of the pandemic and virus containment measures are hurting cross-border migration. The international migrant stock increased to 271.6 million in 2019 from 248.9 million in 2015, of which Asia accounted for about one-third (90.3 million).** The pandemic upended the trend in 2020. Migrants from top source countries in Asia—including India, the PRC, Bangladesh, Pakistan, and the Philippines—were hit hard while job and income losses had dire consequences for their families back home. Mobility and travel restrictions in major destination countries—including the US, the Russian Federation, and Middle East countries—hampered economic activity and led to massive repatriation of unemployed migrants. There were also the concurrent challenges to traveling back home. Outward migration from Asia had steadily increased, with 64.8% of Asian migrants heading outside the region in 2019. This was led by migrants from South Asia (45.3%) and Southeast Asia (24.2%), especially among the region's skilled migrant workers, who continue to prefer developed countries and the Middle East over regional host economies. Meanwhile, intraregional migration remains an important source of international migration, especially for migrants in East Asia, Southeast Asia, Oceania, and the Pacific.

- **The pandemic breaks the growth momentum of international remittance inflows. Global remittance inflows reached $716.7 billion in 2019, up by $21.9 million over 2018.** Asia received $315.3 billion in 2019. Asia's largest remittance sources were the Middle East ($100.4 billion), North America ($78.0 billion), and Europe ($45.6 billion). As these face major economic downturns, recipient countries are bracing for the consequences of lower remittances in 2020—inflows are estimated to decline by 7.4%. The impact is acute—particularly for the economies in Central Asia and the Pacific that rely heavily on remittances, and those who receive the largest remittances in terms of absolute value, including India, the PRC, and the Philippines. Despite the expected drop due to the pandemic-induced global downturn and adverse impact on migrant workers, remittance inflows will likely remain the key source of external financing in Asia, along with other types of financial flows such as FDI and tourism receipts, which are expected to decline more.

- **Tourism has been particularly hard hit by the pandemic; extensive travel restrictions and the fear of infection led to a sharp fall in international tourist arrivals in Asia.** Assuming that most travel restrictions will remain in place until the end of 2020, ADB estimates that international tourist arrivals in Asia will be 82% below 2019 levels. For highly tourism-dependent economies, the sudden fall in tourist arrivals is having severe economic and social consequences, within and beyond the tourism sector. As the recovery to precrisis levels is expected to take years, the survival of large parts of the sector is at risk. Prior to the pandemic, tourism was one of Asia's most vibrant and promising industries and an important driver of growth. Asia's tourism sector outperformed all other regions in the world. While global tourist arrivals increased at an average annual rate of 5.3% from 2010 to 2018, arrivals to Asia grew at an average of 7.2%. Increasing regional integration has also given Asia's tourism sector a strong intraregional component, with the share of Asian visitors traveling within the region rising from 74.0% in 2010 to 79.1% in 2018. Rebuilding tourism will likely follow a staged approach: first promoting domestic tourism, then establishing green corridors to allow safe travel between close partners, and finally a complete reopening to international travel.

Regional Integration Moving Ahead as Measured by Integration Index

- **Latest ARCII estimates indicate that regional integration in Asia rose slightly in 2018, mainly due to a rebound in the money and finance dimension.** Three dimensions of the Asia-Pacific Regional Cooperation and Integration Index (ARCII)—the movement of people, infrastructure and connectivity, and trade and investment—continued to drive regional integration in the region. In 2018, overall regional integration increased for most Asian subregions, with Southeast Asia remaining the most integrated, driven by trade and investment and movement of people. Performance across subregions varied. While weak infrastructure and connectivity weighed on regional integration in the South Asia Subregional Economic Cooperation and Central Asia Regional Economic Cooperation subregions, accelerated infrastructure developments in transport, trade facilitation, and energy trade are poised to spur deeper future integration. Worldwide, Asia remains highly integrated, only less than the EU. The new ARCII framework adds two new dimensions: (i) technology and digital connectivity, and (ii) environmental cooperation and regional public goods. Overall, trends in technology sharing (including regional collaboration in research outputs and patent applications), and digital connectivity (including internet penetration and bandwidth), have improved in Asia over the past 15 years.

- **Geographic factors play a role in how integrated Asian economies are with other economies in the region. Spatial analysis using ARCII suggests that geographic position influences a country's level of regional integration.** An economy's level of regional integration is positively associated with its neighbors' level of regional integration and with its income. In Asia, high levels of regional integration are concentrated in Southeast Asia, whereas clusters of low levels of regional integration are found in geographically disadvantaged economies, such as landlocked countries in Central Asia and sea-locked countries in the Pacific. The significant influence of a neighbor's level of regional integration underscores the importance of positive synergies and spillovers in pursuing regional integration—and calls for closer cross-border coordination and cooperation.

Theme Chapter: Making Digital Platforms Work for Asia and the Pacific

- **Digital platforms are transforming how we work, socialize, and create economic value. A digital platform creates a virtual place for communities to interact and exchange information, goods, and services.** Examples of successful digital platforms include social media such as Facebook, Instagram, LinkedIn, TikTok, and Twitter; search engines and marketing platforms such as Google, Yahoo!, and Baidu; video sharing and music streaming platforms such as YouTube and Spotify; e-commerce such as Amazon and Alibaba; and service-sharing platforms such as Airbnb, Grab, Uber, and GrubHub. These digital platforms use data, search engines, and algorithms to (i) reduce the cost of acquiring and applying information, (ii) bypass intermediaries, (iii) reduce trade barriers, and (iv) use idle assets to lower production and distribution costs.

- **With the rise of digital platforms, new business models have proliferated, offering enormous economic opportunities.** In 2019, digital platform business-to-consumer revenues reached $3.8 trillion, equivalent to 4.4% of global GDP.[b] Asia accounted for about 48% ($1.8 trillion; equivalent to 6% of regional GDP), the US accounted for 22% ($836.7 billion; 3.9%), and the euro area 12% ($445.3 billion; 3.3%). Asia will continue its rise as a major player in the global digital platform market as wider access reaches more users and generates higher revenue growth.

- **The COVID-19 pandemic is accelerating the digital transformation for businesses of all sizes and across all industries.** This accelerated digital transformation can potentially boost global output, trade and commerce, and employment. For example, a 20% increase in the size of the digital sector over the baseline by 2025 will increase global output by an average of $4.3 trillion yearly from 2021 to 2025 (equivalent to 5.4% of the 2020 baseline) or a cumulative impact of $21.4 trillion in 5 years. Asia would reap an economic dividend of more than $1.7 trillion yearly (equivalent to 6.1% of the 2020 regional GDP baseline) or more than $8.6 trillion over the 5 years to 2025. Global trade will increase by roughly $2.4 trillion per year (5.5% of the 2020 global baseline trade) or $11.8 trillion impact in 5 years to 2025. Asia's trade will increase by more than $1.0 trillion per year (6.8% of the 2020 regional baseline trade) or $5 trillion increase in 5 years. There will be about 140 million additional jobs every year (5.0% of the 2020 global baseline employment)—65 million new jobs per year in Asia (or 3.9% of the region's 2020 baseline). By subregion, greater digital use will boost the Pacific island economies most, followed by Central Asian and Southeast Asian economies. The reasons include the potential for (i) digital connectivity to help developing countries overcome challenging geographies; (ii) productivity and economic gains to allow leapfrogging; and (iii) stronger digitally enabled services trade to support inclusive growth.

- **Policy support on multiple fronts can realize the potential gains from the digital economy.** The first is to improve digital infrastructure and connectivity—to deliver affordable mobile and broadband services and expand broadband internet access and coverage. While digital connectivity offers vast opportunities for developing countries to participate in international trade and move up the value chain, traditional trade and logistics related to physical connectivity can remain a significant barrier to the delivery of goods, even when digitally purchased. Notably, the gap in the logistics performance index between the best- and worst-connected countries remains wide. Continued digitization of customs clearance and border procedures is important, along with broadening access to

[b] Based on Statista data covering (i) e-commerce, (ii) online travel, (iii) transportation, (iv) advertising technology (Adtech), (v) e-services, and (vi) digital media.

safe and secure digital financial services. Investing in training for digital skills and literacy by providing access to information and communication technology devices and online teaching platforms is critical. It is important to create a smart, robust, and transparent regulatory system to protect personal data, prevent illegal activities, and strengthen cybersecurity. A coordinated regional and international response is needed to develop digital tax policies and effectively plug tax loopholes in the digital economy.

- **However, several key reform areas should ensure that appropriate policies and regulations are in place to manage undue advantage and unfair disruptions posed by the emergence of digital platforms.** Like any new technology, digital platforms present a disruptive force to existing markets and market players. As they create new ecosystems where producers, service providers, workers, and consumers interact with new distribution channels, the massive network externalities generated disrupt traditional markets and exert dominant market power. While access to unique big data and the ability to use them exclusively offer digital platforms the opportunity to innovate and create new products and services, the immense data advantage can generate monopolistic market power, often raising privacy and cybersecurity issues for users and consumers.

  - **Competition:** Digital platforms are "double-edged." While they can offer access to unprecedented opportunities for micro-businesses, they also tend to create one or very few "winners" due to strong network effects and large-scale economies. Authorities should craft policies that encourage fair competition and ease entry barriers. Authorities should promote interoperability across platforms to help market players collaborate and innovate to the benefit of consumers. Ease in multi-homing should be facilitated and switching cost ought to be lowered to enhance competition.

  - **Labor security and social protection:** As traditional labor relations and conditions no longer apply to digital platforms, online workers are often classified as contractors or self-employed, leaving them without social protection benefits. As youth employment is increasingly short-term intermittent, or involves non-standard work arrangements, the base of social security contributions is running thin. This widens coverage gaps, which could undermine the sustainability of existing social protection schemes and strain public finances as unemployed social assistance balloons. Thus, it is important to create a social protection system that is inclusive and universal, portable, linked to other initiatives, and digitally enabled. Especially in low-income countries, an unconditional cash transfer of uniform amounts to poor and vulnerable families can also help alleviate poverty, expand social protection to the socially excluded, promote social equity, and redistribute digital transformation dividends.

  - **Data access, privacy, and security:** As the data value chain rests on data access, use, and sharing, it is important that regulations foster greater transparency in using, sharing, and creating value from data. It is crucial to uphold data privacy, while ensuring that access to data and information is secure and not used to discriminate against specific groups; and that benefits are fairly and broadly distributed. Continuous cross-border policy coordination is equally important to address cybercrime.

  - **Taxation:** Taxing digital platforms is challenging. There are regulatory gaps and difficulties in identifying taxable digital activities as companies develop their businesses without physical presence within a specific tax jurisdiction, among many other issues. With increasing cross-border digital transactions, it is critically important to strengthen international tax cooperation and harmonization to plug loopholes and properly capture profits generated by the digital economy.

- **Policy makers should be flexible when setting policies and regulations and work together with the private sector to build open and innovative ecosystems for platform businesses; all while ensuring adequate legislation or regulations for data privacy, consumer protection, and cybersecurity.** Regulating rapidly evolving technologies is difficult. Legislating light-touch regulatory approaches to technologies that involve data processing and data protection may be helpful. This could be in the form of best practice guidelines, warnings, and advisories, along with better communication and closer coordination with regulated sectors. This will allow governments to supervise industry development while monitoring how the new technology develops and affects consumers. There are merits in adopting and issuing rules that allow certain, prequalified entities to soft-launch products in controlled environments or regulatory sandboxes. Policies that support innovation-driven entrepreneurship can also nurture platforms and ecosystems for platform-based businesses.

- **Despite rapid advances in technology and digital platforms, large segments of the population remain left behind.** Digital inclusion is crucial for technology and digital platforms to reach all countries and all levels of society. The key is to invest in digital infrastructure and connectivity to broaden physical access to mobile and internet networks and enhance access to education, markets, and other economic opportunities. The pandemic cast a spotlight on the digital divide in many aspects including remote work and distance learning during lockdowns and school closures. There are other significant digital readiness gaps based on location, age, gender, skills, culture, and social norm. Greater efforts should be made to narrow the digital divide within the specific context of each country and community; for example, through strengthening digital literacy and skills training for the poor, rural communities, women, the elderly, and unserved segments of the population. It is important to ensure that the digital divide does not undermine the development of inclusive digital economies during the digital transformation.

- **Upgrading education and labor market policies remains crucial for reaping the benefits of digital platforms and spreading the gains from the digital economy more widely.** Digital platforms hold great promise to scale up the coverage of education and learning—especially helpful in adapting to disruptions such as COVID-19 due to which over 1.5 billion students were unable to attend face-to-face learning. With the rise of online learning amid the COVID-19 outbreak, EdTech tools and approaches can be game changers in education in many ways and it is important to ensure that EdTech can be a catalyst in raising the quality of learning and addressing lags and deficits in learning outcomes. Creating an ecosystem for digital skills development and training, especially in technical and vocational education and training (TVET), will better prepare workers for the future. Developing arrangements for online quality assurance and credentials (such as micro-credentials and digital badges, among others) will help. Digital solutions can also help to provide lifelong learning opportunities for all and facilitate workplace-based training as workers face multiple transitions between jobs.

- **Planning and coordination among key national institutions can help ensure that digital transformation benefits all.** Innovation and digital platforms require new forms of coordination across public policy space and public–private partnerships. Currently, there is scope to better coordinate within government agencies in many economies in the region. Developing and implementing national strategies, enacting laws and regulations governing digital business activities, and adopting standards are all essential. It is important to resolve ambiguity over regulatory coverage. More importantly, governments need to build relationships with various actors involved in creating, diffusing, and utilizing the innovation, data, and services from digital platforms. Coordination is critical to avoid confusion. A responsive information dissemination system can also play a pivotal role in helping micro, small, and medium-sized enterprises understand the rapidly changing digital landscape, reduce costs, and increase market reach.

- **Regional cooperation must be strengthened to better address cross-border issues and challenges.** Cooperation could focus on sharing country lessons and experience, conducting regional policy dialogues, and working together to collect data and produce knowledge products to understand how digital platforms can help or hinder inclusive and sustainable development. It is also crucial for intergovernmental forums and mechanisms to formulate regionally consistent frameworks, strategies, and regulations, especially on cross-border data transfer and international taxation. Finally, with limited fiscal and financial resources, a regional approach to raise finance for technology can support digital transformation. Generally, three key factors can help close the technology funding gap: (i) increasing the pipeline of technology projects; (ii) crowding in private capital; and (iii) mitigating the risks and costs of technology projects. Multilateral institutions can play an important role in building the trust and confidence of public, private, and personal stakeholders in this area of technological development.

1 Managing Globalization and Regional Integration Post-COVID-19

The COVID-19 pandemic tested the resilience of health and economic systems worldwide.

Since it was first reported in December 2019, the coronavirus disease (COVID-19) infected more than 100 million, with more than 2.2 million lives lost (Figure 1.1). Across regions, Europe and North America were hardest hit. Asia initially had the highest number of confirmed cases but was overtaken by other regions in March 2020.[1] As of 4 February 2021, Asia reported 15.8 million confirmed cases.

The virus spread rapidly across the globe, shutting down or affecting almost all spheres of human activity—from travel to education, business, and work, along with social and family life. The pandemic also tested national health systems around the world, straining even the most advanced hospital systems in France, Italy, Germany, and the United States (US), among others.

Figure 1.1: Global COVID-19 Confirmed Cases, By Region (million)

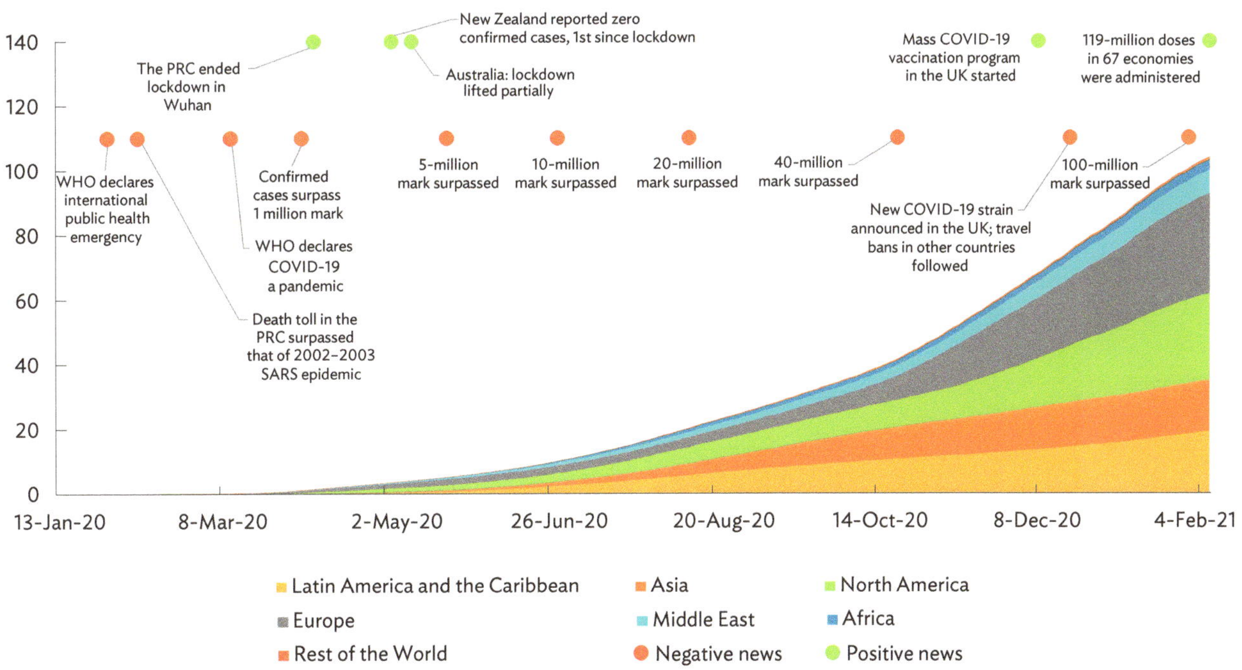

COVID-19 = coronavirus disease, PRC = People's Republic of China, SARS = severe acute respiratory syndrome, UK = United Kingdom, WHO = World Health Organization.

Source: World Health Organization statistics downloaded using CEIC.

[1] Asia refers to the 49 members of the Asian Development Bank (ADB) within Asia and the Pacific, which includes Japan and Oceania (Australia and New Zealand) in addition to the 46 developing Asian economies.

The devastating impact of COVID-19 forced many regional, national, and subnational authorities to implement stringent border controls, lockdowns, and community quarantines to contain the spread of the virus. In Asia, the Oxford COVID-19 Government Response Stringency Index for government response to the pandemic fluctuated from around 20 index points in February, to a high of 76 in April, then falling to 50 index points in October and November before rising in mid-December to 53 index points (Figure 1.2).

Unsurprisingly, the pandemic plunged the world into its deepest recession since the end of the Second World War. In 2020, the global economy was expected to contract by 3.5%, 6.3 percentage points lower than the 2.8% growth in 2019. The International Labour Organization estimated that about 73.7% of workers globally were affected by mobility restrictions as of May 2020, and the Asian Development Bank (ADB) estimated 242 million job losses and foregone wage income of $1.8 trillion (Park et al. 2020).

Figure 1.2: Oxford COVID-19 Government Response Stringency Index—Asia, 2020

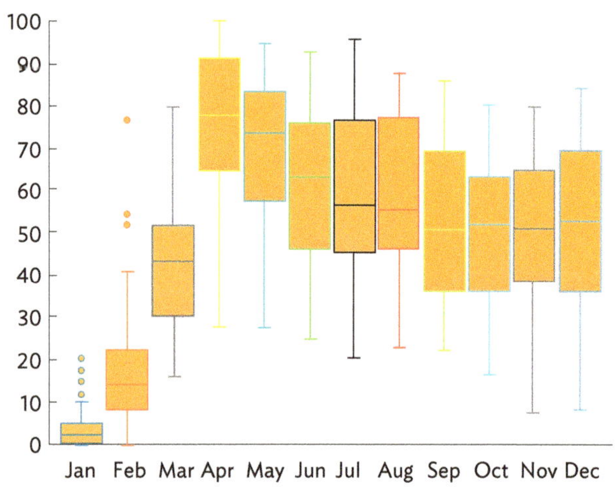

COVID-19 = coronavirus disease.

Notes: The Oxford COVID-19 Government Response Stringency Index is a composite indicator, with a range of 0 to 100 (most restrictive), that captures policy decisions on (i) school closings, (ii) workplace closings, (iii) cancellation of public events, (iv) restrictions on gathering size, (v) public transport closures, (vi) home confinement orders, (vii) restrictions on internal movement, (viii) international travel controls, and (ix) public information on COVID-19. Data as of 21 December 2020. The middle line of the box represents the median. The upper (bottom) line of the box represents the median of the upper (bottom) half. The vertical lines extend from the ends of the box to the minimum and maximum values.

Source: Blavatnik School of Government, University of Oxford. Coronavirus Government Response Tracker. https://www.bsg.ox.ac.uk/research/research-projects/coronavirus-government-response-tracker (accessed December 2020).

The pandemic further tested existing relationships among nations around the world.

Before COVID-19, globalization in trade, investment, finance, and migration was facing headwinds, spurred by geopolitical tensions over trade between the US and the People's Republic of China (PRC), the United Kingdom (UK) "Brexit" vote, along with rising polarization and social inequality. Globalization had been viewed by some countries as a source of insecurity—opening local economies to unwanted migrants, creating unfair competition, contributing to rising inequality, and destabilizing peace, order, and culture. Skeptics said that globalization was also partly responsible for financial cycles that could destabilize capital flows and threaten macroeconomic stability. These negative public perceptions were reinforced by stagnating wages and limited growth in job opportunities.

Thus, it was unsurprising to see that—as global trade and health systems teetered under the COVID-19 strain—the tendency to prioritize self-interest strengthened the questioning of globalization itself. Will it wither and fall? Will it be replaced by stronger regional arrangements? Or will it drift toward a stronger emphasis on sovereignty and nationhood?

The pandemic severely disrupted Asia's cross-border flows and activities.

Border closures, lockdowns, quarantines, and other means to control the virus spread disrupted supply chains and weakened demand, resulting in an overall decline in global trade. Intraregional trade within Asia declined during the first half of 2020, with Central and South Asia subregions reporting large contractions in intraregional trade (Figure 1.3). In South Asia, intraregional trade fell sharply in April as economies entered strict lockdowns. The gradual recovery of global and intraregional trade in the second half of the year reflected the measured reopening of economies and weak demand.

Figure 1.3: Intraregional Trade Value Growth—Asia
(%, y-o-y)

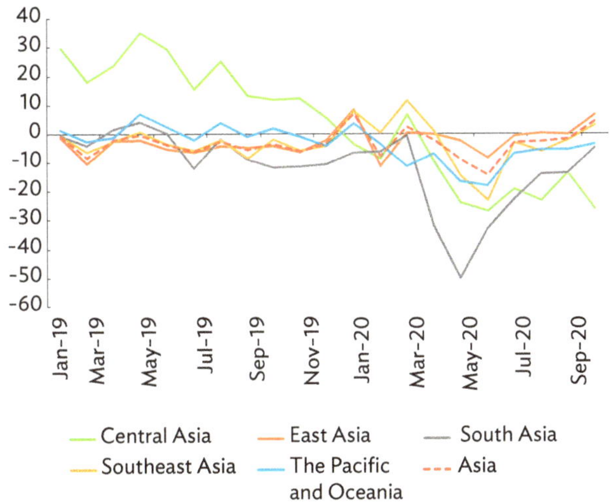

y-o-y = year on year.

Source: ADB staff calculations using data from International Monetary Fund. Direction of Trade Statistics. http://data.imf.org/DOT (accessed December 2020).

Figure 1.4: Foreign Direct Investments—Selected Economies

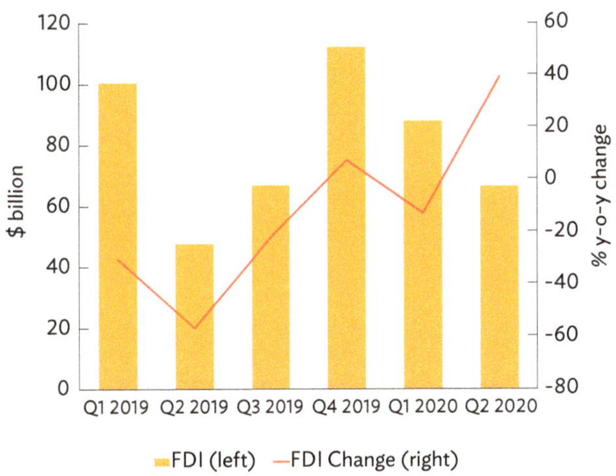

FDI = foreign direct investment, y-o-y = year on year.

Note: Sample includes Bangladesh; Cambodia; Hong Kong, China; India; Indonesia; Kazakhstan; Mongolia; Nepal; the People's Republic of China; the Philippines; the Republic of Korea; Taipei,China; and Thailand.

Source: ADB calculations using national source data accessed through CEIC.

Cross-border investments also contracted in 2020 as multinational enterprises postponed or canceled their planned or ongoing investment projects amid the uncertain prospects of economic recovery, duration of the pandemic, and earnings. Foreign direct investments (FDI) to selected Asian economies declined by over 10% year-on-year (y-o-y) in the first quarter of 2020, with Bangladesh, the PRC, Indonesia, Kazakhstan, and Mongolia dropping by more than 20% (Figure 1.4). The decline in Asia's FDI reflected the region's vulnerability to supply chain disruptions and growing uncertainties on business conditions. Although FDI inflows captured through balance of payments data stalled, firm-level cross-border investment data in the second quarter of 2020 showed early signs of recovery through higher mergers and acquisitions.

Foreign portfolio financial flows reversed in March 2020 as global investor sentiment deteriorated, uncertainties mounted, and liquidity conditions tightened at the height of the COVID-19 outbreak. Nonresident portfolio outflows to the region amounted to $20 billion, mostly equity outflows (Figure 1.5). This coincided with a steep fall in equity prices in March. But monetary, financial, and fiscal support measures were swiftly implemented globally, resulting to an easing of financial conditions and a recovery of asset prices by June 2020, leading to the resumption of nonresident portfolio debt inflows by June 2020. Yet, for some economies in the region, equity prices in the second half of 2020 (H2 2020) were nowhere near their values at the start of year, and the risks of tightening liquidity conditions and corporate insolvencies loomed large toward the end of the year.

Figure 1.5: Nonresident Portfolio Flows—Emerging Asia
($ billion)

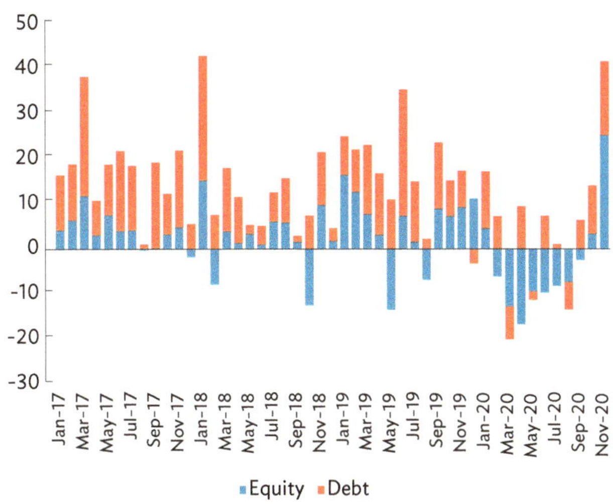

Source: Institute of International Finance. Capital Flows Tracker. https://www.iif.com/Research/Capital-Flows-and-Debt/Capital-Flows-Tracker (accessed December 2020).

International travel ground to a halt in the second quarter of 2020 as 217 destinations, including those in Asia, implemented total or partial border closures, flight suspensions, travel restrictions, and other measures to contain the spread of COVID-19 (Figure 1.6). In Asia, tourist and visitor arrivals in April completely stopped in India, Maldives, Singapore, Sri Lanka, and Thailand, while arrivals fell to a trickle in Cambodia; Hong Kong, China; the Republic of Korea; Taipei,China; and Viet Nam. By H2 2020, travel restrictions were gradually eased. As of 1 November 2020, 152 destinations had eased COVID-19-related travel restrictions, while 59 destinations kept their borders completely closed to international tourism. In Asia, 27 destinations maintained total border closures, while 22 destinations, including 5 small island developing countries, had partial border closures or specific travel restrictions.

Figure 1.6: Growth in Tourist and Visitor Arrivals—Selected Economies (%, y-o-y)

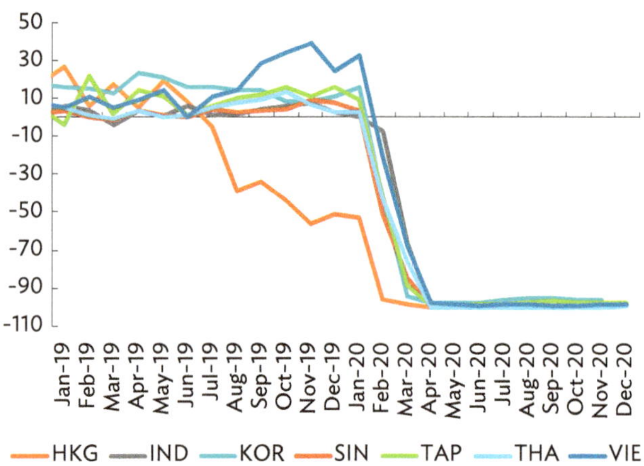

HKG = Hong Kong, China; IND = India; KOR = Republic of Korea; SIN = Singapore; TAP = Taipei,China; THA = Thailand; VIE = Viet Nam; y-o-y = year on year.

Source: ADB calculations using data from Haver Analytics.

Remittance flows to Asia also plunged amid the pandemic, with the drop most severe during the strict lockdown phase in April 2020 (Figure 1.7). For the first half of 2020 (H1 2020), remittances fell by 30% in Kazakhstan, 13% in the Kyrgyz Republic, 17% in Armenia, and 9% in Sri Lanka. While some migrant workers increased their remittances to families in extremely difficult situations back home, the prevailing weak economic situation in host economies also contributed to the sharp decline in remittance inflows. In some economies, this reversed in June as lockdowns began to be lifted in destinations that allowed migrants to remit their accumulated money from previous months—usually over the counter or through money transfers. Some governments in the region also introduced policies to incentivize transfers by reducing compliance checks, restrictions, and transaction fees; as well as undertaking an aggressive promotion campaign to migrants to prop up remittances.

Figure 1.7: Remittances to Selected Countries in Asia, January–November 2020 (% change)

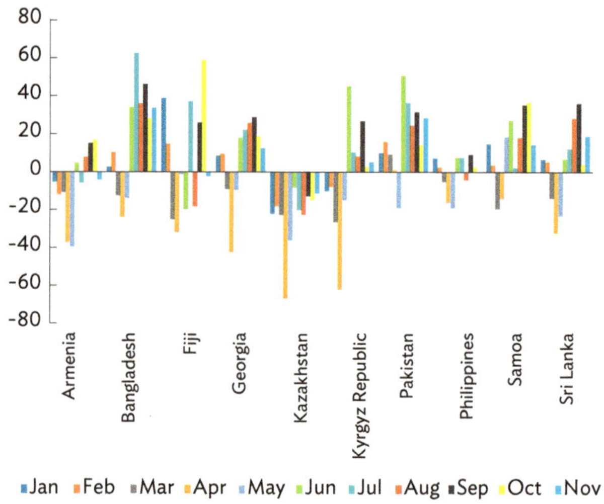

Note: Numbers refer to the year-to-date percent changes (base year 2019) in remittance inflows to selected Asian economies.

Source: ADB calculations using data from the central banks of respective economies (accessed January 2021).

Restraints on cross-border activities and weak demand weakened the region's economic prospects in 2020, with developing Asia likely to contract in 2020 for the first time in 6 decades.

Most economies contracted in H1 2020 due to the strict containment measures that disrupted supply and slowed consumption. The US economy contracted by 4.3% and the euro area by 9.0%. Most economies in Asia also contracted during the period. Based on national data released as of December 2020, the PRC economy shrunk by 1.6%, Indonesia by 1.3%, the Republic of Korea by 0.7%, and the Philippines by 9.3%.

Prospects for a swift and robust recovery waned in H2 2020 as the number of COVID-19 cases continued to rise. Concerns over recurrent "waves" of infections, particularly during the winter season in the northern hemisphere, and reinstating localized lockdowns while slowly reviving economies weighed down growth outlook. Moreover, new virus strain in Europe raised fears of sustained high infection rates in the coming months. Nonetheless, there were signs of an upturn in business and consumer confidence and cross-border transactions, including trade and investment, although still lower than pre-pandemic levels. More importantly, news on the high efficacy of candidate vaccines supported the prospects of sustained economic recovery in 2021.

ADB's *Asian Development Outlook Supplement December 2020* projected that developing Asia's output would contract by 0.4% in 2020 (Figure 1.8)—a significant downward revision from the 2.2% growth forecast in the Asian Development Outlook April 2020 issue. More than two-thirds of the economies in developing Asia are expected to post negative growth rates in 2020, while the rest will grow weakly. Actual GDP growth rates for 2020 indicate that the PRC and Viet Nam grew slowly by 2.3% and 2.9%, respectively; while the Republic of Korea contracted slightly by 1.0%.

Figure 1.8: Economic Growth Forecasts for 2020 (%)

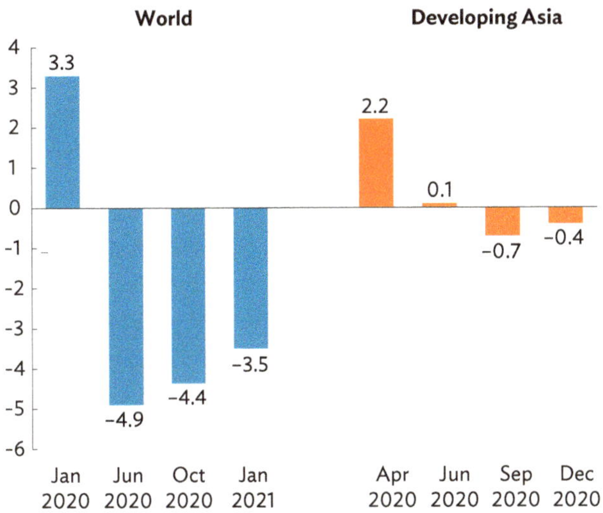

Sources: ADB. Asian Development Outlook (ADO) Series. https://www.adb.org/publications/series/asian-development-outlook; and International Monetary Fund. World Economic Outlook Reports. https://www.imf.org/en/publications/weo (both accessed February 2021).

The COVID-19 pandemic also bared the risks of globalization and global supply chains.

As the COVID-19 pandemic evolved, concerns over the future of global supply chains emerged. A few days after the PRC lockdown of the city of Wuhan on 23 January 2019—later expanded to neighboring cities and provinces—several multinational enterprises in Asia and elsewhere reported that they had to suspend production due to the lack of intermediate inputs produced in the PRC. Around 17% of the PRC's total exports in 2018 were intermediate products used by foreign manufacturers outside the country to produce final goods—such as auto parts, electronic components, and other final goods. The PRC's exports of intermediate goods to South Asia and East Asia and the Pacific accounted for 36% and 18% of its total exports compared with North America, and Europe and Central Asia, which were only 8% and 14%, respectively. These highlight the importance of the PRC in keeping the global supply chains going, as well as the economic interdependence among Asian economies.

The pandemic also exposed several risks to global supply chains—such as the geographic concentration of production and overstretched supply chains of critical goods like medical supplies, and intermediate products, particularly active pharmaceutical ingredients and food ingredients. For instance, generic drug manufacturers in India could not produce medicines without active pharmaceutical ingredients from the PRC. In addition, the concentration of production led to shortages of critical items, particularly of personal protective equipment, sanitizers, and face masks. These demonstrated the drawbacks of "just-in-time" production or of holding significantly fewer inventories—as they could lead to production stoppages once cross-border controls are in place.

These risks to global supply chains highlight the advantages of keeping the production of critical products and supplies within (back-reshoring) or close (near-reshoring) to one's borders; and they strengthen the arguments for reshoring. Before COVID-19, reshoring had been a growing phenomenon motivated by product quality issues, alignment of corporate priorities and values, and flexibility and security of work legislation (Barbieri, Boffelli, and Elia 2020). The pandemic acted as a trigger for company decisions on reshoring production—due to the risk exposure and policy interventions affecting operational continuity and supporting post-crisis manufacturing growth. The future of reshoring will depend on firm-level decisions as well as how supply chains reorganize, which will require more time for preparation.

Yet, globalization will unlikely reverse its course although it may take different shapes.

Asia's value chain linkages with the global economy remain crucial for the region's own supply chain and continued prosperity. While global value chains and FDI will adjust in response to the pandemic, globalization will unlikely reverse course in the region in the near term. Moreover, Asia holds the key to reshaping the global trade and investment landscape, reflecting its greater influence on the post-pandemic trade regimes. The signing of the Regional Comprehensive Economic Partnership (RCEP) among 15 members on 15 November 2020 signifies the region's commitment to pursuing open and inclusive trade and investment regimes and reflects its growing influence in the global multilateral trading system beyond the COVID-19 pandemic.[2]

Developing Asia has benefited greatly from globalization and will most likely continue its economic and trade relations with the rest of the world. In fact, the region's export-driven growth strategy and openness to FDI provided jobs and lifted millions out of poverty. In East Asia, poverty dropped from 33% to 2% of the population in 2 decades as trade openness grew by 7% of total output. In South Asia, poverty declined from 35% to 15% of the population as trade openness increased by 14% of total output (Figure 1.9). These two subregions account for Asia's largest population share.

Figure 1.9: Change in Poverty Headcount and Trade Openness (% points)

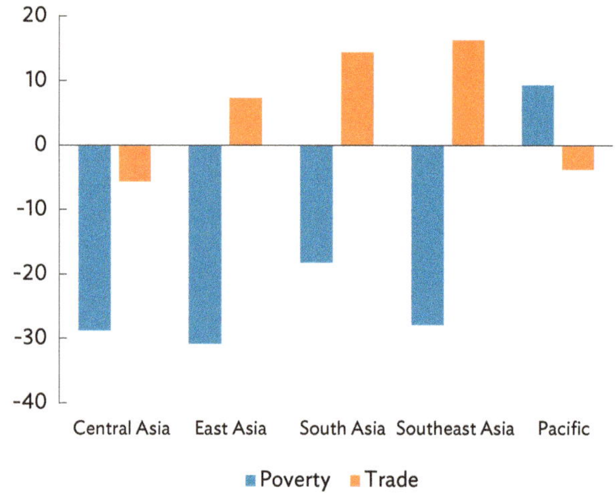

Note: Values refer to the median values of the change in poverty headcount ratio at $1.90 per day (% of population) and the sum of merchandise exports and imports (% of GDP) from 1990–1995 to 2011–2015.

Sources: ADB calculations using data from International Monetary Fund. Direction of Trade Statistics. http://data.imf.org/DOT; and World Bank. World Development Indicators. https://databank.worldbank.org/source/world-development-indicators (all accessed October 2020).

Going forward, the increasing digitalization of global services can facilitate the post-pandemic recovery.

Prior to COVID-19, the services sector was already an important part of the economy and international trade. For instance, services accounted for about 65% of global gross domestic product (GDP) in value-added terms and almost a quarter of global trade in the past 5 years.[3] There was also an increasing pattern of trade in services in developing Asia, particularly in East Asia and Southeast Asia (Figure 1.10).

The services sector was the primary destination for over two-thirds of FDI flows, with its share of global FDI stock more than double that of manufacturing. Services was also the largest and fastest growing employer, contributing to higher female labor force participation

[2] Members include ASEAN (Brunei Darussalam, Cambodia, Indonesia, the Lao People's Democratic Republic, Malaysia, Myanmar, the Philippines, Singapore, Thailand, and Viet Nam), three East Asian economies (Japan, the People's Republic of China, and the Republic of Korea), and Oceania economies (Australia and New Zealand).

[3] The data refer to average annual services share in 2015-2018 for global GDP and 2015-2018 for global trade. Based on data from World Bank. World Development Indicators. https://databank.worldbank.org/source/world-development-indicators (accessed January 2021).

and wages. More importantly, it was a key contributor to productivity growth—as multifactor productivity increased due to innovations (Stephenson 2020).

Figure 1.10: Trade in Services Growth—Developing Asia
(%, y-o-y)

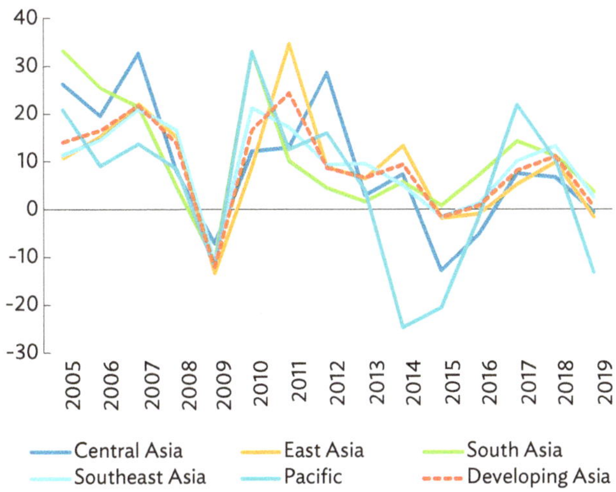

y-o-y = year-on-year.

Source: World Bank. World Development Indicators. https://databank.worldbank.org/source/world-development-indicators (accessed October 2020).

Trade in services is more digitally enabled than trade in goods. For example, McKinsey Global Institute (2016) reported that over 50% of services were digitally enabled compared with only 12% for goods.

Although some services have been adversely affected by travel bans and lockdowns, particularly tourism and hospitality, other digitally enabled services have helped keep the world economy afloat during the pandemic. For instance, most consumers shifted to mobile and online platforms to purchase food and household items, also relying on expanding digital payment systems. Businesses adopted contactless transactions online, through mobile payment applications, and pick-up or home delivery of ordered goods. Similarly, work from home arrangements, online education, tele-health services, online meeting platforms, and recreational streaming services also gained traction during the pandemic. This increasing digitalization of global services can continue to support global economic recovery.

Rapid technological progress will strengthen global connectivity.

While global trade and commerce decelerated due to rising uncertainty and weak global growth, digital connectivity worldwide is progressing at high speed. Rapid progress in infrastructure and transactional technology is creating faster and cheaper connections worldwide. Cross-border data flows grew 45 times between 2005 and 2014. From 2005 to 2017, the amount of cross-border bandwidth use grew 148 times larger. These increased digital connections raised world GDP by 10% over what it would have been in a world without cross-border flows (McKinsey Global Institute 2016).

Asia's digital connections to the world have also increased. From 2010 to 2019, internet bandwidth from Asia to Europe increased 40 times; the US and Canada 12 times; the Middle East 31 times; and Asia 33 times.[4] These rapid increases in bandwidth have contributed to widespread internet use, with an accompanying surge in data flows related to e-commerce and other digital platform activities.

About half of global trade in services depends on access to cross-border data flows (Stephenson 2020). This includes digitally enabled knowledge-intensive services, software, and technologies that help connect firms and consumers through digital platforms and internet services, communications and transportation networks, cloud computing and storage, artificial intelligence, machine learning, and social media. It is likely that these connections will increase further as technological progress continues.

That said, there are also several challenges related to data-intensive businesses. Digital platforms have become powerful business entities due to their first mover advantage and strong network effects. Their virtual presence often "in the cloud" allows them to skirt regulations and taxation. They are also able to employ underutilized assets and a workforce often with little employment or social protection (see Chapter 8: Making Digital Platforms Work for Asia and the Pacific).

4 Based on Telegeography data. See Table 6.2 in Chapter 6. Asia-Pacific Regional Cooperation and Integration Index: Regional Integration Moving Ahead as Measured by Integration Index for more details.

The pandemic presents an opportunity for greater global and regional cooperation.

Although early government actions—such as border controls and controls on the trade of essential commodities at the onset of the pandemic were inevitable, there is now a growing realization that only a collective and coordinated effort can meet the challenges of coping with the current and future pandemics. For one, global efforts to keep supply chains open for medical equipment, medicines, and food supplies, and mobilize resources complemented national efforts to contain and suppress infections. Global and regional cooperation also remain vital to address future pandemics by collaborating on the development, production, and dissemination of vaccines and treatments; and aiding economies in dealing with harmful socioeconomic impacts. More importantly, a range of global and regional initiatives have also been used to fight the pandemic.

For example, on 15 April 2020, the Group of Twenty (G20) finance ministers and central bank governors unveiled a global action plan to fight COVID-19. The comprehensive plan covered health, economic, and financial responses (Table 1.1). There were several critical recommendations:

- Ensure that all elements of the health-care response are fully funded, enhance collaboration, and increase funding to support accelerated research and development for diagnostics, therapeutics, and vaccines.

- Support the vulnerable and maintain conditions for a strong recovery by lifting restrictions as soon as it is safe and provide support to minimize the impact and social damage.

The plan also outlined actions to provide international financial support to help countries combat COVID-19:

- Deliver the International Monetary Fund (IMF) support package and apply tools from regional financial arrangements.

- Swiftly implement support from the World Bank and regional development banks.

- Provide debt service suspension to the poorest economies.

- Ensure efficiency and operational coordination to optimize resource use.

- Welcome actions taken by central banks to support financial stability, including the deployment and expansion of bilateral swap lines and the introduction of repo facilities for sovereign debt.

In addition, various regional initiatives were proposed (Table 1.2):

- On 10 March 2020, the Association of Southeast Asian Nations (ASEAN) economic ministers agreed to collectively work toward mitigating the impact of COVID-19. Some of the key actions included keeping the ASEAN market open for trade and investment; leveraging technologies and digital trade to allow businesses to continue operating amid the outbreak; enhancing ASEAN's economic cooperation with external and development partners to strengthen supply chains; and building on existing trade facilitation platforms such as the ASEAN Single Window to promote supply chain connectivity.[5]

- Subregional initiatives—such as the Central Asia Regional Economic and Integration Cooperation (CAREC) Program, the Greater Mekong Subregion (GMS) Program, and the South Asia Subregional Economic Cooperation (SASEC)—have proposed regional cooperation and integration (RCI) efforts to support the hardest-hit sectors (health, tourism, and trade) (See Chapter 7: Updates on Subregional Cooperation Initiatives for details). Subregional health cooperation was strengthened to boost regional health security, improve access to health services, and develop a health workforce. Specific examples of action plans to boost tourism include, among others, the promotion of domestic and inter-subregional "travel bubbles,"

[5] ASEAN Secretariat. 2020. ASEAN Leaders Vision Statement on a Cohesive and Responsive ASEAN: Rising Above Challenges and Sustaining Growth. 26 June. https://asean.org/storage/2020/06/Final-ASEAN-Leaders-Vision-Statement-on-a-Cohesive-and-Responsive-ASEAN-final.pdf.

joint tourism promotion and marketing strategies, and enhanced use of digital technologies. To facilitate trade during and after COVID-19, CAREC will update its strategic plan to support trade expansion and diversification projects while ensuring safer trade and increased resilience. The GMS Program will utilize electronic customs clearance and invest in cross-border infrastructure to include health screening on top of the current plans of improving customs and immigration security. SASEC also plans to leverage "smart" approaches (for example, automation) to minimize disruptions in the supply chains of essential goods.

Aside from their vital role in addressing COVID-19, global and regional initiatives and cooperation can help shape the post-pandemic world. Global cooperation is thus crucial in reorganizing and sustaining global and regional value chains to secure sustained and inclusive economic growth. Regional cooperation can also help embrace looming opportunities from the potential dispersion of production networks, shortening supply chains, and redirecting trade and investment. For instance, although the decision for reshoring production depends on a single firm, supply chain reorganization is a joint decision among various suppliers and enterprises (Barbieri, Boffelli, and Elia 2020). As it is difficult to attract an entire supply chain within one single economy, there is scope for regional cooperation in near-shoring initiatives. Both can gain advantage through post-pandemic collective action.

Table 1.2: Areas of Subregional Cooperation Efforts to Promote Recovery Post-COVID-19

	ASEAN	CAREC	GMS	SASEC
Health	●	●	●	●
Trade and trade facilitation	●	●	●	●
Tourism	●	●	●	●
Gender/Women empowerment	●	●		
Agriculture and food security	●		●	
Climate change and environmental sustainability	●		●	

ASEAN = Association of Southeast Asian Nations, CAREC = Central Asia Regional Economic Cooperation, COVID-19 = coronavirus disease, GMS = Greater Mekong Subregion, SASEC = South Asia Subregional Economic Cooperation.

Sources: ADB (Central and West Department, South Asia Department, Southeast Asia Department); and ASEAN Secretariat. 2020. ASEAN Leaders Vision Statement on a Cohesive and Responsive ASEAN: Rising Above Challenges and Sustaining Growth. 26 June. https://asean.org/storage/2020/06/Final-ASEAN-Leaders-Vision-Statement-on-a-Cohesive-and-Responsive-ASEAN-final.pdf.

Global cooperation can help build a safer world, but regional support is also needed.

Now more than ever, the global economy faces multiple transnational challenges, including regional connectivity issues, trade frictions, financial contagion, pandemics, natural hazards, climate change, and geopolitical conflicts. These events are becoming more frequent with deeper economic impact. Unilateral approaches will not suffice with these issues better addressed using a cooperative approach.

Table 1.1: G20 Action Plan in Response to the COVID-19 Pandemic

Areas	Description
Health response	• Ensure that health-care responses are fully funded and enhance collaboration to support accelerated research and development for diagnostics, therapeutics, and vaccines
Economic and financial response	• Support the vulnerable and provide support to minimize the impact and social damage
Returning to strong, sustainable, balanced, and inclusive growth once containment measures are lifted	• Share the latest information and country experiences on COVID-19 containment measures • Task international organizations to support members in developing standardized data, analysis, and sharing • Support workers through active labor market, training, and reskilling policies to minimize the loss of human and organizational capital • Re-double efforts to promote quality infrastructure investment and accelerate efforts to mobilize private sources of infrastructure financing
International support to countries in need	• Deliver a comprehensive International Monetary Fund support package and use available tools from regional financial arrangements • Implement swiftly the support proposed by the World Bank and regional development banks • Provide debt service suspension for the poorest economies • Ensure efficiency and operational coordination to optimize the use of resources • Welcome the actions taken by central banks to support financial stability

COVID-19 = coronavirus disease.

Source: G20. 2020. Extraordinary G20 Leaders' Summit: Statement on COVID-19. 26 March. https://www.ilo.org/wcmsp5/groups/public/---dgreports/---dcomm/documents/meetingdocument/wcms_740022.pdf.

In addition, collective regional and global action is needed to address cross-border drug trafficking, money laundering and terrorism, and human slavery, which tend to become more brazen during times of economic crisis.

One key concern about the negative impact of globalization has to do with rising inequality, as higher wage premiums are accorded skilled labor. It is thus essential to strengthen investment in education and skills development and enhance financial inclusion to improve people's access to economic opportunities, particularly for unskilled and informal workers. Improving education and training quality—especially for technical and vocational education—is also critical. Leveraging on digital technology to enhance productivity in agriculture, fishery, and services can also benefit low-income households. For advanced economies, strengthening the middle-class welfare system will help spread the benefits of globalization more broadly across society.

Compensatory benefits and social assistance are also important to ensure that vulnerable members of society can access the financial resources to deal with and adjust to some of the economic challenges that accompany globalization. Flexible labor market policies that foster labor mobility can also be helpful while strengthening social protection, and skills training programs are crucial to support displaced workers between jobs and help them retrain and move on to other gainful employment.

Promoting better governance standards could also help spread the benefits of globalization more widely. By promoting greater accountability and efficiency, good governance saves resources and improves government service delivery to the poor. Similarly, greater transparency and accountability minimizes leakages and improves targeting for social protection programs, thus making the redistribution of benefits more effective. Greater participation and consensus building also ensures that everyone is consulted and considered when making decisions that will affect the greater good.

References

Asian Development Outlook (ADB). Asian Development Outlook (ADO) Series. https://www.adb.org/publications/series/asian-development-outlook (accessed February 2021).

Association of Southeast Asian Nations (ASEAN) Secretariat. 2020. ASEAN Leaders Vision Statement on a Cohesive and Responsive ASEAN: Rising Above Challenges and Sustaining Growth. 26 June. https//asean.org/storage/2020/06/Final-ASEAN-Leaders-Vision-Statement-on-a-Cohesive-and-Responsive-ASEAN-final.pdf.

Blavatnik School of Government. University of Oxford. Coronavirus Government Response Tracker. https://www.bsg.ox.ac.uk/research/researchprojects/coronavirus-government-response-tracker (accessed December 2020).

G20. 2020. Extraordinary G20 Leaders' Summit: Statement on COVID-19. 26 March. https://www.ilo.org/wcmsp5/groups/public/---dgreports/---dcomm/documents/meetingdocument/wcms_740022.pdf.

Institute of International Finance. Capital Flows Tracker. https://www.iif.com/Research/Capital-Flows-and-Debt/Capital-Flows-Tracker (accessed December 2020).

International Monetary Fund. Direction of Trade Statistics. http://data.imf.org/DOT (accessed October and December 2020).

———. World Economic Outlook Reports. https://www.imf.org/en/publications/weo (accessed February 2021).

Barbieri, P., A. Boffelli, and S. Elia. 2020. What Can We Learn about Reshoring after Covid-19?. *Operations Management Research*. https://doi.org/10.1007/s12063-020-00160-1.

McKinsey Global Institute. 2016. Digital Globalization: The New Era of Global Flows. McKinsey and Company.

Park, C.Y., J. Villafuerte, A. Abiad, B. Narayanan, E. Banzon, J. Samson, A. Aftab, and M. C. Tayag. 2020. An Updated Assessment of the Economic Impact of COVID-19. *ADB Briefs*. No. 133. Manila: Asian Development Bank.

Stephenson, S. 2020. Medium and Long-Term Impact of COVID-19 on the Trade Landscape: Focusing on Services and Digital Trade. Presentation at RCI-POD Webinar No. 3: Immediate and Long-Term Impact of COVID-19 on Trade Landscape. 23 June. Manila: Asian Development Bank.

World Bank. World Development Indicators. https://databank.worldbank.org/source/world-development-indicators (accessed October 2020 and January 2021).

2 Trade and the Global Value Chains
The Challenging Trade Environment and Changing Global Value Chain Landscape

Recent Trends in Asia's Trade

Asia's trade growth was hit hard by the pandemic amid contracting global demand; nevertheless, recent high frequency data indicate a tempered yet gradual recovery.

Having peaked in 2017, Asia's trade growth began to slow in the second half of 2018 (Figure 2.1).[6] This came in the wake of rising trade tensions between the United States (US) and the People's Republic of China (PRC) along with continued moderation in global economic growth. Trade volume has since declined, although positive growth returned toward mid-2019 and was recovering by the end of 2019 until January 2020. It fell steeply negative beginning February 2020 as the coronavirus disease (COVID-19) pandemic greatly affected the PRC—a main driver of Asia's trade growth. By May 2020, trade volume contracted by -10.1%, has bottomed out since, returning to positive growth at 5.3% by September 2020.

Trade value growth moved in parallel with trade volume growth, although it has not been positive since February 2019 amid low inflation rates globally.[7] It followed a steep downward trajectory since the pandemic hit, prompting all major economies to impose stringent containment measures, including economic lockdowns and strict social distancing, among others. A steep oil price plunge, due to demand side concerns (a potential disruptive economic "sudden stop"), added to the downside pressure on trade value growth.

Temporary export and import bans on essential medical equipment and further trade restrictions of critical food supplies worsened trade performances both globally and regionally. Port closures—air, sea, and land—along with strengthened border crossing and quarantine procedures impeded the seamless flow of goods, along with temporary disruptions of supply chain networks due to bottlenecks in sourcing resources and deploying key personnel on sites.

With containment policies continuing to disrupt air and sea transport, supply chains, and consumption and investment, global trade value and volume growth rates are expected to continue to trend downward. But as economies began to exit lockdowns, resume economic activity and the mobility of people and goods, some recovery in trade growth is expected—already evident in some economies. First was the PRC, which entered lockdown near the beginning of the year. In contrast to the regional trend, PRC trade value began to rise again beginning April 2020 as it began lifting lockdowns (Figure 2.1). Throughout the second quarter, the PRC's trade value growth steadily recovered from –8.2% in March 2020, its lowest since 2018, to 11.4% growth in November 2020.

6 Asia refers to the 49 members of the Asian Development Bank (ADB) within Asia and the Pacific, which includes Japan and Oceania (Australia and New Zealand) in addition to the 46 developing Asian economies.

7 Crude oil prices had fallen by as much as 75% in June 2020 from their January level. It has partly recovered since, as governments began to lift quarantine measures and global oil supply fell after successful production cuts were coordinated by OPEC+. Moreover, oil price volatility has diminished recently. The Brent crude oil price is forecast to increase slowly, resulting in an average $42.50/barrel in 2020. And as economic activity normalizes and the oil market rebalances, it is forecast to average $50/barrel in 2021 (ADB 2020b).

Figure 2.1: Monthly Trade, by Value and Volume—Asia

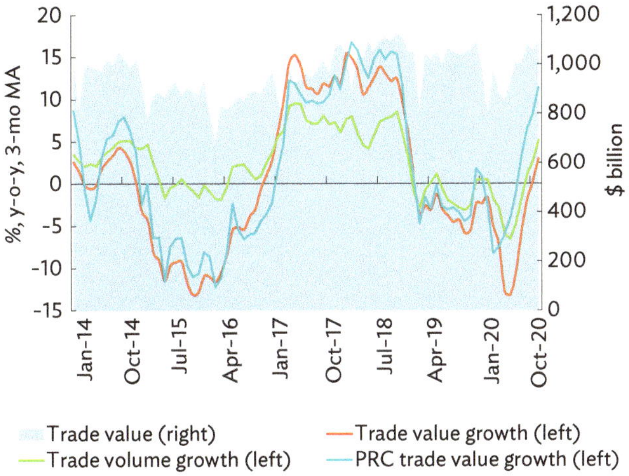

mo = month, MA = moving average, PRC = People's Republic of China, y-o-y = year-on-year.

Notes: Trade volume growth rates were computed using volume indexes. For each period and trade flow type (i.e., imports and exports), available data include indexes for Japan and the PRC, and aggregate indexes for selected Asian economies: (i) advanced economies (excluding Japan) include Hong Kong, China; the Republic of Korea; Singapore; and Taipei,China; and (ii) emerging economies (excluding the PRC) include India; Indonesia; Malaysia; Pakistan; the Philippines; Thailand; and Viet Nam. To come up with an index for Asia, trade values were used as weights for the computations. Trade value levels and growth rates were computed by aggregating import and export values of the same Asian economies.

Sources: ADB calculations using data from CEIC; and CPB Netherlands Bureau for Economic Policy Analysis. World Trade Monitor. https://www.cpb.nl/en/data (accessed January 2021).

The pandemic adversely affected trade growth for all economies in the region, but to varying degrees and at different paces. Changes in the patterns of import and export volumes are similar to the trade value growth trends since the pandemic began (Figure 2.2). Taipei,China continues to stand out as its export and import volume growth were least hurt by the pandemic. Volume growth rates certainly slowed significantly, especially import volumes, but never contracted—export volume growth was 12.7% and import growth was 5.6% in November 2020—with export growth the highest among newly industrialized economies (NIEs). The other NIEs—Hong Kong, China; the Republic of Korea; and Singapore—saw trade volumes contract during the early pandemic period. But their export volume growth rates were already on a recovery trajectory beginning June 2020 for Hong Kong, China; and in July 2020 for the Republic of Korea and Singapore. Compared with export volume growth, import volumes took longer due to deeper declines across the region partly reflecting a tepid recovery in domestic demand.

Asia's export and import volume and value growth trends have generally followed the trajectory of global business confidence until October 2020 (Figure 2.3). The significant uncertainties associated with health risks and economic activities pose constant downside risks to global trade, including Asia's. Although maritime and land transport has been resilient during the pandemic, air freight has been fragile, and various types of travel restrictions and voluntary travel restraints will likely hamper the recovery in international trade. With the COVID-19 pandemic suppressing business confidence and consumer sentiment, the outlook for the region's external demand remains bleak for 2020 (ADB 2020a). Although economies have begun to lift restrictions, without a clear sign of worldwide containment, the global pandemic is expected to continue to upend production, trade, and tourism, both within the region and externally—resulting in suppressed trade growth.[8]

Standardized high frequency indicators—such as global shipping and packaging indexes and port calls—and some monthly indicators suggest global trade bottomed out during the first half of the year. For instance, the Bloomberg and Dow Jones indexes, which declined to as low as below 3 standard deviations below average toward the end of March 2020, recovered steeply during the second quarter, suggesting global trade growth could recover faster than anticipated (Figure 2.4).

[8] In a press release on 20 April 2020, the World Trade Organization (WTO) forecasts that world trade was expected to fall by 13%–32% in 2020 (WTO 2020a). On 22 June, it announced that the volume of merchandise trade shrank by 3% year-on-year in the first quarter (WTO 2020b). Subsequently, the trade growth forecast for 2020 was revised to -9.2% (WTO 2020c). However, looking ahead to 2021, adverse developments, including a second wave of COVID-19 outbreaks, weaker than expected economic growth, or widespread return to trade restrictions, could cause the trade recovery to fall short of projections.

Figure 2.2: Monthly Trade Volume Growth—NIEs, PRC, and Selected ASEAN
(%, y-o-y, 3-month moving average)

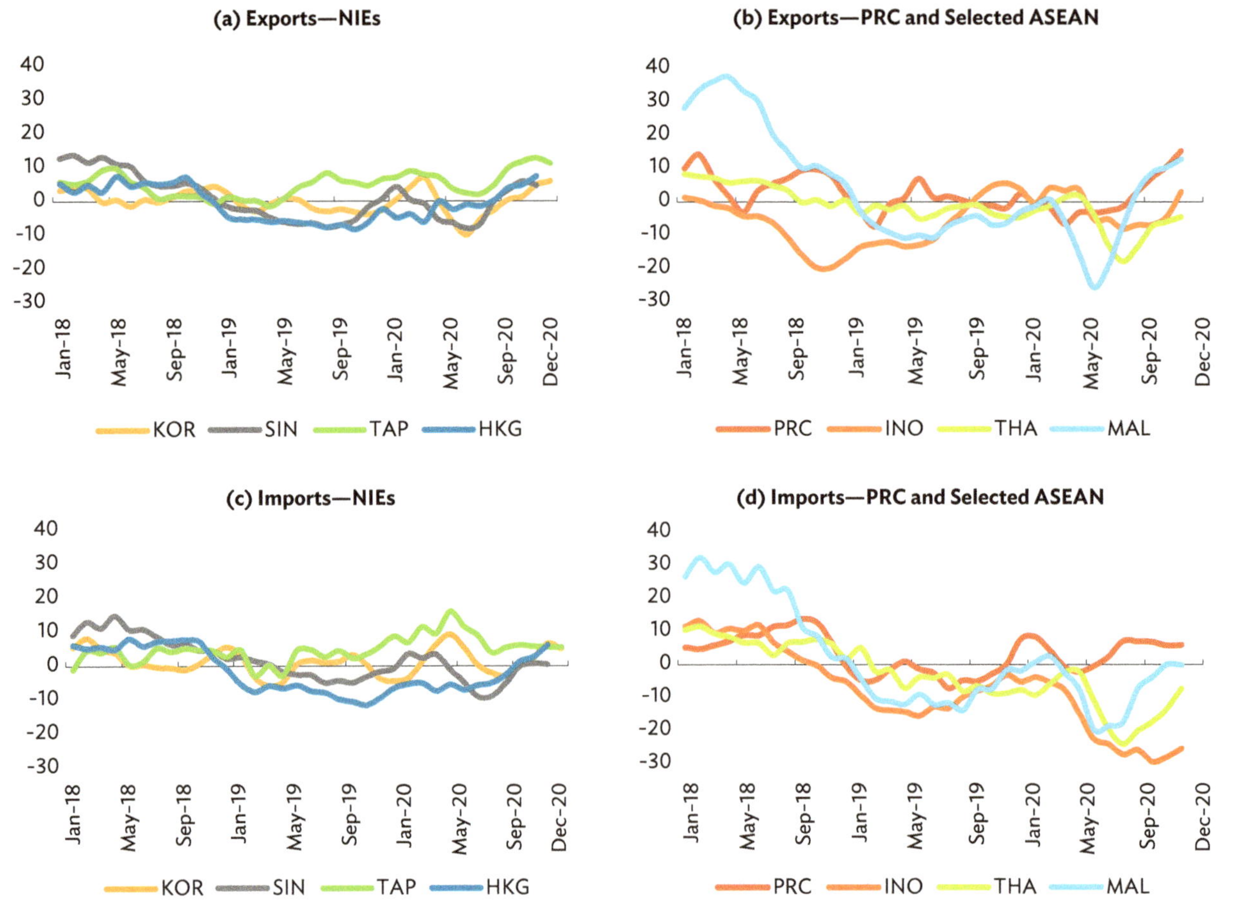

ASEAN = Association of Southeast Asian Nations; HKG = Hong Kong, China; INO = Indonesia; KOR = Republic of Korea; MAL = Malaysia; NIE = newly industrialized economy; PRC = People's Republic of China; SIN = Singapore; TAP = Taipei,China; THA = Thailand; y-o-y = year-on-year.

Notes: Latest data are September 2020 for all economies, except TAP and KOR (October 2020). Data for the PRC refer to the export and import volume index from CPB Netherlands Bureau for Economic Policy Analysis. For the rest, export and import volume is computed by deflating export and import values by their corresponding price indexes.

Sources: ADB calculations using data from CPB Netherlands Bureau for Economic Policy Analysis. World Trade Monitor. https://www.cpb.nl/en/data; and Haver Analytics (accessed January 2021).

Looking at the number of port calls, all regions saw a drop at the beginning of the first quarter—in January and February for Asia and in February for the rest of the world—as major ports in the PRC; Singapore; the Republic of Korea; and Hong Kong, China halted operations during lockdowns (Figure 2.5). The trend recovered for all regions since March. By mid-September, the number of port calls were already around 86% of their pre-pandemic levels.

For the first time since the financial crisis of 2008–2009, Asia's trade contracted in 2019 as external demand declined amid a persistent uncertain trade environment.

Asia's merchandise trade volume declined by –0.5% in 2019 from 4.1% growth in 2018 (Figure 2.6a). Rising trade tensions between the US and the PRC along with the continued slowdown in global economic growth resulted in the decline of the region's trade volume growth. The region's output, on the other hand, continued to grow at 4.6% in 2019, though below the 5.3% in 2018.

Figure 2.3: Global Business Confidence and Asia's Trade Volume Growth

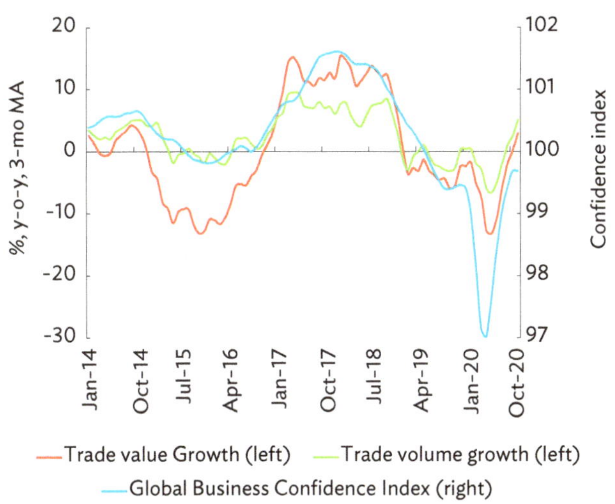

mo = month, ma = moving average, y-o-y = year-on-year.

Notes: Trade volume growth rates were computed using volume indexes. For each period and trade flow type (i.e., imports and exports), available data include indexes for Japan and the People's Republic of China (PRC), and aggregate indexes for selected Asian economies: (i) advanced economies (excluding Japan) include Hong Kong, China; the Republic of Korea; Singapore; and Taipei,China; and (ii) emerging economies (excluding the PRC) include India; Indonesia; Malaysia; Pakistan; the Philippines; Thailand; and Viet Nam. To come up with an index for Asia, trade values were used as weights for the computations. Trade value levels and growth rates were computed by aggregating import and export values of the same Asian economies. Global business confidence index covers Organisation for Economic Co-operation and Development economies.

Sources: ADB calculations using data from CEIC; CPB Netherlands Bureau for Economic Policy Analysis. World Trade Monitor. https://www.cpb.nl/en/data; and OECD. Business confidence index indicator. doi: 10.1787/3092dc4f-en (accessed January 2021).

Figure 2.4: Global Trade—Weekly Indicators (Z-scores)

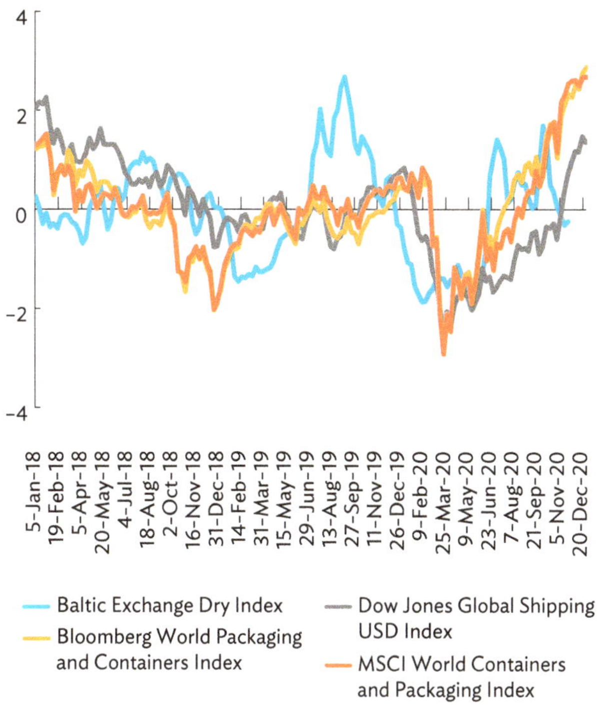

USD = United States dollar.

Notes: The indexes have been normalized using z-scores. Calculated mean and standard deviation of the indexes were for 1 May 2018 to 25 December 2020, except for Baltic Exchange Dry Index, which is only up to 11 November 2020.

Sources: ADB calculations using data from Bloomberg; CEIC; and Freights Baltic Index. https://fbx.freightos.com/ (accessed December 2020).

Figure 2.5: Number of Port Calls by Region

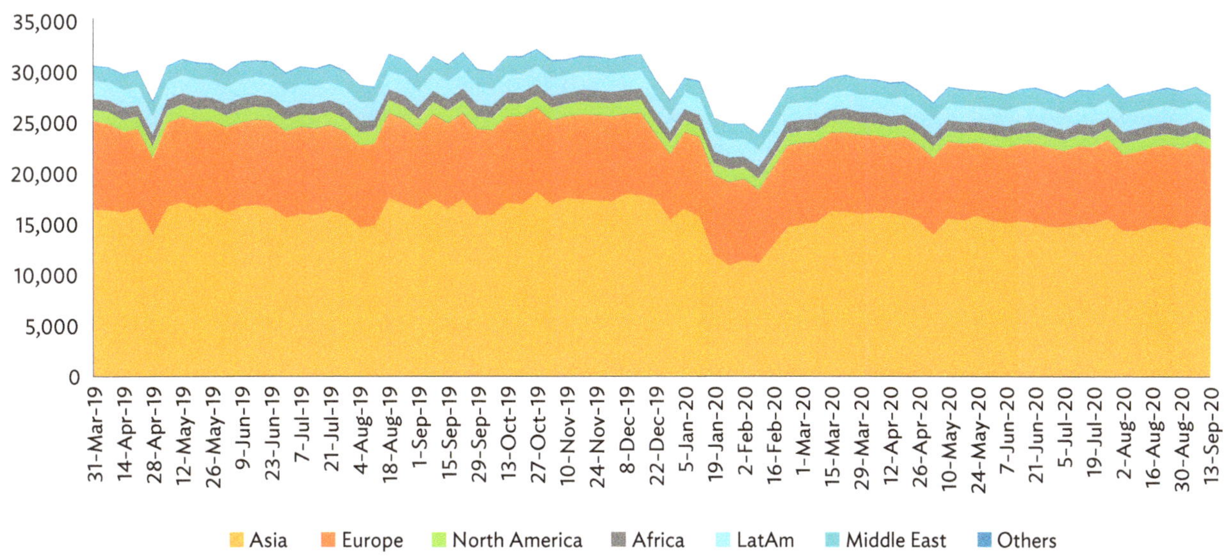

LatAm = Latin America.

Note: Composition of regions follows Asia Regional Integration Center's integration indicators country groupings at https://aric.adb.org/integrationindicators/groupings.

Source: United Nations. Commodity Trade Database: AIS Weekly Port Calls. https://comtrade.un.org/data/monitor#AISPort (accessed November 2020).

Figure 2.6: Merchandise Trade Volume and Real GDP Growth—Asia and World (%, year-on-year)

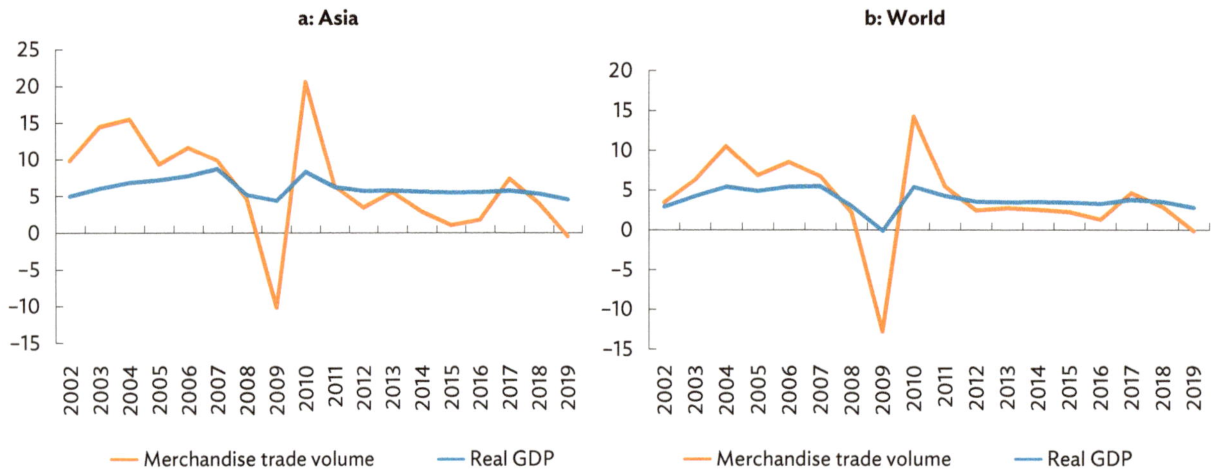

GDP = gross domestic product.

Note: Real GDP growth is weighted using purchasing power parity.

Sources: ADB calculations using data from International Monetary Fund. World Economic Outlook October 2020 Database. https://www.imf.org/en/Publications/WEO/weo-database/2020/October (accessed October 2020); and World Trade Organization. Statistics Database. http://data.wto.org/en (accessed October 2020).

Global trade volume also declined (-0.1%) in 2019 after growing 2.9% in 2018—also the first contraction in global trade since 2009. Despite falling trade volumes, global economic output continued to grow, but at lower rate of 2.8%, compared to 3.5% in 2018 (Figure 2.6b).

The region's export volume barely grew at 0.05% in 2019, a significant drop from the 2018 growth rate of 3.5%. Most major exporter economies in Asia had either negative or decelerating growth rates. Those with negative growth rates included Hong Kong, China (-7.3%); Indonesia (-3.3%); Thailand (-3.0%); Japan (-1.9%); Malaysia (-2.0%); the Republic of Korea (-1.8%); and Singapore (-3.0%). Economies that continued to grow, although at lower rates than in 2018 were Australia (0.5% in 2019 from 5.1% in 2018), the PRC (2.0% from 4.1%), Pakistan (13.7% from 15.9%), Viet Nam (8.6% from 12.3%), India (2.8% from 3.6%), and New Zealand (2.1% from 2.2%). Some economies accelerated growth or recovered from 2018, such as Taipei,China (3.9% from 3.4%); the Philippines (4.3% in 2019 from -1.8% in 2018); Sri Lanka (7.2% from 0.4%); Cambodia (14.9% from 12.3%); Kazakhstan (3.1% from 2.3%); and the Kyrgyz Republic (5.1% from 1.2%).

Compared with exports, Asia's import volume declined by -1.1% in 2019—significantly below 2018 growth of 4.9%. Also similar to export volumes, many major importers in the region contracted: Hong Kong, China (-9.3%); Sri Lanka (-6.0%); Indonesia (-6,4%); Thailand (-5.0%); Malaysia (-3.0%); the Philippines (-2.8%); India (-1.6%); Australia (-1.4%); the Republic of Korea (-1.3%); Singapore (-1.2%); and Pakistan (-0.7%). Import volumes for the PRC (0.2% from 6.4% in 2018), Japan (0.4% from 1.9%), and New Zealand (0.4% from 6.4%), barely grew. Viet Nam had positive growth but at a lower rate of 7.2% (from 9.3% in 2018); while a few economies accelerated like Taipei,China (4.4% from 3.1% in 2018) and Cambodia (19.5% from 15.9% in 2018).

Asia's trade values fell more than trade volumes.

The trade value of the region fell at a rate of -2.8% in 2019, a large turnaround from 10.4% in 2018 (Figure 2.7). The region's trajectory is mirrored by the trend of global trade value, which also fell to -2.8% in 2019 compared with 10.0% in 2018. Whereas global export and import values fell at the same rate (–2.8%), in Asia, imports value declined at –3.7%, larger than the decline of export values at –1.9%.

Figure 2.7: Trade Value—Asia and World

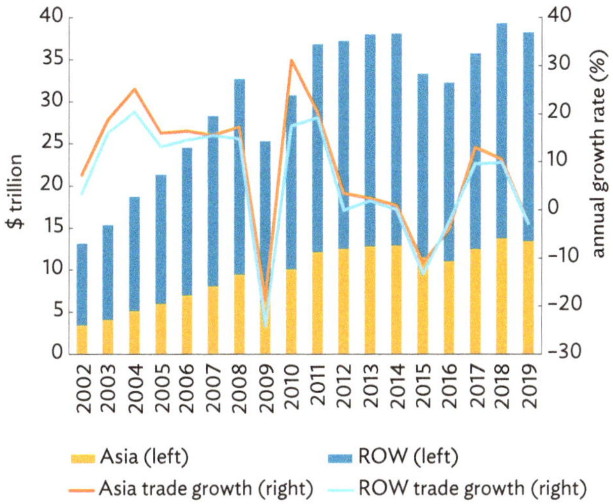

ROW = rest of the world.

Source: ADB calculations using data from World Trade Organization. Statistics Database. http://data.wto.org/en (accessed October 2020).

Asia's Intraregional Trade

Despite the deteriorating global trade environment, Asia continues to show strong intraregional trade linkages.

The region's intraregional trade share remained stable at 57.5% in 2019, still above the 56.5% average for 2012–2018 (Figure 2.8). This remains higher than North America (40.9%) and lower than the European Union (EU) (63.2%).[9] The strong trade linkages among the Asian economies could serve as a buffer for a potential trade growth slowdown or decline. The pandemic, which could diminish the rationale for further expanding globalization or prompt a rationalization or diversification of existing supply chains—optimizing regional trade linkages and strengthening regional trade integration—could help the

Figure 2.8: Intraregional Trade Shares—Asia, European Union, and North America (%)

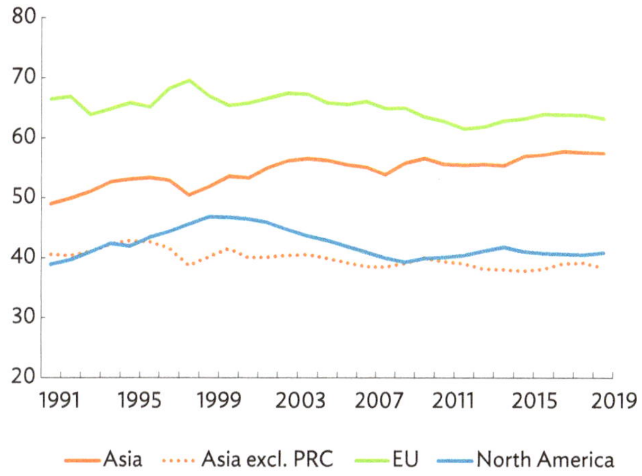

EU = European Union, PRC = People's Republic of China.

Notes: Values expressed as percentage of the region's total merchandise trade (sum of exports and imports). EU refers to the aggregate of 28 members including the United Kingdom. North America covers Canada, Mexico, and the United States.

Source: ADB calculations using data from International Monetary Fund. Direction of Trade Statistics. http://data.imf.org/DOT (accessed December 2020).

region's economies navigate the challenges to sustain trade growth. The region needs to embrace stronger trade liberalization and facilitation regimes, including engaging in regional and bilateral trade agreements and improving trade logistics to continue this momentum.

After 2 years of recovery in 2017 (14.0%) and 2018 (10.4%), Asia's intraregional trade values contracted by –2.7% in 2019. Similarly, Asia's extraregional trade values also fell at a rate of –2.4% in 2019 after having grown by 11.5% in 2018. Taken together, these two factors pulled down the region's intraregional trade share slightly in 2019.

The importance of the PRC as the region's major trading partner has also grown substantially—as shown by the increasing gap of intraregional trade share between Asian economies excluding the PRC and Asia including the PRC (Figure 2.8). By 2019, Asia's trade relations with the PRC contributed about a third to the region's intraregional

[9] The EU refers to the 28 members that include the United Kingdom (UK) in this analysis. (The UK formally withdrew from the EU on 31 January 2020 with the transition effective at the end on 31 December 2020. See Eddington (2020).

trade share. While intraregional trading within Asia excluding the PRC remained relatively stable over the past 30 years—within a 38% to 43% range—the dynamics of the extent of its trade linkages with other regions have changed considerably. The most important trading partner of Asia (excluding the PRC) outside the region was North America in 1990 (24.8%), followed by the EU (17.6%). In the past 3 decades, the share of Asia's (excluding the PRC) regional trade with North America and the EU gradually fell by 2019 to 12.4% and 11.0%, respectively, as the region diversified to other trading partners, mainly the PRC: the regional trade share with the PRC has grown to 24.4% (from 5.8% in 1990) with the share to the rest of the world up modestly to 13.8% (from 13.0% in 1990).

By April 2020, intraregional trade for the EU and North America fell relatively sharply, whereas Asia (including the PRC) remained stable.

Intraregional trade linkages deepened across subregions over the past decade.

From 2010 to 2019, intraregional trade shares increased across all subregions, albeit at varying rates. Central Asia had the highest increase, from 28.7% in 2010 to 35.7% in 2019—a 24% or 7 percentage point increase. This was followed by the Pacific and Oceania with intraregional share growth of 4.2% or 2.9 percentage points from 68.9% in 2010 to 71.8% in 2019. The intraregional share for East Asia barely changed, from 55.2% in 2010 to 55.7% in 2019.

By magnitude, the Pacific and Oceania continued to hold the highest intraregional share in 2019 (71.8%), followed by Southeast Asia (68.4%) and East Asia (55.7%) (Figure 2.9). Despite having increased the most over the past decade, the intraregional trade share for Central Asia and South Asia remained below 40%.

Across subregions, East Asia continues to have the highest intra-subregional trade share (34.7%), followed by Southeast Asia (22.4%). The other subregions all recorded intra-subregional trade shares below 10%—Central Asia (7.8%), the Pacific and Oceania (3.9%), and South Asia (5.6%).

Figure 2.9: Intraregional Trade Shares by Asian Subregions (%)

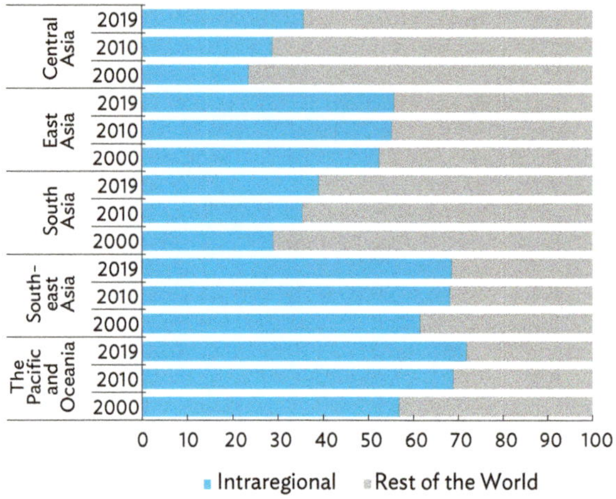

Note: Timor-Leste was recently classified under Southeast Asia, previously it was under the Pacific and Oceania.

Source: ADB calculations using data from International Monetary Fund. Direction of Trade Statistics. http://data.imf.org/DOT (accessed December 2020).

Progress of Global and Regional Value Chains

The expansion of global value chains continued to stagnate with regional value linkages within Asia following a similar trend.

Globally, the rapid increase in cross-border production networks since 2000 slowed significantly in the 2010s, following the recovery from the 2008–2009 global financial crisis (Figure 2.10). Global value chain (GVC) participation peaked between 2011 and 2013 when the share of value-added content comprised three-quarters of the world's gross exports, surpassing the pre-financial crisis rate. Asia's GVC participation, while remaining strong, continues to slow and even declined the past 2 years, mirroring the general global trend of stagnating overall GVC participation. Asia-to-Asia value chains declined in 2018 and 2019. Still, the share of traded intermediate goods for further processing through cross-border production networks remains high at 67.4% of the region's gross exports in 2019, or about the level in 2000 (67.2%).

Asian economies' participation of 47.2% (3-year moving average) in the regional value chain (RVC) has nearly

Figure 2.10: GVC and RVC Participation Rates (%)

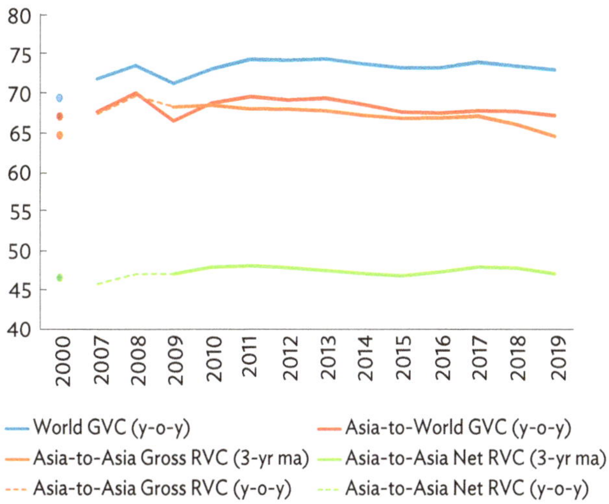

3-yr ma = 3-year moving average, GVC = global value chain, RVC = regional value chain, y-o-y = year-on-year.

Notes: The GVC participation rate is the share of gross exports that involves production in at least two economies using cross-border production networks. The RVC participation rate, on the other hand, is the same as that of GVC, except that it only involves economies of the same region.

Sources: ADB calculations using data from ADB. Multi-Regional Input-Output Tables; and methodology by Wang, Wei, and Zhu (2013).

Figure 2.11: RVC–GVC Intensity—Asia, European Union, and North America

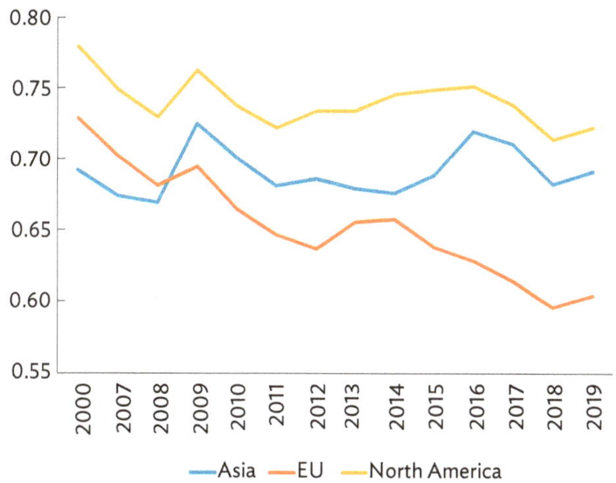

EU = European Union, GVC = global value chain, RVC = regional value chain.

Notes: RVC–GVC intensity is the ratio of RVC participation and GVC participation rates. The EU refers to the aggregate of 28 members including the United Kingdom. North America consists of United States, Canada, and Mexico.

Sources: ADB calculations using data from ADB Multi-Regional Input-Output Tables; and methodology by Wang, Wei, and Zhu (2013).

returned to its 2000 rate (46.7%) after falling from a peak of 48% in 2017. GVC participation is higher than RVC participation. Moreover, the region's intensity of participation in RVCs against GVC participation (the ratio of the two) has been volatile (returning to its 2000 level of 0.69 in 2019) (Figure 2.11).

Asia has relatively strong regional value chain linkages—as measured by the regional value chain to global value chain intensity ratio (Figure 2.11). Asia's RVC-to-GVC participation remains much lower than in North America, but higher than the EU.[10] Asia is gradually closing the gap with North America in terms of RVC–GVC intensity. The EU's RVC–GVC intensity has sharply declined over the past 2 decades while the region's trade networks expanded outside the region.[11]

Cross-border production networks in Asia remain stronger in primary goods, leaving RVC opportunities in higher value-added sectors.

Asia had its highest GVC participation rate (86.6%) in the primary sector—which includes agriculture, mining, and quarrying. Most of this value-added trading is done within the region with an RVC rate of 69.5%, hence the high intensity ratio (Figure 2.12). The low-technology sector also has a relatively high intensity ratio, although it has the lowest GVC participation (50.1%) and RVC participation (36.3%) rates in 2019.[12] Its RVC, however, is high relative to GVC, reflecting a faster increase in value-added factor content trading within the region than outside the region.

10 The EU includes the UK in this analysis (see footnote 6).

11 For instance, a network analysis that maps the evolution of the topology of global production network structure between 2000 and 2017 by Li, Meng, and Wang (2019) shows how the supply hub in Europe, in particular Germany, developed direct linkages to Asia supply hubs like the PRC, especially in the information and communication technology (ICT) and services sector. To a certain extent, this is also observed in the resulting network analysis of demand hubs of trade in value-added for the ICT sector.

12 The low-tech sector consists of the following industries: food, beverages, and tobacco; textiles and textile products; leather, leather products, and footwear; wood and products of wood and cork; pulp, paper, paper products, printing, and publishing; rubber and plastics; manufacturing; recycling; electricity, gas, and water supply; and construction.

Figure 2.12: RVC–GVC Trade Intensity, by Major Sector—Asia

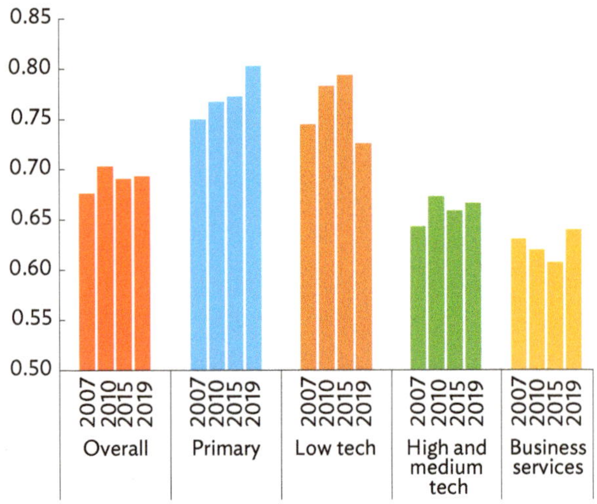

GVC = global value chain, RVC = regional value chain.

Note: Sectoral classification is based on ADB (2015).

Sources: ADB calculations using data from ADB Multi-Regional Input-Output Tables; and methodology by Wang, Wei, and Zhu (2013).

In contrast, intermediate trade linkages within the region relative to the region's GVC trade linkages rose slowly in the medium and high technology and business services sectors. Their GVC participation rates were higher than the low-technology sector at 69.9% and 68.6% in 2019, respectively (although still below primary sector levels). On the other hand, much less intermediate trading in these industries was done within the region, with RVC participation rates in 2019 at 46.6% and 43.9%, respectively, resulting in relatively lower RVC–GVC intensity. These regional trade linkage patterns imply that Asian economies still have room to strengthen their RVC in higher value goods and services. Policies that can improve capacity and relax trade and investment restrictions would help further deepen an economy's participation in global and regional value chains beyond the primary and low tech sectors.

National RVC and GVC participation levels have a high degree of heterogeneity.

In general, economies with higher GVC participation rates also have higher RVC participation rates, while some economies show deeper regional value linkages within the region (Figure 2.13). Economies, such as Hong Kong, China; Mongolia; Pakistan; Nepal; and Brunei Darussalam, have higher RVC participation rates than GVC participation rates.

For Asia, RVC–GVC intensity declined slightly between 2015 and 2019. Cambodia had the biggest decline and the lowest RVC–GVC intensity in 2019. This is partly because its GVC participation rate rose faster than its RVC participation rate.

Other economies—such as Nepal, Bhutan, Sri Lanka, the Kyrgyz Republic, and Mongolia—had stronger RVC participation growth relative to GVC as their intensity ratios rose by at least 8% between 2015 and 2019. But dynamics differ across economies. Nepal, Bhutan, and Sri Lanka had RVC participation rates growing faster than GVC linkages. Singapore and the Kyrgyz Republic had rising RVCs, while GVC participation rates fell. For Mongolia, GVC participation fell more than RVC participation.

Commodity-exporting economies—such as Australia, Brunei Darussalam, Kazakhstan, and Mongolia—tend to have high GVC and RVC participation rates. Most commodity-exports are used as raw materials for producing intermediate and final goods, which is why these economies have high upstream value chain participation. For example, Brunei Darussalam exports most of its fuel and natural gas to Malaysia and Singapore for further processing and export. This also applies to Mongolia, which exports minerals to the PRC, the Lao People's Democratic Republic (Lao PDR) (which exports electricity to Thailand), and Kazakhstan (which exports fuel and metals to the PRC).

Complex regional and global value chains show a different picture.[13] By 2019, complex global value chain participation for the region reached 41.1% of gross exports, still below its pre-financial crisis level but higher than

13 Complex value-added linkages are exports that cross borders two or more times.

Figure 2.13: Overall RVC and GVC Participation—Selected Asian Economies

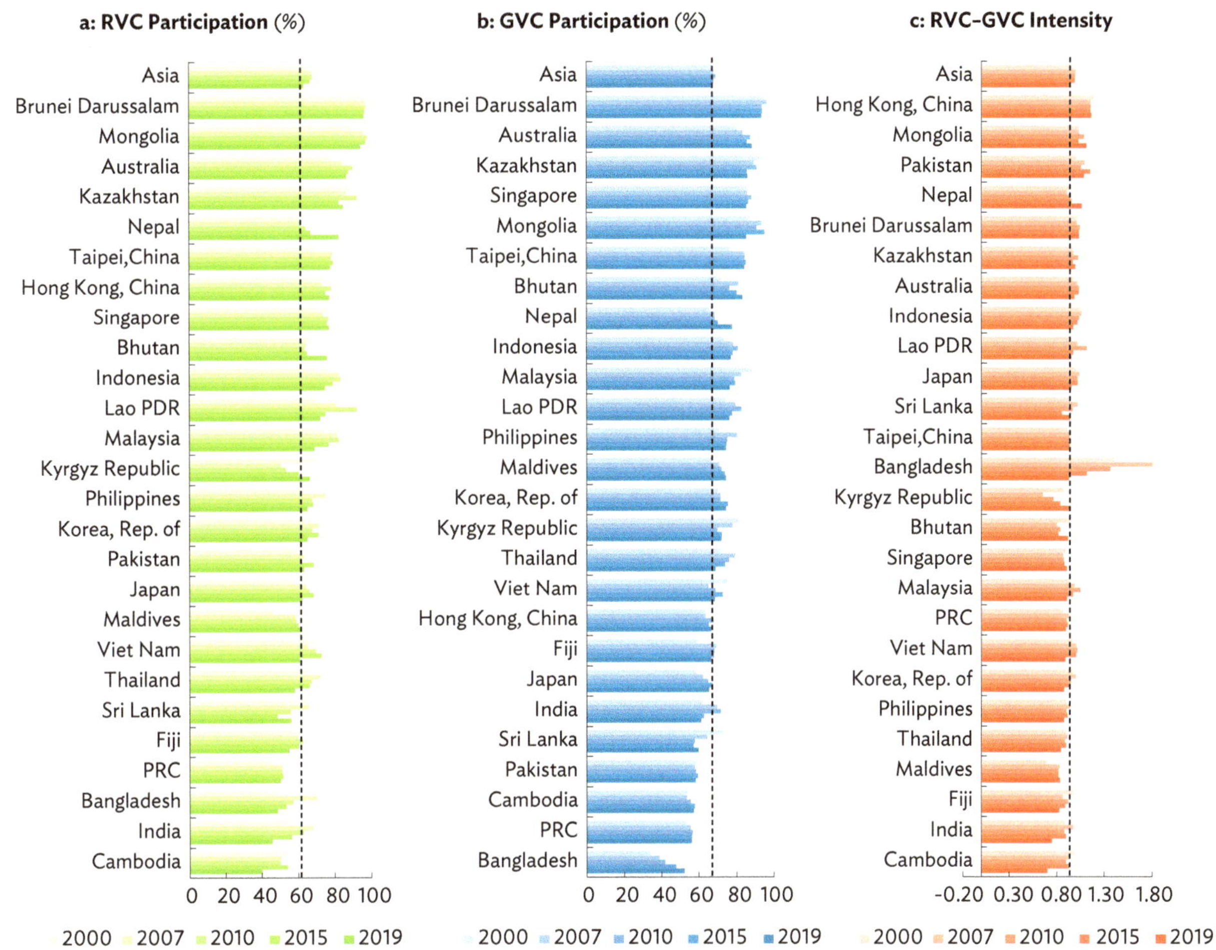

GVC = global value chain, Lao PDR = Lao People's Democratic Republic, PRC = People's Republic of China, RVC = regional value chain.

Notes: RVC–GVC intensity is the ratio of RVC participation and GVC participation rates. The overall GVC participation rate is the share of gross exports that involves production in at least two economies using cross-border production networks. The overall RVC participation rate is the same concept as that of overall GVC, except that it only involves economies of the same region and that the denominator excludes third and fourth partner economies. Economies are ordered by 2019 values from highest to lowest. Vertical line represents the value for Asia for 2019.

Sources: ADB calculations using data from ADB Multi-Regional Input-Output Tables; and methodology by Wang, Wei, and Zhu (2013).

the 2015 slump. In 2019, for economies like Singapore; Taipei,China; Malaysia; Maldives; and the Republic of Korea, at least 50% of global gross exports involve intermediate goods crossing borders more than once (Figure 2.14b). Complex gross regional value-added linkages, however, have been either stagnant or declining since 2010, and now comprise 23.6% of regional gross exports (excluding exports to third and fourth partner economies). Economies such as Taipei,China; and many in Southeast Asia—Singapore, Viet Nam, Malaysia, and the Philippines, have at least 30% of their regional gross exports part of complex value chains (Figure 2.14a). Bangladesh had a large increase in complex GVC and complex gross RVC participation rates between 2015 and 2019. This can be attributed mostly to (i) the rise in intermediate goods exports used to produce intermediate exports for final use exports in third economies, and (ii) the rise in foreign value-added in final use exports.

Complex RVC–GVC intensity ratios increased for some Asian economies since 2000. The highest increase was in the Kyrgyz Republic, which had one of the lowest intensity

Figure 2.14: Complex RVC and GVC Participation—Selected Asian Economies

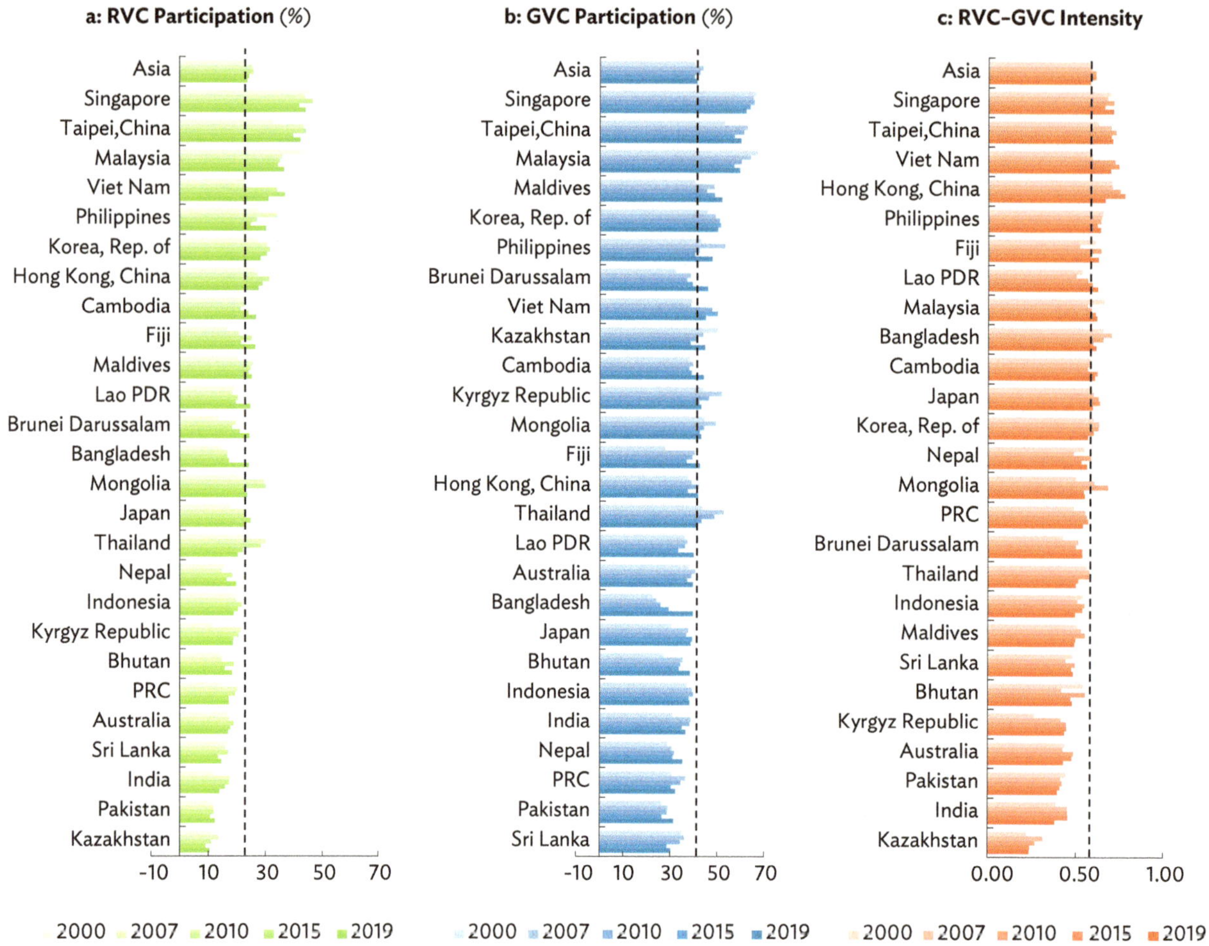

GVC = global value chain, Lao PDR = Lao People's Democratic Republic, PRC = People's Republic of China, RVC = regional value chain.

Notes: RVC–GVC intensity is the ratio of RVC participation and GVC participation rates. The complex GVC participation rate is the share of gross exports that involves production in at least two economies using cross-border production networks but includes only part of the gross exports for which the production entails border-crossing twice or more. The complex RVC participation rate, on the other hand, is the same concept as complex GVC, except that it only involves economies of the same region and that the denominator excludes third and fourth partner economies. Economies are ordered by 2019 values from highest to lowest. Vertical line represents the value for Asia for 2019.

Sources: ADB calculations using data from ADB Multi-Regional Input-Output Tables; and methodology by Wang, Wei, and Zhu (2013).

ratios (0.26) in the region in 2000. Other economies with notable increases were Brunei Darussalam; Viet Nam; the Lao PDR; and Taipei,China. In contrast, economies such as Thailand; Bhutan; Pakistan; Bangladesh; Hong Kong, China; Malaysia; and the Republic of Korea were lower. As of 2019, those with the highest RVC–GVC intensity, at least 0.60, were mostly Southeast Asian and East Asian economies plus Fiji (Figure 2.14c). Most of these are highly embedded into deeper manufacturing production networks in electrical and optical equipment, and transport and transport equipment, which involve complex global and regional value chains.

The Impact of GVC Reshoring

The risk of GVC bottlenecks became clear during the pandemic. Thus, some countries could use reshoring as a means to transfer production back home. However, many could not compensate for all imported intermediate goods over a short span of time due to constraints in domestic production capacity, thus leading to a decline in overall production.

GVC Snapshot

Exported products are either produced using local content or imported intermediate goods (Figure 2.15a). Some intermediate goods used by the exporter come directly from the partner. Of those imported, some are finally consumed by the importer; some eventually return to the exporter; while others are used by the importer to produce goods sold to other countries. Importing countries either consume them domestically or process them further for later export (Figure 2.15b).

GVC Reshoring

When reshoring, the exporter decreases outsourced goods, processing them locally instead. In the backward linkages, the exporter could reshore the production of intermediate goods to be imported. In the forward, the exporter also can reshore the production of goods outsourced to foreign economies.

The success of any reshoring strategy relies on the exporting country's capacity to substitute for its reduction of imported intermediate goods and outsourced production. At best, where the substitution rate is 100%, the country maintains its level of exports. However, if all countries use this strategy, even if all theoretically reach 100%, global exports will decline as demand for intermediate goods decreases.

When the supply chains are reshored by 10%–20%, global exports, imports, and total trade are estimated to decrease by 13%–22%.

The impact of reshoring is estimated under three scenarios: when the capacity of local manufacturers to compensate for the reduction of imported intermediate goods is 100%, 50%, and 30% (Tables 2.1, 2.2, and 2.3). These were then estimated with reshoring at 10%, 20%, and 40%.

The reshoring of supply chain networks to domestic economies, while only partial, could significantly reduce international trade. Based on simulations using ADB's Multi-Regional Input-Output Tables—which can trace spillover impacts across trade supply chains—global trade is estimated to contract by 13%–22% when 10%–20% of overseas supply chains are reshored, and the capacity of the economies to substitute for the reshored products is 50% (Table 2.3).

The Asian subregion with the largest decline is Southeast Asia (14%–25%), followed by Central Asia (13%–23%) and the Pacific and Oceania (12%–21%) (Table 2.3). Central Asia participates heavily in the EU value chain, while Southeast Asia and the Pacific and Oceania connect primarily with Asia's value chain. The Asian economies most affected include Malaysia; Kazakhstan; Brunei Darussalam; Taipei,China; Singapore; Australia; Maldives; and the Republic of Korea.

Figure 2.15a: Backward Global Value Chain Linkages

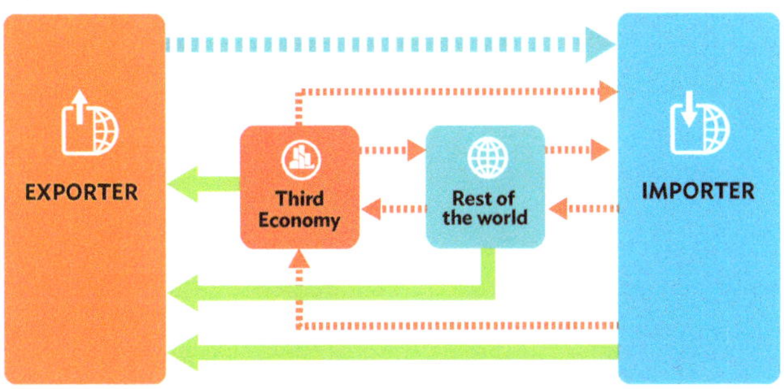

Figure 2.15b: Forward Global Value Chain Linkages

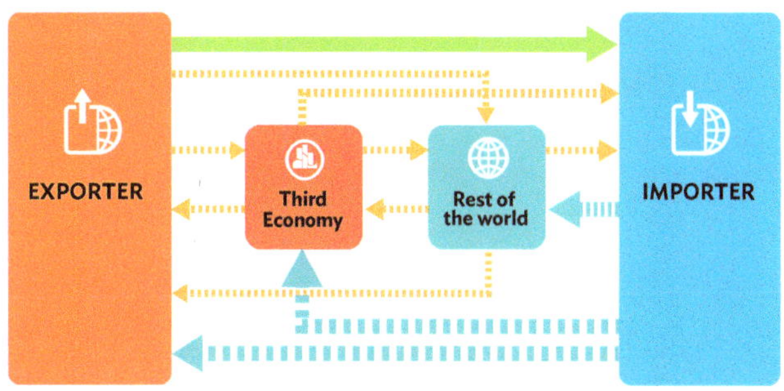

Export of supplies to produce intermediate goods for further processing

Export of goods for final consumption after crossing borders three times during the production chain, originating from the exporter

Export of Intermediate goods used for further processing

Export of final or intermediate goods using processed intermediate goods

Source: ADB staff.

Table 2.1: Impact of Reshoring on Exports (%)

Region/Subregion	100% Substitution Rate			50% Substitution Rate			30% Substitution Rate		
	10% Reshoring	20% Reshoring	40% Reshoring	10% Reshoring	20% Reshoring	40% Reshoring	10% Reshoring	20% Reshoring	40% Reshoring
Asia and the Pacific	**-8.79**	**-14.64**	**-29.29**	**-12.30**	**-20.50**	**-41.01**	**-13.71**	**-22.85**	**-45.70**
Central Asia	-15.60	-26.01	-52.01	-17.68	-29.47	-58.94	-18.51	-30.85	-61.70
East Asia	-8.56	-14.26	-28.53	-11.80	-19.66	-39.32	-13.09	-21.82	-43.64
South Asia	-8.36	-13.93	-27.86	-11.24	-18.74	-37.48	-12.40	-20.66	-41.32
Southeast Asia	-8.31	-13.85	-27.71	-13.31	-22.19	-44.37	-15.31	-25.52	-51.04
The Pacific and Oceania	-13.20	-21.95	-43.90	-15.08	-25.13	-50.26	-15.84	-26.40	-52.81
European Union	**-8.14**	**-13.56**	**-27.12**	**-13.82**	**-23.03**	**-46.07**	**-16.09**	**-26.82**	**-53.64**
Latin America	**-8.89**	**-14.81**	**-29.62**	**-14.12**	**-23.54**	**-47.08**	**-16.22**	**-27.03**	**-54.06**
North America	**-11.11**	**-18.51**	**-37.02**	**-14.08**	**-23.47**	**-46.93**	**-15.27**	**-25.45**	**-50.89**
Rest of the World	**-8.96**	**-14.94**	**-29.88**	**-13.50**	**-22.51**	**-45.01**	**-15.32**	**-25.53**	**-51.06**
World	**-8.92**	**-14.86**	**-29.72**	**-13.34**	**-22.24**	**-44.48**	**-15.11**	**-25.19**	**-50.38**

Notes: Reshoring rate refers to the share of imported intermediate goods and outsourced production that the main exporter will cut off. Substitution rate refers to the capacity of local manufacturers to produce enough intermediate goods to compensate for the cut off of imported intermediate goods and outsourced production.

Sources: ADB calculations using data from ADB. Multi-Regional Input–Output Tables; and methodology by Wang, Wei, and Zhu (2013).

Table 2.2: Impact of Reshoring on Imports (%)

Region/Subregion	100% Substitution Rate			50% Substitution Rate			30% Substitution Rate		
	10% Reshoring	20% Reshoring	40% Reshoring	10% Reshoring	20% Reshoring	40% Reshoring	10% Reshoring	20% Reshoring	40% Reshoring
Asia and the Pacific	**-7.49**	**-12.48**	**-24.96**	**-11.82**	**-19.70**	**-39.39**	**-13.55**	**-22.58**	**-45.17**
Central Asia	-4.86	-8.11	-16.21	-8.89	-14.81	-29.62	-10.50	-17.49	-34.99
East Asia	-6.89	-11.48	-22.95	-11.09	-18.49	-36.97	-12.77	-21.29	-42.58
South Asia	-4.67	-7.79	-15.58	-8.84	-14.74	-29.48	-10.51	-17.52	-35.03
Southeast Asia	-11.42	-19.04	-38.07	-16.21	-27.01	-54.02	-18.12	-30.20	-60.40
The Pacific and Oceania	-4.81	-8.02	-16.04	-9.25	-15.41	-30.83	-11.02	-18.37	-36.75
European Union	**-12.50**	**-20.83**	**-41.67**	**-17.53**	**-29.22**	**-58.44**	**-19.54**	**-32.57**	**-65.15**
Latin America	**-10.35**	**-17.25**	**-34.50**	**-15.32**	**-25.53**	**-51.07**	**-17.31**	**-28.85**	**-57.69**
North America	**-5.00**	**-8.34**	**-16.68**	**-9.42**	**-15.70**	**-31.39**	**-11.18**	**-18.64**	**-37.28**
Rest of the World	**-8.59**	**-14.32**	**-28.65**	**-12.48**	**-20.80**	**-41.60**	**-14.03**	**-23.39**	**-46.78**
World	**-8.92**	**-14.86**	**-29.72**	**-13.34**	**-22.24**	**-44.48**	**-15.11**	**-25.19**	**-50.38**

Notes: Reshoring rate refers to the share of imported intermediate goods and outsourced production that the main exporter will cut off. Substitution rate refers to the capacity of local manufacturers to produce enough intermediate goods to compensate for the cut off of imported intermediate goods and outsourced production.

Sources: ADB calculations using data from ADB. Multi-Regional Input–Output Tables; and methodology by Wang, Wei, and Zhu (2013).

Table 2.3: Impact of Reshoring on Total Trade (%)

Region/Subregion	100% Substitution Rate			50% Substitution Rate			30% Substitution Rate		
	10% Reshoring	20% Reshoring	40% Reshoring	10% Reshoring	20% Reshoring	40% Reshoring	10% Reshoring	20% Reshoring	40% Reshoring
Asia and the Pacific	**-8.15**	**-13.59**	**-27.18**	**-12.07**	**-20.11**	**-40.22**	**-13.63**	**-22.72**	**-45.44**
Central Asia	-10.62	-17.70	-35.41	-13.60	-22.67	-45.34	-14.79	-24.66	-49.31
East Asia	-7.74	-12.91	-25.81	-11.45	-19.09	-38.18	-12.94	-21.56	-43.12
South Asia	-6.30	-10.50	-21.01	-9.90	-16.51	-33.01	-11.34	-18.91	-37.81
Southeast Asia	-9.78	-16.31	-32.61	-14.68	-24.47	-48.94	-16.64	-27.74	-55.47
The Pacific and Oceania	-9.44	-15.73	-31.47	-12.48	-20.80	-41.59	-13.69	-22.82	-45.64
European Union	**-10.23**	**-17.04**	**-34.09**	**-15.60**	**-25.99**	**-51.99**	**-17.75**	**-29.58**	**-59.15**
Latin America	**-9.63**	**-16.05**	**-32.10**	**-14.73**	**-24.55**	**-49.11**	**-16.77**	**-27.95**	**-55.91**
North America	**-7.79**	**-12.99**	**-25.97**	**-11.55**	**-19.25**	**-38.49**	**-13.05**	**-21.75**	**-43.50**
Rest of the World	**-8.77**	**-14.62**	**-29.25**	**-12.98**	**-21.63**	**-43.26**	**-14.66**	**-24.43**	**-48.87**
World	**-8.92**	**-14.86**	**-29.72**	**-13.34**	**-22.24**	**-44.48**	**-15.11**	**-25.19**	**-50.38**

Notes: Reshoring rate refers to the share of imported intermediate goods and outsourced production that the main exporter will stop. Substitution rate refers to the capacity of local manufacturers to produce enough intermediate goods to compensate for the difference. Total trade includes imports and exports.

Sources: ADB calculations using data from ADB. Multi-Regional Input–Output Tables; and methodology by Wang, Wei, and Zhu (2013).

Post-pandemic, economies may consider diversifying upstream production—economies decrease their dependency on their primary source of intermediate goods, acquiring them from other sources. Similarly, they may also diversify downstream production by decreasing dependency on demand from their top importer and export intermediate products to other economies. This strategy could involve different scenarios, such as regionalizing or nearshoring supply chains (Annex 3b). While the trade distribution effect among economies could be minimal under this modest assumption, the exercise could work when analyzing diverse supply chain diversification scenarios.

Figure 2.16: Number of Newly Effective Free Trade Agreements—Asia

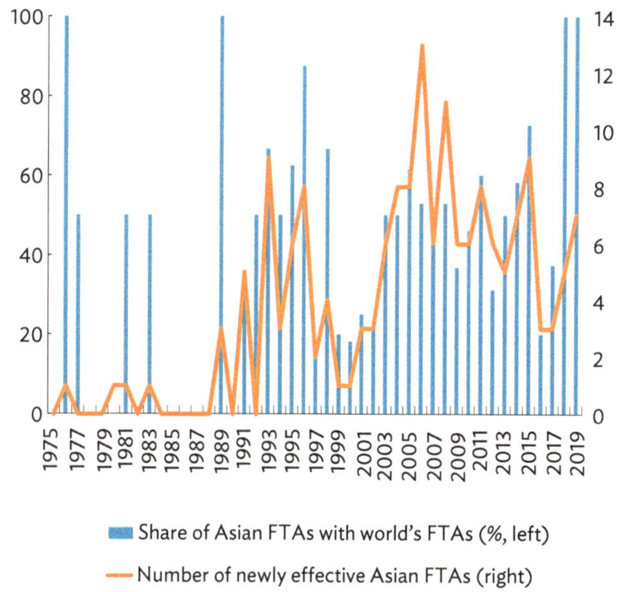

FTA = free trade agreement.

Sources: ADB calculations using data from ADB. Asia Regional Integration Center FTA Database. https://aric.adb.org/fta; and World Trade Organization. Regional Trade Agreement Information System. http://rtais.wto.org (both accessed July 2020).

Updates on Regional Trade Policy

New free trade agreements continue as economies use online conferencing for negotiations.

In the months prior to the COVID-19 pandemic, the number of signed Asian free trade agreements (FTAs) surged. According to the World Trade Organization (WTO) Regional Trade Agreements database, all FTAs that came into force in 2018 and 2019 involved Asian economies (Figure 2.16). This was a huge jump compared with the 38% share of Asian FTAs in 2017. Between August 2019 and October 2020, nine FTAs entered into force. These included the (i) Indonesia–Chile FTA (10 August 2019); (ii) Republic of Korea–Central America (1 November 2019); (iii) Singapore–EU FTA (21 November 2019); (iv) Japan–US FTA (1 January 2020) (v) Australia–Hong Kong, China FTA (17 January 2020); (vi) Australia–Peru FTA (11 February 2020); (vii) PRC–US Economic and Trade Agreement (14 February 2020); (viii) Australia–Indonesia Comprehensive Economic Partnership Agreement (5 July 2020); and (ix) Viet Nam–EU FTA (1 August 2020).

During that time, several FTAs were signed or concluded negotiations. The Republic of Korea–United Kingdom FTA, Indonesia–Mozambique Preferential Trade Agreement (PTA), and Cambodia–PRC FTA were signed, while five FTAs concluded negotiations: (i) Indonesia–Republic of Korea FTA; (ii) Republic of Korea–Israel FTA; (iii) Hong Kong, China–Maldives FTA; (iv) the Regional Comprehensive Economic Partnership Agreement (RCEP); and (v) Bangladesh–Bhutan Preferential Trade Agreement. The accession of Mongolia to the Asia-Pacific Trade Agreement (APTA) on 30 September 2020 was the first expansion of APTA after the accession of the PRC in 2001, a milestone in the progress of APTA toward becoming a modern regional agreement.

Several key trends continue. The region's push for stronger trade ties and greater market access to non-Asian economies was largely unhampered by the ongoing COVID-19 pandemic. While extraregional FTAs dominate Asia's FTA landscape, the region continues to strengthen intraregional trade ties.

FTA negotiations continued despite the imposition of travel restrictions and physical distancing due to the COVID-19 pandemic. In a videoconference in June 2020, Bangladesh and Bhutan concluded negotiations for a preferential trade agreement that aims to liberalize trade in 100 products from Bangladesh and 34 products from Bhutan. The PRC and Cambodia concluded "virtual" trade talks in July 2020, just 6 months after negotiations were launched in January. Several FTAs were also launched, including an Australia–UK FTA and Cambodia–Republic of Korea FTA.

Regional Comprehensive Economic Partnership[14]

After 8 years of negotiations, RCEP was signed on 15 November 2020. RCEP unifies existing FTAs between the Association of Southeast Asian Nations (ASEAN)[15] and existing partners, the so-called "+ 3 economies"—Japan, the PRC, and the Republic of Korea—and Australia and New Zealand (Figure 2.17). Together, these economies account for about 29% ($25.8 trillion) of global gross domestic product (GDP), 30% (2.3 billion) of the world's population, and 25% ($12.7 trillion) of global trade in goods and services.[16]

Figure 2.17: Regional Trade Groupings Involving ASEAN+3

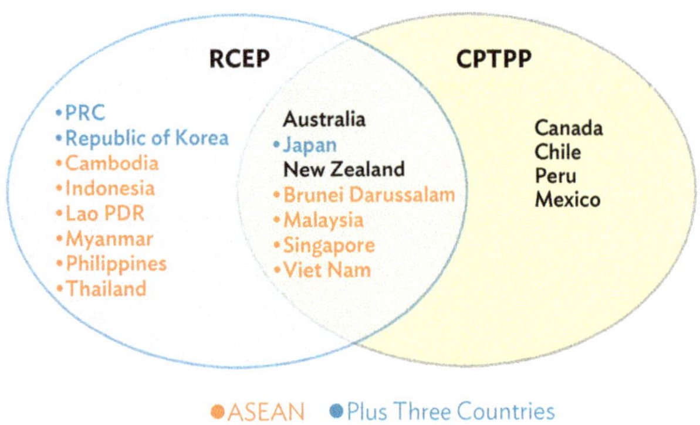

ASEAN = Association of Southeast Asian Nations (includes Brunei Darussalam, Cambodia, Indonesia, the Lao PDR, Malaysia, Myanmar, the Philippines, Singapore, Thailand, and Viet Nam); ASEAN+3 = ASEAN plus Japan, the People's Republic of China and the Republic of Korea; CPTPP = Comprehensive and Progressive Agreement for Trans-Pacific Partnership; Lao PDR = Lao People's Democratic Republic; PRC = People's Republic of China; RCEP = Regional Comprehensive Economic Partnership.

Source: Asian Development Bank.

RCEP will be the world's largest FTA measured by GDP, bigger than the Comprehensive and Progressive Agreement for Trans-Pacific Partnership (CPTPP), the EU, the MERCOSUR trade bloc in South America, and the United States–Mexico–Canada Free Trade Agreement. RCEP is the PRC's first multilateral agreement, the first FTA between the PRC and Japan, and Japan and the Republic of Korea. As the region's economies continue to recover from the unprecedented economic turmoil caused by the COVID-19 pandemic, RCEP is expected to boost growth by ensuring markets remain open and regional supply chains function.

RCEP will enter into force once ratified by at least six ASEAN economies and three non-ASEAN signatories, a process that will take months to start and years to complete. It is open for accession by any economy 18 months after entry into force. India, as an original negotiating state, is exempted from this rule; it can immediately rejoin once the agreement enters into force.

Rules of Origin and Regional Value Chains

One of RCEP's key features is a commitment to common rules of origin for all goods traded (Box 2.1). This means a product that meets RCEP originating criteria is subject to the same rules across all 15 member economies. RCEP's common rules of origin could foster contemporary production processes and trade logistics arrangements. The ease of movement of goods across the region through RCEP members and the use of regional distribution hubs will be enhanced (DFAT 2020).

Following usual practice, the RCEP rules of origin chapter lists the minimal operations and processes considered insufficient to confer originating status on goods using non-originating materials. If a good does not satisfy a change in the tariff classification rule in the annex on product-specific rules, the chapter lays down certain de minimis rules through which the good could still acquire originating status (ASEAN Secretariat 2020).

14 This section draws from Kang et al. (2020).

15 ASEAN includes Brunei Darussalam, Cambodia, Indonesia, the Lao People's Democratic Republic, Malaysia, Myanmar, the Philippines, Singapore, Thailand, and Viet Nam.

16 Based on 2019 data for GDP and population, and 2018 for trade in goods and services. Source: ADB staff calculations using data from World Bank. World Development Indicators. https://databank.worldbank.org/source/world-development-indicators (accessed December 2020).

Box 2.1: Regional Comprehensive Economic Partnership Rules of Origin

Rules of origin for the Regional Comprehensive Economic Partnership (RCEP) will bring under one umbrella countries that until now have had diverse sets of rules. Given the nature of the free trade agreements (FTAs), each RCEP country uses different sets of rules of origin enshrined in its own FTAs with other countries. In other words, not only does the Association of Southeast Asian Nations (ASEAN) apply different rules of origin with each of its dialogue partners, but Australia, Japan, the People's Republic of China (PRC), the Republic of Korea, and New Zealand also rely on diverse sets of rules of origin to trade with FTA partners. While this network of FTAs will continue, RCEP is the first to apply a common trade platform on rules of origin among members.

Thus, the potential to unravel the "spaghetti bowl" of rules governing origin in existing FTAs is among RCEP's key achievements. The agreement does this by expanding the geographic scope of cumulation due to its wider membership. This allows the treatment of intermediate products and inputs from *all participating countries*—including the PRC, Japan, and the Republic of Korea—as originating for defining the origin of the final goods regionally exported.

Empirical research finds that less restrictive cumulation systems in rules of origin (such as diagonal or full cumulation) promote sharing of the production value chain and expand trade in the cumulation zone, which generates greater trade gains than in more restrictive systems such as bilateral cumulation, as explained by Kim, Park, and Park (2013), and Hayakawa (2014). Yet, whereas RCEP provides for diagonal/regional cumulation (paragraph 1 of Article 3.4 of the RCEP Chapter 3), allowance of full cumulation will be negotiated upon RCEP's entry into force (paragraph 2 of Article 3.4 of Chapter 3). Under full cumulation, all operations carried out in the RCEP region are considered in determining whether the origin criterion is fulfilled. In contrast, under diagonal cumulation, only inputs that have already acquired originating status (fulfilled the origin criterion) in the RCEP region can be considered for cumulation purposes when used in further manufacturing processes (World Customs Organization 2017).

RCEP has embraced the concepts of product-specific rules of origin (PSROs) and regional value chain in the same spirit as other trading agreements.[a] Accordingly, goods are recognized as originating in RCEP if they meet product-specific rules of origin listed in the agreement's Annex 3(a). The main criteria used in the annex in determining rules of origin for a product are the regional value content and change of tariff classification (CTC). Depending on the PSROs contained in Annex 3(a), the criteria could be a CTC or an alternative between an regional value chain and a CTC. The formula for regional value content allows as much as 60% of the materials used in production of a good to be non-originating (materials from outside RCEP) and, due to diagonal cumulation, all materials[b] originating in RCEP will not be counted against this threshold. The formula for determining regional value chain is similar to that used in the ASEAN Trade in Goods Agreement, but under RCEP materials from the PRC, Japan, and the Republic of Korea will no longer be counted as non-originating (against the threshold of 60%), making it easier for members to meet the agreement's PSROs.

Given its wider geographic coverage, the possibility for cumulation within RCEP holds the potential to foster significant regional integration and value-chain creation by providing strong incentives to source intermediates within the RCEP region. Yet, turning potential success into reality depends on the timing of tariff phase-outs and, most importantly, the nature of administrative requirements related to origin, including certification, direct consignment, third-country invoicing, and how back-to-back certificates will be handled.

[a] The Comprehensive and Progressive Agreement for Trans-Pacific Partnership and ASEAN Trade in Goods Agreement.

[b] This only refers to materials originating in RCEP (diagonal cumulation), not to the working or processing operations in other RCEP countries (full cumulation).

Source: Kang et al. (2020).

Economic Impact of the RCEP Agreement

The major regional trade groupings involving ASEAN economies are RCEP and the CPTPP. While both are mega trade deals, their breadth and depth are different. Overall, the degree of liberalization within RCEP is not as deep as in the CPTPP, and the coverage is less comprehensive. However, in terms of economic size, RCEP is much bigger. As mentioned, the 15 nations in RCEP account for 29% of global GDP, 25% of global trade, and a population of 2.3 billion, while the 11 nations in CPTPP account for 13% of global GDP, 14% of global trade, and a population of 507.7 million.[17] Further, RCEP is expected to spur renewed momentum for intraregional trade and strengthen value chains among the +3 countries, as well as between them and other members. While RCEP is the first FTA covering the PRC, Japan, and the Republic of Korea at the same time, it is also the first to include two of the world's three largest economies. Unlike the CPTPP, RCEP does not include provisions to harmonize regulatory standards on the environment or labor markets.

Petri and Plummer (2020) estimated economic gains for the global economy from the combination of the CPTPP and RCEP using a computable general equilibrium model. In a business-as-usual scenario which assumed a return to pre-trade warpath, they added the CPTPP and RCEP agreements in sequence, estimating their respective incremental effects. The CPTPP is estimated to increase world real income by $147 billion by 2030 with RCEP adding $186 billion. The potential benefits from these two mega-regional trade agreements for Asia (including nonmembers) far exceed gains the agreements are expected to generate for the rest of the world (Figure 2.18).

RCEP members are projected to gain $174 billion in real income by 2030, equivalent to 0.4% of members' aggregate GDP. The +3 countries will benefit the most, with likely gains of $85 billion for the PRC, $48 billion for Japan, and $23 billion for the Republic of Korea. Other significant RCEP gains will accrue to Indonesia, Malaysia, Thailand, and Viet Nam. RCEP will also create sizable new trade among the +3 countries. ASEAN countries'

Figure 2.18: Potential Benefits of Regional Trade Agreements—Real Income Increases in 2030 ($ billion)

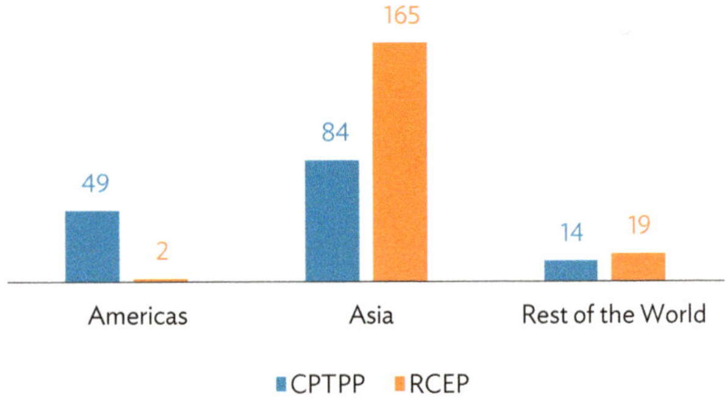

CPTPP = Comprehensive and Progressive Agreement for Trans-Pacific Partnership; RCEP = Regional Comprehensive Economic Partnership.

Notes: Estimates include income effects to non-members of CPTPP and RCEP. Asia includes Oceania (Australia and New Zealand), following ADB definition. Americas and the rest of the world are based on Petri and Plummer (2020).

Source: Petri and Plummer (2020).

FTAs with non-ASEAN member economies precede RCEP, and ASEAN's already-significant economic integration means that any marginal benefit RCEP creates for trade among them would be limited.

Traditional economic modeling exercises forecast that RCEP members, particularly the +3 countries, will gain the most. The largest gains will be due to their sheer economic size and comparative advantage in higher-end, richer value-added segments of industrial production. However, other economies also gain significantly from larger regional trade, stronger regional value-chain linkages, and the opening of more opportunities for foreign investment. As well as reaping benefits from deeper regional economic integration, members could take the regional trading bloc as a springboard to deepen economic reforms and improve industrial competitiveness. These dynamic gains, difficult to capture through economic modeling, more often than not far exceed the numerical economic gains forecast (Kang 2020).

As more detailed information about country and sectoral level market access and tariff concessions is released, further analyses and assessments of RCEP's economic impact are expected to become available in the coming months.

17 Based on 2019 data for GDP and population, and 2018 for trade in goods and services. Source: ADB staff calculations using data from World Bank. World Development Indicators. https://databank.worldbank.org/source/world-development-indicators (accessed December 2020).

The number of nontariff measures imposed on Asia increased significantly over the years, even before the onset of the COVID-19 pandemic (Figure 2.19).

As of 24 August 2020, Asia enacted 36.4% of COVID-19-related trade measures. Some 45.3% of these liberalize trade, while 54.7% are trade restrictive. India leads the region with the greatest number of COVID-19-related trade measures, reflecting its rising number of COVID-19 cases (Figure 2.20). Meanwhile, 63.67% of COVID-19-related trade measures were imposed by non-Asian economies. More than half of these (51.71%) are trade restrictive while 48.29% are trade liberalizing. Outside Asia, Brazil imposes the highest number of COVID-19-related trade measures, given the South American country's recent attempt to contain the rise of COVID-19 cases (Figure 2.21).

Figure 2.19: Number of Nontariff Measures Imposed on Asia

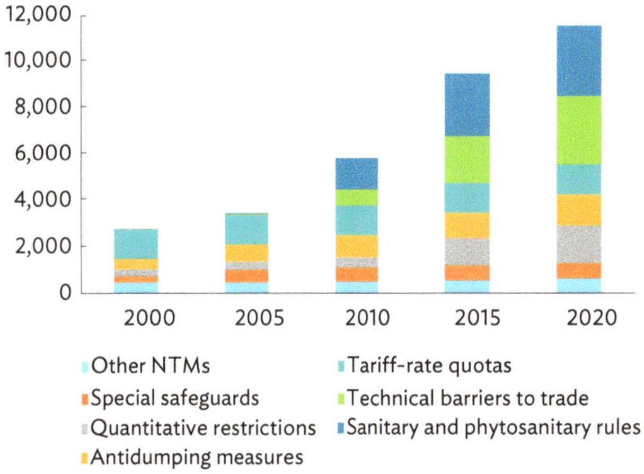

NTM = nontariff measure.

Note: Data cover NTMs in force until December 2020.

Source: ADB calculations using data from World Trade Organization. Integrated Trade Intelligence Portal. https://www.wto.org/english/res_e/statis_e/itip_e.htm (accessed September 2020).

Figure 2.20: Number of COVID-19-Related Measures Imposed by Asia, by Effect on Trade (as of 24 August 2020)

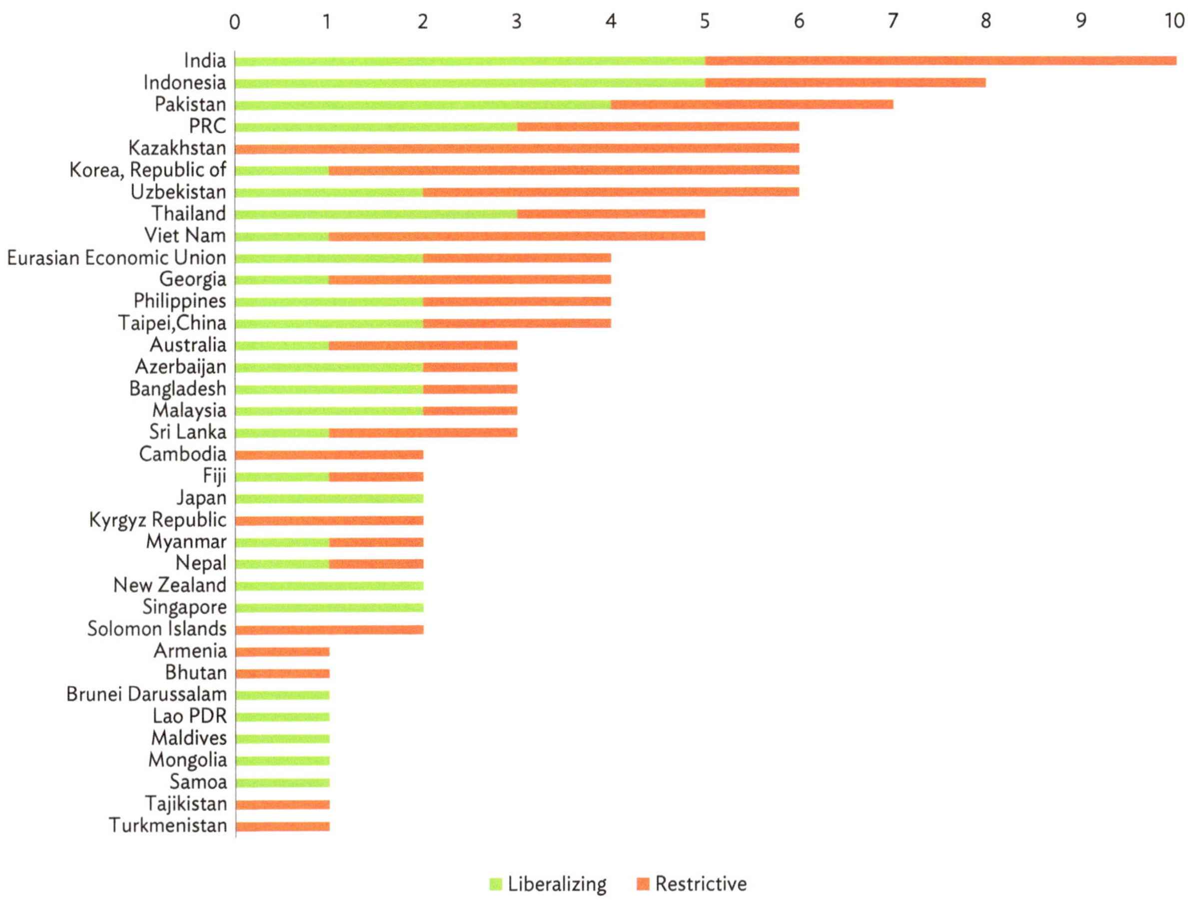

COVID-19 = coronavirus disease, Lao PDR = Lao People's Democratic Republic, PRC = People's Republic of China.

Source: ADB calculations using data from International Trade Centre. https://www.intracen.org (accessed August 2020).

Figure 2.21: Number of COVID-19-Related Measures Imposed by Non-Asian Economies, by Effect on Trade
(as of 24 August 2020)

COVID-19 = coronavirus disease.

Source: ADB calculations using data from International Trade Centre. https://www.intracen.org (accessed August 2020).

Both Asian and non-Asian economies enacted the highest number of COVID-19-related trade measures in March 2020 or at the same period the World Health Organization officially declared COVID-19 a pandemic—and numerous economies worldwide started implementing lockdowns or stay-at-home orders (Figure 2.22). More than 50% of COVID-19-related trade measures enacted are restrictive. The number of COVID-19-related measures enacted began to slow in April 2020 until July 2020.

Medical goods had the highest number of COVID-19-related trade measures (Figure 2.23). About 53% were liberalizing while 47% were trade restrictive. For the rest of the world, the majority of COVID-19-related trade measures imposed on medical goods are trade restrictive. For both Asia and non-Asian economies, agricultural products had the largest share of trade restrictive COVID-19 measures.

Tariff reductions constitute 34.2% of COVID-19-related trade measures enacted in Asia while export prohibition was 31.6%. The same trend is seen in non-Asian economies, with tariff reductions representing 33.7% while export prohibition 26.3%. This shows that both Asia and non-Asian economies relied more on tariff reductions to ensure adequate access to essential goods (Figure 2.24).

Figure 2.22: 2020 Timeline of COVID-19-Related Trade Measures, by Effect on Trade (as of 24 August 2020)

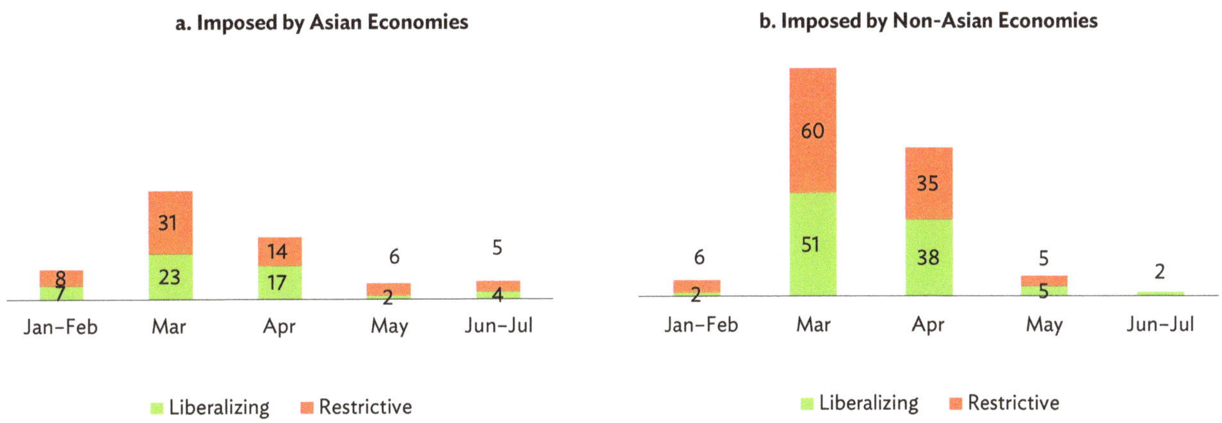

COVID-19 = coronavirus disease.

Source: ADB calculations using data from International Trade Centre. https://www.intracen.org (accessed August 2020).

Figure 2.23: Products Affected by COVID-19-Related Trade Measures, by Effect on Trade (as of 24 August 2020)

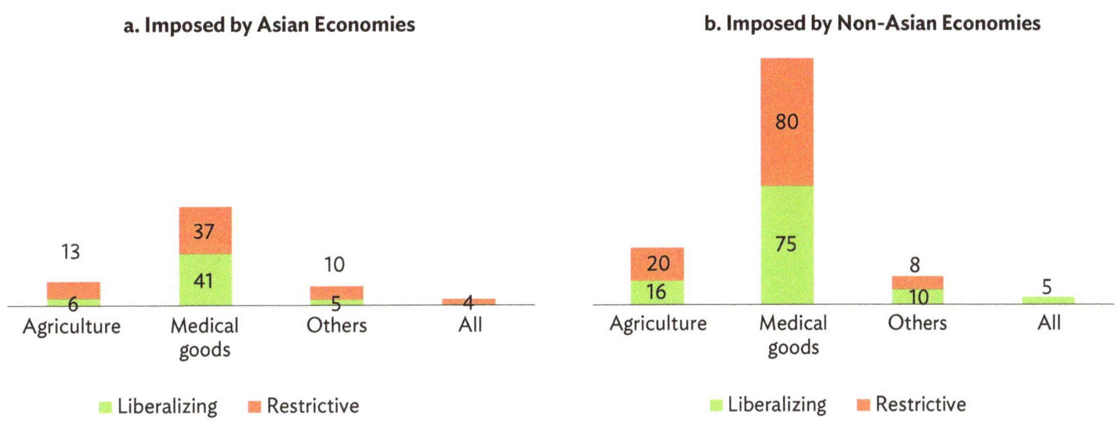

COVID-19 = coronavirus disease.

Source: ADB calculations using data from International Trade Centre. https://www.intracen.org (accessed August 2020).

Figure 2.24: Type of Measures Imposed, by Effect on Trade (as of 24 August 2020)

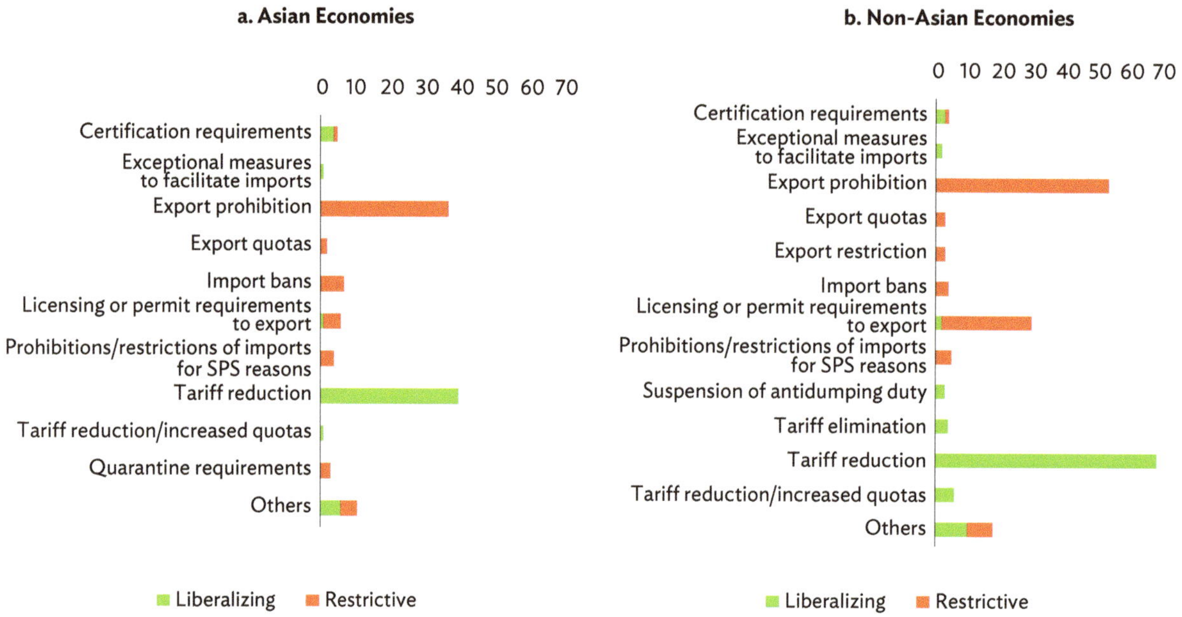

SPS = sanitary and phytosanitary.

Source: ADB calculations using data from International Trade Centre. https://www.intracen.org (accessed August 2020).

Asian economies largely resorted to export prohibition measures to ensure a stable supply of agricultural products (Figure 2.25). The region also used a combination of tariff reduction and export prohibition to ensure adequate access to, and supplies of, medical goods—including protective equipment (such as masks, gloves, and garments), medical equipment (like ventilators), and pharmaceuticals. Non-Asian economies also used both export prohibition and tariff reduction measures to achieve food security during the pandemic (Figure 2.26). The rest of the world also took a trade restrictive approach to meet domestic supply needs for medical goods by implementing many measures prohibiting exports and export licensing or permit requirements.

An agreement is needed to institutionalize international cooperation in securing the trade of essential goods during a pandemic should the world want to ensure undisrupted supplies of key products.

In general, Article XI of the General Agreement on Tariffs and Trade (GATT) 1994 provides the regulatory framework on prohibitions on quantitative restrictions such as export/import bans and export quotas. However, it allows members to use them temporarily to prevent or relieve critical shortages of foodstuff or other essential products. The WTO Agreement on Agriculture requires that members imposing temporary restrictions on foodstuff should accord due consideration to the food security needs of others. WTO rules also contain more general exceptions, which could be used to justify restrictions if they are not a means of arbitrary or unjustifiable discrimination between countries, or a disguised restriction on international trade.

FTAs are another means to regulate quantitative restrictions. They provide a regulatory framework that specifically addresses trading concerns of FTA partners better than the multilateral WTO framework. Fewer economies are involved in FTA negotiations compared with multilateral agreements, creating the possibility for stronger commitments, and devising alternate ways to improve the regulation of quantitative restrictions. Also, recent FTAs respond better to the challenges of a rapidly evolving international trade landscape than WTO laws, which came into force more than 25 years ago.

Figure 2.25: Type of Measures Imposed by Asia, by Product Group and Effect on Trade (as of August 2020)

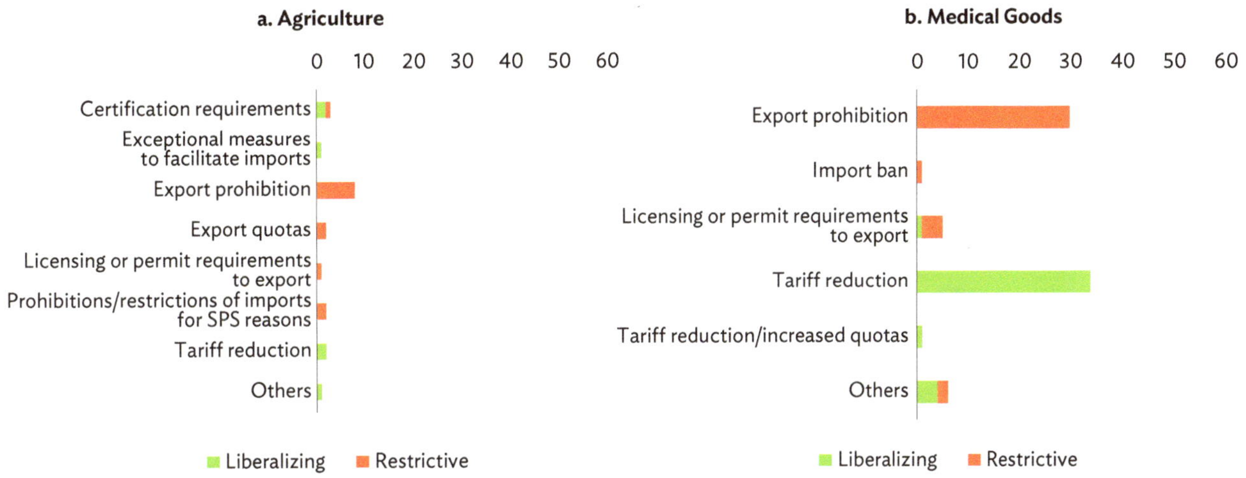

SPS = sanitary and phytosanitary.

Source: ADB calculations using data from International Trade Centre. https://www.intracen.org (accessed August 2020).

Figure 2.26: Type of Measures Imposed by Non-Asia, by Product Group and Effect on Trade (as of August 2020)

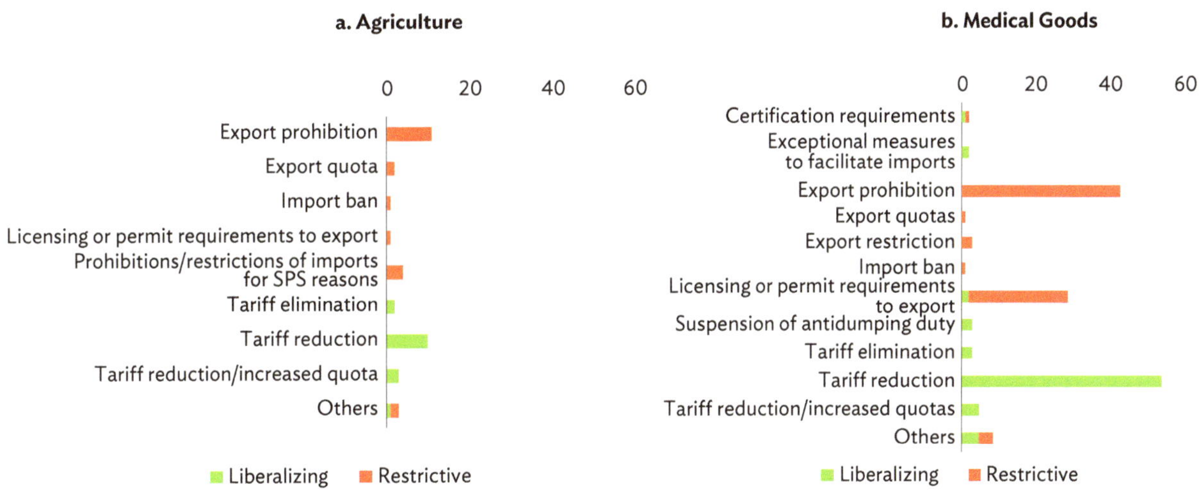

SPS = sanitary and phytosanitary.

Source: ADB calculations using data from International Trade Centre. https://www.intracen.org (accessed August 2020).

An analysis of Asian FTAs in force (with available full texts) shows that 128 of the 135 FTAs (94.8%) contain provisions on quantitative restrictions. However, these provisions are largely heterogeneous and can be grouped into four broad strands (Figure 2.27). First, 41 Asian FTAs (30.4%) contain provisions on quantitative restrictions without reference to WTO laws. Second, stipulations on quantitative restrictions in 46 Asian FTAs (34.1%) explicitly mention relevant WTO laws and agreements without the expression mutatis mutandis. Third, nine Asian FTAs (6.7%) incorporate Article XI based on mutatis mutandis with the last category including other commitments in addition to incorporating Article XI using mutatis mutandis or mutatis mutandis plus provisions (32 Asian FTAs or 23.7%). The plus provisions include stipulations on advance notification, transparency, and consultation, among others.

Figure 2.27: Types of Provisions on Quantitative Restrictions in Asian FTAs (%)

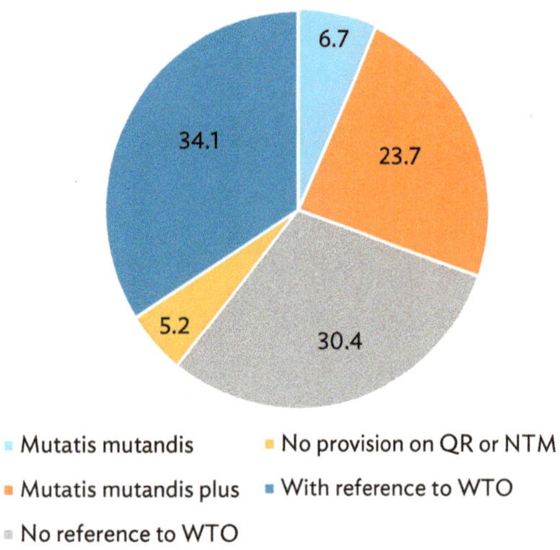

FTA = free trade agreement, NTM = nontariff measure, QR = quantitative restriction, WTO = World Trade Organization.

Note: Mutatis mutandis incorporates relevant WTO laws on quantitative restrictions into the FTA while mutatis mutandis plus provisions include other commitments beyond WTO obligations such as advance notification, transparency, consultation, among others.

Source: ADB calculations using official FTA full texts.

Overall, there is no norm governing the provisions on quantitative restrictions in Asian FTAs. However, this has not always been the case. Of the 32 FTAs in force up to 2000, 26 (or 81.3%) contain provisions on quantitative restrictions without referencing WTO laws—this implies it was the norm prior to 2000 (Figure 2.28). Almost the same number of extraregional and intraregional FTAs contains this type of provision (Figure 2.29). The first decade of the 21st century saw a paradigm shift with the majority of Asian FTA provisions on quantitative restrictions referencing WTO laws. This was driven by a sudden increase in the number of intraregional Asian FTAs with this type of provision. Meanwhile, extraregional FTAs had started incorporating Article XI based on mutatis mutandis together with other commitments beyond WTO obligations, marking the divergence between extra-regional and intraregional Asian FTAs with respect to provisions on quantitative restrictions.

The last decade saw a surge in FTAs containing mutatis mutandis expressions. Some 29 of 46 Asian FTAs (63%) that came into force since 2010 invoke Article XI based on mutatis mutandis (Figure 2.28). Of these, 21 include commitments beyond WTO obligations. This trend is due to a move by extraregional Asian FTAs toward greater harmonization of FTA provisions on quantitative restrictions with WTO law (Figure 2.29). This leads to several conclusions. The evolution of provisions on quantitative restrictions in Asian FTAs shows that the use of Article XI based on mutatis mutandis is a new phenomenon which only gained traction in the last 10 years. This reflects economies' desire to make their FTAs consistent with existing multilateral trade agreements, increasing the institutional relationship with the WTO.

The widespread use of quantitative restrictions as a policy response to secure adequate access to—and supply of—essential goods during the COVID-19 pandemic shows that these measures are under-regulated in WTO law. As shown above, COVID-19-related quantitative restrictions take the form of export restrictions, export licenses, or export quotas. Although Article XI of the GATT stipulates a general prohibition of quantitative export restrictions to trade, the parameters of valid exceptions are not clearly defined—with no

Figure 2.28: Evolution of Provisions on Quantitative Restrictions in Asian FTAs

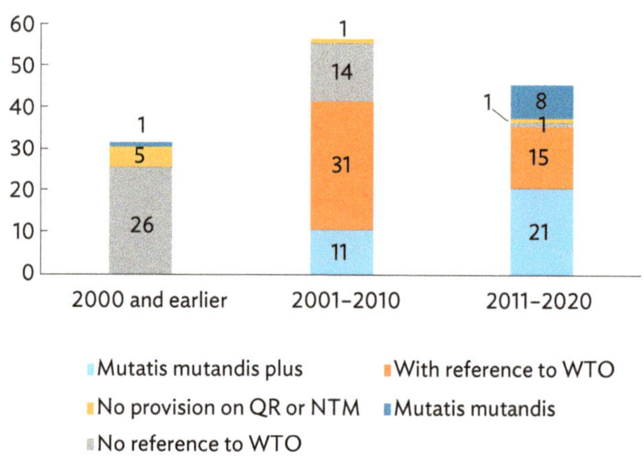

FTA = free trade agreement, NTM = nontariff measure, QR = quantitative restriction, WTO = World Trade Organization.

Note: Mutatis mutandis incorporates relevant WTO laws on quantitative restrictions into the FTA while mutatis mutandis plus provisions include other commitments beyond WTO obligations such as advance notification, transparency, consultation, among others.

Source: ADB calculations using official FTA full texts.

Figure 2.29: Evolution of Provisions on Quantitative Restrictions in Asian FTAs, by Region

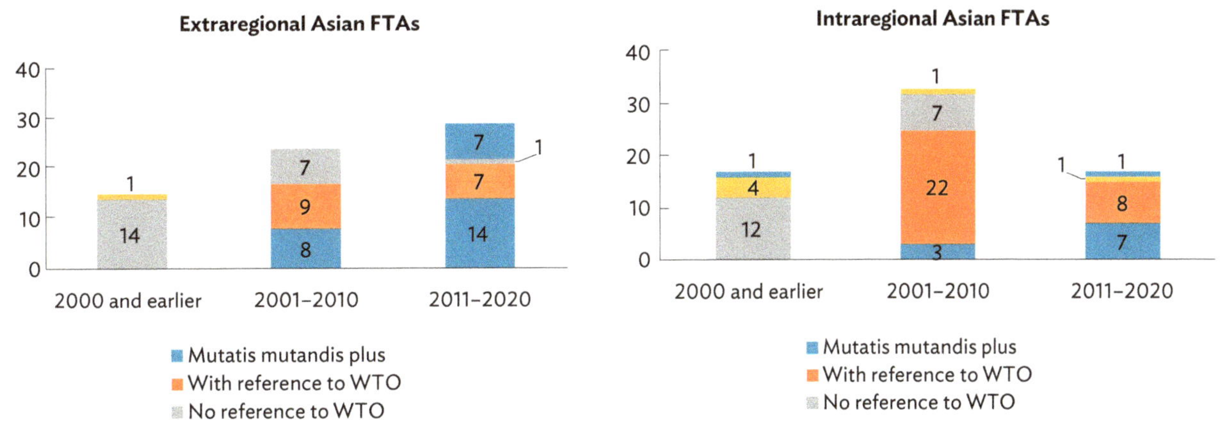

FTA = free trade agreement, WTO = World Trade Organization.

Note: Mutatis mutandis incorporates relevant WTO laws on quantitative restrictions into the FTA while mutatis mutandis plus provisions include other commitments beyond WTO obligations such as advance notification, transparency, consultation, among others.

Source: ADB calculations using official FTA full texts.

definitive WTO case law shedding light on this legal uncertainty. In effect, it remains unclear whether the COVID-19-related quantitative restrictions imposed are inconsistent with WTO law, which might lead to a rise in future trade disputes. While countries have explored other alternatives in improving WTO-based regimes in the context of FTAs, this has contributed to the heterogeneity of approaches in regulating quantitative restrictions.

A plurilateral agreement among like-minded economies to ensure free flow of essential products during a pandemic can help optimize any crisis response. Toward this end, several economies—such as Australia, Brunei Darussalam, Canada, Chile, the Lao PDR, Myanmar, New Zealand, Singapore, and Uruguay—recently signed a Joint Ministerial Statement on Supply Chain Connectivity (JMS). The JMS commits signatories to (i) refrain from imposing export restrictions, tariffs, and nontariff barriers; (ii) remove existing trade restrictive measures on essential goods; and (iii) ensure that critical infrastructure remains open. Since its issuance, New Zealand and Singapore began work on a Declaration on Trade in Essential Goods for Combating the COVID-19 Pandemic. The declaration, which was launched on 15 April 2020, contains commitments to be unilaterally undertaken on a most-favored nation (MFN) basis by New Zealand and Singapore for a list of specified essential goods.

Further, a plurilateral agreement ensuring the free flow of essential goods in times of pandemics or natural disasters could be conceived following the modality of the WTO Information Technology Agreement (Box 2.2). An agreement could also create a homogenous regulatory framework on quantitative restrictions which boosts transparency in applying these measures, strengthening enforcement of existing obligations, and upgrading monitoring mechanisms. It can also include stipulations that clearly define the scope of exception contained in Article XI:2(a) GATT, requiring specific temporal limits and defining parameters for the concept of "essential goods" to achieve an effective solution that will prevent future trade conflicts on the use of quantitative restrictions.

Box 2.2: World Trade Organization Information Technology Agreement

The Information Technology Agreement (ITA) was originally signed on 13 December 1996 by 29 participants at the Singapore Ministerial Conference. It went into effect on 13 March 1997. The ITA is a seminal plurilateral tariff liberalization arrangement negotiated by the World Trade Organization (WTO) after its establishment in 1995. The signatories commit to eliminate tariffs and binding customs duties at zero for all products specified in the Agreement. The ITA covers 97% of world trade in information technology products—such as computers, telecommunication equipment, semiconductors, semiconductor manufacturing and testing equipment, software, scientific instruments, as well as most of the parts and accessories of these products. An expansion of the agreement was concluded by over 50 members at the Nairobi Ministerial Conference in December 2015. The ITA includes an additional 201 products valued at over $1.3 trillion per year. Moreover, the inclusion of ITA concessions in the signatories' WTO schedules of concessions means that tariff eliminations are implemented on a most-favored nation (MFN) basis. This creates a positive spillover effect because even non-ITA signatories can benefit from the trade opportunities generated by ITA tariff elimination.

In the context of value chain integration, ITA-induced tariff reductions simultaneously affect both imports and exports, creating opportunities for ITA signatories to integrate into global value chains (Henn and Gnutzmann-Mkrtchyan 2015). Variations on the ITA impact across economies are driven by differences in reasons for joining the ITA, indicating to a certain extent the initial state of a country's ITA sector. Positions of ITA members along vertically fragmented information and communication technology (ICT) value chains, whether upstream (exporting intermediates) or downstream (importing intermediates/exporting final goods), also help explain why the impact of ITA varies across economies.

The ITA has also shifted trade patterns and market shares of its members (Henn and Gnutzmann-Mkrtchyan 2015). The rise of Asian economies led by the People's Republic of China, and the growing importance of developing economies in ICT global value chains have altered the ITA trade landscape. Several economies with disparate trade and economic backgrounds acceded to the ITA after 1997. This cohort of "late signatories" is grouped into "passive" or "active" signatories. Passive signatories are economies with less developed ITA sector that joined after 1997, largely motivated by policy objectives such as accession to the European Union, WTO, or other trade agreements. All non-passive signatories are grouped into "active" signatories (Henn and Gnutzmann-Mkrtchyan 2015).

Largely attributed to their ITA membership, passive signatories—mostly developing and emerging economies—saw a rapid expansion of global trade in ITA goods during 1996–2015, encroaching on the trade share of developed "active" signatories (box figure).

Overall, by helping lower the price of ITA goods through tariff reductions and elimination, the agreement has spurred the adoption and diffusion of key ICT goods—such as mobile phones, particularly in developing economies. While trade liberalization of ICT products can also come either unilaterally or through free trade agreements, legally binding, WTO-enforceable tariff concessions makes ITA product liberalization harder to reverse than if it were achieved outside the plurilateral agreement. This "commitment effect" creates a stable and predictable trading environment that draws multinational firms to enter and invest in ITA member economies, thereby enhancing their competitiveness and capacity to innovate.

World Market Shares in ITA Products by Type of Accession (%)

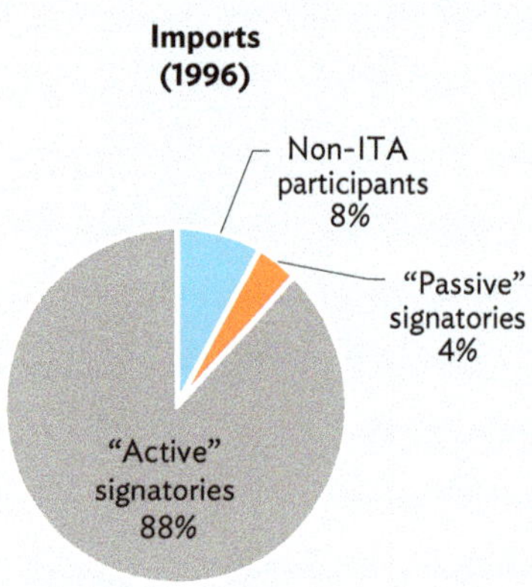

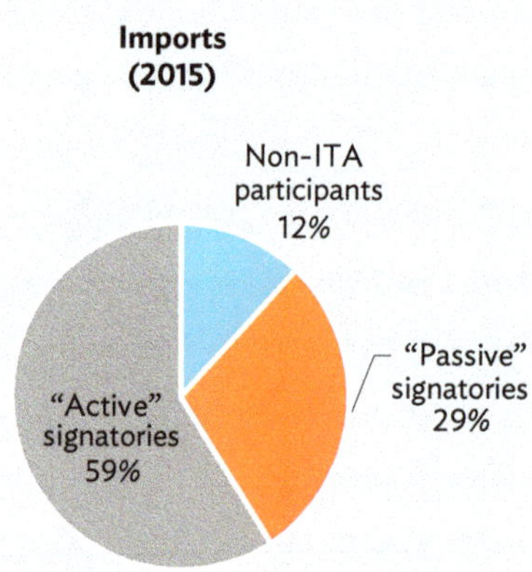

continued on next page

Box 2.2: World Trade Organization Information Technology Agreement *(continued)*

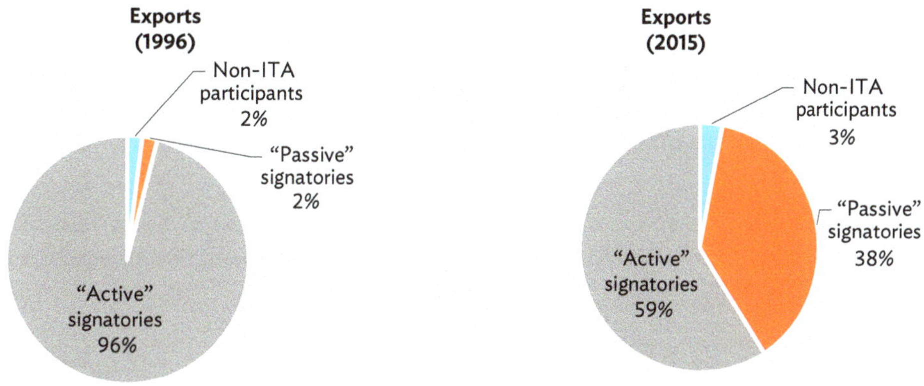

ITA = Information Technology Agreeement.

Notes: "Passive" signatories are economies that signed the ITA after it came into force in 1997 and motivated by an encompassing policy objective. "Active" signatories include ITA original members and/or driven by other considerations.

Source: WTO (2017).

Source: ADB staff based on Henn and Gnutzmann-Mkrtchyan (2015) and WTO (2017).

References

ASEAN Secretariat. 2020. *Summary of the Regional Comprehensive Economic Partnership Agreement.* https://asean.org/storage/2020/11/Summary-of-the-RCEP-Agreement.pdf.

Asian Development Bank (ADB). Asia Regional Integration Center FTA Database. https://aric.adb.org/fta (accessed July 2020).

———. Multi-Regional Input-Output Tables.

———. 2015. *Key Indicators for Asia and the Pacific 2015.* Manila.

———. 2019. Asian Economic Integration Report 2019/2020: Demographic Change, Productivity, and the Role of Technology. Manila.

———. 2020a. *Asian Development Outlook 2020 Supplement: Lockdown, Loosening, and Asia's Growth Prospects*. Manila.

———. 2020b. *Asian Development Outlook 2020 Update: Wellness in Worrying Times.* Manila.

CPB Netherlands Bureau for Economic Policy Analysis. World Trade Monitor. https://www.cpb.nl/en/data (accessed November 2020).

Department of Foreign Affairs and Trade, Australia (DFAT). 2020. *RCEP Outcomes: Goods. Fact Sheet.* 15 November. https://www.dfat.gov.au/sites/default/files/rcep-outcomes-goods.pdf.

Eddington, T. 2020. Brexit: All You Need to Know about the UK Leaving the EU. *BBC News Analyses.* 20 December. https://www.bbc.com/news/uk-politics-32810887.

Freights Baltic Index. https://fbx.freightos.com (accessed December 2020).

Hayakawa, K. 2014. Impact of Diagonal Cumulation Rule on FTA Utilization: Evidence from Bilateral and Multilateral FTAs between Japan and Thailand. *Journal of the Japanese and International Economies.* 32. pp. 1–16.

Henn, C. and A. Gnutzmann-Mkrtchyan. 2015. The Layers of the IT Agreement's Trade Impact. *WTO Working Paper.* ERSD-2015-01. Geneva: World Trade Organization.

International Monetary Fund. Direction of Trade Statistics. http://data.imf.org/DOT (accessed December 2020).

———. World Economic Outlook October 2020 Database. https://www.imf.org/en/Publications/WEO/weo-database/2020/October (accessed October 2020).

International Trade Centre. https://www.intracen.org (accessed August 2020).

Kang, J. W., P. Crivelli, M. C. Tayag, and D. Ramizo. 2020. Regional Economic Partnership: Overview and Economic Impact. *ADB Brief.* No. 164. December. Manila: ADB.

Kang, J. W. 2020. RCEP is a Gargantuan Trade Deal but Will Economies Be Able to Make the Most of It? *Asian Development Blog.* 20 November. https://blogs.adb.org/blog/rcep-gargantuan-trade-deal-will-economies-be-able-make-most-it.

Kim, S., I. Park, and S. Park. 2013. Trade-Creating Regime-wide Rules of Origin: A Quantitative Analysis. *Applied Economics Letters.* 20 (11). pp. 1056–61.

Li, X., B. Meng, and Z. Wang. 2019. Recent Patterns of Global Production and GVC Participation. Chapter 1 in WTO et al. *Global Value Chain Development Report 2019: Technological Innovation, Supply Chain Trade, and Workers in a Globalized World.* Geneva.

Organisation for Economic Co-operation and Development (OECD). Business confidence index indicator. doi: 10.1787/3092dc4f-en (accessed November 2020).

Petri, P. and M. Plummer. 2020. East Asia Decouples from the United States: Trade War, COVID-19, and East Asia's New Trade Blocs. *PIIE Working Paper*. June. Washington, DC: Peterson Institute for International Economics. https://www.piie.com/system/files/documents/wp20-9.pdf.

United Nations. Commodity Trade Database: AIS Weekly Port Calls. https://comtrade.un.org/data/monitor#AISPort (accessed November 2020).

Wang, Z., S. J. Wei, and K. Zhu. 2013. Quantifying International Production Sharing at the Bilateral and Sector Levels. *NBER Working Paper.* No. 19677. Cambridge, MA: National Bureau of Economic Research.

World Bank. World Development Indicators. https://databank.worldbank.org/source/world-development-indicators (accessed December 2020).

World Customs Organization. 2017. *Comparative Study on Preferential Rules of Origin*. Brussels. http://www.wcoomd.org/-/media/wco/public/global/pdf/topics/origin/instruments-and-tools/reference-material/170130-b_comparative-study-on-pref_roo_master-file_final-20_06_2017.pdf?db=web.

World Trade Organization (WTO). Integrated Trade Intelligence Portal. https://www.wto.org/english/res_e/statis_e/itip_e. htm (accessed September 2020).

———. Statistics Database. http://data.wto.org/en (accessed October 2020).

———. 2017. *20 Years of Information Technology Agreement*. Geneva.

———. 2020a. Trade Statistics and Outlook: Trade Set to Plunge as COVID-19 Pandemic Upends Global Economy. Press Release. No. 855. 8 April. https://www.wto.org/english/news_e/pres20_e/pr855_e.htm.

———. 2020b. Trade Statistics and Outlook: Trade Falls Steeply in First Half of 2020. Press Release. No. 858. 23 June. https://www.wto.org/english/news_e/pres20_e/pr858_e.htm.

———. 2020c. Trade Statistics and Outlook: Trade Shows Signs of Rebound from COVID-19, Recovery Still Uncertain. Press Release. No. 862. 6 October. https://www.wto.org/english/news_e/pres20_e/pr862_e.htm.

Annex 2a: Analytical Framework of GVC and RVC

A new framework for understanding global value chain (GVC) and regional value chain (RVC) participation is introduced here to better track Asia's progress in its global and regional trade linkages. The world's gross exports can be divided into two: (i) exports that cross borders once as final goods (represented by the blue area in Annex Figure 2a); and (ii) exports that go through two or more economies for further production (yellow area in Annex Figure 2a). World-to-world GVC is the share of the world's total GVC terms to its gross exports. Asia-to-world GVC is the share of Asia's total GVC terms to its gross exports. Asia-to-Asia gross RVC is the share of Asia's intraregional GVC terms to its intraregional gross exports, excluding all non-Asian third economies.[1] Asia-to-Asia net RVC is similar to gross RVC, except that its denominator, total intraregional exports, includes non-Asian third economies.

Annex Figure 2a: Analytical Framework of GVC and RVC

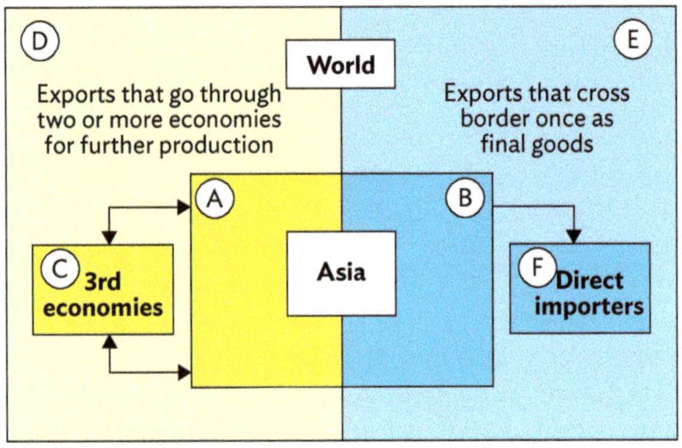

Participation Rates:

(1) World GVC $= \frac{A + C + D}{A + B + C + D + E + F}$

(2) Asia-to-World GVC $= \frac{A + C}{A + B + C + F}$

(3) Asia-to-Asia Gross RVC $= \frac{A}{A + B}$

(4) Asia-to-Asia Net RVC $= \frac{A}{A + B + C}$

GVC = global value chain, RVC = regional value chain.

Source: ADB (2019).

1 Third economies are those that indirectly participate in a GVC transaction. For example, Singapore exports intermediate goods used by the People's Republic of China (PRC) to produce and export final goods to Malaysia. From Singapore's point of view, the PRC is the direct partner, while Malaysia is the third economy.

Annex 2b: GVC Diversification—Backward Linkages

Under the diversification scenario, the exporter decides to increase its import of intermediate goods from its secondary sources, while it simultaneously decreases its imports from its top source. In this case, the exporter reduces its import of intermediate goods from its top source by 30% and then sources it instead from its top 2 and top 3 sources equally (Annex Figure 2b.1a). Going further upstream, the top sources of intermediate goods are interconnected with one another (Annex Figure 2b.1b). The top source indirectly supplies the exporter through the top 2 and top 3 sources (Annex Figure 2b.1c). Likewise, some of the intermediate goods exported by the top 2 and top 3 sources are used by the top source to produce supplies needed by the exporter (Annex Figure 2b.1d and Annex Figure 2b.1e). Aside from the top sources, which are affected by the exporter's diversification strategy, other economies which supply goods to those countries will be affected as well (Annex Figure 2b.1f).

Annex Figure 2b.1a: Direct Impact of Diversification to Backward Linkages

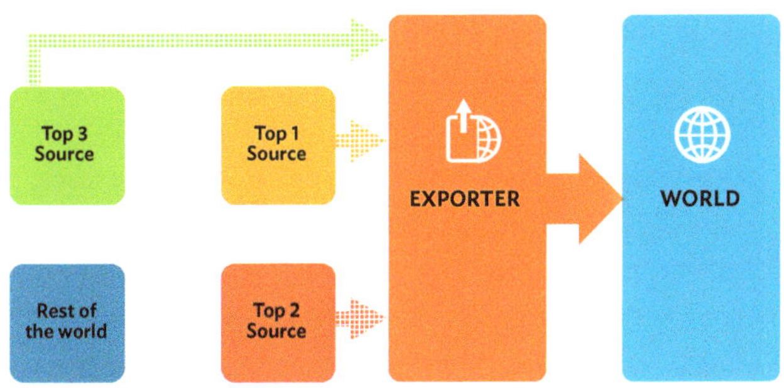

Annex Figure 2b.1b: Direct and Indirect Impact of Diversification to Backward Linkages

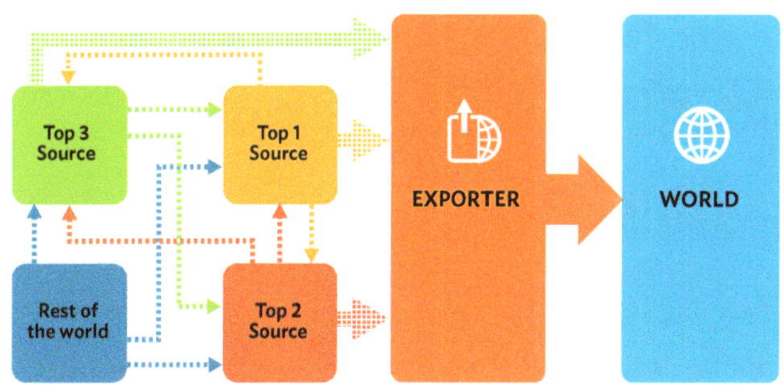

Annex Figure 2b.1c: Impact to Top Source

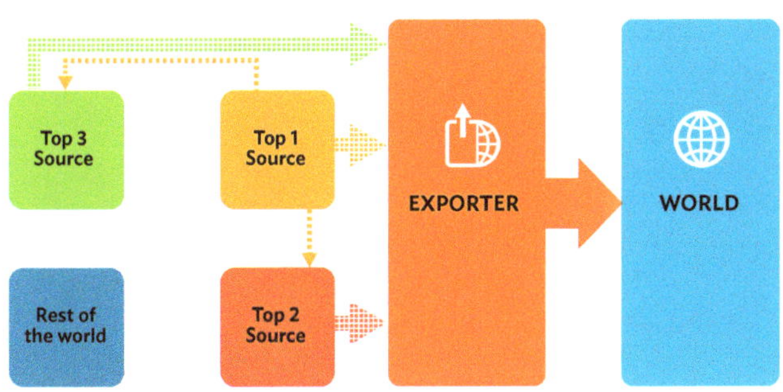

Annex Figure 2b.1d: Impact to Top 2 Source

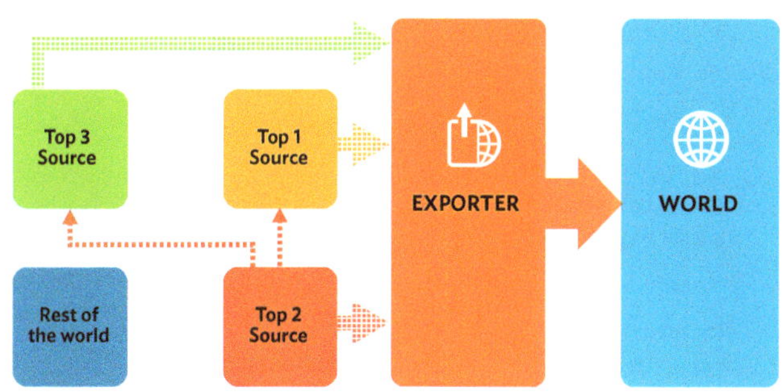

continued on next page

Figures continued

Annex Figure 2b.1e: Impact to Top 3 Source

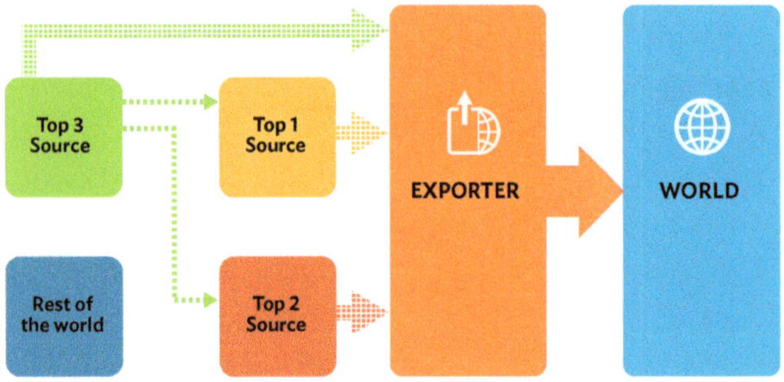

Annex Figure 2b.1f: Impact to the Rest of the World

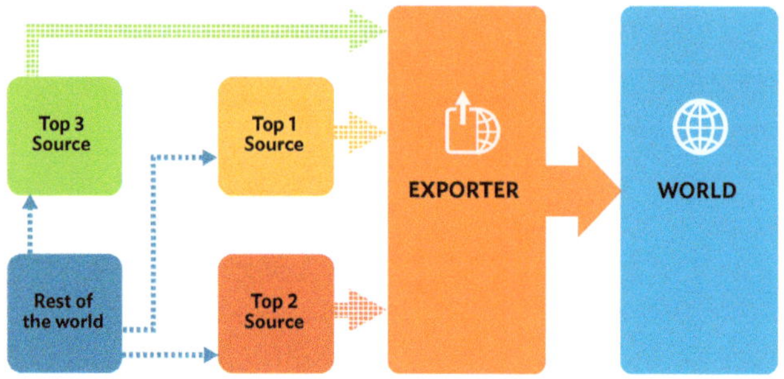

Notes: Indirect supply refers to the exported intermediate goods that goes through further processing by a middle country before reaching its destination. Direct supply refers to the exported intermediate goods which go straight to its destination.

Source: ADB staff.

When all economies decrease their dependency from their primary source by 30%, and then import intermediate goods from the next two sources, total trade for Asia gains by 1.2%, while total trade for the EU and North America declines.

This diversification scenario in backward linkages is applied on a global scale using the 62-country data set from the ADB Multi-Regional Input–Output Tables (MRIO) for 2019. The main contributor for Asia's increase in trade is East Asia, specifically Japan and the People's Republic of China (PRC). Japan sees increase in trade with Asia and Latin America, while the PRC sees increasing trade with the European Union (EU). The EU trade declines as economies decrease trading with their primary partners within their region and increase trade with Asia instead. North America also sees a decline as its primary partners in the EU and Latin America diversify to Asia as well. The world's total trade does not change as the magnitude of the decline in exports by primary sources is offset by the increase in exports from secondary sources (Annex Table 2b.1).

Annex Table 2b.1: Impact of Diversification on Backward Linkages (%)

Region	Impact on Exports		Impact on Imports	Impact on Total Trade
	Direct	Adjusted		
Asia and the Pacific	**1.23**	**1.17**	**1.29**	**1.23**
Central Asia	1.37	1.48	1.04	1.28
East Asia	1.75	1.65	1.84	1.74
South Asia	0.06	0.04	0.05	0.04
Southeast Asia	0.06	0.07	0.13	0.10
The Pacific and Oceania	1.28	1.37	1.28	1.33
European Union	**-0.41**	**-0.36**	**-0.34**	**-0.35**
Latin America	**0.79**	**0.66**	**0.79**	**0.73**
North America	**-4.37**	**-4.25**	**-3.90**	**-4.06**
Rest of the World	**0.98**	**0.94**	**0.94**	**0.94**
World	**0.00**	**0.00**	**0.00**	**0.00**

Notes: The direct impact on total exports includes only the top sources which were directly impacted by the exporter's diversification strategy. The adjusted impact on total exports includes all the economies which have contributed to the top sources' supply of intermediate goods to the exporter.

Sources: ADB calculations using data from ADB. Multi-Regional Input-Output Tables; and methodology by Wang, Wei, and Zhu (2013).

GVC Diversification—Forward Linkages

In this strategy, the exporter decreases its export of intermediate goods to its primary destination and exports those goods instead to its secondary destinations, the top 2 and top 3, equally (Annex Figure 2b.2a). This will create a ripple effect for the downstream production until it affects the final consumers (Annex Figure 2b.2b).

The decreasing supply of intermediate goods to the top destination will affect its exports (Annex Figure 2b.2c), as well as top 2 and 3's downstream production of exported goods (Annex Figure 2b.2d). Likewise, the increase of supply to the top 2 and top 3 destinations (Annex Figures 2b.2e and 2b.2g) may also increase the top destination's downstream production (Annex Figures 2b.2f and 2b.2h).

Annex Figure 2b.2a: Direct Impact of Diversification to Forward Linkages

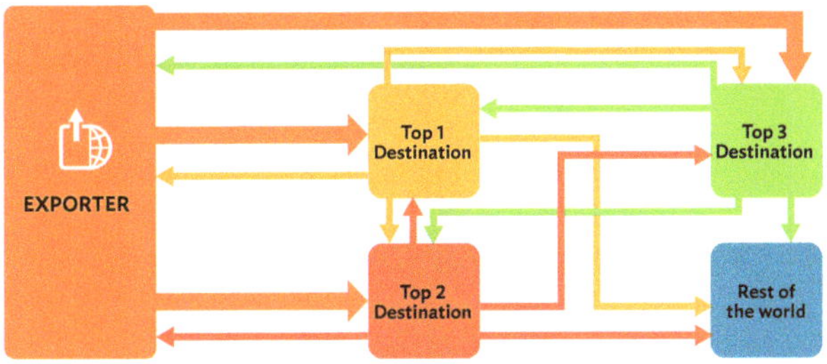

Annex Figure 2b.2b: Direct and Indirect Impact of Diversification to Forward Linkages

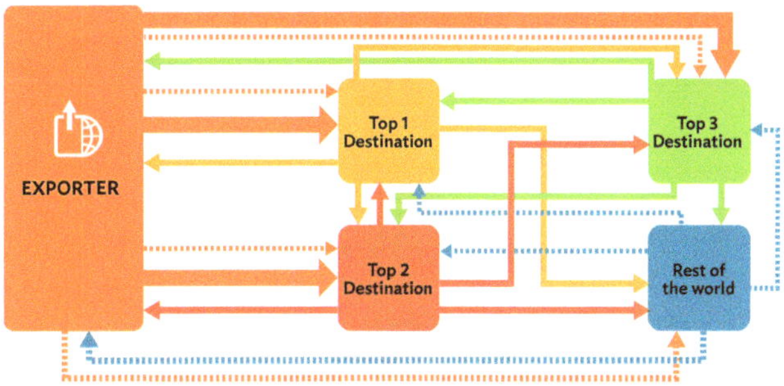

Annex Figure 2b.2c: Impact to Top Destination

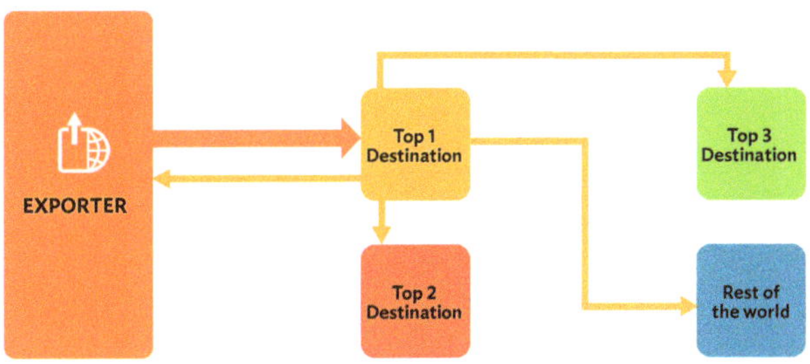

Annex Figure 2b.2d: Spillover of Impact to Top Destination

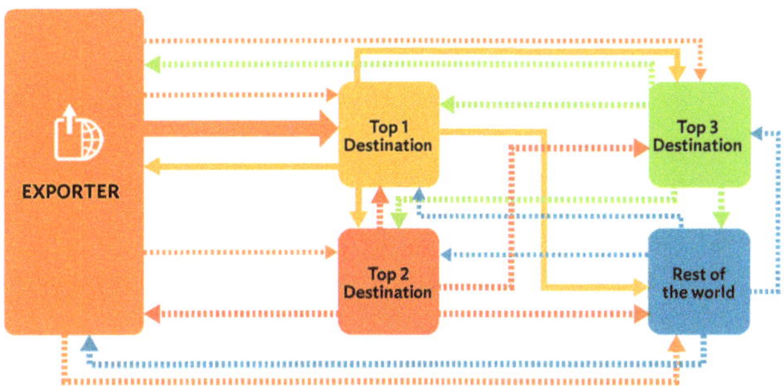

Annex Figure 2b.2e: Impact to Top 2 Destination

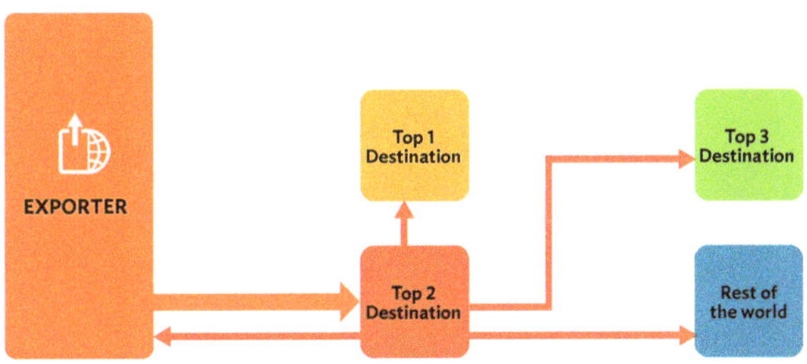

Annex Figure 2b.2f: Spillover of Impact to Top 2 Destination

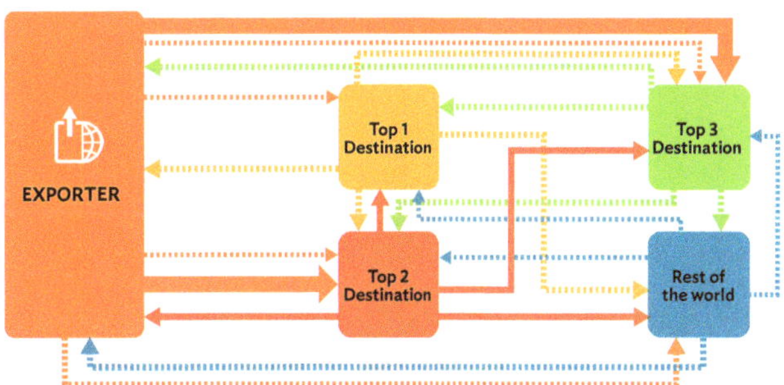

continued on next page

Figures continued

Annex Figure 2b.2g: Impact to Top 3 Destination

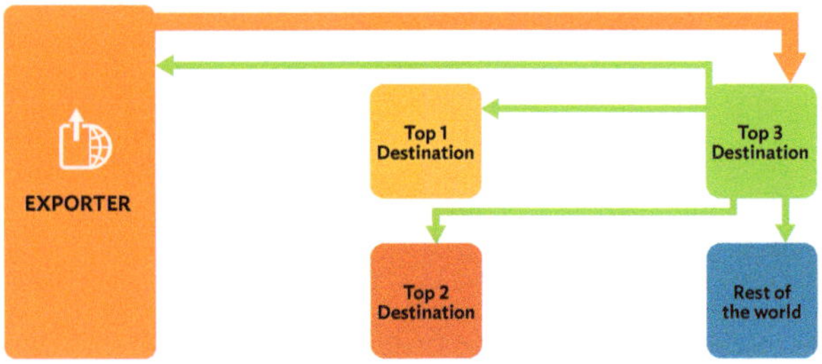

Annex Figure 2b.2h: Spillover of Impact to Top 3 Destination

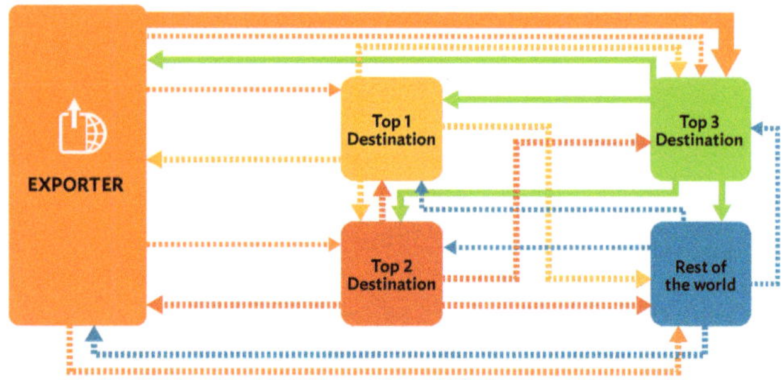

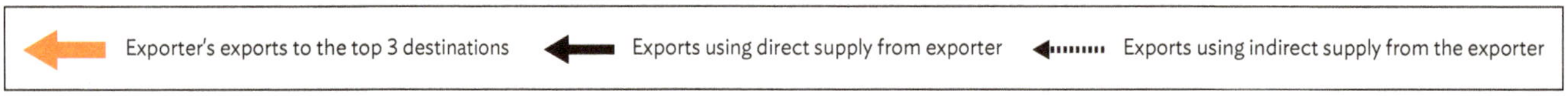

Notes: Indirect supply refers to the exported intermediate goods that goes through further processing by a middle country before reaching its destination. Direct supply refers to the exported intermediate goods which go straight to its destination.

Source: ADB staff.

Applying this diversification strategy on forward linkages globally using data from ADB's MRIO shows that Asia's total trade decreases both from the direct and adjusted impact on exports.

Some economies such as Japan and Viet Nam see exports increasing as their supply of intermediate goods coming from Asia increases as well. However, the magnitude is greater for the decrease in exports of economies such as the Republic of Korea, the PRC, and Malaysia. Latin America's exports also decrease as North America decreases its supply of intermediate goods to Mexico. The EU's exports increase as it gains more supplies from North America and Asia, while North America gains more supplies from Asia. The impact of this strategy, however, is not as significant compared with the impact of trade diversification in the backward linkages (Annex Table 2b.2).

Annex Table 2b.2: Impact of Diversification on Forward Linkages (%)

	Exports		Imports		Total Trade	
Country	Direct	Adjusted	Direct	Adjusted	Direct	Adjusted
Asia and the Pacific	**-0.13**	**-0.12**	**-0.13**	**-0.04**	**-0.13**	**-0.08**
Central Asia	0.00	0.00	-0.01	-0.01	0.00	-0.01
East Asia	-0.22	-0.19	-0.20	-0.04	-0.21	-0.12
South Asia	0.00	-0.01	0.00	-0.05	0.00	-0.03
Southeast Asia	0.04	0.03	0.03	-0.04	0.03	0.00
The Pacific and Oceania	-0.01	0.00	-0.01	0.00	-0.01	0.00
European Union	**0.25**	**0.23**	**0.26**	**0.10**	**0.25**	**0.17**
Latin America	**-2.91**	**-2.76**	**-2.67**	**-0.18**	**-2.79**	**-1.45**
North America	**0.22**	**0.21**	**0.18**	**-0.22**	**0.20**	**-0.02**
Rest of the World	**0.08**	**0.08**	**0.07**	**0.07**	**0.08**	**0.08**
World	**0.00**	**0.00**	**0.00**	**0.00**	**0.00**	**0.00**

Notes: The direct impact on total exports includes only the top destinations which were directly impacted by the exporter's diversification strategy. The adjusted impact on total exports includes all the economies which have contributed to the top sources' supply of intermediate goods to the exporter.
Sources: ADB calculations using data from ADB. Multi-Regional Input–Output Tables; and methodology by Wang, Wei, and Zhu (2013).

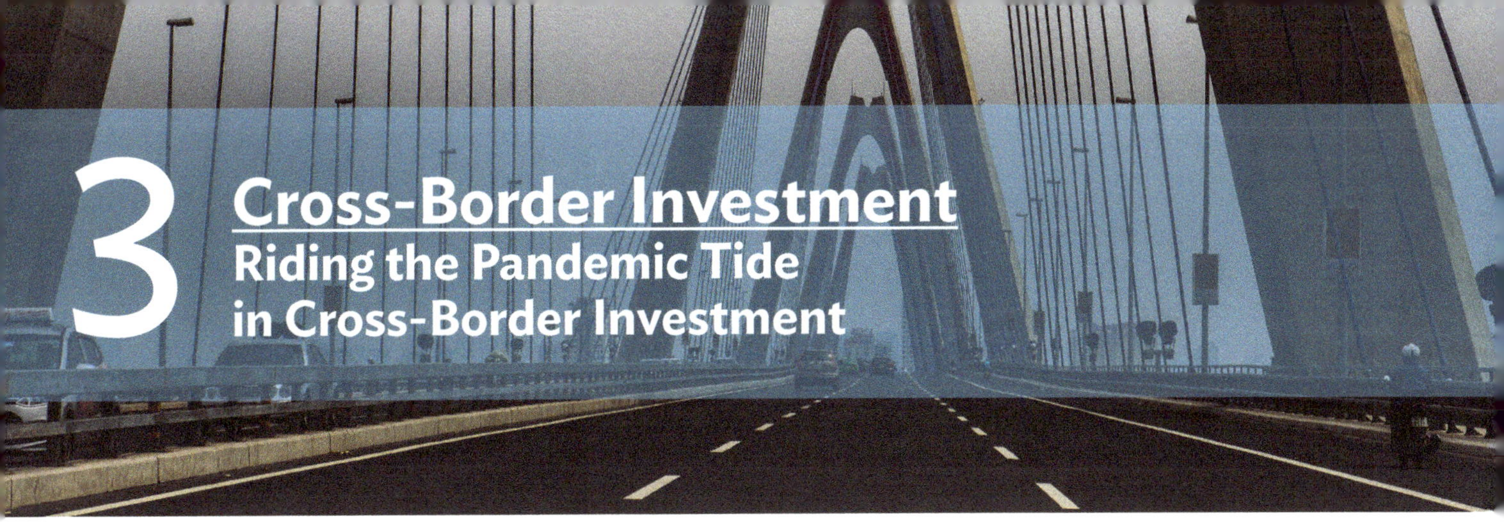

3 Cross-Border Investment
Riding the Pandemic Tide in Cross-Border Investment

Updates on Foreign Direct Investment During the COVID-19 Pandemic

Although cross-border investment inched higher in 2019, global foreign direct investment is expected to decline in 2020 and 2021 as the COVID-19 pandemic could weaken corporate earnings, and investors might take a more cautious approach.

The coronavirus disease (COVID-19) pandemic has had a significant effect on the global economy. Efforts in containing the virus continue to weigh on economic activities, whether in the supply or demand side. The region's bleak growth outlook will negatively affect inward foreign direct investment (FDI) flows.

FDI edged up by 3.0% in 2019, after a 12.1% downturn in 2018. Global inward FDI rose to $1.54 trillion in 2019 from $1.50 trillion in 2018 (Figure 3.1).[18] Inward FDI to Asia slid by 7.7% from $553.3 billion in 2018 to $510.5 billion in 2019.[19] Despite the dip in inward levels, the region remained an important FDI destination, accounting for 33.1% of total global FDI. The drop in Asia's inward FDI in 2019 resulted mainly from weakening global demand for electronics and automotive products, as well as persistent trade tensions between the United States (US) and the People's Republic of China (PRC). Yet in 2019 Asia's intraregional FDI share remained stable at 51.7%.

Figure 3.1: Global Inward Foreign Direct Investment, by Destination ($ trillion)

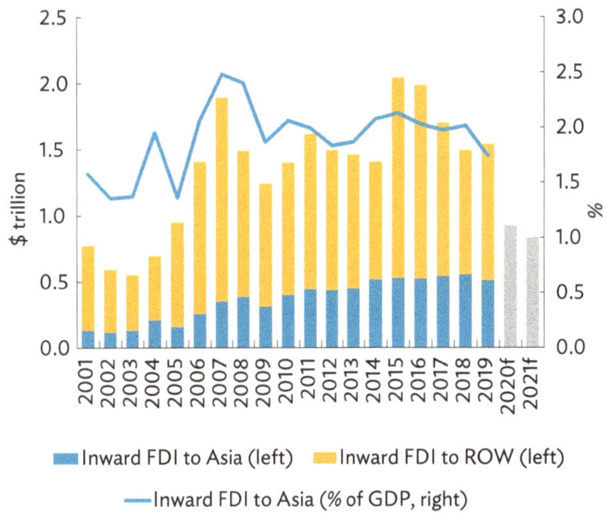

f = forecast, FDI = foreign direct investment, GDP = gross domestic product, ROW = rest of the world.

Notes: Bars for 2020 and 2021 represent estimates from the United Nations Conference on Trade and Development's World Investment Report 2020. Estimate for 2020 is based on a forecasted 40% decline from 2019 levels, with 2021 based on a forecasted 5% decline from 2020 levels.

Source: ADB calculations using data from United Nations Conference on Trade and Development. World Investment Report 2020 Statistical Annex Tables. http://unctad.org/en/Pages/DIAE/World%20Investment%20Report/Annex-Tables.aspx (accessed June 2020).

Although FDI recovered slightly in 2019, inward investment has been trending down since peaking at $2.0 trillion in 2015. The decline is expected to continue into 2020 and 2021, exacerbated by the COVID-19 pandemic.

[18] The World Investment Report excludes the Caribbean financial centers from the total. These include Anguilla, Antigua and Barbuda, Aruba, the Bahamas, Barbados, British Virgin Islands, the Cayman Islands, Curaçao, Dominica, Grenada, Montserrat, Saint Kitts and Nevis, Saint Lucia, Saint Vincent and the Grenadines, Saint Maarten, and the Turks and Caicos Islands.

[19] Asia refers to the 49 members of the Asian Development Bank (ADB) within Asia and the Pacific, which includes Japan and Oceania (Australia and New Zealand) in addition to the 46 developing Asian economies.

According to the United Nations Conference on Trade and Development's 2020 World Investment Report, global FDI inflows for 2020 may decline by as much as 40.0% in 2020, bringing FDI below $1.0 trillion for the first time since 2005. Moreover, FDI may continue to decline in 2021 by about 5% to 10%. Even as investment is likely to recover in 2022, forecasts indicate that inflows for 2022 may still be below the $1.2 trillion trough seen during the global financial crisis.

FDI flows are expected to fall in 2020, with immediate effects apparent within the first quarter of the year. A foreseen decline in reinvested earnings may bring about this fall in FDI inflows, according to the Organisation for Economic Co-operation and Development's (OECD) estimates. A fall in reinvested earnings during the pandemic is an expected outcome. During the financial crisis, reinvested earnings fell from almost 50% of earnings in 2007 to roughly a quarter over the succeeding couple of years. The share of reinvested earnings started to recover in 2010 and has been on the uptrend since 2013. However, enterprises are expected to respond in the same way they did in the global financial crisis, leading to the possible dip in reinvested earnings (OECD 2020a).

The first quarter of 2020 saw firm-level investment activity decline (Figures 3.2a and 3.2b). Greenfield investment from January to March of this year amounted to $126.8 billion globally, which is a 27.0% decline compared with the same period in 2019. Mergers and acquisitions (M&As) fared worse during the first quarter, with only $208.9 billion in deals pushing through. This level is less than half of that recorded in the first quarter of 2019. Delays and postponement of projects due to the COVID-19 pandemic negatively impacted greenfield investment, while cautionary measures due to an expected downturn in corporate earnings hampered M&As.

Asian economies were among the hardest hit globally in the first quarter of 2020. Greenfield investment in the PRC declined most in the first quarter of 2020, with FDI to the country dropping over $10.0 billion, due largely to the steep decline in investments in the coal, oil, and gas sector. The pandemic also damaged the Philippine economy during the quarter. Greenfield FDI to the Philippines slid by $6.6 billion, due to declines in travel-dependent sectors such as hotels and tourism. The United Kingdom (UK) saw the third-largest decline in greenfield FDI globally, with investment to the country slipping by $4.5 billion as investment in both renewable energy and electronic components fell.

Meanwhile, M&A deals suffered greatly in the US, as the value of deals in the first quarter (Q1) of 2020 declined by $87.5 billion. Substantial losses in deals in financial services, software and information technology (IT) services, and communications resulted in the steep drop

Figure 3.2: Global Inward FDI, First Quarter Estimates, 2003–2020—Greenfield and M&As ($ billion)

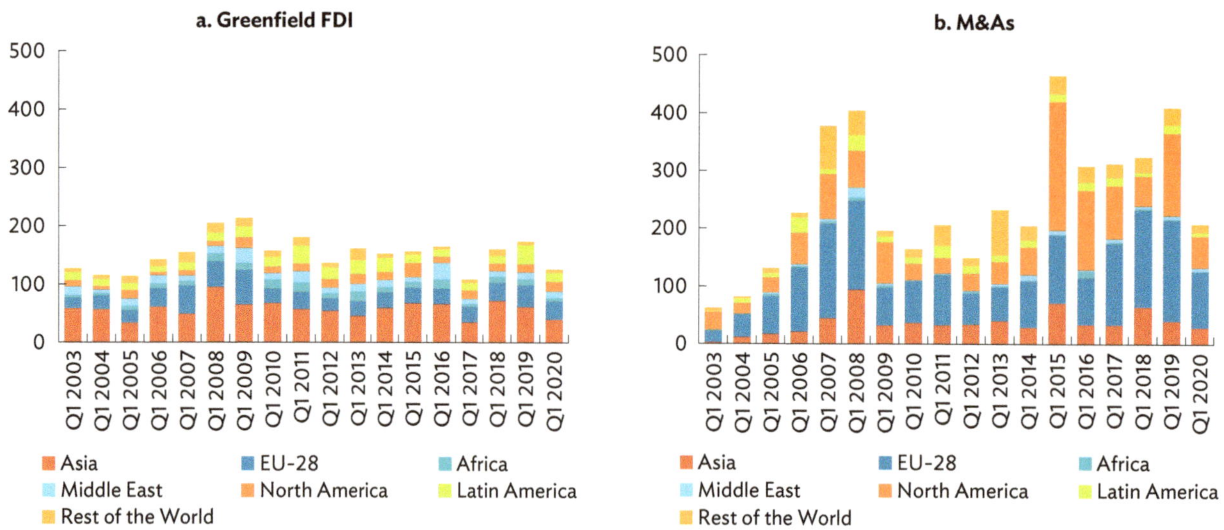

EU = European Union, FDI = foreign direct investment, M&A = merger and acquisition.

Sources: ADB calculations using data from Bureau van Dijk. Zephyr M&A Database; and Financial Times. fDi Markets (both accessed August 2020).

in the country's M&As in Q1 2020. Countries in Europe were also among the badly hit, with deals in the UK (down $58.3 billion) and Italy (down $13.8 billion) falling in the first quarter.

In Asia, M&As in the PRC dropped the most, from $12.6 billion in Q1 2019 to $8.3 billion in Q1 2020. Losses in deals in software and IT services, as well as in real estate, drove the decline. Deals in Indonesia also slid during the quarter (down $2.4 billion) because M&As in financial services and rubber sectors decreased.

Greenfield investment declined in almost all regions in the first quarter of 2020, barring North America (up 20.6%). Regions with the largest declines in greenfield investment were Latin America (down 52.3%), Africa (down 45.1%), and Asia (down 35.2%). In Latin America, four countries accounted for roughly three-fourths of the total decline in the region: Brazil, Bolivia, Cuba, and Peru. Meanwhile, two countries in Africa accounted for over 80% of the total decline in greenfield FDI in the region: Algeria and Kenya.

For M&As, all regions had been negatively impacted by the COVID-19 pandemic, with North America (down 61.8%) and Latin America (down 53.4%) among the hardest hit regions. The downturn in M&As in North America is due largely to the $87.5 billion decline in M&As in the US. In Latin America, decreased M&A volumes in Bermuda (51.9% of total), Brazil (30.9%), and Barbados (15.6%) accounted for almost all decline in the region.

Greenfield FDI and M&As in Asia similarly declined in the first quarter of 2020 (Figures 3.3a and 3.3b). Greenfield investments in Asia declined by 35.2% in the quarter compared with the first quarter of 2019. Despite this decline, the region continues to be an attractive and important destination for foreign investment.

Among Asian subregions, greenfield investment fell most in East Asia (down 56.4%) and Central Asia (down 51.6%). In East Asian economies, declines were recorded in Hong Kong, China; the PRC; and Taipei,China. In Central Asia, losses in greenfield FDI in Kazakhstan, Tajikistan, and Uzbekistan affected the region most. Meanwhile, M&As in the region declined by 27.8%, with the largest in Central Asia (down 76.8%) and Southeast Asia (46.5%). In Southeast Asia, large declines in M&As were recorded in Indonesia (down 82.8%) and Myanmar (down 63.6%).

Outward investment also declined in the first quarter of 2020 (Figures 3.4a and 3.4b). Global outward greenfield investment amounted to $126.8 billion compared with the previous year's first quarter outward investment of $173.7 billion. This translates to a 27.0% year-on-year decline in the first quarter of 2020.

Figure 3.3: Asian Inward FDI, First Quarter Estimates, 2003–2020—Greenfield and M&As ($ billion)

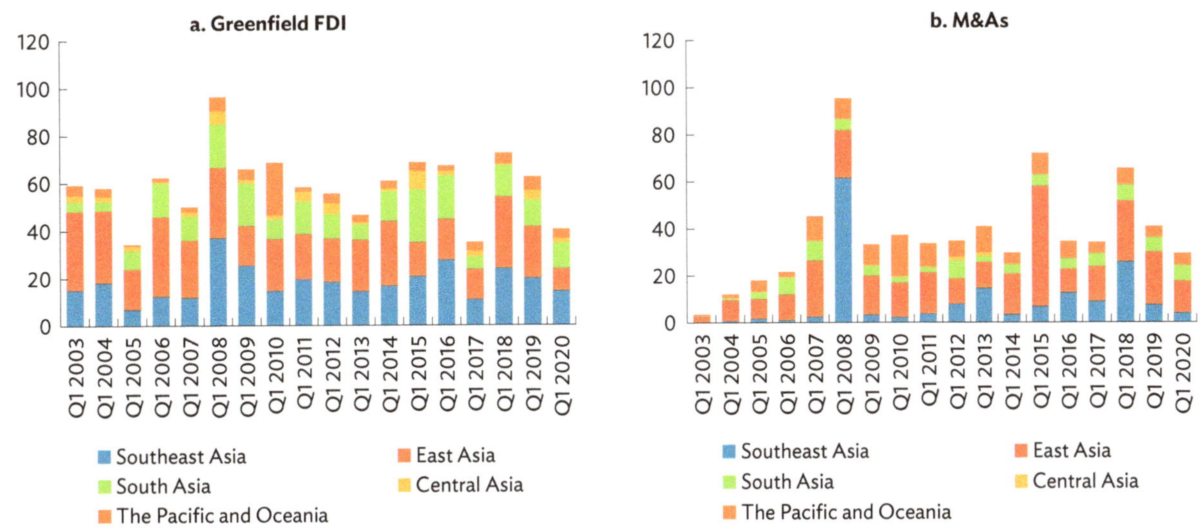

FDI = foreign direct investment, M&A = merger and acquisition.

Sources: ADB calculations using data from Bureau van Dijk. Zephyr M&A Database; and Financial Times. fDi Markets (both accessed August 2020).

Figure 3.4: Global Outward FDI, First Quarter Estimates, 2003–2020—Greenfield and M&As ($ billion)

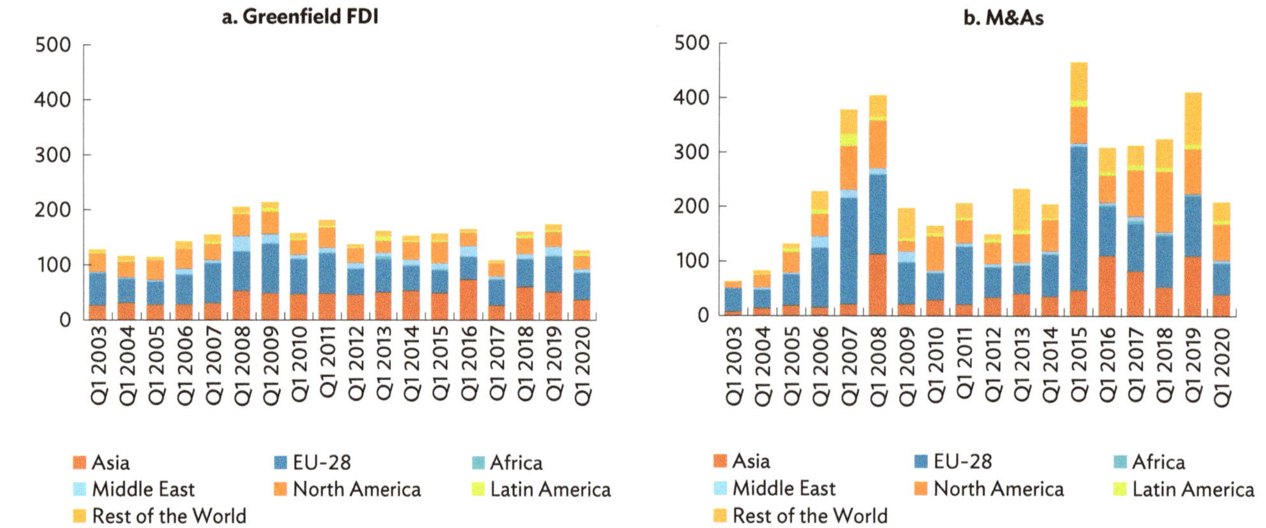

EU = European Union, FDI = foreign direct investment, M&A = merger and acquisition.

Sources: ADB calculations using data from Bureau van Dijk. Zephyr M&A Database; and Financial Times. fDi Markets (both accessed August 2020).

In terms of outward greenfield investment, FDI from the PRC, Saudi Arabia, and Germany recorded the largest declines. Greenfield FDI from the PRC fell by $8.4 billion in the first 3 months of 2020, as the country invested less in cross-border projects in transportation and warehousing, chemicals, and electronic components. Meanwhile, investment from Saudi Arabia fell by $8.3 billion as investment activities in coal, oil, and gas took a backseat in the first quarter. In Germany, steep falls in its outward investment in renewable energy; coal, oil, and gas; and plastics drove the $8.2 billion decline.

Deals from Japanese firms took a backseat in the first quarter of 2020, with M&As from the country declining by $59.3 billion. Most of the decline came with pharmaceutical activity being focused on developing treatments and vaccines for the virus, rather than consolidation. Deals from firms in Switzerland also recorded a $54.0 billon decrease, as deals in the communications, financial services, and software and IT services dipped. By region, in the first quarter of 2020, greenfield investment from the Middle East (down 65.0%) and Africa (down 36.8%) declined most.

Meanwhile, outward M&As fell by almost half in the first quarter of 2020, from $410.8 billion in the first quarter of 2019 to $208.9 billion. Despite a significant increase in M&As from the Middle East (from $500 million in Q1 2019 to $4.4 billion in Q1 2020), downturns in other regions drove down M&As. M&As from Asia (down 64.3%) and Africa (down 60.6%) slid most. M&As from South Africa (down $2.4 billion) and Mauritius (down $619.9 million) took the biggest hit.

Greenfield investment from Asia amounted to $37.9 billion in the first quarter of 2020, a 27.0% decline from the first quarter of 2019 (Figures 3.5a and 3.5b). Greenfield investment from Oceania (down 69.9%) and Central Asia (down 53.7%) declined the most.

M&As from Asia in the first quarter of 2020 was only about a third of the level in the first quarter of 2019 (Figure 3.5). This amounted to $39.4 billion, compared with the previous M&A value of $110.2 billion. Apart from large declines in M&As from South Asia (down 97%), East Asia (down 67.1%), and Southeast Asia (down 51.6%), no M&As had been recorded for Central Asia and the Pacific in the first 3 months of 2020.

M&As from India suffered most in South Asia, with mergers amounting to only $157.2 million in Q1 2020 compared with $5.2 billion in the same quarter a year earlier. In East Asia, the value of M&As by Japan firms declined by $59.3 billion, accounting for 99.1% of

Figure 3.5: Asian Outward FDI, First Quarter Estimates, 2003–2020—Greenfield and M&As ($ billion)

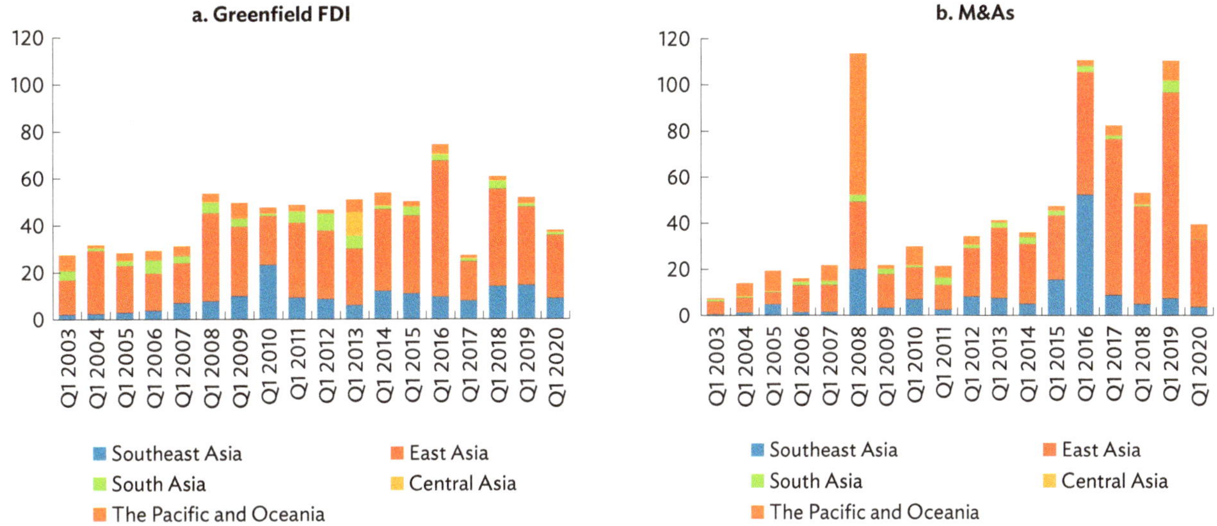

FDI = foreign direct investment, M&A = merger and acquisition.

Sources: ADB calculations using data from Bureau van Dijk. Zephyr M&A Database; and Financial Times. fDi Markets (both accessed August 2020).

the total decline in the region. Meanwhile, losses of $3.0 billion in M&As from Singapore and $500 million from Thailand led the decreased M&As from Southeast Asia. Lower greenfield FDI and M&As from Asian investors hint at the more cautious stance as the region continues to battle the COVID-19 pandemic.

Sector-wise, the pandemic affected industries disproportionately. Early on, consumption in some activities such as travel, leisure, and entertainment took a hit, as minimum health standards such as physical distancing and cross-border policies such as travel bans were implemented.

Activity moved similarly in greenfield investment and M&As. Globally speaking, greenfield investment in the coal, oil, and gas sector plunged $13.6 billion year-on-year in the first quarter of 2020, due in part to slowing demand and earnings. Meanwhile, greenfield FDI in hotels and tourism in the first quarter of 2020 also fell, by $8.0 billion, followed by real estate (down $4.9 billion), leisure and entertainment (down $4.5 billion), and transportation and warehousing (down $3.5 billion). Lockdown measures impacted movement of people and goods greatly in these sectors, which led to sharp falls in foreign investment.

In Asia, the coal, oil, and gas sector was also among the largest decliners in Q1 2020. Greenfield investment to the sector fell $10.8 billion. Asia's hotels and tourism sector also took a big hit, with FDI in the sector declining by $8.1 billion that quarter. Investment in real estate also declined by $2.6 billion. Greenfield FDI in the automotive original equipment manufacturing sector also declined by $2.2 billion in Q1 2020, as production and demand slowed.

Meanwhile, global deals in pharmaceuticals declined by $62.4 billion in the first quarter of 2020. As the world started to grapple with the effects of the pandemic, pharmaceutical companies redirected resources to developing treatments and vaccines, taking attention away from M&As. As in greenfield investment, M&As in coal, oil, and gas also dropped by $18.0 billion year-on-year in Q1 2020. Deals in the financial services sector slipped by $17.4 billion in the first 3 months of 2020. M&As also declined in the first quarter of 2020 in the medical devices (down $16.8 billion) and software and IT services (down $16.6 billion) sectors.

M&As in Asia declined the most in the communications industry, where deals dropped by $4.8 billion in Q1 2020. This is followed by software and IT services (down $2.7 billion), ceramics and glass (down $2.4 billion), business services (down $1.7 billion), and pharmaceuticals (down $1.7 billion).

Firm-level activity showed some signs of recovery in the second and third quarters, as countries started to reopen and ease some pandemic-related restrictions.

Despite the sharp drop in inward FDI during the first quarter, Q2 2020 showed some signs of recovery, especially for M&As (Table 3.1). While greenfield FDI decreased to $115.3 billion in Q2 2020 from $126.8 billion in Q1, capital expenditure for projects recovered in some regions. Greenfield investment in the European Union (EU)–28 countries increased by $3.7 billion in the second quarter, most notably in the UK (up $9.3 billion) and France (up $2.2 billion). Meanwhile, greenfield FDI in North America also recovered in the second quarter (up $6.3 billion) due to increased investment in the US (up $8.5 billion), which cushioned the decline in greenfield FDI in Canada in the same quarter. In the UK, much of the recovery was in renewable energy, along with transportation and warehousing, while FDI growth in the US was driven by investment in semiconductors and chemicals.

While greenfield FDI decreased overall in Asia, some countries saw increased FDI in the second quarter. Greenfield investment in Indonesia increased by almost $9.0 billion between the first and second quarter, largely in FDI to the country's chemicals and real estate sectors. Australia saw a $4.8 billion increase in FDI in the second quarter, due to projects in the coal, oil, and gas sector. Meanwhile, increased FDI in the real estate sector primarily drove Japan's growth in the second quarter.

M&As appear to have recovered in the second quarter. Attractive valuations due to lower equity prices and weakened currencies helped the recovery. Global M&As increased $152.2 billion over the first quarter. Large increases in M&A deals were seen in North America (up $74.9 billion), the EU-28 (up $40.5 billion), and Asia (up $28.9 billion). Second-quarter deals in the US more than doubled those in the first quarter ($50.8 billion to $120.2 billion). Meanwhile, deals in Ireland (up $63.7 billion) drove M&As up among EU-28 countries. In the US, deals in the communications, semiconductors, and automotive components sectors paved the way for FDI recovery. Meanwhile, pharmaceutical M&As drove recovery in Ireland.

In Asia, M&As recovered in India (up $15.6 billion) and Australia (up $9.6 billion). India recorded higher M&A values in the communications, food and beverages, and electronic components sectors. In Australia, M&As in food and beverages; paper, printing, and packaging; and real estate supported growth in the second quarter.

Among Asian subregions, overall firm-level investment activities picked up among countries in Oceania (up $15.1 billion), South Asia (up $7.0 billion), and Southeast Asia (up $5.1 billion), as shown in Table 3.2. Greenfield investment increased most in Oceania (up $5.6 billion) due to an uptick in Australia (up $4.8 billion). Large gains in greenfield FDI in Japan (up $2.1 billion) and other countries offset the sizable decline in FDI in the PRC (down $2.6 billion), resulting in an increased greenfield investment in East Asia (up $800 million). Meanwhile, M&As increased largely in South Asia (up $15.7 billion)

Table 3.1: Global Inward Investment by Destination Region, Q1 to Q3 2020—Greenfield FDI and M&As ($ billion)

	Greenfield FDI			M&As		
Region	**Q1 2020**	**Q2 2020**	**Q3 2020**	**Q1 2020**	**Q2 2020**	**Q3 2020**
Asia	40.5	38.5	18.1	29.6	58.4	42.8
EU-28	32.0	35.8	23.1	97.7	138.0	90.4
Africa	5.9	5.7	3.0	1.4	5.0	0.6
Middle East	11.1	1.8	10.3	5.3	9.4	11.7
North America	16.2	22.5	10.7	54.5	129.4	20.4
Latin America	15.7	8.3	7.1	6.7	8.9	2.8
Rest of the World	5.3	2.7	3.2	13.7	12.1	27.9
Total	**126.8**	**115.3**	**75.5**	**208.9**	**361.1**	**196.6**

EU = European Union, FDI = foreign direct investment, M&A = merger and acquisition.

Sources: ADB calculations using data from Bureau van Dijk. Zephyr M&A Database; and Financial Times. fDi Markets (both accessed November 2020).

because deals in India recovered significantly. Increased M&A deals in Australia brought about an increase in M&As in Oceania (up $9.4 billion), while gains in Indonesia (up $2.8 billion), Viet Nam (up $1.6 billion), and Singapore (up $1.3 billion) drove up M&As in Southeast Asia (up $4.9 billion).

While greenfield FDI continued to decline globally in the second quarter, some sectors saw increased activity. Global greenfield investment in semiconductors recovered, from $276.6 million in the first quarter to $12.7 billion. Renewable energy greenfield investment increased from $19.8 billion to $30.9 billion. Other sectors that posted recoveries between the first two quarters of 2020 were ceramics and glass, communications, and engines and turbines.

In Asia, second-quarter greenfield investment grew most in the chemicals sector, to $10.9 billion from $5.4 billion in the first quarter. Greenfield FDI also recovered in coal, oil, and gas (up $2.8 billion); real estate (up $1.9 billion); renewable energy (up $1.4 billion); and semiconductors (up $571.6 million).

M&As fared better in the second quarter of 2020 than in the first, largely because of gains in global pharmaceuticals deals (up $64.6 billion). Deals in communications also revived, with M&As growing by $51.0 billion globally. M&As increased in the food and services sector, from $6.0 billion in the first quarter to $19.1 billion in the second quarter. Increases in M&As were also recorded in electronic components (up $8.9 billion) and semiconductors (up $8.6 billion).

M&As in Asia in the food and beverages sector leapt in the second quarter compared with the first, from $1.3 billion to $15.6 billion. Communications also rebounded, from $3.0 billion to $11.5 billion. Deals in electronics components (up $3.5 billion), financial services (up $2.7 billion), and chemicals (up $2.6 billion) also increased in the second quarter.

Overall, outward FDI followed the same trend as inward FDI in the second quarter of 2020. Outward greenfield FDI slid further, by $11.5 billion, with the largest decline in outward greenfield investment from the EU-28 countries (down $9.7 billion), particularly in France (down $5.7 billion) and Spain (down $3.0 billion). This was followed by North America, as greenfield FDI from the region slid $5.1 billion between the first and second quarters. Meanwhile, Asia's outward greenfield FDI recovered, though modestly, by $1.3 billion. Large declines in financial hubs such as Japan, the PRC, and Singapore were offset by a $17.0 billion increase in greenfield investment from Taipei,China.

As greenfield FDI dove further in the second quarter, outward M&As recovered overall by $152.2 billion. The EU-28 and North America were at the forefront, as M&As from EU-28 countries increased by $96.1 billion, while those from North America increased by $61.6 billion. M&As from Asia also recovered in the second quarter, as deals from the region ticked upward by $8.9 billion.

Compared with Q2 2020, Q3 2020 indicated some steam lost in firm-level investment (see Table 3.1). Greenfield FDI continued a descent, globally pulling in only $75.5 billion in Q3 2020 compared with

Table 3.2: Asian Inward Investment by Destination Region, Q1 to Q3 2020—Greenfield FDI and M&As ($ billion)

	Greenfield FDI			M&As		
Asian Subregions	Q1 2020	Q2 2020	Q3 2020	Q1 2020	Q2 2020	Q3 2020
Southeast Asia	14.6	14.8	0.4	4.0	9.0	0.0
East Asia	9.5	10.3	8.8	13.7	11.1	27.6
South Asia	10.8	2.2	1.9	6.5	22.2	7.2
Central Asia	1.9	2.0	3.2	0.0	1.6	2.8
The Pacific and Oceania	3.8	9.3	3.9	5.3	14.7	5.2
Total	**40.5**	**38.5**	**18.1**	**29.6**	**58.4**	**42.8**

FDI = foreign direct investment; M&A = merger and acquisition.

Sources: ADB calculations using data from Bureau van Dijk. Zephyr M&A Database; and Financial Times. fDi Markets (both accessed November 2020).

$115.3 billion in Q2 2020. Greenfield investment declined in Asia (down $20.4 billion), totaling $18.1 billion in Q3 2020 compared with $38.5 billion in Q2 2020. Large declines were also recorded in the EU (down $12.7 billion) and North America (down $11.8 billion). Meanwhile, greenfield investment saw a bright spot in the Middle East during Q3 2020, as it increased to $10.3 billion from $1.8 billion in Q2 2020.

After a steep growth in Q2 2020, M&As retracted some of its recovery momentum in Q3, with the largest loss recorded in North America (down $109.0 billion). However, M&A trend was still quite robust in Asia. M&A deals in Asia also grew on year-on-year basis, recording $42.8 billion in Q3 2020 compared with $35.7 billion in Q3 2019 (see Table 3.1).

M&As in East Asia rebounded in Q3 2020. After dipping to only $11.1 billion in Q2 2020, M&As in the subregion totaled $27.6 billion in Q3 (see Table 3.2).

Despite uncertainties around the prolonged impact of the pandemic, FDI is expected to have continued its recovery trend in Q4 2020 in Asia, driven by the region's relatively better performance in containing the pandemic and resilience in industrial production capacities.

The COVID-19 pandemic is expected to continue weighing on foreign direct investment.

Some efforts to contain the coronavirus such as business and establishment closures—especially those of manufacturing plants and construction sites—have caused delays in the implementation of projects. While some fixed operational expenditures continued, other forms of capital expenditure were blocked. In addition, as governments rightly divert their attention to addressing the ongoing crisis, the approval of some planned mergers have been delayed.

Some countries have also tightened FDI screening measures to safeguard key establishments and sectors from possible predatory takeovers. While this policy response is not new in the time of the pandemic, measures such as these are expected to have a long-term effect on incoming FDI. In addition, shortages early in the pandemic also highlighted the need for supply chain resilience and autonomy, especially for critical supplies, such as medicine and personal protective equipment. In some cases, this has resulted in diversion, divestment, and reshoring.

Policy Updates: Regulatory Restrictions and Screening in Foreign Direct Investments

FDI regulatory restrictiveness across the world increased in recent years.

Countries regulate incoming investments in one way or another. More than assuring that investments are beneficial to their economy and meet best practices, some regulations are intended to address issues related to national security. Policies include entry and establishment regulations such as business permits, approval requirements, and, in some cases, limitations on foreign investment in some sectors. Restrictions play a role in how open a country is to FDI, and this degree of openness, in turn, affects its attractiveness as a destination for investment.

An index from the OECD helps measure a country's regulatory restrictiveness. The index measures four regulatory areas: foreign equity limitations, discriminatory screening or approval mechanisms, foreign employment restrictions in key positions, and other operational restrictions. Values range between 0 and 1, with zero indicating openness (OECD 2010).

Globally, the FDI regulatory restrictiveness index had been rising since 2006, reaching its peak in 2014 at 0.144 (Figure 3.6).[20] It declined for several years, before increasing again and settling at 0.142 in 2019. The increase and eventual peak of the restrictiveness index coincided with a

[20] Economies included in the index were classified as Asia and non-Asia. Asia includes Armenia, Australia, Azerbaijan, Brunei Darussalam, Cambodia, Georgia, India, Indonesia, Japan, Kazakhstan, the Republic of Korea, the Kyrgyz Republic, the Lao People's Democratic Republic, Malaysia, Mongolia, Myanmar, New Zealand, the PRC, the Philippines, Singapore, Tajikistan, Thailand, Uzbekistan, and Viet Nam. Non-Asia includes Albania, Algeria, Argentina, Austria, Belarus, Belgium, Bosnia and Herzegovina, Brazil, Canada, Chile, Colombia, Costa Rica, Croatia, Czechia, Denmark, Egypt, Estonia, Finland, France, Germany, Greece, Hungary, Iceland, Ireland, Israel, Italy, Jordan, Kosovo, Latvia, Lebanon, Libya, Lithuania, Luxembourg, Mexico, Moldova, Montenegro, Morocco, Netherlands, North Macedonia, Norway, Peru, Poland, Portugal, Romania, the Russian Federation, Saudi Arabia, Serbia, Slovakia, Slovenia, South Africa, Spain, State of Palestine, Sweden, Switzerland, Tunisia, Turkey, Ukraine, the UK, the US, and Uruguay.

Figure 3.6: FDI Regulatory Restrictiveness Index versus FDI—World

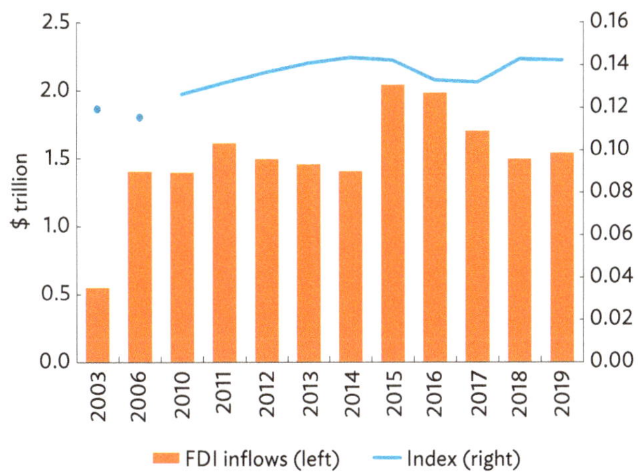

FDI = foreign direct investment.

Notes: The FDI Regulatory Restrictiveness Index measures statutory restrictions on FDI in 22 sectors. The index considers restrictions on four main areas: foreign equity limitations, discriminatory screening or approval mechanisms, foreign employment restrictions in key positions, and other operation restrictions. The index ranges in value from 0 to 1, with 0 being more open and 1 being more closed.

Sources: ADB calculations using data from Organisation for Economic Co-operation and Development. FDI Regulatory Restrictiveness Index. https://stats.oecd.org/Index.aspx?datasetcode=FDIINDEX# (accessed September 2020); and United Nations Conference on Trade and Development. World Investment Report 2020 Statistical Annex Tables. http://unctad.org/en/Pages/DIAE/World%20Investment%20Report/Annex-Tables.aspx (accessed June 2020).

trough in global inward FDI in 2014, valued at $1.4 trillion. Restrictions eased starting in 2015, and global FDI also recovered; however, global inward investments since seem to be on a downtrend, while restrictiveness is on an uptrend.

By region, FDI restrictiveness has been generally higher in Asian countries, also reaching a peak in 2014, at around 0.276 (Figure 3.7a). Regulatory restrictions have since eased, with the 2019 index valued at 0.195. A rise in FDI to Asia coincided with this ease.

Meanwhile, regulatory restrictions in countries outside of Asia seem to be lower, hovering along the 0.085 line across the years (Figure 3.7b). Available data indicate a peak in 2003 at 0.087, quickly reaching a trough in 2010 at 0.079. The Regulatory Restrictiveness Index reached another peak in 2012 and had declined until 2016. It has since picked up, with a value of 0.083 in 2019. While policy movements in non-Asian countries seem to be minimal, movement in inward FDI are more pronounced. Together with more lax restrictions came an influx of investment in 2015. Declines in FDI to non-Asian countries also coincide with an uptick in restrictiveness since 2017.

Figure 3.7: FDI Regulatory Restrictiveness Index versus FDI—Asia and Non-Asia

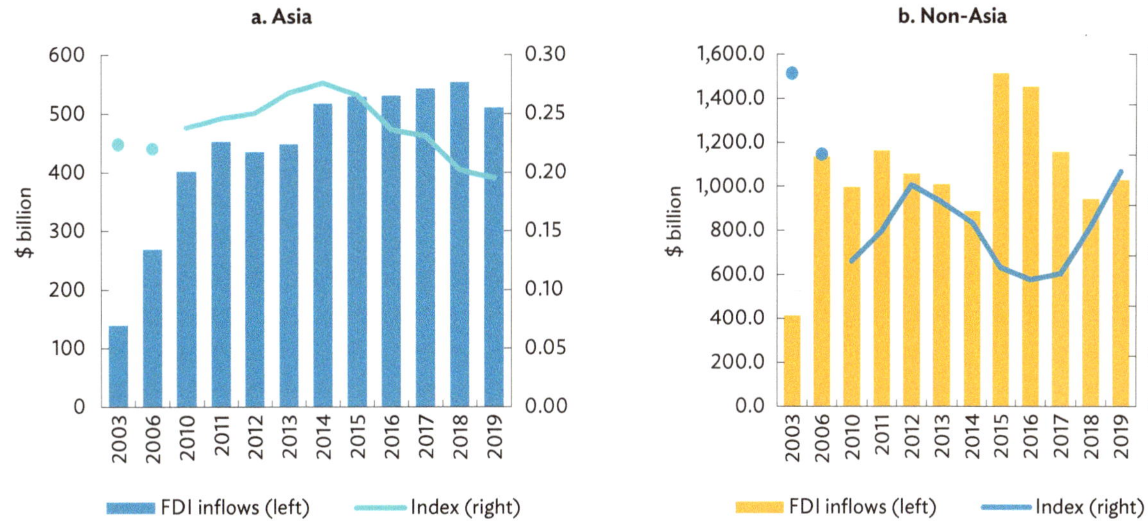

FDI = foreign direct investment.

Notes: The FDI Regulatory Restrictiveness Index measures statutory restrictions on FDI in 22 sectors. The index considers restrictions on four main areas: foreign equity limitations, discriminatory screening or approval mechanisms, foreign employment restrictions in key positions, and other operation restrictions. The index ranges in value from 0 to 1, with 0 being more open and 1 being more closed.

Sources: ADB calculations using data from Organisation for Economic Co-operation and Development. FDI Regulatory Restrictiveness Index. https://stats.oecd.org/Index.aspx?datasetcode=FDIINDEX# (accessed September 2020); and United Nations Conference on Trade and Development. World Investment Report 2020 Statistical Annex Tables. http://unctad.org/en/Pages/DIAE/World%20Investment%20Report/Annex-Tables.aspx (accessed June 2020).

Recent years have seen some screening mechanisms gain popularity worldwide. These mechanisms are aimed at screening foreign investments which may impede national security and other public interest.

Countries typically employ three types of screening mechanisms, usually in combination—cross-sector screening, sector-specific screening, or entity-specific mechanism. Cross-sector and sector-specific screening mechanisms are the most used, and typically employed in conjunction (UNCTAD 2019).

Sector-specific mechanisms initially regulated potential investments in the military and defense sectors, but these have since developed to protect other sectors deemed to be of domestic importance, with several countries specifying sectors of particular interest. These sectors include infrastructure such as energy supply and production, media, and telecommunications. Screening mechanisms may also include investments acquiring technology such as artificial intelligence, robotics, and aerospace technologies. In addition, the access of foreign investors to sensitive data on locals is also under consideration for screening in some countries.

Some countries have also implemented policies employing various FDI screening criteria (Table 3.3), with the majority focusing on defense, national security, public order, or public safety. These criteria and concerns have evolved into criteria besides national security. Some countries have included criteria on the possible effects of foreign investment on their respective economies, such as the economy's smooth operation, financial system stability, and steady economic growth, among others. Social costs, such as effects on the environment, health, and quality of life, are also of interest in some countries.

Mechanisms such as these are implemented across sectors and assessments are made whether potential investment impinge on specified criteria. However, even in the presence of cross-sector reviews, certain sectors or activities could be targeted through other restrictions such as lower relevant thresholds and other specific screening criteria.

Although legitimate from policy objective perspectives, some measures are expected to exert a negative impact on foreign investment.

For example, the US implemented tax reforms in 2017, which resulted in a repatriation of earnings of some multinational enterprises. Foreign investment from the US slumped to negative $90.6 billion in 2018 from $300.4 billion in 2017. Such measures continued to affect US outward investment in 2019. FDI to the US also declined by $194.5 billion in 2017, and continued to decline by $23.7 billion in 2018, and by $7.3 billion in 2019. On the inward FDI front, the US expanded the jurisdiction of the Committee on Foreign Investment in the United States through the Foreign Investment Risk Review Modernization Act of 2018. The implemented reforms were aimed at resolving "growing national security concerns over foreign exploitation of certain investment structures which traditionally have fallen outside of Committee's jurisdiction" (US Department of Treasury 2018).

In March 2019, the EU established a framework to screen inward FDI to shield the region from some predatory M&A practices and risks to security or public order (EU 2019). Early in 2020, the ongoing crisis saw the EU adding to its guidelines, enjoining member states to protect health-related companies and important assets. The COVID-19 pandemic has brought a fresh round of national security concerns, not only in the EU but in some Asian countries as well.

In April 2020, India moved to establish FDI rules to guard against opportunistic takeovers of companies hurt in the pandemic. Instead of being automatically approved, investors from border states must first seek government approval (BloombergQuint 2020). Australia also enacted some temporary measures in its FDI screening regime, lowering existing monetary review thresholds to $0, in effect subjecting all incoming foreign investment to review from March 29 onward (The Guardian 2020). The review schedule was also extended from 30 days to up to 6 months. The country implemented the temporary policy to "ensure appropriate oversight over all proposed foreign investment during [the pandemic]."

Table 3.3: FDI Screening Criteria—Select Economies

Economies	Screening Criteria
Australia	National interest
Austria	Public policy and public security, including services of public interest and crisis prevention, which affect a basic interest of society
Belgium (Flanders)	Strategic interests of the Flemish Community or the Flemish Region
Canada	Net benefit, national security
European Union	Security or public order
Finland	Key national interest: national defense, public order and security, fundamental interests of society
France	Public order, public security, or national defense
Germany	Public order or security, essential security interests
Hungary	Security interests
Iceland	National security, public order, public safety, or public health or in the event of serious economic, social, or environmental difficulties in particular economic sectors or particular areas
Italy	Defense interests, national security, essential interests of the State, public order
Japan	National security, public order, public safety; smooth operation of the economy
Latvia	National security
Lithuania	National security
New Zealand	Business experience and acumen, financial commitment, good character of an investor
Norway	National security
People's Republic of China (PRC)	National security, impact on the core key technological innovation development capabilities in important areas of the PRC, national steady economic growth, basic social living order, the research and development capacity of key technologies involving national security
Poland	Independence and territorial integrity, safeguarding human rights and freedoms, security and public order, environmental protection, ensuring the needs of the population to protect health and lives, prevention of activities and social and political phenomena disturbing international relations or impeding responsibilities of NATO membership
Portugal	Defense, national security, security of supply in services fundamental to the national interest
Republic of Korea	National security, national safety and public order, public hygiene, or the environmental preservation; Korean morals and customs
Romania	National security
Russian Federation	Defense, security
South Africa	National security
United Kingdom (UK)	Public interest, national security, stability of the UK financial system, accurate presentation of news, free expression of opinion
United States	National security

FDI = foreign direct investment, NATO = North Atlantic Treaty Organization, PRC = People's Republic of China, UK = United Kingdom.

Source: UNCTAD (2019).

The pandemic has also highlighted some downsides to increasing reliance on a more globalized supply chains and some countries may move to reshore or diversify their production. Such decisions will not only impact trade and production, they may also impact investment flows.

Bilateral Investment Treaties and Foreign Direct Investment

International investment agreements (IIAs) are an important policy tool to attract FDI by safeguarding the economic interests of both the recipient economies and international investors. Investment treaties govern a set of circumstances that includes the scope of investment, treatment received by foreign investors, and dispute settlement and compensation mechanisms. Investment treaties grant international legal protection to foreign investors from adverse actions by governments of host states. States, on the other hand, often support investment treaties for their perceived role in attracting investment flows. Investment agreements can signal a stable and predictable environment for investment. In addition, they are believed to play a role in promoting good governance standards and, by making host states liable, encourage administrative and judicial reforms.

In recent years, however, some concerns arose that IIAs impose costs to states and do not always fully deliver their objectives. Increasing cross-border investment flows in the past 15 years have been followed by a rise in the number of investor–state disputes (ISD), more concentrated in middle-income economies. Strategies by multinationals to structure investments by resorting to investment treaties have exacerbated this trend.[21]

While the design and negotiation of IIAs can be complex, new approaches are emerging to compare the design, structure, and economic impact of these agreements (Bergstrand and Egger 2013, Konrad 2017). Among these efforts is ADB's development of a comprehensive database of IIAs in Asia, including both bilateral investment treaties (BITs) and investment chapters of free trade agreements, to create a granular classification of provisions enforced by Asian economies.[22]

The purpose of this section is threefold: first, to characterize the existent bilateral investment treaties in Asia, with a focus on existing and new investment provisions. Second, to present a more granular analysis on the impact of BIT provisions in Asia's investment flows, emphasizing differences by entry mode and sector allocation. Third, to present a taxonomy of policy responses where countries resort to investment treaties to mitigate the effects of COVID-19 on FDI, and to assess their past and their potential role after the pandemic.

Trends in BITs and Investor–State Dispute Cases in Asia

As of 2020, nearly 3,000 IIAs, including BITs and preferential trade agreements, had been signed globally —of which around one-third involve Asian economies. Since the early 1990s, Asia started to engage more actively in bilateral investment treaties, both within and outside the region, with the number of agreements decreasing in the last decade (Figure 3.8a). The regional composition of Asian BITs has also evolved, with emerging regions (Africa, Latin America, and the Middle East) becoming more present from the mid-1990s (Figure 3.8b.2).

---

21 A number of multinationals have adopted a "treaty shopping" strategy allowing investors from a home state to incorporate a subsidiary in a third state, use that subsidiary as corporate vehicle to make investments in the host state, and claim the protection of an investment treaty between the third state and the home state. This type of triangulation poses challenges for identifying the jurisdiction in investment disputes and exposes host states to arbitration claims.

22 The database codifies into 15 provisions, as follows: (i) definition of investment, (ii) admission versus establishment, (iii) national treatment, (iv) most-favored nation clause, (v) fair and equitable treatment, (vi) direct and indirect expropriation, (vii) free transfer of investment-related funds, (viii) noneconomic standards, (ix) investor–state dispute mechanism, (x) umbrella clause, (xi) temporal scope of application, (xii) performance requirements (xiii) transparency mechanisms, (xiv) public interest obligations, and (xv) exception clause.

Figure 3.8: Number of Enforced Asian BITs and Regional Distribution, by Year

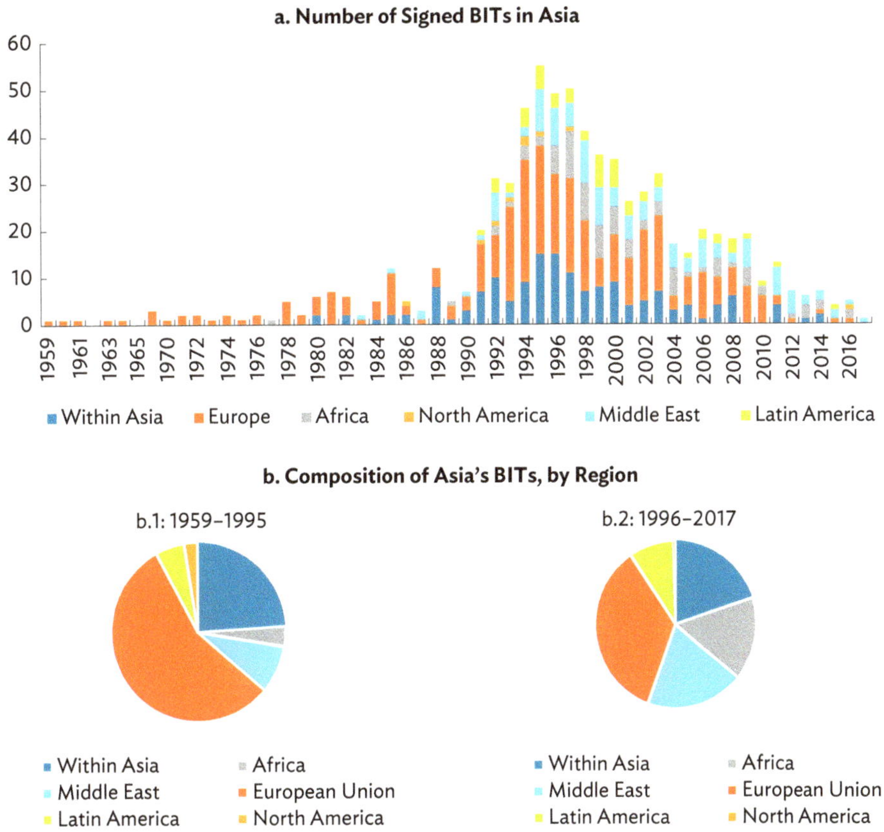

BIT = bilateral investment treaty.

Source: ADB (Regional Cooperation and Integration Division, Economic Research and Regional Cooperation Department). International Investment Agreement Database.

ISDs have increased steadily in number over the past 2 decades, both globally and in Asia. Whereas before 2000 Asian economies were involved in very few cases, the caseload has gradually increased. The World Bank's International Center for Settlement of International Disputes database, which covers a significant portion of ISDs worldwide (both conciliation and arbitration), reports 673 cases globally (both ongoing and concluded) since 2003, of which 83 concern Asian economies (Figure 3.9a). Disputes involving Asian states increased by 57% between 2000–2010 and 2011–2020. Sector concentration is high. Most cases are concentrated in the oil, gas and mining, and electricity sectors (Figure 3.9b). About 60% of the cases worldwide have invoked BITs as the basis of consent to establish taking action (ICSID 2020).

Characterization of BIT Provisions in Asian Treaties

The ADB BIT database characterizes 15 provisions across 1,012 investment treaties in Asia. It allows firms to compare IIAs directly across countries where they may locate affiliates, and for policy makers to identify provisions that could be incorporated in other treaties or multilateralized. Building on an existent database for BITs in Asia (Chaisse and Bellak 2015), five new provisions are included in the new database: public interest obligation, exception clause, performance requirements, access to arbitration, and transparency in investor–state arbitration (Figure 3.10).

Figure 3.9: Trends in Investor–State Disputes in Asia

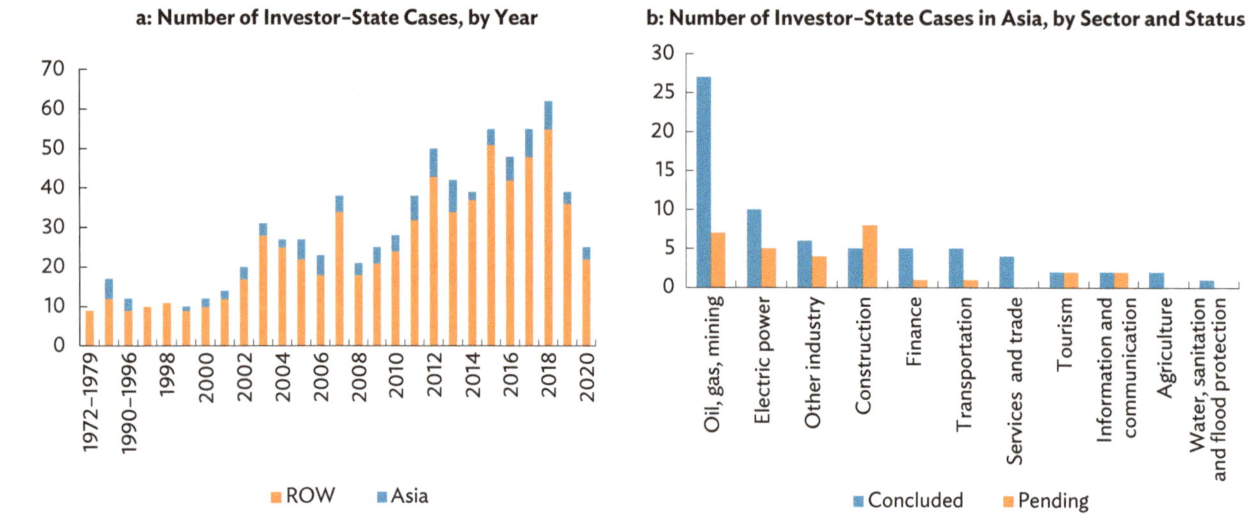

ROW = rest of the world.

Source: ADB calculations using data from World Bank. International Center for Settlement of International Disputes (ICSID). ICSID Cases Database. https://icsid.worldbank.org/cases/case-database (accessed July 2020).

Figure 3.10: Description of New BIT Provisions in ADB Database

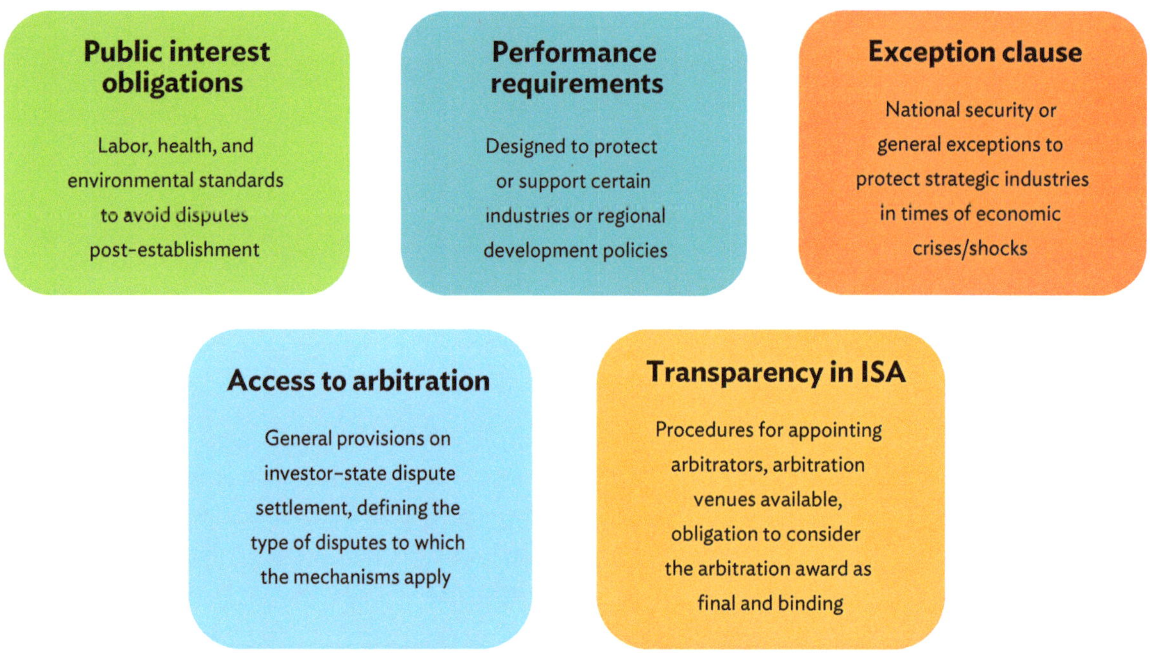

BIT = bilateral investment treaty, ISA = investor–state arbitration.

Source: ADB (forthcoming).

A first glance at the distribution of BIT provisions in Asian investment treaties (Figure 3.11) confirms the heterogeneity among treaties, and that certain provisions (i.e., expropriation, definition of investment, exception clause) are more common than others (i.e., national treatment, performance requirements, transparency in investor–state arbitrations). While certain provisions are fundamental to any bilateral treaty, many are not part of Asian treaties in force today.

Figure 3.11: Average Score for BIT Provisions in Asia's Bilateral Investment Treaties

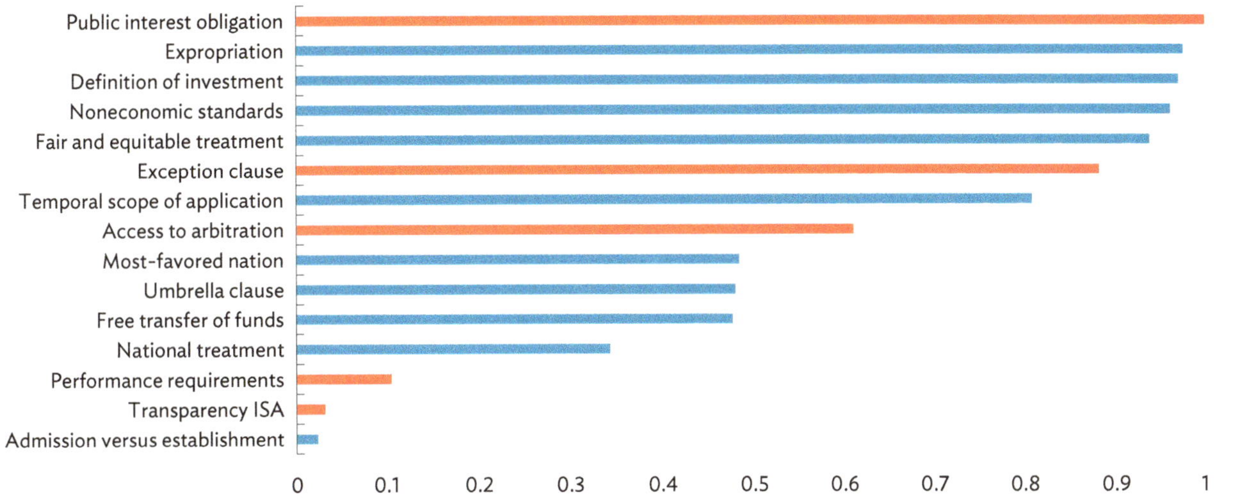

BIT = bilateral investment treaty, ISA = investor-state arbitration.

Notes: Bars in red denote additional provisions included in the ADB International Investment Agreement Database. For all provisions, the higher the value the more likely will the treaty foster foreign direct investment.

Source: ADB (Regional Cooperation and Integration Division, Economic Research and Regional Cooperation Department). International Investment Agreement Database.

Provisions in intra-Asian bilateral investment treaties tend to differ from those between Asia and the rest of the world (ROW), with possible implications for foreign investment.

Comparison of intra-Asian (Asia–Asia) and extra-Asian (Asia–ROW) agreements shows that certain provisions are standard (e.g., definition of investment, expropriation, fair and equal treatment), while others differ between intra and extraregional Asian BITs (Figure 3.12). Examples include the free transfer of funds and the umbrella clause. Clauses on transfer payments are particularly important for investors, and about half of Asia's BITs stipulate that a wide range of payments and other investment-related funds can be transferred out of the host state in a freely convertible currency. The umbrella clause extends the scope of the application of a BIT to any dispute relating to investments and offers more protection to the investor. The template or model of an investment treaty can have implications for both investors and states. In the case of free transfer of funds and umbrella clause, Asian investors tend to be less protected than investors from outside the region. Having less access to arbitration mechanisms could also deter intra-Asian investors. In general, extra-Asian agreements tend to include more favorable provisions for investors.

Figure 3.12: BIT Provisions for Intraregional (Asia–Asia) and Extraregional (Asia–ROW) Agreements

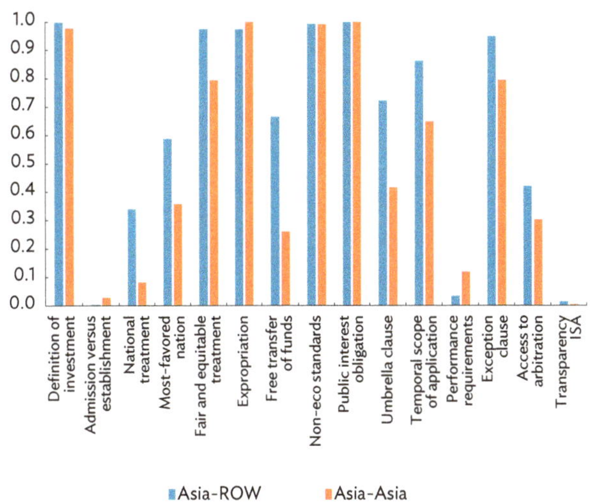

BIT = bilateral investment treaty, ISA = investor-state arbitration, MFN = most-favored nation, ROW = rest of the world.

Note: For all provisions, the higher the value the more likely is the treaty to foster FDI.

Source: ADB (Regional Cooperation and Integration Division, Economic Research and Regional Cooperation Department). International Investment Agreement Database.

Incorporation of certain BIT provisions in Asian treaties has also increased over time, highlighting new priorities for investors and host economies.

A mapping of the incorporation of BIT provisions over time shows a small group of provisions constitutes the backbone of most agreements: definition of investment, fair and equal treatment, expropriation (Figure 3.13). Other provisions have become more prominent; in particular, performance requirements and transparency in investor–state arbitration. Performance requirements have been used as an instrument of regional development policy or to protect certain industries, but their use has been more limited in recent years as they challenge World Trade Organization obligations. Transparency rules in ISD mechanisms, on the other hand, have become more common, with some treaties stipulating public arbitration. Noticeably, the number of agreements including provisions on free transfer of funds and the umbrella clause has decreased. The change in composition of provisions stresses the need for considering the interrelations among investment provisions, as studied in the following section.

Figure 3.13: Average BIT Provisions by Year of Signature or Enforcement

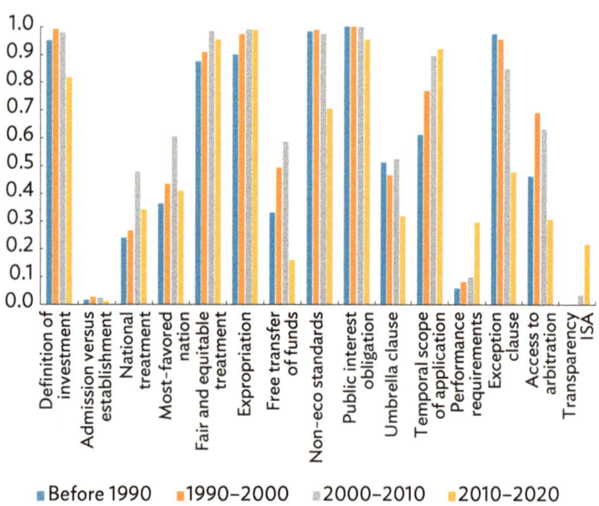

BIT = bilateral investment treaty, ISA = investor–state arbitration, MFN = most-favored nation.

Note: For all provisions, the higher the value the more likely will the treaty foster foreign direct investment.

Source: ADB (Regional Cooperation and Integration Division, Economic Research and Regional Cooperation Department). International Investment Agreement Database.

Liberalization and Antidiscrimination Indicators

Two original indicators are estimated at the country level from the ADB database to assess Asian economies' stance on BIT provisions. The Liberalization Quality Indicator captures the openness of an economy to foreign investment, or, conversely, the degree of control maintained by a state over foreign investment. The indicator is based on the coding of three provisions related to entry: the regulation of foreign investment entry (admission clause), the regulation of transfer of investment-related funds out of the host state, and the presence of noneconomic standards.[23] The index provides a proxy for an economy's stance on FDI capital transfers (equity, reinvested earnings, or profit shifting) and long-term capital movements. Results suggest that economies with a low score (i.e., Myanmar, the PRC, and Viet Nam) tend to have a more restrictive approach toward foreign investors, whereas economies with a high score (e.g., Vanuatu, India, and Pakistan) are more open to foreign investment (Figure 3.14). Some scores are also explained by treaties having been signed before the expansion of cross-border investments in the 1990s.

Figure 3.14: Liberalization Quality Indicator

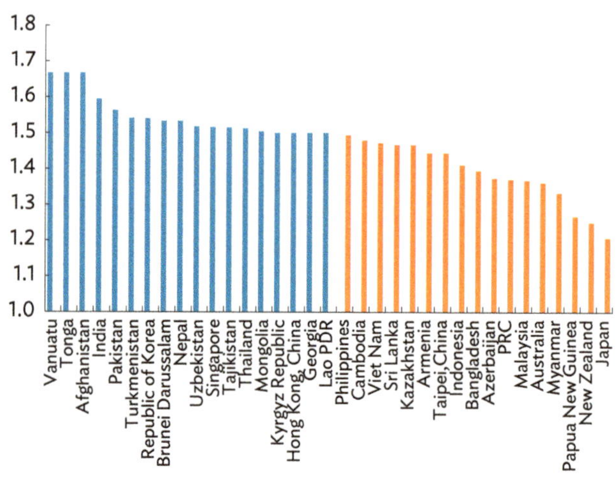

Lao PDR = Lao People's Democratic Republic, PRC = People's Republic of China.

Note: The Liberalization Quality Indicator measures the degree of openness of an economy to foreign investment, or alternatively, the degree of control still maintained by a state over foreign investment.

Source: ADB (Regional Cooperation and Integration Division, Economic Research and Regional Cooperation Department). International Investment Agreement Database.

[23] For more information, see ADB IIA Toolkit for a Comparative Analysis of Concluded IIAs (ADB forthcoming).

The Antidiscrimination Quality Indicator measures the level of equal treatment and absence of discrimination between domestic and foreign investment and how provisions bring about equal treatment for investors (Figure 3.15). The indicator is based on the most-favored nation and national treatment provisions. Economies with a high Antidiscrimination Quality Indicator score indicate that they protect foreign investors from discriminatory practices. On the flip side, these economies can be more vulnerable to facing investment disputes by investors.

Figure 3.15: Antidiscrimination Indicator

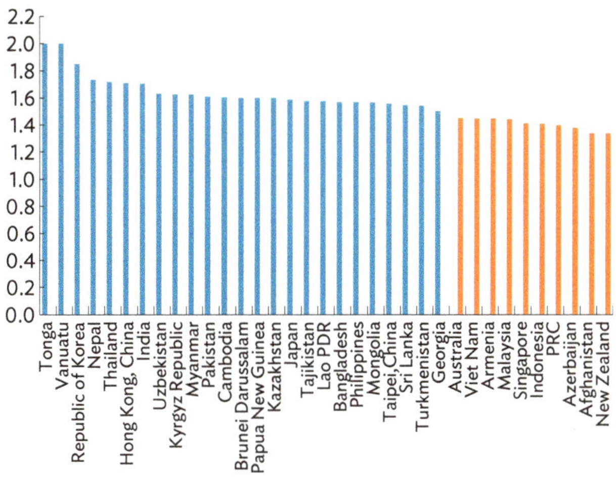

Lao PDR = Lao People's Democratic Republic, PRC = People's Republic of China.

Note: The Antidiscrimination Indicator measures the degree to which international investment agreements ensure a certain degree of equality for foreigners (among themselves and/or relative to nationals).

Source: ADB (Regional Cooperation and Integration Division, Economic Research and Regional Cooperation Department). International Investment Agreement Database.

Assessing the Impact of BIT Provisions on Foreign Investment Flows

To assess the role of BIT provisions on foreign investment, an empirical analysis is proposed, building on ADB's previous work and the relevant literature. The following econometric specification is estimated using a global investment data set of FDI (M&As and Greenfield) over 2003–2019 in a Poisson Pseudo-Maximum Likelihood gravity setting:

$$FDI_{ijk} = exp[\alpha + \beta \mathbf{BIT\_prov}_{ij} + \theta \mathbf{Grav}_{ij} + \delta_i + \delta_j + \delta_k]\varepsilon_{ijk}$$

where FDI_{ijk} denotes investment flows from country i to country j in subsector k, $\mathbf{BIT\_prov}_{ij}$ is a vector with the BIT provisions between countries i and j, $\mathbf{Grav}_{ij}$ is a vector of dyadic control variables in a standard gravity model (distance, gross domestic product origin and destination, common language, contiguity, colonial relationship, governance quality), and δ are fixed-effects for countries and sector. The dependent variable is defined by different measures of FDI flow: M&As (number of deals and deal value in millions of US dollars) and greenfield (number of projects and capital investment in millions of US dollars). The use of Poisson Pseudo-Maximum Likelihood in the estimation has several advantages in this context: it takes into account the heteroskedasticity of errors; it is relatively robust to different variance process scenarios; and it performs well when the proportion of zeros is large, as in this study.

Preliminary results (Table 3.4) for individual provisions confirm the association between BIT provisions and FDI inflows. A comparison of the extensive margin (number of deals and projects) by entry mode (M&As versus greenfield) indicates that most provisions tend to have a positive impact on greenfield investments than for M&A investments. Overall, results are more significant for the extensive margin variables (number of deals and projects) than intensive margin (deal value and investment). The results suggest that investment provisions could capture long-term factors and established attributes of the origin and recipient countries, to which greenfield investments are more sensitive, whereas M&As could be more dependent on short-term fluctuations, including macroeconomic and financial risks (Davies and Desbordes 2018).

As some BIT provisions cover similar areas of investment policy, provisions can be analyzed individually or aggregated in five broad families, as defined in Annex Table 3a.1. Preliminary results for the model above using the broad families of BIT provisions for the full sample and by sector (primary, manufacturing, and services) are presented in Table 3.5. Results suggest that *entry* provision rules (which describe entry rules for foreign investors in domestic markets) and

Table 3.4: M&A and Greenfield Variables, and BIT Provisions

	Dependent Variable			
	M&A		Greenfield	
	Number of Deals	Deal Allocated	Projects	Investment
BIT	0.098	0.221	0.412***	0.227**
	(0.146)	(0.179)	(0.090)	(0.104)
Definition of investment	-0.015	0.062	0.153***	0.053
	(0.068)	(0.084)	(0.043)	(0.048)
Admission versus establishment	0.036	0.113	0.248***	0.064
	(0.126)	(0.151)	(0.085)	(0.086)
National treatment	-0.039	0.127	0.240***	0.107
	(0.086)	(0.130)	(0.053)	(0.065)
Most-favored nation	0.004	0.120	0.215***	0.092
	(0.083)	(0.108)	(0.047)	(0.057)
Fair and equitable treatment	0.027	0.075	0.204***	0.096**
	(0.059)	(0.082)	(0.037)	(0.048)
Expropriation	-0.018	0.068	0.160***	0.067
	(0.069)	(0.085)	(0.044)	(0.049)
Free transfer	0.040	0.087	0.212***	0.072
	(0.095)	(0.101)	(0.045)	(0.057)
Noneconomic standards	-0.026	0.064	0.159***	0.069
	(0.070)	(0.085)	(0.044)	(0.049)
Public interest	-0.020	0.155	0.294***	0.119
	(0.143)	(0.175)	(0.088)	(0.097)
Umbrella clause	0.016	0.139	0.218***	0.087
	(0.073)	(0.098)	(0.042)	(0.053)
Temporal scope	0.014	0.022	0.194***	0.090*
	(0.062)	(0.081)	(0.039)	(0.048)
Performance requirements	0.340	-0.623**	0.033	-0.207
	(0.218)	(0.302)	(0.260)	(0.227)
Exception	-0.036	0.070	0.140***	0.059
	(0.077)	(0.090)	(0.047)	(0.050)
Arbitration	0.144	0.235	0.280***	-0.036
	(0.158)	(0.189)	(0.076)	(0.094)
ISA	0.637	-0.299	-0.479	-0.490
	(0.443)	(0.628)	(0.454)	(0.468)
Observations	2,715	2,715	2,715	2,715

*** Significant at 1%, **Significant at 5%, *Significant at 10%. Standard errors in parentheses.

BIT = bilateral investment treaty, ISA = investor-state arbitration, M&A = merger and acquisition.

Notes: Poisson Pseudo-Maximum Likelihood estimates. Robust standard errors clustered by country pair. Baseline control variables (average from 2004–2019) include log(distance), log(gross domestic product [GDP] origin country), log(GDP destination country), contiguity, common language, colonial relationship, common colonizer, and governance indicators. Dependent variable is taken as the total from 2004–2019.

Sources: ADB calculations using data from Bureau van Dijk. Zephyr M&A Database; Financial Times. fDi Markets; Centre d'Études Prospectives et d'Informations Internationales (the French Research Center in International Economics). GeoDist Database. http://www.cepii.fr/CEPII/en/cepii/cepii.asp (all accessed June 2020); and ADB (Regional Cooperation and Integration Division, Economic Research and Regional Cooperation Department). International Investment Agreement Database.

expropriation provisions could be more favorable to greenfield investments in the manufacturing sector (the base sector in Table 3.5). The effects of *treatment* and investor–state dispute mechanism provisions are less conclusive. These results point to an heterogeneous effect of BIT provisions in explaining M&A and greenfield investment flows, so as among economic sectors, which is coherent with a strand of the literature (Berger et al. 2010, Urata 2015, and Desbordes 2016). They also call for further analysis of ADB's IIA database to understand the role of provisions in explaining FDI recent trends in developing Asia.

Policy Implications under COVID-19

Asian economies have taken different steps to mitigate the disruptive effects of the COVID-19 pandemic on foreign investment.

Measures toward investment facilitation, enlarged services of investment promotion agencies related to COVID-19, and incentives for investment in essential sectors have been introduced. Examples of policy measures in the region include alleviating administrative

Table 3.5: M&A and Greenfield (Number of Deals/Projects), by BIT Family and Sector

Dependent Variable = Number of M&A deals	Independent Variables = BIT and BIT Families					
	BIT	ENTRY	TREAT	SCOPE	EXPR	ISDM
BIT	-0.077	-0.043	-0.071	-0.063	-0.057	-0.077
	(0.177)	(0.123)	(0.107)	(0.104)	(0.089)	(0.132)
Prov x Primary	-0.253	-0.182	-0.131	-0.144	-0.094	-0.142
	(0.334)	(0.213)	(0.196)	(0.188)	(0.164)	(0.241)
Prov x Services	-0.365***	-0.247***	-0.214***	-0.212***	-0.177***	-0.238***
	(0.110)	(0.074)	(0.067)	(0.064)	(0.053)	(0.081)
Observations	5,027	5,027	5,027	5,027	5,027	5,027
Pseudo R2	0.610	0.610	0.610	0.610	0.610	0.609
Dependent Variable = Greenfield Investments	**Independent Variables = BIT and BIT Families**					
	BIT	**ENTRY**	**TREAT**	**SCOPE**	**EXPR**	**ISDM**
BIT	0.291*	0.175*	0.159	0.149	0.137*	0.080
	(0.157)	(0.106)	(0.097)	(0.092)	(0.078)	(0.098)
Prov x Primary	-0.266	-0.165	-0.109	-0.122	-0.075	-0.081
	(0.285)	(0.187)	(0.176)	(0.165)	(0.141)	(0.194)
Prov x Services	-0.442***	-0.286***	-0.256***	-0.240***	-0.206***	-0.244**
	(0.142)	(0.093)	(0.091)	(0.084)	(0.072)	(0.101)
Observations	5,027	5,027	5,027	5,027	5,027	5,027
Pseudo R2	0.579	0.579	0.579	0.579	0.579	0.577

*** Significant at 1%, **Significant at 5%, *Significant at 10%. Standard errors in parentheses.

BIT = bilateral investment treaty, EXPR = expropriation, ISDM = investor–state dispute mechanism, M&A = merger and acquisition, TREAT = treatment.

Notes: Poisson Pseudo-Maximum Likelihood estimates. Robust standard errors clustered by country pair. Baseline control variables (average from 2004–2019) include log(distance), log(gross domestic product [GDP] origin country), log(GDP destination country), contiguity, common language, colonial relationship, common colonizer, and governance indicators. Dependent variable is taken as the total from 2004–2019. Includes main effects of the variables in the interaction.

Sources: ADB calculations using data from Bureau van Dijk. Zephyr M&A Database; Centre d'Etudes Prospectives et d'Informations Internationales (the French Research Center in International Economics). GeoDist database. http://www.cepii.fr/CEPII/en/cepii/cepii.asp; and Financial Times. fDi Markets. (all accessed June 2020); ADB (Regional Cooperation and Integration Division, Economic Research and Regional Cooperation Department). International Investment Agreement Database.

burdens for firms to speed up production during the pandemic (e.g., Myanmar, the PRC, and Thailand) and the use of online and e-government services. Countries have also strengthened partnerships between domestic and foreign investors (e.g., Indonesia). Investment incentives have also been introduced in Asia during the crisis, including, for example, support for the rapid development of medical equipment (e.g., the Republic of Korea) and the conversion of production lines toward essential sectors (e.g., India) (UNCTAD 2020b).

At the international level, there is a fear that governments' response to the COVID-19 crisis could trigger an upsurge of investor-states disputes.

International investment tribunals might have to play a role in the review of states' measures to tackle the COVID-19 pandemic, and calls for a moratorium on all treaty-based ISD arbitration for COVID-19-related measures have emerged (CCSI 2020). From the perspective of IIAs, policy measures by governments can be grouped in four broad areas: (i) foreign investors operating conditions; (ii) market access, transparency, and fairness in global trade; (iii) due process issues; and (iv) other indirect measures (Table 3.6) (Chaisse 2020). A possible increase in the number of ISDs does not mean these claims will be successful; the general perception is that most breaches of investment treaties could be justified, particularly given the emergency situation caused by the COVID-19 pandemic.

Should investment claims increase, some BIT provisions will become important for the recovery.

States and investors have been confronted with economic downturns, political crises, disasters, and other major events. Recent examples in the region include investor claims in cases of expropriation of mining leases and nationalization in the banking sector. Certain BIT provisions have been and will be particularly important in the context of post-COVID-19 investment claims. A critical provision is Fair and Equitable Treatment, which could represent the main entry point for investors against states after the pandemic. Also, provisions on expropriation could play a role in future COVID-19 disputes. Expropriation occurs when an investor can prove that the legal system has been changed in breach of a legitimate expectation the investor had at the time of making an investment. To better respond to a crisis such as COVID-19, Asian governments should continue strenghtening provisions in their BITs to ensure that they are flexible and balanced (Table 3.7).

Table 3.6: International Investment Agreements and Types of COVID-19 Measures

Type of Measures	Measures
Foreign investors operating conditions	Suspension of utility payments
	Compelling production/supply
	Deliveries/supplies limitation
Market access, transparency, and fairness in global trade	Price controls
	Export controls
	Other potentially WTO-inconsistent measures
Due process issues and procedural irregularities	Private property seizure
	Courts closure
	Extraordinary powers to government
Other measures with indirect impact	Other measures with indirect impacts
	COVID-19 tax measures
	Arbitral institutions

COVID-19 = coronavirus disease, WTO = World Trade Organization.

Sources: ADB compilation based on Chaisse (2020) and UNCTAD (2020a).

Table 3.7: Recommendations for Improving BIT Provisions in the Post-COVID-19

BIT Provision	Definition	Post COVID-19 Recommendation
National treatment	Provision describes the obligation to grant foreign investors treatment no less favorable than domestic investors.	Maintain a degree of flexibility with regard to national treatment. Exempt specific policy areas and vital economic sectors to meet both current and future regulatory or public policy needs.
Fair and equitable treatment (FET)	Provision describes if an IIA stipulates equal treatment between foreign/domestic investment for accessing national courts and agencies, imposing taxes, and dealing with domestic regulation.	Clarify scope and obligations of FET standards; FET does not preclude states from adopting good-faith regulatory measures that pursue legitimate policy objectives.
Expropriation	Provision describes arrangements for host government to take over foreign assets. It can be direct (asset appropriation) or indirect (no economic benefit for foreign investors due to loss of management, depreciation, and so on.)	Set out criteria that should not be considered an expropriation, e.g., legitimate regulation taken in exceptional circumstances for the public interest.
Most-favored nation clause	Provision describes the nondiscrimination of foreign investment. The more favorable treatment provided to previous agreements is applied to current agreement.	Maintain a degree of flexibility with regard to MFN. Exclude specific areas and vital economic sectors to meet regulatory or public policy needs.
Free transfer of investment-related funds	Provision describes modalities for repatriation of investment (including profits, benefits, capital gain), proceeds from liquidation or sale, payments.	Provide list of covered payments or transfers and include exceptions in case of serious balance-of-payments difficulties or serious economic crisis.
Non-economic standards	Provision describes protection to investors that covers non purely economic issues, including labor regulations, environmental standards, health, and human rights.	Set out investor obligations by raising the obligation to comply with domestic laws and corporate social responsibility clauses.
Access to arbitration	Provision describes access to arbitration mechanisms, including the International Centre for Settlement of Investment Dispute or others. Existence can be an incentive to invest by providing access to a neutral jurisdiction.	Consider ISD reform: a standing ISDS tribunal replacing the ad hoc investor–state arbitration, limited ISDS, more state control over ISDS, opening proceedings to the public and third parties, enhancing the suitability and impartiality of arbitrators, and replacing ISDS by settling disputes in domestic courts or state–state dispute settlement.
Transparency in ISA	Provision describes existence of *ISDM-specification* transparent mechanisms (more transparent) or *ISDM provisions* for the appointment of arbitrators, obligations of parties, and enforcement (more restrictive).	

BIT = bilateral investment treaty, COVID-19 = coronavirus disease, FET = fair and equitable treatment, IIA = international investment agreement, ISDM = Investor–State Dispute Mechanism, ISDS = investor–state dispute settlement, MFN = most-favored nation.

Sources: ADB compilation based on Chaisse (2020) and UNCTAD (2020b).

In the long-term, a balance between adopting policy measures that prioritize national interest while keeping treaty compliance will be important.

Some reforms to the international investment regime have been implemented gradually to allow states to respond to crisis episodes. In recent years, countries have been more aware of investor–state dispute mechanisms, in particular regarding transparency of settlement procedures, the suitability and selection of arbitrators, and possible resolutions through state–state dispute settlement. Early warning systems for potential disputes are also being developed (UNCTAD 2020b, 2020c). Finally, an important effort in capacity development of government officials responsible for investment policy is needed. Investment treaties could lead to losses—both in the policy space and pecuniary—where host countries lack legal capacity to ensure implementation. Government capacity will play an important role in mediating the impact of investment treaties' disputes in the aftermath of the COVID-19 crisis.

References

Asian Development Bank (ADB). Forthcoming. *ADB International Investment Agreements Toolkit: Technical Report and Database.* Manila: ADB.

Berger, A., M. Busse, P. Nunnenkamp, and M. Roy. 2010. Do Trade and Investment Agreements Lead to More FDI? Accounting for Key Provisions Inside the Black Box. *Kiel Working Papers.* No. 1647. Kiel: Kiel University.

Bergstrand, J. and P. Egger. 2013., What Determines BITs?. *Journal of International Economics.* 90 (1). pp. 107–122.

BloombergQuint. 2020. FDI Policy: Investors from Border States Need Government Approval to Invest in Indian Companies. 18 April. https://www.bloombergquint.com/law-and-policy/fdi-policy-investors-from-border-states-need-government-approval-to-invest-in-indian-companies.

Centre d'Études Prospectives et d'Informations Internationales (the French Research Center in International Economics). GeoDist Database. http://www.cepii.fr/CEPII/en/cepii/cepii.asp (accessed June 2020).

Chaisse, J. 2020. Both Impossible and Improbable: Could the COVID-19 Measures Give Rise to Investor–State Disputes?. *Contemporary Asia Arbitration Journal.* 13 (1). pp. 99–184.

Chaisse, J. and C. Bellak. 2015. Navigating the Expanding Universe of International Treaties on Foreign Investment—Creation and Use of a Critical Index. *Journal of International Economic Law.* 18 (1). pp. 79–115.

Columbia Center on Sustainable Investment (CCSI). 2020. Call for ISDS Moratorium During COVID-19 Crisis and Response. *Columbia Center on Sustainable Investment Memos and Briefing Notes.* May. http://ccsi.columbia.edu/2020/05/05/isds-moratorium-during-covid-19.

Davies, R. and R. Desbordes. 2018. Greenfield Versus Merger and Acquisition FDI: Same Wine, Different Bottles?. *Canadian Journal of Economics.* 51 (4). pp. 1151–90.

Desbordes, R. 2016. A Granular Approach to the Effects of Bilateral Investment Treaties and Regional Trade Investment Agreements on Foreign Direct Investment. Background paper prepared for Asian Economic Integration Report 2016 theme chapter on "What Drives Foreign Direct Investment in Asia and the Pacific?." Manuscript.

European Union. 2019. Regulation (EU) 2019/452 of the European Parliament and of the Council of 19 March 2019: Establishing a Framework for the Screening of Foreign Direct Investments into the Union. *Official Journal of the European Union.* L79 I/1.

Eurostat. Balance of Payments. http://ec.europa.eu/eurostat/web/balance-of-payments/data/database (accessed July 2020).

The Guardian. 2020. Australian Authorities to Check Every Proposed Foreign Investment during Coronavirus Crisis. 29 March. https://www.theguardian.com/world/2020/mar/29/australian-authorities-to-check-every-proposed-foreign-investment-during-coronavirus-crisis.

International Centre for Settlement of Investment Disputes (ICSID). 2020. The ICSID Caseload–Statistics. Issue 2020-1. Washington, DC: World Bank. https://icsid.worldbank.org/sites/default/files/publications/Caseload%20Statistics/en/The%20ICSID%20Caseload%20Statistics%20%282020-1%20Edition%29%20ENG.pdf.

Konrad, K. A. 2017. Large Investors, Regulatory Taking and Investor-State Dispute Settlement. *European Economic Review.* 98. pp. 341–53.

Organisation for Economic Co-operation and Development (OECD). FDI Regulatory Restrictiveness Index. http://stats.oecd.org/Index.aspx?datasetcode=FDIINDEX# (accessed September 2020).

———. 2010. *OECD's FDI Restrictiveness Index: 2010 Update.* Paris. https://www.oecd-ilibrary.org/docserver/5km91p02zj7g-en.pdf?expires=1598956630&id=id&accname=guest&checksum=2E2E0E0DA64D5D40CDA6BE1B41384AD8.

———. 2020a. *Foreign Direct Investment Flows in the Time of COVID-19.* Paris. https://www.oecd.org/coronavirus/policy-responses/foreign-direct-investment-flows-in-the-time-of-covid-19-a2fa20c4/.

———. 2020b. *Investment Screening in Times of COVID-19 and Beyond.* Paris. http://www.oecd.org/coronavirus/policy-responses/investment-screening-in-times-of-covid-19-and-beyond-aa60af47/.

United Nations Conference on Trade and Development (UNCTAD). 2020a. *World Investment Report 2020: International Production Beyond the Pandemic.* Geneva.

———. *World Investment Report 2020,* Statistical Annex Tables. Geneva. https://unctad.org/en/Pages/DIAE/World%20Investment%20Report/Annex-Tables.aspx (accessed June 2020).

———. 2020b. *Investment Policy Monitor—Special Issue: Policy Responses to the COVID-19 Pandemic.* Geneva. https://unctad.org/en/PublicationsLibrary/diaepcbinf2020d3_en.pdf.

———. 2020c. *International Investment Agreements Reform Accelerator.* Geneva. https://unctad.org/system/files/official-document/diaepcbinf2020d8_en.pdf (accessed January 2021).

———. 2019. *Investment Policy Monitor: National Security-Related Screening Mechanisms for Foreign Investment.* Geneva. https://unctad.org/en/PublicationsLibrary/diaepcbinf2019d7_en.pdf.

Urata, S. 2015. Impacts of FTAs and BITs on the Locational Choice of Foreign Direct Investment: The Case of Japanese Firms. *RIETI Discussion Paper Series.* 15-E-066.

United States Department of Treasury. 2018. Summary of the Foreign Investment Risk Review Modernization Act of 2018. Washington, DC. https://www.treasury.gov/resource-center/international/Documents/Summary-of-FIRRMA.pdf.

World Bank. International Center for Settlement of International Disputes (ICSID). ICSID Cases Database. https://icsid.worldbank.org/cases/case-database (accessed July 2020).

———. World Development Indicators. https://databank.worldbank.org/source/world-development-indicators (accessed July 2020).

———. World Governance Indicators. https://info.worldbank.org/governance/wgi (accessed July 2020).

Annex 3a: Supplementary Charts and Table on BITs and the Liberalization and Antidiscrimination Indicators

Annex Table 3a.1: BIT Provisions by Category

Dimension	Definition	BIT Provisions Included
Entry	Describes entry rules for foreign investors	• Admission versus establishment • Noneconomic standards • Investment-related funds
Treatment	Describes treatment given to foreign investors against domestic ones	• National treatment • Most-favored nation • Public interest obligation*
Scope	Describes definition of investment, jurisdiction, and duration of treaty	• Definition of investment • Umbrella clause • Temporal scope of application • Exception clause* • Performance requirements*
Expropriation	Arrangements for host states to take over foreign assets	• Fair and equitable treatment • Direct and indirect expropriation
Dispute mechanism		• Access to arbitration* • ISA transparency*

BIT = bilateral investment treaty, ISA = investor–state arbitration.

*New available provisions in ADB's (Regional Cooperation and Integration Division, Economic Research and Regional Cooperation Department) International Investment Agreement Database, not covered in Chaisse and Bellak (2015).

Sources: ADB compilation based on Desbordes (2016) and Chaisse (2020).

Annex Figure 3a.1: Liberalization and Antidiscrimination Indicators in Asia

GDP per Capita

Liberalization Indicator and GDP per Capita

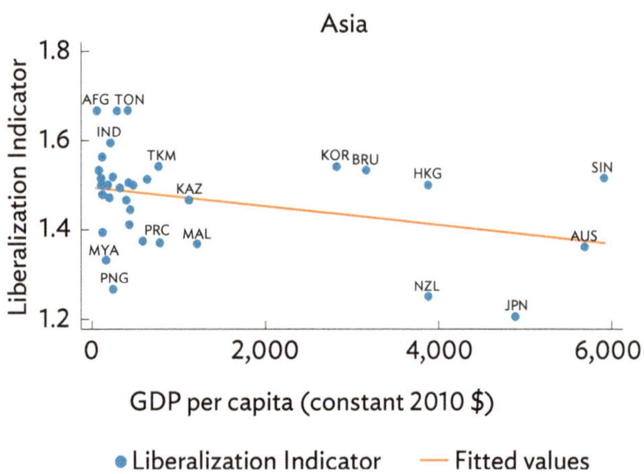

Antidiscrimination Indicator and GDP per Capita

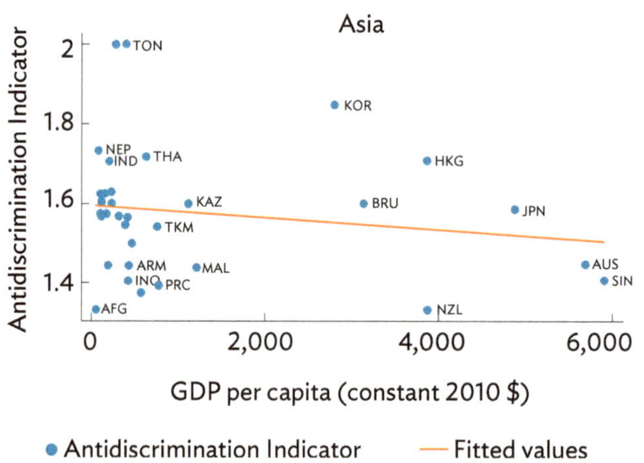

continued on next page

Figure continued

FDI Regulatory Restrictiveness Index

Liberalization Indicator and FDI Regulatory Restrictiveness Index

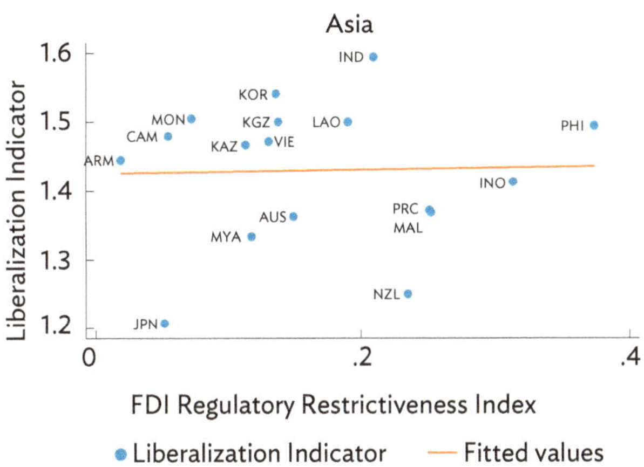

Antidiscrimination Indicator and FDI Regulatory Restrictiveness Index

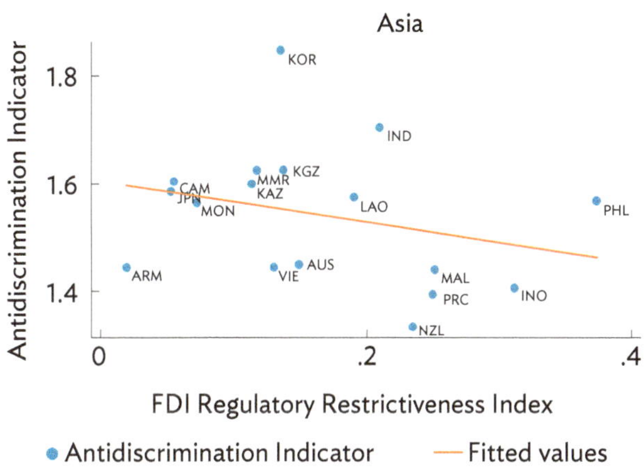

World Governance Indicator (Regulatory Quality)

Liberalization Indicator and Regulatory Quality

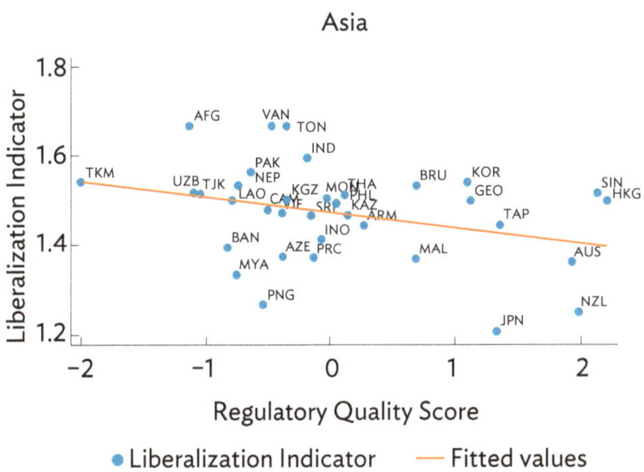

Antidiscrimination Indicator and Regulatory Quality

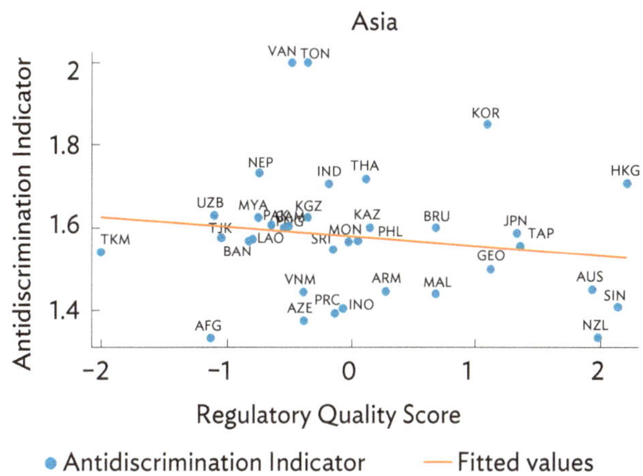

AFG = Afghanistan; ARM = Armenia; AUS = Australia; AZE = Azerbaijan; BAN = Bangladesh; BRU = Brunei Darussalam; CAM = Cambodia; FDI = foreign direct investment; GDP = gross domestic product; GEO = Georgia; HKG = Hong Kong, China; IND = India; INO = Indonesia; JPN = Japan; KAZ = Kazakhstan; KGZ = Kyrgyz Republic; KOR = Republic of Korea; LAO = Lao People's Republic of China; MAL = Malaysia; MON = Mongolia; MYA = Myanmar; NEP = Nepal; NZL = New Zealand; OECD = Organisation for Economic Co-operation and Development; PAK = Pakistan; PHI = Philippines; PNG = Papua New Guinea; PRC = People's Republic of China; SIN = Singapore; SRI = Sri Lanka; TAJ = Tajikistan; TAP = Taipei,China; THA = Thailand; TKM = Turkmenistan; TON = Tonga; UZB = Uzbekistan; VAN = Vanuatu; and VIE = Viet Nam.

Sources: ADB calculations using data from Organisation for Economic Co-operation and Development. FDI Regulatory Restrictiveness Index. https://stats.oecd.org/Index.aspx?datasetcode=FDIINDEX#; World Bank. World Development Indicators. https://databank.worldbank.org/source/world-development-indicators; World Bank. World Governance Indicators. http://info.worldbank.org/governance/wgi (all accessed July 2020); and ADB (Regional Cooperation and Integration Division, Economic Research and Regional Cooperation Department). International Investment Agreement Database.

4 Financial Integration
Heightened Financial Vulnerabilities amid the Pandemic

The onset of the COVID-19 pandemic led to a spike in global financial volatility, a deterioration in investor sentiment, and tighter liquidity conditions in March 2020.

As the World Health Organization declared the coronavirus disease (COVID-19) outbreak a global pandemic on 11 March 2020, investor sentiment deteriorated quickly. The Chicago Board Options Exchange's volatility index (VIX), a measure of risk aversion, reached levels last seen during the 2008 global financial crisis (Figure 4.1). The index rose sharply in early March as economies implemented strict quarantine measures, and its peak in the week of 10 March was slightly higher than the peak reached in October of 2008.

The pandemic and related containment measures hit the economies hard around the world. As risk-off sentiment spread globally, emerging market assets were sold off. Sovereign credit default swaps (CDS) spreads of selected Asian economies widened sharply (Figure 4.2). Amid massive unwinding of risky assets and flight to safety, short-term dollar funding markets tightened (Figure 4.3). Offshore dollar funding costs in emerging market economies, likewise, rose sharply amid disruptions of the dollar supply. The cross-currency basis swap versus the United States (US) dollar widened in mid-March, particularly for the won and ringgit, and to a much greater degree than it did for major currencies, such as the euro, pound sterling, or yen (Figure 4.4).

Figure 4.1: Volatility Index

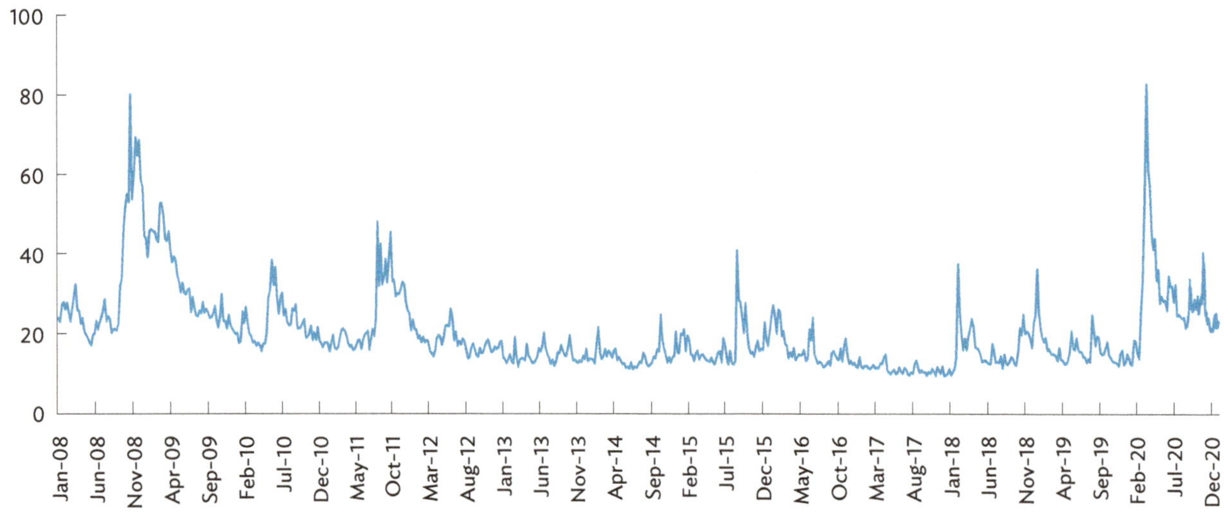

Note: The volatility index refers to the adjusted close value.

Source: Chicago Board Options Exchange. Volatility Index. http://www.cboe.com/vix (accessed January 2021).

Figure 4.2: Credit Default Swaps—Selected Asian Economies (spreads index, 2 January 2020 = 100)

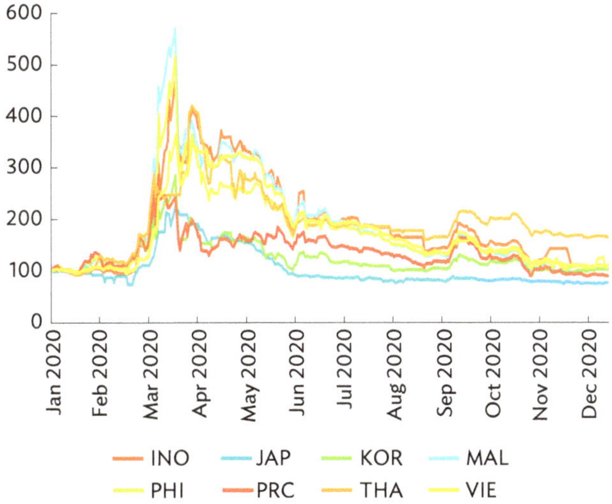

INO = Indonesia, JPN = Japan, KOR = Republic of Korea, MAL = Malaysia, PHI = Philippines, PRC = People's Republic of China, THA = Thailand, VIE = Viet Nam.

Notes: A credit default swap is a financial derivative that insures against the risk of default by one party. A higher index value reflects a higher spread, which is associated with higher default risk.

Source: ADB calculations using data from Bloomberg.

Figure 4.3: LIBOR-OIS Spread—Global Financial Crisis versus COVID-19 (basis points)

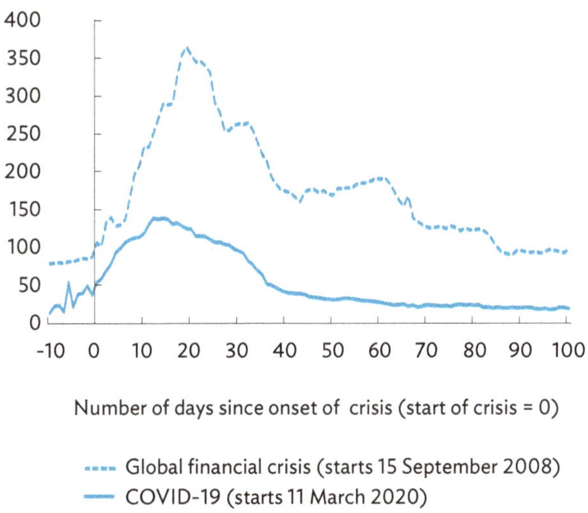

COVID-19 = coronavirus disease, LIBOR = London Inter-Bank Offered Rate, OIS = Overnight Index Swap.

Source: ADB calculations using data from Bloomberg.

Figure 4.4: Cross-Currency Basis Swap Spread against the United States Dollar (basis points)

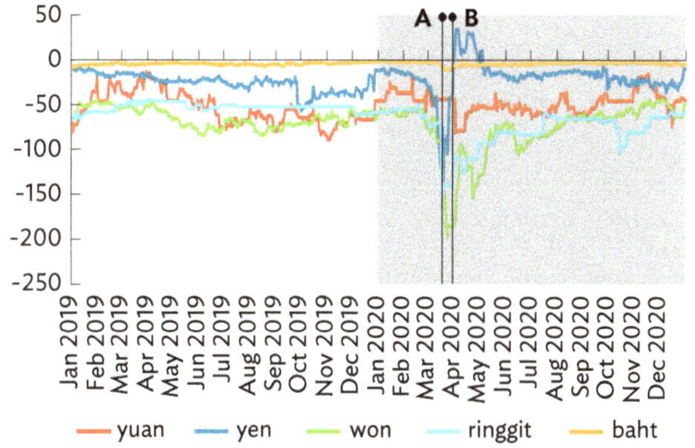

A (19 March 2020): US Federal Reserve established nine temporary dollar liquidity swap lines

B (30 March 2020): US Federal Reserve introduced temporary foreign and international monetary authorities repo facility

US = United States.

Note: 3-month cross-currency basis swap for the yen, ringgit, and yuan; 6 months for the baht; and 3 months for the won versus 6 months for the US dollar.

Source: Bloomberg.

The deterioration in investor sentiment and tighter liquidity conditions, due to the COVID-19 pandemic and its impact on economic and financial conditions led to financial market stress around the world. Financial stress indexes climbed in the euro area, the United Kingdom and the US. In Asia, they spiked in India, Indonesia, Japan, the Philippines, Singapore, and Thailand (Figures 4.5a and 4.5b).

Equity prices in the region plunged in mid-March 2020, along with the region's currencies and a sharp reversal in portfolio equity flows.

Asset prices in the region dropped significantly in March. Benchmark stock prices in India; Indonesia; Japan; the Republic of Korea; the Philippines; Singapore; Thailand, and Viet Nam lost more than 30% of their values on 2 January 2020 by mid-March (Figure 4.6). But the slump in the region's benchmark equity prices from the onset of the pandemic was less severe in 2020 than during the 2008 global financial crisis (Figure 4.7).

Figure 4.5a: Financial Stress Index—Euro Area, the United States, and the United Kingdom

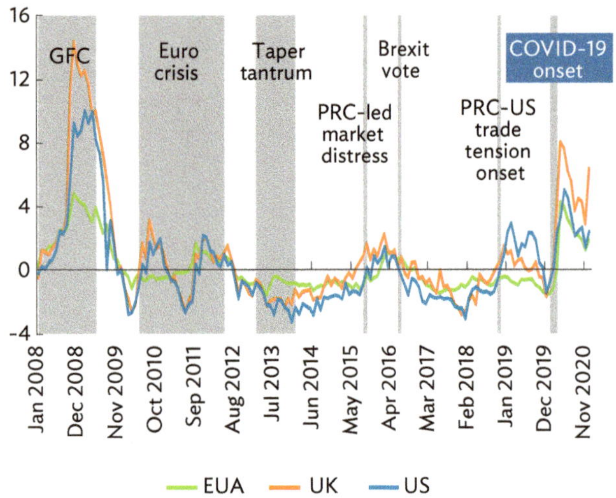

EUA = euro area, GFC = global financial crisis, PRC = People's Republic of China, UK = United Kingdom, US = United States.

Notes:

(i) Based on principal components analysis on data from 4 major finance sectors: the banking sector, debt, equity, and foreign exchange markets.

(ii) Principal components are based on the banking sector price index, sovereign yield spreads, stock market volatility, stock price index return, and exchange market pressure index.

Sources: ADB calculations using data from Bloomberg; CEIC; Haver Analytics; the International Monetary Fund. International Financial Statistics. http://data.imf.org/IFS (accessed January 2021); and methodology by Park and Mercado (2014).

Figure 4.5b: Financial Stress Index—Selected Asian Economies

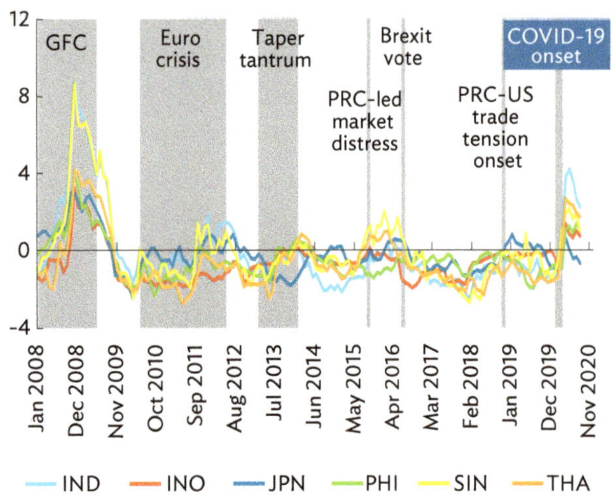

GFC = global financial crisis, IND = India, INO = Indonesia, JPN = Japan, PHI = Philippines, PRC = People's Republic of China, SIN = Singapore, THA = Thailand, US = United States.

Notes:

(i) Based on principal components analysis on data from 4 major finance sectors: the banking sector, debt, equity, and foreign exchange markets.

(ii) Principal components are based on the banking sector price index, sovereign yield spreads, stock market volatility, stock price index return, and exchange market pressure index.

Sources: ADB calculations using data from Bloomberg; CEIC; Haver Analytics; the International Monetary Fund. International Financial Statistics. http://data.imf.org/IFS (accessed January 2021); and methodology by Park and Mercado (2014).

Figure 4.6: Stock Price Index—Selected Asian Economies
(2 January 2020 = 100)

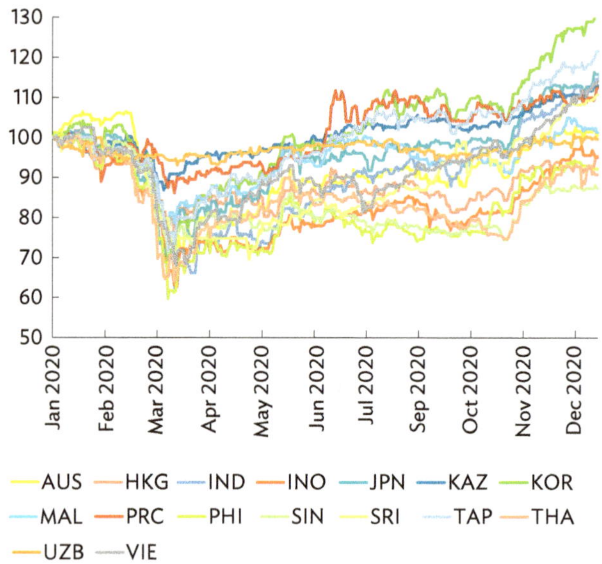

AUS = Australia; HKG = Hong Kong, China; IND = India; INO = Indonesia; JPN = Japan; KAZ = Kazakhstan; KOR = Republic of Korea; MAL = Malaysia; PHI = Philippines; PRC = People's Republic of China; SIN = Singapore; SRI = Sri Lanka; TAP = Taipei,China; THA = Thailand; UZB = Uzbekistan; VIE = Viet Nam.

Source: ADB calculations using data from Bloomberg.

Figure 4.7: Comparison of Equity Market Slump—Selected Economies

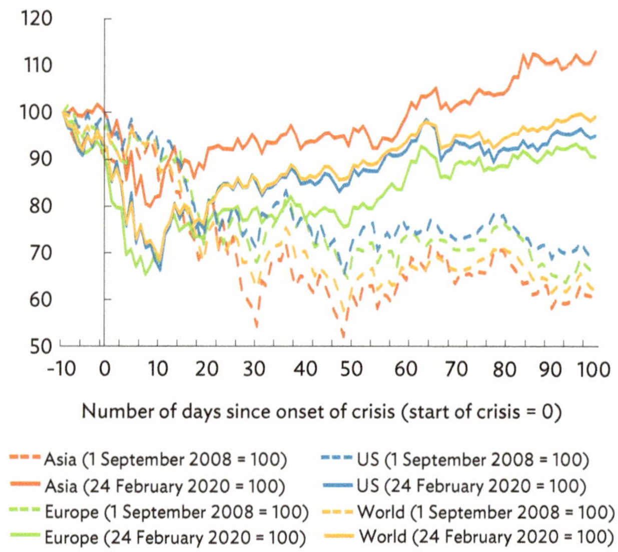

US = United States.

Note: Onset of the crises is defined as follows: Collapse of Lehman Brothers 15 September 2008 (global financial crisis); and imposed lockdown in Italy 9 March 2020 (COVID-19 pandemic).

Sources: ADB calculations using data from Google Finance. http://google.com/finance; Investing.com. https://www.investing.com/indices/msci-world-historical-data; MSCI. MSCI World Index. https://www.msci.com/eqb/esg/performance/106.0.all.xls; and S&P Dow Jones Indices. Dow Jones Industrial Average Index. https://us.spindices.com/indices/equity/dow-jones-industrial-average (all accessed August 2020).

The drop in equity prices was accompanied by nonresident portfolio outflows in the region last March (Figure 4.8). Reported nonresident portfolio equity outflows reached $19 billion in the week of 13 March, and this accounted for a large share of the overall portfolio outflows to emerging market economies in that week. The recorded nonresident portfolio outflows repeated a familiar pattern of nonresident capital flow retrenchment or flight to safety as asset prices fall during episodes of financial stress.

Figure 4.8: Nonresident Portfolio Flows—Selected Asian Economies ($ billion)

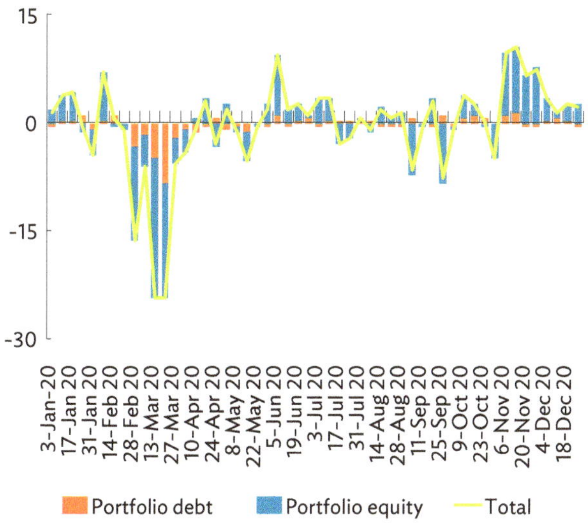

Sources: ADB calculations using data from the Institute of International Finance and national sources.

Total nonresident financial flows to selected Asian economies dropped by 34% in the first quarter (Q1) of 2020, compared with the previous quarter, to reach $138 billion (Figure 4.9). Nonresident portfolio equity outflows in Q1 2020 amounted to $57 billion, which is a significant turnaround from equity inflows of about $40 billion in Q4 2019. Aside from nonresident portfolio equity outflows, trade credit and advances also reported outflows, amounting to $39 billion. The drop in trade credits and advances was also observed during the 2008–2009 global financial crisis. However, there were increases in some of the components of capital inflows in Q1 2020. Currency and deposits grew by 50% in the same quarter to $66 billion, from $44 billion in Q4 2019, implying nonresident investors' move to more liquid assets. Loan inflows increased to $52 billion, suggesting higher cross-border demand for credit.

Figure 4.9: Nonresident Capital Flows—Selected Asian Economies ($ billion)

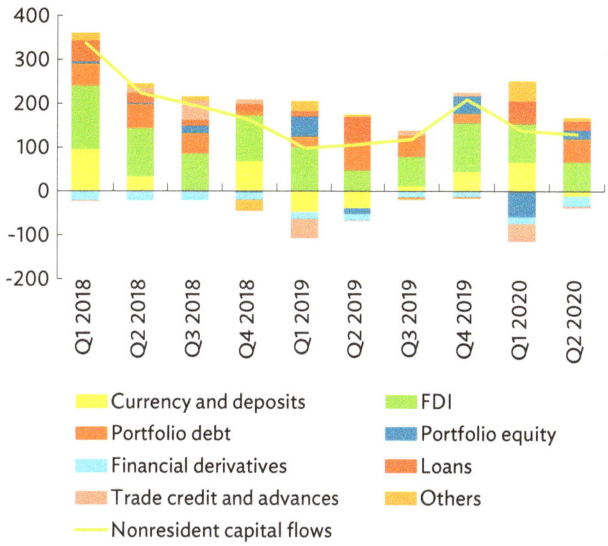

FDI = foreign direct investment.

Note: Asia includes Bangladesh; Cambodia; Hong Kong, China; India; Indonesia; Kazakhstan; Mongolia; Nepal; the People's Republic of China; the Philippines; the Republic of Korea; Taipei,China; and Thailand.

Source: ADB calculations using data from the International Monetary Fund. Balanced of Payments. Accessed from CEIC.

Regional currencies also weakened during the onset of the COVID-19 global pandemic, but to varying degrees (Figure 4.10). The Australian dollar, rupiah, and tenge lost more than 10% of their values on 2 January 2020 by mid-March. The Brunei dollar, Indian rupee, won, ringgit, Singapore dollar, and baht lost about 5%, while the yuan, peso, Sri Lanka rupee, and dong lost less than 5% of their values.

Swift policy responses across the region and elsewhere helped ease liquidity conditions and restored investor sentiment by June 2020.

In response to the COVID-19 pandemic and subsequent financial market stress, authorities implemented measures to navigate economic overhang and ease financial strains. These included fiscal support, policy rate cuts, liquidity support, and credit provisions, among others. For instance, central banks in Asia slashed policy rates, on average, by around 50 basis points from March to May 2020 (Figure 4.11). In response to exchange rate pressures and volatility, and to support foreign

Figure 4.10: Exchange Rate, $/LCU—Selected Asian Currencies (2 January 2020 = 100)

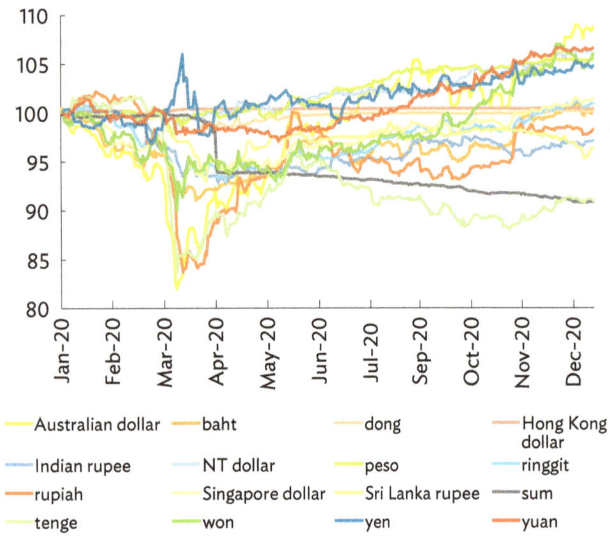

LCU = local currency unit.

Source: ADB calculations using data from Bloomberg.

Figure 4.11: Policy Rate Cuts—Selected Asian Economies

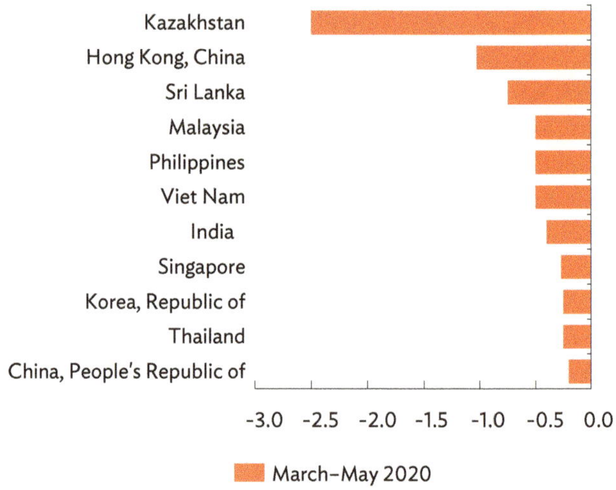

Source: ADB calculations using data from CEIC.

exchange liquidity, central banks or monetary authorities entered into bilateral currency swap arrangements with the US Federal Reserve and/or with other central banks with international currency, including the Bank of Japan.[24] Moreover, some emerging market central banks, including some in the region, implemented unconventional monetary policy measures through local currency bond purchase programs, including government securities, either to support monetary policy or market liquidity. Initial assessment of this measure suggests their success as local currency bond yields fell with minimal effect on the exchange rate (Arslan, Drehmann, and Hofmann 2020).

These swift policy actions by authorities, within and outside the region, eased financial conditions greatly and restored investor sentiment by June 2020. Equity prices and exchange rates trended upward after April 2020 (Figures 4.6 and 4.10). In fact, stock prices in Australia; India; Japan; Kazakhstan; the People's Republic of China (PRC); the Republic of Korea; Malaysia; Sri Lanka; Taipei,China; and Viet Nam traded above their start-of-the-year values as of the end of December. However, for some economies in the region, shares have yet to reach their start-of-the-year values in 2020. The Australian dollar, yen, won, ringgit, peso, NT dollar, and baht surpassed their start-of-the-year values as of the end of December, but several regional currencies did not. The extent to which regional exchange rates reacted was significantly more moderate than during the 1997 Asian financial crisis and the global financial crisis. Nonresident portfolio equity outflows stopped, and debt inflows resumed by June 2020 (Figure 4.8).

But risks of financial volatility remained at large in the rest of 2020.

Although financial conditions improved as early as June 2020, rising cases of COVID-19 infections, the possibility of localized or wider lockdowns and border closures being reimposed, and weak economic prospects in the second half of the year continued to fuel uncertainties and test investor risk sentiment. The VIX remained elevated as of the end of December 2020, along with financial stress indexes for selected advanced and Asian economies (Figures 4.1, 4.5a, and 4.5b). Moreover, dollar funding costs remained high; and equity prices remained below their start-of-the-year values for some economies in the region (Figures 4.4 and 4.6). Total nonresident financial

24 In addition to the US Federal Reserve's standing swap lines with major central banks, the establishment of nine temporary dollar liquidity swap lines (19 March 2020), including with regional central banks in Australia, New Zealand, the Republic of Korea, and Singapore, as well as the introduction of the temporary foreign and international monetary authorities repo facility (31 March 2020) to a broader group of foreign central banks and other international monetary authorities were effective in arresting panic in the US dollar funding market.

flows to selected Asian economies slipped lower to $130 billion in Q2 2020, down by 6% from Q1 2020 (Figure 4.9). Although portfolio equity inflows resumed, other components of capital inflows declined in Q2 2020, including currency and deposits; and loan inflows. Should investor sentiment deteriorate, renewed financial market turbulence and tighter liquidity conditions may resurface.

Given the global nature of the ongoing pandemic and associated economic impact, the share of global shocks in the variation of Asian asset price returns rose sharply and remained larger than the share of regional shocks.

The share of global shocks that explain the variation of equity returns in Asia rose to around 20% in Q1 2020, which was almost double the share reported in in the final trimester of 2019 (Figure 4.12). The global share further rose to around 28% for the rest of the year, reflecting the global nature of the pandemic and its associated economic and financial uncertainties. In contrast, the proportion of regional shocks initially slipped to around 7% in Q1 2020, which was slightly lower than that was reported in the previous period. But, like global shares, the share of regional shocks increased to 9.3% for the rest of 2020. Across subregions of Asia, East Asia's equity markets showed the strongest sensitivity to global and regional shocks at the start of the COVID-19 pandemic, followed by Oceania.

Similarly, the proportion of global shocks that explain the variation of bond returns rose to almost 11% in Q1 2020 (Figure 4.13). This was also higher than the share registered in the final trimester of 2019. The global share increased further to 17% for the rest of 2020. The proportion of regional shocks, likewise, increased from January to March 2020, compared with September to December 2019, and remained stable for the rest of the year. Across subregions, the increase in the share of global shocks was highest for Oceania during the onset of the pandemic, while the increase in the proportion of regional shocks was strongest for South Asia.

Compared with the 2008–2009 global financial crisis, the shares of global and regional shocks that account for the variations in equity returns were considerably lower during the onset of the COVID-19 pandemic, while the share of domestic

Figure 4.12: Variance Decomposition—Equity Returns

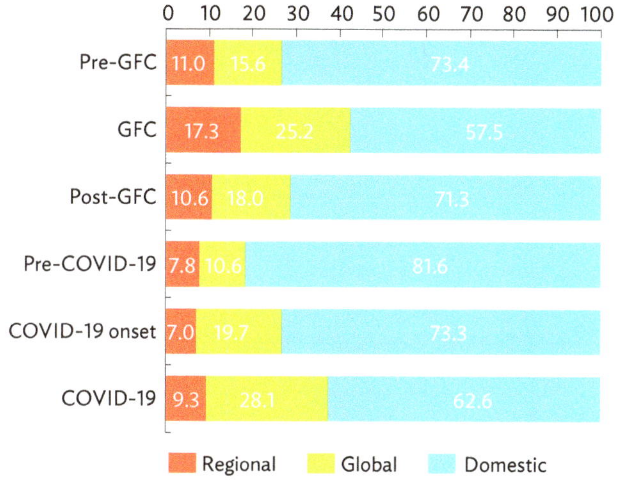

COVID-19 = coronavirus disease, GFC = global financial crisis.

Note: Pre-GFC = January 1999 to September 2007, GFC = October 2007 to June 2009, Post-GFC = July 2009 to December 2015, Pre-COVID-19 = September to December 2019, COVID-19 onset = January to March 2020, COVID-19 = April to December 2020.

Asia includes Australia; Bangladesh; Cambodia; Georgia; Hong Kong, China; India; Indonesia; Japan; Kazakhstan; the Kyrgyz Republic; the Lao People's Democratic Republic; Malaysia; Mongolia; Nepal; New Zealand; Pakistan; the People's Republic of China; the Philippines; the Republic of Korea; Singapore; Sri Lanka; Taipei,China; Thailand; Uzbekistan; and Viet Nam.

Sources: ADB calculations using data from Bloomberg; CEIC; and methodology by Lee and Park (2011).

Figure 4.13: Variance Decomposition—Bond Returns

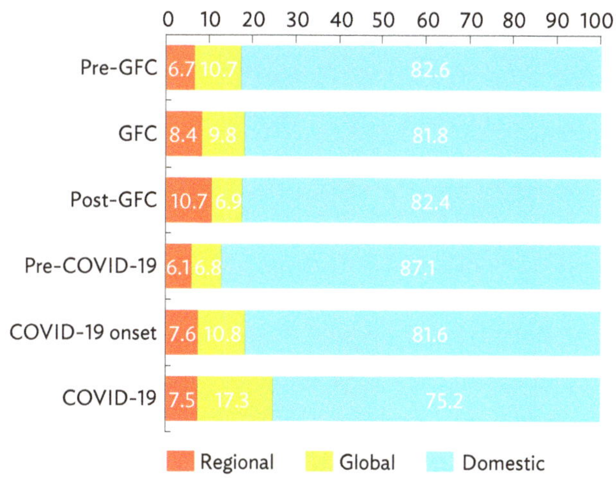

COVID-19 = coronavirus disease, GFC = global financial crisis.

Note: Pre-GFC = January 1999 to September 2007, GFC = October 2007 to June 2009, Post-GFC = July 2009 to December 2015, Pre-COVID-19 = September to December 2019, COVID-19 onset = January to March 2020, COVID-19 = April to December 2020.

Asia includes Australia; Hong Kong, China; India; Indonesia; Japan; Kazakhstan; Malaysia; the People's Republic of China; the Philippines; the Republic of Korea; Singapore; Thailand; and Viet Nam.

Sources: ADB calculations using data from Bloomberg; CEIC; and methodology by Lee and Park (2011).

Figure 4.14: Cross-Border Assets—Asia

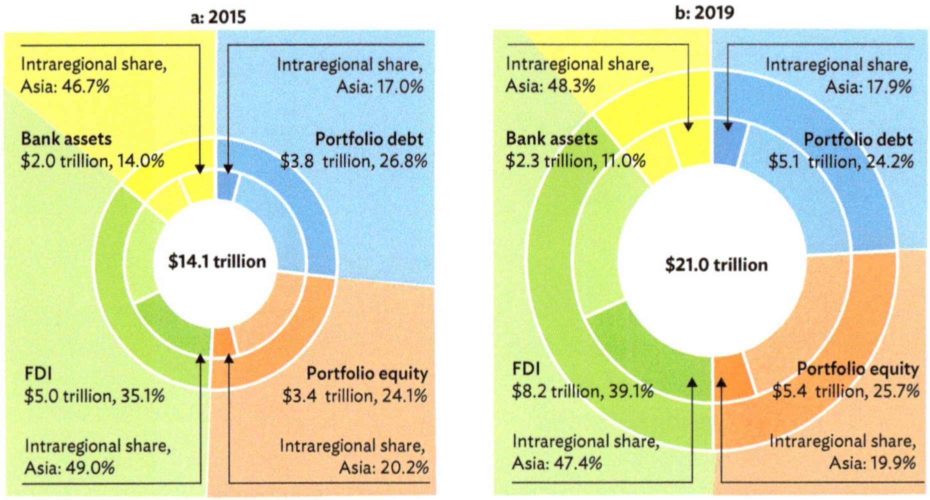

FDI = foreign direct investment.

Notes: FDI assets refer to outward FDI holdings. Bank assets refer to bank claims and limited to loans and deposits. Asia includes ADB regional members for which data are available.

Sources: ADB calculations using data from the Bank for International Settlements. Locational Banking Statistics. https://www.bis.org/statistics/bankstats.htm (accessed October 2020); International Monetary Fund (IMF). Coordinated Direct Investment Survey. http://cdis.imf.org (accessed December 2020); and IMF. Coordinated Portfolio Investment Survey. http://cpis.imf.org (accessed September 2020).

shocks were higher (Figures 4.12 and 4.13). The stronger impact of global and regional shocks in 2008 and 2009 reflected the financial nature of the global crisis, whereas the ongoing COVID-19 pandemic is a global health crisis.

Recent Trends in Asia's Cross-Border Financial Assets and Liabilities

Asian investors continued to hold considerably more non-regional assets and liabilities than regional ones.[25]

Asia's total cross-border financial asset holdings reached $21.0 trillion at the end of 2019, which was significantly greater than $14.1 trillion registered at the end of 2015 (Figure 4.14).[26] Most of the region's investment holdings in the 2019 amount took the form of direct investment assets ($8.2 trillion), followed by portfolio equity ($5.4 trillion) and portfolio debt ($5.1 trillion), and then banking sector loan and deposit holdings ($2.3 trillion). But around two thirds of Asia's asset holdings were placed in non-regional economies, and about one-third in regional economies.

Asia's outward portfolio debt holdings increased from $4.5 trillion in 2018 to $5.1 trillion in 2019, recording a 12% increase while continuing the trend over the past years.[27] The Asian investors' outward portfolio equity holdings rebounded strongly to $5.4 trillion in 2019, after declining to $4.5 trillion in 2018. Meanwhile, Asia's cross-border total bank claims (including loans, deposits, debt securities, and other instruments) continued to rise in 2019 to $6.6 trillion, from $6.3 trillion in 2018.

25 Asia's reporting economies include Australia; Bangladesh; Hong Kong, China; India; Indonesia; Japan; Kazakhstan; Malaysia; Mongolia; New Zealand; Pakistan; Palau; the People's Republic of China; the Philippines; the Republic of Korea; Singapore; and Thailand.

26 The values reported for total cross-border assets, liabilities, and net position do not reflect total values in the International Investment Position. This is because reported values include only those with available bilateral breakdown to decompose regional and non-regional holdings and liabilities. Throughout this chapter, cross-border investment holdings include foreign direct investment (FDI), portfolio equity, portfolio debt, and banking sector loan and deposit assets (claims) and liabilities. Unlike previous editions of this report, banking sector cross-border claims and liabilities refer to loans and deposits instead of total claims and liabilities, which include debt securities and other instruments.

27 The overall increase or decrease in stock portfolio holdings and liabilities is attributed to changes in flows and valuation changes of existing portfolio holdings and liabilities.

The region's total external financial liabilities also inched higher to $20.9 trillion by the end of 2019, up from $15.7 trillion for 2015 (Figure 4.15). Most of the region's liabilities at the end of 2019 were foreign direct investments ($9.3 trillion), followed by portfolio equity ($5.6 trillion), portfolio debt ($3.2 trillion), and then banking sector loan and deposit liabilities ($2.8 trillion). Two-thirds of these liabilities were held by non-regional economies, and one-third by regional economies. As two-thirds of Asia cross-border investment holdings and liabilities were placed in non-regional economies and in the form of direct investments, the region remained exposed to changing non-regional profit earnings outlook, investor sentiment, and liquidity conditions (Box 4.1).

Inward debt portfolio investment grew to $3.2 trillion in 2019, from $2.9 trillion in 2018, while the value of inward equity portfolio investment rose considerably to $5.6 trillion, after dropping to $4.7 trillion in 2018. The intraregional share of inward portfolio debt holdings increased to 28.8% in 2019 from 27.1% in 2018, and that of inward portfolio equity investment rose to 19.0% from 18.3% in the same period. Asia's banking sector cross-border liabilities (including loans, deposits, debt securities, and other instruments) slightly increased in 2019 to $3.8 trillion from $3.7 trillion in 2018. The fact that Asian banks' cross-bank claims exceed their cross-border liabilities highlights the region's role as a net global lender, while the downward trending intraregional shares imply Asian banks' increasing integration within the global banking network.

As the region held more debt assets than debt liabilities, but more equity liabilities than equity assets, it retained its long debt, short equity position as of the end of 2019. The net debt position rose from $1.2 trillion at the end of 2015 to $1.5 trillion at the end of 2019, while the net equity position improved from −$2.8 trillion in 2015 to -$1.3 trillion in 2019. The major share of its long debt and short equity positions were with non-regional economies, as of the end of 2019, mirroring the regional breakdown of its international investment assets and liabilities. Annex 4a provides additional discussions on trends in Asia's cross-border assets and liabilities.

Figure 4.15: Cross-Border Liabilities—Asia

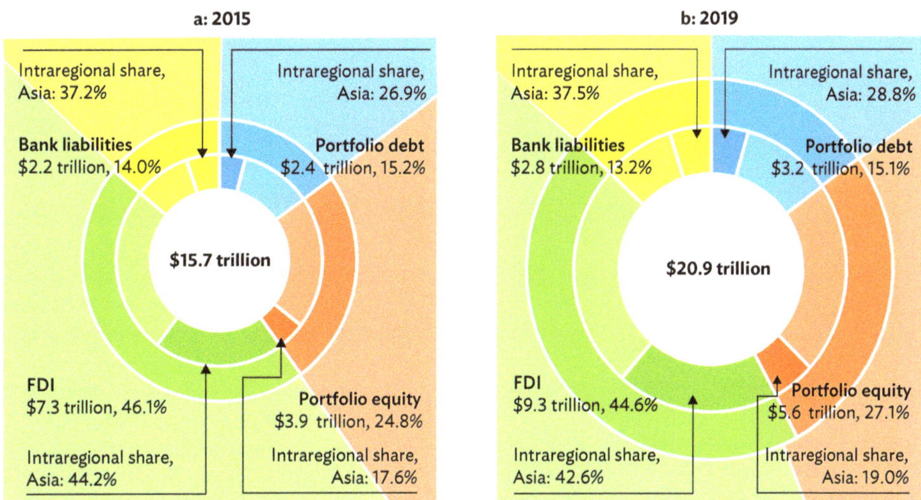

FDI = foreign direct investment.

Notes: FDI assets refer to outward FDI holdings. Bank assets refer to bank claims and limited to loans and deposits. Asia includes ADB regional members for which data are available.

Sources: ADB calculations using data from the Bank for International Settlements. Locational Banking Statistics. https://www.bis.org/statistics/bankstats.htm (accessed October 2020); International Monetary Fund (IMF). Coordinated Direct Investment Survey. http://cdis.imf.org (accessed December 2020); and IMF. Coordinated Portfolio Investment Survey. http://cpis.imf.org (accessed September 2020).

Box 4.1: Global Financial Risk and Banking Sector Flows

Asia and the Pacific rely heavily on the banking sector for cross-border financial intermediation. Yet cross-border bank flows or transactions, either within or outside the region, are channels through which policies and risks spill over across economies. They depend on a host of factors, including similarities and familiarities, economic linkages, and transaction costs. Based on the asset trade literature, it is expected that economies closer to one another tend to have greater economic ties; lower information asymmetries and transaction costs; and are more similar compared with those that are farther apart.[a] Banks are, likewise, expected to lend more to international customers about whom information is easily obtained and monitoring costs are lower. Consequently, cross-border bank flows tend to be greater among economies with closer geographic proximity. The empirical literature offers a wide range of evidence showing the inverse relationship between cross-border banking flows and information asymmetries (Brei and von Peter 2018; Herrmann and Mihaljek 2013).

As bilateral bank flows tend to decline as information asymmetries increase, it is of interest to assess how this relationship evolves during episodes of global financial uncertainty. For example, both the 2008 global financial crisis and onset of the COVID-19 pandemic in 2020 led to heightened investor risk aversion, as measured by the Chicago Board Options Exchange's volatility index (VIX). Do these and similar episodes of global financial uncertainties exacerbate information asymmetries, leading to a greater decline in bilateral bank flows between economies that are more distant? Or do banks reduce transactions more with economies that are closer or with less information asymmetries?

Box Figure: Conditional Marginal Effects of CBOE VIX with 95% CIs

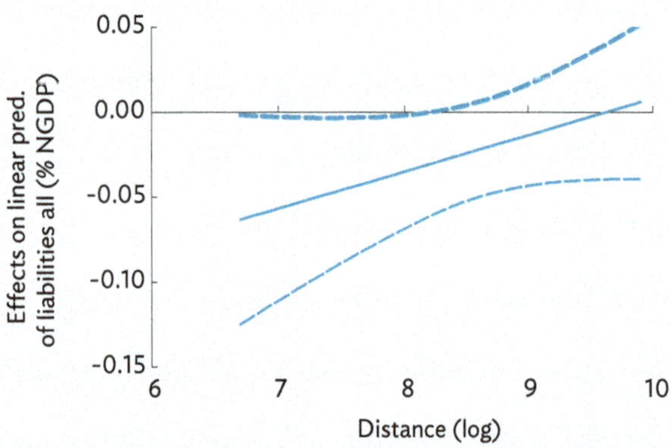

CBOE = Chicago Board Options Exchange, CIs = confidence intervals, NGDP = nominal gross domestic product.

Sources: ADB calculations using data from the Bank for International Settlements. Locational Banking Statistics. https://www.bis.org/statistics/bankstats.htm; Centre d'Etudes Prospectives et d'Informations Internationales (the French Research Center in International Economics). GeoDist database. http://www.cepii.fr/CEPII/en/welcome.asp; and International Monetary Fund. Direction of Trade Statistics. https://data.imf.org/DOT (all accessed August 2020).

To address this question, quarterly adjusted bilateral banking sector data were used, ranging from the first quarter of 2004 to the first quarter of 2020 for 44 Asia and Pacific economies and their bilateral regional and non-regional counterparty economies using the Bank for International Settlements' Locational Banking Statistics. Adjusted values were used to capture banking sector cross-border flows.[b] The data refer to total banking liabilities based on reported values of counterparty economies. A gravity equation was estimated including bilateral factors such as distance, trade, colonial relationship, common spoken language, and common legal origins. Country, partner, and year fixed effects were also included. VIX and an interaction term between VIX and distance were added.[c] But since the interacted variables are both continuous, we report marginal effects of an increase in VIX on bilateral banking sector liabilities at different levels of distance.[d]

The conditional marginal effects suggest that the region's bilateral bank inflows decline more for economies that are closer to one another when global risk aversion rises. In contrast, it decreases less or even increases at some point for more distant economies when global risk increases. For instance, log distance 9 and 10 reflect the distance between East Asia with Europe and the Americas. Hence, we do not find any evidence that global risks exacerbate information asymmetries, based on our sample. On the contrary, we provide more evidence that global financial risks can have greater regional impact, in line with Mercado (2020). This finding may reflect the limited degree of regional banking integration in the region and offers support on the importance and significance of regional financial safety net initiatives.

[a] See Choi, Rhee, and Oh (2014), Portes, Rey, and Oh (2001), and Portes and Rey (2005) on portfolio flows; Brei and von Peter (2018), Herrmann and Mihaljek (2013), and Papaioannou (2009) on bank flows; di Giovanni (2005) on mergers and acquisitions; and Daude and Fratzscher (2008) and Mercado (2020) on all types of foreign- and domestic-driven investment flows.

[b] The values were adjusted by exchange rate changes as well as structural breaks from the bilateral holdings data.

[c] See Mercado (2020) for similar approach using total bilateral capital flows.

[d] Distance were in log values, and bilateral banking liabilities flows are in percent of an economy's annual nominal GDP.

Source: Asian Development Bank.

The currency compositions of Asia's international investment assets and liabilities indicate the prominence of the US dollar.[28]

Almost half of Asia's international asset holdings were denominated in US dollars (USD) as of the end of 2019, followed by other currencies (OTH) at 18% and then euros (EUR) at 11%. In contrast, almost two-thirds of its external liabilities were dominated in local currencies (LCU), followed by USD at 25% (Figure 4.16). Consequently, the region had a foreign currency net asset position and local currency net liabilities position. As the currency shares remained largely stable over the past decade, these are unlikely to change considerably, at least in the short term (Figure 4.17). Asia's foreign and local currency net positions suggest that a uniform movement of regional currencies versus all currencies will generate welfare effects through valuation gains or losses. But the size of the effects will depend on the individual economy's degree of financial integration, such that the greater the financial integration measure, the stronger the valuation gains or losses will be, and, hence, the corresponding welfare effects. Moreover, the dominance of the US dollar implies that changes in the exchange rate versus the dollar will have stronger valuation and welfare impacts compared with other currencies.

Across types of investments, equity-type assets, which include FDI equity and portfolio equity, were mostly denominated in other currencies as it is assumed that currency composition of these investments closely track geographic positions. Equity-type liabilities were denominated in local currency as foreign direct and portfolio equity ownerships are mostly denominated in the host country currency (Figure 4.18a). The currency compositions of debt-type investments highlight the

Figure 4.16: Currency Composition of Asia's International Investment Positions (%)

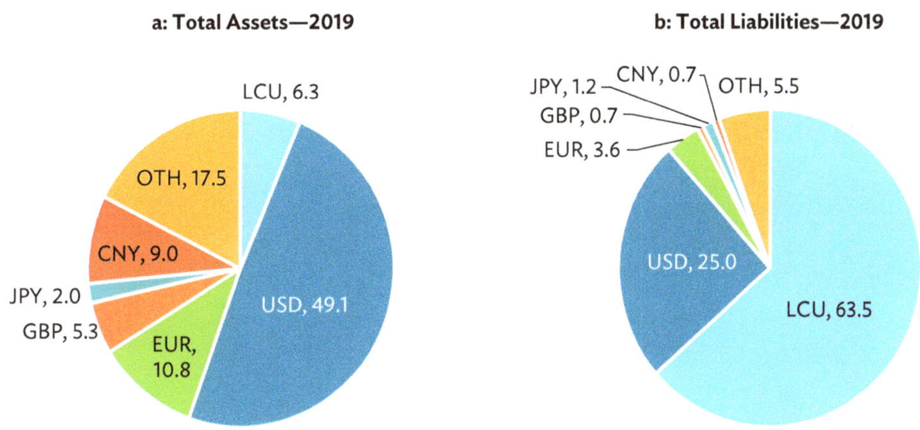

CNY = yuan, EUR = euro, GBP = pound, JPY = yen, LCU = local currency unit, OTH = other currencies, USD = United States dollar.

Notes:

(i) CNY and JPY are classified as LCU for the People's Republic of China and Japan, respectively.

(ii) Values were estimated using currency weights for 2017 and International Investment Positions for 2019, and shown as percent of total.

(iii) OTH shares were derived as residual values.

(iv) Asia includes Australia; Hong Kong, China; India; Indonesia; Japan; Malaysia; New Zealand; Pakistan; the People's Republic of China; the Philippines; the Republic of Korea; Singapore; Sri Lanka; and Thailand.

Sources: ADB calculations using data from Bénétrix et al. (2019); and International Monetary Fund. Balance of Payments and International Financial Statistics. http://data.imf.org/IIF (accessed September 2020).

[28] In this analysis, we use the currency decomposition of the International Investment Position (IIP), which reports the total external assets and liabilities of all sectors across all types of instruments, providing comprehensive analysis on currency breakdown. The primary data set used comes from Bénétrix et al. (2019) and includes the IMF Survey on currency composition of IIP for selected economies, including those from the Asia and Pacific region. Their data set updated the currency composition data set of Lane and Schambaugh (2010a), Lane and Schambaugh (2010b), and Bénétrix, Lane, and Schambaugh (2015) by adding institutional surveys and national sources.

Figure 4.17: Currency Shares of Asia's International Investment Assets and Liabilities (share of total)

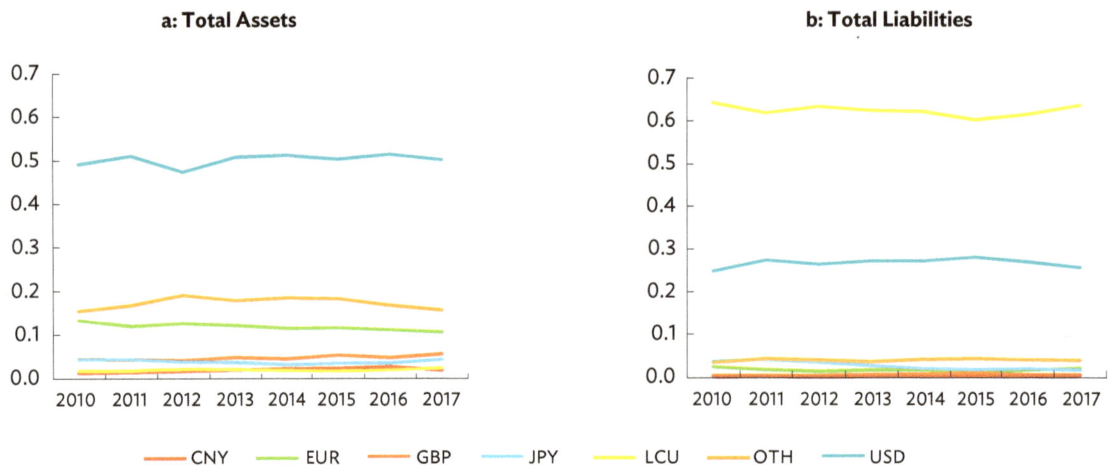

CNY = yuan, EUR = euro, GBP = pound, JPY = yen, LCU = local currency unit, OTH = other currencies, USD = United States dollar.

Notes:

(i) CNY and JPY are classified as LCU for the People's Republic of China and Japan, respectively.

(ii) OTH shares were derived as residual values.

(iii) Data refer to annual median shares of individual economies.

(iv) Asia includes Australia; Hong Kong, China; India; Indonesia; Japan; Malaysia; New Zealand; Pakistan; the People's Republic of China; the Philippines; the Republic of Korea; Singapore; Sri Lanka; and Thailand.

Sources: ADB calculations using data from Bénétrix et al. (2019); and International Monetary Fund. Balance of Payments and International Financial Statistics. http://data.imf.org/IIF (accessed September 2020).

Figure 4.18a: Currency Composition of Asia's International Equity Investments (%)

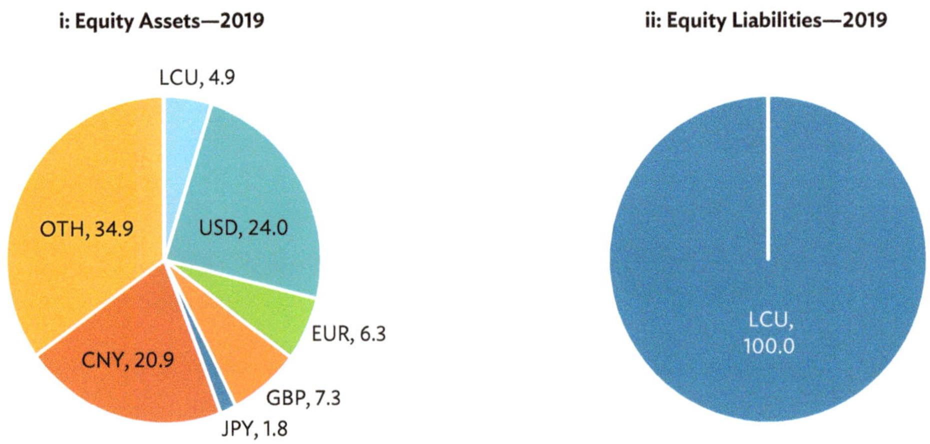

CNY = yuan, EUR = euro, GBP = pound, JPY = yen, LCU = local currency unit, OTH = other currencies, USD = United States dollar.

Notes:

(i) CNY and JPY are classified as LCU for the People's Republic of China and Japan, respectively.

(ii) Values were estimated using currency weights for 2017 and International Investment Positions for 2019, and shown as percent of total.

(iii) OTH shares were derived as residual values.

(iv) Equity investments include foreign direct investment equity and portfolio equity.

(v) Asia includes Australia; Hong Kong, China; India; Indonesia; Japan; Malaysia; New Zealand; Pakistan; the People's Republic of China; the Philippines; the Republic of Korea; Singapore; Sri Lanka; and Thailand.

Sources: ADB calculations using data from Bénétrix et al. (2019); and International Monetary Fund. Balance of Payments and International Financial Statistics. http://data.imf.org/IIF (accessed September 2020).

dominance of the US dollar. For debt assets, which include FDI debt, portfolio debt, other investments, and official reserves, about 63% were denominated in the US dollar, followed by the euro (13%) and other currencies (9%). In contrast, half of debt liabilities, including FDI debt, portfolio debt, and other investments, were denominated in US dollars, followed by local currency (28%), and other currencies (10%) (Figure 4.18b).

The dominance of the US dollar is more pronounced on the region's trade invoices.

Recent studies have shown the dominant role of the US dollar in the pricing of merchandise exports and imports, despite the relatively lower share of the US on bilateral trade (Adler et al. 2020; Boz et al. 2020; Gopinath 2015; and IMF 2019a). For instance, exports of an economy are mostly priced in US dollars even if it trades with economies other than the US. The dominant currency pricing paradigm implies when a country's exchange rate depreciates, its import prices rise in the short term, leading to lower imports. But prices faced by export partners will not change because their exchange rate relative to dominant currency remains unchanged. Consequently, the country's exports remain the same (Adler et al. 2020). Hence, under dominant currency pricing, a depreciation of the domestic exchange rate leads to lower imports, and muted response of export volume in the short term.

In Asia, most recent available data indicate that around 87% of the region's merchandise good exports were invoiced in the US dollar, although the US accounted for only about 9% of the region's merchandise exports (Figure 4.19). A similar pattern emerges for merchandise good imports. Around 77% of the region's imports were invoiced in the US dollar, but the US accounted for only about 5% of the region's merchandise imports. The dominance of the US dollar in the region's trade invoicing was striking when compared with other economies (Figure 4.20). For other emerging and developing economies, around 57% of exports and 48% of imports were invoiced in US dollar; and a significant share was in euros.

Figure 4.18b: Currency Composition of Asia's International Debt Investments (%)

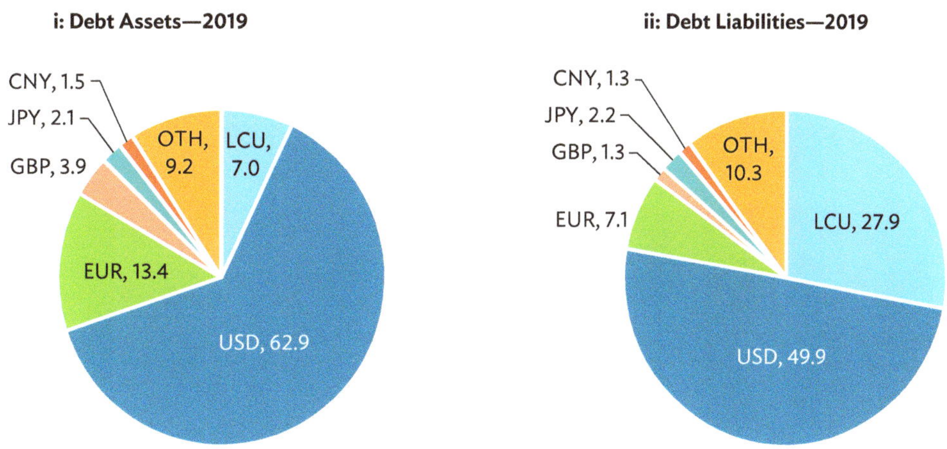

CNY = yuan, EUR = euro, GBP = pound, JPY = yen, LCU = local currency unit, OTH = other currencies, USD = United States dollar.

Notes:

(i) CNY and JPY are classified as LCU for the People's Republic of China and Japan, respectively.

(ii) Values were estimated using currency weights for 2017 and International Investment Positions for 2019, and shown as percent of total.

(iii) OTH shares were derived as residual values.

(iv) Equity investments include foreign direct investment equity and portfolio equity.

(v) Asia includes Australia; Hong Kong, China; India; Indonesia; Japan; Malaysia; New Zealand; Pakistan; the People's Republic of China; the Philippines; the Republic of Korea; Singapore; Sri Lanka; and Thailand.

Sources: ADB calculations using data from Bénétrix et al. (2019); and International Monetary Fund. Balance of Payments and International Financial Statistics. http://data.imf.org/IIF (accessed September 2020).

Figure 4.19: Asia's Trade with the United States and US Dollar Invoicing (%)

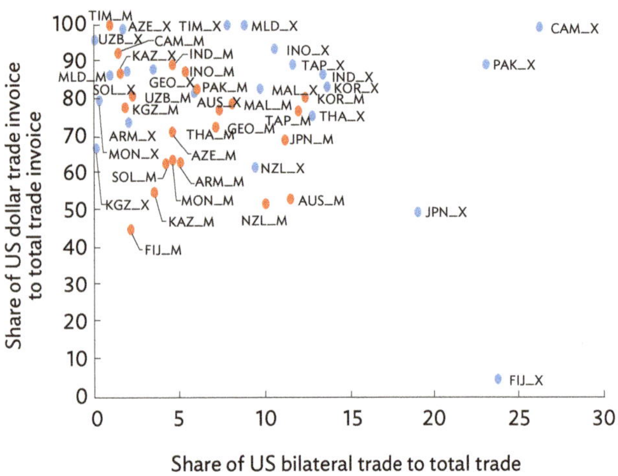

ARM = Armenia; AZE = Azerbaijan; CAM = Cambodia; FIJ = Fiji; GEO = Georgia; KAZ = Kazakhstan; KGZ = Kyrgyz Republic; IND = India; INO = Indonesia; JPN = Japan, KOR = Korea, Republic of; MAL = Malaysia; MLD = Maldives; MON = Mongolia; NZL = New Zealand; PAK = Pakistan; SOL = Solomon Islands; TAP = Taipei,China; TIM = Timor-Leste; THA = Thailand; US = United States; UZB = Uzbekistan; _X = merchandise exports; _M = merchandise imports.

Notes: Values are relative shares to total. Values refer to latest year data are available.

Sources: ADB calculations using Boz et al. (2020) data set; and International Monetary Fund. Direction of Trade Statistics. http://data.imf.org/DOT (accessed September 2020).

Figure 4.20: United States Dollar and Other Currency Trade Invoicing (%)

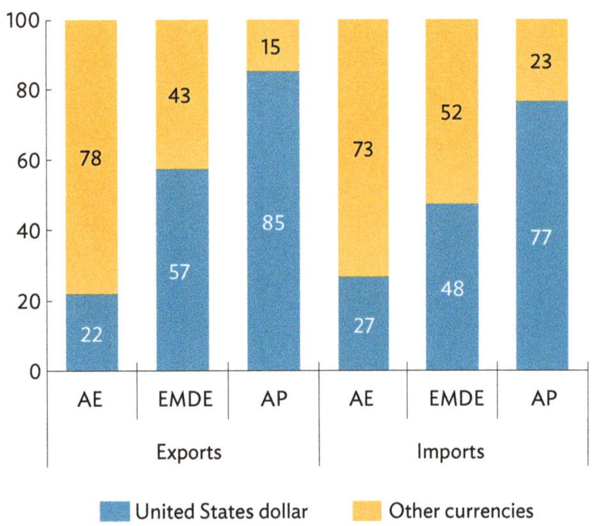

AE = advanced economies, AP = Asia and Pacific economies, EMDE = other emerging and developing economies.

Notes: Asia and Pacific economies include Armenia; Azerbaijan; Cambodia; Fiji; Georgia; India; Indonesia; Japan; Kazakhstan; the Republic of Korea; the Kyrgyz Republic; Malaysia; Maldives; Mongolia; New Zealand; Pakistan; Solomon Islands; Taipei,China; Thailand; Timor-Leste; and Uzbekistan. Data refer to the average of regional annual median values from 2000 to 2019.

Source: ADB calculations using Boz et al. (2020) data set.

The US dollar share of trade invoicing varies across the region. For merchandise exports, dollar trade invoicing was highest for Southeast Asia, followed by Central Asia and India. For merchandise imports, the share was largest in India followed by Southeast Asia. Among the subregions, the Pacific and Oceania reported the lowest US dollar trade invoicing, although it was still significantly higher than for non-Asian economies for merchandise exports. Moreover, the region's US dollar share of trade invoicing was stable over the past 2 decades (Figure 4.21). The high share of US dollar trade invoicing in Asia may reflect the importance of strategic same-currency pricing with competitors; as well as the use of imported US-dollar-priced intermediate inputs of the region's exporters.

A high US dollar trade invoicing entails several policy concerns in the short-term horizon. First, dominant currency pricing weakens external rebalancing mechanism. Specifically, the muted response of export volumes to exchange rate movements implies that much of the external rebalancing takes place through import compression. Second, unilateral movement of the US dollar against all other currencies may cause

Figure 4.21: Currency Shares of Asia's Trade Invoice (%)

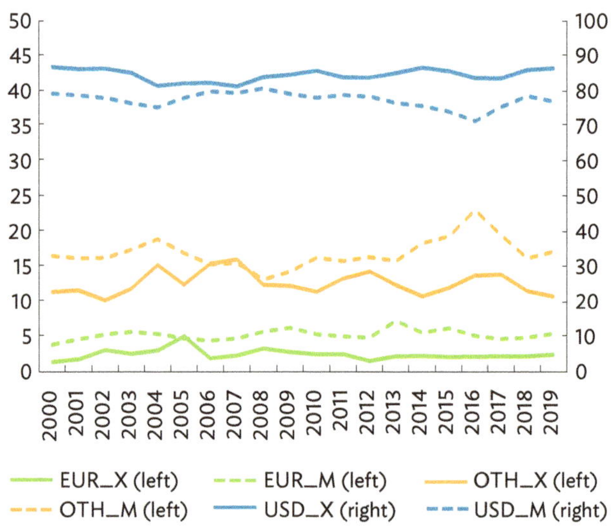

EUR = euro, OTH = other currencies, USD = United States dollar, _M = imports, _X = exports.

Note: Asia includes Armenia; Azerbaijan; Cambodia; Fiji; Georgia; India; Indonesia; Japan; Kazakhstan; the Kyrgyz Republic; Malaysia; Maldives; Mongolia; New Zealand; Pakistan; the Republic of Korea; Solomon Islands; Taipei,China; Thailand; Timor-Leste; and Uzbekistan.

Source: ADB calculations using data from Boz et al. (2020).

contractionary or expansionary effect on global trade. For instance, an appreciation of the US dollar versus all other currencies will raise domestic prices of imports for other economies. This, in turn, will lower import demand, which will lead to less global trade (Adler et al. 2020). Third, the dominant currency pricing is intertwined with dominant currency financing, whereby the US dollar is commonly used in cross-border corporate external financing (Figure 4.18b). The dominance of the US dollar in trade invoicing leads to a larger demand for US dollar deposits, which makes US dollar funding cheaper than other currencies (Gopinath and Stein 2018). This reinforces US dollar dominance in both trade pricing and financing.

Looming Financial Risks Stemming from COVID-19

COVID-19 has unraveled global financial markets, putting Asia's financial resilience to a test and raising the specter of financial volatility and instability in the region. Although financial market jitters were quickly quelled through swift and aggressive policy interventions around the globe, it still reveals several looming financial risks that policy makers need to consider. Already high levels of debt, both sovereign and private, will inevitably increase, with the possibility that a deterioration of debt quality in the aftermath of the pandemic will threaten regional banking sector stability. Furthermore, the pandemic exposed the Asian banking sector's structural vulnerability given the liquidity mismatches associated with increased international activity and a reliance on US dollar funding by non-US banks.

The COVID-19 pandemic poses an ongoing challenge to regional economies with elevated debt levels as large-scale policy responses could entail further debt accumulation.

A decade of historically low interest rates since the global financial crisis has resulted in elevated debt-to-GDP ratios globally. This pattern also played out in Asia, as emerging economies exhibit particularly high and rising debt levels (Figure 4.22), with Hong Kong, China; the PRC; the Republic of Korea; and Singapore exhibiting strong increases as of 2020 compared with 2010. While public debt levels have increased throughout Asia since 2010, especially in Japan, private debt (i.e., corporate and household) has risen considerably in developing Asia, most notably in Hong Kong, China; the PRC; the Republic of Korea; Singapore; and Thailand. The current pandemic could expose the already heavily indebted economies in the region to additional challenges, as large-scale policy responses to COVID-19 will inevitably result in increased debt. The increase is expected to materialize across all sectors, amid (i) fiscal spending at large scale, (ii) accommodative monetary policy resulting in low interest rates for firms and households, and (iii) revenue reduction due to lackluster economic growth. It is estimated that Asia's public debt-to-GDP ratio could rise from 56.7% in 2019 to 65.8% in 2020, and to 69.4% by 2021 (IMF 2021). Transiting toward normalized fiscal balances post-COVID-19 will be crucial to assuring debt sustainability in the region moving forward.

Looming risks of high debt levels could weaken Asia's banking and corporate sectors.

In case interest rates would normalize, interest payments and debt rollover risks may arise. A possible sluggish economic recovery, combined with ballooning debt levels, could prompt credit rating agencies to downgrade certain economies' creditworthiness, further lifting interest rates and exacerbating these risks. As for private sector debt, the risks are similar as weaker corporate earnings and worsening credit conditions could result in insolvencies weighing on banking sector resilience and producing adverse social effects.

This in turn could spell trouble for Asian banks and corporations, particularly micro, small, and medium-sized enterprises (MSMEs), due to the looming risk of debt quality deterioration. Given the dominant role of banks in Asia's financial systems, this could

Figure 4.22: Sectoral Debt, 2010 versus 2020*—Asia (% of GDP)

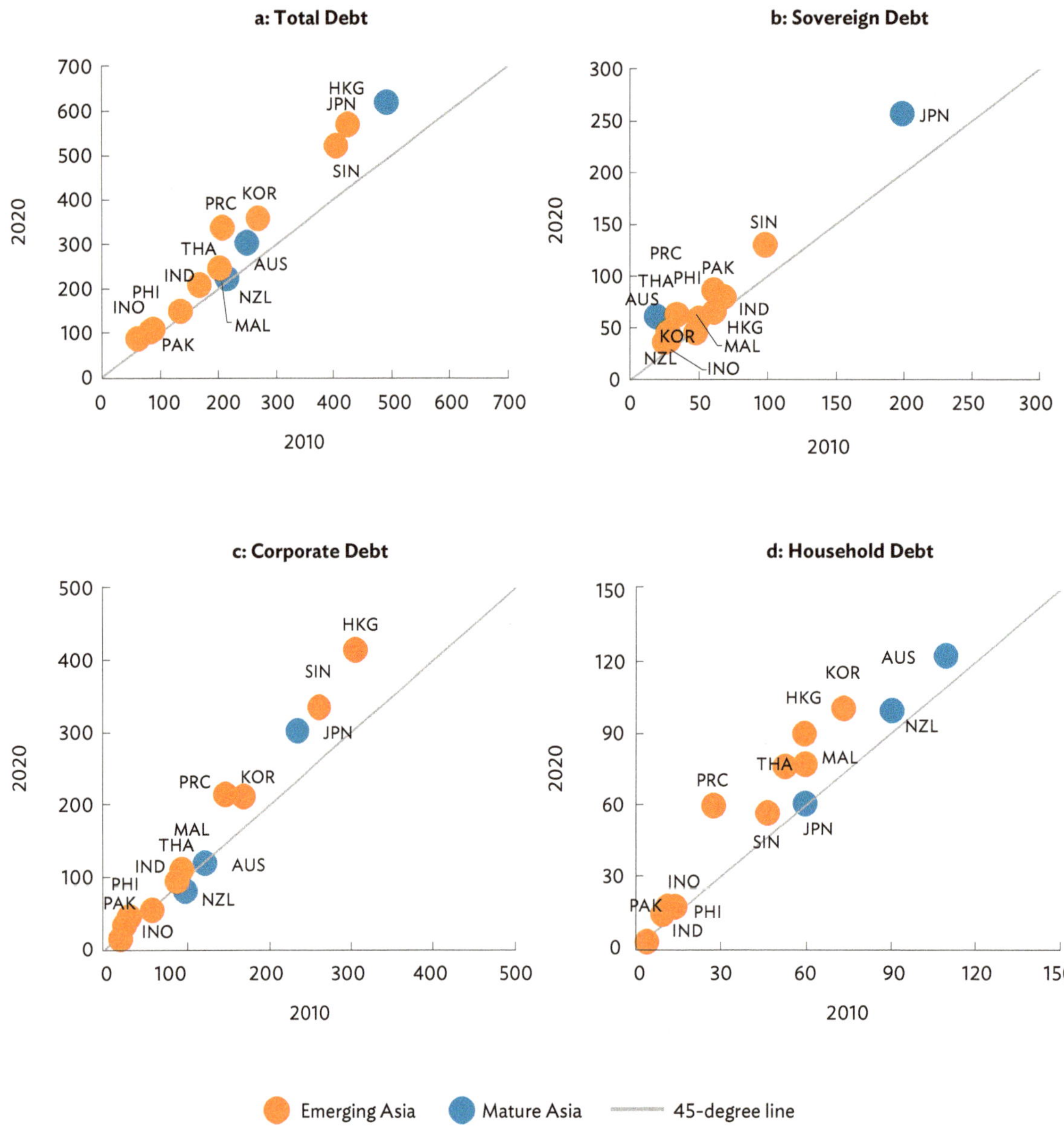

* = As of Q3 2020.

AUS = Australia; GDP = gross domestic product; HKG = Hong Kong, China; IND = India; INO = Indonesia; JPN = Japan, KOR = Republic of Korea; NZL = New Zealand; PAK = Pakistan; PHI = Philippines; PRC = People's Republic of China; SIN = Singapore; THA = Thailand.

Notes: Economy grouping based on Institute of International Finance definition. Emerging Asia includes HKG, IND, INO, KOR, MAL, PAK, PHI, PRC, SIN, and THA. Mature Asia includes AUS, JPN, and NZL.

Source: Institute of International Finance. Global Debt Monitor December 2020. https://www.iif.com/Research/Capital-Flows-and-Debt/Global-Debt-Monitor (accessed January 2021).

breed widespread financial instability and drag on economic recovery. As banks remain the biggest source of corporate financing in emerging Asia (Figure 4.23), safeguarding banking sector health is a prerequisite for sustained economic development and recovery post-COVID-19.

Figure 4.23: Corporate Financing—Emerging Asia (% of GDP)

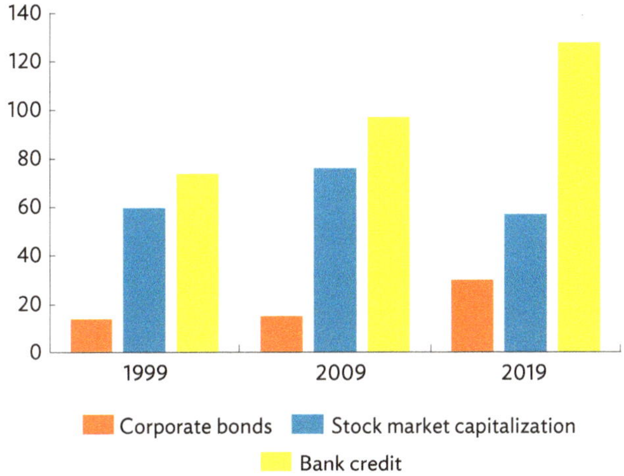

GDP = gross domestic product.

Notes:

(i) Emerging Asia includes India, Indonesia, the Republic of Korea, Malaysia, the People's Republic of China, the Philippines, Thailand, and Viet Nam.

(ii) 1999 corporate bond data for the Republic of Korea, Malaysia, the Philippines, Thailand, and Viet Nam as of 2000; and 1999 stock market capitalization data for Viet Nam as of 2000.

(iii) 2009 corporate data as of 2010 for India; and 2009 stock market capitalization data for Indonesia as of 2010.

Sources: AsianBondsOnline; CEIC; Haver Analytics; and national sources (all accessed April 2020).

Credit conditions could tighten when temporary financial relief extended to the corporate sector is lifted and regulatory forbearance phased out, highlighting risks of rising nonperforming loans (NPLs).

Should corporate earnings fall, corporations will face challenges in their debt servicing capacity, possibly resulting in defaults. Thus far, large-scale fiscal stimulus helped considerably to prevent the occurrence of corporate defaults, while regulatory forbearance has relieved pressure from banks in addressing NPLs. Ample liquidity has been provided to the corporate sector to avoid an insolvency crisis. However, when temporary relief is lifted and regulatory forbearance tapers off, corporate defaults may materialize, and banks could become exposed to rising NPLs. This, in turn, could contribute to a deterioration in banks' balance sheets and therefore impede their capacity for financial intermediation, and thus result in negative macrofinancial effects. In addition, financial instability and an economic downturn could disproportionately affect MSMEs, which typically do not have access to capital markets, further amplifying adverse social effects. Usually, MSMEs, representing the backbone of the economies, would be the most vulnerable in case credit conditions tighten. It is therefore important to prepare for a smooth transition, to monitor financial health of banks and assure sufficient credits to solvent MSMEs.

Deterioration of banking and corporate sector debt quality could undermine economic recovery and weaken future growth.

Past crises have shown that problems associated with debt quality can have long-lasting effects on the finance sector, still weighing on banks' balance sheets years after the crisis. In Asia, more than 2 decades after the Asian financial crisis, NPL ratios in the region have stabilized at a considerably lower level than during crisis periods, also due to strong postcrisis reforms, a combination of micro- and macroprudential policies, and sound macroeconomic conditions. However, in some Central, East, and South Asian economies, NPL ratios have been rising recently (Figure 4.24). Although moderate relative to levels during the Asian financial crisis, increasing NPL

Figure 4.24: Development of NPLs, 2015 versus 2019—Selected Asian Economies (NPL ratio, %)

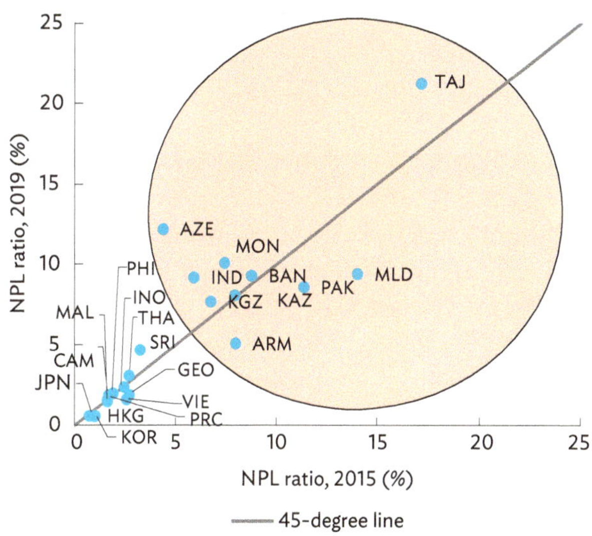

ARM = Armenia; AZE = Azerbaijan; BAN = Bangladesh; CAM = Cambodia; GEO = Georgia; HKG = Hong Kong, China; IND = India; INO = Indonesia; JPN = Japan; KAZ = Kazakhstan; KGZ = Kyrgyz Republic; KOR = Republic of Korea; MAL = Malaysia; MON = Mongolia; MLD = Maldives; NPL = nonperforming loan; PAK = Pakistan; PHI = Philippines; PRC = People's Republic of China; SRI = Sri Lanka; TAJ = Tajikistan; THA = Thailand; VIE = Viet Nam.

Source: ADB calculations using data from Bank of Mongolia; CEIC; the International Monetary Fund. Financial Soundness Indicators. https://data.imf.org; and World Bank. World Development Indicators. http://databank.worldbank.org/data/reports.aspx?source=world-development-indicators (all accessed July 2020).

ratios, alongside the buildup of debt and default risks, pose challenges to financial stability in the region. Given the nature and persistence of NPLs, these challenges may last beyond the actual COVID-19 pandemic.

Experiences of other regions, like the European sovereign debt crisis, illustrates the long-lasting effects of deteriorating debt quality. The global financial crisis and succeeding European sovereign debt crisis reversed a downward trend in NPL ratios in the euro area, with certain economies, mainly in Southern Europe, severely affected. In spite of a gradual decline to 3.6% in 2019, the euro area NPL ratio remained three times higher than equivalent ratios in the US and the United Kingdom in that year, and precrisis levels have not yet been reached. This underlines the strong persistence of NPL ratios and the sustained impact they have on banking sector health.

The significance of banking sector instability and a rise in distressed assets is further underscored by the macrofinancial feedback effects of NPLs. Empirical investigation of the determinants and effects of bank-specific NPLs in Asia points to the effect NPLs have on the real economy and financial variables. In particular, a rise in NPL ratio prompts a reduction in gross domestic product, a tightening of credit supply, and an increase in unemployment rate (ADB 2017; Lee and Rosenkranz 2020).

The growing interconnectedness of Asian and global financial markets, moreover, highlights the risks of cross-border spillovers and contagion effects triggered by global shocks and financial distress.

Previous financial crises demonstrated how weaknesses in finance sectors can spread to neighboring economies. Analysis of direct and indirect banking sector exposure of emerging economies to crisis-afflicted economies points to the elevated risk of contagion in the form of capital outflows due to increased interlinkages during crisis periods (ADB 2017; Park and Shin 2017, 2018, 2020a, 2020b). At a time of such heightened interconnectedness, a buildup in NPLs can further heighten global banking instability, owing to their macrofinancial and possible spillover effects (Park and Shin 2020a).

Empirical evidence shows that emerging market borrowers could suffer a significant increase in capital outflows if the NPL ratios of both lenders and borrowers rise. This has been evidenced from 2000 to 2017, as globally active lenders withdrew capital from emerging market borrowers when they experienced a rise in NPL ratios. Park and Shin (2020a) find that international banks withdraw funds from emerging economies in response to the increase in the NPL ratios of either advanced or emerging economies, or both (Table 4.1). Given the looming risk of a rise in credit risk in the wake of the COVID-19 pandemic, regional policy makers need to carefully monitor financial conditions and take preemptive action today.

Table 4.1: Impact of Nonperforming Loans on Banking Outflows from Emerging Market Economies
(LBS total cross-border foreign claims)

Variables	(1)	(2)	(3)	(4)	(5)
NPL ratio lender	0.851*** [0.088]	0.909*** [0.114]	0.688*** [0.118]	0.875*** [0.119]	0.696*** [0.121]
NPL ratio borrower		0.519*** [0.044]	0.481*** [0.045]	0.587*** [0.051]	0.495*** [0.049]
Year fixed effects	No	No	Yes	No	Yes
R-squared	0.008	0.03	0.084	0.049	0.111
Observations	11,113	6,176	6,176	4,428	4,428

LBS = locational banking statistics, NPL=nonperforming loan.

Notes: The dependent variable is the growth rate of banking outflows calculated using BIS LBS total cross-border foreign claims. Columns (1), (2) and (4) are estimated by pooled ordinary least squares. Year fixed effects are added in columns (3) and (5) but the coefficients are not reported. Columns (4) and (5) include the following non-reported additional regressors: Increase in current account; Real exchange rate change; Increase in credit; Reserve/M2; GDP growth; Inflation; and Rule of law. The sample period is from 2000 to 2017. Numbers in brackets are robust standard errors. The asterisks denote significance levels. *** at 1%, ** at 5%, and * at 10%.

Source: Park and Shin (2020b).

Amid flight to safety, global demand for the US dollar soared, threatening local financial stability in emerging Asian economies which remain heavily exposed to US dollar funding risks.[29]

At the peak of the COVID-19 pandemic in March, the fear of economic recession and the risk-off sentiment unraveled global financial markets, putting Asia's

[29] This section draws from Park, Rosenkranz, and Tayag (2020).

financial resilience to a test and making Asian banks vulnerable to US dollar funding activities. While multiple factors are behind the surge in demand, it has been a global rush to unwind carry trades that have driven a rise in global US dollar funding costs, also resulting in capital outflows as discussed above.

Asian banks' cross-border assets and liabilities have risen considerably since the aftermath of the global financial crisis (Figure 4.25), with the majority denominated in foreign currency (83.5% of cross-border claims and 75.6% of cross-border liabilities as of Q2 2020, primarily in US dollars), and cross-border banking operations of Asian banks having considerably expanded both in claims and liabilities.

Figure 4.25: US Dollar Cross-Border Bank Holdings by Non-US Banks ($ trillion)

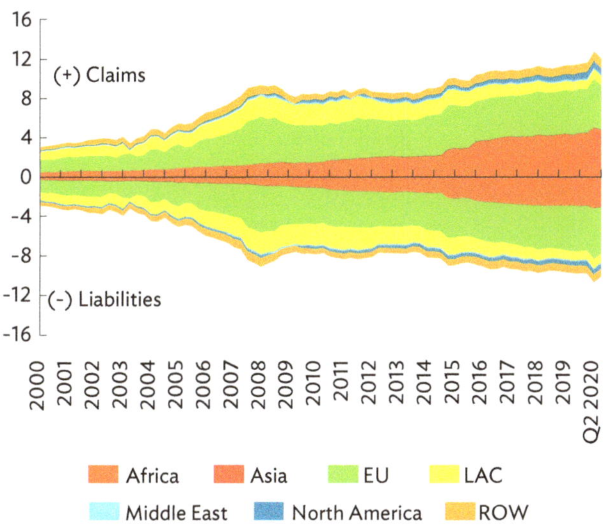

EU = European Union, LAC = Latin America and the Caribbean, ROW = rest of the world, US = United States.

Notes: Africa includes South Africa (beginning Q3 2009). Asia includes Australia; Hong Kong, China (beginning Q4 2014); India (beginning Q4 2001); Japan; the People's Republic of China (beginning Q4 2015); the Philippines (beginning Q4 2016); the Republic of Korea (beginning Q1 2005); and Taipei,China (beginning Q4 2000). EU includes Austria (beginning Q4 2013), Belgium, Cyprus (beginning Q4 2008), Denmark, Finland, France (beginning Q1 2010), Germany, Greece (beginning Q4 2003), Ireland, Italy (beginning Q2 2012), Luxembourg, the Netherlands (beginning Q4 2014), Portugal (beginning Q1 2012), Spain (beginning Q1 2014), Sweden, and the United Kingdom. Latin America and the Caribbean includes the Bahamas, Brazil (beginning Q4 2002), Cayman Islands, Chile (beginning Q4 2002), Mexico (beginning Q4 2003), and Panama (beginning Q4 2002). Middle East includes Bahrain. North America includes Canada. ROW includes Bermuda (beginning Q4 2002); Guernsey (beginning Q4 2001); Isle of Man (beginning Q4 2001); Jersey (beginning Q4 2001); Macau, China (beginning Q4 2013); Norway (beginning Q1 2014); the Russian Federation (beginning Q4 2015); and Switzerland.

Sources: ADB calculations using data from the Bank for International Settlements. Locational Banking Statistics. https://www.bis.org/statistics/bankstats.htm (accessed October 2020); and Park, Rosenkranz, and Tayag (2020).

The landscape of non-US global banks' activities in US dollar funding has changed since the global financial crisis. Severely hit by the global financial crisis and the European sovereign debt crisis, European banks have reduced their cross-border US dollar assets. Meanwhile, non-European, non-US banks—particularly in Australia, Canada, Japan, and Singapore—came to pick up the slack left by European banks (Remolona and Shim 2015; IMF 2019b). As a result, since Q4 2016, Asia has accounted for the highest share of cross-border claims denominated in US dollars by non-US global banks, highlighting the growing role of Asian banks in the global US dollar funding market.

In line with global trends, Asian banks have also been increasingly engaged with nonbank counterparts in cross-border banking activities, with 58.6% of Asian banks' claims and 38.1% of their liabilities being on nonbanks (e.g., life insurers, pension funds, or hedge funds) as of Q2 2020 (Figure 4.26). While the cross-border activities of foreign banks have remained largely stable in recent years, activities with nonbanks have ballooned. This pattern stems from financial regulatory reforms following the global financial crisis aimed to limit excessive risk taking and leverage of global banks. Consequently, nonbank financial institutions, such as pension funds or life insurers, have emerged to assume a greater share of dollar-denominated cross-border activities. As the nonbanks are less stringently regulated and have higher market concentration, BIS (2020) points toward the possible risk of them acting as an amplifier of global financial conditions and market volatility, thus threatening financial stability.

This rising exposure to foreign currency-denominated activities yields several risks as global banks not based in the US (non-US global banks) need to rely on foreign exchange swaps, given their limited access to a stable US dollar deposit base or US monetary policy operations. The fact that currency hedging mechanisms and instruments remain underdeveloped in the region further highlights associated vulnerabilities. As discussed on page 70, interbank money markets came under severe strain in March 2020 and the price for obtaining US dollars through a cross-currency basis swap—in a way an emergency US dollar liquidity

Figure 4.26: Gross Cross-Border Bank Claims and Liabilities—Asia ($ trillion)

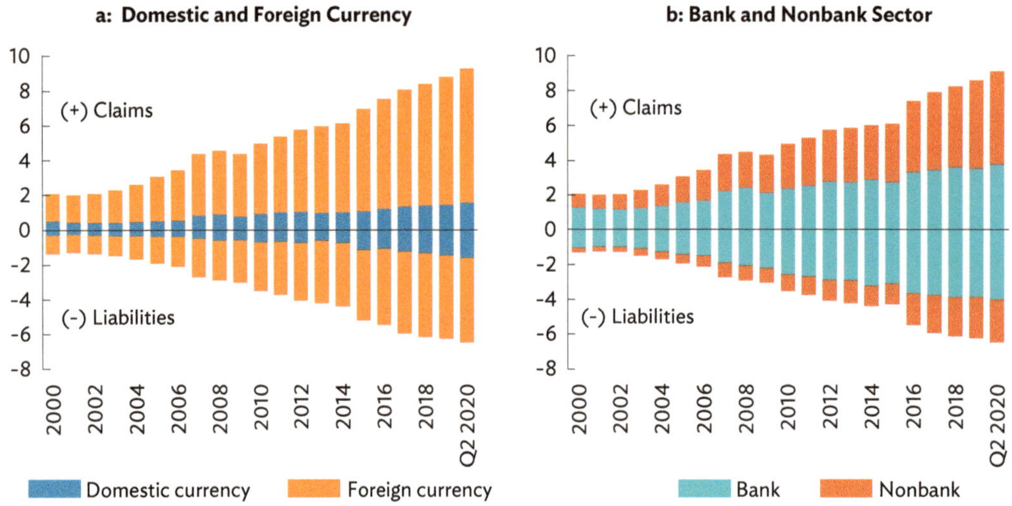

Notes: Asia includes Australia; Hong Kong, China; Indonesia; India; Japan; Malaysia; the People's Republic of China (PRC); the Philippines; the Republic of Korea; Singapore; and Taipei,China. Data for Indonesia beginning 2010, India beginning 2001, Malaysia 2007, the PRC beginning 2015, the Philippines beginning 2016, and the Republic of Korea beginning 2005. For total claims, domestic currency for Hong Kong, China (2000–2012) and Malaysia were deduced by subtracting foreign currency claims from total claims. For total liabilities, domestic currency for Hong Kong, China (2000–2012); Malaysia; and Singapore were deduced by subtracting foreign currency liabilities from total liabilities.

Sources: ADB calculations using data from Bank for International Settlements. Locational Banking Statistics. https://www.bis.org/statistics/bankstats.htm (accessed October 2020); and Park, Rosenkranz, and Tayag (2020).

facility—spiked for several emerging Asian currencies (Figures 4.3 and 4.4).

Asian banks' reliance on US dollar funding markets exposes the structural vulnerability of the region's financial systems during times of crisis, and so poses risks to regional financial stability as a sudden squeeze in global dollar liquidity can have significant destabilizing effects. In particular, financial stress by global non-US banks can trigger a sharp contraction in cross-border international lending, even while emerging Asian economies maintain overall solid financial conditions. Additionally, as the US dollar appreciates sharply because of its safe asset quality, emerging Asian borrowers will face difficulties in repaying or rolling over their US-dollar-denominated debt. A depreciation of the bilateral exchange rate against the US dollar is linked to a worsening of balance sheets of US dollar-indebted economies and the tightening of financial conditions through a financial channel of the exchange rate (ADB 2017, 2019; Hoffmann, Shim, and Shin 2017, 2019).

An empirical analysis reveals that the exposure of the domestic banking system to US dollar funding (i) is significantly and positively associated with a widening cross-currency basis swap, and (ii) also amplifies the effect of financial stress on the cross-currency basis swap. The cross-currency basis swap is, moreover, particularly costly during crisis periods—especially for emerging market economies. In turn, a widening in the cross-currency basis swap—i.e., a higher marginal dollar funding cost—is also significantly and positively related to nonresident capital outflows, especially driven by debt and bank flows (Figure 4.27). Consequently, the financial vulnerability experienced by non-US global banks due to their US dollar activities rises with their exposure. This is especially valid for emerging economies.

Figure 4.27: Determinants of the Cross-Currency Basis Swap and Effect on Nonresident Capital Outflows

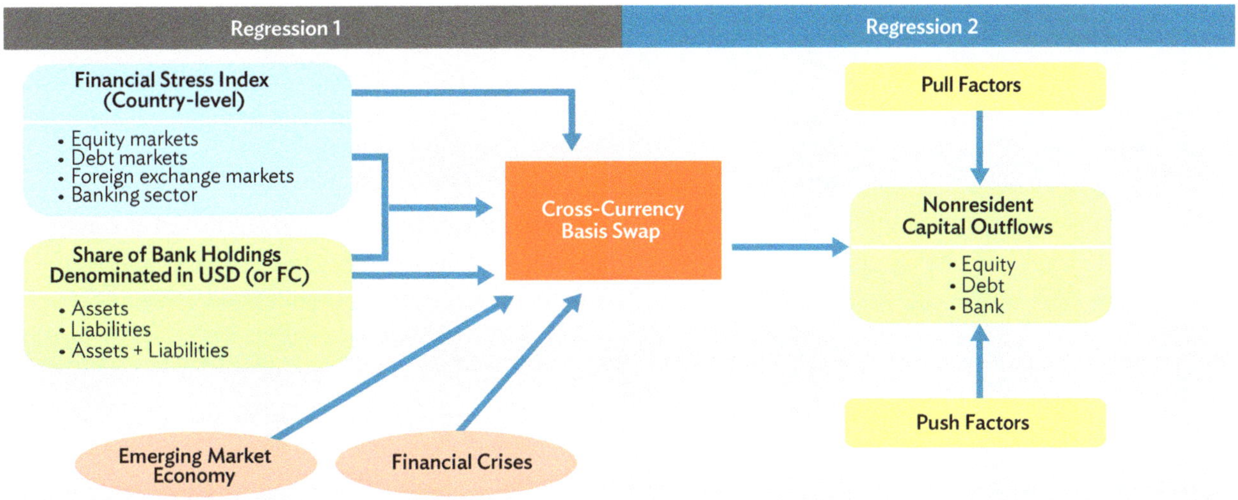

FC = foreign currency, USD = United States dollar.

Note: Park, Rosenkranz, and Tayag (2020) includes more detailed discussion of the regression results illustrated in this figure.

Source: Park, Rosenkranz, and Tayag (2020).

The COVID-19 pandemic offers an opportunity to regain reform momentum and strengthen regional financial cooperation. The recent agreement reached by ASEAN+3 finance ministers on enhancing the Chiang Mai Initiative Multilateralization (CMIM) underpins the region's commitment to strengthen the regional financial safety net.

While marking the 10th anniversary of the original CMIM agreement this year, in September 2020, ASEAN+3 finance ministers agreed to enhance CMIM by (i) increasing the IMF de-linked portion from 30% to 40%, (ii) clarifying the conditionality framework for the IMF de-linked portion, and (iii) institutionalizing voluntary and demand-driven local currency contributions. These measures will strengthen the crisis responsiveness by CMIM through giving more discretion to ASEAN+3 countries and CMIM's regional surveillance unit, AMRO. Amid increasingly interconnected financial markets, both regionally and globally, these efforts underpin the complementary role of the regional financial safety net (e.g., CMIM and AMRO) with global layers, such as provided by the IMF.

Regional policy makers need to remain vigilant against the potential impact of COVID-19 on financial stability, collectively working on risk identification, mitigation, and response.

It is important to sustain market confidence and ensure adequate liquidity. While the region's macrofinancial positions so far remained sound during the pandemic, policy makers should remain vigilant against financial market distress and tightening liquidity conditions. Therefore, maintaining sound macrofinancial policies that are supportive of the economy and help stabilize financial markets is key. Given that Asia's financial system remains largely bank-based, it is important to safeguard banking sector resilience, including through action to prevent corporate defaults that would weigh on banks' balance sheet quality.

The ongoing COVID-19 pandemic provides impetus for strengthening regional financial cooperation. Deeper regional and global financial interconnectedness can result in faster transmission of shocks across borders, highlighting the risk of financial contagion. These patterns have been apparent during past crisis episodes. Consequently, the ongoing COVID-19 calls for collective action, which is crucial in safeguarding regional financial stability and resilience.

Asia needs to further strengthen its regional financial safety nets. The latest reform of CMIM in September 2020 contributed to enhanced financial resilience. Yet, several options can further bolster the region's financial safety nets, including an increase in the CMIM's capacity (e.g., through paid-in capital) or a possible widening of the CMIM's mandate such as the recapitalization of systemically important financial institutions. While the operability of the CMIM has yet to be tested, 10 successful test runs have been completed. AMRO's surveillance function during COVID-19 also plays an important role in monitoring and safeguarding financial stability in Asia. In addition, under the current pandemic, multilateral institutions' financial crisis support has been significant, highlighting their complementary role in the global and regional financial safety net. ADB, for example, has committed a $20 billion COVID-19 response package, including through its crisis-related policy-based lending toolkit.

The region should continue developing and nurturing vibrant local currency bond markets to help address the structural vulnerabilities inherent in Asian financial systems such as reliance on their strong dollar dependency as well as to alleviate the reliance on bank-based finance. Greater availability of local currency long-term securities can reduce short-term needs for US-dollar liquidity and reduce currency and maturity mismatches. Also, the investor base needs to be broadened, including through encouraging more domestic investors such as government pension funds and regional life insurers to buy long-term securities. Given that these investors would have their liabilities primarily denominated in domestic currency, they would not be compelled to withdraw funds from the region because of currency mismatches on their balance sheets. As a result, large swings in capital flows could be mitigated. In that regard, the ASEAN+3 Multi-Currency Bond Issuance Framework (AMBIF), a policy initiative under the Asian Bond Markets Initiative, supported the creation of a corporate bond market in Cambodia in 2018, which even preceded the formation of a sovereign bond market in Cambodia.

The current pandemic has seen the substantial elevation of public debt levels, which may rise further as the pandemic continues. Unwinding and managing these levels sustainably will remain a priority beyond COVID-19, and public spending should be productive and well-targeted to support the most vulnerable and provide the investment needed for a sustainable recovery. Strong international leadership is, moreover, vital to mitigating further debt problems, which threaten to unfold once policy stimulus begins to unwind, if not sufficiently addressed early on.

Domestic resource mobilization will play an important role in that regard, which necessitates both strengthened domestic tax systems and regional cooperation in international taxation. Policies need to take into consideration an acceleration of the digitalization of the global economy amid COVID-19.

High and rising NPLs require early and preemptive measures. A sharp increase in NPLs could destabilize regional financial systems and compromise swift post-pandemic economic recovery. Growing cross-border banking activities and the rise of big regional financial institutions—of potentially systemic importance—underpin the risk of financial contagion in the region in the event of a surge in NPLs, which could not only compromise economic recovery, but also threaten regional financial stability. Consequently, early and preemptive action is needed to prevent corporate defaults, strengthen NPL resolution mechanisms, and develop distressed asset markets; allowing banks and financial institutions to swiftly dispose of NPLs as they arise.

References

Adler, G., C. Casas, L. Cubeddu, G. Gopinath, N. Li, S. Meleshchuk, C. Osorio Buitron, D. Puy, and Y. Timmer. 2020. Dominant Currencies and External Adjustment. *IMF Staff Discussion Note*. SDN/20/05. Washington, DC: International Monetary Fund (IMF).

Arslan, Y., M. Drehmann, and B. Hofmann. 2020. Central Bank Bond Purchases in Emerging Market Economies. *BIS Bulletin No. 20*. Basel: Bank for International Settlements (BIS).

Asian Development Bank (ADB). 2017. *Asian Economic Integration Report 2017: The Era of Financial Interconnectedness—How Can Asia Strengthen Financial Resilience?* Manila.

———. 2019. *Asian Development Outlook: Strengthening Disaster Resilience*. Manila.

AsianBondsOnline. https://asianbondsonline.adb.org (accessed April 2020).

Bank for International Settlements (BIS). Locational Banking Statistics. https://www.bis.org/statistics/bankstats.htm (accessed August and October 2020).

———. 2020. US Dollar Funding: An International Perspective. *Committee on the Global Financial System Papers*. No. 65. Basel: BIS.

Bénétrix, A., D. Gautam, L. Juvenal, and M. Schmitz. 2019. Cross-Border Currency Exposures. New Evidence Based on an Enhanced and Updated Dataset. *IMF Working Paper No. 19/299*. Washington, DC: International Monetary Fund (IMF).

Bénétrix, A., P. R. Lane, and J. C. Schambaugh. 2015. International Currency Exposures, Valuation Effects and the Global Financial Crisis. *Journal of International Economics*. 96 (1). pp. 98–109.

Brei, M. and G. von Peter. 2018. The Distance Effect in Banking and Trade. *Journal of International Money and Finance*. 81. pp. 116–137.

Boz, E., C. Casas, G. Georgiadis, G. Gopinath, H. Le Mezo, A. Mehl, and T. Nguyen. 2020. Patterns in Invoicing Currency in Global Trade. *IMF Working Paper No. 20/126*. Washington, DC: IMF.

Cayman Compass. 2018. Cayman's Value Highlighted to Chinese Investors. Cayman Compass. 30 October. https://www.caymancompass.com/2018/10/30/caymans-value-highlighted-to-chinese-investors.

Central Bank of Mongolia. https://www.mongolbank.mn/eng (accessed July 2020).

Centre d'Études Prospectives et d'Informations Internationales (the French Research Center in International Economics). GeoDist database. http://www.cepii.fr/CEPII/en/welcome.asp (accessed August 2020).

Chicago Board Options Exchange. Volatility Index. http://www.cboe.com/vix (accessed January 2021).

Choi, C., D.-E. Rhee, and Y. Oh. 2014. Information and Capital Flows Revisited: The Internet as a Determinant of Transactions in Financial Assets. *Economic Modelling*. 40. pp. 191–98.

di Giovanni, J. 2005. What Drives Capital Flows? The Case of Cross-Border M&A Activity and Financial Deepening. *Journal of International Economics*. 65. pp. 127–149.

Daude, C. and M. Fratzscher. 2008. The Pecking Order of Cross-Border Investment. *Journal of International Economics*. 74. pp. 94–119.

Google Finance. http://google.com/finance (accessed August 2020).

Gopinath, G. 2015. The International Price System. *NBER Working Paper 21646*. Cambridge, MA: National Bureau of Economic Research.

Gopinath, G. and Jeremy C. Stein. 2018. Banking, Trade, and the Making of a Dominant Currency. *Harvard and NBER paper*. Cambridge, MA: Harvard University and National Bureau of Economic Research.

Herrmann, S. and D. Mihaljek. 2013. The Determinants of Cross-Border Bank Flows to Emerging Markets. *Economics of Transition*. 21 (3). pp. 479–508.

Hoffmann, B., I. Shim, and H. S. Shin. 2017. Sovereign Yields and the Risk-Taking Channel of Currency Appreciation. *BIS Working Papers*. No. 538. Basel: BIS.

———. 2019. Bond Risk Premia and the Exchange Rate. *BIS Working Papers*. No. 775. Basel: BIS.

Institute of International Finance. Global Debt Monitor December 2020. https://www.iif.com/Research/Capital-Flows-and-Debt/Global-Debt-Monitor (accessed January 2021).

International Monetary Fund (IMF). Balance of Payments and International Investment Position Statistics. http://data.imf.org/IIF (accessed September 2020).

———. Coordinated Direct Investment Survey. http://data.imf.org/CDIS (accessed December 2020).

———. Coordinated Portfolio Investment Survey. http://data.imf.org/CPIS (accessed September 2020).

———. Direction of Trade Statistics. http://data.imf.org/DOT (accessed September 2020).

———. Financial Soundness Indicators. http://data.imf.org/FSI (accessed July 2020).

———. International Financial Statistics. http://data.imf.org/IFS (accessed September 2020).

———. 2019a. *External Sector Report: The Dynamics of External Adjustment*. Washington, DC.

———. 2019b. *Global Financial Stability Report: Lower for Longer*. October. Washington, DC.

———. 2021. *Fiscal Monitor Update*. January. Washington, DC.

Investing.com. https://www.investing.com/indices/msci-world-historical-data (accessed August 2020).

Lane, P. R. and J. C. Shambaugh. 2010a. Financial Exchange Rates and International Currency Exposures. *American Economic* Review. 100 (1). pp. 518–540.

———. 2010b. The Long or Short of It: Determinants of Foreign Currency Exposure in External Balance Sheets. *Journal of International Economics*. 80 (1). pp. 33–44.

Lee, J. and P. Rosenkranz. 2020. Nonperforming Loans in Asia: Determinants and Macrofinancial Linkages. In B. N. Jeon and J. Wu, eds. Emerging Market Finance: New Challenges and Opportunities. *International Finance Review*. Vol. 21. Bingley: Emerald Publishing Group.

Lee, J. W. and C. Y. Park. 2011. Financial Integration in Emerging Asia: Challenges and Prospects. *Asian Economic Policy Review*. 6 (2). pp. 176–198.

Mercado, R. 2020. Bilateral Capital Flows: Gravity, Push, and Pull. *IFC Bulletin*. No. 52. Irving Fisher Committee on Central Bank Statistics.

MSCI. MSCI World Index. https://www.msci.com/eqb/esg/performance/106.0.all.xls (accessed August 2020).

———. https://www.investing.com/indices (accessed September 2020).

Papaioannou, E. 2009. What Drives International Financial Flows? Politics, Institutions and Other Determinants. *Journal of Development Economics.* 88. pp. 269–281.

Park, C. Y. and R. Mercado. 2014. Determinants of Financial Stress in Emerging Market Economies. *Journal of Banking and Finance.* 45. pp 199–224.

Park, C. Y., P. Rosenkranz, and M. Tayag. 2020. COVID-19 Exposes Asian Banks' Vulnerability to US Dollar Funding. *ADB Briefs.* No. 146. Manila: ADB.

Park, C. Y. and K. Shin. 2017. A Contagion through Exposure to Foreign Banks during the Global Financial Crisis. *ADB Economics Working Paper.* No. 516. Manila: ADB.

———. 2018. Global Banking Network and Regional Financial Contagion. *ADB Economics Working Paper.* No. 546. Manila: ADB.

———. 2020a. Contagion through National and Regional Exposures to Foreign Banks during the Global Financial Crisis. *Journal of Financial Stability.* 46.

———. 2020b. The Impact of Nonperforming Loans on Cross-Border Bank Lending: Implications for Emerging Market Economies. *ADB Briefs.* No. 136. Manila: ADB.

Portes, R. and H. Rey. 2005. The Determinants of Cross-Border Equity Flows. *Journal of International Economics.* 65. pp. 269–296.

Portes, R., H. Rey, and Y. Oh. 2001. Information and Capital Flows: The Determinants of Transactions in Financial Assets. *Journal of International Economics.* 45. pp. 783–796.

Remolona, E. and I. Shim. 2015. The Rise of Regional Banking in Asia and the Pacific. *BIS Quarterly Review.* September. Basel: BIS.

S&P Dow Jones Indices. Dow Jones Industrial Average Index. https://us.spindices.com/indices/equity/dow-jones-industrial-average (accessed August 2020).

World Bank. World Development Indicators. http://databank.worldbank.org/data/reports.aspx?source=world-development-indicators (accessed July 2020).

Yahoo! Yahoo! Finance. https://finance.yahoo.com/quote/GD.AT/history?period1=788918400&period2=1600214400&interval=1d&filter=history&frequency=1d (accessed September 2020).

Annex 4a: Updates on Asia's Cross-Border Financial Assets and Liabilities

International portfolio debt holdings of Asian economies continued to increase in 2019 as cross-border portfolio equity holdings rebounded sharply in 2019, after a considerable decline in 2018.

Asia's cross-border portfolio debt asset holdings increased from $4.5 trillion in 2018 to $5.1 trillion in 2019, recording an 11.6% increase and continuing its upward trend over the past years (Annex Figure 4a.1a).[1] The value of the region's cross-border portfolio equity asset holdings, likewise, grew in 2019 (Annex Figure 4a.1b). After declining from $4.8 trillion in 2017 to $4.5 trillion in 2018, cross-border equity asset holdings rebounded sharply to $5.4 trillion in 2019. The increase in the value of Asia's total cross-border portfolio asset holdings in 2019, which amounted to $1.5 trillion, was primarily due to the increase in the value of Japan's total cross-border portfolio asset holdings, which grew by $542 billion, underpinning its important role as global portfolio investor.

The value of Asia's cross-border portfolio debt assets increased by $526 billion in 2019 (Annex Figure 4a.2a). The increase in the value of US bond holdings, amounting to $242 billion, accounted for the bulk of the total increase, amid rising US interest rates in the first half of 2019. This was in contrast to 2018 when the value of the region's cross-border portfolio debt asset in the US declined by $12 billion. The amount of the region's holdings of European Union (EU) debt securities, likewise, increased by $106 billion in 2019, which was more than the $86 billion increase in 2018. The bulk of the increase reflected improvements in the value of Japan's holdings of debt securities from France, Spain, and Germany. As in past years, Asian investors, specifically from Japan; Australia; and Hong Kong, China, saw the value of their portfolio debt holdings in the Cayman Islands rise, by around $29 billion in 2019. The value of the region's intraregional portfolio debt assets, likewise, grew by $110 billion, more than thrice the 2018 increase of $30 billion.

Annex Figure 4a.1: International Portfolio Assets—Asia

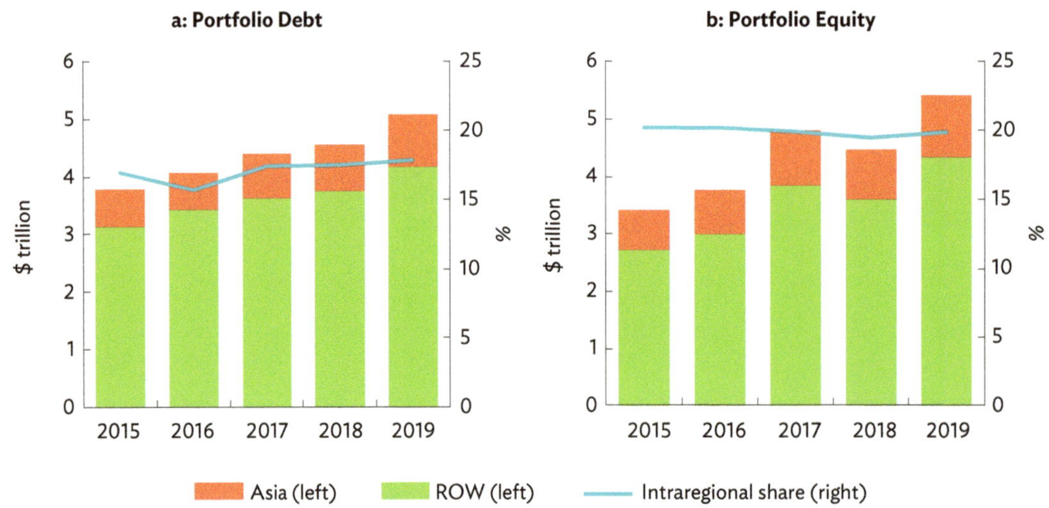

ROW = rest of the world.

Note: Asia includes ADB regional members for which data are available.

Source: ADB calculations using data from the International Monetary Fund. Coordinated Portfolio Investment Survey. http://data.imf.org/CPIS (accessed September 2020).

[1] The overall increase or decrease in stock portfolio holdings and liabilities is attributed to changes in flows and valuation changes of existing portfolio holdings and liabilities.

Annex Figure 4a.2: Change in International Portfolio Assets—Asia ($ billion)

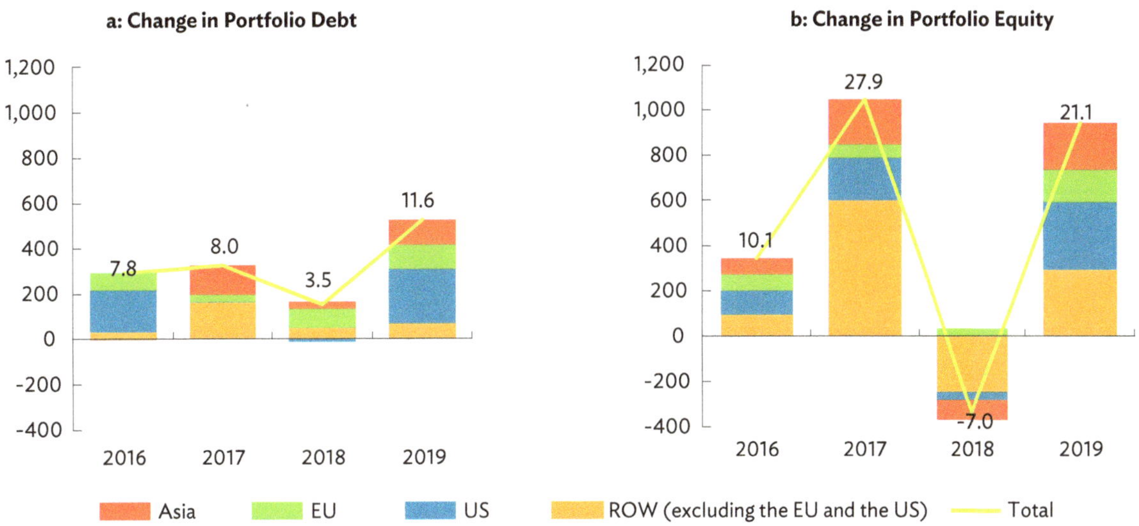

EU = European Union, ROW = rest of the world, US = United States.

Notes: Asia includes ADB regional members for which data are available. Labels refer to year-on-year percentage change.

Source: ADB calculations using data from the International Monetary Fund. Coordinated Portfolio Investment Survey. http://data.imf.org/CPIS (accessed September 2020).

The value of the region's cross-border portfolio equity holdings grew by $942 billion in 2019 (Annex Figure 4a.2b). Holdings of US equities gained attraction in 2019, rising by $297 billion in 2019 amid better-than-expected performance of US stock markets. Holdings of equities in global financial hubs such as Japan (with $132 billion), Australia ($59 billion), and the Republic of Korea ($37 billion) accounted for large shares of the increase in the value of the region's US equity investments. The amount of Asia's cross-border portfolio equity assets with the rest of the world (ROW) also rose. In particular, portfolio holdings in the Cayman Islands increased by $262 billion, with investments from Hong Kong, China accounting for $150 billion and from Japan $61 billion. Although these figures indicated increased risk appetite, some part of the increase may also be attributed to favorable rules in the People's Republic of China (PRC) and PRC investors' preference for Cayman Islands' equity securities with investment routed through Hong Kong, China (Cayman Compass 2018). Increased risk appetite also entails betting on the region's equity markets. The value of the region's intraregional equity investment grew by $206 billion, after declining by $87 billion in 2018.

While the growth in the region's international portfolio debt liabilities remained subdued, the value of its cross-border portfolio equity liabilities increased in 2019 after falling in 2018.

Asia's cross-border portfolio debt liabilities rose to $3.2 trillion in 2019, from $2.9 trillion in 2018, while the value of its portfolio equity liabilities increased to $5.6 trillion, after dropping to $4.7 trillion in 2018 (Annex Figure 4a.3). This pattern mirrored Asia's robust economic and financial performance in 2019 and the associated appetite for Asian securities, specifically equities. Hence, one can observe investors' appetite for returns, characterized by significantly larger increases in Asian equity holdings. The trend also reflected the increase in the amount of the region's intraregional portfolio liabilities. The value of the region's interregional portfolio debt liabilities increased by $98 billion in 2019, while the amount of its interregional portfolio equity liabilities, likewise, increased by $705 billion in the same year.

Annex Figure 4a.3: International Portfolio Liabilities—Asia

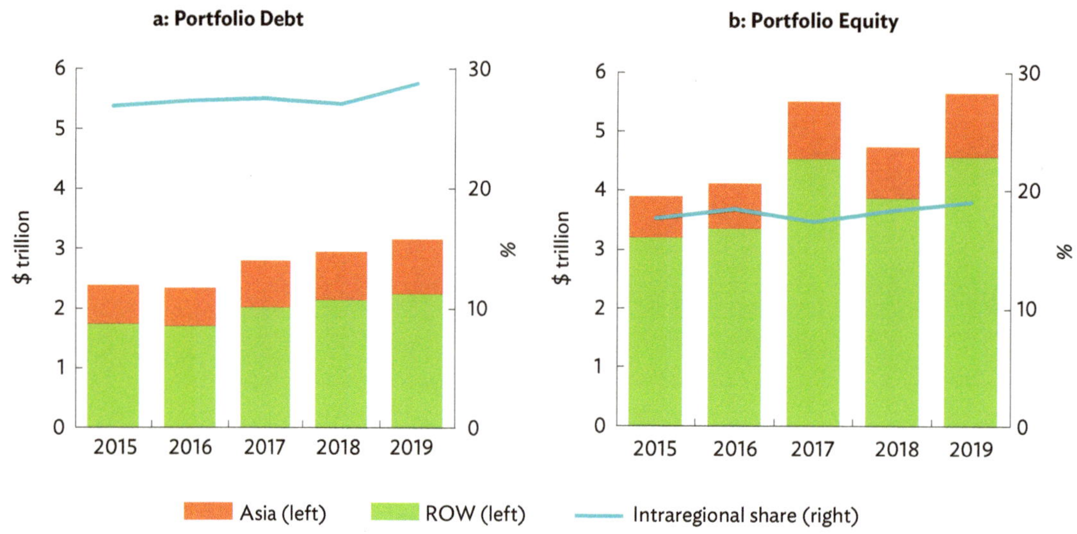

ROW = rest of the world.

Note: Asia includes ADB regional members for which data are available.

Source: ADB calculations using data from the International Monetary Fund. Coordinated Portfolio Investment Survey. http://data.imf.org/CPIS (accessed September 2020).

Annex Figure 4a.4: Change in International Portfolio Liabilities—Asia ($ billion)

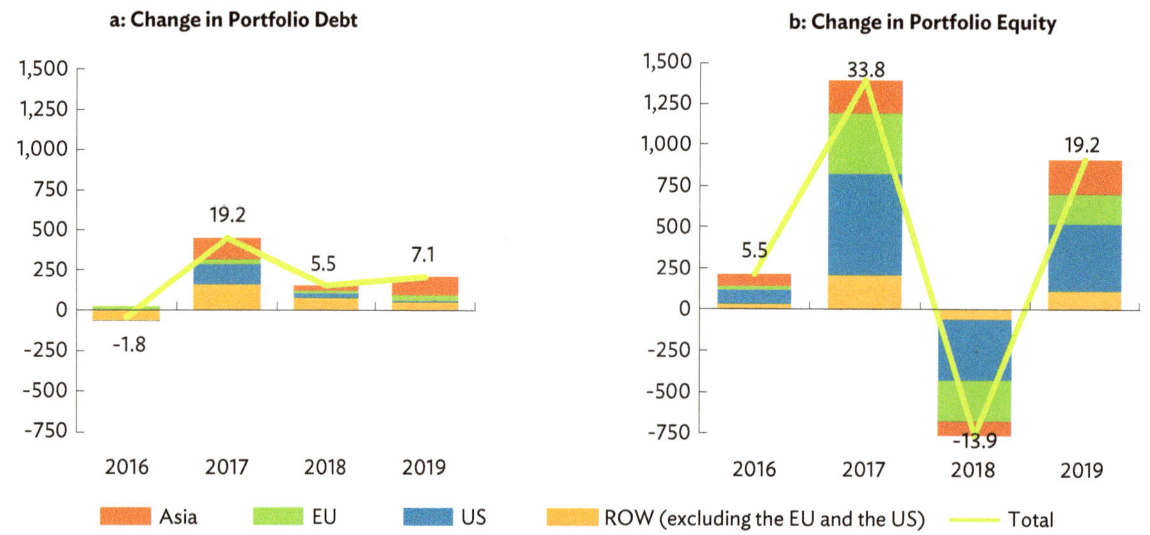

EU = European Union, ROW = rest of the world, US = United States.

Notes: Asia includes ADB regional members for which data are available. Labels refer to year-on-year percentage change.

Source: ADB calculations using data from the International Monetary Fund. Coordinated Portfolio Investment Survey. http://data.imf.org/CPIS (accessed September 2020).

The increase in the value of Asia's cross-border portfolio debt liabilities was primarily driven by the increase in the amount of portfolio debt liabilities in Asia, as the amount of intraregional debt liabilities grew by $110 billion in 2019, more than thrice the increase in 2018 (Annex Figure 4a.4a). The PRC's bond market was the most appealing even intraregionally. Besides considerable cross-border trading and holdings between Hong Kong, China and the PRC, the demand for bonds issued in the PRC grew after JP Morgan announced in September 2019 the inclusion of PRC bonds in its government bond index for emerging markets.

The noticeable increase in value of international investors' holdings of Asian equities in 2019 was driven by the increase in the value of US investors' equity holdings in the region, which grew by $407 billion, after declining significantly in 2018 (Annex Figure 4a.4b). The EU's holdings of Asian equities also bounced back, with an increase of $182 billion in 2019, after declining by $247 billion in 2018. Specifically, the value of EU equity holdings of Japanese equities grew by $45 billion in 2019.

East Asia continued to be the main driver of intraregional portfolio debt and equity investments.

As a source, the share of East Asia's portfolio debt holdings decreased from 73% in 2015 to 68% in 2019 (Annex Figure 4a.5). As a destination, East Asia's portfolio debt liabilities share remained at 55% in 2019. While East Asia still accounts for half of intraregional portfolio debt investments, Southeast Asia had been an increasingly attractive debt destination as its portfolio debt liabilities share increased to 16% in 2019 from 14% in 2015.

As a source, the share of East Asia's portfolio equity investment increased to 55% from 57%, with Japan, the PRC, and the Republic of Korea continuing to be the most prominent investors in the region (Annex Figure 4a.6). Southeast Asia also remained the second top investor, with a share of 32% in 2019, as Singapore continues to play a dominant role as a regional financial hub. As a destination, East Asia continued to attract almost three-fourths of the region's investment, followed by Southeast Asia.

Annex Figure 4a.5: Intraregional Portfolio Debt Investment—Asia, by Subregion

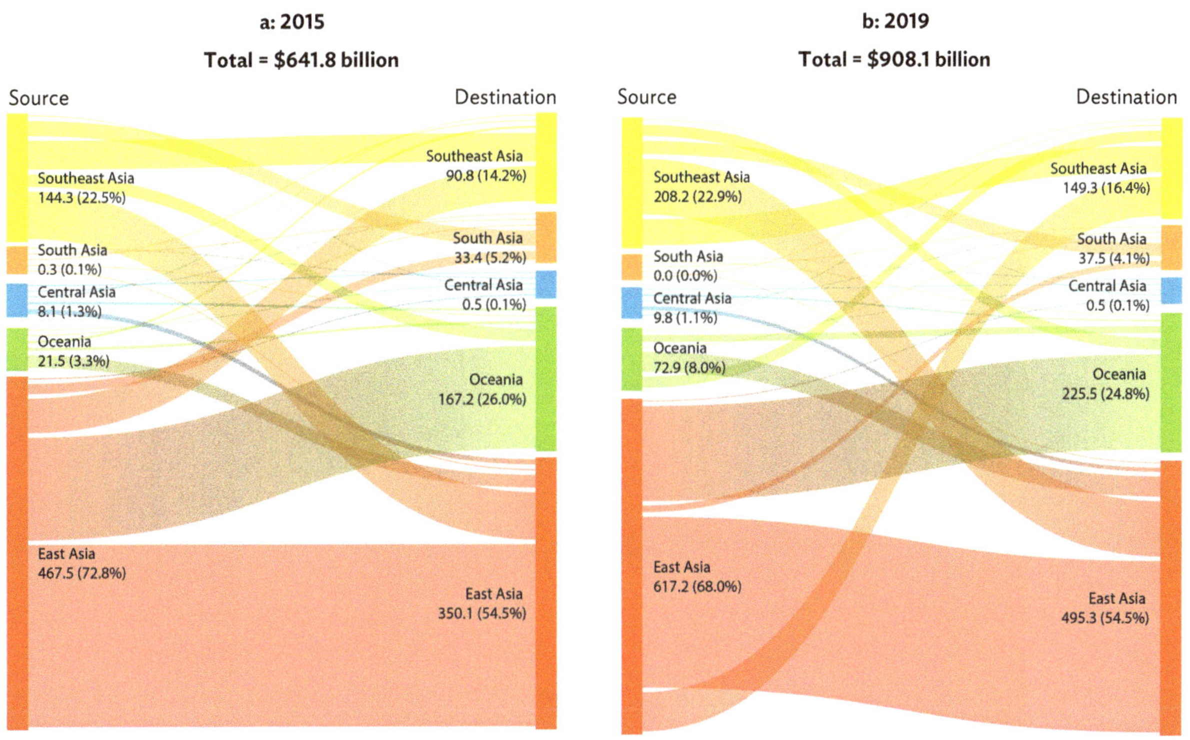

Notes: Asia includes Central Asia, East Asia, Oceania, South Asia, and Southeast Asia. Central Asia includes Kazakhstan. East Asia includes Hong Kong, China; Japan; Mongolia; the People's Republic of China; and the Republic of Korea. Oceania includes Australia and New Zealand. South Asia includes Bangladesh, India, and Pakistan. Southeast Asia includes Indonesia, Malaysia, the Philippines, Singapore, and Thailand.

Source: ADB calculations using data from the International Monetary Fund. Coordinated Portfolio Investment Survey. http://data.imf.org/CPIS (accessed September 2020).

Annex Figure 4a.6: Intraregional Portfolio Equity Investment—Asia, by Subregion

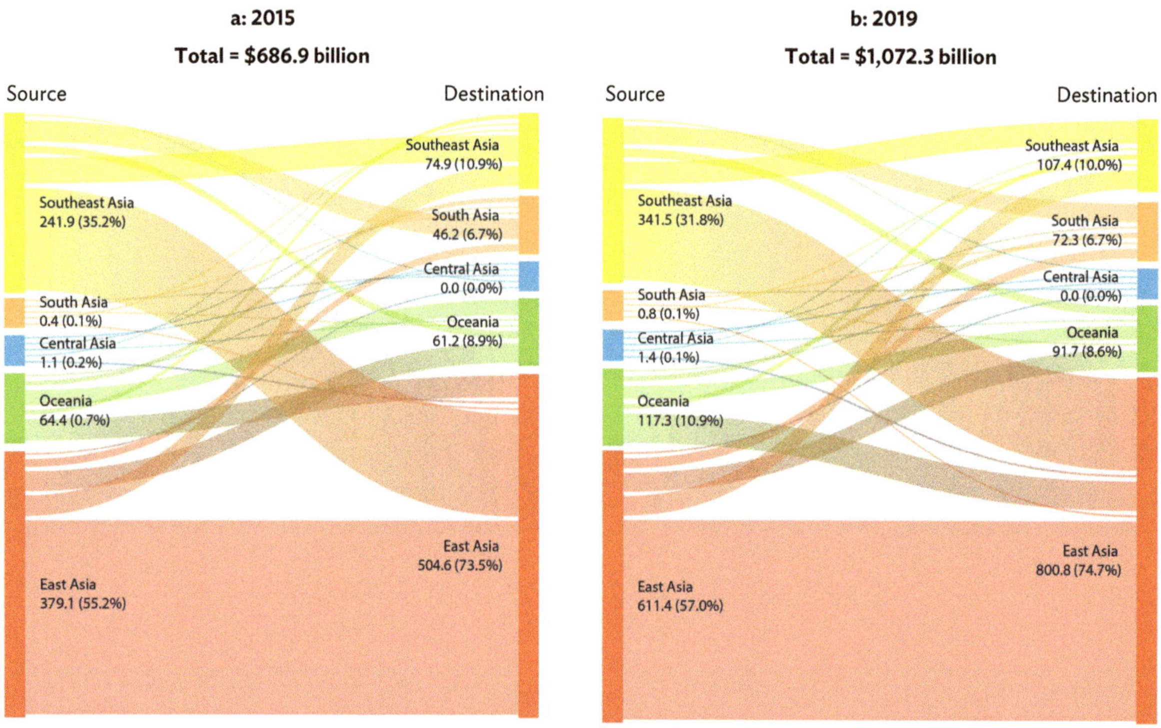

Notes: Asia includes Central Asia, East Asia, Oceania, South Asia, and Southeast Asia. Central Asia includes Kazakhstan. East Asia includes Hong Kong, China; Japan; Mongolia; the People's Republic of China; and the Republic of Korea. Oceania includes Australia and New Zealand. South Asia includes Bangladesh, India, and Pakistan. Southeast Asia includes Indonesia, Malaysia, the Philippines, Singapore, and Thailand.

Source: ADB calculations using data from the International Monetary Fund. Coordinated Portfolio Investment Survey. http://data.imf.org/CPIS (accessed September 2020).

Asia's cross-border banking activities continued to rise in 2019, as foreign bank claims reached $6.6 trillion and foreign bank liabilities hit $3.8 trillion, highlighting the Asian banks' role as net lender globally.

Asia's cross-border total bank claims continued to rise in 2019 to $6.6 trillion from $6.3 trillion in 2018, while Asian banks' cross-border liabilities slightly increased in 2019 to $3.8 trillion from $3.7 trillion in 2018 (Annex Figure 4a.7). Intraregional shares fell slightly for cross-border claims (from 32% in 2018 to 30% in 2019) and liabilities (from 38% in 2018 to 37% in 2019). The slightly downward trending intraregional shares over the past few years may suggest that Asian banks are becoming increasingly integrated with the global banking network.

The value of the region's bank claims on the US increased by $137 billion in 2019, while those on EU counterparts grew by $119 billion (Annex Figure 4a.8a). These gains offset the slight decline of $21 billion in the value of intraregional bank claims recorded in 2019. Japanese banks' cross-border claims were driving these trends, as the values of their bank claims on the EU, the US, and ROW (excluding the EU and the US) registered considerable increases of about $76 billion, $105 billion, and $80 billion, respectively, while the value of their intraregional bank claims declined by $29 billion. As of the first quarter (Q1) of 2020, the value of Asia's cross-border bank claims on the US and the EU surged by $293 billion and $181 billion, respectively. In Q2 2020, the region's cross-border bank claims lost value as economies went into lockdown to contain the spread of COVID-19, investor sentiment deteriorated, and liquidity conditions tightened.

Annex Figure 4a.7: Cross-Border Bank Holdings—Asia

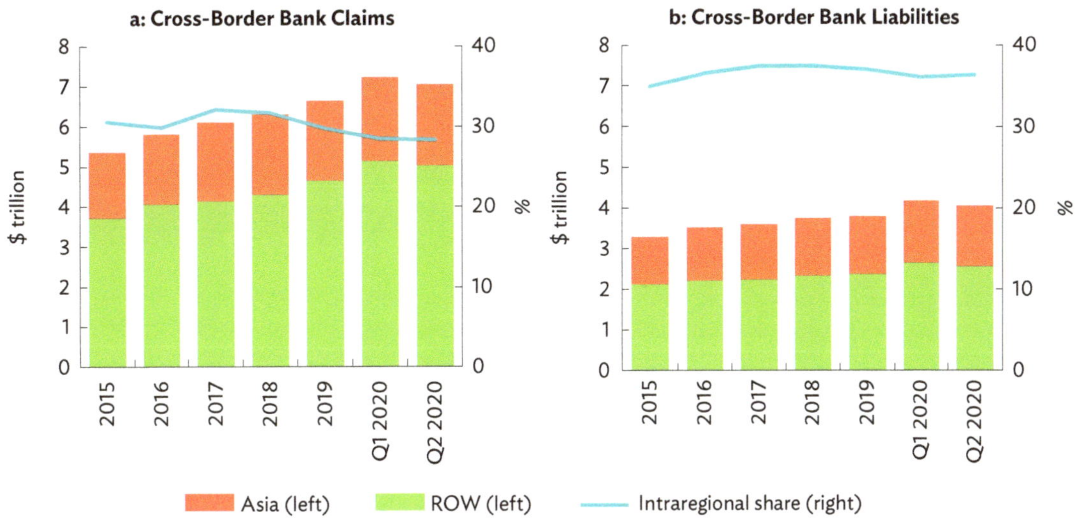

ROW = rest of the world.

Note: Asia includes ADB regional members for which data are available.

Source: ADB calculations using data from the Bank for International Settlements. Locational Banking Statistics. https://www.bis.org/statistics/bankstats.htm (accessed October 2020).

Annex Figure 4a.8: Change in Cross-Border Bank Holdings—Asia ($ billion)

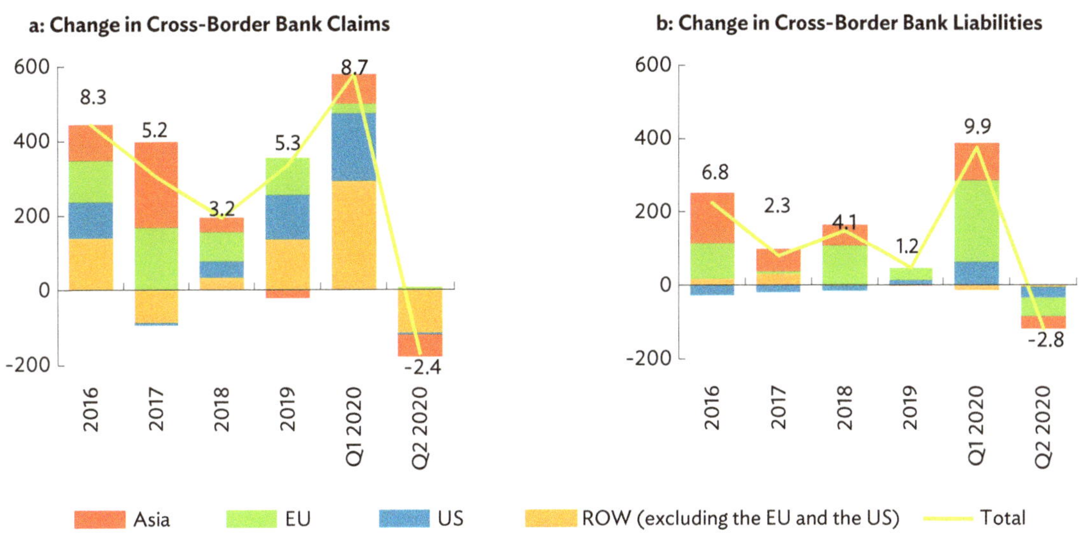

EU = European Union, ROW = rest of the world, US = United States.

Notes: Asia includes ADB regional members for which data are available. Labels refer to year-on-year percentage change.

Source: ADB calculations using data from the Bank for International Settlements. Locational Banking Statistics. https://www.bis.org/statistics/bankstats.htm (accessed October 2020).

In 2019, the value of Asia's cross-border bank liabilities to the US and the EU grew by $14 billion and $33 billion, respectively (Annex Figure 4a.8b), while intraregional bank liabilities lost value by $0.1 billion. In Q1 2020, the amount of Asia's cross-border bank liabilities rose as the amount of bank liabilities to the EU grew by $223 billion, while that for the region increased by $100 billion. Asia's cross-border bank liabilities lost value in the Q2 2020.

5 Movement of People
People Mobility Hampered by the Pandemic and Virus Containment Measures

Migration

The number of Asian migrants stood at 90.3 million in 2019 out of 271.6 million migrants worldwide. The coronavirus disease pandemic affected their lives via health, socioeconomic, and protection crises.[30]

In 2019, the stock of international migrants worldwide reached 271.6 million, up 9.2% from 2015 (Figure 5.1).[31] International migrants accounted for around 3.5% of the global population in 2019. The migrant stock continued to grow across all regions from 2015.[32] Global migrants from Asia grew 7.6% to 90.3 million in 2019 from 84.0 million in 2015. During the same period, growth was highest in the Middle East (16.8%) and Africa (12.5%).

Asia remains the largest source of migrants—one in three migrants (33.3%) worldwide. India had the largest number of outward migrants in 2019 (17.5 million) and has been the top source of Asian outmigrants since 1995

Figure 5.1: International Migrant Stock and Share of Migrants from Asia

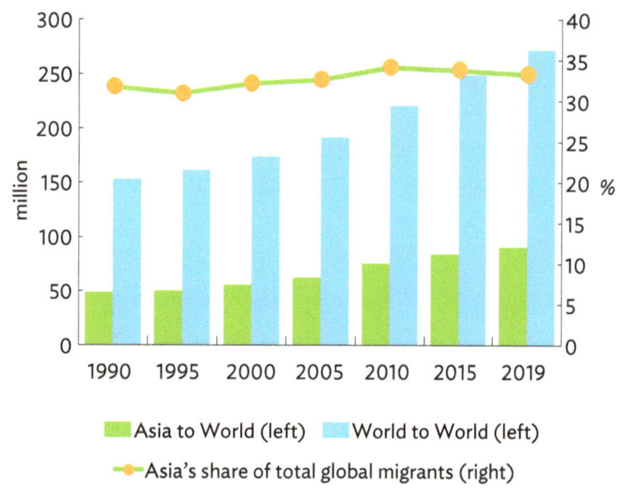

Note: Asia's share of total global migrants is computed as (migrants from the region / total global migrants) x 100.

Source: ADB calculations using data from United Nations. Department of Economic and Social Affairs, Population Division. International Migrant Stock: The 2019 Revision. https://www.un.org/en/development/desa/population/migration/data/estimates2/estimates19.asp (accessed May 2020).

30 Asia refers to the 49 members of the Asian Development Bank (ADB) within Asia and the Pacific, which includes Japan and Oceania (Australia and New Zealand) in addition to the 46 developing Asian economies.

31 United Nations (UN) recommendations on statistics of international migration define the "stock of international migrants present in a country" as "the set of persons who have ever changed their country of usual residence, that is to say, persons who have spent at least one year of their lives in a country other than the one in which they live at the time the data are gathered" (UN 1998). International migrant stock consists of persons crossing borders for various reasons—for employment, family reunification, study, and flight from conflict and violence. Some involve the creation of new borders, generating large numbers of international migrants—as during the 1991 dissolution of the Soviet Union.

32 With the exit of the United Kingdom (UK) from the European Union on 31 January 2020, the UK's immigration policy will shift from free movement to a points-based system which would reduce overall levels of migration and prioritize skills and talent: scientists, engineers, academics and other highly-skilled workers (Government of the United Kingdom 2020). In the United States (US), nonimmigrant admissions grew by 5.4% from 77.1 million in 2016 to 81.3 million in 2018, while those granted lawful permanent residence declined from 1.2 million in 2016 to 1.1 million in 2018 (Government of the US Department of Homeland Security. Immigration Data and Statistics). In 2020, the US Citizenship and Immigration Services (USCIS) raised its fees as one way to slow legal migration (Government of the US Department of Homeland Security. USCIS).

(7.2 million). Other Asian countries with large diaspora populations include the People's Republic of China (PRC) (10.7 million), Bangladesh (7.8 million), Pakistan (6.3 million), and the Philippines (5.4 million) (Figure 5.2).

Figure 5.2: Top 10 Sources of Migrants, 2019—Asia (million)

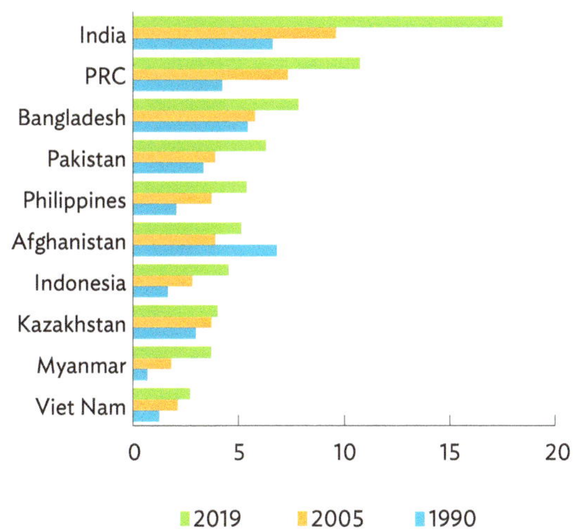

PRC = People's Republic of China.

Source: ADB calculations using data from United Nations. Department of Economic and Social Affairs, Population Division. International Migrant Stock: The 2019 Revision. https://www.un.org/en/development/desa/population/migration/data/estimates2/estimates19.asp (accessed May 2020).

Mobility Restrictions and Challenges in 2020

Border closures, travel restrictions, and quarantine measures imposed to mitigate the spread of the coronavirus significantly limited mobility and disproportionately impacted international migrants.

The coronavirus disease (COVID-19) pandemic significantly affected people's movement, halted many industries, and disproportionately imposed huge costs on migrants and their families. Restrictions on mobility and travel to curtail COVID-19 infections disrupted economic activity, created massive unemployment, and led to a global economic crisis. As the number of confirmed cases began to rise, many countries quickly imposed lockdowns, the first in late January and becoming most stringent in late March and April (Figure 5.3). Some measures were gradually eased in late April and May but remained restrictive relative to precrisis conditions as social distancing and partial lockdowns continued. Mobility restrictions were more stringent in the top 10 destination countries for migrants—including the US, the Russian Federation, and Middle East countries—where more than 60% of Asia's migrants reside. It became challenging for migrant workers to travel back home.

Figure 5.3: Mobility Restrictions during the COVID-19 Pandemic—2020 Oxford Government Stringency Index

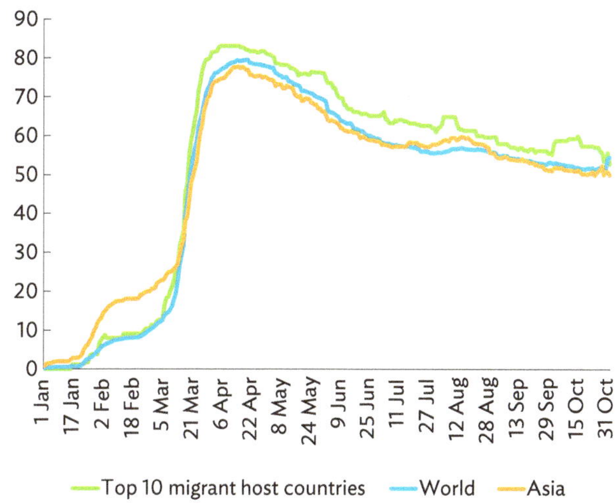

COVID-19 = coronavirus disease.

Notes: The Oxford COVID-19 Government Response Stringency Index is a composite indicator, with a range of 0 to 100 (most restrictive), that captures policy decisions on (i) school closings, (ii) workplace closings, (iii) cancellation of public events, (iv) restrictions on gathering size, (v) public transport closures, (vi) home confinement orders, (vii) restrictions on internal movement, (viii) international travel controls, and (ix) public information on COVID-19. The top 10 migrant host countries for 2019 include the United States, Saudi Arabia, the Russian Federation, the United Arab Emirates, India, Australia, Thailand, Canada, Pakistan, and Malaysia.

Source: ADB calculations using data from Hale et al. (2020a).

The pandemic and ensuing lockdowns put many migrant jobs in jeopardy. The International Labour Organization (ILO 2020b) reported that low-skilled migrants and seasonal workers were likely to be laid off first, but last to get tested or treated. They are often excluded from government policy responses, such as wage subsidies, unemployment benefits or social security, and social protection measures. With limited or no social protection, no savings, without adequate food and shelter, and no financial means to return to their home countries, thousands of migrants were stranded. Working migrants sent home continue to face uncertainty over their future employment prospects.

Thailand's closure of 18 border points from 23 March resulted in the sudden, unexpected outflow of migrant workers from Cambodia, the Lao People's Democratic Republic (Lao PDR), and Myanmar traveling back to their home countries and communities (Table 5.1).[33] Nepal expects around 500,000 workers who lost their jobs abroad to return home, mainly from the Middle East and Malaysia, while Bangladesh has repatriated about 400,000 of its migrants. India's Vanda Bharat mission flights have repatriated at least 1 million workers. Between February and December 2020, at least 300,000 Filipino migrant workers have been repatriated. Australia's travel ban for noncitizens and nonresidents, and the temporary suspension of its visa-exemption facilities, put Indonesian migrant workers and working professionals in limbo as they were either locked in or out of Australia for indefinite periods.[34] Indonesians in the southern Philippines had to appeal for food assistance from their government in Jakarta. Malaysia's movement control order barred its citizens from traveling abroad—including 300,000 workers who commute to Singapore daily.[35] Migrants from Asia crucial to the Middle East workforce were confronted with the sudden loss of income and unemployment, particularly low-skilled workers. In Qatar, migrant construction workers were quarantined in overcrowded labor dormitories, creating a higher risk of COVID-19 exposure (Pattison and Sedhai 2020).

Table 5.1: Number of Return Migrants during the COVID-19 Pandemic

	Return Migrants			
Country of Origin	Number	% Outmigrant Stock (2019)	Repatriated Mainly from	As of
Armenia	60,000	6.2	Russian Federation, Europe	30 June
Azerbaijan	20,000	1.7	Russian Federation	29 May
Bangladesh	408,408	5.2	Middle East	31 December
Cambodia	100,000	9.1	Thailand	06 August
India	1,666,496	9.5	Middle East, US, Europe, Asia	31 December
Indonesia	130,000	2.9	Malaysia, Middle East	Mid-June
Lao PDR	119,401	8.9	Thailand	17 June
Myanmar	135,469	3.7	Thailand, PRC, Lao PDR	15 June
Nepal	51,441	2.3	India	12 October
Philippines	327,511	6.1	Middle East, Asia, US, Europe	31 December
Samoa	1,000	0.8	New Zealand	5 August
Tonga	3,000	4.0	New Zealand	26 August
Uzbekistan	500,000	25.3	Russian Federation	29 May
Vanuatu	1,000	13.6	New Zealand	26 June

COVID-19 = coronavirus disease, Lao PDR = Lao People's Democratic Republic, PRC = People's Republic of China, US = United States.

Sources: ADB calculations using data from United Nations. Department of Economic and Social Affairs, Population Division. International Migrant Stock: The 2019 Revision. https://www.un.org/en/development/desa/population/migration/data/estimates2/estimates19.asp (accessed May 2020); Ahamad (2021); Engblom, Lephilibert, and Baruah (2020); Eurasianet.org (2020); Global Knowledge Partnership for Migration and Development (2020); Government of India, Ministry of External Affairs. https://www.mea.gov.in/vande-bharat-mission-list-of-flights.htm (accessed January 2021); Government of the Philippines, Department of Foreign Affairs (2021); International Organization for Migration (2020a, 2020b, 2020c, 2020d); Massing (2020); Millard (2020); Olsen and Vorn (2020); Pannier (2020); Pollock and Paing (2020); Prasain (2020); Radio New Zealand (2020a, 2020b).

33 As of December 2019, there were 2.8 million registered migrant workers in Thailand and an unknown number of undocumented migrant workers. Around 700,000 migrant workers in Thailand, who worked mostly in tourism, services, and construction industries, have lost their jobs since the lockdown started in late March 2020.

34 According to Government of Australia, Department of Home Affairs, from 20 March 2020, travel restrictions have been in place prohibiting travel to Australia of all foreign nationals, unless exempt.

35 Martinus (2020) reported that the Singapore government then made accommodations for Malaysian workers to continue working as usual.

Among the safety nets provided to returning Asian migrants were cash grants, subsidies for housing and transportation, as well as free access to COVID-19 testing and treatment. Subsidies were offered to help businesses retain employees, and social insurance contributions were deferred for employers (Testaverde 2020). Placement services were deployed, and regulations adjusted to protect migrants. Regulations and taxes on remittance were also reduced.

Returning Philippine migrants were given cash ($200) and transportation assistance (Government of the Philippines, Department of Labor and Employment 2020). In Bangladesh, returning migrants received a stipend of Tk5,000 upon arrival at the airport and were eligible for government loans ranging from Tk500,000 to Tk700,000 if they invested in economic activities, especially in agriculture (BenarNews.org 2020). Viet Nam used apps that record a person's health status and symptoms to expedite the return of migrant workers or those traveling within the country (Bismonte 2020). In the Republic of Korea, a disaster relief fund that began in March 2020 was expanded to include all migrants, provided they have been living in the capital city for at least 90 days. Using prepaid cards, the measure provided relief to migrants who had lost their jobs and were unable to return to their home countries due to travel restrictions (The Workers Rights 2020). In New Zealand, migrant workers were allowed to take sick leave given assistance for lost work due to lockdowns. Free COVID-19 testing and treatment was provided in Kazakhstan and the Republic of Korea. Singapore canceled levies for hiring foreign workers to help employers of foreign workers. The PRC also developed an online platform to facilitate job placement and recruitment as well as skills development.

Overview of Migration to and from Asia

Outward migration has steadily increased, especially those headed outside Asia.

In recent years, the stock of Asian migrants across the world has grown faster than the number of migrants residing within the region (Figure 5.4), suggesting that extraregional migration remains the preferred route. Although the number of intraregional migrants within Asia has increased since 1990, the share has been trending downward.

Figure 5.4: Migration to and from Asia, by Region (million)

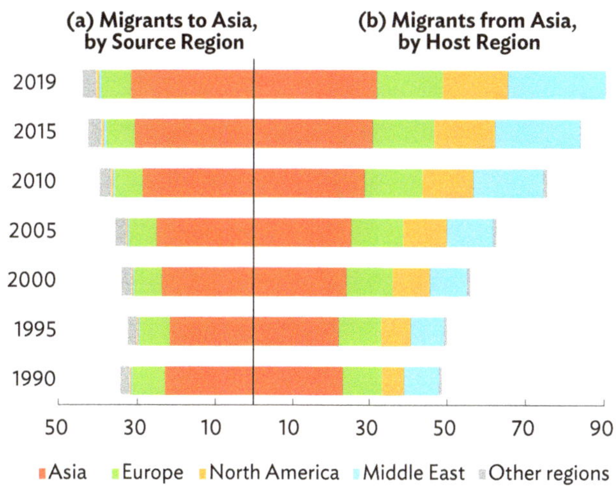

Source: ADB calculations using data from United Nations. Department of Economic and Social Affairs, Population Division. International Migrant Stock: The 2019 Revision. https://www.un.org/en/development/desa/population/migration/data/estimates2/estimates19.asp (accessed May 2020).

By subregion, South Asia (45.3%) and Southeast Asia (24.2%) account for the largest shares of Asian outmigrants (Figure 5.5). Around 50% of migrants from South Asia move to the Middle East while 28.9% remain within Asia. Southeast Asian migrants tend to stay within Asia, although 24.9% reside in North America. Central Asian migrants are found mostly in Europe, particularly the Russian Federation.

Outmigration is also common in the Pacific. In Fiji, Samoa, and Tonga, outmigrants comprise about 35.4% of the population—and are affected by Oceania's migration policies. New Zealand's Recognized Seasonal Employer (RSE) scheme and Australia's Pacific Labour Scheme allow for the employment of migrants from the Pacific. The RSE cap for 2020–2021 is 14,400, while the Pacific Labour Scheme is uncapped.[36] Nationals from Niue and the Cook Islands, as concurrent New Zealand citizens, can

[36] Government of New Zealand, Ministry of Business, Innovation and Employment. https://www.immigration.govt.nz/about-us/research-and-statistics/research-reports/recognised-seasonal-employer-rse-scheme (accessed September 2020); and Government of Australia, Department of Foreign Affairs and Trade. https://www.dfat.gov.au/geo/pacific/engagement/pacific-labour-mobility (accessed September 2020).

live and work in New Zealand without restriction.[37] In Central Asian economies such as Armenia, Georgia, and Kazakhstan, outmigrants comprise at least 20% of the population.

Figure 5.5: Asian Outmigrants by Subregion and Their Regional Destination, 2019 (number of international migrants)

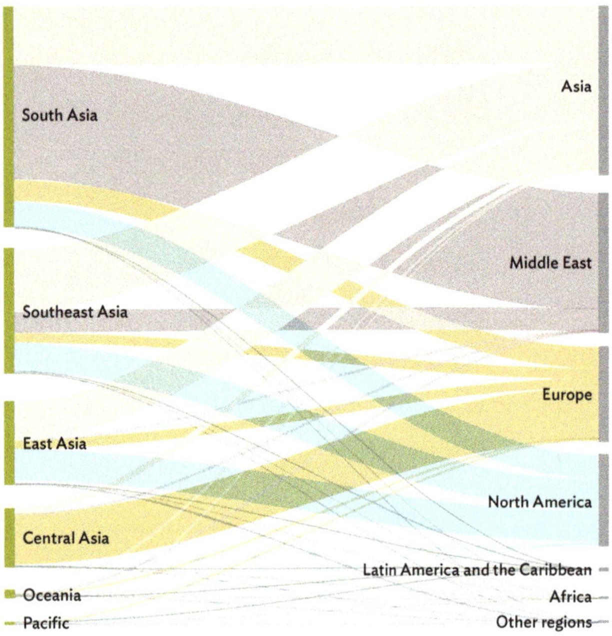

Source: ADB calculations using data from United Nations. Department of Economic and Social Affairs, Population Division. International Migrant Stock: The 2019 Revision. https://www.un.org/en/development/desa/population/migration/data/estimates2/estimates19.asp (accessed May 2020).

Many low-skilled migrants from Asia were hit hard by the pandemic, forcing them to return home, while high-skilled migrant workers in sectors vital to developed host countries stayed on.

Migrants from Asia are in 186 different economies, with more than 40% concentrated in the US, Saudi Arabia, the Russian Federation, the United Arab Emirates, and Canada (Table 5.2). These non-Asian destinations also collectively account for about one-third of the confirmed COVID-19 cases globally. Among the top host countries in Asia, India had 12.3% share of confirmed coronavirus cases.

Skills and the relative importance of certain types of migrant occupations in host countries basically determined how much pressure was applied for migrants to return to their home countries. In the Middle East, where foreign workers account for up to 80% of the labor force, many low-skilled migrant workers in construction, tourism, retail services, and as domestic workers either lost their jobs or were stranded and had to return home with no clear prospects of reemployment. The same was true for migrants in the Russian Federation, where 80% have only low- to medium-level skills (Figure 5.6).

Table 5.2: Top 10 Economies Hosting Migrants from Asia and COVID-19 Cases

	Number of Asian Migrants	Share of Total	Number of Confirmed COVID-19 Cases[a]	Share of Global Total
United States	13,177,721	14.4%	19,968,087	23.9%
Saudi Arabia	9,167,287	10.0%	362,741	0.4%
Russian Federation	6,806,668	7.5%	3,127,347	3.7%
United Arab Emirates	6,517,803	7.1%	207,822	0.2%
India	5,097,377	5.6%	10,266,674	12.3%
Australia	3,713,494	4.1%	28,425	0.0%
Thailand	3,617,946	4.0%	7,163	0.0%
Canada	3,307,678	3.6%	584,409	0.7%
Malaysia	3,186,689	3.5%	113,010	0.1%
Pakistan	3,180,724	3.5%	482,178	0.6%
Top 10 total	**57,773,387**	**64.0%**	**35,147,856**	**42.1%**

COVID-19 = coronavirus disease.

[a] The number of confirmed COVID-19 cases are as of 31 December 2020; the number of global cases totaled 83,427,446.

Sources: ADB calculations using data from Roser et al. (2020); and United Nations. Department of Economic and Social Affairs, Population Division. International Migrant Stock: The 2019 Revision. https://www.un.org/en/development/desa/population/migration/data/estimates2/estimates19.asp (accessed May 2020).

[37] Outward migrants from Niue and the Cook Islands were proportional to 170.3% and 63.3% of their respective populations in 2019.

For high-skilled migrants working in Australia, Canada, Saudi Arabia, and the UK, there was far less pressure to return to their home countries. Migrants working in industries key to the pandemic response, such as health workers, were relatively insulated from being repatriated. In Canada, for example, 26% of doctors are foreign-trained workers.[38] In Qatar and the United Arab Emirates, at least 90% of doctors are foreign-born workers. In Bahrain, Oman, Qatar and Saudi Arabia, at least 47% of nurses are migrants. Kuwait, where 96% of nurses are migrants, recently hired at least 500 doctors and nurses from Pakistan, is preparing for a second wave of the coronavirus (Al Sherbini 2020).

Figure 5.6: Employment Distribution of Migrants by Level of Skills (%)

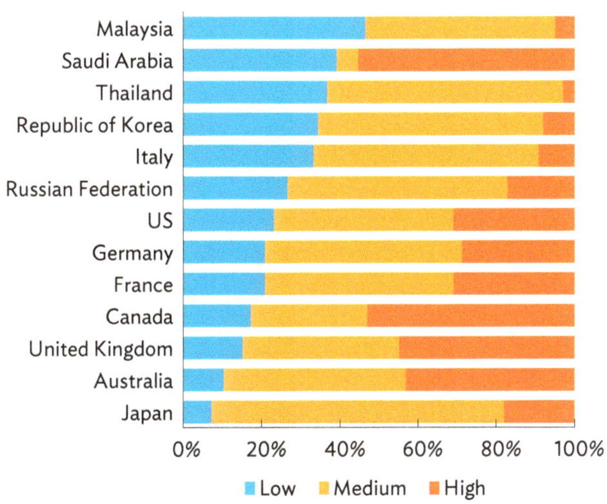

US = United States.

Note: Data are from latest available year.

Source: International Labour Organization. ILOSTAT. https://ilostat.ilo.org/data/ (accessed September 2020).

In the US, incoming migrants faced new entry restrictions. The US immigration services were suspended in April 2020 and the issuance of H-1B and other work visas were suspended until 31 December 2020, banning the entry of foreign workers who present a risk to the labor market. Exemptions were made for public health or health-care professionals, and researchers directly engaged in alleviating the effects of the COVID-19 pandemic or engaged in research with substantial public health benefits.[39] This temporary ban affected migrants, especially those in professional occupations (16.9%), elementary occupations (23.3%), and sales and service workers (18.6%).[40] In the UK, skilled tier visas accounted for 50% of all visa applications, a category dominated by migrants from India (46.4%) and, to a lesser extent, the Philippines (7.2%) and Australia (3.8%).[41] As part of the continuing national effort to fight the pandemic, doctors, nurses, and paramedics had their work visas automatically extended for 1 year free of charge. This benefited the source countries for medical workers, such as the Philippines, the largest source of migrant nurses worldwide (Ladrido 2020). Migrants account for at least 25% of employed professionals in the UK.[42]

Many Asian migrants continue to seek (re)employment prospects in Saudi Arabia and the United Arab Emirates. The global economic contraction is forecast to reverse short-term growth prospects in the Middle East; and policies on the nationalization of labor have begun to affect the flow of low-skilled migrants. In Bangladesh, for example, between 2017 and 2019, the flow of migrant workers to Saudi Arabia declined by 27.6%, to the United Arab Emirates by 19.8%, and to Qatar by 38.7%.[43] Notwithstanding these domestic-oriented labor policies, the demand for migrant labor in the Middle East will likely continue as the region pursues post-pandemic diversification (Ghosh 2020).

38 See World Health Organization. National Health Workforce Accounts. https://apps.who.int/nhwaportal/ (accessed January 2021).

39 See Government of the United States, Department of State–Bureau of Consular Affairs (2020).

40 International Labour Organization. ILOSTAT. https://ilostat.ilo.org/data/ (accessed September 2020).

41 Visa applications for the year ending September 2019 totaled 63,510—29,482 from India; 4,576 from the Philippines; and 2,401 from Australia.

42 ILOSTAT data set on employment of migrants by occupation. https://ilostat.ilo.org/data/ (accessed September 2020).

43 Government of Bangladesh. Bureau of Manpower, Employment and Training. http://www.old.bmet.gov.bd/BMET/stattisticalDataAction (accessed September 2020).

Intraregional Migration

Intraregional migration remains an important part of international migration from the region.

Around 35% of Asian migrants stay within the region, varying by subregion (Figure 5.7). The absolute number of intraregional Asian migrants during 2015–2019 rose 3.3%—from 30.8 million to 31.8 million. Most intraregional migrants come from the PRC (5.4 million), Bangladesh (3.7 million), Myanmar (3.3 million), India (3.2 million), and Indonesia (1.9 million). Intraregional PRC migrants move to Japan (14.6%), Australia (12.0%), and the Republic of Korea (11.6%), but Hong Kong, China (42.3%) remains the top destination. At least 80% of Bangladeshi migrants move to India while 57% of those from Myanmar reside in Thailand.

Figure 5.7: Migration from Asia by Subregion
(% of total outmigrants)

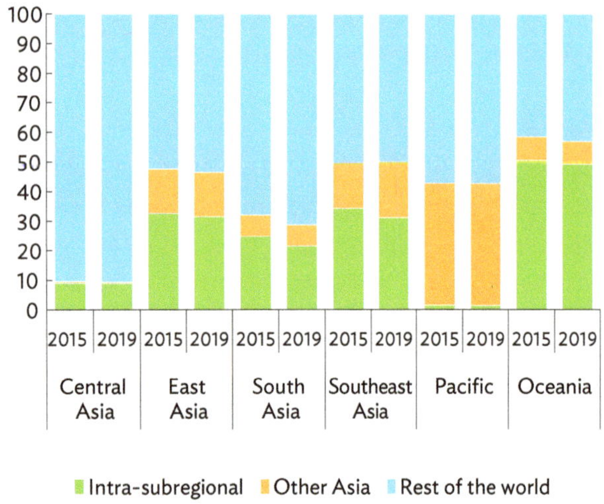

Notes:

(i) Intra-subregional refers to migrants from subregion i as a percentage of migrants from subregion i to the world.

(ii) Other Asia refers to migrants from subregion i to other Asian subregions as a percentage of migrants from subregion i to the world.

(iii) Rest of the world refers to migrants from subregion i to the rest of the world as a percentage of migrants from subregion i to the world.

Source: ADB calculations using data from United Nations. Department of Economic and Social Affairs, Population Division. International Migrant Stock: The 2019 Revision. https://www.un.org/en/development/desa/population/migration/data/estimates2/estimates19.asp (accessed May 2020).

Among the top economies hosting intraregional migrants are India (5.1 million), Australia (3.7 million), Thailand (3.6 million), Malaysia (3.2 million), and Pakistan (3.2 million). Intraregional migrants to India largely come from neighboring countries such as Bangladesh (3.1 million), Pakistan (1.1 million), and Nepal (0.5 million). Australia hosted migrants primarily from the PRC (0.6 million), New Zealand (0.6 million), and India (0.6 million), while Thailand hosted those from nearby countries such as Myanmar (1.9 million), the Lao PDR (0.9 million), and Cambodia (0.7 million).

Inter-subregional migration remains high among ADB's Pacific developing member countries (41.2%). New Zealand—through its Recognized Seasonal Employer (RSE) scheme—allows in horticulture and viticulture workers from Fiji, Kiribati, Nauru, Papua New Guinea, Samoa, Solomon Islands, Tonga, Tuvalu, and Vanuatu. Australia's Pacific Labour Scheme allows workers from Fiji, Kiribati, Nauru, Papua New Guinea, Samoa, Solomon Islands, Timor-Leste, Tonga, Tuvalu, and Vanuatu to take up nonseasonal low- and semi-skilled work in rural Australia in growth sectors such as health care, social assistance, and hospitality.[44] As the pandemic battered tourism across Pacific countries, the Pacific Labour Scheme is one way migrant workers can continue to send remittances to their home country (McDonald 2020).

East Asia and Southeast Asia also have relatively high migrant mobility within their subregions. Intra-subregional migrants in East Asia, primarily from the PRC (3.7 million) and the Republic of Korea (0.7 million) were double their inter-subregional migrants (2.1 million) in 2019. Still, migrants from Indonesia, the Philippines, and Viet Nam continue as the top migrants to East Asia. These economies have labor arrangements—such as a bilateral labor agreement with the Republic of Korea and the Philippines[45] and a memorandum of cooperation for specified skilled workers between Japan and the Philippines (Japan International Trainee and Skilled Worker Cooperation Organization 2019)—to ensure their migrants have worker protection.

[44] The Pacific Labour Scheme—built on the success of the Seasonal Worker Programme—gave more Australian employers access to a reliable seasonal workforce drawn from the Pacific and Timor-Leste.

[45] The Republic of Korea's Employment Permit System has memoranda of understanding with Bangladesh, Cambodia, Indonesia, the Kyrgyz Republic, Myanmar, Mongolia, Nepal, Pakistan, the PRC, the Philippines, Sri Lanka, Thailand, Timor-Leste, Uzbekistan, and Viet Nam.

In Southeast Asia, 31.3% (6.9 million) of migrants remained intra-subregional in 2019. This relatively large number of migrants within the subregion makes intraregional government support and cooperation essential for migrant protection and safety. For example, in 2017, the Association of Southeast Asian Nations (ASEAN) approved a Consensus on the Protection and Promotion of the Rights of Migrant Workers, a framework of cooperation on intraregional migrant workers.

A Call for Bolder Regional Cooperation

As with previous crises, the COVID-19 pandemic has led to many calls for greater regional cooperation.

Health systems and related infrastructure should be upgraded and strengthened to make mobility "pandemic-proof." Across the region, health systems need to better respond to future health emergencies—with improved medical facilities and more-skilled personnel. The pandemic has underscored the need for better, more accessible sanitation and water supply infrastructure.[46]

A regional migrant information infrastructure can leverage new technology to provide efficient information sharing. The exchange of timely, accurate, and reliable information is essential to manage crises. Establishing a shared regional migrant information infrastructure will allow the exchange of accurate, relevant, and timely migrant information and help apply migration best practices among countries (KNOMAD 2017). It can address data gaps on migration and remittances, and provide a monitoring system to spot any abrupt changes requiring policy intervention. The system could also facilitate coordination and cooperation during emergencies and help policy makers better assess migration issues.

Enhanced regional dialogue can explore new ways to legalize or regularize migration, promote labor standards, protect migrants, and ensure remittance inflows. Regional cooperation and integration initiatives can ease migrant deployment and remittance flows. There is a need to coordinate on issues such as formalizing unregistered migrants, the costs of migration, ethical recruitment, promoting international labor standards and social protection for migrant workers, and enhancing mutual recognition of skills.[47]

Better coordination on education and training can improve capabilities, sharpen competencies, and expand skills. Asian migrants provide vital skills that benefit both source and destination countries. The pandemic highlighted the key role migrant workers play in medicine and as medical front liners in many advanced countries. Source countries need to invest in quality education and relevant training to develop human capital.

Remittances

The COVID-19 pandemic disrupted the growth momentum of remittance inflows to Asia—which reached $315.3 billion in 2019.

In 2019, global remittance inflows reached $716.7 billion—$21.9 million more than in 2018 (Figure 5.8).[48] From 2010 to 2018, global remittance inflows grew by an average 4.9% annually. However, the growth of inflows

46 At the 36th ASEAN Summit in June 2020, leaders discussed regional comprehensive post-pandemic recovery plans. They established the ASEAN COVID-19 response fund, a reserve for medical supplies to meet urgent needs during the pandemic, and ASEAN standard procedures for epidemic response in case of health emergencies (ASEAN 2020).

47 For example, a multi-stakeholder policy dialogue held in February 2020 discussed implementation of the ASEAN Consensus on the Protection and Promotion of the Rights of Migrant Workers, emphasizing the need for more collaborative, multi-stakeholder approaches to the protection of migrant workers (Philippine News Agency 2020).

48 The World Bank defines personal remittances as the sum of personal transfers and compensation of employees. Personal transfers include all current transfers in cash or in kind between resident and nonresident individuals, independent of the source of income of the sender (and regardless of whether the sender receives income from labor, entrepreneurial or property income, social benefits, and any other types of transfers; or disposed assets) and the relationship between the households (regardless of whether they are related or unrelated individuals). Compensation of employees refers to the income of border, seasonal, and other short-term workers who are employed in an economy where they are not resident and of residents employed by nonresident entities.

Figure 5.8: Remittance Inflows to Asia and the World

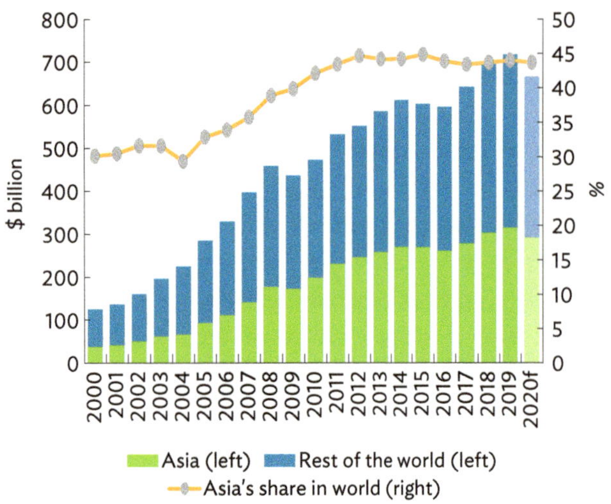

f = forecast.

Source: ADB calculations using data from Global Knowledge Partnership on Migration and Development (KNOMAD). http://www.knomad.org/data/remittances (accessed November 2020).

in 2019 moderated to 3.2% because of the economic slowdown in Europe, local currency depreciation against the US dollar in some major remittance-source countries such as the Russian Federation, and lower oil prices and production cuts in the Middle East.

In 2020, the World Bank estimated the impact of the pandemic-induced global economic slowdown, the uncertain job market for migrants, weak oil prices, and unfavorable exchange rates could result in a $50 billion drop in remittance inflows globally. Inflows to low- and middle-income countries are expected to fall by 7.2% with remittances to Asia dropping 7.4%—more than twice the drop in inflows during the 2008–2009 global financial crisis and the largest contraction since the Asian financial crisis. Other major remittance recipients in Europe and Africa can expect deep cuts in the growth of remittances in 2020.[49]

Remittances to Europe grew the slowest in 2019 due to the economic slowdown in major European outflow countries, the lower price of oil, and the depreciation of the euro against the US dollar. Estimates suggest that the region will suffer a $16.3 billion loss in remittance inflows in 2020 as the impact of the pandemic further weakens major economies (Table 5.3). Latin America and the Caribbean, the top recipient region of remittances from the US, is estimated to have 0.2% lower remittances in 2020, a sharp downturn compared with the 8.1% remittance growth it had in 2019, the year inflows hit $98.1 billion, its highest on record. Around 77% of these inflows came from the US, one of the worst-hit remittance source economies.

Table 5.3: Remittance Inflows by Recipient Region

Region	Share of Total, 2019	Remittance Inflows ($ billion)		Growth		Level Change ($ billion)	
		2019	2020e	2019	2020e	2019	2020e
Asia	44.0%	315.3	291.8	3.9%	-7.4%	12.0	-23.4
Europe	24.5%	175.8	159.5	0.20%	-9.3%	0.3	-16.3
Latin America and the Caribbean	13.7%	98.1	97.9	8.1%	-0.2%	7.4	-0.2
Middle East	4.2%	30.1	27.5	1.7%	-8.6%	0.5	-2.6
North America	1.1%	8.1	7.5	1.1%	-6.7%	0.1	-0.5
Africa	12.0%	85.9	78.4	1.8%	-8.7%	1.5	-7.5

e = estimate.

Source: ADB calculations using data from Global Knowledge Partnership on Migration and Development (KNOMAD). http://www.knomad.org/data/remittances (accessed November 2020).

49 Based on World Bank estimates released in October 2020, remittance inflow growth was expected to fall across all regions, most notably Europe and Central Asia (−16.1%), followed by East Asia and the Pacific (−10.5%), sub-Saharan Africa (−8.8%), the Middle East and North Africa (−8.5%), South Asia (−3.6%), and Latin America and the Caribbean (−0.2%). Based on weighted averages, remittance growth in Asia is forecast to contract by 8.4% in 2020 and 7.5% in 2021.

Remittance Inflows by Asian Subregion

Except for Oceania, subregional remittance inflows grew in 2019 (Table 5.4). South Asia accounted for 44% ($139.8 billion) of the Asian total—up 6.1% in 2019. Growth fell from the 12.3% growth in 2018, as lower oil prices slowed economic activity in the Middle East (the source for 59.1% of South Asian remittances). Inward-looking labor policies in the Middle East have started to affect migrant flows.[50] Growth in inflows to other Asian regions were relatively subdued in 2019. Remittances to Southeast Asia rose by 2.8%—yet inflows to major recipients Indonesia, the Philippines, and Viet Nam grew by 4% or more.

Lower inflows are expected across all subregions in 2020. Remittances to Central Asia, which depends on the Russian Federation for at least 75% of its inflows, are estimated to drop by 17.4%. Inflows to Southeast Asia will likely drop by 8.4%, down $6.5 billion as large numbers of workers were repatriated and remittances slowed from the Middle East, North America, and the Russian Federation. Inflows to South Asia are expected to contract by similar amounts.

A gradual and prolonged decline in remittance inflows will hurt the region's top remittance recipients (Figure 5.9). India, the PRC, and the Philippines accounted for 59.3% ($186.9 billion) of remittances to Asia and 26.1% of remittances globally ($716.7 billion). Inflows to these economies will collectively drop by $18.1 billion in 2020, equivalent to 77.4% of the projected decline in Asia.

Figure 5.9: Top 10 Remittance Recipients in Asia, 2019
($ billion)

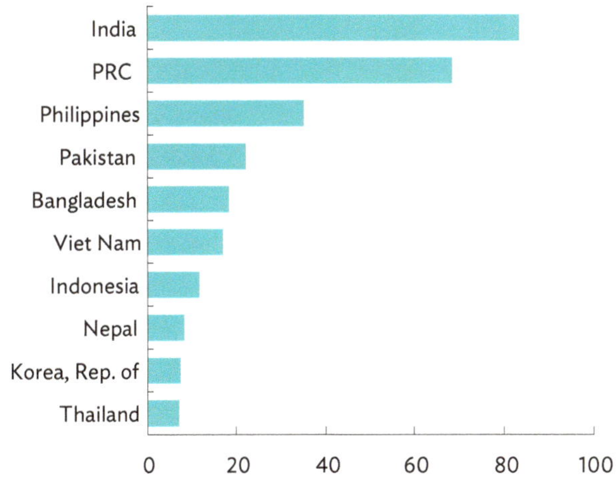

PRC = People's Republic of China.

Source: ADB calculations using data from Global Knowledge Partnership on Migration and Development (KNOMAD). http://www.knomad.org/data/remittances (accessed November 2020).

Table 5.4: Remittance Inflows to Asian Subregions and Growth

Subregion	Amount in $ billion (share of total)		Growth	
	2019	2020e	2019	2020e
Central Asia	14.5 (4.6%)	11.9 (4.1%)	3.70%	-17.4%
East Asia	81.2 (25.7%)	72.1 (24.7%)	1.7%	-11.2%
South Asia	139.8 (44.4%)	134.7 (46.2%)	6.1%	-3.6%
Southeast Asia	76.9 (24.4%)	70.4 (24.1%)	2.8%	-8.4%
Oceania	2.2 (0.7%)	2.0 (0.7%)	-5.5%	-9.2%
Pacific	0.8 (0.2%)	0.7 (0.2%)	0.7%	-4.3%

e = estimate.

Source: ADB calculations using data from Global Knowledge Partnership on Migration and Development (KNOMAD). http://www.knomad.org/data/remittances (accessed November 2020).

50 Data on overseas employment by destination from the Government of Pakistan, Bureau of Emigration and Overseas Employment (https://beoe.gov.pk/reports-and-statistics) show that in 2018, the number of Pakistani overseas workers deployed in Oman declined by 35.8%, in Saudi Arabia by 29.6%, and in the United Arab Emirates by 24.3%. The Government of Bangladesh, Bureau of Manpower Employment and Training (http://www.old.bmet.gov.bd/BMET/viewStatReport.action?reportnumber=16) indicated that in 2019, the number of workers deployed had dropped by 55.5% in Kuwait (to 12,299) and 34.3% in Qatar (to 50,292).

The drop in remittances in 2020 will also affect economies with lower absolute amounts but with higher impact on gross domestic product (GDP). In Nepal, the fourth largest remittance recipient by share of GDP (Figure 5.10a), remittance inflows are 10 times larger than official aid, 9 times more than exports, and 67 times FDI (Pandey 2020). Its remittances derive mostly from the Middle East (44.6%) and Asia (43.8%), particularly India and Malaysia where 50% of Nepali emigrant population reside. A significant drop in remittance inflows could hurt Nepal's external balance and foreign exchange liquidity in its economy. Remittance inflows are also essential to several Pacific countries with GDP shares ranging from 10% to as high as 36% (Figure 5.10b). Per capita remittances are high in Tonga, Samoa, the Marshall Islands, and Fiji—and a prime source of foreign exchange. These economies are also largely dependent on tourism, devastated by global travel restrictions. Hurricane Harold also damaged Fiji, Solomon Islands, Tonga, and Vanuatu in April 2020 (IMF 2020a).

Quarantine measures to contain the spread of COVID-19 hampered migrants' ability to send money home to their families.

As the number of confirmed COVID-19 cases began increasing, governments began imposing a variety of mobility restrictions to contain the spread of the virus. In January and February, when restrictions were just starting, migrants were still able to send money home without discernible difficulty. Remittance inflows to 11 selected Asian economies even grew by 6.2% in January and 7.0% in February (Figure 5.11). However, stringency measures jumped sharply in March 2020 and peaked in April when almost all economies imposed border and travel restrictions in one form or another. In many remittance-sending countries, remittance service providers were not considered essential businesses and were closed during these months. On average, remittance inflows to Asia fell by 5% in March. A sharp downturn in inflows occurred in April (–17.5%) and May (–18.3%) before recovering by 24.3% in June and 26.7% in July, as the restrictions on movement gradually eased.

Figure 5.10: Top 10 Remittance Recipients in Asia, 2019

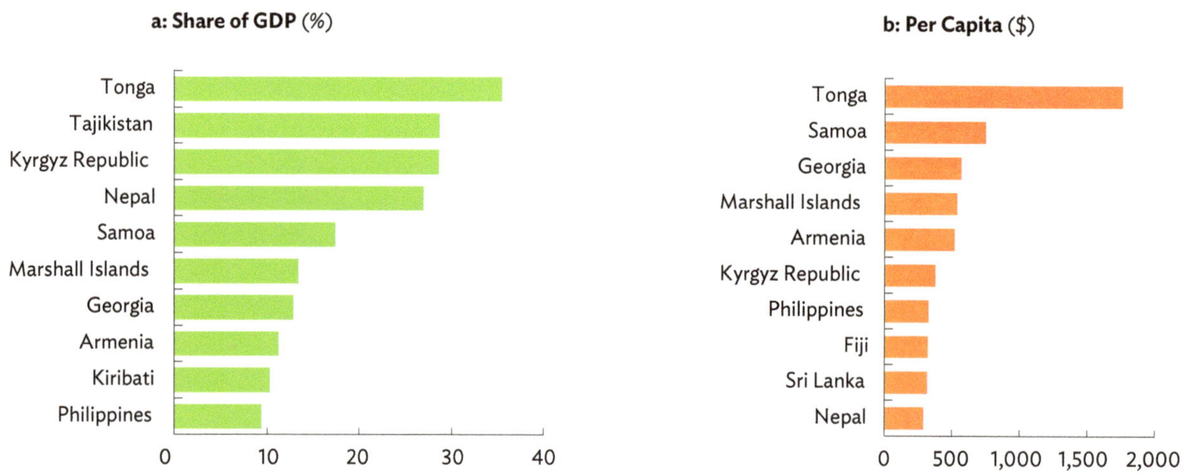

GDP = gross domestic product.

Note: 2019 figures are not available for some countries.

Sources: ADB calculations using data from Global Knowledge Partnership on Migration and Development (KNOMAD). http://www.knomad.org/data/remittances (accessed November 2020); International Monetary Fund. World Economic Outlook Database. https://www.imf.org/en/Publications/WEO/weo-database/2020/October (accessed November 2020); and United Nations. Department of Economic and Social Affairs, Population Division. World Population Prospects 2019. https://population.un.org/wpp/Download/Standard/Population/ (accessed April 2020).

Figure 5.11: Stringency Measures and Remittance Growth, 2020

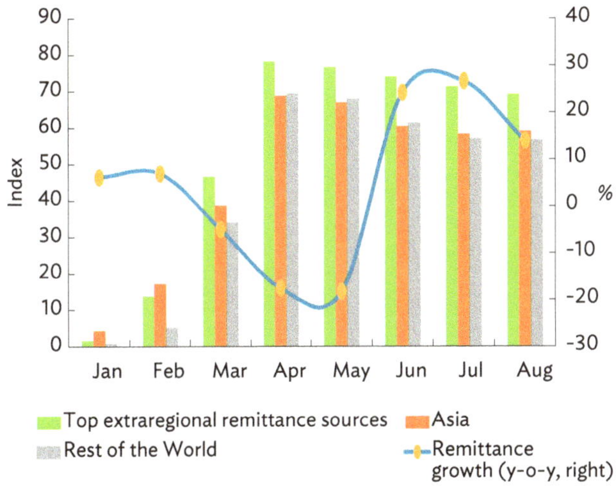

Notes: Data refer to the average of sample countries. Stringency measures refer to the Oxford COVID-19 Government Response Stringency Index that ranges from 0 (no restriction) to 100 (most restrictive). The top extraregional remittance senders to Asia include the United States, Saudi Arabia, the United Arab Emirates, the Russian Federation, the United Kingdom, Qatar, Canada, Oman, and Italy. Remittance growth is based on the year-on-year growth of aggregate remittance inflows to Armenia, Bangladesh, Bhutan, Fiji, Georgia, Kazakhstan, the Kyrgyz Republic, Pakistan, the Philippines, Samoa, and Sri Lanka.

Sources: ADB calculations using data from Hale et. al (2020a); and the central banks of Armenia, Bangladesh, Bhutan, Fiji, Georgia, Kazakhstan, the Kyrgyz Republic, Pakistan, the Philippines, Samoa, and Sri Lanka (all accessed in December 2020).

Despite the large drop, remittances to Asia will likely remain a relatively stable source of external financing compared with other types of financial flows.

In past crises, remittance flows showed signs of resilience to shocks relative to other financial flows. However, this pandemic is different as economies in both source and recipient countries suffered from a sudden, sharp slowdown. The road to recovery is expected to be long and slow. The pandemic is a harder test of the countercyclical character of remittances despite that inflows to some developing Asian countries have started to bounce back (Box 5.1). This could have implications on the growing role remittances play, particularly compared with other inflows such as foreign direct investment (FDI) and tourism. Remittances accounted for 20.5% of financial flows, behind FDI (47.8%, $646 billion) and tourism (26.6%, $359 billion) during 2014–2018 (Figure 5.12a). Asia's remittance share relative to other financial flows has also been rising over the past decade (Figure 5.12b). By subregion, South Asia and Central Asia have seen rapid increases in the relative

Figure 5.12: Financial Flows to Asia (% of total financial flows)

a: By Type and Subregion, 2018

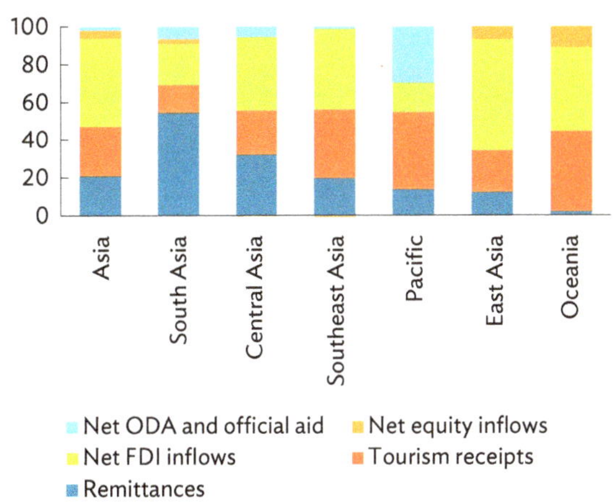

b: Remittance Shares by Subregion
(5-year moving average)

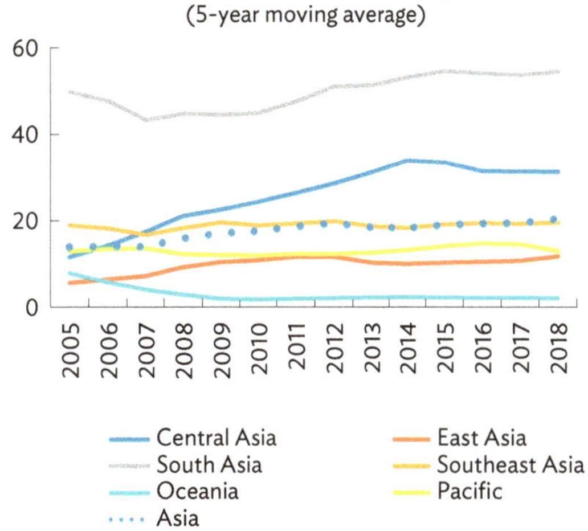

FDI = foreign direct investment, ODA = official development assistance.

Sources: ADB calculations using data from Global Knowledge Partnership on Migration and Development (KNOMAD). http://www.knomad.org/data/remittances (accessed November 2020); World Bank. World Development Indicators Database. https://databank.worldbank.org/source/world-development-indicators (accessed October 2020); UNWTO (2020); and International Monetary Fund (2019).

economic contribution of remittances. South Asia is heavily reliant on remittances for external financing, accounting for more than 50% of total financial flows, followed by Central Asia, where remittance inflows account for one-third of financial flows.

Box 5.1: Remittances and COVID-19—A Test of Resilience

Since 2000, remittance inflows to the region have declined twice—in 2009 during the global financial crisis and in 2016 due to weak economic growth in the Russian Federation and the Middle East (box figure). Remittance inflows fell 2.7% in 2009 (foreign direct investment [FDI] fell 20%) with Central Asia, East Asia, and Oceania hit hard. In 2016, remittance inflows to the region fell by 3.1% (FDI fell 10%) as the oil price collapse weakened economic growth in the Middle East and the Russian Federation.[a] The impact on remittance inflows was more severe in South Asia and Central Asia in 2016 than other subregions, as the two subregions rely on the oil-producing regions as their principal source of inflows.

Remittance inflows during past crises, however, recovered rapidly, surpassing precrisis levels the following year. Resilient and stable inflows relative to other financial flows (like FDI) highlight the key role remittances play in reducing volatility in output, consumption, and investment. Even in extreme cases, remittances reduce the probability of financial crises (IMF 2005; Singer 2008; Ratha and Sirkeci 2010; Rajan and Narayana 2012; Sirkeci, Ratha, and Cohen 2012):

- Remittance inflows to countries in South Asia and Southeast Asia continued to grow as the subregions diversified migrant destinations.
- Remittances are countercyclical—migrants tend to send more money, responding to the needs of their families during crises or natural disasters.
- Existing migrants adjust to the income shock by reducing their own consumption (to continue sending money home).
- Foreign exchange rate movements cause a surge in investment-oriented remittances as local currencies of recipient countries depreciate sharply.

While the two past health crises—the severe acute respiratory syndrome in 2002–2004 and the Middle East respiratory syndrome in 2012—had limited impact on remittances, the COVID-19 pandemic is fundamentally different. Its economic impact is so wide and deep across all source and destination countries, resulting in job and income losses for existing and new migrants, and the mass repatriation of migrants. Thus, remittances as an economic hedge against shocks will likely have limited effect during the pandemic.

Trend in Remittance Inflows

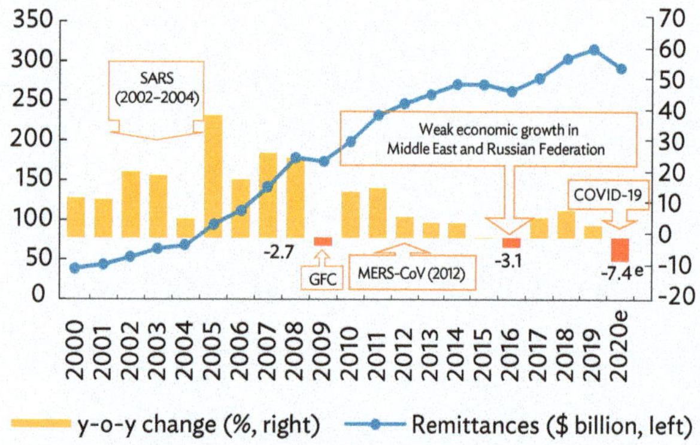

Remittance Inflows Growth (%)

	2009	2016	2020e
Asia	**-2.7**	**-3.1**	**-7.4**
Central Asia	-22.5	-11.1	-17.4
East Asia	-12.8	-3.2	-11.2
South Asia	4.5	-5.9	-3.6
Southeast Asia	5.9	3.6	-8.4
Pacific	7.7	-0.8	-4.3
Oceania	-14.5	-5.4	-9.2

COVID-19 = coronavirus disease, e = estimate, GFC = global financial crisis, MERS-CoV = Middle East respiratory syndrome coronavirus, SARS = severe acute respiratory syndrome, y-o-y = year-on-year.

Source: ADB calculations using data from Global Knowledge Partnership on Migration and Development (KNOMAD). http://www.knomad.org/data/remittances (accessed November 2020).

[a] The Russian Federation in 2016 also suffered a sharp fall in its exchange rate, a balance of payment crisis, and economic sanctions by the United States and the European Union.

Source: Asian Development Bank.

Intraregional and Extraregional Remittance Flows

As major source countries face a significant economic downturn, recipient subregions in Asia brace for the consequences of lower remittances in 2020.

Asia's largest source of remittances remains the Middle East—the inflows of $100.4 billion in 2019, 5.3% ($5.0 billion) more than in 2018 (Figure 5.13). Almost all outflows went to two Asian subregions, South Asia (82.3%) and Southeast Asia (17.4%)—around 50% (about 21 million) of migrants from South Asia and 20% (about 4 million) from Southeast Asia reside in the Middle East. India, Pakistan, and the Philippines received a total of $76.6 billion, equivalent to 76.3% of Middle East outflows to Asia and 53.1% of its outflows worldwide. Year-to-date remittances in the second quarter (Q2) of 2020 grew in India (3.5% y-o-y) and Pakistan (8.8%), suggesting the pandemic had not affected remittance-sending behavior.

In 2019, there were $6.2 billion more inflows from North America and $3.0 billion more from Europe. Those from North America ($78.0 billion) accounted for 24.7% of total inflows to Asia—to Southeast Asia (33.8%), East Asia (37.3%), and South Asia (27.5%). The PRC, India, the Philippines, Viet Nam, and the Republic of Korea received a combined $67.6 billion, equivalent to 86.6% of North America's total remittances to Asia. Remittance inflows from North America to these economies are expected to slow due to widespread infections in the US, business closures, and the resulting drop in economic activity. Inflows from Europe grew to $45.6 billion in 2019, up by 7.2% from 2018. Led by outflows from the UK and the Russian Federation, the top subregion recipients were South Asia (India and Pakistan) and Central Asia (Uzbekistan, the Kyrgyz Republic, and Tajikistan). Countries within Asia also contributed to remittance inflows—though $1.4 billion less than in 2018—as Asia's intraregional remittance share declined marginally to 26.9% in 2019 from 28.6% in 2018. By economy, the US, Saudi Arabia, the United Arab Emirates, and the Russian Federation were among the top sources of remittance inflows to the region. Together these economies sent $146.9 billion to the region, the equivalent of 46.5% of global remittances to Asia. Top intraregional remitters include Hong Kong, China; Australia; and Japan, which together sent $41.2 billion, or 48.4% of intraregional remittances received.

Figure 5.13: Intraregional and Extraregional Remittance Flows to Asia ($ million)

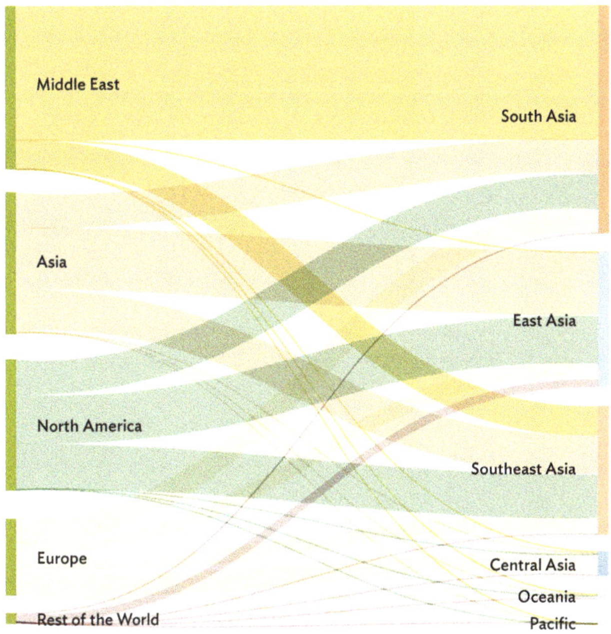

Source: ADB calculations using data from Global Knowledge Partnership on Migration and Development (KNOMAD) staff estimates. Bilateral Remittance Matrix 2020 (May).

Declining remittance inflows also threaten economies dependent on remittances.

In 2019, around 26.9% ($85.0 billion) of inflows to Asia came from migrant host countries within the region—around 64.5% were from East Asia and Southeast Asia; another 34% from Oceania and South Asia (Figure 5.14). Malaysia, India, Singapore, and Thailand figure prominently among the major intraregional remittance sources. Thus, the pandemic will have varying impact on the livelihood and incomes of the Asian migrant workers they host.

Among subregions, the Pacific stands out by its dependence on Asia for at least 55% of remittances. Oceania is the source for at least 50% of global remittances to Fiji, Kiribati, Samoa, Solomon Islands, and Tonga. Economic recovery in Australia and New Zealand will benefit countries in the Pacific, which rely on Oceania for employment and remittance inflows. However, the deep cut in tourism across the Pacific suggests that recovery will depend on the resumption of global travel and tourism alongside a rebound in remittances.

In 2019, Central Asia (93.5%), South Asia (84.9%), and Oceania (61.0%) received higher proportions of remittances from outside Asia, as the bulk of their migrant workers work in the Russian Federation, the United Arab Emirates, Saudi Arabia, the US, and the UK. East Asia's remittance profile showed a slight increase (to 52.8% from 49.1% in 2015) in remittance receipts from non-Asian sources. Over the same period, Southeast Asia showed an increase over other Asian subregions.

Figure 5.14: Subregional Remittance Sources in Asia (%)

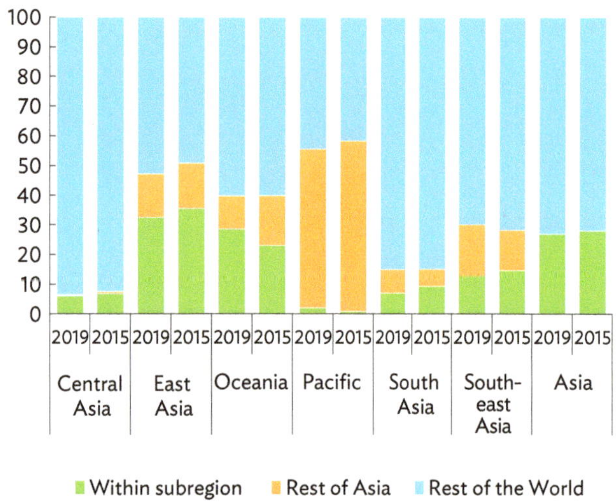

Notes:

(i) Within subregion refers to remittances within subregion *i* as a percentage of remittances from the world to subregion *i*.

(ii) Rest of Asia refers to the remittances from other Asian subregions to subregion *i* as a percentage of remittances from the world to subregion *i*.

(iii) Rest of the World refers to remittances from non-Asian economies to subregion *i* as a percentage of remittances from the world to subregion *i*.

Sources: ADB calculations using data from Global Knowledge Partnership on Migration and Development (KNOMAD). http://www.knomad.org/data/remittances (accessed December 2019); and KNOMAD staff estimates. Bilateral Remittance Matrix 2020 (May).

Technology, Digitalization, and Remittance Costs

Digital technology will likely play a more important role as traditional remittance channels are constrained by limited mobility.

Many conventional money transfer businesses closed during the height of government-mandated border and mobility restrictions, particularly in April and May 2020. This opened many opportunities for technology-driven money transfer companies. As people resorted to cashless payment systems, the use of digital remittances grew at an unprecedented rate. People began accessing alternative means of sending remittances—such as mobile money, internet banking, and other non-cash digital and electronic channels. The US payment service company, PayPal, gained 21.3 million new customers in Q2 2020, increasing nearly 140% y-o-y (Manila Standard 2020).

The lockdowns showcased the role digital channels will play in future remittances. They influenced migrant behavior in their choice of remittance channel. But many core problems with accelerating digitalization of remittances continue. By Q3 2020, the average cost of remitting to Asia remains far higher than the Sustainable Development Goal target of 3%—it costs 6.1% from anywhere in the world and 4.6% from any of the top remittance-sending countries to Asia.[51] There are significant variations in remittance costs across Asian subregions—a $200 cash remittance is cheaper to send to Central Asia (1.0% to Azerbaijan) and South Asia (4.1% to Bangladesh), while remitting to the Pacific remains the costliest, ranging from 8.1% (Fiji) to 10.8% (Tonga).

Several nations and organizations issued a call to action in May 2020 calling on policy makers to declare remittance services as essential and facilitate the scaling up of digital remittance channels.[52] The biggest policy reinforcements should focus on three areas: (i) providing digital infrastructure, internet connectivity, and technological innovations to extend

[51] World Bank. Remittance Prices Worldwide. https://remittanceprices.worldbank.org/en (accessed November 2020).

[52] Led by the UK and Swiss authorities, a call to action is a plea for countries across the globe to ease access to international money transfers and support the scaling of digital channels to ensure funds keep flowing to developing markets during the pandemic.

the coverage of money transfer services across national and currency borders, while simultaneously lowering costs; (ii) executing the necessary legal, regulatory, and oversight reforms to allow more nonbank remittance service providers (especially in rural areas), including consumer and investor protection, know-your-customer and anti-money laundering compliance costs; and (iii) supporting government-led knowledge-sharing campaigns to improve financial literacy among migrants and their beneficiaries—to further inclusion in the formal financial system.

Way Forward through Regional Cooperation

As economies recover, the region could benefit from policies and regional cooperation mechanisms that ensure the flow and growth of remittances in a post-pandemic environment.

There are several ways regional cooperation could benefit remittance flows. First, there needs to be stronger government commitment to develop remittance infrastructure, including expanding internet access to rural and remote areas to increase remittances channeled formally and help bring down costs. By expanding rural access to digital technology, remittances could support rural development and create new jobs and opportunities. Ensuring interoperability between mobile financial services will also improve remittance inflows through mobile accounts.

Second, governments and development partners can expand financial and digital literacy campaigns to improve the use of modern remittance channels. This will help migrants with limited experience in accessing formal financial services and those used to sending remittances through informal channels.

Third, public institutions and remittance service providers could collaborate on helping transition migrants and their families to open bank accounts, enhance saving habits, and help build household financial resilience. This will also improve family access to savings, credit, and insurance products, and provide digital solutions via mobile phone apps.

Fourth, harmonizing regulations will help unlock access to digital remittance channels. Reducing the application time for companies to obtain licenses from central banks, having clearer regulations on cross-border partnerships of financial service providers, and promoting innovative know-your-customer solutions to include migrants and their families will encourage digital service providers to open and partner with existing remittance service providers to expand markets.

And fifth, a broader international remittance agenda for the long term must include innovation in the global remittances market and leveraging remittances for consumer and business lending, micro-saving and micro-insurance, improving country risk ratings, and accessing international capital markets through securitization and the issuance of diaspora bonds (Mohieldin and Ratha 2020).

Tourism

The COVID-19 pandemic hit tourism in Asia abruptly and deeply. A recovery to precrisis levels will likely take years, endangering the survival of large parts of the sector.

Impact of COVID-19 on International Visitor Arrivals

The imposition of travel restrictions and fear of infection during travel caused a steep fall in international arrivals.

Asia had become a major destination for international tourism over the past 2 decades.[53] The COVID-19 pandemic brought this trend to an abrupt halt. Many

[53] According to the 2008 International Recommendations for Tourism Statistics (United Nations Statistical Commission 2007) that the UNWTO adopts when compiling tourism statistics, *tourism* refers to the activity of *visitors*. A *visitor* is a traveler taking a trip to a main destination outside his/her usual environment, for less than a year, for any purpose (business, leisure, or other personal purpose) other than to be employed by a resident entity in the country or place visited. A *visitor* is classified as a *tourist* (or overnight visitor), if his/her trip includes an overnight stay, or as a *same-day visitor* (or excursionist) otherwise. There are no significant differences between the number of visitors and tourists in many countries except for the PRC where some 60% of visitors are same-day visitors arriving from Hong Kong, China; and Macau, China.

governments in the region introduced enhanced travel controls in February 2020 and extended them to full travel bans within 2 months (Figure 5.15). As of October 2020, most bans were still in place, with only a few governments deciding to slowly ease travel restrictions.

The extensive travel restrictions led to the grounding of airline fleets worldwide. Apart from a sudden slump in the supply of transportation, demand for tourism quickly contracted as many people became afraid to travel. An International Air Transport Association (IATA) survey on consumer travel confidence in April 2020 indicated that 40% of respondents would wait 6 months or more before traveling again—this rose to 55% in the June edition of the survey (IATA 2020a). Consumer travel confidence remained unfavorable in the most recent version of the survey in September, with more than half of respondents planning to travel no sooner than in 6 months (IATA 2020b).

Monthly international tourist arrivals fell dramatically for selected economies in four subregions from January 2019 to September 2020 (Figure 5.16). The drop first occurred in East Asia, where the pandemic originated and where travel restrictions were first imposed. Southeast Asia followed, then South Asia and the Pacific, as the pandemic spread to those subregions.

Figure 5.15: International Travel Restrictions, 2020

Lao PDR = Lao People's Democratic Republic.

Notes: Data refer to policy applied to foreign travelers, not citizens. No data were available for the following: Armenia, the Cook Islands, the Federated States of Micronesia, Kiribati, Maldives, the Marshall Islands, Nauru, Niue, Palau, Samoa, Tonga, and Tuvalu.

Source: ADB calculations using data from Hale et al. (2020b).

Figure 5.16: Monthly International Tourist Arrivals by Subregion (January 2019 = 100)

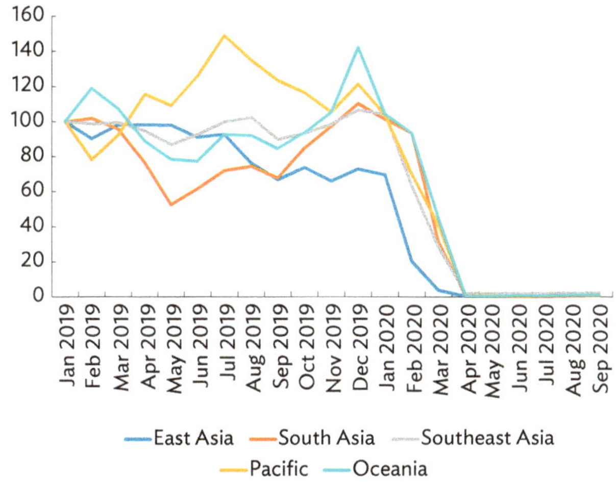

Notes: Only economies with complete data from January 2019 to June 2020 were included in estimating the value for each subregion. For some economies with missing data between July and September 2020, international tourist arrivals were obtained from the previous 3-month average. East Asia includes Hong Kong, China; Japan; the Republic of Korea; and Taipei,China. South Asia includes India, Maldives, Nepal, and Sri Lanka. Southeast Asia includes Cambodia, Indonesia, the Lao People's Democratic Republic, Malaysia, Myanmar, the Philippines, Singapore, Thailand, and Viet Nam. The Pacific includes Fiji, Palau, Samoa, Solomon Islands, and Vanuatu. Oceania includes Australia and New Zealand.

Sources: ADB calculations using data from CEIC; Government of Fiji, Bureau of Statistics. htttps://www.statsfiji.gov.fj (accessed October 2020); Government of the Lao PDR People's Democratic Republic, Ministry of Information, Culture, and Tourism. International Tourist Arrivals January–March 2020. Unpublished; Government of Malaysia, Ministry of Tourism and Culture. Tourist Arrivals Data. http://mytourismdata.tourism.gov.my; Government of Palau. Visitor Arrivals. https://www.palaugov.pw/visitor-arrivals/; Government of the Republic of Korea, Tourism Organization. https://kto.visitkorea.or.kr; Government of Samoa, Samoa Tourism Board. http://www.samoatourism.org; Government of Singapore, Department of Statistics. https://www.tablebuilder.singstat.gov.sg (all accessed October 2020); Government of Solomon Islands, Ministry of Finance and Treasury. Government (2020); Government of Vanuatu, Ministry of Finance and Economic Management, National Statistics Office (2019); Haver Analytics; and International Monetary Fund (2020b, 2020c, 2020d).

As international arrivals fell to historic lows, economies heavily dependent on tourism were particularly hard hit. For example, arrivals to Thailand (which reported the first COVID-19 case outside the PRC in January 2020) subsequently fell from 10.8 million in the first quarter (Q1) of 2019 to 6.7 million in Q1 2020. After the government introduced a strict travel ban by the end of March, Thailand recorded zero tourist arrivals throughout Q2 2020 and Q3 2020. Following the same pattern, other Southeast Asian countries, such as Cambodia (-98.1%), Myanmar (-97.5%), the Philippines (-97.8%), Singapore (-99.3%), and Viet Nam (-99.0%) saw near shutdowns for Q2 2020. Similar trends continued in Q3 2020. According to IMF (2020d), arrivals to the Pacific island countries contracted 22.7% in Q1 2020, further slumping by 99.5% in Q2 2020 and 99.4% in Q3 2020. For example, between April and September, Samoa, Tonga, and Vanuatu had no international arrivals. Noting that these countries are among the top 10 recipients of tourism receipts as a percent of GDP in the Asia and Pacific region, numerous people lost their jobs and domestic economies suffered significant losses.

A quick recovery in tourism seems unlikely as an end to the pandemic is not yet in sight. The prolonged gloomy prospects for tourism could become a drag on the economic recovery, especially in highly tourism dependent economies.

With a slump in international arrivals, many economies expect a substantial decrease in tourism receipts. If Q4 2020 will see similarly low levels of international tourist arrivals, tourism receipts are expected to decline by 83.2% in Thailand ($11.9 billion from $70.5 billion, year-on-year [y-o-y]) and 79.6% in Cambodia ($1.1 billion from $5.2 billion, y-o-y) (Figure 5.17). In 21 selected Asian economies, the contributions of international tourism receipts to GDP are forecast to plunge by an average of 80.8% in 2020 y-o-y. In terms of absolute change, it will be most severe for Maldives, where tourism is one of the main pillars of the economy. From an estimated 61.2% contribution to GDP in 2019, it is expected to fall to 19.1% in 2020. A similar drop is forecast for Vanuatu (9.2% from 45.4%, y-o-y), Palau (9.7% from 45.6%, y-o-y), Samoa (3.2% from 25.6%), and Fiji (5.7% from 28.1%, y-o-y).

Pre-COVID-19 Performance of International Tourism

Prior to the COVID-19 outbreak, tourism had been one of the world's most vibrant and promising economic sectors. In many economies in Asia, tourism was an important pillar of growth and a reliable source of development.

Global tourism showed phenomenal growth over the past 10 years. In 2019, the number of international arrivals had risen to 1.5 billion, up from 949.6 million a decade earlier (United Nations World Tourism Organization 2020e).

Figure 5.17: Outlook for Tourism Receipts in Selected Asian Economies (% of GDP)

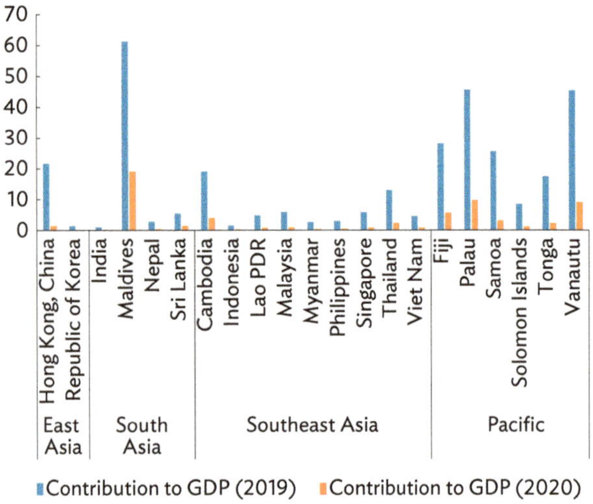

GDP = gross domestic product, Lao PDR = Lao People's Democratic Republic.

Notes: Only economies with available data on tourism arrivals up to September 2020 were included in estimating contributions of international tourism receipts to GDP. Estimates for receipts (2019 and 2020) were produced under the assumption that international tourism receipts per capita remain at 2018 levels. Estimates for international arrivals (October to December 2020) were produced under assumptions that Q4 2020 arrivals follow Q3 2020 trends, and international movements in the remaining months of the year remain restrictive. Estimates for GDP (2020) were according to the projections of the Asian Development Outlook Update.

Sources: Asian Development Bank calculations using data from Asian Development Bank (2020); CEIC; Haver Analytics; International Monetary Fund (2020b, 2020c); United Nations World Tourism Organization. Tourism Satellite Accounts. http://statistics.unwto.org/ (accessed October 2020); and World Bank. World Development Indicators. https://databank.worldbank.org/source/world-development-indicators (accessed September 2020).

Figure 5.18: Global Visitor Arrivals by Region of Destination

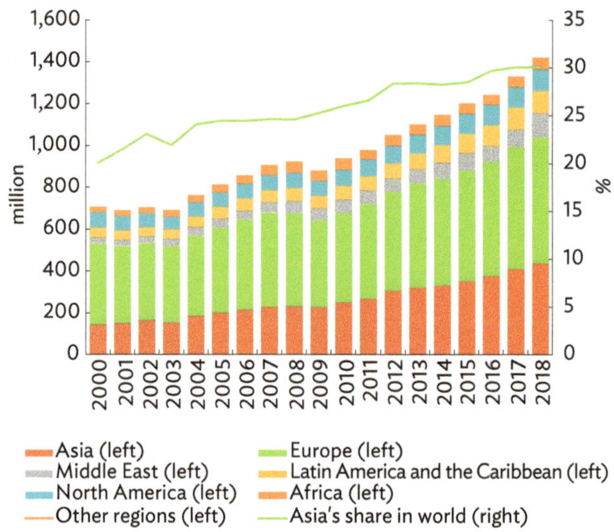

Source: ADB calculations using data from United Nations World Tourism Organization. Tourism Satellite Accounts. http://statistics.unwto.org/ (accessed October 2020).

International visitor arrivals grew by 3.8% in 2019 and marked the tourism sector's 10th consecutive year of growth.[54] Asia has outperformed other regions with its share of global arrivals rising from around 20% in the early 2000s to 30.1% in 2018 (Figure 5.18).

The number of international travelers to Asia increased by 6.9% in 2018 to reach 439.5 million. Growth in the number of travelers to Europe was 3.2% in 2018, though it continued to attract the largest number of arrivals (603.9 million visitors) and had the largest share of the global total (43.3% on average since 2010). The number of arrivals to North America rose by 2.9% to 100.9 million visitors, the highest growth since 2016. The rapid increase in number of travelers to Asia in 2018 continued an ongoing trend. While global arrivals increased at an average annual rate of 5.3% from 2010 to 2018, arrivals to Asia grew an average 7.2%, faster than North America (3.6%), Europe (4.4%), and Latin America and the Caribbean (6.2%).

Various factors were behind the strong growth of tourism in Asia. A long period of broad-based economic growth gave an increasing part of the population the financial means to travel domestically and internationally. In addition, an increasingly liberalized air transport market led to many low-cost carriers offering inexpensive flights. For example, ASEAN established the Multilateral Agreement on Air Services in 2008 and the Multilateral Agreement for the Full Liberalization of Passengers Air Services in 2010, which led to an increase in open routes between different cities in the region and allowed greater market penetration for low-cost carriers (Leonir and Laplace 2016). In addition, visa requirements were reduced, especially within the region, easing travel still further.

[54] Based on data from United Nations World Tourism Organization. https://www.unwto.org/global-and-regional-tourism-performance (accessed September 2020).

Intraregional tourism has been an increasingly important component of Asia's tourism sector.

As regional integration increased, tourism in Asia has developed a strong intraregional component. Of 439.5 million total arrivals in 2018, the number of intraregional arrivals (the number of Asian visitors traveling to Asian destinations) topped 347.7 million (Figure 5.19). The intraregional arrival share rose from 74.0 % in 2010 to 79.1 % in 2018. There were 9.8 million more arrivals in East Asia and 7.7 million more in Southeast Asia. The sharpest relative increase was in Central Asia, where intraregional tourism increased by 42.6%, to 22.2 million in 2018. This strong growth underscores opportunities to help operationalize the Central Asia Regional Economic Cooperation (CAREC) Tourism Strategy 2030.

Extraregional visitors to Asia had also been growing since 2010, reaching 91.8 million in 2018, up from 88.6 million in 2017. Some 40% came from Europe, around 20% from North America, with one-third from other regions. Visitors from Europe and North America—led by Canada, Germany, France, the Russian Federation, the UK and the US—preferred East Asian and Southeast Asian destinations, notably Japan, the PRC and Thailand.[55]

Figure 5.19: Visitors to Asia (million)

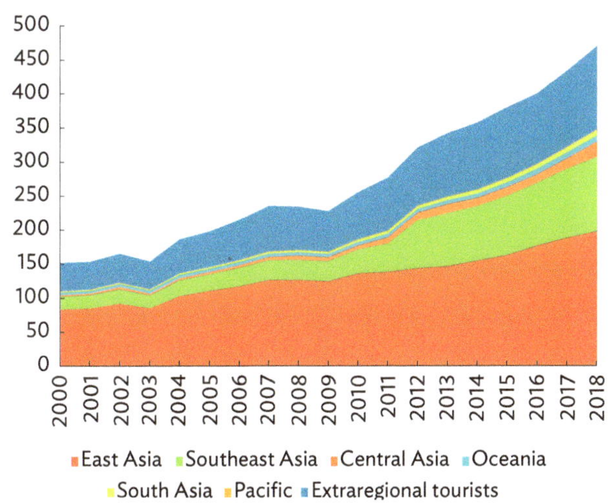

Source: ADB calculations using data from United Nations World Tourism Organization. Tourism Satellite Accounts. http://statistics.unwto.org/ (accessed October 2020).

Outbound tourist expenditures from Asia nearly doubled between 2010 and 2018, with the PRC taking the lead.

Asian tourist expenditures continuously grew in nominal terms by an average annual growth rate of 11.2% between 2010 and 2018, reaching $546.1 billion in 2018 (Figure 5.20). Throughout the period, spending by East Asian travelers accounted for 63.6% on average. The PRC remained the top spender at $227.3 billion, equivalent to at least half of tourism expenditures in the region.

Figure 5.20: Tourism Expenditure by Asian Economies

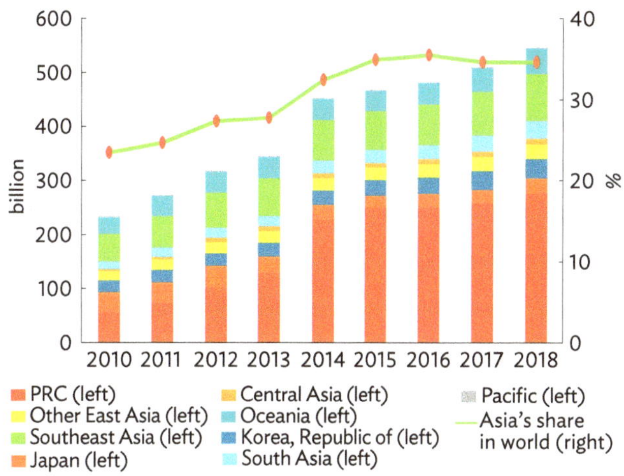

PRC = People's Republic of China.

Sources: ADB calculations using data from World Bank. World Development Indicators Database. https://databank.worldbank.org/source/world-development-indicators (accessed October 2020); and United Nations World Tourism Organization (2020f).

Although outbound tourism expenditures for the region has been on an upward trend since 2010, spending per capita has been declining, from $1,306.9 in 2015 to $1,212.2 in 2018 (Figure 5.21a). Compared with 2015, average per capita tourist spending in 2018 declined in many economies and in all subregions except Oceania. These downward trends may be attributable to the rising popularity of budget travel and the increasing availability of low-cost flights. For instance, outbound tourists from Southeast Asia almost tripled between 2010 and 2018, reaching 97.6 million in 2018, but per capita spending fell by 42.9% to an average of $879.9.

55 Around 96% of extraregional visitors from other regions were visitors from Macau, China to the PRC.

Figure 5.21: Tourism Expenditure per Outbound Tourist ($'000)

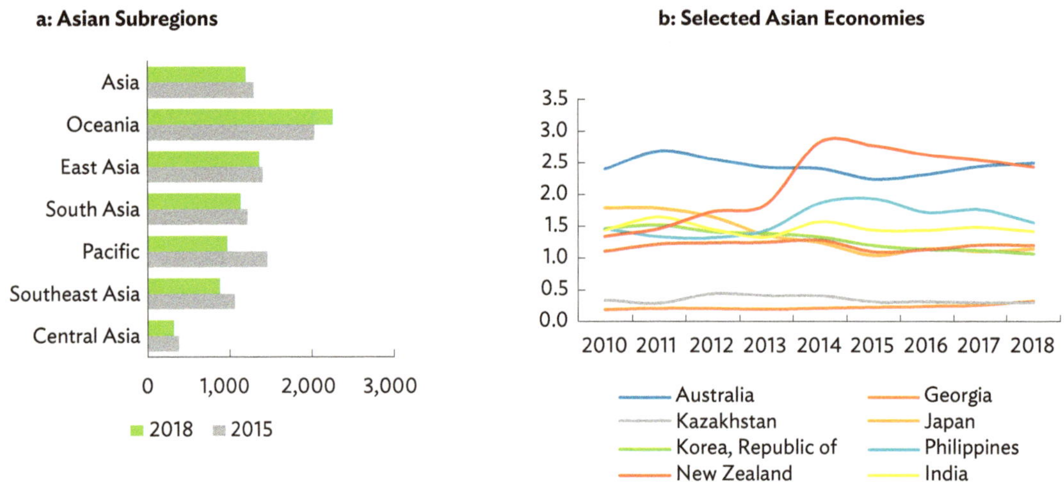

Note: 2018 data were not available for some economies with substantial tourism expenditures.

Sources: ADB calculations using data from United Nations World Tourism Organization. Tourism Satellite Accounts. http://statistics.untwo.org/ (accessed October 2020); United Nations World Tourism Organization (2020f); and World Bank. World Development Indicators. https://databank.worldbank.org/source/world-development-indicators (accessed October 2020).

Figure 5.22: International Tourism Receipts by Major Geographic Region, 2018

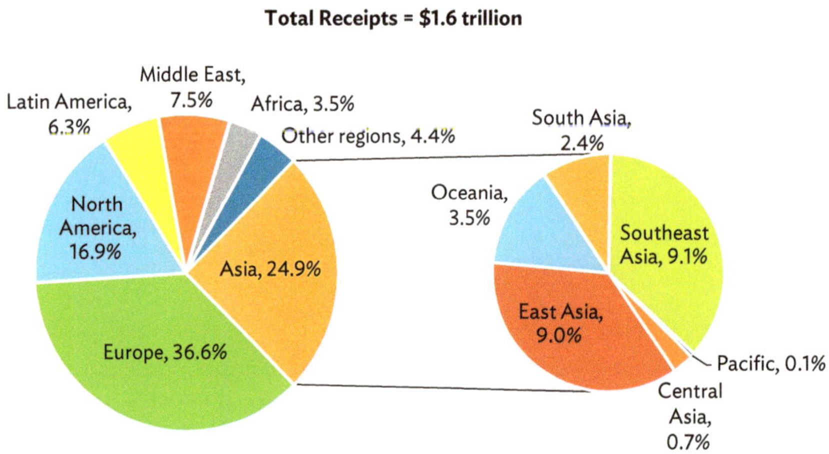

Sources: ADB calculations using data from International Monetary Fund (2019); United Nations World Tourism Organization (2020e, 2020f); and World Bank. World Development Indicators Database. https://databank.worldbank.org/source/world-development-indicators (accessed October 2020).

Asia's international tourism receipts increased by 10.2%, to a record $411.2 billion in 2018.

Reflecting the robust growth in the number of visitors to the region, international tourism receipts increased to a record $411.2 billion in 2018. Global tourism brought in $1.6 trillion in international tourism receipts, 7.4% more than in 2017. Europe (36.6%) and Asia (24.9%) maintained their shares as the two largest recipients, but tourism receipts to Asia grew 10.1%. (Figure 5.22). Significant tourism receipts helped expand employment opportunities and strengthen local business.

The upward trend in receipts particularly benefited tourism-dependent economies in the Pacific and Southeast Asia.

In 2018, receipts in all Asia's subregions increased. The two subregions with the largest shares of international arrivals also earned the largest share of the region's tourism receipts—Southeast Asia (36.6%) and East Asia (36.0%) (Table 5.5). In Southeast Asia, Thailand received the highest share ($65.2 billion), while Cambodia ($4.8 billion) had the highest y-o-y growth (20.1%). In East Asia, Japan reported both the highest tourism receipts ($45.3 billion) and growth (22.4%).

Oceania had fewer but relatively high value tourists—most visitors to Oceania are from countries with relatively high tourism expenditures. In 2018, the PRC was Australia's biggest source of tourists followed by New Zealand, the US, the UK, Japan, and Singapore. New Zealand had a similar pattern of tourists from developed countries, with 40% from Australia and the next 30% from the PRC, the US, the UK and Germany.

In terms of the largest absolute contribution of tourism receipts to GDP, Thailand ranked first with $65.2 billion, followed by Australia and Japan (Figure 5.23a). As a share of tourism receipts in GDP, Maldives was the most tourism-dependent economy in Asia, deriving 57.4% of its 2018 GDP from tourism (Figure 5.23b). Tourism receipts are important to many countries in the Pacific, averaging at least 16% of GDP. In Central Asia, tourism income was proportional to 20% of GDP in Georgia and 9.9% in Armenia. In Cambodia and Thailand, tourism also contributes a significant share of GDP.

Tourism receipts per visitor arrival varied across subregions.

International tourism receipts per international visitor rose 3.0% to $956.2 in 2018 but differed across subregions (Figure 5.24). Oceania earned the most per arrival in 2018 at $4,472.8, as Australia ($5,120.8) ranked first in tourism receipts per arrival in the region. The second highest per capita income in the region was South Asia at $2,506.7—India ($2,767.3), Sri Lanka ($2,403.0), and Maldives ($2,058.6) contributed to the high level of per capita receipts in the subregion. In contrast, Central Asia recorded the lowest earnings per arrival at $379.0 in 2018. Among the countries in Central Asia, the Kyrgyz Republic had the lowest receipts per arrival at $70.4, which was only 7.4% of Asia's average. Nevertheless, the subregion is tapping its strong potential to promote safe, sustainable, and inclusive tourism under the CAREC Tourism Strategy 2030. This includes regional initiatives for improved advertising and branding, additional investments in tourism services and critical infrastructure, jointly developing tourist products, and advocating harmonization and relaxation of visa regimes.[56]

Table 5.5: Tourism Arrivals and Receipts in Asia by Subregion, 2018

	International Tourism Receipts		International Arrivals	
Subregion	$ million	% of total Asia	million	% of total Asia
Central Asia	12,208	3.0	32.2	7.3
East Asia	147,914	36.0	245.6	55.9
Oceania	58,288	14.2	13.0	3.0
Pacific	2,438	0.6	1.6	0.4
South Asia	39,895	9.7	15.4	3.5
Southeast Asia	150,369	36.6	131.7	30.0
Total	**411,112**	**100.0**	**439.5**	**100.0**

Sources: ADB calculations using data from International Monetary Fund (2019); United Nations World Tourism Organization (UNWTO). Tourism Satellite Accounts. http://statistics.untwo.org/ (accessed September 2020); UNWTO (2020e and 2020f); and World Bank. World Development Indicators Database. https://databank.worldbank.org/source/world-development-indicators (accessed October 2020).

56 CAREC Program. https://www.carecprogram.org (accessed December 2020).

Figure 5.23: Top 10 Recipients of Tourism Receipts, 2018

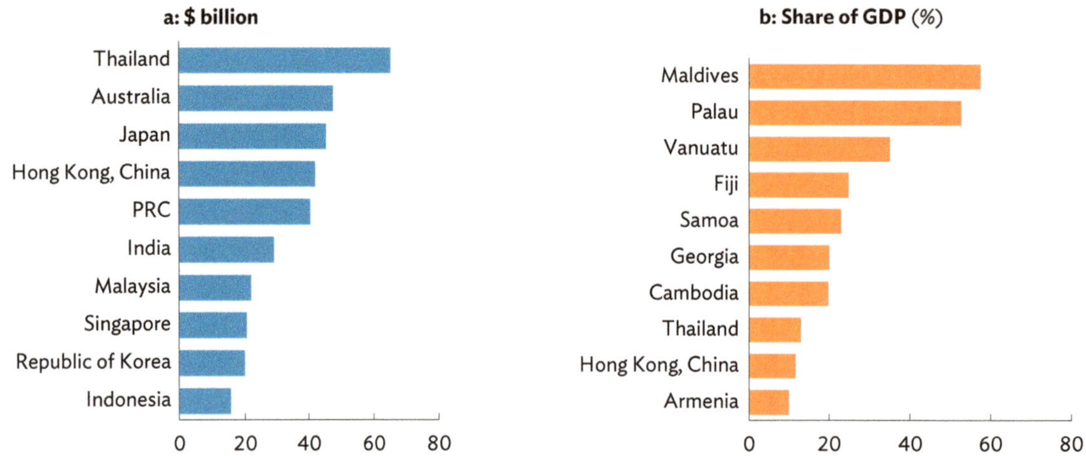

GDP = gross domestic product, PRC = People's Republic of China.

Note: Some economies with incomplete or no time-series data on international tourism receipts (such as Federated States of Micronesia; Niue; Taipei,China; Turkmenistan; and Tuvalu) were not included in the data set used to generate these charts.

Sources: ADB calculations using data from International Monetary Fund. World Economic Outlook Database. https://www.imf.org/en/Publications/WEO/weo-database/2020/October (accessed November 2020); International Monetary Fund (2019); UNWTO (2020f); and World Bank. World Development Indicators. https://databank.worldbank.org/source/world-development-indicators (accessed October 2020).

Figure 5.24: Tourism Receipts per Arrival

PRC = People's Republic of China.

Sources: ADB calculations using data from International Monetary Fund (2019); United Nations World Tourism Organization (UNWTO). Tourism Satellite Accounts. http://statistics.untwo.org/ (accessed September 2020); UNWTO (2020e, 2020f); and World Bank. World Development Indicators Database. https://databank.worldbank.org/source/world-development-indicators (accessed October 2020).

Comparing 2018 with 2015, receipts per arrival in Asia slightly declined by 1.6%—tourism revenues per visitor arrival fell by 14.7% in Central Asia and 8.7% in East Asia, despite rising numbers of international arrivals. This could be due to changing travel behavior involving more frequent budget trips that last for shorter periods.

Prior to the COVID-19 pandemic, tourism was an important driver of income for many economies.

According to the World Travel and Tourism Council (WTTC) (2020), tourism contributed $8.9 trillion to global GDP and accounted for 28.3% of global services exports. As the tourism sector spans various industries—including transportation, accommodation, and food—it has generated large amounts of employment and business. The WTTC estimates that around 330 million people were employed in the sector and accounted for one in every four new jobs created in the 5 years prior to COVID-19 (WTTC 2020).

Many Asian economies counted on the tourism sector not only for its effect on income and jobs, but also for its impact on poverty reduction—and tourism's ability to raise the level of community engagement and social integration (Box 5.2). An ILO (2020b) study using selected countries in Asia indicated that tourism employment accounts for 5.1% of total employment (5.9% among women and 4.7% among men). In Fiji, where tourism contributes significantly to GDP, tourism's share in total employment was 10.2%; in Samoa, it was 12.2%. By providing jobs and income opportunities to the informal sector, tourism also helps alleviate poverty.[57]

Box 5.2: Tourism Dependency of the Pacific

The Pacific is particularly dependent on tourism for jobs and growth. In the case of Palau, tourism employment accounts for almost half of the island's total employment. In the Cook Islands and Niue, a third of those employed work in the tourism sector, making substantial contributions to GDP. Papua New Guinea is the Pacific country that is least dependent on tourism, as both tourism employment and receipts hover at just 1%.

The box figure shows that Samoa and Vanuatu enjoy high levels of receipts, considering their moderate tourism employment rates. Fiji has the greatest number of international tourists among the Pacific island countries, accounting for approximately half of total visitors. Prior to the COVID-19 pandemic, the Fijian government recognized tourism as a pillar in the country's National Development Plan—it targeted tourism industry growth from $1.9 billion in 2017 to $2.2 billion by the end of 2021.[a]

Contribution of Tourism to Employment and GDP in the Pacific

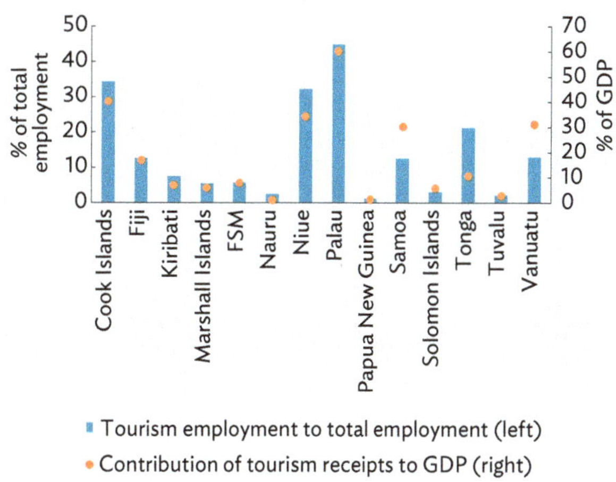

FSM = Federated States of Micronesia, GDP = gross domestic product.

[a] Government of Fiji, Ministry of Commerce, Trade, Tourism & Transport. https://www.mcttt.gov.fj/divisions/tourism-unit/programmes/fijian-tourism-2021/ (accessed October 2020).

Notes: Calculations were done using latest available data for employment (2014 for the FSM and Nauru; 2015 for the Marshall Islands and Samoa; 2016 for the Cook Islands and Tuvalu; 2017 for Kiribati and Solomon Islands; and 2018 for Fiji, Niue, Palau, Papua New Guinea, Tonga, and Vanuatu).

Sources: ADB calculations using data from South Pacific Tourism Organization (2019, 2020); and World Bank. World Development Indicators. https://databank.worldbank.org/source/world-development-indicators (accessed October 2020).

57 As noted by Lemma (2014) and Faber and Gaubert (2019), despite the important and fast-growing role of the tourism sector, the link between tourism and development outcomes remains understudied, especially in developing countries.

Tourism has also triggered the development of large infrastructure projects with positive spillover effects across sectors and beyond borders. For example, to meet increasing tourism demand, Solomon Islands has a long pipeline of priority projects for improved airports, roads, wharves, water and sanitation, solid waste management, energy, and information and communication technology. In Papua New Guinea, ADB financed a comprehensive national airport development program to expand safe and secure access to centers throughout the country that are inaccessible by road (Everett, Simpson, and Wayne 2018). Tourism development has played an integral part in the national strategic development framework of many economies in the region, especially those where tourism receipts are significant, either in absolute terms or as a proportion of GDP (see Figure 5.24).

Reviving and Rebuilding the Tourism Sector

The COVID-19 pandemic has hit tourism particularly hard with governments struggling to provide a lifeline for the sector.

Tourism has been one of the most severely hit sectors by the COVID-19 pandemic. With the end of the pandemic not yet in sight, it is highly unlikely tourism will recover in 2021. IATA (2020c) estimates international flights to reach precrisis levels no earlier than 2024. With estimates of up to 120 million direct tourism jobs at risk, $900 billion to $1.2 trillion in export earnings, and a global GDP loss ranging from 1.5% to 2.8% (UNWTO 2020g), the stakes in successfully restarting the tourism sector are very high.

Box 5.3: Government Measures to Support Tourism in Selected ADB Developing Members

Tourism is important for many economies in Asia. Governments in the region have used stimulus packages to mitigate the pandemic impact and assist businesses and workers in the travel and tourism industry:

The Government of **Cambodia** has implemented measures to support the tourism industry and its workers, including tax breaks, tax exemptions, and financial aid. It allocated up to $2.0 billion to combat the economic disruption caused by the coronavirus disease (COVID-19) outbreak. Suspended employees from the tourism sector were eligible to receive a monthly subsidy ranging from $15 to $40. Hotels, guesthouses, restaurants, and travel agencies in Phnom Penh, Siem Reap, Sihanoukville, Kep, Kampot, and Bavet, were exempted from paying taxes until the end of 2020. The government is also paying 20% of the minimum wage of hospitality workers. Workers are required to attend a short course delivered by the Ministry of Tourism before payments can be made through the National Social Security Fund. Also, the government granted tax exemptions to airlines until December 2020.

In **Georgia**, the government prepared an economic stimulus package worth GEL1.0 billion (~$330.0 million) in response to the negative COVID-19 impact on the economy—which includes infrastructure spending and tax exemptions until November 2020 to aid the tourism industry (about GEL100.0 million (~$33.0 million). Tourism-related businesses are exempt from property and income taxes, covering about 18,000 companies and more than 50,000 employees. Georgia's Tourism Recovery and Anti-Crisis Plan includes support for tax deferment and tax exemption for businesses, and allowances and subsidies for employees. Banks are restructuring the debts of individuals and businesses, especially those in tourism. Interest rate subsidies, bank guarantees, and credit guarantees are also designed for tour operators, hotels, food and beverage business, travel agencies and guides.

In **Indonesia**, the government has applied fiscal measures for all sectors, including tourism: a 6-month tax break for employees and companies starting April 2020; delay of individual and corporate income tax collection to stimulate the economy; and income tax relief for workers in specific sectors. In October 2020, the Tourism and Creative Economy Minister committed to disburse Rp3.3 trillion (~$224.0 million) in grants for tourism-related businesses and local administrations to counter the impact of the COVID-19 pandemic. Of the allocated grants, 70% will be for businesses with the remaining 30% for local administrations.

The **Republic of Korea** made available W300 billion (~$243.0 million) to support the tourism sector. As part of the program, the government allocated W100 billion (~$81.0 million) to provide access to temporary

continued on next page

Box 5.3: Government Measures to Support Tourism in Selected ADB Developing Members *(continued)*

unsecured low interest loans for small and medium-sized tourism companies. In addition, it has granted loan extensions or deferments for 1 year on previous loans up to a total of W200 billion (~$162.0 million). Other financial, fiscal, and tax relief measures for the tourism sector include an emergency relief fund for affected small and medium-sized enterprises (SMEs), tax cuts for businesses, and employment support. To encourage local tourism, the government issued domestic travel and tourism vouchers, and increased the "vacation bonus subsidy" program.

In **Malaysia**, the government launched three economic stimulus packages worth RM260.0 billion (~$59.9 billion) to fulfill three main strategies of protecting social welfare, supporting businesses, and strengthening the economy. Initiatives that target tourism-related businesses include moratoriums on loans, postponement of monthly tax installments, exemption from payment of service tax, discounts up to 50% on monthly electricity bills, additional tax deductions for training expenses, and deferment of income tax installment payments for SMEs. To boost domestic tourism, the government provided travel discount vouchers in partnership with airlines, resorts, and hotels worth RM100 (~$22) per visitor, and offered an individual income tax relief worth RM1,000 (~$226) per visitor for expenses at tourist attractions and accommodation registered with the Ministry of Tourism.

The Government of **Samoa** launched a stimulus package to assist the tourism sector to cope with the unprecedented impact of the COVID-19 pandemic, such as freezing payments for the Samoa National Provident Fund (SNPF) worth ST2.6 million (~$1.0 million) and the Accident Compensation Corporation (ACC) worth ST1.0 million (~$400,000) for 6 months. Under the SNPF, its assistance includes postponing contribution payments for employers in the hospitality sector. ACC assistance includes a 50% reduction in hotels' daily fixed rate, exemption from paying rent for all businesses operating within the Faleolo Airport, provision of interest relief on loans, extension of due dates on income taxes, and waiving registration and late fees for transport.

In **Thailand**, the government issued stimulus packages worth B22.4 billion (~$718.0 million) to support the tourism industry. The initiatives are named "We Travel Together" and "Moral Support." Available from July to October 2020, benefits include subsidized hotel accommodation, airline tickets, car rental fees, bus fares, and facilities in tourist destinations around the country. A total of B20.0 billion (~$641.0 million) was allocated under the "We Travel Together" stimulus package. Some B18.0 million (~$577.0 million) was set aside to subsidize 40% of normal room rates at hotels to eligible travelers, capped at B3,000 (~$96) per night for up to five nights. The other B2.0 million (~$64.0 million) is to subsidize 2 million airline tickets, priced at B2.0 (~$64) per person. The government also allocated B2.4 billion (~$77.0 million) for its "Moral Support" stimulus package, aimed to fund holiday travel expenses of around 1.2 million health workers and volunteers from sub-district hospitals. The subsidy is limited to B2,000 (~$64) per person for a 2-day and 1-night trip. Additionally, the government launched special tourist visas (STV), which allows foreign tourists to stay in Thailand for more than 200 days, as long as they abide by health protocols and insurance requirements. STV applications started in October 2020 and are scheduled to end in September 2021. The government aims to attract 1,200 tourists each month, generating some B12.0 billion (~$380.0 million) in revenue.

Sources: Medina (2020a, 2020b, 2020c, 2020d, 2020e, and 2020f); Organisation for Economic Co-operation and Development (2020); Parama (2020); and United Nations World Tourism Organization (2020d).

Governments are using various fiscal, monetary, and industry-specific measures to help their economies cope with the socioeconomic impact of the pandemic—and its impact on tourism (Box 5.3). Despite these substantive efforts, it is unlikely that the entire tourism sector will be able to revive until the end of the pandemic. And it will likely shrink as some businesses will be unable to survive. One important government objective should be to maintain a critical level of tourism infrastructure so the sector can bounce back quickly once demand returns.

Governments should use a phased approach for tourism recovery.

With the priority to protect the health of travelers and residents, governments have little choice but to rebuild tourism in stages: (i) by promoting domestic tourism; (ii) then by establishing green corridors (or "bubbles") that allow safe travel between partners; and (iii) finally, a full return to international travel. Here we analyze this phased approach.

Jumpstarting Domestic Tourism to Reboot the Tourism Sector

Many governments have started to promote domestic tourism, mainly by providing subsidies for domestic tourists. Stimulating domestic tourism typically responds to actual demand, as many people still yearn to travel but prefer to stay closer to home and avoid mass transportation. Furthermore, international travel restrictions have made it difficult to visit foreign countries.

Early evidence, however, shows that fully mobilizing all outbound travelers to vacation within the country can be difficult. First, in several countries, local lockdowns—such as those previously in Metro Manila, Philippines, and Melbourne, Australia—make it impossible to travel domestically. Second, due to the severe economic downturn and heavy job losses, overall demand for tourism has declined. One also needs to note that the tourism industry is often no longer able to operate at full capacity due to social distancing and other containment measures. This includes actions such as urging airlines to keep middle seats empty. Furthermore, in analyzing demand, some travelers may have lost interest in domestic destinations, and are more interested in exploring new places abroad. Domestic tourism might also be limited by the fact that some people might not want to travel at all because of fear of infection.

Another limitation of domestic tourism might be a mismatch between international and domestic demand. Some countries had been successful in attracting high-income travelers from abroad before the pandemic. However, those international travelers are no longer visiting, and the number of domestic tourists able to afford high-end tourism services might be limited. In the worst case, domestic tourist demand for lower cost travel services might go unmet.

In summary, as domestic tourism is relatively easier to promote than international tourism, it has become a short-term objective for many governments in the region (Box 5.4). In some economies where the number of foreign tourists exceeds the number of outbound tourists, stimulating domestic tourism has proven a viable strategy to help the industry survive. For example, in the Republic of Korea, 2020 has seen a boom in domestic tourism, especially during times when new COVID-19 cases were low. During May 2020, the number of tourists almost reached the 2019 level, when both domestic and international tourists could visit. Similarly, in Viet Nam, domestic tourism has shown a clear upward trend since the lockdown was eased on 11 May 2020. However, in countries with a large surplus in tourism infrastructure, domestic tourism, even if fully mobilized, is not enough. Governments then need to decide on how best to support the sector.

Establishing Travel Bubbles

In the second stage, many governments have tried to restart tourism by establishing so-called travel bubbles or green corridors. Travel bubbles are agreements to open borders to the nationals of the partner economy. Travel bubbles can be for business travel only or also include leisure travel. They often specify provisions on health protocols that need to be followed when leaving and entering the territory. Access can be reciprocal or unilateral. They can be formed between two or more partners.

The first travel bubble in Asia was established between the PRC and the Republic of Korea in early May 2020. The agreement is limited to business travelers, who need to be invited by a company in the other country. And they need to follow a strict health protocol. After this first travel bubble, several others have followed with similar arrangements allowing for essential travel. The exact definition of essential travel varies and can include diplomats, commuters, or expatriates (Table 5.6). As only a limited number of visitors qualify for travel under these arrangements, the increase in international arrivals has so far been small.

Box 5.4: The Potential of Domestic Tourism and Travel Bubbles

To gauge the potential of domestic tourism and travel bubbles, Helble and Fink (2020) provide a detailed scenario analysis. To gauge the potential of domestic tourism, they assume that due to the pandemic all tourists that traveled internationally in 2018 would decide to vacation in their home country. As box figure 1 illustrates the results and shows that across Asia, in more than half the cases, domestic tourism technically has the potential to fully replace foreign visitors. For example, in Armenia, before the pandemic, outbound tourists exceeded the number of inbound foreign tourists by 30%. Armenia thus stands a good chance to fill a substantial part of the gap left by international tourists by domestic guests. However, in economies that are highly dependent on tourism, such as Fiji, Maldives, or Thailand, domestic tourism, even when fully mobilized, will not be enough.

1: Scenario Analysis of Domestic Replacing Foreign Tourists, Based on Number of Tourists (%)

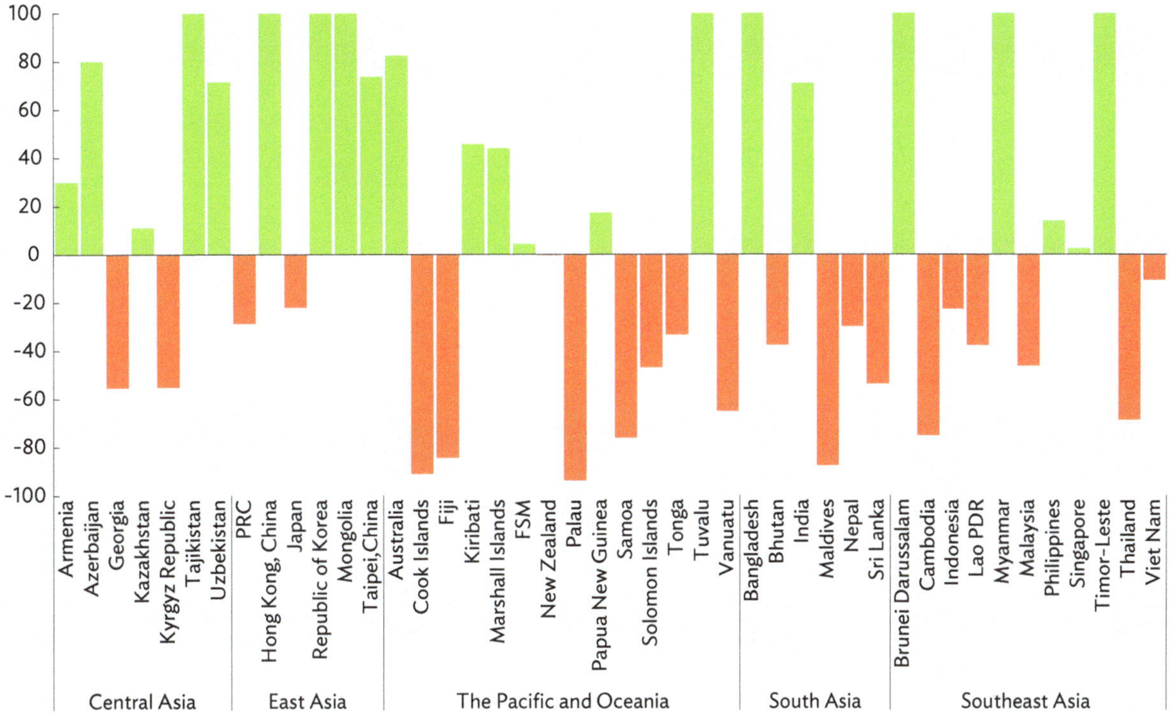

FSM = Federated States of Micronesia, Lao PDR = Lao People's Democratic Republic, PRC = People's Republic of China.

Note: These are ratios of difference between domestic tourist departures and international tourist arrivals, to international tourist arrivals. Using data from 2018 tourist arrivals, a value of zero suggests an economy's domestic tourists are sufficient to compensate for international tourist arrivals. Economies with green bars indicate the potential of domestic tourism is higher than the gap left by the absence of international tourists. Economies including Bangladesh; Brunei Darussalam; Hong Kong, China; Mongolia; Myanmar; the Republic of Korea; Tajikistan; Timor-Leste; and Tuvalu have values that surpass 100%, suggesting these economies' domestic tourists were more than double their international tourists in 2018. Economies with red bars indicate a gap in arrivals even with mobilization of domestic tourists.

Source: Helble and Fink (2020).

To estimate the potential of travel bubbles, Helble and Fink (2020) assume that such agreements would allow travelers to move in both directions and that the volume would reach the pre-pandemic level and that all bubbles would happen simultaneously. If one country, such as the People's Republic of China (PRC), is the largest source of tourists for various partners, the tourist flows would reach the 2018 level across all pairs (box figure 2).

Bilateral travel bubbles obviously help most economies highly dependent on tourism from one source country. For example, the gap for Fiji would drop from 84% to 44% if it entered a bilateral agreement with Australia.

continued on next page

Box 5.4: The Potential of Domestic Tourism and Travel Bubbles *(continued)*

Thailand would see an improvement from −68% to −46% if it established an agreement with the PRC. While these are significant improvements, they still leave these economies with large deficits. In addition, it is unlikely that bilateral tourism would quickly reach precrisis levels. As with domestic tourism, social distancing and other containment measures would limit supply. Furthermore, traveling in bubbles often requires multiple testing, which comes at a cost that deters some people from traveling abroad.

2: Scenario Analysis of Tourism Bubble with Largest Partner, Based on Number of Tourists (%)

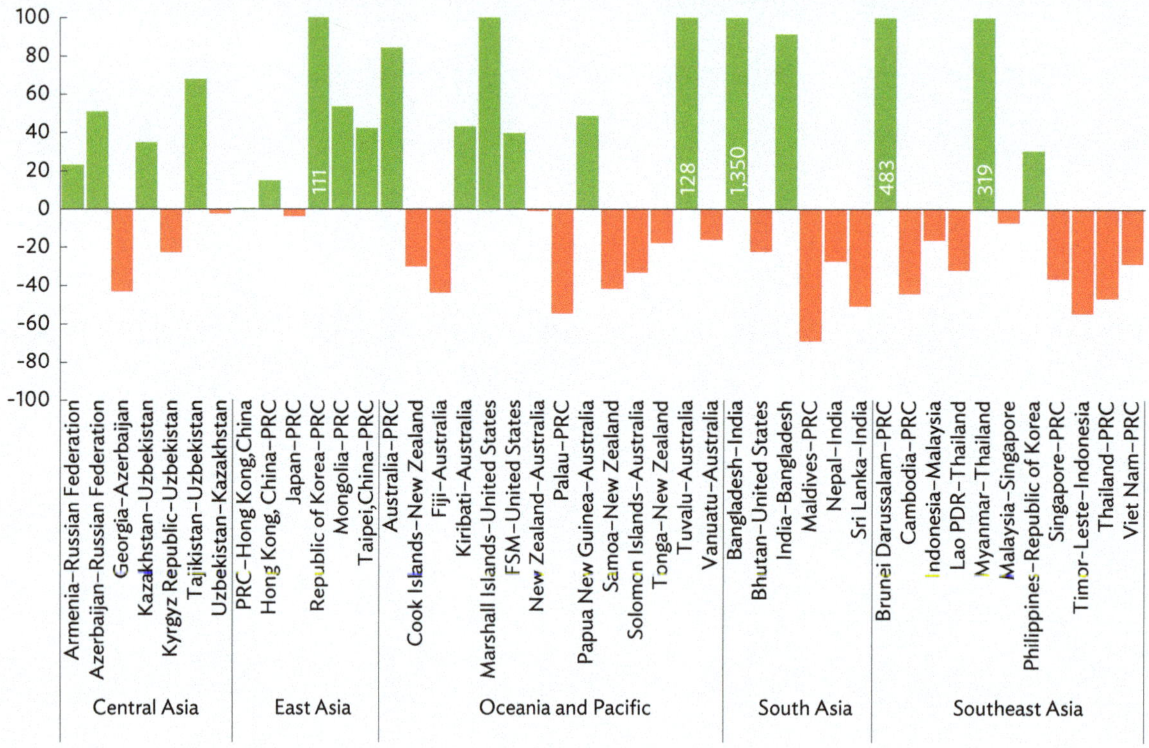

FSM = Federated States of Micronesia, Lao PDR = Lao People's Democratic Republic, PRC = People's Republic of China.

Notes:

(i) Using 2018 data, in this scenario we assumed that domestic tourists who would otherwise leave the economy would stay at home. We then got the difference between international tourist arrivals, and the sum of inbound tourists from the economy's preferred partner and its own domestic tourists. We then divided this figure by the total international tourist arrivals to get the ratio.

(ii) The green bars indicate by how much the combined domestics tourists from an economy and its preferred partner would surpass the number of international tourists. Some economies and their preferred—including Bangladesh, Brunei Darussalam, the Marshall Islands, the Republic of Korea, Tuvalu, Myanmar—have values that surpass 100%, which suggests that their combined tourists are more than double their 2018 international tourist arrivals. Economies with red bars indicate a gap in arrivals, even with mobilization of domestic tourists and arrivals from their preferred partner.

(iii) Arrival data for 2017 were used for the Marshall Islands, Tonga, and Tuvalu, while 2016 was used for the FSM and 2014 for Bangladesh. There was no arrival data available for Afghanistan, Pakistan, Turkmenistan, and Tuvalu for any year.

Source: Helble and Fink (2020).

Table 5.6: Travel Bubbles in Asia

Economies involved (type of agreement)	Effective Date	Purpose		Testing Requirements		Quarantine Requirement	Sponsor Needed	Contact-Tracing App
		Business/ Official	Leisure	Before Departure	Upon Arrival			
PRC–Republic of Korea	1 May 20	√		√	√	Wait until negative test result	√	
PRC–Singapore	8 Jun 20	√		√	√	Wait until negative test result	√	√
Japan–Thailand; Japan–Viet Nam (Residence Track)	29 Jul 20	√		√	√	14 days	√	√
Singapore- Malaysia (RGL)	17 Aug 20	√		√	√	Wait until negative test result	√	√
Singapore- Malaysia (PCA)	17 Aug 20	√		√	√	7 days	√	√
Singapore–Brunei Darussalam (RGL)	1 Sep 20	√		√	√	Wait until negative test result	√	√
Singapore–Republic of Korea (RGL)	4 Sep 20	√		√	√	Wait until negative test result	√	√
Japan–Malaysia; Japan–Myanmar; Japan–Cambodia; Japan–Lao PDR; Japan–Taipei,China (Residence Track)	8 Sep 20	√		√	√	14 days	√	√
Japan–Singapore (Business Track)	18 Sep 20	√		√	√	Singapore: Wait until negative test result Japan: none	√	√
Japan–Singapore (Residence Track)	30 Sept 20	√		√	√	14 days	√	√
Japan–Republic of Korea (Business Track)	8 Oct 20	√		√	√	none	√	√
Japan- Republic of Korea (Residence Track)	8 Oct 20	√		√	√	14 days	√	√
Australia–New Zealand	16 Oct 20	√	√			none		
Singapore–Indonesia (RGL/TCA)	26 Oct 20	√		√	√	Wait until negative test result	√	√

Lao PDR = Lao People's Democratic Republic, PCA= Periodic Commuting Arrangement, PRC = People's Republic of China, RGL = Reciprocal Green Lane, TCA = Travel Corridor Arrangement.

Notes:
(i) The Reciprocal Green Lane and Travel Corridor Arrangement are reserved for short, business-related travel.
(ii) The Periodic Commuting Arrangement is especially for Singapore or Malaysian citizens with working visa who previously frequently crossed the Johor–Singapore border. Under this arrangement, the workers must spend 90 days in the country of work before they can return home.
(iii) Residence Track, usually used by bubbles involving Japan, is for noncitizen long-term residents with working visa, including their families.
(iv) Business Track, usually used by bubbles involving Japan, is for short business trips.
(v) Testing requirements refer to the COVID-19 polymerase chain reaction (PCR) test. Time allowed to take the test prior to departure varies between bubbles.
(vi) Quarantine requirement refers to quarantine upon arrival. "Wait until negative test result" indicates the number of days required to wait in isolation for the result of the PCR test to become available. Travelers wait in either a self-sourced or government provided location.
(vii) Sponsor refers to a business or government agency who would need to sponsor documents such as a travel pass or visa that would grant entry into the country.
(viii) The Australia–New Zealand Bubble only opens travel in one direction—from New Zealand to Australia. Travelers to Australia can only visit New South Wales and the Northern Territory which are considered as safe travel zones. Upon return to New Zealand, the traveler will be subject to a COVID-19 PCR test and 14-day quarantine in a government facility.

Sources: Government of Australia, Department of Home Affairs. https://covid19.homeaffairs.gov.au; Government of Brunei Darussalam, Ministry of Foreign Affairs. http://www.mfa.gov.bn/Shared%20Documents/Annex.pdf; Government of Cambodia, Ministry of Foreign Affairs and International Cooperation. http://www.cambodianembassy.jp/web2/; Government of Indonesia, Ministry of Foreign Affairs. https://kemlu.go.id/singapore/id; Government of Japan, Ministry of Foreign Affairs. https://www.mofa.go.jp; Government of the Lao PDR, Ministry of Foreign Affairs. http://www.mofa.gov.la; Government of Malaysia, Immigration Department of Malaysia. https://www.imi.gov.my/; Government of New Zealand, Ministry of Business, Innovation and Employment. https://www.immigration.govt.nz/; Government of the People's Republic of China, Ministry of Foreign Affairs of the People's Republic of China. https://www.fmprc.gov.cn/mfa_eng/; Government of the Republic of Korea, Ministry of Foreign Affairs. http://www.mofa.go.kr/eng/ and http://overseas.mofa.go.kr/sg-en/index.do; Government of Singapore, Ministry of Foreign Affairs. https://safetravel.ica.gov.sg; Government of Thailand, Ministry of Foreign Affairs. http://site.thaiembassy.jp/en/; and Government of Viet Nam, Ministry of Foreign Affairs. https://vnembassy-jp.org/en/ (all accessed November 2020).

Economic incentives and trust between partners have proven the decisive factors in establishing travel bubbles. Particularly interesting is the arrangement between Singapore and Malaysia. Because of geographic proximity and close economic ties, these two economies agreed on a so-called Periodic Commuting Arrangement for workers who regularly cross the border. However, the arrangement does not allow for a daily commute, but those who cross will have to spend at least 90 days in their country of employment before they can return home. Overall, the reciprocal travel arrangements signed so far show that economic considerations beyond tourism have become the primary driving force (Table 5.6).

Negotiations on establishing travel bubbles that would allow for leisure travel started in mid-2020. For example, Australia and New Zealand initiated negotiations on a "Trans-Tasman" travel bubble. Given the strong economic and cultural links between the two countries, the agreement was expected to boost tourism in both economies. However, the negotiations stalled due to a COVID-19 outbreak in the Australian state of Victoria in June 2020. In October 2020, authorities agreed to open a quarantine-free, one-way corridor from New Zealand to limited parts of Australia. In a similar effort to open borders to leisure tourists, Fiji's government proposed to form a travel bubble with Australia and New Zealand the so-called "Bula bubble" in June 2020. Recurrent waves of coronavirus infections have been a common tipping point for these travel negotiations to advance.

One critical requirement to establish travel bubbles is that the pandemic is under control across partner countries. While some governments were able to quickly limit the pandemic spread, others have struggled or continue to struggle to contain the disease. Recently, some countries were also confronted with a second wave of infections. Apart from public health considerations, the epidemiological situation affects a tourist's willingness to travel and a country's willingness to receive tourists. The opportunity to open bilateral tourism typically only arises once both parties are well beyond their peak of new infections.

In addition to the epidemiological situation, pandemic preparedness is another important consideration for tourists. As new outbreaks can never be excluded, countries need to demonstrate their capacity to handle them when they do. However, pandemic preparedness varies significantly. As of October 2020, very few countries in the region could demonstrate both: a full control of new infections as well as adequate pandemic preparedness. This is the main reason that, despite the strong interest in travel bubbles, few have materialized so far and the ones agreed upon cover only essential travel.

In sum, restoring public trust in safe travel is key to reviving Asia's tourism sector; by promoting coordinated, seamlessly executed, responsible, and safety-oriented travel measures, multilateral development banks such as ADB, regional cooperation initiatives, as well as regional policy forums and dialogues can help bring back tourism's long-term sustainable potential.

The results of an IATA (2020a) survey revealed that fear of catching the virus while traveling is a major factor keeping them from returning to their old travel habits—only 45% expressed interest in traveling again once the pandemic subsides, while 64% will postpone travel until the general economic environment has improved. Furthermore, stringent travel requirements deter travelers—83% revealed that they will not travel if there is a chance of compulsory quarantine after arrival (IATA 2020b).

With the uncertain outlook, the survival of tourism-related businesses is at risk, along with millions of jobs. Government stimulus packages to cushion the socioeconomic impact of the pandemic may vary, but measures that target the tourism sector typically include marketing campaigns, tax relief, subsidies, and special incentives to boost demand. Furthermore, many governments have established detailed health and sanitary protocols.

Many governments have been looking to domestic tourism to help stimulate economic recovery. For those with existing strong domestic tourism markets, promoting domestic tourism can provide a lifeline. However, for highly dependent tourism economies, including small island developing states such as Fiji, the Cook Islands, Palau, and Maldives, domestic tourism markets are too small to be a viable option for filling the gap left by international arrivals. Furthermore, promoting domestic tourism is not straightforward. Many people have less disposable income for leisure activities, and social distancing as well as other containment measures may make it difficult or less appealing. Equally, in countries where the tourism attractions are geared toward foreign markets it may take time to reorientate toward domestic preferences. In many cases, there is also a clear difference in spending between domestic and foreign tourists.

Establishing bilateral travel bubbles is another option to revive tourism. The growing number of travel agreements between countries is a testament to this. Economies which are highly dependent on tourism from one source country would particularly benefit. A bilateral bubble between Fiji and Australia would reduce the gap in Fiji by half compared with relying on domestic tourism. Agreements are, however, subject to rapidly changing epidemiological circumstances. If potential bilateral pairings are analyzed according to pandemic preparedness and whether they appear to be past their peak of outbreaks, very few bilateral parings were feasible. Currently existing agreements are not yet targeted to conventional tourists, but allow for essential travel, such as business travel or expatriates returning to work.

As more and more travel bubbles are being put into place, we will certainly witness the emergence of subregional travel bubbles soon. Regional communities in Asia have a history of cooperation on tourism and travel facilitation and many are in discussions to help respond to the crisis. Subregional travel bubbles are, however, only a better solution to bilateral bubbles when there is a large degree of intra-subregional travel. Epidemiological considerations may also become even more complex. One of the most important policy implications for subregional bubbles is the establishment of harmonized protocols for travel and tourism. This should consider the full customer journey from their taxi to the airport to their arrival at their accommodation and visits to attractions and sites. ADB is currently working with international travel and tourism organizations to contribute to this process.

Another important consideration when considering travel bubbles is the ability to conduct cross-border and regional contact tracing. Countries have adopted different tools for contact tracing, from centralized to decentralized systems as well as different technologies, such as quick response (QR) codes or Bluetooth. Varying systems across economies make it difficult to utilize contact tracing apps for cross-border movement. Harmonized systems which can share information would be particularly helpful for subregional travel bubbles which have a high frequency of cross-border movement. This should be based on shared and transparent agreements on data privacy. In a similar vein health insurance needs to cover COVID-19-related costs of travelers. Within the Greater Mekong Subregion, for example, ADB is seeking to trial innovative approaches to contact tracing and mobile insurance in special economic zones located in border areas.

It is also important to remember that travel bubbles are only a second-best option. If the pandemic allows, a nondiscriminatory approach should be preferred. Several countries have chosen this option. Maldives, for example, is open for international tourism. They have established guidelines around health checks for inbound tourists and exacting health protocols in the event of an outbreak. They are supported by their "one island one resort" tourism model, which affords some natural social distancing.

As the pandemic situation further evolves, we might see the emergence of global mobile phone apps, such as CommonPass, or of vaccine passes that would greatly facilitate international travel. Again, harmonized standards around recognition of vaccination certificates will be critical to freedom of international movement. Promoting tourism is and will therefore be first and foremost a joint undertaking and makes regional cooperation more needed than ever.

Tourism post-COVID-19 will be different: more than beautiful sights and cheap flights, it will be about health and safety. Governments may also want to use the crisis as an opportunity to "build back better" and increase the long-term sustainability of their tourism sector. Leveraging on innovative solutions, technological advancements, and regional cooperation, it is high time to rethink the future of tourism.

References

Ahamad, R. 2021. Four Lakh People Working Abroad Return to Bangladesh amid Pandemic Fallout. *New Age*. 5 January. https://www.newagebd.net/article/126273/four-lakh-migrant-workers-return.

Al Sherbini, R. 2020. 500 Pakistani Medics to Arrive in Kuwait to Fight. COVID-19. Gulf News. 6 September. https://gulfnews.com/world/gulf/kuwait/500-pakistani-medics-to-arrive-in-kuwait-to-fight-covid-19-1.73664524#.

Asian Development Bank (ADB). 2020. *Asian Development Outlook 2020 Update: Wellness in Worrying Times.* Manila.

Association of Southeast Asian Nations (ASEAN). 2020. Chairman's Statement of the 36th ASEAN Summit. https://asean.org/storage/2020/06/Chairman-Statement-of-the-36th-ASEAN-Summit-FINAL.pdf.

BenarNews.org. 2020. Region's Migrants Struggle with Job Losses, Hunger Caused by COVID-19. 15 April. https://www.benarnews.org/english/news/indonesian/migrant-covid-04152020165752.html.

Bismonte, C. 2020. The Disproportionate Effect of COVID-19 on Migrant Workers in ASEAN. *The Diplomat*. 22 May. https://thediplomat.com/2020/05/the-disproportionate-effect-of-covid-19-on-migrant-workers-in-asean/.

CAREC Program. 2020. Tourism. https://www.carecprogram.org/?page_id=13250 (accessed September 2020).

Engblom, A., N. Lephilibert, and N. Baruah. 2020. COVID-19: Impact on Migrant Workers and Country Response in Thailand. International Labour Organization. 3 July. https://www.ilo.org/wcmsp5/groups/public/---asia/---ro-bangkok/---sro-bangkok/documents/briefingnote/wcms_741920.pdf.

Eurasianet.org. 2020. Hundreds of Azerbaijanis Languish on Russian Border. 16 June. https://eurasianet.org/hundreds-of-azerbaijanis-languish-on-russian-border.

Everett, H., D. Simpson, and S. Wayne. 2018. Tourism as a Driver of Growth in the Pacific. *Issues in Pacific Development*. No. 2. Manila: ADB.

Faber, B. and C. Gaubert. 2019. Tourism and Economic Development: Evidence from Mexico's Coastline. *American Economic Review*. 109 (6). pp. 2245-93.

Ghosh, B. 2020. The Impact of Coronavirus on Foreign Workers. 7 July. Bloomberg Quint. https://www.bloombergquint.com/view/world-bank-expert-explains-coronavirus-impact-on-foreign-workers.

Global Knowledge Partnership on Migration and Development (KNOMAD) staff estimates. Bilateral Remittance Matrix 2020 (May).

Global Knowledge Partnership on Migration and Development (KNOMAD). http://www.knomad.org/data/remittances (accessed December 2019 and November 2020).

———. 2017. Migration and Remittances Recent Developments and Outlook. Migration and Development Brief No. 28. Washington, DC: World Bank Group. https://www.knomad.org/sites/default/files/2017-12/Migration%20and%20Development%20Report%2012-14-17%20web.pdf.

———. 2020. Phase II: COVID-19 Crisis through a Migration Lens. *Migration and Development Brief 33*. Washington, DC: World Bank Group. https://www.knomad.org/publication/migration-anddevelopment-brief-33.

Government of Australia, Department of Foreign Affairs and Trade. https://www.dfat.gov.au/geo/pacific/engagement/pacific-labour-mobility/Pages/default (accessed September 2020).

Government of Australia, Department of Home Affairs. Inwards Travel Restrictions Operation Directive. https://www.homeaffairs.gov.au/covid-19/Documents/inward-travel-restrictions-operation-directive.pdf (accessed September 2020).

———. https://covid19.homeaffairs.gov.au/new-zealand-safe-travel-zone (accessed November 2020).

Government of Bangladesh, Bureau of Manpower, Employment and Training. Statistical Reports. http://www.old.bmet.gov.bd/BMET/stattisticalDataAction (accessed September 2020).

———. Overseas Employment and Remittances (1976 to 2020). http://www.old.bmet.gov.bd/BMET/viewStatReport.action?reportnumber=16 (accessed September 2020).

Government of Brunei Darussalam, Ministry of Foreign Affairs. http://www.mfa.gov.bn/Shared%20 Documents/Annex.pdf (accessed November 2020).

Government of Cambodia, Ministry of Foreign Affairs and International Cooperation. Royal Embassy of Cambodia in Japan. http://www.cambodianembassy.jp/web2 (accessed November 2020).

Government of Fiji, Bureau of Statistics. Tourism and Migration Statistics. https://www.statsfiji.gov.fj/latestreleases/tourism-and-migration/visitor-arrivals (accessed October 2020).

Government of Fiji, Ministry of Commerce, Trade, Tourism & Transport. https://www.mcttt.gov.fj/divisions/tourism-unit/programmes/fijian-tourism-2021/ (accessed October 2020).

Government of India, Ministry of External Affairs. https://www.mea.gov.in/vande-bharat-mission-list-of-flights.htm (accessed January 2021).

Government of Indonesia, Ministry of Foreign Affairs. Embassy of Indonesia in Singapore. https://kemlu.go.id/singapore/id (accessed November 2020).

Government of Japan, Ministry of Foreign Affairs. https://www.mofa.go.jp (accessed November 2020).

Government of the Lao People's Democratic Republic (Lao PDR), Ministry of Foreign Affairs. http://www.mofa.gov.la (accessed November 2020).

Government of the Lao People's Democratic Republic, Ministry of Information, Culture, and Tourism. International Tourist Arrivals January–March 2020. Unpublished.

Government of Malaysia, Immigration Department. https://www.imi.gov.my (accessed November 2020).

Government of Malaysia, Ministry of Tourism & Culture. Tourist Arrivals data. http://mytourismdata.tourism.gov.my (accessed October 2020).

Government of New Zealand, Ministry of Business, Innovation and Employment. New Zealand Immigration. https://www.immigration.govt.nz/about-us/research-and-statistics/research-reports/recognised-seasonal-employer-rse-scheme (accessed September 2020).

———. https://www.immigration.govt.nz (accessed November 2020).

Government of Palau. Visitor Arrivals. https://www.palaugov.pw/visitor-arrivals/ (accessed October 2020).

Government of Pakistan, Bureau of Emigration and Overseas Employment. https://beoe.gov.pk/reports-and-statistics.

Government of the People's Republic of China, Ministry of Foreign Affairs. https://www.fmprc.gov.cn/mfa_eng/ (accessed November 2020).

Government of the Philippines, Department of Foreign Affairs. 2021. DFA Repatriates 327,511 Overseas Filipinos in 2020. 4 January. https://dfa.gov.ph/dfa-news/dfa-releasesupdate/28480-dfa-repatriates-327-511-overseas-filipinos-in-2020.

Government of the Philippines, Department of Labor and Employment. Overseas Workers Welfare Administration (OWWA). 2020. OWWA Cash Aid to OFWs Affected by Travel Ban Reached P81M. https://owwa.gov.ph/index.php/news/central/83-owwa-cash-aid-to-ofws-affected-by-travel-ban-reached-p81m.

Government of the Republic of Korea, Ministry of Foreign Affairs. http://www.mofa.go.kr/eng/ (accessed November 2020).

———. Embassy of the Republic of Korea to Singapore. http://overseas.mofa.go.kr/sg-en/index.do (accessed November 2020).

Government of the Republic of Korea, Tourism Organization. Monthly Statistics of Tourism. https://kto.visitkorea.or.kr (accessed October 2020).

Government of Samoa, Samoa Tourism Board. Total Visitor Arrivals by Country/Year. http://www.samoatourism.org (accessed October 2020).

Government of Singapore, Department of Statistics. https://www.tablebuilder.singstat.gov.sg (accessed October 2020).

Government of Singapore, Ministry of Foreign Affairs. Immigration and Checkpoints Authority. https://safetravel.ica.gov.sg (accessed November 2020).

Government of Solomon Islands, Ministry of Finance and Treasury. Solomon Islands National Statistics Office. 2020. Visitor Arrivals Statistics. *Statistical Bulletin.* No. 08/2020. https://www.solomonchamber.com.sb/media/1908/visitor-arrivals-statistics_1stquarter-2020-002.pdf.

Government of Thailand, Ministry of Foreign Affairs. Thailand Embassy in Tokyo. http://site.thaiembassy.jp/en/(accessed November 2020).

Government of the United Kingdom. 2020. The UK's Points-Based Immigration System: Policy Statement. 19 February. https://www.gov.uk/government/publications/the-uks-points-based-immigration-system-policy-statement/the-uks-points-based-immigration-system-policy-statement.

Government of the United States, Department of State–Bureau of Consular Affairs. 2020. National Interest Exceptions to Presidential Proclamations (10014 & 10052) Suspending the Entry of Immigrants and Nonimmigrants Presenting a Risk to the United States Labor Market During the Economic Recovery Following the 2019 Novel Coronavirus Outbreak. *US Visas News.*12 August. https://travel.state.gov/content/travel/en/News/visas-news/exceptions-to-p-p-10014-10052-suspending-entry-of-immigrants-non-immigrants-presenting-risk-to-us-labor-market-during-economic-recovery.html.

Government of the United States, Department of Homeland Security. https://www.dhs.gov/immigration-statistics/yearbook/2018/table3 (accessed September 2020).

———. US Citizenship and Immigration Services (USCIS). https://www.uscis.gov/archive/our-fees (accessed September 2020).

Government of Vanuatu, Ministry of Finance and Economic Management, National Statistics Office. 2019. October 2019 Provisional Highlights. *Tourism News.* 31 December. https://vnso.gov.vu/images/Public_Documents/Statistics_by_Topic/Economics/Tourism/2019/IVA_10_October_2019.pdf.

Government of Viet Nam, Ministry of Foreign Affairs. Embassy of Viet Nam in Japan. https://vnembassy-jp.org/en/ (accessed November 2020).

Hale, T., S. Webster, A. Petherick, T. Phillips, and B. Kira. 2020a. Oxford COVID-19 Government Response Tracker. Blavatnik School of Government. https://github.com/OxCGRT/covid-policy-tracker/raw/master/data/timeseries/OxCGRT_timeseries_all.xlsx (accessed 3 November 2020).

Hale, T., N. Angrist, E. Cameron-Blake, L. Hallas, B. Kira, S. Majumdar, A. Petherick, T. Phillips, H. Tatlow, and S. Webster. 2020b. Oxford COVID-19 Government Response Tracker. Blavatnik School of Government. https://www.bsg.ox.ac.uk/research/research-projects/coronavirus-government-response-tracker.

Helble, M. and A. Fink. 2020. Reviving Tourism Amid the COVID-19 Pandemic. *ADB Briefs* No. 150. Manila: ADB.

International Air Transport Association (IATA). 2020a. *Air Passenger Market Analysis – May 2020.* Montreal. https://www.iata.org/en/iatarepository/publications/economic-reports/airpassenger-monthly-analysis---may-2020/.

———. 2020b. *Air Passenger Market Analysis–August 2020.* Montreal. https://www.iata.org/en/iata-repository/publications/economicreports/air-passenger-monthly-analysis---august-2020/.

———. 2020c. COVID-19 Puts Over Half of 2020 Passenger Revenues at Risk. Press Release. No. 29. 14 April. https://www.iata.org/en/pressroom/pr/2020-04-14-01/.

———. 2020d. Recovery Delayed as International Travel Remains Locked Down. Press release. 28 July. https://www.iata.org/en/pressroom/pr/2020-07-28-02/.

International Labour Organization (ILO). 2020a. COVID-19 and Employment in the Tourism Sector: Impact and Response in Asia and the Pacific. Thematic Brief. 24 April. https://www.ilo.org/wcmsp5/groups/public/---asia/---ro-bangkok/documents/briefingnote/wcms_742664.pdf.

———. 2020b. COVID-19: Impact on Migrant Workers and Country Response in Myanmar. https://www.ilo.org/wcmsp5/groups/public/---asia/---ro-bangkok/---ilo-yangon/documents/briefingnote/wcms_749466.pdf.

———. 2020c. COVID-19 and Employment in the Tourism Sector: Impact and Response in Asia and the Pacific.

International Labour Organization. ILOSTAT. https://ilostat.ilo.org/data/ (accessed September 2020).

International Monetary Fund (IMF). 2005. *World Economic Outlook: Globalization and External Balances*. https://www.imf.org/en/Publications/WEO/Issues/2016/12/31/Globalization-and-External-Imbalances.

———. 2019. Republic of Palau: 2018 Article IV Consultation-Press Release; Staff Report; and Statement by the Executive Director for the Republic of Palau. *IMF Country Report.* No. 19/43. https://www.imf.org/en/Publications/CR/Issues/2019/02/05/Republic-of-Palau-2018-Article-IV-Consultation-Press-Release-Staff-Report-and-Statement-by-46582.

———. 2020a. Pacific Islands Threatened by COVID-19. 27 May. https://www.imf.org/en/News/Articles/2020/05/27/na-05272020-pacific-islands-threatened-by-covid-19.

———. 2020b. Tourism Tracker Asia & Pacific Edition. Issue 6. 25 August. https://www.imf.org/en/Countries/ResRep/PIS-Region.

———. 2020c. Tourism Tracker Asia & Pacific Edition. Issue 7. 22 September. https://www.imf.org/en/Countries/ResRep/PIS-Region.

———. 2020d. Tourism Tracker Asia & Pacific Edition. Issue 8. 27 October. https://www.imf.org/en/Countries/ResRep/PIS-Region.

———. World Economic Outlook Database. https://www.imf.org/en/Publications/WEO/weo-database/2020/October (accessed November 2020).

International Organization for Migration. 2020a. Return of Undocumented Afghans. Weekly Situation Report. 24–30 May. https://afghanistan.iom.int/sites/default/files/Reports/iom_afghanistan-return_of_undocumented_afghans-_situation_report_24-30_may_2020.pdf.

———. 2020b. COVID-19 Impact on Stranded Migrants. *Issue Briefs*. 30 September. https://reliefweb.int/sites/reliefweb.int/files/resources/issue_brief_return_task_force.pdf.

———. 2020c. COVID-19 Analytical Snapshot #54: Returning Migrants Update. 8 September. https://www.iom.int/sites/default/files/documents/covid-19_analytical_snapshot_54-_returning_migrants_update.pdf.

———. 2020d. COVID-19 Response. IOM Mission in Cambodia Situation Report. 13 April–15 May. https://www.iom.int/sites/default/files/situation_reports/file/covid-19_response_iom_cambodia_sitrep_13apr-15may_2020.pdf.

Japan International Trainee & Skilled Worker Cooperation Organization. 2019. Conclusion of Memorandum of Cooperation (MOC) on Specified Skilled Workers between the Governments of Japan and the Philippines. https://www.jitco.or.jp/en/news/article/588/.

Ladrido, P. 2020. How the Philippines Became the Biggest Supplier of Nurses Worldwide. *CNN Philippines*. 6 May. https://www.cnnphilippines.com/life/culture/2020/5/6/ofw-nurses.html.

Lemma, A. 2014. Tourism for Poverty Reduction in South Asia: What Works and Where Are the Gaps? July 2014. https://assets.publishing.service.gov.uk/media/57a089eee5274a27b2000323/Tourism_for_Poverty_Reduction_in_South_Asia_A_Lemma.pdf.

Leonir, N. and I. Laplace. 2016. Liberalization in Southeast Asia: Who Is Capturing the Markets?. WCTR 2016, World Conference on Transport Research. Shanghai, People's Republic of China. July 2016. Shanghai, China. https://hal.archives-ouvertes.fr/hal-01727424/document.

Manila Standard. 2020. PayPal Posts Strongest Growth as Consumers Shift to Digital Payments. 12 September. https://manilastandard.net/index.php/business/corporate/333966/paypal-posts-strongest-growth-as-consumers-shift-to-digital-payments.html.

Martinus, M. 2020. Shielding ASEAN Migrant Workers. *Bangkok Post*. 8 May. https://www.bangkokpost.com/opinion/opinion/1914580/shielding-asean-migrant-workers.

Massing, A. 2020. NZ Seasonal Workers Repatriation a Success. *Daily Post*. 26 June. https://dailypost.vu/news/nz-seasonal-workers-repatriation-a-success/article_d61179d8-b731-11ea-ade8-8b52547959da.html?fbclid=IwAR3nn3dWLCU6H9EdIRslEteGLX97rLZhxU8VhQzRb_ru8Kq7Em0Np7xnsgg.

McDonald, J. 2020. Australia to Open Travel Corridor for Seasonal Workers. *The Diplomat*. 24 August. https://thediplomat.com/2020/08/australia-to-open-travel-corridor-for-seasonal-workers/.

Medina, A. F. 2020a. Malaysia Issues Stimulus Package to Combat COVID-19 Impact. *ASEAN Briefing*. 19 March. https://www.aseanbriefing.com/news/malaysia-issues-stimulus-package-combat-covid-19-impact.

———. 2020b. More Incentives, Obligations Announced for Businesses in Cambodia in Tourism, Garment Industries. *ASEAN Briefing*. 7 May. https://www.aseanbriefing.com/news/incentives-obligations-announced-businesses-cambodia-tourism-garment-industries/.

———. 2020c. Thailand Issues Stimulus Packages to Boost Domestic Tourism. *ASEAN Briefing*. 9 July. https://www.aseanbriefing.com/news/thailand-issues-stimulus-packages-boost-domestic-tourism/.

———. 2020d. Cambodia Issues Additional Support for Workers and to Revive Economy. *ASEAN Briefing*. 5 August. https://www.aseanbriefing.com/news/cambodia-issues-additional-support-for-workers-and-to-revive-economy/.

———. 2020e. Thailand Issues Special Tourist Vias to Help Revive Economy. *ASEAN Briefing*. 7 October. https://www.aseanbriefing.com/news/thailand-issues-special-tourist-visas-to-help-revive-economy/.

———. 2020f. Cambodia Extends Incentives to Support Private Sector and Economy. *ASEAN Briefing*. 8 October. https://www.aseanbriefing.com/news/cambodia-extends-incentives-to-support-private-sector-and-economy/.

Millard, R. 2020. Millions of Migrant Workers Head Home Due to Virus: UN. *The Jakarta Post*. 25 June. https://www.thejakartapost.com/news/2020/06/25/millions-of-migrant-workers-head-home-due-to-virus-un.html.

Mohieldin, M. and D. Ratha. 2020. How to Keep Remittances Flowing. *Brookings Future Development Blog*. 11 June. https://www.brookings.edu/blog/future-development/2020/06/11/how-to-keep-remittances-flowing/.

Olsen, A. and V. Vorn. 2020. COVID-19: Impact on Cambodian Migrant Workers. *ILO Briefing Note*. Bangkok: International Labour Organization.

Organisation for Economic Co-operation and Development (OECD). 2020. *Tourism Policy Responses to the Coronavirus*. https://read.oecd-ilibrary.org/view/?ref=124_124984-7uf8nm95se&title=Covid-19_Tourism_Policy_Responses.

Pandey, P. R. 2020. COVID-19 and Remittance Inflows in Nepal. Center for International Private Enterprise. 4 September. https://www.cipe.org/wp-content/uploads/2020/09/PoshRajPandey_09042020.pdf.

Pannier, B. 2020. Uzbekistan's Coronavirus 'Success Story' Rapidly Falls Apart. *Radio Free Europe/Radio Liberty*. 30 June. https://www.rferl.org/a/uzbekistan-s-coronavirus-success-story-rapidly-falls-apart/30756514.html.

Parama, M. 2020. Govt to Disburse Rp3.3 Trillion Grant for Hard-Hit Tourist Industry. *The Jakarta Post*. 14 October. https://www.thejakartapost.com/news/2020/10/14/govt-to-disburse-rp3-3-trillion-grant-for-hard-hit-tourist-industry.html.

Pattison, P. and R. Sedhai. 2020. Covid-19 Lockdown Turns Qatar's Largest Migrant Camp into 'Virtual Prison'. *The Guardian*. 20 March. https://www.theguardian.com/global-development/2020/mar/20/covid-19-lockdown-turns-qatars-largest-migrant-camp-into-virtual-prison.

Philippine News Agency. 2020. PH Hosts 3rd Asean Meet on Tourism Professionals. 7 September. https://www.pna.gov.ph/articles/1114571.

Pollock, J. and A. T. Paing. 2020. COVID-19: Impact on Migrant Workers and Country Response in Myanmar. https://www.ilo.org/wcmsp5/groups/public/---asia/---ro-bangkok/---ilo-yangon/documents/briefingnote/wcms_749466.pdf.

Prasain, S. 2020. All Repatriation Flights Called Off for an Indefinite Period. *The Kathmandu Post*. 13 October. https://kathmandupost.com/national/2020/08/17/all-repatriation-flights-called-off-for-an-indefinite-period.

Radio New Zealand. 2020a. Quarantine Overload Forces Samoa Repatriation Pause. 5 August. https://www.rnz.co.nz/international/pacific-news/422842/quarantine-overload-forces-samoa-repatriation-pause.

———. 2020b. RSE Workers Stranded in NZ: "Tonga Needs to Look After Its Own Citizens" – Employer. 26 August. https://www.rnz.co.nz/news/country/424500/rse-workers-stranded-in-nz-tonga-needs-to-look-after-its-own-citizens-employer.

Rajan, S. I. and D. Narayana. 2012. The Financial Crisis in the Gulf and Its Impact on South Asian Migration Remittances. In S. Kelegama, R. Adhikari, P. Sharma, and P. Kharel, eds. *Regional Economic Integration: Challenges for South Asia during Turbulent Times (Edited volume)*. Kathmandu: South Asia Watch on Trade, Economics and Environment.

Ratha, D. and I. Sirkeci. 2010. Remittances and the Global Financial Crisis. *Migration Letters*. 7 (2). pp. 125–131. https://papers.ssrn.com/sol3/papers.cfm?abstract_id=1831716.

Ratha, D., S. De, E. J. Kim, S. Plaza, G. Seshan, and N. D. Yameogo. 2020. Migration and Development Brief 33: Phase II: COVID-19 Crisis through a Migration Lens. Washington, DC: KNOMAD-World Bank.

Roser, M., H. Ritchie, E. Ortiz-Ospina, and J. Hasell. 2020. Coronavirus Pandemic (COVID-19). OurWorldInData.org. https://ourworldindata.org/coronavirus (accessed January 2021).

Singer, D. 2008. Migrant Remittances, Financial Globalization, and Exchange Rate Regimes in the Developing World. Presented at the Federal Reserve Bank of Atlanta Conference on Remittances and the Macroeconomy. Atlanta. 21–22 February. https://www.frbatlanta.org/-/media/Documents/news/conferences/2008/08remittances/Singer.pdf.

Sirkeci, I., D. Ratha, and J. Cohen. 2012. Introduction: Remittance Flows and Practices during the Crisis. https://www.researchgate.net/publication/282217656_Introduction_Remittance_Flows_and_Practices_during_the_Crisis.

South Pacific Tourism Organization. 2019. *2018 Annual Visitor Arrivals Report*. Suva.

———. 2020. *Pacific Tourism: COVID 19 Impact & Recovery*. May. https://corporate.southpacificislands.travel/wp-content/uploads/2020/05/Pacific-Tourism-Sector-Status-report-Final.pdf.

Testaverde. 2020. Social Protection for Migrants During the COVID-19 Crisis: The Right and Smart Choice. *World Bank Blogs*. 28 April. https://blogs.worldbank.org/voices/social-protection-migrants-during-covid-19-crisis-right-and-smart-choice.

The Workers Rights. 2020. Seoul Announces Relief Fund for Migrant Workers. 1 September. https://www.theworkersrights.com/seoul-announces-relief-fund-for-migrant-workers/.

United Nations. Department of Economic and Social Affairs, Statistics Division. 1998. Recommendations on Statistics of International Migration. *Statistical Papers*. Series M, No. 58, Rev. 1. New York.

United Nations. Department of Economic and Social Affairs, Population Division. International Migrant Stock: The 2019 Revision. https://www.un.org/en/development/desa/population/migration/data/estimates2/estimates19.asp (accessed May 2020).

———. World Population Prospects 2019. https://population.un.org/wpp/Download/Standard/Population/ (accessed April 2020).

United Nations Statistical Commission. 2007. *2008 International Recommendations for Tourism Statistics*. New York/Madrid.

United Nations World Tourism Organization (UNWTO). 2020a. Tourism Satellite Accounts. https://www.unwto.org/statistics (accessed September 2020).

———. 2020b. *COVID-19 Related Travel Restrictions. A Global Review for Tourism.* https://webunwto.s3.eu-west-1.amazonaws.com/s3fs-public/2020-04/TravelRestrictions%20-%2028%20April.pdf.

———. 2020c. *The Impacts of COVID-19 on Tourism.* Manila.

———. 2020d. COVID-19: Measures to Support Travel and Tourism. https://www.unwto.org/covid-19-measures-to-support-travel-tourism.

———. 2020e. *World Tourism Barometer.* 18 (4). July 2020 Update. https://www.e-unwto.org/doi/epdf/10.18111/wtobarometereng.2020.18.1.4.

———. 2020f. Compendium of Tourism Statistics Dataset (Electronic data updated 21 September 2020). Madrid.

———. 2020g. Global and Regional Tourism Performance. https://www.unwto.org/global-and-regionaltourism-performance (accessed September 2020).

World Bank. 2020. COVID-19: Remittance Flows to Shrink 14% by 2021. Press release. 29 October. https://www.worldbank.org/en/news/press-release/2020/10/29/covid-19-remittance-flows-to-shrink-14-by-2021.

———. World Development Indicators Database. https://databank.worldbank.org/source/world-development-indicators (accessed October 2020).

———. Remittances Prices Worldwide. http://remittanceprices.worldbank.org (accessed November 2020).

World Health Organization. National Health Workforce Accounts. https://apps.who.int/nhwaportal/ (accessed September 2020).

World Travel & Tourism Council (WTTC). 2020. Economic Impact Reports. https://wttc.org/Research/Economic-Impact (accessed August 2020).

6 Asia-Pacific Regional Cooperation and Integration Index

Regional Integration Moving Ahead as Measured by Integration Index

The Asia-Pacific Regional Cooperation and Integration Index (ARCII) is a broad-based, multidimensional measure of regional integration. The index, established in 2017, tracks progress on a set of relevant dimensions of regional integration, and identifies strengths and weaknesses at regional, subregional, and national levels. The ARCII is composed of 26 indicators that measure regional integration along six dimensions: (i) trade and investment, (ii) money and finance, (iii) regional value chains, (iv) infrastructure and connectivity, (v) movement of people, and (vi) institutional and social integration (Huh and Park 2018). The index covers Asian Development Bank (ADB) member countries in Asia, which include 46 developing member economies along with Japan, Australia, and New Zealand.[58]

Figure 6.1: Overall ARCII and Dimensional Indexes—Asia

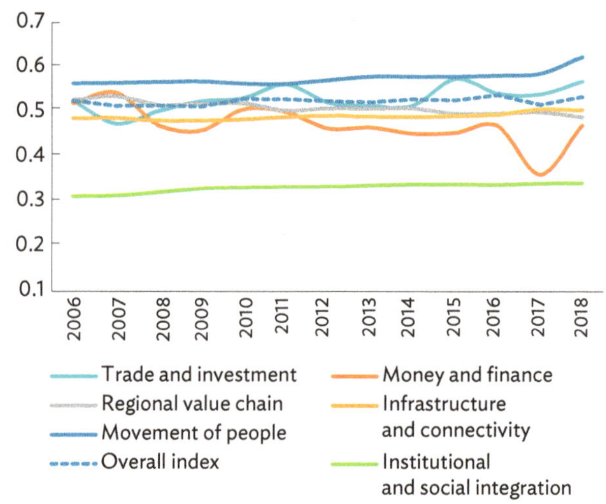

ARCII = Asia-Pacific Regional Cooperation and Integration Index.

Source: ADB. Asia-Pacific Regional Cooperation and Integration Index Database. https://aric.adb.org/database/arcii (accessed October 2020).

Key Regional Integration Trends in Asia

Latest ARCII estimates indicate that regional integration in Asia rose slightly in 2018, due mainly to the rebound in the money and finance dimension (Figure 6.1). Regional monetary and financial integration plunged in 2017 due to fluctuations in two indicators: interest rates dispersion and cross-border equity liabilities. The dispersion in regional interest rates is explained by increases in global interest rates since 2016, mainly led by the United States (US) Federal Reserve (Federal Reserve Bank of New York 2020), without corresponding surges in Asian economies, particularly East Asia, Oceania, and the Pacific. Gradual interest rate hikes in Asia along with global interest rates came in 2018, leading to less regional dispersion and higher financial integration.[59] Likewise, a noticeable dip followed by a recovery during 2017–2018 was observed in cross-border equity liabilities for Central Asia, Oceania, and South Asia.

Meanwhile, movement of people, infrastructure and connectivity, and trade and investment continued to drive regional integration in Asia (Figure 6.2). The contribution of indicators for each of the six dimensions remained

[58] For a more information on the ARCII database, methodology, and definitions, see ADB. Asia Regional Integration Center. ARCII. https://aric.adb.org/database/arcii. Asia refers to Asia and the Pacific.

[59] The contribution of this indicator to the money and finance dimension doubled from 9% to 18% during the same period.

broadly stable, with a slight increase in the contribution of the proportion of intraregional countries that do not require an entry visa, in the movement of people dimension, from 19% in 2017 to 22% in 2018.

Figure 6.2: Dimensional Contribution to the ARCII

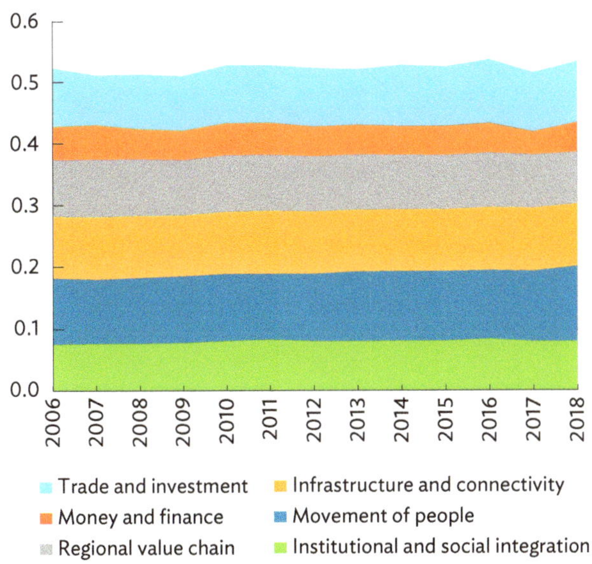

ARCII = Asia-Pacific Regional Cooperation and Integration Index.

Note: Dimensional contribution is computed as the weight of the dimension multiplied by the dimensional score.

Source: ADB. Asia-Pacific Regional Cooperation and Integration Index Database. https://aric.adb.org/database/arcii (accessed October 2020).

In 2018, overall regional integration in Asia increased for almost all subregions (Figure 6.3a). Southeast Asia remains the most integrated subregional group within the entire Asian region. Meanwhile, the slight drop in East Asia's overall regional integration could partly be due to policy challenges in the infrastructure and connectivity dimension, including the need to improve cross-border transit with the Central Asia Regional Economic Cooperation (CAREC) Program and the Greater Mekong Subregion (ADB 2019b).

Asian subregions continued to display wide-ranging performance in regional integration across dimensions (Figure 6.3b). For instance, East Asia scored highest in the dimensions of money and finance, infrastructure and connectivity, regional value chain, and institutional and social integration. East Asia's prominence in the regional value chain dimension may be explained by strong and well-integrated regional production networks in manufacturing (ADB 2019b). Meanwhile, Southeast Asia outperformed other subregions in trade and investment and movement of people. Southeast Asia's performance in trade and investment may be driven by trade intensity with regional partners, considering that approximately 60% of its trade were with economies in Asia (UNESCAP 2018).

Finally, South Asia and Central Asia trailed the other subregions in most dimensions (Figure 6.3b). However, ongoing initiatives promoting energy trade and enhancing multimodal transport networks in South Asia are poised to generate direct benefits and spillover effects for countries within the region. For instance, the construction of a pipeline corridor between Bangladesh and India is expected to boost energy trade and supply of crude oil. South Asian countries have also allotted sizable investments in developing ports and airports to increase capacity (ADB 2019b). While the ARCII does not cover the Russian Federation and Islamic Republic Iran, important economic partners of Central Asian economies, the index may underestimate the degree of regional cooperation and integration in Central Asia. The construction of a Eurasia index aims to address this and provide a more complete picture for this subregion (Box 6.1).

The ARCII also shows the degree of regional cooperation and integration (RCI) in Asia's subregional initiatives across the six RCI dimensions. The Association of Southeast Asian Nations (ASEAN) exhibits the highest degree of subregional cooperation and integration, particularly strong in trade and investment and movement of people (Figure 6.4). Ongoing projects promoting border economic zones support the subregion's efforts to establish effective RCI linkages between the People's Republic of China (PRC) and ASEAN, aimed at improving mobility of goods and services, as well as people (ADB 2019b).[60] Initiatives to improve the tourism sector have also taken place, particularly to improve the mobility of tourism professionals and high-potential tourism market segments such as gastronomy and cruise tourism) (ASEAN Secretariat 2019).

60 Several of these ADB-funded projects include the Guangxi RCI Promotion Investment Program, the Yunnan Lincang Border Economic Cooperation Zone Development project, and the Mongolia's Regional Improvement of Border Services (RIBS) project.

Figure 6.3: Overall ARCII—Asia Subregions

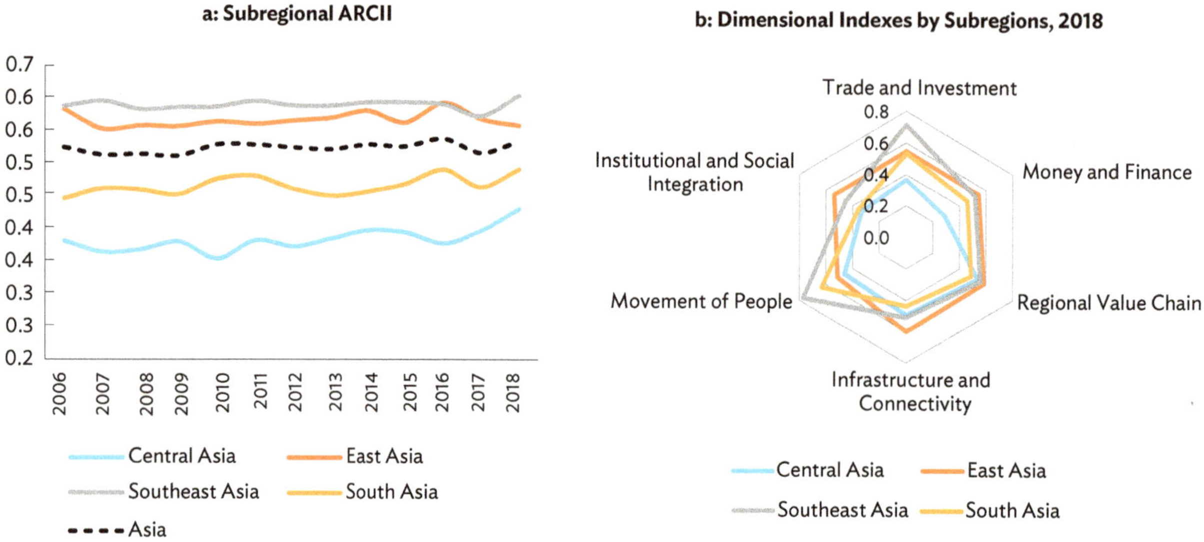

ARCII = Asia-Pacific Regional Cooperation and Integration Index.

Source: ADB. Asia-Pacific Regional Cooperation and Integration Index Database. https://aric.adb.org/database/arcii (accessed October 2020).

The Greater Mekong Subregion (GMS) shows a similar trajectory to ASEAN. Connectivity in this subregion is expected to be further strengthened by initiatives such as the Ha Noi Action Plan 2018–2020 and the GMS Transport Sector Strategy 2030. South Asia Subregional Economic Cooperation (SASEC)—driven mainly by movement of people, trade and investment, and regional value chains—comes third. For this subregional initiative, improvements in transport linkages with nearby subregions are expected from joint initiatives with the South Asian Association for Regional Cooperation and the Bay of Bengal Initiative for Multi-Sectoral Technical and Economic Cooperation (ADB 2019a). Finally, CAREC appears to be the least regionally integrated initiative. This is especially clear in the trade and investment dimension, where CAREC member countries exhibit more volatility (del Rosario 2019). Addressing connectivity gaps, trade linkages, and boosting tourism (e.g., relaxing visa policies) remain a priority for countries in these subregional initiatives (ADB 2019b). Recent developments for CAREC suggest a more encouraging picture, including the region surpassing its Transport and Trade Facilitation Strategy 2020 targets, increasing port capacity, and higher energy trade flows in the Central Asian Power System (ADB 2019b).

Regional integration indexes were also constructed for other regions worldwide. As expected, the European Union (EU) remains the global leader in regional integration (Figure 6.5). The EU was strongest in institutional and social integration, given its solid economic and monetary union institutions, highly integrated labor markets, and established institutional framework for education, research and innovation, security, agriculture and environmental

Figure 6.4: Dimensional Subindexes by Subregional Cooperation Initiatives, 2018

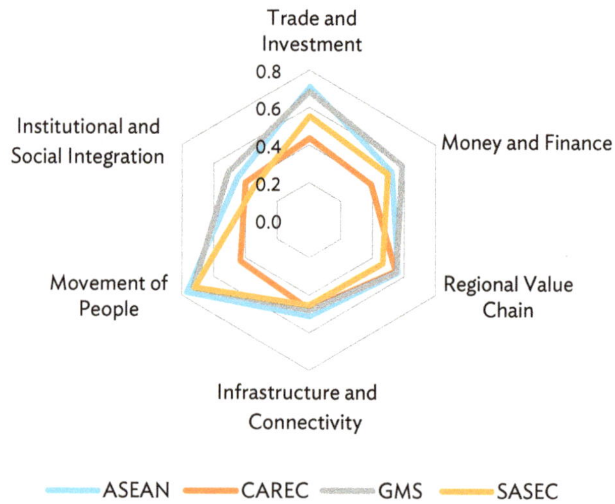

ASEAN = Association of Southeast Asian Nations, CAREC = Central Asia Regional Economic Cooperation, GMS = Greater Mekong Subregion, SASEC = South Asia Subregional Economic Cooperation.

Source: ADB. Asia-Pacific Regional Cooperation and Integration Index Database. https://aric.adb.org/database/arcii (accessed October 2020).

Figure 6.5: Regional Integration Index, 2018—Asia versus Other Regions

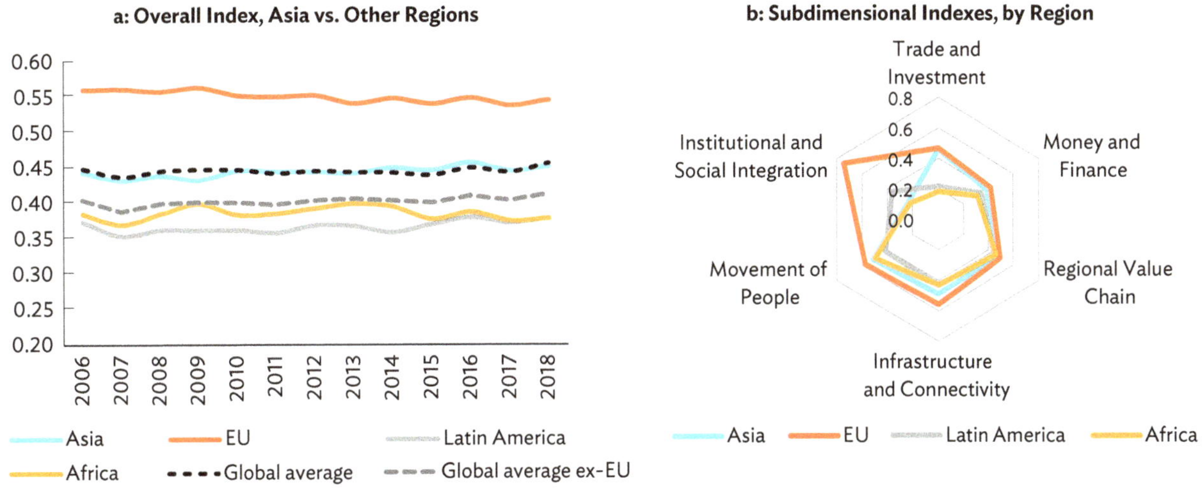

EU = European Union.

Source: ADB. Asia-Pacific Regional Cooperation and Integration Index Database. https://aric.adb.org/database/arcii (accessed October 2020).

regulation, which position the EU at the forefront of regional cooperation and integration (European Commission 2019). Meanwhile, Asia comes second to the EU and coincides with the global average. In particular, Asia's dimensional scores on trade and investment and regional value chains equal those of the EU over time. The main Asia–EU gaps are on the monetary and financial dimension—where some convergence has occurred in recent years—and infrastructure and connectivity. Latin America outperformed Asia in institutional and social integration, while Africa continued to score the lowest in almost all dimensions.

The Enhanced ARCII Framework

The index structure has been strengthened to accommodate new approaches to the measurement of regional cooperation and integration in Asia.

Key Messages

- The channels of regional cooperation and integration are changing. While countries in Asia have made significant progress in RCI, the nature and pillars of regional cooperation and integration are evolving.
- Digital technologies are determining new forms of connectivity with significant impacts on regional integration. Trends in indicators of technological sharing and digital connectivity show that Asia is increasingly integrated through these channels.
- Regional public goods (RPGs) are also increasingly important, particularly in the area of environmental cooperation, which is evolving, for example, through the inclusion of environmental provisions in trade and investment agreements and environmental goods trade.

Rationale for a new framework. As the channels of regional cooperation and integration expand, the enhanced ARCII framework aims to reflect these by including new relevant dimensions and new indicators to existing ones (Figure 6.6). Two new dimensions are now part of the enhanced ARCII framework: (i) technology and digital connectivity, and (ii) environmental cooperation/regional public goods (Figure 6.7). The technology and digital dimension naturally responds to the growing role of digital technologies in economic activity, which had not been fully captured in other dimensions; it also aims to reflect regional progress in research and technological exchange. The environmental cooperation/RPGs dimension, on the other hand, provides a basis for assessing regional environmental performance

Box 6.1: Emerging Trends in Regional Integration in Eurasia: The Eurasia Integration Index

Whereas indexes provide an overview of regional and subregional performance in regional cooperation and integration (RCI), understanding the underlying factors involves a more comprehensive assessment of historical, institutional, and political factors behind these trends. To improve their interpretation and comparability, RCI metrics should consider different initial conditions, economic systems, production structures, and even extraregional linkages (Huh and Park 2020).

As a pilot to improve the usefulness of the Asia-Pacific Regional Cooperation and Integration Index (ARCII) in a subregional context, the Eurasia Integration Index (EII) applies the ARCII methodology to the subregion covering the three countries of the South Caucasus (Armenia, Azerbaijan, and Georgia), the five Central Asia countries (Kazakhstan, the Kyrgyz Republic, Tajikistan, Turkmenistan, and Uzbekistan), and the Russian Federation (which is not an Asian Development Bank member).

Several developments have driven RCI in Eurasia in recent years: First, the establishment of the Eurasian Economic Union in 2015 by Armenia, Belarus, Kazakhstan, the Kyrgyz Republic, and the Russian Federation provided a framework for the free movement of goods, services, capital, and labor among the member countries and policy coordination in areas that included macroeconomic management, foreign trade, agriculture, industry, transport, energy, and investment (Eurasian Economic Commission 2019). Second, the creation in 2011 of the Commonwealth of Independent States free trade area between Armenia, Kazakhstan, the Kyrgyz Republic, the Russian Federation, Tajikistan, and Uzbekistan—along with Belarus, Moldova, and Ukraine—was also a major step toward higher integration in the Eurasia region. Third, regional integration between Eurasia and the People's Republic of China (PRC) has advanced considerably in recent years. The Eurasian Economic Union and the PRC concluded a trade and economic cooperation agreement in 2019. Eurasian countries have supported projects of the Belt and Road Initiative of the PRC.[a] They collaborate within the framework of regional organizations and programs including the Central Asia Regional Economic Cooperation (CAREC) Program and the Shanghai Cooperation Organization (SCO).

Following the methodology of Park and Claveria (2018), the Eurasia Integration Index was estimated for 2006–2017. The estimation generated intraregional scores for Asia (inclusive of Eurasia) and intra-subregional scores for Eurasia alone. To ensure coverage, the index excludes the money and finance dimension due to lack of financial indicators data.

Preliminary results are broadly consistent with recent developments described above. In general, Eurasian countries became more engaged in RCI both within Eurasia and the Asian region over 2006–2017 (box table). Increases in RCI scores in Armenia, Kazakhstan, the Russian Federation, Tajikistan, and Uzbekistan within Eurasia reflect the effect of regional cooperation mechanisms such as the Eurasian Economic Union and the Commonwealth of Independent States free trade area. Increases in most Eurasian countries' scores for RCI within Asia are due largely to increasing integration between Eurasia and the PRC, with some countries, including Georgia and Turkmenistan, reorienting their trade linkages in this direction.

Eurasia Integration Index, based on ARCII Methodology

	Overall Integration			
	With Asia		Within Eurasia	
	2006	2017	2006	2017
Armenia	0.327	0.353	0.496	0.543
Azerbaijan	0.306	0.342	0.481	0.555
Georgia	0.341	0.372	0.579	0.544
Kazakhstan	0.381	0.464	0.639	0.653
Kyrgyz Republic	0.379	0.39	0.645	0.603
Tajikistan	0.338	0.399	0.524	0.612
Turkmenistan	0.215	0.316	0.483	0.399
Uzbekistan	0.443	0.431	0.515	0.646
Russian Federation	0.391	0.451	0.324	0.423
Eurasia	0.347	0.391	0.521	0.553

ARCII = Asia-Pacific Regional Cooperation and Integration Index.

Source: ADB (forthcoming).

These preliminary results suggest that, over the past decade, Eurasian countries made major strides in regional integration. Furthermore, as reflected by the index scores within Asia, RCI between Eurasian countries and the PRC increased significantly. An in-depth analysis of the underlying data will allow to assess how accurately the index scores capture different aspects of RCI in Eurasia. Such an analysis will help determine future improvements on the methodology and data sources to make the index more useful to researchers and policy makers monitoring RCI.

[a] See Kohli, Linn, and Zacker (2020) for a review of Belt and Road Initiative projects in Central Asia and the South Caucasus.

Source: ADB (forthcoming).

Figure 6.6: Proposed ARCII Enhanced Framework

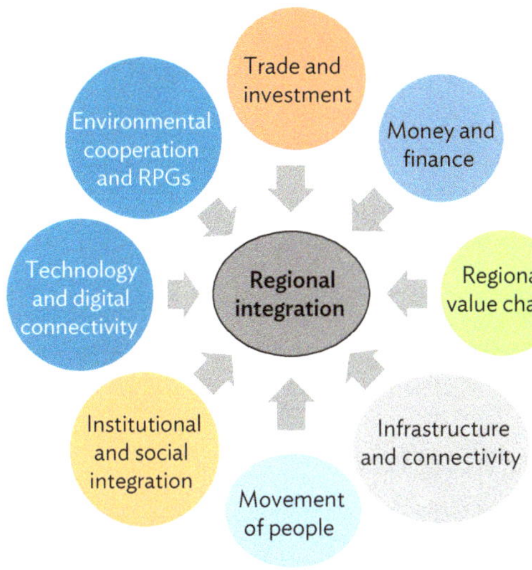

ARCII = Asia-Pacific Regional Cooperation and Integration Index, RPGs = regional public goods.

Source: ADB (2020).

Figure 6.7: Proposed New Dimensions in the ARCII Enhanced Framework

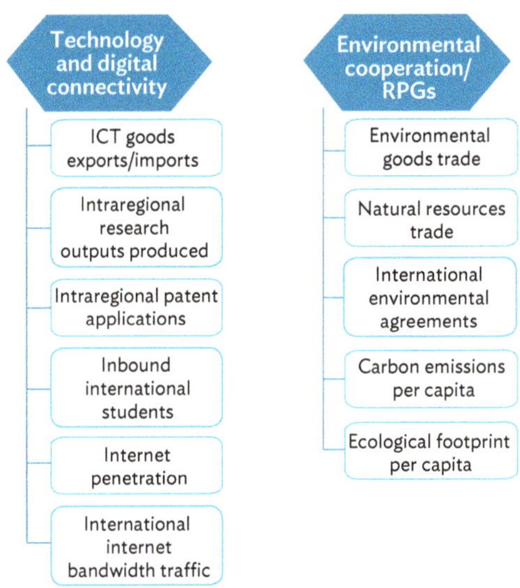

ARCII = Asia-Pacific Regional Cooperation and Integration Index, ICT = information and communication technology, RPGs = regional public goods.

Source: ADB (2020).

in the context of regional cooperation. In a similar vein, UNESCAP (2020) proposes a framework for measuring sustainable regional integration and digital economy integration in the Asian region. In line with the theme chapter of this year's report, this section introduces only a subgroup of indicators in the digital dimension.

Improving indicators in existing dimensions. To ensure that ARCII dimensions adequately capture the underlying RCI dynamics, new indicators are included into existing dimensions (Figure 6.8). New indicators in the money and finance dimension ensure better coverage for Asian countries and aim to capture regional financial vulnerabilities and exchange rate co-movement. Including the Chinn-Ito index as a measure of capital account openness allows the index to determine how lesser restrictions on capital movements affect financial integration, while a measure of exchange rate co-movements provides information on regional synchronization and transmission channels. The regional value chain dimension will be strengthened by a value-added indicator that captures the region's participation in global value chains. A new indicator of international flight passengers is incorporated into the infrastructure and connectivity dimension to account for the role of air transport connectivity in promoting greater access to the global economy, which could further enable economic integration. Indicators for trade on cultural goods and services, trademark applications, and intergovernmental organizations are now also part of the framework.

The enhanced ARCII framework will allow for more flexibility in the inclusion or exclusion of dimensions and indicators. The original six-dimensional ARCII, from now on referred to as the baseline index, will still be reported and shall serve as a comparable series to previous releases, whereas the proposed eight-dimensional ARCII will be an extended version. In addition, the ARCII will be customized for specific needs and priorities of subregions or country groups, including for relevant indicators. Table 6.1 provides the complete list of dimensions and indicators in the enhanced framework. Meanwhile, Box 6.2 provides a description of current ADB initiatives to improve RCI measurement.

Figure 6.8: Proposed New Indicators for Existing Dimensions in the ARCII Enhanced Framework

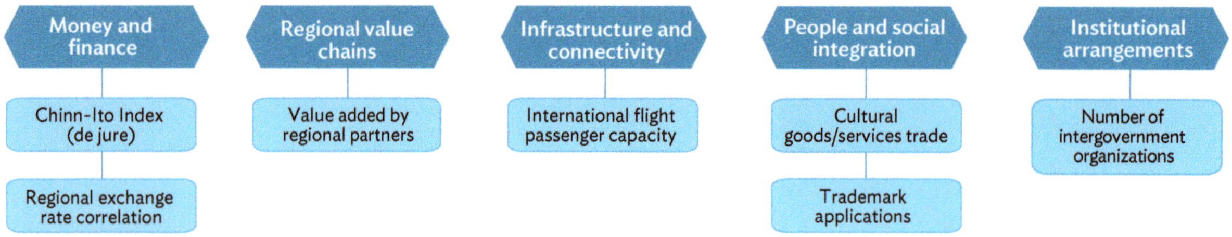

ARCII = Asia-Pacific Regional Cooperation and Integration Index.

Source: ADB (2020).

Table 6.1: Dimensions and Indicators under the Proposed Enhanced ARCII Framework

Dimension	Indicator	
I. Trade and Investment Integration	I-a	Proportion of intraregional goods exports to total goods exports
	I-b	Proportion of intraregional goods imports to total goods imports
	I-c	Intraregional trade intensity index
	I-d	Proportion of intraregional FDI inflows to total FDI inflows
	I-e	Proportion of intraregional FDI inflows plus outflows to total FDI inflows plus outflows
II. Money and Finance Integration	II-a	Proportion of intraregional cross-border equity liabilities to total cross-border equity liabilities
	II-b	Proportion of intraregional cross-border bond liabilities to total cross-border bond liabilities
	II-c	Pair-wise dispersion of deposit rates averaged regionally relative to that averaged globally
	II-d*	Capital account openness: Chinn–Ito Index (de jure)
	II-e	Correlations of exchange rates vis-à-vis US dollar averaged regionally minus those averaged globally
III. Regional Value Chain	III-a	Ratio between the averaged trade complementarity index over regional trading partners and the averaged trade complementarity index over all trading partners
	III-b	Ratio between the averaged trade concentration index over regional trading partners and the averaged trade concentration index over all trading partners
	III-c	Proportion of intraregional intermediate goods exports to total intraregional goods exports
	III-d	Proportion of intraregional intermediate goods imports to total intraregional goods imports
IV. Infrastructure and Connectivity	IV-a	Ratio between the averaged trade cost over regional trading partners and the averaged trade cost over all trading partners
	IV-b	Ratio between the averaged liner shipping connectivity index over regional trading partners and the averaged liner shipping connectivity index over all trading partners
	IV-c	Proportion of passenger seats sold on regional flights to those sold on all international flights
	IV-d*	Logistics Performance Index (overall)
	IV-e*	Doing Business Index (overall)
V. Technology and Digital Connectivity	V-a	Proportion of intraregional ICT goods exports to total ICT exports
	V-a.2	Proportion of intraregional ICT goods imports to total ICT imports
	V-b	Research outputs with intraregional collaborators relative to research outputs with all international collaborators
	V-c	Patent applications made with intraregional residents relative to patent applications made with all foreign residents
	V-d	Proportion of inbound international students within the region relative to all inbound international students
	V-e*	Proportion of persons using the internet
	V-f*	International internet bandwidth
	V-g	Ratio between the average internet bandwidth with intraregional countries and the average internet bandwidth with all countries

continued on next page

Table 6.1 continued

Dimension	Indicator	
VI. People and Social Integration	VI-a	Proportion of intraregional outbound migration to total outbound migration
	VI-b	Proportion of intraregional tourists to total tourists (inbound plus outbound)
	VI-c	Proportion of intraregional remittances to total remittances
	VI-d	Cultural proximity with interregional countries relative to that with all other countries
	VI-e	Proportion of intraregional cultural goods trade (exports plus imports) to all cultural goods trade
	VI-f	Trademark applications made with intraregional residents relative to trademark applications made with all foreign residents
VII. Institutional Arrangements	VII-a	Proportion of intraregional countries that have signed FTAs with
	VII-b	Proportion of intraregional countries that have an embassy
	VII-c	Proportion of intraregional countries that have signed business investment treaties with
	VII-d	Proportion of intraregional countries that have signed double taxation treaties with
	VII-e*	Number of international intergovernment organizations in which a country is a member
	VII-f	Proportion of intraregional countries that do not require an entry visa to the total number of intraregional countries
VIII. Environmental Cooperation	VIII-a	Proportion of intraregional environmental goods trade (exports plus imports) to total intraregional goods trade
	VIII-b	Proportion of interregional natural resources trade (exports plus imports) to total intraregional goods trade
	VIII-c*	Number of international environmental agreements ratified
	VIII-d*	Carbon emissions (metric tons per capita)
	VIII-e*	Ecological footprint of imports and exports as a share of biocapacity

ARCII = Asia-Pacific Regional Cooperation and Integration Index, FDI = foreign direct investment, FTA = free trade agreement, ICT = information and communication technology, US = United States.

Notes: Highlighted cells indicate new dimensions or indicators included in the enhanced ARCII framework. Indicators marked with an asterisk are national-level indicators.

Source: Asian Development Bank.

Box 6.2: Recent Initiatives among Subregional Programs for Improving RCI Measurement

The Asian Development Bank regional departments and subregional programs are producing metrics of regional cooperation and integration (RCI) to help monitor progress and address the gaps and challenges specific to each subregion.

In 2017, the Greater Mekong Subregion (GMS) established a statistical database that includes economic and sector indicators to monitor RCI.[a] The Brunei Darussalam–Indonesia–Malaysia–Philippines East ASEAN Growth Area and the Indonesia–Malaysia–Thailand Growth Triangle have also developed statistical working groups to institutionalize the data collection process with national statistics offices. The GMS is developing a new statistical framework with sector groups, including energy and education, to improve the availability of RCI indicators. There are also efforts aimed toward improving the quality of existing RCI indicators by ensuring consistency, strengthening database management, and institutionalizing mechanisms for data production and dissemination. These have helped improved data comparability across years and countries.

Operational indicators, as well as contract awards and disbursements, are used in South Asia Subregional Economic Cooperation (SASEC) to measure RCI progress. National indicators with implications for cross-border connectivity have also been used. For example, for trade facilitation projects, indicators include improvements in cargo clearance time. Transport, energy, and economic corridor development indicators focus on national targets (e.g., increases in traffic of project roads and electricity access rates). Regional indicators include intraregional trade share, customs revenues in the subregion, and growth of cross-border power flows. SASEC is also taking a sector approach to RCI indicators. In transport, examples include connectivity measures, such as the length (in kilometers) of SASEC corridor roads meeting AH1 standards, the use of regional ports to handle cargo, and the number of flying passengers between regional airports. In trade facilitation, trade efficiency is measured through regional trade agreements (e.g., negative list of products) and mutual recognition indicators.

continued on next page

Box 6.2: Recent Initiatives among Subregional Programs for Improving RCI Measurement *(continued)*

For Central Asia Regional Economic Cooperation (CAREC), the CAREC Regional Integration Index (CRII) was developed and used as a measure to monitor progress on the CAREC 2030 Strategy. CRII results suggest that policies promoting trade openness, regulatory reforms to formalize informal trade, and financial reform must be put in place.

In the case of the Pacific countries, common RCI issues involve the fisheries, environment, trade, and tourism sectors. Current data gaps, particularly in the money and finance dimension, pose an issue in capturing the level of financial development. To resolve this, the subregion is continuously improving the collection of the data to address these gaps.

[a] Greater Mekong Subregion Statistical Database. https://www.greatermekong.org/stats/index-static.php (accessed November 2020).

Source: ADB (2020).

Technology and Digital Connectivity: A New Lens for Exploring Recent Integration Trends

Key Messages

- Trends in technology sharing in Asia have improved over the past 15 years, with an increase in regional collaboration in research outputs and patent applications.

- Improvements in digital connectivity in Asia are remarkable over the same period, with overall increasing internet penetration and well-established intraregional bilateral bandwidth among countries in the region. Still, the gaps in access and quality remain important for a number of countries.

Asia has made significant progress toward regional integration, driven by trade and investment, increasing participation in global production networks and better infrastructure. As in other spheres, digital technologies are redefining these same channels and creating new ones. Technology sharing and collaboration on research and development are, for instance, driving innovation. E-commerce and digital trade are adapting to consumer behavior and the coronavirus disease (COVID-19) is marking a turning point for the digital transformation (see Chapter 8: Making Digital Platforms Work for Asia and the Pacific). The following section describes some of the indicators in the enhanced ARCII framework that intended to capture these effects.

Asian economies have improved on their regional collaboration through research outputs. Research collaboration and innovation among regional partners can have beneficial effects (Guerrero Bote, Olmeda-Gómez, and Moya-Anegón 2013). Indicators on technology transfer through research in Asia and the Pacific show a steady increasing trend since 2006, with the Pacific and Southeast Asia having the highest share of research outputs produced with intraregional collaborators relative to its total, followed by South Asia and Central Asia. Meanwhile, research collaboration among regional peers is lower in Oceania and in East Asia, which is explained by higher extraregional research collaboration in these subregions (Figure 6.9).

At the subregional level, research collaboration has gradually increased in subregional initiatives, including CAREC, GMS, and SASEC subregional programs. In 2018, around half of the total research output produced from international collaboration were made with regional collaborators (Figure 6.9). In comparison to some subregions, collaboration within CAREC, SASEC, and GMS seems to be stronger. Individual country performance also suggests large heterogeneity in research outputs across Asia. The PRC and Australia have encouraged collaboration among local researchers within Asia, with the PRC producing

Figure 6.9: Research Outputs with Intraregional Collaboration
(% of total international collaboration)

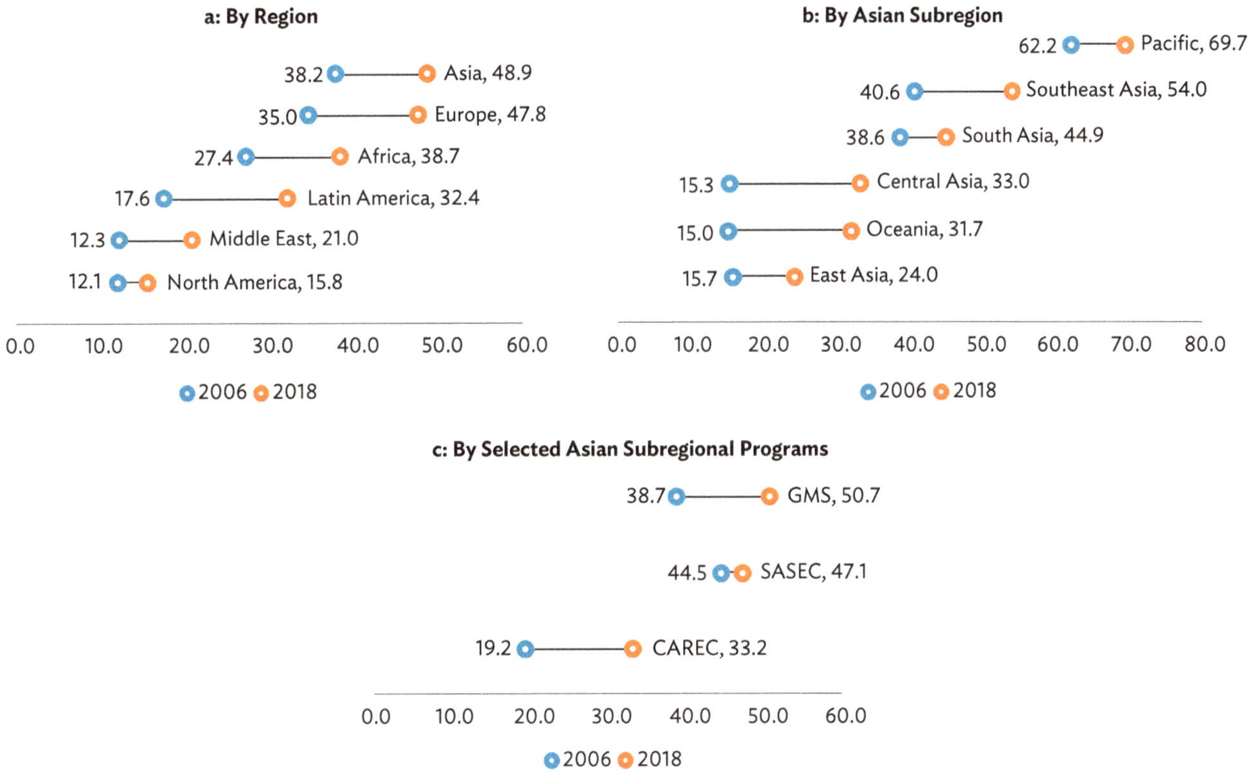

CAREC = Central Asia Regional Economic Cooperation, GMS = Greater Mekong Subregion, SASEC = South Asia Subregional Economic Cooperation.

Source: ADB calculations using data from Clarivate Analytics. Web of Science Database. https://www.webofknowledge.com (accessed August 2020).

an average of more than 27,000 research outputs, and Australia more than 17,000, from 2015 to 2018. Other countries in Asia (e.g., Japan, the Republic of Korea, India, Singapore) have also enlarged the pool of intraregional research outputs (Figure 6.10).[61]

Intraregional patent applications in Asia have been consistently high, with clear gaps among subregions. Patterns of registration of patent applications can reflect synergies for research production and innovation at the regional level applications.[62] Europe's share has gradually declined from 19% to 4% between 2006 and 2018. Meanwhile, Asia has maintained its share within the 80% to 95% range over the same period (Figure 6.11). Within Asia, East Asia has filed the greatest number of intraregional patent applications relative to its total, with Southeast Asia's share catching up in recent years. The top three countries in the region are all from East Asia, led by the PRC with almost more than 1.4 million applications filed in 2018 (Figure 6.12).

61 In the ARCII methodology, intraregional research is defined as research outputs produced with intraregional collaborators considering the author's affiliation rather than nationality. For instance, a publication produced by an Asian researcher affiliated with an institution in the United States counts in favor of the United States. Meanwhile, if an Asian researcher based in the United States coauthored a paper with a researcher in Canada, this counts as an intraregional research output for the US (North America region). The equivalent ARCII indicator is computed as a ratio between the number of research outputs with intraregional collaborators relative to research outputs with all international collaborators.

62 The ARCII indicator is computed as the number of patent applications made with intraregional residents relative to patent applications made with all foreign residents.

Figure 6.10: Number of Intraregional Research Outputs in Asia

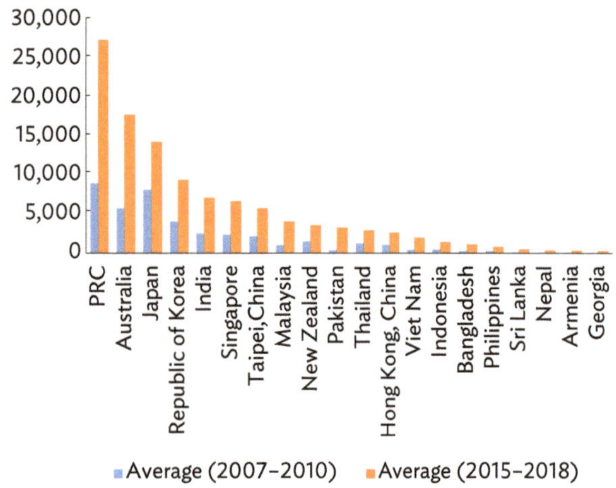

PRC = People's Republic of China.

Note: Refer to research outputs from the Science Citation Index Expanded collection, with all languages, and all research output included.

Source: ADB calculations using data from Clarivate Analytics. Web of Science Database. https://www.webofknowledge.com (accessed August 2020).

Figure 6.12: Number of Intraregional Patent Applications in Selected Asian Economies ('000)

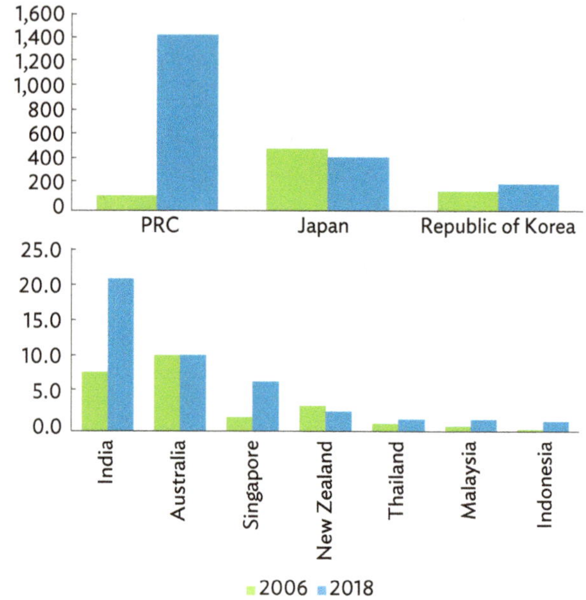

PRC = People's Republic of China.

Source: ADB calculations using data from World Intellectual Property Organization (WIPO). WIPO Statistics Database. https://www3.wipo.int/ipstats/ (accessed May 2020).

Figure 6.11: Intraregional Patent Applications
(% of total patent applications made with all foreign residents)

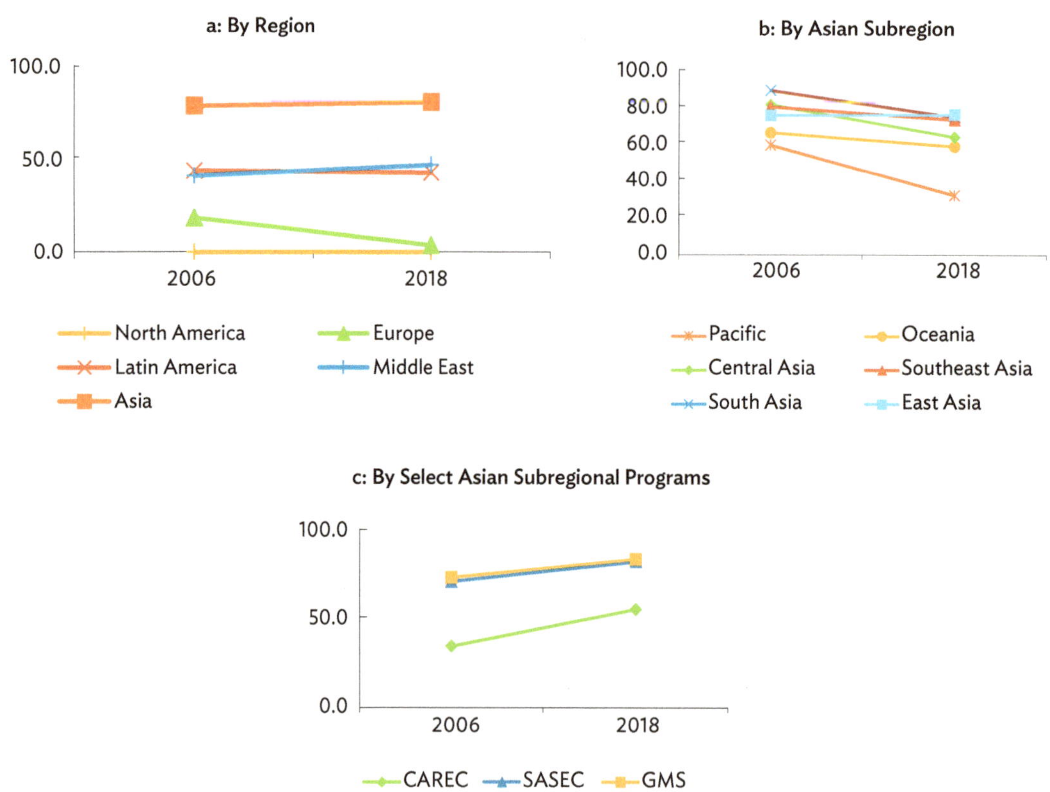

CAREC = Central Asia Regional Economic Cooperation, GMS = Greater Mekong Subregion, SASEC = South Asia Subregional Economic Cooperation.

Source: ADB calculations using data from World Intellectual Property Organization (WIPO). WIPO Statistics Database. https://www3.wipo.int/ipstats/ (accessed May 2020).

Digital connectivity in Asia has increased, with rising internet penetration, but large subregional gaps persist. Greater access to online resources through internet connectivity allows consumers, businesses, and governments to gain wider and better access to goods and services beyond geographic borders. Overall, global trends in internet penetration show a steady increase over the last decade, with significant gaps among regions (Figure 6.13). However, looking at the proportion of the population using the internet, Asia lags behind most regions. More than half of the populations of North America, Europe, and the Middle East had access to the internet by 2013, whereas for Asia, only in 2018 did the region reach the same level.

Within Asia, progress on digital connectivity varies across economies, with a significant improvement over the past decade (Figure 6.14). While economies like Australia; Hong Kong, China; Japan; New Zealand; and the Republic of Korea have an average internet penetration rate of more than 85%, the Pacific countries—including Kiribati, Papua New Guinea, and Solomon Islands—continue to struggle, with fewer than 15% of their populations having internet access.

Figure 6.13: Internet Penetration (% of population)

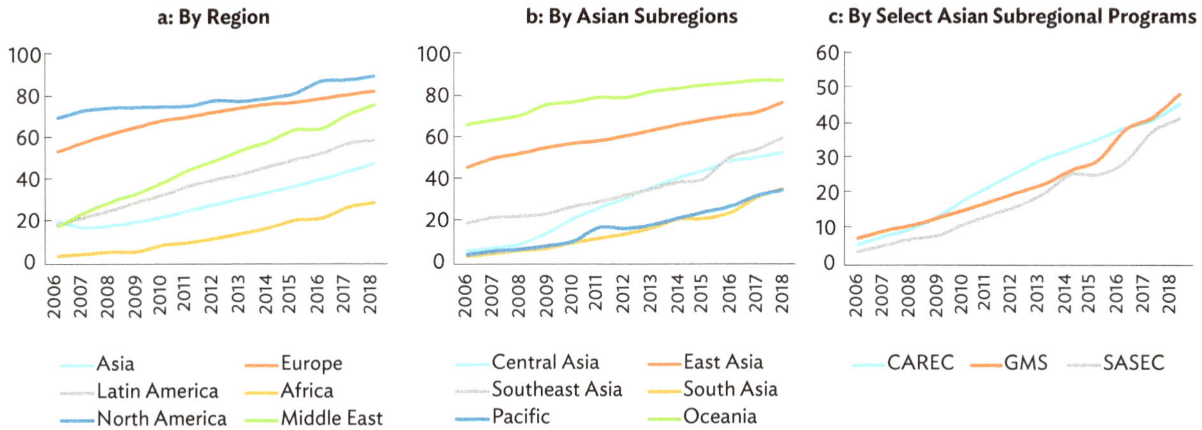

CAREC = Central Asia Regional Economic Cooperation, GMS = Greater Mekong Subregion, SASEC = South Asia Subregional Economic Cooperation.

Source: ADB calculations using data from ITU (2019).

Figure 6.14: Internet Penetration for Select Asian Economies (% of population)

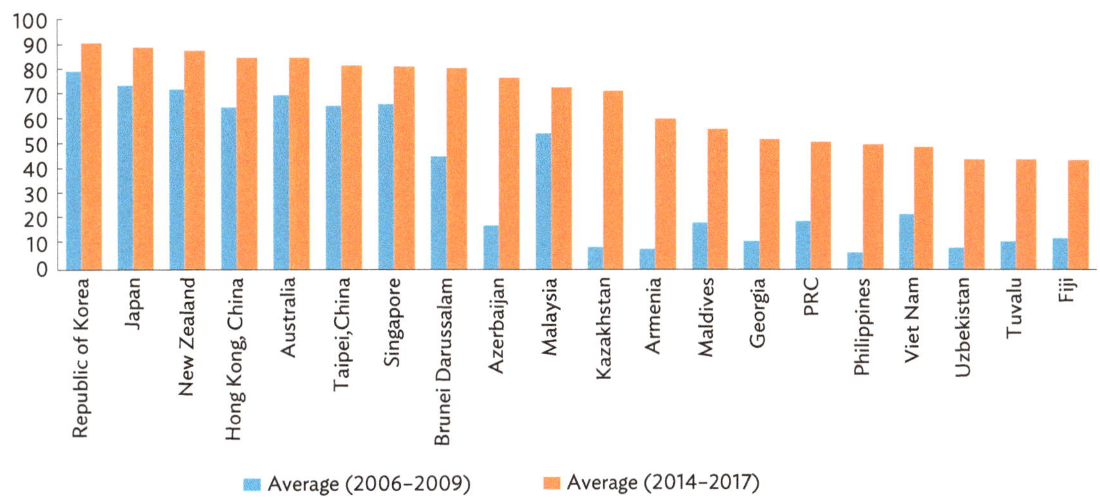

PRC = People's Republic of China.

Source: ADB calculations using data from ITU (2019).

Asia's bilateral internet bandwidth performs better regionally than with the rest of the world. Asia's intraregional internet bandwidth capacity has improved considerably over the last decade, in contrast to the region's bandwidth with other regions (Table 6.2).[63] The share of bandwidth to North America dropped from 49% in 2010 to almost 25% in 2019. A possible explanation for this trend could be the growing efforts of key content providers such as Google and Facebook in augmenting their proprietary bandwidth across the Pacific to connect their data centers and to push their content closer to end users (TeleGeography 2019). As a result, there is little incentive for Asian carriers to operate a high-capacity link to North America. Crucially, the significant share of international internet bandwidth capacity within Asia reflects high internet traffic among Asian countries and shows that digital connectivity is well-established within the region (Figure 6.15). For instance, internet traffic between Indonesia and Singapore rose from 2.4 Gbps in 2006 to 7,041.6 Gbps in 2019 (Table 6.3).

Table 6.2: International Internet Bandwidth by Regional Routes

		Gbps		Share to Total (%)	
Origin	Destination	2010	2019	2010	2019
Asia	Asia	1,776	58,019	37.8	54.0
Asia	US and Canada	2,314	26,729	49.2	24.9
Asia	Europe	499	20,150	10.6	18.7
Asia	Middle East	81	2,480	1.7	2.3
Asia	Africa	32	112	0.7	0.1
Asia	Latin America	0	0	0.0	0.0

Gbps = gigabyte per second, US = United States.

Notes: Values refer to the internet bandwidth connected across international borders as of 30 June 2020. The order of region pairs does not imply directionality. Domestic routes are excluded. Regional totals may differ from the sum of connected regions due to rounding.

Source: ADB calculations using data from Telegeography. Global Internet Geography.

Figure 6.15: Intraregional Internet Bandwidth (% of total internet bandwidth traffic)

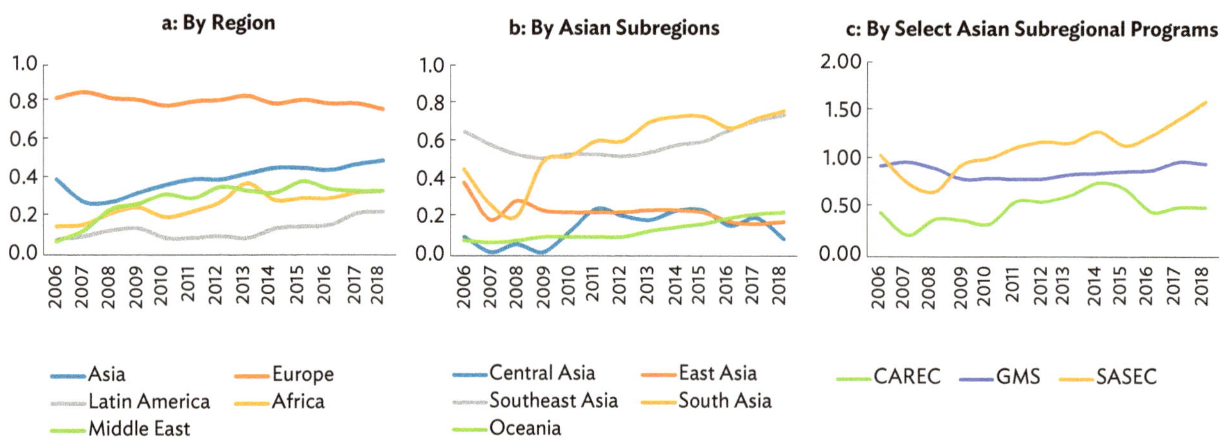

CAREC = Central Asia Regional Economic Cooperation, GMS = Greater Mekong Subregion, SASEC = South Asia Subregional Economic Cooperation.

Note: Values refer to the average internet bandwidth with economies belonging to the same region/subregion/subregional program, expressed as ratio to the average internet bandwidth with all economies worldwide.

Source: ADB calculations using data from Telegeography. Global Internet Geography.

63 The reported indicator builds on ARCII Indicator V-f. International internet bandwidth traffic. TeleGeography defines internet bandwidth capacity as the amount of data transmitted in the public internet, which includes general internet traffic through email, webpages, video streaming, voice over internet protocol (VOIP) calls, and corporate IP VPN traffic over a given period. The values in Table 6.2 present the internet bandwidth capacity measured in gigabytes per second (Gbps) within Asia (intraregional) and across other regions (interregional).

Table 6.3: International Internet Bandwidth Traffic for Selected Asian Economies (Mbps)

Origin	Destination	2006	2012	2019
Indonesia	Singapore	2,437	159,406	7,041,643
India	Singapore	6,153	241,969	5,537,849
People's Republic of China	Singapore	14,337	373,804	5,069,763
People's Republic of China	Viet Nam	3,265	194,729	5,069,000
People's Republic of China	Japan	51,489	745,156	4,800,856
Singapore	Thailand	417	87,223	4,313,075
Malaysia	Thailand	90	21,272	2,600,000
Singapore	Viet Nam	977	32,443	2,351,000
Malaysia	Singapore	4,377	154,524	2,316,755
Japan	Singapore	10,427	265,912	2,297,443
People's Republic of China	Taipei,China	38,033	323,234	2,011,201
People's Republic of China	Republic of Korea	26,212	267,608	1,382,555
People's Republic of China	Malaysia	2,782	99,546	1,176,155
Japan	Republic of Korea	32,174	174,042	1,095,266
Australia	New Zealand	2,862	43,193	1,022,864

Mbps = megabyte per second.

Notes: Values refer to the internet bandwidth connected across international borders as of 30 June 2019. The order of region pairs does not imply directionality. Domestic routes are excluded. Regional totals may differ from the sum of connected regions due to rounding.

Source: ADB calculations using data from TeleGeography. Global Internet Geography Report.

Figure 6.16: Intraregional ICT Goods Exports and Imports, 2018 (% of total exports and imports)

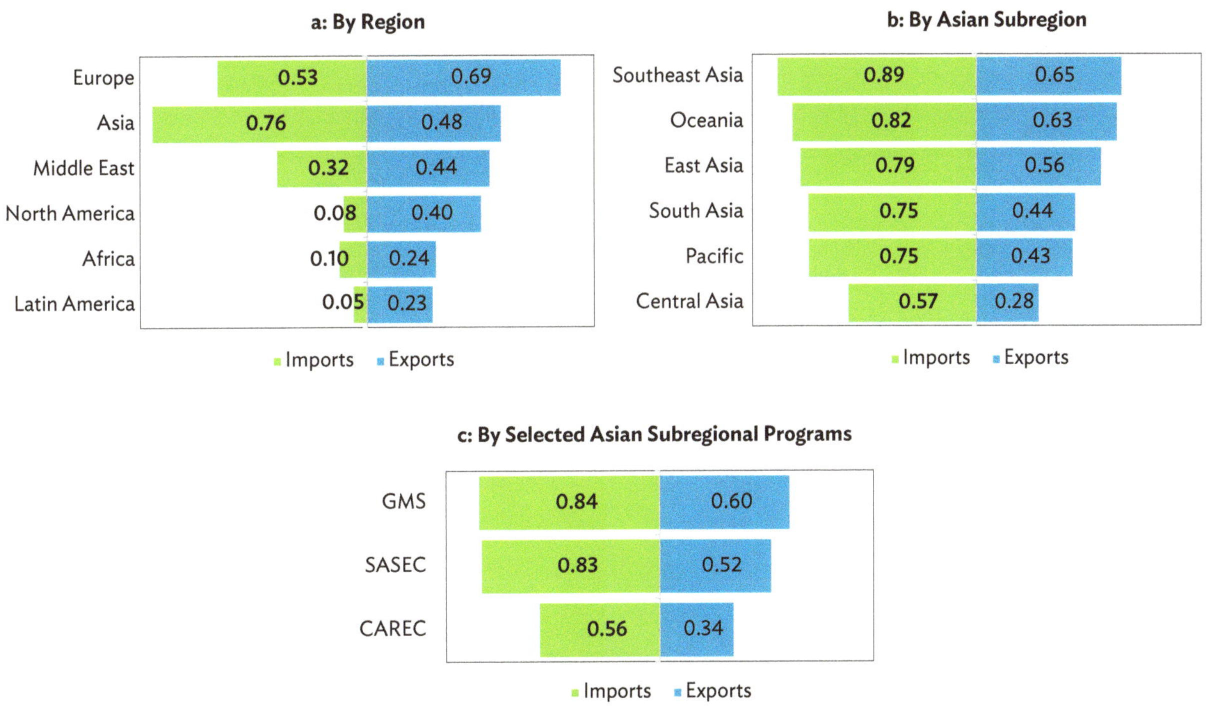

CAREC = Central Asia Regional Economic Cooperation, GMS = Greater Mekong Subregion, ICT = information and communication technology, SASEC = South Asia Subregional Economic Cooperation.

Source: ADB calculations using data from United Nations Conference on Trade and Development. ICT goods categories and composition. https://unctadstat.unctad.org/en/Classifications/DimHS2017Products_Ict_Hierarchy.pdf (accessed June 2020).

Box 6.3: Extending the Research Agenda

The new indicators of regional integration collected for the Asia-Pacific Regional Cooperation and Integration Index (ARCII) enhanced framework should allow extension of the current research agenda and investigation of new areas in the future. Some of these include: first, assessing the contribution and trade-offs of the two new dimensions, Digital connectivity and Environmental cooperation, on patterns of regional integration. Second, using new available indicators to further assess some dimensions. For instance, new indicators of financial integration in regions where data were previously not available, and the air transportation indicator for movement of people. And third, subregional analyses on the determinants of regional cooperation and integration where new indicators may capture idiosyncratic features of subregional integration, as illustrated in the case of the Eurasia Index, could be implemented in other subregions.

Source: ADB (2020).

Asia's production networks reflect high regional integration in ICT exports and imports. Indicators on intraregional trade of ICT goods show that the share of intraregional exports relative to total ICT exports is higher in Europe than in Asia (Figure 6.16). In the case of imports, Asia outperforms Europe. Within Asia, intraregional imports of ICT goods comprise more than 70% of total ICT imports. At the subregional level, Southeast Asia leads in the proportion of intraregional ICT goods exports and imports, whereas Central Asia tends to perform lower than the rest of the region. This could reflect higher backward and forward linkages in Southeast Asian industries (e.g., Cambodia, Myanmar) compared with other subregions (e.g., Central Asia, the Pacific).

Regional Integration in Asia: To What Extent Does Location Matter?

Key Messages

- Regional integration in the Asian region tends to exhibit positive spatial autocorrelation: economies with low (high) levels of regional integration tend to be surrounded by economies with low (high) levels of regional integration.
- Clusters of low regional integration can be found in geographically disadvantaged economies such as landlocked countries in Central Asia and sea-locked countries in the Pacific.
- An economy's level of regional integration is positively associated with its neighbors' level of regional integration and with its income.

An economy's geographic location can play an important role in its ability to forge linkages with other economies in the region. For instance, geographically disadvantaged economies are no doubt at the low end of the regional integration spectrum. Landlocked economies have no territorial access to the sea, limited border crossings, and transit dependence. Due to their remoteness, landlocked countries are dependent on neighboring transit countries for their external trade and suffer from high transaction costs. Therefore, it comes as no surprise that Central Asia remains the subregion least integrated with Asia. Meanwhile, sea-locked economies face greater risk of marginalization due to their small size, remoteness from large markets, and high economic vulnerability to economic and natural shocks.

At the same time, an economy's level of regional integration tends to depend on its neighbors' levels of regional integration. As evident in Figure 6.17, economies with low ARCII scores seem to be near one another, and those with high ARCII scores are clustered in the same manner. This is not surprising, given that the ARCII dimensions likewise depict that neighboring economies generally have similar index scores (Figure 6.18). This suggests that countries might influence their neighbors' integration potential through certain dimensions of regional integration such as trade, investment, and movement of people.

Indeed, spatial analysis using the ARCII confirms that an economy's location influences its level of regional integration (Table 6.4). A significantly positive (negative) statistic from a Global Moran's I test shows clustering of economies with similar (dissimilar) levels of regional integration for the whole Asia and the Pacific. In this regard, results confirm that economies with low (high) levels of overall regional integration tend to be surrounded by economies with low (high) levels of regional integration. The same is true for most of the individual dimensions of regional integration included in the index.

Table 6.4: Results for Global Moran's I Statistic for the ARCII and Dimensional Subindexes

	Moran's I Statistic
Overall ARCII	0.386**
Trade and investment	0.211**
Regional value chain	0.281**
Infrastructure and connectivity	0.054
Movement of people	0.297**
Institutional and social integration	0.191**

ARCII = Asia-Pacific Regional Cooperation and Integration Index.

Notes: ** indicates significance at 5% level. A significantly positive (negative) Moran's I statistic indicates the presence of positive (negative) spatial autocorrelation. Positive (negative) spatial autocorrelation implies that neighboring economies tend to have the same (different) levels of regional integration.

Source: ADB calculations using data from ADB. Asia-Pacific Regional Cooperation and Integration Index Database. https://aric.adb.org/database/arcii (accessed October 2020).

Figure 6.17: Spatial Distribution of the ARCII, 2018

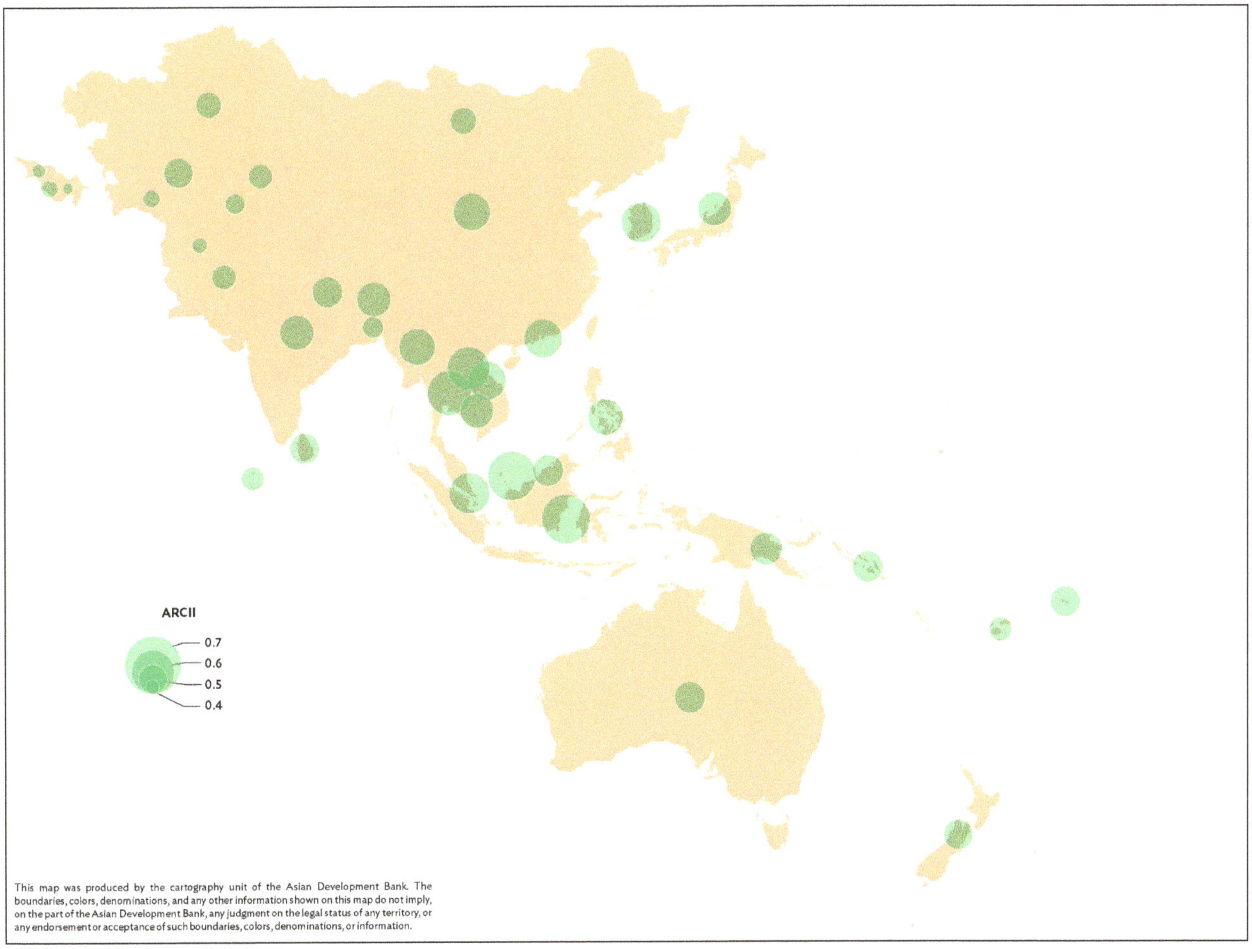

ARCII = Asia-Pacific Regional Cooperation and Integration Index.

Notes: The green circles represent the ARCII score of each country. Large circles translate to a higher ARCII score, while smaller circles mean a lower score.

Source: ADB. Asia-Pacific Regional Cooperation and Integration Index Database. https://aric.adb.org/database/arcii (accessed October 2020).

Figure 6.18: Spatial Distribution of ARCII Dimensions, 2018

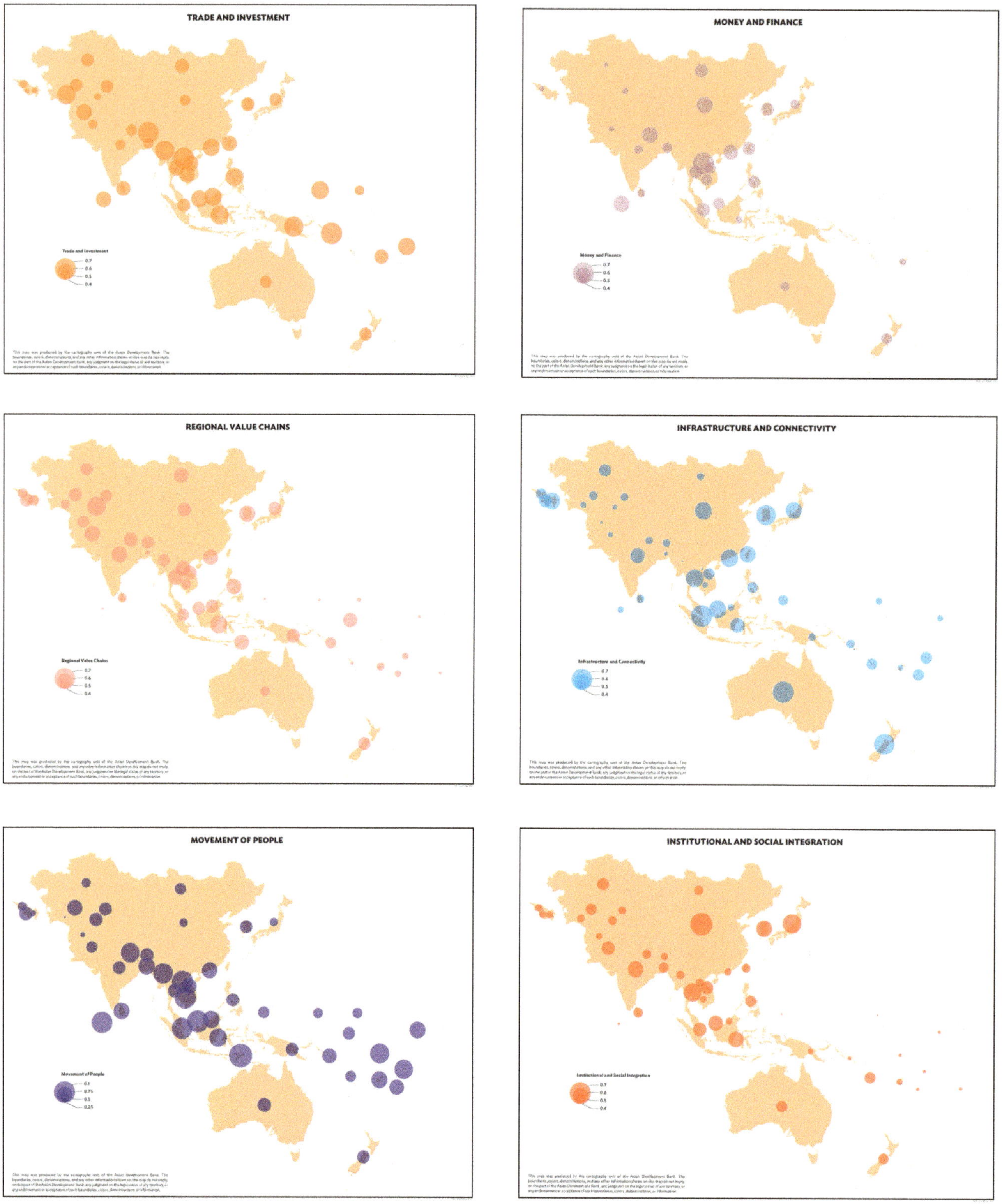

ARCII = Asia-Pacific Regional Cooperation and Integration Index.

Notes: The colored circles represent the ARCII dimensional score of each country. Large circles translate to a higher score for the specified dimension, while smaller circles mean a lower score.

Source: ADB. Asia-Pacific Regional Cooperation and Integration Index Database. https://aric.adb.org/database/arcii (accessed October 2020).

To assess the nature of clustering among the subregions in Asia, the localized version of Moran's I test was employed.[64] The test assesses the presence of clusters of economies with high levels (hot spots) and low levels (cold spots) of regional integration. In general, and as expected, geographically disadvantaged economies such as landlocked countries in Central Asia and sea-locked countries in the Pacific appear to be cold spots of regional integration in Asia, whereas high levels are clustered in Southeast Asia.

The previous findings suggest the presence of spatial autocorrelation in countries' RCI scores. Looking forward, as a first step to analyze the drivers of regional integration using the ARCII, the spatial effects can be corrected through a Spatial Autoregressive model or a Spatial Error Model. As a second step, the analysis could be extended not only to understand the determinants of regional integration but also to evaluate the impact of regional integration on development outcomes including economic growth, income inequality (Park and Claveria 2018, Huh and Park 2020), or income convergence. The spatial component provides a viable instrument to address the potential endogeneity between these outcomes and the ARCII scores.

The significant influence exerted by neighboring economies' regional integration underscores the importance of understanding the spatial effects of regional cooperation. As the role of regional public goods, including environmental and health initiatives, is being discussed today, exploring further the contribution of spatial factors to specific dimensions of regional integration will be essential.

64 The global Moran's I test provides a single measure of spatial autocorrelation in regional integration for the whole Asia. Meanwhile, the local Moran's I test decomposes the global version, thereby providing a measure of spatial autocorrelation within subregions.

References

Asian Development Bank (ADB). Asia Regional Integration Center. Asia-Pacific Regional Cooperation and Integration Index Database. https://aric.adb.org/database/arcii (accessed October 2020).

———. 2019a. *Maritime Cooperation in SASEC*. Manila. https://doi.org/10.22617/SPR190418-2.

———. 2019b. *Asian Economic Integration Report 2019/2020: Demographic Change, Productivity, and the Role of Technology*. Manila. https://doi.org/10.22617/TCS190461-2.

———. 2020. New Approaches to Measuring and Assessing Regional Cooperation and Integration: Workshop Highlights. https://dx.doi.org/10.22617/TCS200310-2.

———. Forthcoming. *Tracking Progress in Regional Cooperation and Integration: The Eurasia Integration Index*. Manila: ADB.

Association of Southeast Asian Nations (ASEAN) Secretariat. 2019. *ASEAN Integration Report 2019*. Jakarta: ASEAN. https://asean.org/storage/2019/11/ASEAN-integration-report-2019.pdf.

Clarivate Analytics. Web of Science Database. https://www.webofknowledge.com (accessed August 2020).

del Rosario, T. 2019. *CAREC Regional Integration Index (CRII): Interpretation and Policy Implications*. Urumqi, Xinjiang: Central Asia Regional Economic Cooperation Institute. https://www.carecinstitute.org/wp-content/uploads/2019/12/CI-CRII-Interpretation-and-Policy-Perspective-27-Dec-2019.pdf.

Eurasian Economic Commission. 2019. Eurasian Economic Union: Facts and Figures. Moscow.

European Commission. 2019. *The EU in 2018—General Report on the Activities of the European Union*. Brussels: European Union. p. 154.

Federal Reserve Bank of New York. 2020. *Federal Reserve Board—Open Market Operations*. 16 March. https://www.federalreserve.gov/monetarypolicy/openmarket.htm.

Greater Mekong Subregion Statistical Database. https://www.greatermekong.org/stats/index-static.php (accessed November 2020).

Guerrero Bote, V. P., C. Olmeda-Gómez, and F. de Moya-Anegón. 2013. Quantifying the Benefits of International Scientific Collaboration. *Journal of the American Society for Information Science and Technology*. 64 (2). pp. 392–404. https://doi.org/10.1002/asi.22754.

Huh, H.-S. and C.-Y Park. 2018. Asia-Pacific Regional Integration Index: Construction, Interpretation, and Comparison. *Journal of Asian Economics*. 54. pp. 22–38. https://doi.org/10.1016/j.asieco.2017.12.001.

Huh, H.-S. and C.-Y. Park. 2020. A New Index of Globalisation: Measuring Impacts of Integration On Economic Growth and Income Inequality. *The World Economy*. 2020 (00). pp. 1–35.

International Telecommunication Union. 2019. *World Telecommunication/ICT Indicators Database, 2019 Edition*. Geneva.

Kohli, H., J. Linn, and L. Zacker, eds. 2020. *China's Belt and Road Initiative: Potential Transformation of Central Asian and the South Caucasus*. New Delhi: SAGE Publishing India.

Park, C.Y. and R. Claveria. 2018. Does Regional Integration Matter For Inclusive Growth? Evidence From The Multidimensional Regional Integration Index. *ADB Economics Working Paper No. 559*. Manila: ADB.

TeleGeography. 2019. *Global Internet Geography Report*. https://www2.telegeography.com/global-internet-geography.

United Nations Conference on Trade and Development. ICT goods categories and composition. https://unctadstat.unctad.org/en/Classifications/DimHS2017Products_Ict_Hierarchy.pdf (accessed June 2020).

United Nations Economic and Social Commission for Asia and the Pacific (UNESCAP). 2018. *Asia-Pacific Trade and Investment Report 2018: Recent Trends and Developments*. Bangkok: United Nations.

———. 2020. Regional Integration for Sustainable Development in Asia and the Pacific: ESCAP Digital and Sustainable Regional Integration Index and Indicator Framework. Bangkok: United Nations.

World Intellectual Property Organization (WIPO). WIPO Statistics Database. https://www3.wipo.int/ipstats/ (accessed May 2020).

7 Updates on Subregional Cooperation Initiatives

The Asia and Pacific region is home to a wide variety of subregional cooperation initiatives, ranging from the Pacific Islands Forum in the east to the Central Asia Regional Economic Cooperation (CAREC) Program in the west. Generally, they all seek greater cooperation and economic integration in transport and trade, access to global value chains, markets, and tourism, along with economic corridor and shared resource development. The key is connectivity and easing border crossings for both people and cargo.

Nothing is more anathema to this than a highly infectious viral pandemic. The coronavirus disease (COVID-19) led to lockdowns, border closings, and strict limits on people's mobility. Yet, for many subregional initiatives, the crisis brought officials together to share information on the pandemic response, to determine how to safely reopen borders, trade, and tourism, among others.

This chapter examines three well-established initiatives and how they have progressed over the past year. And it describes two areas where cooperation offers heightened benefits in a post-pandemic "new normal," whether pooling resources to provide vaccines or in accelerating adaptation to digital technology. The discussions highlight contributions of the Asian Development Bank (ADB) in promoting subregional cooperation through inclusive, sustainable cross-border development.

Central and West Asia: Central Asia Regional Economic Cooperation Program[65]

The CAREC Program includes Afghanistan, Azerbaijan, Georgia, Kazakhstan, the Kyrgyz Republic, Mongolia, Pakistan, the People's Republic of China (PRC), Tajikistan, Turkmenistan, and Uzbekistan. The CAREC 2030 strategy aims to create an open and inclusive regional cooperation platform to help connect people, policies, and projects for shared and sustainable development.[66] Building on 20 years of progress in transport, energy, and trade connectivity (Table 7.1), CAREC is expanding cooperation into new areas—including economic and financial stability, agriculture and water, and human development. The evolving COVID-19 pandemic poses significant challenges to the region. CAREC members more than ever need to work in unison to restore economic activity and renew progress toward the prosperity and the well-being of their citizens.

65 Contributed by Saad Abdullah Paracha, CAREC unit head, Central and West Asia Department (CWRD), Asian Development Bank (ADB); Xinglan Hu, principal regional cooperation specialist, CWRD; and Ronaldo Oblepias, CAREC consultant, CWRD, ADB.

66 The CAREC 2030 Strategy focuses on five operational clusters: (i) economic and financial stability; (ii) trade, tourism, and economic corridors; (iii) infrastructure and economic connectivity; (iv) agriculture and water; and (v) human development.

Table 7.1: Selected Economic Indicators, 2019—CAREC

	Population (million)	Nominal GDP ($ billion)	GDP Growth (2015 to 2019, average, %)	GDP per Capita (current prices, $)	Trade Openness (total trade, % of GDP)
Afghanistan	38.0	19.6	2.4	514	39.1
Azerbaijan	10.0	47.3	0.4	4,706	70.5
China, People's Republic of	1,433.8	14,140.2	6.7	9,862	32.3
Georgia	4.0	17.7	4.4	4,439	72.5
Kazakhstan	18.6	179.3	2.9	9,667	53.6
Kyrgyz Republic	6.4	8.5	4.2	1,319	81.2
Mongolia	3.2	13.6	4.2	4,229	98.3
Pakistan	216.6	282.5	4.5	1,305	26.1
Tajikistan	9.3	8.1	7.0	870	62.6
Turkmenistan	5.9	44.4	6.3	7,465	30.2
Uzbekistan	33.0	57.9	5.8	1,756	62.6
CAREC	**1,778.9**	**14,819.1**	**6.6**	**8,331**	**32.8**

CAREC = Central Asia Regional Economic Cooperation, GDP = gross domestic product.

Notes: CAREC's average GDP growth rate is weighted using nominal GDP. Total trade refers to the sum of exports and imports.

Sources: ADB calculations using data from ADB (2020a); CEIC; International Monetary Fund. http://data.imf.org; and World Bank. World Development Indicators. http://databank.worldbank.org/ (all accessed June 2020).

Overview

Investments in CAREC continued to grow strongly prior to the onset of COVID-19.

As of 30 September 2020, CAREC investments included 208 regional projects valued at $39.3 billion, increased 6% from $36.9 billion in 2018. Of the total, $14.7 billion was financed by the Asian Development Bank (ADB), $15.8 billion by other development partners, and $8.8 billion by CAREC governments (Figure 7.1). Transport held the biggest share, with about 76%, or $29.9 billion; energy accounted for 22%, or $8.7 billion; with trade accounting for 2%, or $0.6 billion (Figure 7.2).

Figure 7.1: CAREC Investments by Funding Source, as of 30 September 2020 ($ billion)

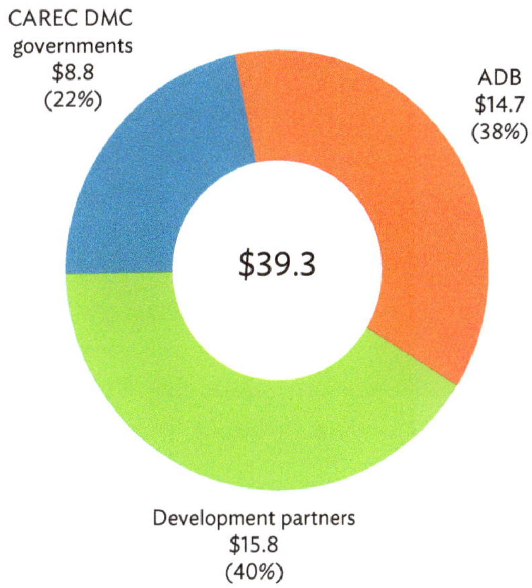

ADB = Asian Development Bank, CAREC = Central Asia Regional Economic Cooperation, DMC = developing member country.

Source: ADB (2019b). CAREC Program Portfolio.

CAREC continues to actively respond to the COVID-19 pandemic.

The CAREC region has been seriously affected by the pandemic. Unprecedented disruptions caused by prolonged lockdowns, border closures, and suspended economic activity significantly lowered domestic output across countries, affected global and regional

Figure 7.2: CAREC Investments by Sector, as of 30 September 2020 ($ billion)

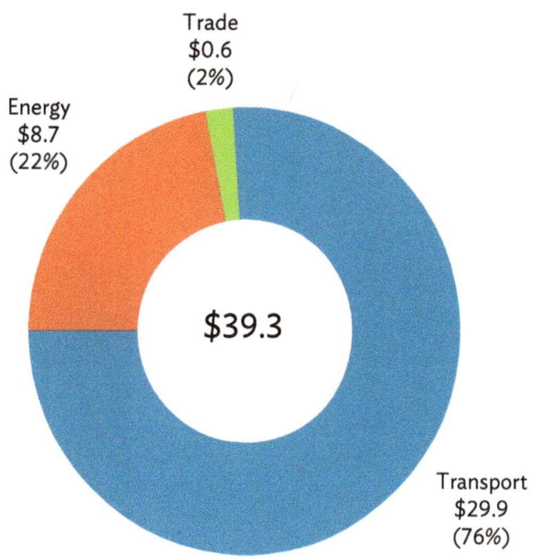

CAREC = Central Asia Regional Economic Cooperation.

Source: ADB (2019b). CAREC Program Portfolio.

supply chains, tourism, remittances, and financial flows, among others (Aleksanyan and Liepach 2020). Since the pandemic began, CAREC members have actively—and jointly—responded to the crisis. They report new cases daily, share experience in fighting COVID-19, and provide medical teams and relief equipment to those in need (such as from the PRC and Kazakhstan to other members). Central Asian leaders communicate proactively with each other to share pandemic information and discuss joint actions to keep borders open for the free flow of food, medical equipment, and humanitarian aid. CAREC countries are also working together to keep international railway freight traffic operating within and across the region following strict disinfection measures.

ADB has stepped up its budget support and emergency assistance through its Countercyclical Support Facility—specifically its COVID-19 Pandemic Response Option (CPRO)—to help CAREC countries mitigate the health, social, and economic impacts of the pandemic. As of 31 December 2020, a total of $3.16 billion emergency and CPRO assistance in loans and grants were committed by ADB to support CAREC countries in response to COVID-19 (Table 7.2).

Table 7.2: ADB Support for CAREC Countries in Response to COVID-19 Loans and Grants Committed as of 31 December 2020

Country	Amount ($ million)
Afghanistan	140.0
Georgia	306.5
Kazakhstan	1,080.6
Kyrgyz Republic	70.0
Mongolia	102.5
Pakistan	802.0
Tajikistan	52.5
Uzbekistan	603.0
Total	**3,157.1**

CAREC = Central Asia Regional Economic Cooperation, COVID-19 = coronavirus disease.

Source: ADB project database.

Performance and Progress over the Past Year

Implementation of CAREC 2030 continues amid COVID-19.

COVID-19 has significantly affected implementation of CAREC 2030 across all five operational clusters, resulting in the cancellation and/or delay of planned meetings and project-related field activities including CAREC's 20th anniversary celebration. Despite the challenges and difficulties, progress continues with support from CAREC countries and development partners, with most programs and activities undertaken virtually.

Economic and Financial Stability. Activities under this cluster continue to promote policy dialogue among CAREC countries to strengthen information sharing on economic and financial challenges facing the region and discuss policy options. On 28 October 2020, a CAREC High-Level Virtual Panel on Countercyclical Fiscal Measures for Recovery was jointly organized with the International Monetary Fund and the World Bank. The panel discussed fiscal policy measures for economic recovery for the CAREC countries in response to the COVID-19 pandemic. A CAREC High-Level Policy Dialogue on COVID-19 and Financial Stability Implications was held on 14 December 2020, which discussed challenges to the economies and financial systems caused by the pandemic in CAREC countries and coordinated solutions at regional and global levels with regional cooperation platform playing a significant role. CAREC is continuing implementation of the regional technical assistance (TA) on "Developing a Disaster Risk Transfer Facility in the CAREC Region," which aims at building countries' physical and financial resilience to infectious disease outbreaks, such as COVID-19, and natural hazards.

Trade, Tourism, and Economic Corridors. The Regional Trade Group and Customs Cooperation Committee met virtually in September 2020 and highlighted the importance of keeping trade open and maintaining the momentum of regional cooperation under the CAREC Integrated Trade Agenda (CITA) 2030 (ADB 2018a). Azerbaijan and Uzbekistan have renewed negotiations for World Trade Organization (WTO) accession, while Turkmenistan gained observer status. Regional Improvement of Border Services projects in Mongolia, the Kyrgyz Republic, and Tajikistan continue to upgrade their border crossing points, and Tajikistan launched its national single window system. Uzbekistan acceded to the International Plant Protection Convention (IPPC) as part of its reforms to improve phytosanitary measures and became the first CAREC country to implement IPPC's e-Phyto system. As part of post-pandemic economic recovery, CAREC countries welcomed the initiatives on expanding services trade and developing e-commerce following the recommendations of completed studies and series of webinars in May to September 2020. Capacity-building activities were organized at various levels such as the forum between CAREC and South Asia Subregional Economic Cooperation customs agencies in October 2019, tailor-made training for Kazakhstan's hosting of the WTO's 12th Ministerial Conference, and the food safety pilot project for Turkmenistan was launched in November 2019. A $1.2 million ADB TA was approved in August 2020 to strengthen knowledge and capacities for the design and implementation of free trade agreements in CAREC.

A $2 million ADB TA to support the formulation of CAREC Tourism Strategy 2030 has made substantial progress. Several milestone activities were undertaken to promote tourism development in CAREC and prepare a CAREC tourism strategy leading to 2030. These include (i) a high-level dialogue on "Promoting Sustainable Tourism Development in the CAREC Region through Public–Private Partnerships" held during the 18th CAREC Ministerial Conference in November 2019; (ii) an inception workshop of the CAREC tourism expert group held in December 2019, which discussed the vision, objectives, and components of the strategy; and (iii) consultations with the CAREC countries held virtually in August–September 2020. The CAREC Tourism Strategy 2030, accompanied by a regional tourism investment framework 2021–2025, aims to promote sustainable, safe, and more inclusive tourism development in the CAREC region to support countries' socioeconomic recovery, help restore jobs and livelihoods, and achieve sustainable growth going forward.

The pilot Almaty–Bishkek Economic Corridor (ABEC) made good progress. The ABEC Tourism Master Plan was adopted to guide tourism development, and a business plan for a regional tourism skilling center has been completed. The governments of Kazakhstan and the Kyrgyz Republic agreed to work together to improve border crossing points (BCPs), develop a modern agricultural wholesale market network, and develop joint health laboratories in the next 2–3 years. An ABEC video and website was launched in November 2019 for better dissemination of ABEC. An additional $750,000 cofinancing was mobilized by ADB to continue supporting ABEC. The road map for the Shymkent–Tashkent–Khujand Economic Corridor (STKEC) development among Kazakhstan, Uzbekistan, and Tajikistan has been finalized and published. ADB has mobilized $1 million additional financing to support the implementation of the STKEC road map. ADB is also implementing a TA project to support the Government of Pakistan on economic corridor planning to reap expanded regional cooperation and integration benefits.

Infrastructure and Economic Connectivity. The CAREC Transport Sector Strategy 2030 is being implemented with ADB TA support including training and workshops for CAREC countries on key transport issues such as the railway sector assessment, road asset management systems, and performance-based contracting. Progress also continues in other transport subsectors including the conduct of several key studies: (i) a scoping study on CAREC ports and logistics has been completed which identified opportunities and challenges in port and logistics cooperation; (ii) railway assessments for all CAREC countries are being conducted, which analyze key railway aspects and contribute to the development of potential CAREC railway projects; and (iii) a study of the COVID-19 impact on CAREC aviation which examined global trends, market recovery strategies, technological changes, and possible applications in CAREC countries has been completed. There were also increased consultations with CAREC countries to effectively implement cross-border transport agreements, improve corridor performance measuring and monitoring, strengthen road safety, road asset management, and cross-border trade facilitation.

The CAREC Energy Strategy 2030 is being implemented through a $2.5 million in new ADB TA to support (i) the establishment of a new regional transmission cooperation association, (ii) promote market reforms, (iii) establish a financing vehicle for green energy projects, and (iv) develop a CAREC energy outlook and a women-in-energy program. CAREC's large regional energy and infrastructure projects have been on track including the flagship Turkmenistan–Uzbekistan–Tajikistan–Afghanistan–Pakistan Power Interconnection Framework and Central Asia–South Asia Electricity Transmission and Trade Project. The Uzbekistan–Afghanistan 500-kilovolt Power System Interconnection Project agreement—under the Afghanistan Energy Supply Improvement Investment Program—was signed on 20 October 2020, which will help strengthen the sustainability of Afghanistan's power sector, and promote cross-border trade in energy. Also, the first phase of the Turkmenistan–Afghanistan–Pakistan–India Natural Gas Pipeline project is planned to be launched in 2021. A regional flagship TA project for five Central Asian countries, which determined the financial savings through regional cooperation in integrating large volumes of renewable energy into the grid, was successfully completed in June 2020.

To mitigate the infrastructure gap in the CAREC region and jumpstart regional projects, the CAREC Secretariat is embarking on developing a CAREC Regional Infrastructure Projects Enabling Facility. A TA project has been approved to help prepare the concept for examining its scope, eligibility criteria, structure, governance, and financing instruments and modalities; and identifying a potential project pipeline that could be supported by such a facility. The facility will ultimately support CAREC governments in preparation of regional projects and readiness, initial design, and application of appropriate financial solutions while promoting knowledge exchange and capacity development. This vehicle is expected to become an important tool in enhancing private sector participation and expanding project financing using innovative approaches.

Agriculture and Water. Progress has been made under this new cluster, with two new TA programs launched in 2020. The first TA supports international food safety standards in agricultural value chains, which aims to improve public health and agro-food trade facilitation in CAREC countries through enabling regulatory environment reforms, enhancing laboratory infrastructure and capacity, strengthening capacity in the value chain, and advancing network linkages and peer-to-peer institutional cooperation. The second TA supports the development of the CAREC water pillar, through analysis of economic aspects and sustainable financing of water resource management including cross-border water resource management through regional cooperation, with a focus on climate change and disaster risk management.

Human Development. Activities in the health sector were initiated, with a scoping study on CAREC health cooperation completed after a regional consultation workshop held virtually on 15 October 2020. The study proposes measures for regional health cooperation going forward, including (i) strengthening regional health security, (ii) supporting national health systems through regional cooperation, and (iii) improving health services for migrants, mobile populations, and border communities. To jumpstart the implementation of recommendations, a TA project has been approved that will help CAREC countries address public health threats, including from COVID-19, as well as support the formulation of a CAREC health strategy leading to 2030. A scoping study on strengthening cross-border community collaboration in the CAREC region assessed how CAREC can promote closer economic and social cooperation and people-to-people contacts among border communities, and proposed directions and opportunities for scaling up cross-border community development initiatives in the region. To implement recommendations from an education scoping study in 2019, ADB is mobilizing financing for a regional TA to support CAREC higher education and technical and vocational education and training.

The **CAREC 2030 Results Framework** has been developed which includes concrete indicators, baseline data, data sources, and output levels that will ensure regular monitoring and evaluation of CAREC 2030 Strategy's goals and objectives.

Prospects

New CAREC gender and tourism strategies will promote inclusive development to mitigate the COVID-19 impact.

In the CAREC region, quarantines and mobility restrictions have greatly weakened economic activity. Domestic demand and production plummeted, plunging global economic activity slashed external demand, amid a collapse in global commodity prices. As a result, gross domestic product (GDP) growth in the CAREC region (excluding the PRC) is forecast to contract by 1.1% in 2020. Hardest hit are small and medium-sized enterprises (SMEs) in tourism, hospitality, education, and other services. In addition to existing gender disparities, the pandemic has also had a disproportionate effect on women due to increased unpaid care work and intensified home-based violence from lockdown measures; and acute vulnerabilities due to insecure labor markets and informal economy where women often work.

With trade, transport, and energy strategies being implemented, CAREC is advancing into areas that promote human development—particularly those supporting increased women's capacity to have equal access to economic opportunities in the region, and through regional tourism development. The CAREC Gender Strategy 2030 was formulated to reduce gender disparities and to promote gender equality in the region. The strategy promotes gender mainstreaming across all five clusters of CAREC 2030 through four strategic pillars: (i) promote women's access to economic activities; (ii) contribute to women's social empowerment; (iii) support women's regional networks and policy reform for women's empowerment; and (iv) enhance women's access to information and communication technology (ICT). Virtual consultations on the CAREC gender strategy were held with CAREC countries in September-October 2020. The CAREC Tourism Strategy 2030 adopts a holistic approach to promote safe and sustainable tourism destinations in the region through five pillars: (i) connectivity and infrastructure, (ii) quality and standards, (iii) skills development, (iv) marketing and branding, and (v) market intelligence. The strategy also mainstreams six crosscutting themes including health, safety and security, digitalization, gender equality, environmental sustainability, private sector participation, and universal access to tourism services. Both new strategies were endorsed at the 19th CAREC Ministerial Conference held virtually on 7 December 2020.

Policy Challenges

CAREC needs to revive growth while containing and mitigating the impact of the COVID-19 pandemic.

Amid COVID-19 pandemic, prospects are uncertain with no significant relaxation on restrictions across the region. It is critical that CAREC countries maintain the right policy balance between restoring economic activities and protecting public health. Regional cooperation can help keep the hardest-hit sectors (such as trade, tourism, and health) functioning, while preparing for a full recovery during post-pandemic time.

In these challenging and uncertain times, maintaining trade flow is essential to save lives and livelihoods. CAREC countries can work together to reduce restrictions on trading medical equipment, food, and other products that help save lives and ensure food security. Gradually easing restrictions offers opportunities for countries to reopen borders and restore travel and tourism by initially creating tourism "bubbles." CAREC members can jointly develop a harmonized set of health and safety protocols for travel and tourism, through multisector collaboration among airlines, hotels, and other tourism services. The CAREC Tourism Strategy 2030 provides a timely platform to help reboot tourism in the region.

Ensuring a safe and healthy environment is a precondition for restoring economic activity across all sectors. Thus, cooperation on health issues is critical for mitigating public health risks as countries gradually reopen. The CAREC health scoping study calls for strengthening health cooperation to fight public health threats (such as COVID-19), secure regional health security, and build resilient health systems for the future. CAREC countries can step up regional health cooperation to provide a solid basis for economic revival through mitigating COVID-19 impacts and other regional health threats.

Southeast Asia: Greater Mekong Subregion Program[67]

Cambodia, the PRC (Yunnan Province and Guangxi Zhuang Autonomous Region), the Lao People's Democratic Republic (Lao PDR), Myanmar, Thailand, and Viet Nam comprise the Greater Mekong Subregion (GMS). ADB houses the GMS Program secretariat. In its 28 years of cooperation, the GMS has created an interconnected subregion that continues to improve economic growth amid enhanced connectivity and competitiveness. From the program's launch in 1992 to 2020, 107 investment projects amounting to $26.6 billion have been approved. Of this, ADB contributed $12.2 billion, GMS governments $6 billion, and other development partners/private sector $8.3 billion. These projects have built, upgraded, or improved over 11,000 kilometers (km) of roads and over 500 km of railways; installed over 2,600 km of power transmission and distribution lines; and added almost 3,000 megawatts (MW) of power generation to bring electricity to almost 150,000 households.

Overview

GMS economies are expected to contract amid the COVID-19 pandemic.

The GMS Program supports subregional projects in agriculture, energy, the environment, health, tourism, transport connectivity, transport and trade facilitation, and urban development. In 2019 and prior to the 2020 pandemic, the subregion's aggregate growth rate rose from 6% (2014–2018) to 6.2% (2015–2019), led by strong growth in Cambodia; Viet Nam; and Yunnan Province, PRC. Thailand's growth continued to improve from a low of 1% in 2014. However, with the COVID-19 pandemic, the GMS economies are expected to contract, in particular tourism-driven segments in Thailand and Cambodia. ADB has provided countercyclical budget support to Cambodia, Myanmar, and Thailand. In addition to responding to the COVID-19 pandemic, GMS countries are working together on subregional health cooperation, strengthening various aspects of regional health security and border areas.

Prior to the pandemic, regional interconnectedness had been strengthening continuously, particularly in intraregional trade and tourism. By 2019, intraregional trade had grown to $552 billion, or 10% of the subregion's total trade (up from 5.7% in 2009). However, excluding the PRC, intraregional trade for GMS countries was only 1.5% of the total, underscoring the critical importance of the PRC to intraregional trade growth. Trade with GMS partners was particularly significant for Cambodia (43% of total trade), the Lao PDR (88%), and Myanmar (50%). While trade remains a significant driver of growth across most of

[67] Contributed by the GMS Secretariat, Southeast Asia Department, ADB.

the subregion—as shown by the high degree of trade openness (trade as a percentage of GDP)—trade's share of GDP is dropping slightly. However, foreign direct investment (FDI) is beginning to contribute more to GDP, with its percentage of GDP increasing slightly across much of the GMS, especially in Cambodia and Viet Nam (Table 7.3). In addition, the subregion is becoming increasingly interconnected through tourism. By 2018, intra-GMS tourism accounted for nearly 23% of overall GMS tourism.

Performance and Progress over the Past Year

A long-term strategic framework to 2030 is being developed for the GMS Program.

In 2019, the GMS Program continued to implement the Ha Noi Action Plan (2018–2022)—endorsed by GMS leaders in March 2018—which outlines the strategic directions and operational priorities for subregional integration. The plan operates under the Regional Investment Framework 2022 (RIF 2022), a medium-term pipeline of priority GMS projects supported by national governments, the private sector, development partners, and ADB. The RIF 2022: Third Progress Report and Update for 2020—endorsed by GMS ministers in November 2020—described progress made on 210 investment and TA projects, with a pipeline valued at $78.3 billion. By November 2020, 71% of the pipeline projects had identified financing, with 16% of projects completed, 42% ongoing, and 42% of projects yet to start.

Under the direction from the GMS leaders and in response to the evolving global environment, work began in early 2019 and continued through the COVID-19 pandemic on a new long-term strategic framework for the GMS Program up to 2030. The secretariat is leading this work, with inputs from GMS members, development partners, the private sector, and subregional think tanks. The GMS Strategic Framework 2030 will be considered by GMS ministers at the 24th GMS Ministerial Meeting, and then by GMS leaders at the 7th GMS Leaders' Summit in March 2021.

Table 7.3: Selected Economic Indicators, 2019—Greater Mekong Subregion

	Nominal GDP ($ billion)	GDP Growth (2015 to 2019, average, %) and Trend	GDP per Capita (current prices, $)	Trade Openness (total trade, % of GDP)	% Change in FDI (2015 to 2019)[a]	FDI Openness (total FDI Inflows, % of GDP)[a]
Cambodia	27	7.1 ↓	1,621	141	47.9	13.7
Guangxi Zhuang Autonomous Region, PRC	308	7.1 ↓	6,210	22	-64.9	0.1
Yunnan Province, PRC	337	8.8 ▪	6,933	10	0.0	0.3
Lao PDR	19	6.5 ↓	2,668	69	41.1	6.9
Myanmar	66	6.4 ↓	1,221	54	-30.1	3.5
Thailand	544	3.4 ↑	7,807	84	118.1	1.1
Viet Nam	262	6.8 ↑	2,715	198	27.9	6.2
GMS	**1,562**	**6.1 ▪**	**4,568**	**75**	**28.7**	**2.0**

FDI = foreign direct investment, GDP = gross domestic product, GMS = Greater Mekong Subregion, Lao PDR = Lao People's Democratic Republic, PRC = People's Republic of China.

Notes: Average GDP growth rate for GMS is weighted using nominal GDP. Total trade refers to the sum of exports and imports.

[a] 2017 for Yunnan, PRC and 2018 data for the Lao PDR.

Sources: CEIC; Greater Mekong Subregion (GMS). GMS Statistics Database. www.greatermekong/statistics; International Monetary Fund. World Economic Outlook April 2020 Database. https://www.imf.org/external/pubs/ft/weo/2020/01/weodata/index.aspx; and United Nations Conference on Trade and Development. World Investment Report 2019. https://unctad.org/Sections/dite_dir/docs/WIR2019/WIR19_tab01.xlsx (all accessed August 2020).

The GMS Program has shown significant progress and benefits to its members.

The GMS Program's performance has further strengthened the competitiveness, connectivity, and community within the GMS itself and, increasingly, creates new links to other subregions.

Cross-Border Transport Connectivity and Economic Corridor Development. Further strengthening regional connectivity infrastructure continued to be a priority. An extensive medium-term pipeline of transport projects are in various stages of development under RIF 2022. According to the RIF 2022 2nd Progress Report and Update, transport projects had an estimated value of $77 billion, or 83% of the RIF pipeline total. Several of these were recently completed—such as the Road and Border Crossing Infrastructure at Mae Sot–Myawaddy, linking Myanmar and Thailand; the Coastal Terminal Development Project of Laem Chabang Port in Thailand; and the Bus and Truck Drivers Training and Testing Center in Cambodia.

With the shift to multimodal transport under the GMS Transport Sector Strategy 2030, the Greater Mekong Railway Association (GMRA) continued to work on the feasibility and investment requirements of nine priority GMS railway links. The GMRA is also working on a Framework Agreement on Cross-Border Railway Transport Connectivity that covers the software side of railway connectivity in the subregion. A new ADB TA will support the strengthening of the GMRA; prepare a plan to develop a modern GMS railway network; update the GMS railway strategy; and update and refine rail demand projections. Some GMS countries (Viet Nam) are also preparing logistics studies and development plans along with projects that establish logistics complexes (Cambodia) that support transport efficiency.

A study was completed identifying ways to cooperate and transform a key sub-corridor of the North–South Economic Corridor between the PRC and Myanmar—NSEC-5 (Kunming–Muse–Mandalay–Yangon–Thilawa)—into a full-fledged economic corridor that increases investment, employment, and incomes within and around the sub-corridor in an inclusive and sustainable manner. The study results were presented at the 11th Economic Corridors Forum in October 2020.

The GMS Subregional Transport Forum has also been focusing more on the softer but important aspects of transport development, and initiated studies on road asset management and road safety, for example.

Transport and Trade Facilitation. In 2019, and prior to the 2020 COVID-19 outbreak, cross-border trade and transport facilitation under the Early Harvest implementation of the GMS Cross-Border Transport Facilitation Agreement were progressing well. Officials were trained, transport operators briefed, administrative circulars distributed, GMS transport permits and temporary admission documents (TADs) issued, and national registers compiled and exchanged with other members. Supporting documents such as permits, TADs, training and outreach materials, and implementation guides were prepared and published online. In 2019, the Joint Committee of the GMS Cross-Border Transport Facilitation Agreement agreed to extend cooperation in several key areas to continue advancing the transport facilitation agenda. These include (i) expanding the permitted cross-border route network and border crossing points; (ii) circulating and sharing national registers of permits and TADs; (iii) regularly monitoring cross-border trade agreement implementation; (iv) sharing transport and trade facilitation data; (v) developing country handbooks that identify key host-county traffic rules and specifying permissible routes and places for passenger (dis)embarkation and cargo (un)loading; and (vi) facilitating foreign operators' access to national customs transit systems.

To ease increased barriers to transport and trade due to the COVID-19 pandemic, GMS countries continued to coordinate and exchange information on the status of border crossing points and the new measures applied in respective countries. The National Transportation Facilitation Committee—which leads the implementation of the GMS Cross-Border Transport Facilitation Agreement—met on 22 June 2020 to help GMS countries better coordinate and cooperate to ensure the safe movement of goods and passengers across GMS borders. Some of the agreed immediate to medium-term recovery measures include (i) an information platform to facilitate interagency and cross-border information exchange between officials; (ii) a portal to keep businesses and the public informed on border crossing issues; and (iii) accelerating the publication of country handbooks agreed on in 2019, specifying host county traffic rules (for example, maximum permissible weights and dimensions, speed limits, vehicle markings, and third party insurance providers, among others), and specifying the permissible routes and places for passenger (dis)embarkation and cargo (un)loading.

Energy. Power trade has entered Stage 2 (country-to-country power trade) as cooperation remains a priority of the Regional Power Trade Coordination Committee (RPTCC). The working groups for (i) planning and operation (formerly, performance standards and grid codes); and (ii) regulatory issues focus on enhancing and deepening Stage 2 of GMS power trade. GMS members continue to work on power grid interconnection, power trade with neighboring countries, and the future development of the power sector. The Nam Ngiep 1 Hydropower Project in the Lao PDR, funded by private sector investments, began operations in September 2019 with an installed capacity of 272 MW—with some sold to the Electricity Generating Authority of Thailand as well as to Electricité du Laos. Also in September 2019, the Lao PDR, Malaysia, and Thailand agreed to expand a trilateral power deal, under which the Lao PDR will sell electricity to Malaysia via Thailand's grid—raising capacity from 100 MW to 300 MW. Cambodia also signed a power purchase agreement with the Lao PDR in September 2019, with 195 MW of electricity transmitted to Cambodia beginning in January 2020.

As power trade continues to grow, revitalizing the Regional Power Coordination Center is crucial to maximize the potential for future GMS power trade. Work needs to accelerate for the regional body to coordinate the application of grid codes, performance standards, and regional regulatory functions.

Tourism. In 2019, GMS recorded nearly 80 million international tourist arrivals. They contributed $101 billion in tourism receipts (15.9% of the economy) and sustained over 18 million jobs in the subregion. Tourism contributed significant shares to the national economies of Thailand (20% of GDP), Cambodia (12% of GDP), Viet Nam (12%), and the Lao PDR (9%). Overland intraregional tourism arrivals reached 83% of total arrivals in the Lao PDR, 59% in Myanmar, 31% in Cambodia, and 14% of arrivals in Thailand. Following the spread of COVID-19 and the subsequent ban on international arrivals and restrictions on domestic movement, tourism fell significantly in the first quarter of 2020 before stopping completely in the second quarter. In the third quarter, economies began to promote domestic tourism to support the sector. However, in Thailand and Cambodia where 71% and 77%, respectively, of tourism spending in 2019 was from international tourism,[68] the tourism economy continues to struggle.

During the initial COVID-19 response and mitigation phase, the Mekong Tourism Coordinating Office and the Tourism Working Group website, https://www.mekongtourism.org/, served as an information platform and portal, connecting travelers with vital, rapidly changing information. It also provided a resource for tourism operators on various government relief and support efforts. A clear source of information on the status and safety of travel will continue to be needed as public confidence returns to resume travel. The Tourism Working Group also works with destination management organizations and tourism suppliers to adapt and strengthen electronic supply chains between producers and end users, and create social media and tourism marketing initiatives to promote a return to tourism.

Urban and Border Area Development. GMS countries have increased their focus on urban development investments for planning smart and livable cities, and on urban development for riverine and coastal cities and towns—as these related to healthy regional oceans and waterways.

[68] World Travel and Tourism Council. https://wttc.org/ (accessed June 2020).

The GMS Urban Development Working Group discussed the ADB Ocean Financing Initiative (under The Action Plan for Healthy Oceans and Sustainable Blue Economies) as well as the ASEAN Smart City Initiative. Suggestions for possible projects in GMS countries to be supported by ADB's urban sector investments or the oceans action plan include solid waste management for cities along the Mekong River and Irrawaddy basin; improving transportation infrastructure links between towns and regions; managing urban growth through public–private partnerships or by deploying new technologies; creating more integrated urban planning and solid waste and wastewater management; and integrating coastal zone planning and coastal adaptation planning to address rapid erosion issues and increase resilience of coastal cities. Under the ASEAN Smart City Initiative, the Urban Development Working Group recommended implementing smart city pilots in selected cities, with the first batch starting in 2020.

Healthy Oceans and ASEAN Smart Cities components are expected to be incorporated into future GMS urban sector investments, including a Livable Cities Investment Project in Cambodia in 2021, which will focus on enhancing urban planning, building community resilience, and providing infrastructure to improve livability in Cambodia's secondary cities such as Battambang, Bavet, Kampot, and Poipet.

Health and Other Human Resources Development. The GMS Health Cooperation Strategy 2019–2023 was endorsed by GMS countries in 2019 and is accompanied by a strategic results framework to monitor and evaluate its implementation and effectiveness. Furthermore, the GMS Health Cooperation Working Group is preparing a regional action plan to operationalize the strategy and support its three pillars: (i) strengthening national health systems to address transnational health threats and health security as a regional public good; (ii) respond to the health challenges and health impacts as a result of connectivity and mobility; and (iii) health workforce development.

The GMS Regional Health Security Project in Cambodia, the Lao PDR, Myanmar, and Viet Nam is progressing as it strengthens public health security mechanisms by improving regional and cross-border communicable disease control services; disease surveillance and outbreak response; hospital infection prevention and control; and laboratory quality and biosafety. The region is also preparing a GMS Healthy Border Special Economic Zones Project for Cambodia, the Lao PDR, and Myanmar to strengthen health care for migrant workers in border areas, develop knowledge partnerships between Thailand and its GMS neighbors, and develop a regional communicable disease control center for regional monitoring and surveillance of outbreaks.

Ongoing GMS health projects and the Working Group on Health Cooperation enabled the GMS Program to respond immediately to COVID-19. As early as February 2020, $2 million in additional financing was approved to support capacity for epidemic response—including investigation, surveillance, prevention, and control—by adding funds to the ongoing technical assistance project, Strengthening Regional Health Cooperation in the GMS. In the same month, the Working Group on Health Cooperation convened a virtual meeting to explore areas of national and regional financial and technical support. So far, as a result of these early actions, nearly $60 million has been mobilized through GMS Health Cooperation in Cambodia, the Lao PDR, Myanmar, and Viet Nam. The support includes additional financing of $20 million in the Lao PDR and $30 million in Myanmar under the GMS Health Security Project; and ongoing project funds direct for procuring $860,000 for thermal scanners, personnel protective equipment, real-time polymerase chain reaction machines, and infrared thermometers for the Lao PDR; $270,000 for thermal scanners for border screening in Cambodia; $6.6 million for thermal scanners, personnel protective equipment, laboratory equipment, and intensive care unit respiratory ventilators in Myanmar; and $500,000 to support emergency response activities in Viet Nam provinces.

As part of the continuing support over the medium- and long-term, pipeline projects such as the GMS Healthy Border Special Economic Zones project are being adjusted to address COVID-19 needs as well as build pandemic resiliency. The technical assistance for Strengthening Regional Health Cooperation in the GMS is also funding "One Health" assessments to strengthen prevention in areas where animal and human health interconnect, such as healthy livestock.

Agriculture. Regional technical assistance on the GMS Sustainable Agriculture and Food Security Program (2020–2025) was approved in December 2019 to support the Strategy for Promoting Safe and Environment-Friendly Agro-Based Value Chains and Siem Reap Action Plan for 2018–2022. The program focuses on (i) green agribusiness supply chains and agribusiness financing; (ii) crop and livestock safety and quality; and (iii) climate-adaptive agriculture in the context of the water–food–energy nexus.

The GMS Climate-Friendly Agribusiness Value Chains Sector Project is underway in Cambodia, the Lao PDR, and Myanmar to harmonize safety and quality standards for agricultural products and strengthen institutional and technical capacity for safety and quality testing. The project will also support rural livelihoods and job creation through rehabilitating and upgrading infrastructure, all instrumental in post-COVID-19 recovery efforts. The GMS Cross-Border Livestock Health and Value Chains Improvement Project is being prepared to help Cambodia, the Lao PDR, and Myanmar better prepare for and prevent future outbreaks of transboundary animal disease, zoonoses, and antimicrobial resistance, as well as improve livestock value chains and COVID-19 responses.

Further, discussions on the COVID-19 response are underway, including (i) GMS response and recovery efforts in agriculture and food security, (ii) digital technologies for greening pandemic-responsive agribusiness supply chains, and (iii) livestock health management.

Environment. A regional technical assistance on the GMS Climate Change and Environmental Sustainability Program was approved in December 2019 to help implement the GMS Core Environment Program Strategic Framework for 2018–2022. The program will focus on (i) climate and disaster resilience, and low carbon transitions; (ii) climate-smart landscapes and environmental sustainability, including pollution control and waste management; and (iii) green technologies and climate and disaster risk financing instruments.

There are ongoing discussions with GMS countries on (i) COVID-19 response and recovery efforts and impacts on environmental sustainability, (ii) opportunities for making COVID-19 recovery efforts green and climate-resilient, (iii) biodiversity conservation and wildlife management in the wake of COVID-19, and (iv) sustainable waste management of COVID-19 related waste.

A technical assistance program for Thailand, Climate Change Adaptation in Agriculture for Enhanced Recovery and Sustainability of Highlands, began in early 2020, and aims to reduce vulnerability of highland communities and ecosystems to cope with climate change impacts. The project will focus on (i) assessing climate change vulnerability of highland agriculture; (ii) prioritizing gender-responsive, climate-smart agriculture practices; (iii) enhancing agricultural product quality, value addition, and market linkages; and (iv) strengthening the capacity of local governments and communities to address climate change.

Prospects

A GMS medium-term COVID-19 recovery plan is in the works.

While GMS members have done well in containing the spread of COVID-19 both nationally and regionally, economic growth has been disrupted and is expected to contract given the significant drop in demand for goods and services worldwide and the cessation of international tourist arrivals across the GMS. More than 8 million people have lost jobs with a further 8 million people pushed below the poverty line.[69]

69 These estimates are made by ADB from March to June 2020 from various briefing materials and are indicative only. They do not include data from Guangxi Zhuang Autonomous Region and Yunnan Province.

Although COVID-19 has drastically affected the GMS economy, it also highlighted the value of having established regional cooperation mechanisms to respond quickly to emerging needs, like regional health cooperation and trade facilitation. Regional tourism cooperation also provides support to sustain tourism and foster dialogue on effective mechanisms for reopening the sector, first to domestic travel, then to regional or bubble tourism in the medium term, before returning to global travel and tourism. Other regional dialogues on the environment and agriculture offer guidance and options on a "green recovery," methods to sustain livelihoods through regional agriculture value chains, and building safe and resilient cross-border livestock trade.

In the medium term, these will be guided by the GMS COVID-19 Response and Recovery Plan 2021–2023, to be presented to the GMS leaders for endorsement in March 2021. GMS members are now developing national medium-term recovery plans (2021–2023) aimed at rebuilding their local economies, the regional economy, and their engagement in the global economy. The GMS is a unique association well-suited to collaborating with other GMS members to address the regional cooperation and integration constraints on this medium-term recovery plan.

In the long term, the GMS is working on developing a long-term strategy to guide countries through 2030. GMS 2030 will be presented for GMS leader adoption at the GMS Summit in early 2021.

Policy Challenge

Subregional cooperation and coordination will be critical in responding to COVID-19.

COVID-19 response plans require multisector coordination to ensure economies and borders can reopen safely, that people's health and the environment are safeguarded, and that vulnerable communities are protected and included in recovery efforts. In particular, the working groups on transport and trade facilitation, tourism, agriculture and health will need to work closely and coordinate activities. Cooperation and coordination across countries will also be critical, particularly in areas where policies and regulations must harmonize with immediate neighbors and the GMS more broadly. The GMS Secretariat and working group secretariats will be coordination points when requested.

East Asia: Support for Regional Cooperation and Integration Initiatives under the CAREC and GMS Subregional Programs and Knowledge-Sharing Activities[70]

The PRC and Mongolia are both active members of the CAREC Program, and ADB, through its East Asia Department (EARD), are committed to supporting regional cooperation and expanding knowledge- and experience-sharing opportunities within and across subregional platforms. In particular, EARD leads the implementation and monitoring of the CITA 2030 and its 3-year Rolling Strategic Action Plan for the 11 CAREC members. EARD also facilitates and supports participation of the PRC in the GMS Program, with specific focus on the North–South Economic Corridor, and the Northern Economic Corridor connecting the PRC with the Lao PDR, Myanmar, Thailand, and Viet Nam.

Overview

East Asia embarked on coordinated investments in the PRC and Mongolia to fully realize the potential benefits of increased physical connectivity and policy coordination between the two countries as part of broader regional economic corridor development. Among these are parallel projects to develop a cross-border economic cooperation zone that will link

[70] Contributed by the Regional Cooperation and Integration (RCI) team of ADB's East Asia Department.

the Erenhot pilot zone in the PRC's Inner Mongolia Autonomous Region (IMAR) and Mongolia's Zamyn-Uud free zone. These investments are part of a wider framework of regional cooperation and trade facilitation projects traversing CAREC corridor 4B.

Enhancing knowledge- and experience-sharing for regional cooperation remains a high priority for East Asia, involving collaboration with the CAREC Institute and under the Regional Knowledge Sharing Initiative (RKSI), among others. Trade facilitation, upgrading sanitary and phytosanitary measures, and regional cooperation have become more important than ever for the PRC, Mongolia, and their trading partners—not only to expand and diversify trade but to ensure food safety and improve resilience to ongoing and future transboundary health threats.

Performance and Progress over the Past Year

ADB continues to support projects in Mongolia and the PRC related to CAREC and the GMS.

In June 2019, the PRC and Mongolia signed a bilateral agreement to develop an economic cooperation zone under the framework of their bilateral strategic partnership and regional cooperation initiatives. ADB support includes a $30 million concessional loan for Mongolia's Developing the Economic Cooperation Zone Project, which was approved in June 2020 (ADB 2020c).[71] The project will develop the physical infrastructure and operationalize the Zamyn-Uud free zone, promote sustainability, and support seamless transit to and from the PRC's Erenhot zone in IMAR.

The Inner Mongolia Sustainable Cross-Border Development Investment Program for the PRC—a $420 million multitranche financing facility (approved in October 2020)—will install smart ports with one-stop inspection systems to improve customs clearance between the two zones and establish a regional cooperation mechanism for better coordination between the PRC and Mongolia zones.[72] Estimated at $196.3 million, tranche 1 will also upgrade key infrastructure and services in border areas; promote the use of high-level technology for ecological restoration within the cooperation zone; create income-generating opportunities by establishing inclusive agricultural value chains and improving access to finance for SMEs; and improve border infrastructure in the Mandula port.

ADB also approved $27 million in additional financing for Mongolia's Regional Improvement of Border Services Project in 2019 to upgrade border crossing points in Bichigt, bordering the PRC in the east; and Borshoo, which borders the Russian Federation in the west (2019a). This will replicate the development initiatives of the ongoing project, which is already upgrading facilities and equipment at the crossing points in Altanbulag and Sukhbaatar, located in the northern part of Mongolia, and enhancing the Customs Automated Information System toward creating a single window. Construction works start in 2020 to upgrade laboratories, quarantine and inspection facilities under Mongolia's $15 million Regional Upgrades of Sanitary and Phytosanitary Measures for Trade Project, approved in 2016.

The PRC's Guangxi Regional Cooperation and Integration Promotion Investment Program Tranche 2—approved in 2018 for $180 million—continued to strengthen SMEs, develop cross-border e-commerce platforms, and upgrade infrastructure and services for border economic zones (ADB 2018b). The Yunnan Lincang Border Economic Cooperation Zone Development Project—approved in 2018 for $250 million—became effective in July 2019 and is making robust headway toward building trade and logistics capacity, and developing border zones. A new TA for policy research and capacity building in the PRC's Yunnan and Guizhou provinces will promote sustainable trade and investment facilitation and economic linkages between the two provinces and the GMS, by integrating environment, social, and governance principles; and introducing innovations in mobilizing green finance.

71 See ADB. Projects. Mongolia: Developing the Economic Cooperation Zone Project. https://www.adb.org/projects/51410-001/main.

72 See ADB. Projects. China, People's Republic of: Inner Mongolia Sustainable Cross-Border Development Investment Program. https://www.adb.org/projects/51192-001/main.

ADB drives coordination with knowledge-sharing platforms.

ADB continues to work closely with the development partners including the CAREC Institute to undertake research and capacity-building initiatives supporting the CITA 2030. Building on a regional workshop on environmental readiness for e-commerce (December 2018 in Shanghai, PRC), a technical study initiated by ADB and the CAREC Institute in 2019 evaluated CAREC countries' legislative and regulatory frameworks (CAREC Institute 2020). In May 2020, a virtual workshop organized by ADB, the CAREC Institute, ADB Institute, and the Asia-Pacific Finance and Development Institute, explored policy options and discussed examples from other countries in developing e-commerce. In September 2020, a CAREC webinar on e-commerce and paperless trade underscored the need to align domestic legislations with international standards and the role of cross-border connectivity and improved customs services for e-commerce development. The next phase of the research will focus on e-commerce infrastructure—including e-payments, logistics, and information and communication technology for business-to-business and business-to-consumer transactions. ADB and the CAREC Institute are also jointly assessing phytosanitary certification systems in CAREC countries to determine the feasibility of an electronic certification system to support harmonization within the region and will deliver training modules for improving border services and capacity building on free trade agreements from 2020 to 2021.

In 2019, ADB and the CAREC Institute initiated a 5-year collaborative partnership for implementation and dissemination of the CAREC corridor performance measurement and monitoring (CPMM) mechanism. It will also design and deliver an enhanced set of CPMM products, including annual reports, midyear updates, country-specific analysis, and policy briefs. The partnership will leverage the CAREC Institute's growing network of research and knowledge institutions to expand the current CPMM methodology and outputs, optimize data collection and validation, and more effectively promote the use of CPMM data and analysis in policy-related decision-making and independent research.

Since 2012, the PRC's Ministry of Finance and ADB have been jointly implementing the RKSI program to facilitate exchange of development-related knowledge among ADB's developing members. RKSI and its partners organized, among others, the 14th ASEAN–China Forum on Social Development and Poverty Reduction; the 5th CAREC Think Tank Forum; the Special Economic Zones as Catalysts for Economic Corridors, Value Chains and Production Networks Training for ASEAN and PRC Officials; and the 2020 North-East Asia Development Forum, which fostered analytical discussions on policies and practices of development cooperation, and identified potential areas of collaboration among northeast Asian countries in global public goods, including health, disaster preparedness, and response. Despite the ongoing pandemic, the RKSI program continued to deliver timely and relevant lecture and webinar series on international development and on the PRC's experience in COVID-19.

Prospects

ADB supports cross-border investment in regional cooperation and integration (RCI).

ADB continues to support PRC investments in RCI through the preparation of tranche 2 ($118.4 million) of the Inner Mongolia Sustainable Cross-Border Development Investment Program for approval in 2022, which will expand economic opportunities and better living conditions along IMAR–Mongolia border areas. Tranche 2 will provide climate-resilient infrastructure and services, improve targeted ecological areas through forestation and desert restoration, as well as promote green SME business development services.

Furthermore, the Guangxi RCI Promotion Investment Program will prepare its third and final tranche—$140 million for 2021 approval—which anticipates expanding RCI benefits along border areas of the Guangxi Zhuang Autonomous Region and northern Viet Nam. Subprojects are expected to develop cold-chain logistics systems, update industrial park facilities in the border economic zone, and enhance road networks at border crossings. Tranche 3 will also explore and develop sustainable regional tourism opportunities.

Policy Challenges

Enhancing resilience to transboundary health risks will sustain economic growth and promote integration with global and regional economies.

ADB mobilized a comprehensive pandemic response, including $100 million in countercyclical budget support to Mongolia, support for the procurement of emergency medical equipment, and technical assistance for the region's pandemic response.

The unprecedented disruption caused by the COVID-19 pandemic and increasing global trade tensions significantly reduced the subregion's exports during 2020–2021 and resulted in economic slowdown. Facilitating international trade therefore remains crucial to the post-pandemic economic recovery of the PRC and Mongolia. This will require policies that make cross-border movement of goods and people safer and more efficient. Worldwide travel restrictions, border closures, and stricter border controls have highlighted the importance of strengthening resilience against transboundary health risks and future pandemics. Effective resilience will require cooperation and collaboration among border agencies, such as customs, inspection, immigration, and health agencies under a "One Health" approach. Transparency, data-sharing, use of technology and stronger systems among these agencies can help coordinate risk management and improve traceability of people and goods crossing borders.

Greater resilience will further enhance the region's participation in global agriculture value chains. The seamless movement of agricultural products (including animal and meat products) will help diversify trade while at the same time ensure food security in the PRC, Mongolia, and beyond. Robust policies will help countries intensify cooperation in modernizing sanitary and phytosanitary measures to address food safety, transboundary plant pests and animal diseases, and risks to human health. Compliance with international instruments and initiatives—such as those of the WTO, World Customs Organization, World Health Organization, and the World Organisation for Animal Health—and creating synergies with regional initiatives such as the CAREC program and partnerships with neighboring countries will help achieve harmonized, responsive, and relevant policy reform.

ADB's pipeline projects for approval in 2021 include a $200 million loan to strengthen health security for the PRC. It covers capacity building to enhance cross-border information-sharing for timely response to outbreaks and establish a regional platform for technical forums and continuing education. A proposed $30 million project for Mongolia will strengthen integrated early warning systems and disaster preparedness to facilitate regional pandemic monitoring and surveillance. These will be complemented by technical assistance for knowledge-sharing on digital actions for sustainable and resilient food systems and managing the risk of food insecurity during and after the COVID-19 crisis.

South Asia: South Asia Subregional Economic Cooperation[73]

The ADB-supported South Asia Subregional Economic Cooperation (SASEC) program had a landmark year in 2019. Five RCI projects—with cumulative ADB assistance of $1,205 million—were committed during the year, significantly more than the three projects committed in 2018 with $350 million in ADB assistance. The 2019 SASEC projects included two transport connectivity projects (in Nepal and Sri Lanka) with $495 million in ADB financing to improve key international trade corridors and improve freight logistics. The others were a rail project (Bangladesh) with $400 million in ADB financing, a trade facilitation project with ADB financing of $10 million (Maldives), and a power transmission project with $300 million in ADB financing (Bangladesh). As of the end of 2019, 60 ADB-financed projects worth $13.77 billion had been committed, of which ADB had extended $7.81 billion in loan/grant assistance. SASEC

73 Contributed by Ronald Antonio Q. Butiong, Chief of Regional Cooperation and Integration Thematic Group, Sustainable Development and Climate Change Department (formerly director, Regional Cooperation and Operations Coordination Division [SARC] of ADB's South Asia Department); Dongxiang Li, lead regional cooperation specialist, SARC; Aileen Pangilinan, senior regional cooperation officer, SARC; Jesusito Tranquilino, ADB consultant, SARC; and Leticia de Leon, ADB consultant, SARC.

members—Bangladesh, Bhutan, India, Maldives, Myanmar, Nepal, and Sri Lanka—have earnestly pursued SASEC Vision flagship initiatives in energy and revamped the SASEC Operational Plan (SASEC OP) 2016–2025 to prioritize narrowing gaps in the subregion's transport and energy networks.

Overview

In 2019, SASEC focused on expanding the scope of multimodal connectivity to include maritime and inland water transport.

Bangladesh, Bhutan, India, and Nepal established SASEC in 2001 to strengthen subregional economic cooperation and address development challenges—such as persistent poverty and expanding demographics (Table 7.4). Maldives and Sri Lanka joined in 2014, followed by Myanmar in 2017, increasing opportunities to enhance cross-border connectivity, intraregional trade, and RCI. ADB is lead financier, secretariat, and development partner, financing investments and technical assistance.

By the end of 2019, 60 ADB-financed projects ($13.77 billion) had been committed (Figure 7.3), with an additional $128.15 million in 97 technical assistance grants. Investments in infrastructure connectivity accounted for the largest share (39 projects, $10.64 billion), with power generation, transmission, and cross-border electricity trade second (13 projects, $2.33 billion). Investments in economic corridor development, trade facilitation, and ICT development amounted to $798.46 million (Figure 7.4). ADB financed over $7.81 billion in investments ($5.34 billion from ordinary capital resources and $2.48 billion in concessional finance), while SASEC members and cofinanciers contributed over $5.96 billion (Figure 7.5).

Figure 7.3: SASEC Investment, Cumulative by Sector and Volume, 2001–2019 ($ million)

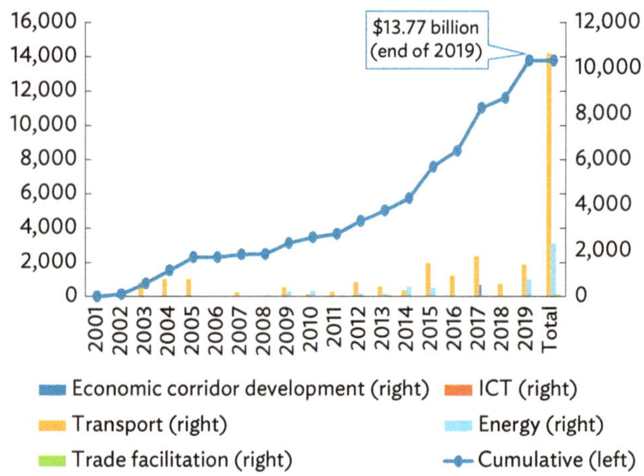

ICT = information and communication technology, SASEC = South Asia Subregional Economic Cooperation.

Source: ADB (2019c). SASEC Project Portfolio 2019.

Table 7.4: Selected Economic Indicators, 2019—SASEC

	Population (million)	Nominal GDP ($ billion)	GDP Growth (%, 2015–2019, average)	GDP per Capita (current prices, $)	Trade Openness (total trade, % of GDP)
Bangladesh	163.0	302.5	7.4	1,855.5	30.2
Bhutan	0.8	2.5	5.6	3,276.1	129.2
India	1,366.4	2,868.9	6.7	2,099.6	28.1
Maldives	0.5	5.8	5.8	10,856.0	52.8
Myanmar	54.0	68.6	6.3	1,270.1	53.5
Nepal	28.6	30.7	5.2	1,072.8	45.5
Sri Lanka	21.8	84.0	3.7	3,852.5	38.8
SASEC	**1,635.2**	**3,363.0**	**6.7**	**2,056.6**	**29.3**

GDP = gross domestic product, IMF = International Monetary Fund, SASEC = South Asia Subregional Economic Cooperation.

Notes: Average GDP growth rate for Myanmar covers 2017 onward. SASEC average GDP growth rate is weighted using nominal GDP, based on IMF staff estimates. Total trade refers to the sum of exports and imports.

Sources: ADB (2020a, 2020b); International Monetary Fund (IMF). Direction of Trade Statistics. https://www.imf.org; IMF. World Economic Outlook October 2020 Database. https://www.imf.org/en/Publications/WEO/weo-database/2020/October; and World Bank. Data. Population Total. https://data.worldbank.org/indicator/SP.POP.TOTL (all accessed November 2020).

Figure 7.4: SASEC Projects by Sector, as of 2019

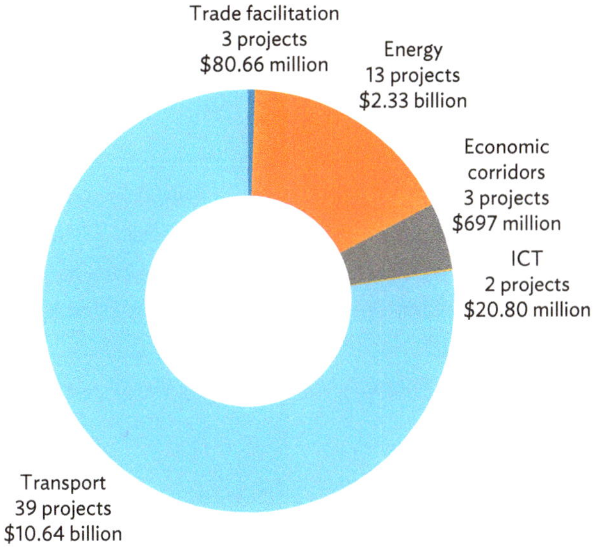

ICT = information and communication technology, SASEC = South Asia Subregional Economic Cooperation.

Source: ADB (2019c). SASEC Project Portfolio 2019.

Figure 7.5: SASEC Investment by Sector, Volume, and Financier 2001–2019 ($ million)

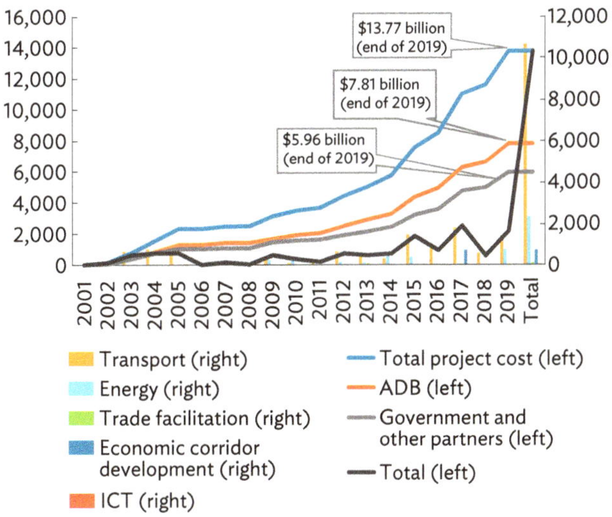

ICT = information and communication technology, SASEC = South Asia Subregional Economic Cooperation.

Source: ADB (2019c). SASEC Project Portfolio 2019.

Refocusing SASEC's operational priorities under the SASEC OP 2016-2025 (ADB 2016b) will enhance multimodal transport networks, especially in linking road and rail corridors with seaports. This will also improve land and maritime-based trade facilitation and logistics, expand the scope of regional energy trade and clean energy efforts, and reinforce value chains in economic corridors. The SASEC Vision adopted in New Delhi in 2017 (ADB 2017) is now guiding the SASEC OP in leveraging resource-based industries, expanding regional value chains, and strengthening gateways and hubs to accelerate economic growth across the subregion. Energy cooperation has been expanded to include oil and gas, both covered by SASEC Vision flagship initiatives.

Performance and Progress over the Past Year

The SASEC Nodal Officials and Working Groups meeting (NOM-WG) held in Seoul, Republic of Korea in March 2019 adopted a streamlined SASEC OP 2016–2025, which prioritizes projects based on their preparedness and role in filling gaps in transport and energy networks. The SASEC OP pipeline was trimmed to 111 projects (over 200 earlier) with required financing of $58.7 billion ($121.5 billion earlier).

Transport. Completing sections of the identified multimodal transport networks (linking main industrial centers with key nodes) continued. Nepal's SASEC Mugling–Pokhara Highway Improvement Phase I Project ($254.0 million) feeds into SASEC corridors 1 and 4 to provide Nepal greater access to international markets. Sri Lanka's SASEC Port Access Elevated Highway Project ($702.9 million) is an elevated toll highway linking Colombo's city center and port with SASEC Corridor 6, enhancing last-mile port connectivity and providing better logistics services for freight operations. The Bangladesh SASEC Chittagong (Chattogram)-Cox's Bazar Railway Project, Phase 1 ($450.0 million), part of the Trans-Asia Railway network, will boost rail service between major Bangladeshi ports and Bhutan, Nepal, and India's northeastern region.

The Seoul NOM-WG agreed to advance maritime cooperation and endorsed regional technical assistance on developing port community systems and addressing legal and regulatory issues, among others.

Trade Facilitation. SASEC assistance has continued to simplify trade processes, promote border agency automation, develop "through transport" agreements, build trade-related infrastructure, and provide capacity building. ADB support for Maldives' National Single Window project ($12.0 million) is designed to improve efficiency of the country's border control procedures. ADB approved $1.5 million in technical assistance to prepare the Bangladesh SASEC Integrated Trade Facilitation Sector Development Program ($200.0 million included in ADB's 2021 pipeline) to improve the country's border infrastructure and trade facilitation environment. ADB assistance supports the SASEC customs subgroup and its national and subregional projects on exchanging trade documents, automating transit, and promoting customs best practices and international standards.

Energy. The Indian government issued revised guidelines on cross-border electricity trade (CBET) in March 2019, expanding coverage to applicable tripartite agreements, along with transmission planning, connectivity, operation, pricing, and access issues, among others.[74] Nepal also recently issued its Transmission System Development Plan, specifying the main trunk lines of India–Nepal connections based on the generation and load estimates to 2040.[75] ADB continues to support hydropower projects in Bhutan and transmission projects in Bangladesh and Nepal. Bangladesh's Dhaka and Western Zone Transmission Grid Expansion ($750 million) will enable dispatch of power imports from India, via the Bheramara substation, to consumers in the western zone of the country. The meeting of the SASEC Cross-Border Power Trade Working Group (SPT-WG) in November 2019 reviewed the draft of the proposed intergovernmental SASEC Regional Power Trade Framework Agreement (RPTFA) to provide a broad framework for enhanced cooperation in power trade and interconnections. The SASEC Regional Gas and Petroleum Working Group (RGP-WG), established in September 2018, is reviewing prospects for enhancing SASEC's gas and fuel supply chain.

Prospects

After the launch of the SASEC Vision in 2017, there has been growing consensus among members on the need for regular SASEC finance ministers meetings (FMMs) to demonstrate greater commitment to the SASEC program. Upgrading the program's oversight reflects members' desire to accelerate regional integration through faster implementation of projects and initiatives.

Enhancing the SASEC's institutional arrangements will expedite implementation of priority initiatives of the SASEC OP and Vision.

At the SASEC 2019 NOM-WG in Seoul, India suggested, and SASEC countries agreed to, convening regular meetings of SASEC finance ministers (the first to be held in India). This would add impetus to new initiatives and commitments to action in partnership with the private sector and development partners. The SASEC FMM can add the political commitment needed to implement the required policy change and resource allocation. A proposed 3-year Action Plan for SASEC Initiatives, to be presented at the First SASEC FMM, will outline the concrete actions to be taken on high-priority projects and new initiatives during 2021–2023.

Policy Challenges

SASEC cooperation must adjust to the "new normal" brought about by the COVID-19 pandemic.

The COVID-19 pandemic, which closed borders and disrupted businesses, has slowed economic growth and increased unemployment in SASEC countries. Its effects will be long-lasting. Poverty reduction could be set back without

[74] Government of India, Central Electricity Regulatory Commission. http://www.cercind.gov.in/2019/regulation/CBTE-Regulations2019.pdf (accessed July 2020).

[75] Nepal in Data. https://nepalindata.com/resource/transmission-system-development-plan-nepal/ (accessed July 2020).

appropriate mitigation measures. Fortunately, instead of resorting to isolationist pressures, the countries of South Asia have banded closer together using existing (and new) platforms. A virtual South Asian Association for Regional Cooperation (SAARC) Summit was held on 15 March 2020 to explore ways to jointly combat the disease, resulting in the launch of a COVID-19 emergency fund, with an initial contribution of $10 million from India. As of July 2020, it has $21.6 million contributed by all SAARC members. The summit was followed by virtual meetings of senior health professionals, trade officials, and health ministers in March and April, which considered various ways to collectively combat the pandemic, including adopting a telemedicine framework, joint diagnostic and therapeutic research, and applying pragmatic solutions to promote trade.

SASEC members have also outlined their approach to economic revival and recovery post-pandemic. It comprises stimulus packages and public investment to promote trade and expand credit, among other measures. In the "new normal," public spending on transport, energy, and trade facilitation will continue as important SASEC areas, but may be affected by shifts in each member's national economic strategy. Strengthening SASEC's cooperation mechanisms will revolve around addressing these needs. Virtual SASEC platforms may be increasingly utilized to oversee projects and determine actions to advance new priorities and initiatives. In transport and trade facilitation, for instance, smart approaches (like automation) and common protocols may be used to minimize disruptions in supply chains for essential goods and enhance the overall resiliency of trading systems.

The Pacific: Crossing "the Last Mile"[76]

The Systems Strengthening for Effective Coverage of New Vaccines in the Pacific project will use pooled procurement and pooled resources to help introduce critical vaccines, improve health management, and promote community awareness about vaccination in Samoa, Tonga, Tuvalu, and Vanuatu. Their small population sizes constrain purchasing power and implementing capacity, and remote locations lead to higher transport costs. The project represents a significant step in safeguarding public health through regional action. It also promotes regional knowledge transfer as the four countries will meet periodically and have access to a pool of experts that will work across countries and throughout the project duration.

Overview

A regional approach will be key to broadening immunization coverage in the Pacific.

Geographic remoteness and limited resources constrain Pacific health systems to effectively deliver comprehensive health services to the population. Individually, these countries lack the purchasing power and capacity to procure adequate supplies of critical vaccines for human papillomavirus (HPV), pneumococcal conjugate (PCV), and rotavirus, as well as the equipment and training needed to store and administer these properly.

ADB has approved a project to address this gap by pooling procurement and capacity building to provide these vaccines to four Pacific developing member countries. It will also strengthen health management and reporting, collaborating with local organizations to build awareness about vaccination and promote better health-seeking behavior at the community level.

The Case for Ensuring Regional Health Security

Long-standing health issues and growing threats. The Pacific comprises mostly small island countries scattered over vast stretches of ocean. High levels of migration within borders and abroad leave these

[76] Contributed by Cara Tinio, associate economics officer; Rommel Rabanal, public sector economist; Inez Mikkelsen-Lopez, health specialist; and Ki-Fung Lam, young professional of ADB's Pacific Department. In this section, Pacific economies include the Cook Islands, the Federated States of Micronesia, Fiji, Kiribati, the Marshall Islands, Nauru, Niue, Palau, Papua New Guinea, Samoa, Solomon Islands, Tonga, Tuvalu, and Vanuatu.

countries highly vulnerable to regional health threats, including communicable diseases.

Routine immunization coverage (for tuberculosis, hepatitis B, polio, measles-rubella, and tetanus) in the Pacific is mostly lower than the international threshold target of over 90% (Figure 7.6). A marked overall decline occurred over recent years, prior to the region's late 2019 measles outbreak (which spurred vaccination drives). Samoa, with over 5,600 cases and 80 deaths, was particularly hard hit (BBC News 2019). Most fatalities were infants and young children.

Worldwide, pneumonia and diarrhea are the two main causes of death among children under age 5, accounting for 12% and 8% of under-5 child deaths, respectively (UNICEF 2019). In Tonga, the incidence of pneumococcal disease—which can lead to blood poisoning and meningitis as well as pneumonia—was reported at 113 per 100,000 children under 2 years old. Of these cases, 25.0% resulted in death, much higher than the 8.7% global fatality rate (ADB 2018c).

Cervical cancer, caused mainly by HPV, is occurring more frequently in the Pacific and has become the second leading cause of death among women in most countries in the region (ADB 2018c). About 1,257 new cases and up to 706 deaths are reported each year (ADB 2018d).

The Pacific's exposure to disease is exacerbated by vulnerability to natural hazards and the adverse impact of climate change. Damage caused by climatic events, and the subsequent strain on limited resources and logistical chains, can increase risk of disease (IFRC 2020). Outbreaks of dengue fever in the Marshall Islands and in countries affected by Tropical Cyclone Harold (Fiji, Solomon Islands, Tonga, Vanuatu), as well as risks from COVID-19, further highlight the need to bolster health-care systems that could easily become overwhelmed if preventive measures are not taken and disease spreads unchecked.

Barriers to adequate health-care coverage. Many Pacific governments subsidize and deliver health services; where services are not free, any user fees charged are generally low relative to global benchmarks (Figure 7.7).

However, available facilities may be inadequate and difficult to access; especially for patients who must travel from remote outer islands to the nearest major urban center—or even abroad—to seek treatment.

Figure 7.6: Routine Immunization Coverage
(% of children, 2000–2018)

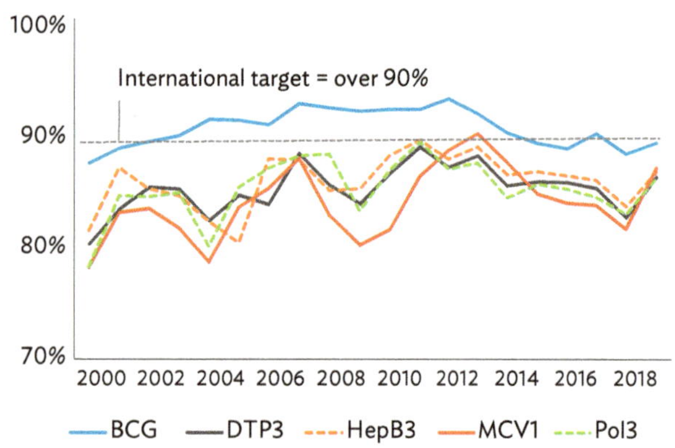

Notes: This figure shows average coverage in ADB's Pacific developing member countries. Vaccines included are BCG (for tuberculosis), DTP3 (for diphtheria, pertussis/whooping cough, and tetanus), HepB3 (for hepatitis B), MCV1 (for measles), and Pol3 (for polio). The BCG, HepB3, MCV1, and Pol3 vaccines are administered to 1-year-old children, while the DTP3 vaccine is administered to those aged between 12-23 months.

Source: United Nations International Children's Fund. Vaccine and Immunization Statistics. Immunization coverage by antigen (country, regional and global trends) https://data.unicef.org/topic/child-health/immunization (accessed July 2020).

Figure 7.7: Composition of Domestic Health Expenditure
(% of current expenditure, average for 2000–2017)

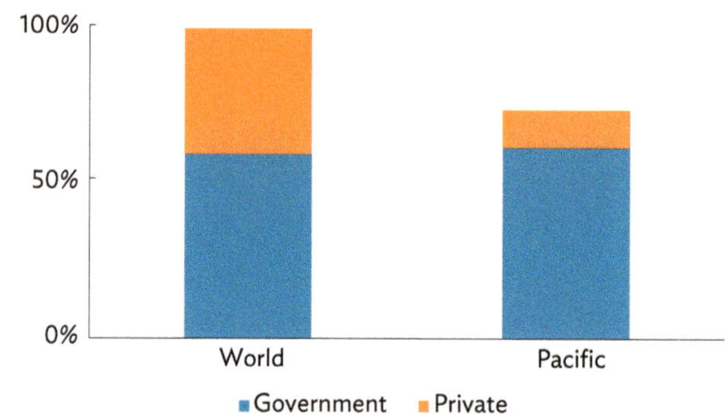

Notes: Data for the Pacific cover ADB developing member countries except for the Cook Islands and Niue. Government expenditure excludes those funded through external sources, such as direct foreign transfers and foreign transfers distributed by government.

Source: World Bank. Health Nutrition and Population Statistics July 2020. https://databank.worldbank.org/source/health-nutrition-and-population-statistics (accessed July 2020).

Further, in most Pacific countries, health workers lack the training to diagnose and treat common childhood diseases, including pneumonia and diarrhea, resulting in unnecessary referrals to district and tertiary centers, at additional costs for families. Screening and treatment for cervical cancer have been especially challenging due to resource, logistical, and follow-up constraints. In addition, many governments face shrinking fiscal resources. Development partners continue to provide critical support in key areas of health care such as human resources, vaccines, and specialist services.

Most national immunization programs in the Pacific procure vaccines through the Vaccine Independence Initiative (VII) under the United Nations Children's Fund. However, the VII has mainly focused on coverage for traditional vaccines. New vaccines such as HPV, PCV, and rotavirus vaccines are much more expensive than traditional ones, and small island Pacific countries lack the individual purchasing power and capacity to procure and administer them. Among ADB's developing member countries in the region, only four have introduced these vaccines: Fiji, and the three North Pacific countries (the Federated States of Micronesia, the Marshall Islands, and Palau) who receive grant support under their Compacts of Free Association with the United States (ADB 2018d). Most Pacific countries are ineligible for immunization financing mechanisms for low-income countries, such as the subsidized prices offered by the Vaccine Alliance (ADB 2018d).

Further, significant investments are required to upgrade cold-chain equipment and supply-chain management for the safe delivery, storage, and management of vaccine stocks, training of vaccinators and related health workers to administer and monitor at routine and outreach immunization, and strengthening risk communication on the benefits of immunization through community engagement and minimize vaccine hesitancy. The wide dispersal of islands within a Pacific country also adds significant costs and logistical challenges to take these vaccines through "the last mile" to remote communities.

A Regional Approach to Strengthening Health-Care Systems

Given these specific and severe constraints, a regional health support mechanism is essential. Pooled resources and collective action will make it easier to purchase supplies and make the necessary investments to broaden vaccine coverage, as well as help Pacific countries build the capacity to provide primary health care and channel local resources toward more sustainable, cost-effective measures. Pacific leaders recognize that cooperation and collective action is key to fighting cervical cancer, identified as a regional development priority (ADB 2018d; Pacific Islands Forum 2016).

In November 2018, ADB approved a Systems Strengthening for Effective Coverage of New Vaccines in the Pacific Project. Over the next 5 years, it will support public health in Samoa, Tonga, Tuvalu, and Vanuatu in several ways:

- **Strengthen vaccine procurement in the region** by funding the purchase, through the VII, of the HPV, PCV, and rotavirus vaccines, and related cold-chain equipment and supplies. The project will work with at least 90% of health facilities in planning the rollout of these vaccines to selected priority communities, using vaccine forecasting to ensure adequate supplies nationwide even in times of emergency. It will also build the capacity of these facilities for more effective planning and procurement of health-related commodities.

- **Strengthen local health systems** by providing support to (i) update immunization and cold-chain policies, guidelines, and training materials; (ii) train health workers to administer vaccines, as well as manage supply chains and conduct preventive maintenance, among others, to help ensure adequate vaccine stocks are available nationwide; (iii) build health staff capacity in evidence-based planning and bottom-up budgeting; (iv) report and integrate sex-disaggregated immunization data in the broader health information system; and (v) conduct nationwide surveys on immunization coverage and other related matters to assess the quality and equity of vaccine management.

- **Improve community awareness about vaccinations** by assisting ministries of health—in partnership with other stakeholders such as civil society and church groups—to heighten public awareness on the efficacy of vaccinations (vaccine acceptance).

Toward More Responsive Health Systems in the Pacific

The project is in the early stages of implementation, but represents a significant step in safeguarding public health through regional action. Pooling procurement through the VII will allow Pacific countries to benefit from establishing a regional buffer stock of vaccines across Samoa, Tonga, Tuvalu, and Vanuatu in case of health emergencies, such as an outbreak. These countries will also benefit from bulk purchasing prices, quality products, and technical expertise toward broadening vaccine coverage, particularly those critically important to women and children under 5 years.

Further, the regional approach will help lower project implementation costs while enhancing the efficiency, sustainability, and accessibility to immunization and primary health services across multiple countries. Improving primary care over the course of the project should help countries better respond to emergencies such as COVID-19. Engaging local stakeholders will also help spread important information on disease prevention and treatment, and promote better health-seeking behavior in communities.

The project directors in the four beneficiary countries have come together annually to discuss the project design features and implementation, and more regular meetings are anticipated as the project activities are stepped up. Under the project, the four countries share a pool of experts in health financing, gender, monitoring and evaluation, procurement, and public health. Besides providing project implementation support to the individual ministries, these experts will also enable sharing of knowledge across countries throughout project duration.

Unlocking the Potential of Digital Platform Economies

Digital platforms can be strong catalysts for economic value, as they significantly lower the cost of acquiring and using information, thereby lowering transaction and production costs. They are seen as an important means for stronger growth, and their ability to minimize human physical contact makes them a valuable tool in ensuring markets continue working during a pandemic.

During the COVID-19 pandemic, ICT plays an increasingly critical role in keeping people and services connected despite the unprecedented lockdowns and virtual suspension of social and economic activities. It allows activities to go online (such as schooling, shopping, virtual meetings, and socializing) and could make the option of "working and learning from home" standard. Digital technology also helps countries respond to the pandemic more effectively by enabling e-medicine (online consultations and diagnostics) and e-tracing (patients and their contacts) along with other services (such as hospital automation). Social and business videochat applications and collaborative platforms are proving increasingly indispensable during the pandemic, and will likely become essential venues in a post-pandemic era. For example, ICT drives e-commerce, which boosts efficiency, enhances market access for businesses and consumers, and generates substantial spillover effects.

A Digital Future for Central Asia

CAREC countries are pursuing national digital strategies and modernizing infrastructure to boost international and local connectivity. Network coverage is wide with costs lower than the world average. Although internet use varies widely, e-commerce is gaining momentum through international digital platforms.

CAREC 2030 promotes integration of ICT use across all CAREC operational clusters to raise the quality and efficiency of public services and support private sector growth. CAREC members, despite uneven levels of integrated ICT solutions, are on average sufficiently prepared to increasingly use improved ICT to mitigate the COVID-19 impact and promote national and regional economic recovery. Challenges remain, however, including outmoded laws on e-transactions and customs rules, preference for cash payments, insufficient e-banking services, and inadequate delivery systems. CAREC countries still need to bridge the digital divide, to fully harness ICT potential in the region. ICT investment and knowledge services are needed to address the key challenges of inadequate internet connectivity and limited access to the latest technologies, and a shortage of support programs to promote digital technology initiatives.

ADB is providing a $1 million TA to help CAREC countries apply digital technologies with strengthened ICT capacities; and better prepare for a new normal—continuously containing the COVID-19 virus while supporting economic revival. The TA supports the digital transformation and start-up ecosystem development in the region.

- Digital transformation of the CAREC Program will be supported through (i) assessing current integration of digital technologies and ICT in member countries and through CAREC clusters, and (ii) developing a CAREC Digital Strategy 2030. New digital mechanisms, tools, and needed equipment will be provided to facilitate virtual dialogue and enable remote collaboration and information exchange among CAREC countries. Virtual training activities, workshops, and seminars will be used to strengthen the required skill set to effectively apply ICT. These efforts will feed into the development of the CAREC Digital Strategy 2030 setting out a vision and a plan toward 2030.

- The start-up ecosystem will be supported through knowledge-sharing and capacity-building activities. A regional platform will be established to harness innovative ideas and digital solutions by encouraging participation in collaborative projects that address the problems posed by the pandemic. Strengthening partnerships between private and public initiatives including government officials, financial institutions, start-ups, incubators, accelerators, and universities, and increasing access to global centers of innovation and start-up excellence—particularly from Japan, Malaysia, the PRC, the Republic of Korea, Singapore, European countries, the United Arab Emirates, and the United States—will accelerate knowledge transfer.

Banking on ICT for GMS Trade Facilitation and Border Opening

As intraregional trade and overland tourism—as well as intraregional labor migration—continue to be major drivers of the GMS economy, the use of digital platforms (such as e-customs clearance and digital contracting technology) will offer a safe way for GMS countries to reopen their land borders. Due to the virus outbreak, travel restrictions, border closures, and mobility restrictions will increase trade costs for industries linked to global supply chains by 1%–2% (Park et al. 2020). Digital platforms can help mitigate these increased costs. For example, in trade facilitation, ADB has been supporting a feasibility study in Cambodia to assess the use of an ICT-based cargo tracking system that allows automated surveillance systems to monitor cargo movement. This cargo tracking system—along with an information platform that allows interagency and cross-border information exchange between officials and electronic customs clearance—can ease the trade of goods across the subregion.

Similarly, as the COVID-19 infection rate remains low and well contained across the subregion, GMS countries could use a digital contact tracking and tracing platform to allow the freer movement of people across GMS borders. With 23% of GMS tourism arrivals from intraregional tourism, and overland arrivals reaching as high as 83% of total tourism in the Lao PDR and 59% in Myanmar, GMS economies could benefit greatly by safely opening land border crossings.

The E-Readiness of East Asia

Of the world's 70 largest digital platforms, the PRC accounts for 22% (by market capitalization). They include companies such as Alibaba, Tencent, JD.com, and Baidu. Government policy, private sector participation, and a large ICT manufacturing base have created the world's largest telecommunications and e-commerce market—and one of the most advanced intelligent connectivity systems. Although not at the same stage as the PRC, Mongolia also has a liberalized and competitive telecommunications market, a developed backbone network, and is improving connectivity with the PRC. Businesses use existing platforms and cloud-hosted software and data services to cater to more than 65% of online shoppers (Delger et al. 2020). The PRC and Mongolia are advancing their efforts in enhancing their regulatory frameworks on e-commerce. The PRC has enacted its Electronic Signature Law and E-Commerce Law in 2019 and is a signatory to the United Nations (UN) Framework Agreement on Facilitation of Cross-Border Paperless Trade in Asia and the Pacific. Meanwhile, the Parliament of Mongolia has on 15 May 2020 passed the legislation to accede to the UN Convention on the Use of Electronic Communications in International Contracts.

SASEC Program to Harness Benefits and Address Challenges of Digital Platforms

E-commerce is expected to become a key driver of growth in South Asia, potentially enhancing competition and productivity, and encouraging production and export diversification (World Bank 2020). Its online trade potential can help integrate the region into international value chains and strengthen commercial linkages between countries. However, while e-commerce has grown, it pales relative to other regions. Online sales, as a proportion of total retail sales, is below 2% in India and Bangladesh, compared with 15% in the PRC and 14% globally.

South Asia, with a large proportion of young people highly receptive to digital technology, could greatly expand e-commerce.[77] SASEC countries face many barriers to e-commerce, including poor logistics and trade processes, restrictive digital regulations and inadequate ICT infrastructure. Cross-country coordination to lower these barriers is being addressed under SASEC's trade facilitation platform. Its efforts to automate and streamline border trade processes will go a long way to enhance digital service platforms. The SASEC platform can also help synchronize government efforts to address related issues such as digital inclusion, cybersecurity, copyright violations, and tax capture, among others.

[77] The World Bank (2020) noted that removing regulatory and logistical challenges to e-commerce would increase SME exports, employment, and productivity by as much as 20%–30%.

References

Aleksanyan, L. and W. E. Liepach. 2020. It's Time for Central Asia to Do Whatever It Takes to Minimize the Pandemic's Economic Impact. *Asian Development Blog*. 24 April. https://blogs.adb.org/time-for-central-asia-to-do-whatever-it-takes-to-minimize-pandemic-s-economic-impact.

Asian Development Bank (ADB). 2016a. *Report and Recommendation of the President for Mongolia's Regional Upgrades of Sanitary and Phytosanitary Measures for Trade Project.* Manila.

———. 2016b. *South Asia Subregional Economic Cooperation Operational Plan 2016–2025.* Manila.

———. 2017. *SASEC Powering Asia in the 21st Century.* Manila.

———. 2018a. *Central Asia Regional Economic Cooperation Integrated Trade Agenda 2030 and Rolling Strategic Action Plan 2018-2020.* Manila.

———. 2018b. *Report and Recommendation of the President for the People's Republic of China Guangxi Regional Cooperation and Integration Promotion Investment Program.* Manila.

———. 2018c. *Report and Recommendation of the President to the Board of Directors: Proposed Loan and Grants to the Independent State of Samoa, Kingdom of Tonga, Tuvalu, and Republic of Vanuatu for the Systems Strengthening for Effective Coverage of New Vaccines in the Pacific Project.* Manila.

———. 2018d. *Report and Recommendation of the President to the Board of Directors: Proposed Loan and Grants to the Independent State of Samoa, Kingdom of Tonga, Tuvalu, and Republic of Vanuatu for the Systems Strengthening for Effective Coverage of New Vaccines in the Pacific Project.* Regional Diagnostic Report (accessible from the list of linked documents in Appendix 2). Manila.

———. 2019a. *Report and Recommendation of the President for Mongolia's Regional Improvement of Border Services Project (Additional Financing).* Manila.

———. 2019b. CAREC Project Portfolio 2019. Manila.

———. 2019c. SASEC Project Portfolio 2019. Manila.

———. 2020a. *Asian Development Outlook 2020: What Drives Innovation in Asia?.* Manila.

———. 2020b. *Asian Development Outlook 2020 Update: Wellness in Worrying Times.* Manila.

———. 2020c. *Report and Recommendation of the President for Mongolia's Developing the Economic Cooperation Zone Project.* Manila.

BBC News. 2019. *Samoa Lifts State of Emergency over Measles Epidemic.* 29 December. https://www.bbc.com/news/world-asia-50938250.

CAREC Institute. 2020. Regulatory Framework for e-Commerce Development in CAREC. *Policy Brief.* April. Urumqi.

Delger O., M. Tseveenbayar, E. Namsrai, and G. Tsendsuren. 2020. Current State of E-Commerce in Mongolia: Payment and Delivery. In J. S. Pan, J. Li, P. W. Tsai, and L. Jain, eds. *Advances in Intelligent Information Hiding and Multimedia Signal Processing: Smart Innovation, Systems and Technologies.* Vol. 156. Singapore: Springer.

Greater Mekong Subregion (GMS). GMS Statistics Database. www.greatermekong/statistics (accessed August 2020).

Government of India, Central Electricity Regulatory Commission. http://www.cercind.gov.in/2019/regulation/CBTE-Regulations2019.pdf (accessed July 2020).

International Federation of Red Cross and Red Crescent Societies (IFRC). 2020. *Dengue Fever Another Blow for the Pacific Islands.* 19 May. https://media.ifrc.org/ifrc/2020/05/19/dengue-fever-another-blow-pacific-islands/.

International Monetary Fund (IMF). http://data.imf.org (accessed June 2020).

———. Direction of Trade Statistics. https://data.imf.org/DOT (accessed November 2020).

———. World Economic Outlook April 2020 Database. https://www.imf.org/external/pubs/ft/weo/2020/01/weodata/index.aspx (accessed August 2020).

———. World Economic Outlook October 2020 Database. https://www.imf.org/en/Publications/WEO/weo-database/2020/October (accessed November 2020).

Nepal in Data. https://nepalindata.com/resource/transmission-system-development-plan-nepal/ (accessed July 2020).

Pacific Islands Forum. 2016. Forum Communiqué. Pohnpei.

Park, C.Y., J. Villafuerte, A. Abiad, B. Narayanan, E. Banzon, J. Samson, A. Aftab, and M.C. Tayag. 2020. An Updated Assessment of the Economic Impact of COVID-19. *ADB Briefs*. No. 133. May. Manila: Asian Development Bank.

United Nations International Children's Fund (UNICEF). 2019. *Levels & Trends in Child Mortality: Report 2019.* New York.

———. Vaccine and Immunization Statistics. Immunization Coverage by Antigen (country, regional, and global trends). https://data.unicef.org/topic/child-health/immunization (accessed 2020).

———. World Investment Report 2019. https://unctad.org/Sections/dite_dir/docs/WIR2019/WIR19_tab01.xlsx (accessed August 2020).

World Bank. 2020. *Unleashing E-Commerce for South Asian Integration.* Washington, DC.

———. Data. Population Total. https://data.worldbank.org/indicator/SP.POP.TOTL (accessed November 2020).

———. Health Nutrition and Population Statistics July 2020. https://databank.worldbank.org/source/health-nutrition-and-population-statistics (accessed July 2020).

———. World Development Indicators. http://databank.worldbank.org/ (accessed June 2020).

8 THEME CHAPTER
Making Digital Platforms Work for Asia and the Pacific

Introduction

The last decade has seen the rise of digital platforms as a primary mechanism for organizing a vast set of human activities, including economic, sociocultural, and political interactions (Kenney and Zysman 2016). Access to digital technology gives individuals and households greater convenience and wider choices, triggering changes in purchasing and consumption behavior. Digital platforms help micro, small, and medium-sized enterprises (MSMEs) conduct their online business, and afford them global reach.

Platforms have been transformative, drastically challenging traditional business models. Digital platform-enabled companies have radically reduced the market shares of traditionally dominant firms and generated modern forms of employment like cloud work, "gig" work or local on-demand work, and informal entrepreneurial work.

Platforms have enabled consumers to become goods and services providers. Traditionally, household production was limited to a few industries, such as agriculture, household services, and real estate. But, as a result of the rise of platforms, households have also become providers of transportation services, food and accommodation, and culture and recreational services, earning income on the side.

By combining data and algorithm, digital platforms can also help address market failure and inefficiencies often associated with the provision of social services such as health, education, water, and sanitation. Usually, asymmetric information is the cause of high delivery costs and low access, and digital technology can bridge this information gap.

However, as with any technology or innovation, the platform economy has desirable and undesirable consequences. It raises issues on competition, data privacy, social and labor protection for platform workers, safety and security for customers, and taxation for the government—all of which require a reevaluation of existing laws and regulations. It may also amplify existing development challenges including inequalities.

The challenge for governments and society more broadly is to harness the potential benefits from digital platforms while minimizing their potential costs.

Rise of Digital Platforms in Asia[78]

Understanding Digital Platforms and the Platform Economy

Economies are undergoing digitalization. This transformation is largely due to the evolution and growing use of information and communication technology (ICT) such as electronic tools, systems, devices, audiovisuals, and storage that generate, store, or process data. Digitalization may also be viewed as the "incorporation of data and the internet into production processes and products, new forms of household and government consumption, fixed-capital formation,

[78] Asia refers to the 49 members of the Asian Development Bank (ADB) within Asia and the Pacific, which includes Japan and Oceania (Australia and New Zealand) in addition to the 46 developing Asian economies.

cross-border flows, and finance" (IMF 2018). Although the pace of digitalization varies among countries, these trends in transformation are reflected in the massive growth of digital data that provide business intelligence and opportunities for development policy (Albert et al. 2019; Martinez and Albert 2018).

The digital economy has core, narrow, and broad scopes. Following Bukht and Heeks (2017), the core and narrow scopes relate to the ICT-producing sector; they comprise various digital services (e.g., business processing outsourcing services) as well as platform economy services such as Facebook and Google (Figure 8.1). The broad scope includes the use of digital technologies for activities such as e-commerce, automation, and artificial intelligence, as well as the sharing and gig economies.

Figure 8.1: Three Dimensions of Digital Transactions

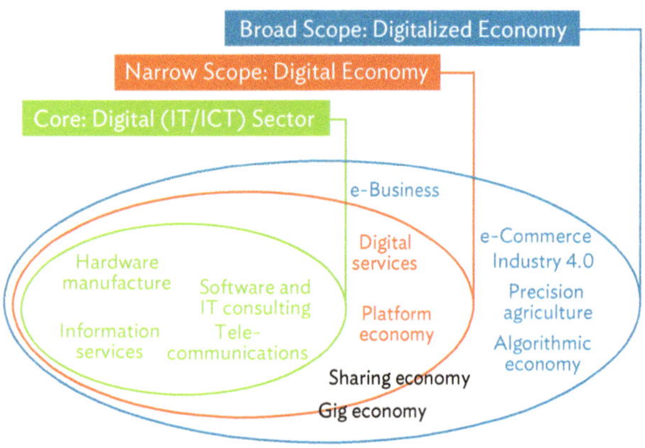

IT = information technology, ICT = information and communication technology.
Source: Bukht and Heeks (2017).

The digital economy can also be defined by the nature of digital transactions. Fortanier and Matei (2017) suggested the following possible criteria for distinguishing digital transactions: (i) the nature of the transaction—if it is digitally ordered, enabled or delivered; (ii) the transacted product—goods, services or data; and (iii) the partners or actors involved in the transaction—consumer, business, or government. Thus, a working definition of digital transactions, though not equivalent to the Organisation for Economic Co-operation and Development (OECD) definition of e-commerce,[79] includes those that are digitally ordered, digitally delivered, or platform-enabled.

Quite often the platform economy (which pertains to activities in business, politics, and social interaction powered by platforms as described in Kenney and Zysman 2016, for instance) is not separated from the wider digital (also called internet) economy, which involves anything powered by digital technologies (Bukht and Heeks 2017), or other new economy models. The latter include the sharing economy, which focuses on the sharing of underutilized assets such as accommodations and rides (Botsman and Rogers 2010; Sundararajan 2016; Cheng, Fu, and de Vreede 2018) and the gig economy, which pertains to labor participation and income generation through "gigs," i.e., single projects or tasks for which a worker is hired, as noted by Friedman (2014) and Berg et al. (2018).

There are no widely accepted standard definitions of the digital sector, the platform economy, and other new economy models. The sharing economy could have a broad definition to include the supply of work for small jobs in open labor platforms as well as crowd funding in financial platforms, or a narrow definition (Eurostat 2018) to include only the supply of underused assets (Figure 8.2).

Digital platforms are digital matchmakers. They provide a mechanism for consumers and suppliers to exchange information, match demands, and pay and receive and deliver goods and services. Platforms differ in their role and in the "products" they "exchange" (Table 8.1).

[79] According to OECD (2011), an e-commerce transaction is "the sale or purchase of goods or services, conducted over computer networks by methods specifically designed for the purpose of receiving or placing of orders. The goods or services are ordered by those methods, but the payment and the ultimate delivery of the goods or services do not have to be conducted online. An e-commerce transaction can be between enterprises, households, individuals, governments, and other public or private organizations. To be included are orders made over the web, extranet or electronic data interchange. The type is defined by the method of placing the order. To be excluded are orders made by telephone calls, fax or manually typed e-mail."

Figure 8.2: Various Senses of the Platform Economy

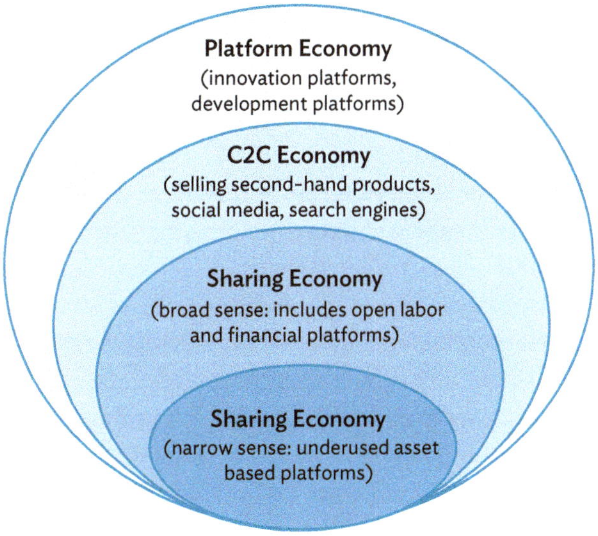

C2C = customer-to-customer.

Source: Heerschap, Pouw, and Atmé (2018).

Key Characteristics

Most digital platforms generally exhibit three basic characteristics: They (i) are mediated through technology; (ii) link user groups; and (iii) allow these groups to perform particular things (Koskinen, Bonina, and Eaton 2019). The major strength of a platform is its ability to mediate peer-to-peer services while eliminating intermediaries or trade barriers using a digital mode to facilitate transactions in goods, services, or data. The digital infrastructure in a platform increases the ease and speed of interactions, transforms transactions from local to global, enlarges the choice possibilities, lowers the transaction costs of interactions, and provides benefit to users and the platform itself (Heerschap, Pouw, and Atmé 2018). While in many cases platform companies do not own the means of production, they create the means of

Table 8.1: Selected Definitions of the Digital Platform

Source	Definitions
Heerschap, Pouw, and Atmé (2018)	A digital service based on a technological, sociocultural, and economic infrastructure for the facilitation and organization of online social (interactions) and economic (transactions) traffic between two or more distinct but interdependent groups of providers and users, with data as fuel (citing van Dijck, Poell, and De Waal 2016; OECD 2018a). Providers and users can be both individuals and businesses as well as science organizations and government.
Kenney and Zysman (2016)	A set of online digital arrangements whose algorithms serve to organize and structure economic and social activity; a set of shared techniques, technologies, and interfaces that are open to a broad set of users who can build what they want on a stable substrate; a set of digital frameworks for social and marketplace interactions. Catalyst that allows value to be created through interactions between various groups of market participants.
Koh and Fichman (2014)	Two-sided networks ... that facilitate interactions between distinct but interdependent groups of users, such as buyers and suppliers.
Langley and Leyshon (2017)	A distinct mode of socio-technical intermediary and business arrangement that is incorporated into wider processes of capitalization. Intermediaries between two or more groups of participants with interdependent demands, ..., (with a) ... main market function ... typically described as the facilitation of interactions and transactions between producers of goods on one side and buyers or users on the other.
OECD (2019a)	Digital services that facilitate interactions between two or more distinct but interdependent sets of users (whether firms or individuals) who interact through the service via the internet.
Pagani (2013)	Multisided platform ... exists wherever a company brings together two or more distinct groups of customers (sides) that need each other in some way, and where the company builds an infrastructure (platform) that creates value by reducing distribution, transaction, and search costs incurred when these groups interact.
Tan et al. (2015)	A commercial network of suppliers, producers, intermediaries, customers ... and producers of complementary products and services termed "complementors" ... that are held together through formal contracting and/or mutual dependency.
WEF (2017a)	Technology-enabled business models that create value by facilitating exchanges and interactions.

Note: The definitions were taken directly from the sources indicated.

Source: Albert (2020).

connection between suppliers and consumers. Two-sided platforms, such as ride-hailing platforms, link two diverse types of participants more readily and enable them to gain through trade or other interaction (Evans and Schmalensee 2007). Multisided platforms, like Facebook, bring together more than two types of participants (Evans 2018), such as users, advertisers, third-party game or content developers, and affiliated third-party sites.

Network effects distinguish platforms from other business models and are one of the main drivers of value creation in the platform economy (Evans 2016). The value and size of a platform rises with its repeated and broader use. Network effects may either be direct (where more users attract more users on the same side of the platform) or indirect (where more users on one side of the platform attract more users on the other side). As participants increase in number, the likelihood that platforms expand the services offered also rises, creating greater value to patrons.

At least three distinct but interdependent actors, namely, sellers or providers (supply side), buyers or clients (demand side), and the platform (intermediary) itself, are always active within the platform ecosystem. The providers offer goods (e.g., Shopee and Lazada), skills or services (e.g., MyKuya, Grab, and Netflix), and/or information (e.g., Google and Facebook) that can be delivered either physically or digitally to (potential) users. The platform itself is another actor in the ecosystem, as it supports price discovery and transactions between the provider and client, could process payments between buyers and sellers, and sometimes is used to distribute the product. Advertisers, which subsidize the value of the attention in the platform, constitute a fourth set of actors. This distributed network of people is the social infrastructure of platforms, and the set of economic and social activities encouraged is referred to as the platform economy.

Some platforms involve switching costs. There are some cases where users cannot easily transfer to other platforms. When investments, such as time and effort, are tied not only to a particular platform but to an entire ecosystem of linked platforms, users are less willing to switch. Positive network effects, economies of scale and scope, especially for first-mover advantages and significant switching costs, can entrench the market positions of the platform giants, and so stifle competition.

Platform-enabled companies, like other firms, gather and generate data. Platforms can use big data to build detailed profiles of their providers and clients which can then be sold as commodities. Most platforms use these digital footprints only to improve their own services, but others can leverage data (usage trends and user demographics) for their growth strategies to maximize value creation (by way of targeted content and advertising, attracting users and increasing platform use, or developing new services). However, this data capture has given rise to monopolistic market power as well as privacy and security issues.

Platform companies can scale faster and at lower cost than traditional firms (World Bank 2019). Since in many cases platforms do not incur the costs of production, they can scale up as fast as they can add partners. The Chinese multinational company Alibaba, which specializes in e-commerce, retail, the internet, and technology, reached 1 million platform users in 2 years and accumulated more than 9 million online merchants and garnered annual sales of $700 billion in 15 years. In contrast, IKEA, the Swedish multinational group that designs and sells ready-to-assemble furniture, kitchen appliances, and home accessories, took more than 7 decades to generate global annual sales of $42 billion.

Typology of Platforms and Measurement Challenges

There are many typologies used in discussing platforms, based on the type of interactions, roles, overall scope and structure, participation strategies or profit motive (Table 8.2). Nevertheless, it is difficult to have categories that are mutually exclusive, as some platforms, especially superplatforms, have features from several categories. Furthermore, functional typologies get archaic as platforms evolve quickly, necessitating periodic adjustments in the typologies.

Table 8.2: Examples of Platform Typologies

Defining Feature	Examples
Type of interaction	Matchmaking platforms; external exchange platforms like classified ad websites and product marketplaces; and maker platforms
Role in the ecosystem	Platforms supporting other platforms, transaction platforms, innovation platforms, integration platforms, and investment platforms
Overall scope and structure	Superplatforms (e.g., WeChat and Facebook), platform constellations (e.g., Google's main platforms), and stand-alone platforms
Revenue source	Subscription platforms (e.g., Netflix or Spotify), advertising-based platforms (e.g., YouTube or Facebook); and pay-to-access platforms such as those for content or app developers (e.g., iPhone or Android app stores)
Factor of production being harnessed	Capital platforms (e.g., Airbnb), labor platforms (e.g., CrowdFlowers and Microworkers), and hybrid platforms like transportation platforms that tap drivers and cars (e.g., Grab)

Sources: Ardolino, Saccani, and Perona (2016); Evans and Gawer (2016); Kenny and Zysman (2016); OECD (2019a); and van Gorp and Batura (2015).

A number of measurement challenges hamper giving a clear and integrated portrait of the role, nature, and size of the digital platform economy:

- Digital platforms (and providers) may not be physically located in the same country of either the buyer or seller, thus their economic transactions are not directly captured in local economic statistics.

- There is no specific economic activity code for platforms. Digital platforms could be active in several sectors, making it difficult to fit them into current statistical classifications. For instance, while the Philippine Standard Industrial Classification (PSIC) includes a sub-class code [47913] for "retail sale via internet," there is no comparable sub-class code for digital platforms beneath specific services sectors (PSA n.d.). For now, the provisional guidance is that digital intermediation platforms should be classified according to the activity they intermediate (if they intermediate services) and to ISIC 47.91 (Retail sale via mail order houses or via internet) if they intermediate sales and purchases of goods (OECD, WTO, and IMF 2019).

- Transactions are not always financial. In social media platforms, transactions are about data and information, the valuation of which can be challenging. Revenue and employment are also difficult to trace, and so likely are underestimated in traditional surveys, since platforms spread supply across small-scale nonprofessional providers. Many digital platforms also do not publish their accounts or disaggregate these data across country boundaries.

The economic activities of digital platforms are not fully captured in the current economic statistics framework. The economic activities of digital platforms are already partly captured in the national accounts. However, a distinction has to be made between market and nonmarket transactions since only market transactions are valued in national accounts. For example, even as the trading of second-hand goods involves a replacement value for the economy, this is not part of national accounts valuation. Annex 8a enumerates a list of indicators needed to measure the digital platform economy appropriately.

There is valid criticism that the gross domestic product (GDP) does not accurately capture the benefits received from unpriced goods, such as data and knowledge, resulting from increasing digitalization. Income from household production in the platform economy is not operationally accounted for. The International Telecommunication Union (ITU) warns that "current measurement efforts do not always reflect the socioeconomic impact of the digital transformation or the upstream and downstream consequences on the economy as a whole as opposed to just the digital share."

International organizations such as the United Nations Conference on Trade and Development (UNCTAD), the International Monetary Fund (IMF), and the OECD have set up work programs to advance the statistical and conceptual frameworks that will help national statistical offices to measure the digital economy in a consistent manner. This work involves defining the digital economy and other new economy models, and testing ways to capture the associated welfare benefits in the System of National Accounts (European Commission et al. 2009). These international organizations have also organized knowledge activities to look at various measurement issues. Dedicated surveys should possibly be coordinated at regional levels by international organizations for developing economies to address these measurement challenges.

Figure 8.3: Technologies Shaping the Digital Platform

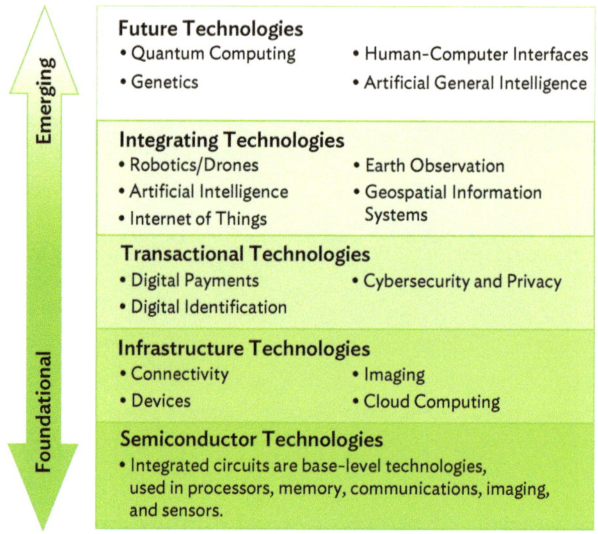

Source: Abell (2020).

Contribution to Growth and Development

Key Technologies Critical to Growth of Digital Platforms and the Digital Economy

Digital platforms are the driving force of future economic growth, and they rely on a few enabling technologies. Investments in these key technologies and effective design of regulations and policy are critical drivers of success.

As noted by Abell (2020), the key technologies that are driving the digital economy (based on digital platforms) can be categorized into five groups (Figure 8.3): (i) *semiconductor* technologies, (ii) *infrastructure* technologies, (iii) *transactional* technologies, (iv) *integrating* technologies, and (v) *future* technologies. All are evolving rapidly, so development planning needs to look far into the future.[80]

Size of the Market

The combined value of digital platform companies in 2017—those with a market capitalization of over $100 million—was estimated at more than $7 trillion, or 20% of global GDP (UNCTAD 2019a). In 2019, seven out of the eight largest companies in the world are platform companies—Apple, Microsoft, Alphabet, Amazon, Facebook, Alibaba, and Tencent. Based on Statista data (Statista 2020a, 2020b) and covering the six major sectors, business-to-consumer (B2C) digital platform revenues reached $3.8 trillion in 2019 equivalent to 4.4% of global GDP (Figure 8.4). E-commerce accounted for over half of these revenues (more than $1.9 trillion globally) of which $1.1 trillion were generated in Asia.

By geographic location, Asia accounts for about 48% of total sales revenue or $1.8 trillion, equivalent to 6% of its regional GDP.[81] Within Asia, 68% or $1.2 trillion in revenues are generated in the People's Republic of China (PRC), which is equivalent to 8.8% of the latter's GDP. On a per capita basis, the United States (US) leads with spending of about $2,542 on digital platforms, while it is only $432 in Asia (Table 8.3). However, Asia outpaced the digital platform revenue growth in other economies in 2018–2019, growing by over 16% on the strength of turnover in the developing economies in the region (Table 8.4).

[80] Annex 8b provides details on technologies that are critical to digital platform growth.

[81] For the market overview, six major digital platform subsectors were used in compiling the sales revenue figures: e-commerce, online travel, AdTech, transportation, e-services, and digital media.

Figure 8.4: Digital Platform Revenues—World and Asia, 2019 ($)

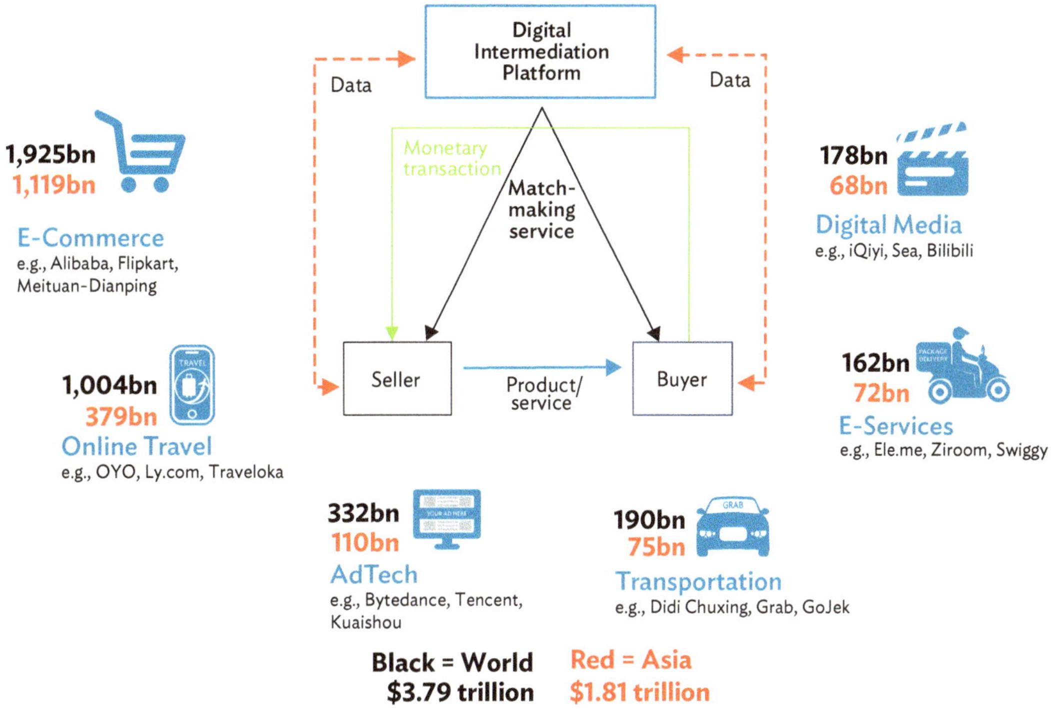

bn = billion, tn = trillion.

Note: Asia refers to Asia and the Pacific, which comprises the 49 ADB regional member economies where data are available.

Sources: ADB calculations using data from Statista (2020a, 2020b); and Organisation for Economic Co-operation and Development, World Trade Organization, and International Monetary Fund (2019).

Table 8.3: Digital Revenue by Region, 2019 ($ million)

Sector	World	Asia	Dev Asia (ex-PRC)	PRC	ANZ + Japan	Euro Area	US	ROW
Digital Media	177.5	67.6	13.8	35.0	18.9	17.3	57.6	35.0
E-Commerce	1,924.9	1,119.2	143.3	862.6	113.3	196.0	343.1	266.5
E-Services	161.8	71.7	16.3	47.0	8.4	15.0	42.8	32.3
Online Travel	1,003.8	379.5	127.8	179.8	71.9	173.5	199.1	251.8
AdTech	331.7	110.4	15.4	71.4	23.6	29.2	129.9	62.2
Transportation	190.3	75.4	19.8	48.8	6.8	14.2	64.2	36.5
Total	**3,790.0**	**1,823.7**	**336.3**	**1,244.6**	**242.8**	**445.3**	**836.7**	**684.3**
% of GDP	4.4%	6.1%	3.7%	8.8%	3.6%	3.3%	3.9%	3.3%
Per capita spend	513.9	432.3	121.1	863.6	1,547.6	1,308.2	2,542.5	275.1

ANZ+Japan = Australia, New Zealand, and Japan; Dev Asia = developing Asia; GDP = gross domestic product; PRC = People's Republic of China; ROW = rest of the world; US = United States.

Notes: Dev Asia includes Armenia; Azerbaijan; Bangladesh; Bhutan; Brunei Darussalam; Cambodia; Fiji; Georgia; Hong Kong, China; India; Indonesia; Kazakhstan; the Kyrgyz Republic; the Lao People's Democratic Republic; Malaysia; Mongolia; Myanmar; Nepal; Pakistan; Papua New Guinea; the People's Republic of China; the Philippines; the Republic of Korea; Singapore; Sri Lanka; Tajikistan; Thailand; Timor-Leste; Turkmenistan; Uzbekistan; and Viet Nam. Euro area includes Austria, Belgium, Cyprus, Estonia, Finland, France, Germany, Greece, Ireland, Italy, Latvia, Lithuania, Luxembourg, Malta, the Netherlands, Portugal, Slovakia, Slovenia, and Spain. Asia includes Dev Asia and ANZ+Japan.

Sources: ADB calculations using data from Statista (2020a, 2020b) and World Bank. World Development Indicators. https://databank.worldbank.org/source/worlddevelopment-indicators (accessed July 2020).

Table 8.4: Growth of Digital Revenue, 2019 (% by sector)

	World	Asia	Dev Asia (ex-PRC)	PRC	ANZ + Japan	US	Euro Area	ROW
Digital Media	6.3	7.1	11.0	8.8	1.6	5.3	5.6	6.8
E-Commerce	16.4	19.6	28.3	19.7	9.7	11.0	10.4	14.8
E-Services	16.0	18.8	22.8	18.7	12.3	10.0	15.5	18.3
Online Travel	7.2	9.1	10.2	10.7	3.3	6.0	5.6	6.6
AdTech	14.4	14.3	15.4	16.2	8.5	15.6	11.9	13.3
Transportation	8.0	12.4	12.4	13.6	4.7	4.3	6.9	6.6
Total	**12.7**	**16.1**	**18.3**	**17.5**	**6.9**	**9.5**	**8.4**	**10.8**

ANZ+Japan = Australia, New Zealand, and Japan; Dev Asia = developing Asia; PRC = People's Republic of China; ROW = rest of the world; US = United States.

Notes: Dev Asia includes Armenia; Azerbaijan; Bangladesh; Bhutan; Brunei Darussalam; Cambodia; Fiji; Georgia; Hong Kong, China; India; Indonesia; Kazakhstan; the Kyrgyz Republic; the Lao People's Democratic Republic; Malaysia; Mongolia; Myanmar; Nepal; Pakistan; Papua New Guinea; the People's Republic of China; the Philippines; the Republic of Korea; Singapore; Sri Lanka; Tajikistan; Thailand; Timor-Leste; Turkmenistan; Uzbekistan; and Viet Nam. Euro area includes Austria, Belgium, Cyprus, Estonia, Finland, France, Germany, Greece, Ireland, Italy, Latvia, Lithuania, Luxembourg, Malta, the Netherlands, Portugal, Slovakia, Slovenia, and Spain. Asia includes Dev Asia and ANZ+Japan.

Source: ADB calculations using data from Statista (2020a, 2020b).

Table 8.5: Digital Revenue, 2019 (% share of region in segment)

Sector	Asia	Dev Asia (ex-PRC)	PRC	ANZ + Japan	Euro Area	US	ROW
Digital Media	38.1	7.8	19.7	10.6	9.7	32.4	19.7
E-Commerce	58.1	7.4	44.8	5.9	10.2	17.8	13.8
E-Services	44.3	10.1	29.1	5.2	9.3	26.5	20.0
Online Travel	37.8	12.7	17.9	7.2	17.3	19.8	25.1
AdTech	33.3	4.6	21.5	7.1	8.8	39.2	18.7
Transportation	39.6	10.4	25.6	3.6	7.5	33.8	19.2
Total	**48.1**	**8.9**	**32.8**	**6.4**	**11.7**	**22.1**	**18.1**

ANZ+Japan = Australia, New Zealand, and Japan; Dev Asia = developing Asia; PRC = People's Republic of China; ROW = rest of the world; US = United States.

Notes: Dev Asia includes Armenia; Azerbaijan; Bangladesh; Bhutan; Brunei Darussalam; Cambodia; Fiji; Georgia; Hong Kong, China; India; Indonesia; Kazakhstan; the Kyrgyz Republic; the Lao People's Democratic Republic; Malaysia; Mongolia; Myanmar; Nepal; Pakistan; Papua New Guinea; the People's Republic of China; the Philippines; the Republic of Korea; Singapore; Sri Lanka; Tajikistan; Thailand; Timor-Leste; Turkmenistan; Uzbekistan; and Viet Nam. Euro area includes Austria, Belgium, Cyprus, Estonia, Finland, France, Germany, Greece, Ireland, Italy, Latvia, Lithuania, Luxembourg, Malta, the Netherlands, Portugal, Slovakia, Slovenia, and Spain. Asia includes Dev Asia and ANZ+Japan.

Source: ADB calculations using data from Statista (2020a, 2020b).

Asia leads in generating digital revenues in all sectors, except in advertising technology (which includes Google and Facebook) where the US dominates (Table 8.5). In e-commerce, Asia accounts for over 58% of total sales revenue. The PRC is the most active country in the region, accounting for over 44.8% of the sales in e-commerce, 29.1% of the sales in e-services, and a quarter of the sales in transportation. The market in developing Asia (excluding the PRC) is also vibrant; its shares in all sectors except digital media and advertising technology are higher than those of Australia, New Zealand, and Japan (ANZ+Japan). By segment, e-commerce and digital travel dominate (Figure 8.5). In Asia, e-commerce generated over 61% of the digital platform revenues while digital travel generated roughly 21%.

Figure 8.5: Digital Revenue in Asia, 2019 (% by Sector)

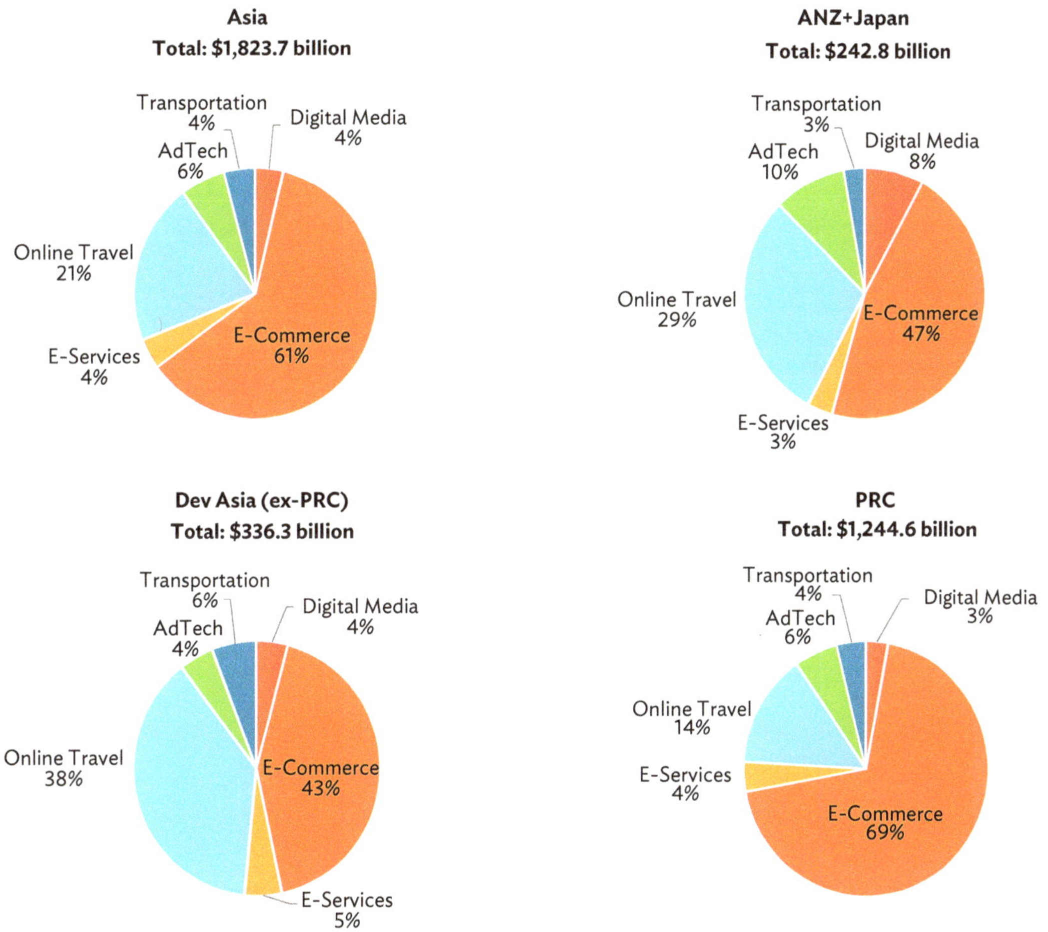

ANZ+Japan = Australia, New Zealand, and Japan; Dev Asia = developing Asia; PRC = People's Republic of China.

Notes: Dev Asia includes Armenia; Azerbaijan; Bangladesh; Bhutan; Brunei Darussalam; Cambodia; Fiji; Georgia; Hong Kong, China; India; Indonesia; Kazakhstan; the Kyrgyz Republic; the Lao People's Democratic Republic; Malaysia; Mongolia; Myanmar; Nepal; Pakistan; Papua New Guinea; the People's Republic of China; the Philippines; the Republic of Korea; Singapore; Sri Lanka; Tajikistan; Thailand; Timor-Leste; Turkmenistan; Uzbekistan; and Viet Nam. Asia includes Dev Asia and ANZ+Japan.

Sources: ADB calculations using data from Statista (2020a, 2020b).

Another indicator of digital platforms is the growing number of users (Table 8.6). It is estimated that AdTech-exposed internet users (who include those using social media apps such as Facebook and Google) are about 4.1 billion, of which more than half are in Asia. E-commerce user accounts number close to 3.2 billion, of which about 60% are in Asia. Meanwhile, accounts in digital media that include Spotify, Netflix, e-services, and online travel and transportation register more than 1.4 billion, about 775 million are in Asia. In terms of penetration rate and per capita spending, however, developing Asia still trails the developed economies (Figure 8.6).

Within the region, the PRC is the biggest market for digital platforms. The PRC accounts for about $1.2 trillion in revenue or 68.2% of Asia's total in 2019. The amount also represents roughly 8.8% of the PRC's GDP. Digital platform activity is similarly vibrant in the other East Asian economies. Revenues in East Asia (excluding the PRC and Japan) surpassed $290 billion in 2019 or about 4% of the combined GDP. South Asia follows, with a market size of about $130.4 billion in 2019, equivalent to 3.6% of its GDP (Table 8.7).

Figure 8.6: Digital Market Users, 2019 (million)

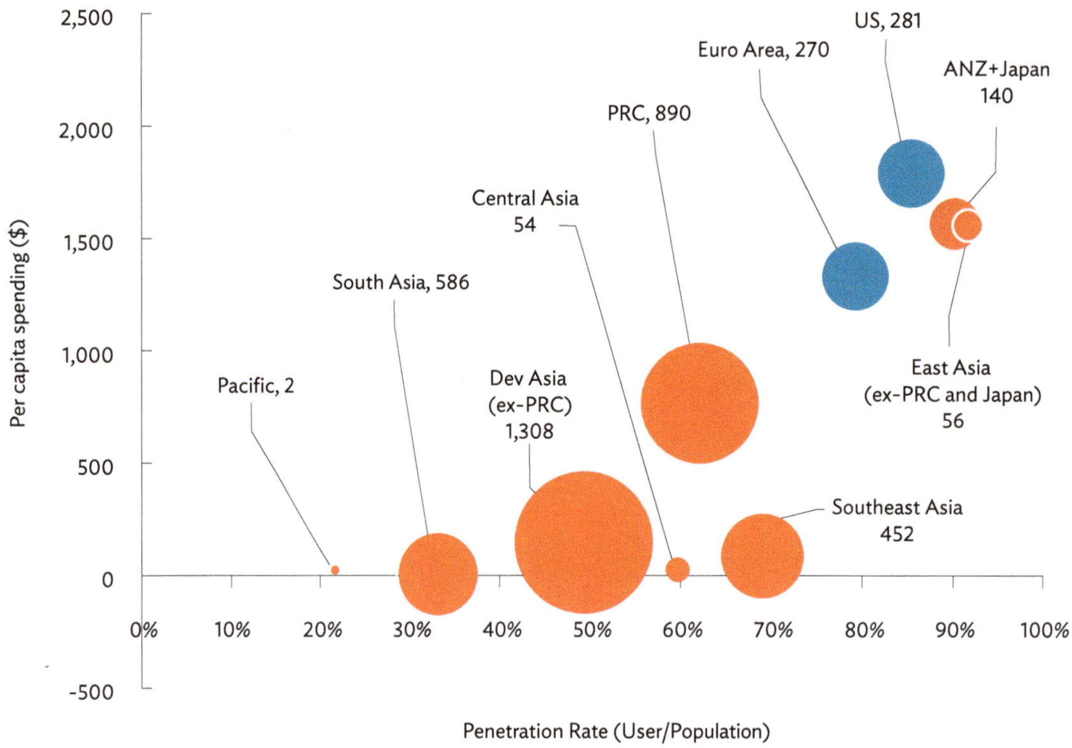

ANZ+JPN = Australia, New Zealand, and Japan; Dev Asia = developing Asia; PRC = People's Republic of China; US = United States.

Notes: Dev Asia includes Central Asia, East Asia ex-Japan, South Asia, Southeast Asia and the Pacific. Central Asia includes Armenia, Azerbaijan, Georgia, Kazakhstan, the Krygyz Republic, Tajikistan, Turkmenistan and Uzbekistan. East Asia includes Hong Kong, China; Mongolia; Japan; the PRC; and the Republic of Korea. South Asia includes Bangladesh, Bhutan, India, Nepal, Pakistan and Sri Lanka. Southeast Asia includes Brunei Darussalam, Cambodia, Indonesia, the Lao People's Democratic Republic, Malaysia, Myanmar, the Philippines, Singapore, Thailand and Viet Nam. Pacific includes Fiji, Papua New Guinea, and Timor-Leste. Euro area includes Austria, Belgium, Cyprus, Estonia, Finland, France, Germany, Greece, Ireland, Italy, Latvia, Lithuania, Luxembourg, Malta, the Netherlands, Portugal, Slovakia, Slovenia, and Spain. Users refer to the AdTech-exposed internet users.

Sources: ADB calculations using data from Statista (2020a, 2020b) and World Bank. World Development Indicators. https://databank.worldbank.org/source/worlddevelopment-indicators (accessed July 2020).

Table 8.6: Total Users in 2019 and Growth Rate in 2018–2019

	World		Asia	
Sector	**Number** (million)	**Growth Rate** (%)	**Number** (million)	**Growth Rate** (%)
Digital Media	1,438.3	6.1%	774.8	6.5%
E-Commerce	3,170.8	15.4%	1,876.4	17.9%
E-Services	815.4	12.1%	463.6	13.6%
Online Travel	987.6	2.5%	540.4	2.8%
Transportation	632.6	2.8%	403.9	3.2%
AdTech-exposed internet users	4,119.5	9.2%	2,338.0	11.9%

Notes: Users (except in AdTech) refer to the number of accounts that made at least one purchase in the last 12 months. Asia includes Armenia; Australia; Azerbaijan; Bhutan; Brunei Darussalam; Cambodia; Fiji; Georgia; Hong Kong, China; India; Indonesia; Japan; Kazakhstan; the Kyrgyz Republic; the Lao People's Democratic Republic; Malaysia; Mongolia; Myanmar; Nepal; New Zealand; Pakistan; Papua New Guinea; the People's Republic of China; the Philippines; the Republic of Korea; Singapore; Sri Lanka; Tajikistan; Thailand; Timor-Leste; Turkmenistan; Uzbekistan; and Viet Nam.

Sources: ADB calculations using data from Statista (2020a, 2020b).

Table 8.7: Digital Revenue by Asian Subregion, 2019 ($ billion)

Sector	ANZ+Japan	PRC	East Asia (ex-PRC and Japan)	Southeast Asia	Central Asia	South Asia	Pacific	Asia
Digital Media	2.3	35.0	22.4	4.2	0.4	3.4	0.02	67.6
E-Commerce	25.2	862.6	153.9	37.8	1.9	37.7	0.11	1,119.2
E-Services	3.4	47.0	8.7	3.3	0.1	9.1	0.004	71.7
Online Travel	20.3	179.8	76.4	32.5	2.6	67.8	0.06	379.5
AdTech	8.2	71.4	21.9	4.4	1.0	3.3	0.07	110.4
Transportation	3.4	48.8	7.4	6.5	0.3	9.1	0.01	75.4
Total	**62.6**	**1,244.6**	**290.6**	**88.8**	**6.4**	**130.4**	**0.28**	**1,823.7**
% of GDP	4.0%	8.8%	4.1%	2.9%	1.7%	3.6%	0.9%	6.1%
Per capita spend	2,086.0	863.6	1,540.3	134.4	70.9	72.6	25.6	247.3

ANZ+Japan = Australia, New Zealand, and Japan; GDP = gross domestic product; PRC = People's Republic of China.

Notes: Asia includes Armenia; Australia; Azerbaijan; Bhutan; Brunei Darussalam; Cambodia; Fiji; Georgia; Hong Kong, China; India; Indonesia; Japan; Kazakhstan; the Kyrgyz Republic; the Lao People's Democratic Republic; Malaysia; Mongolia; Myanmar; Nepal; New Zealand; Pakistan; Papua New Guinea; the People's Republic of China; the Philippines; the Republic of Korea; Singapore; Sri Lanka; Tajikistan; Thailand; Timor-Leste; Turkmenistan; Uzbekistan; and Viet Nam.

Sources: ADB calculations using data from Statista (2020a, 2020b) and World Bank. World Development Indicators. https://databank.worldbank.org/source/worlddevelopment-indicators (accessed July 2020).

Macroeconomic Impact of Digitalization in Asia: Estimating Potential Future Growth

The digital economy in Asia is expected to grow further, providing opportunities to bolster economic growth, build business, create jobs, and address socioeconomic challenges. To estimate the macroeconomic benefits of increased usage of digital technology, a scenario that leads to a 20% increase from the baseline by 2025 is analyzed (Figure 8.7). This scenario represents the digital transformation that has occurred during the coronavirus disease (COVID-19) outbreak as evident from the shift to work from home, online education, tele-health, e-commerce, and reliance on digital media. The digital transformation scenario is implemented by increasing investment in the digital sector which in turn contributes to higher output of sectors that use digital inputs more intensively and raises the overall productivity in the economy. Overall, the size of the global digital sector is expected to increase by an average of roughly $617 billion annually from baseline levels, or $3.1 trillion in total from 2021 to 2025, while the digital sector in Asia is modeled to rise by about $184 billion annually from baselines, or about $919 billion in 5 years. Box 8.1 provides the details of the simulation exercise.

Figure 8.7: Size of the Digital Sector in Asia and the World, 2021–2025 ($ trillion)

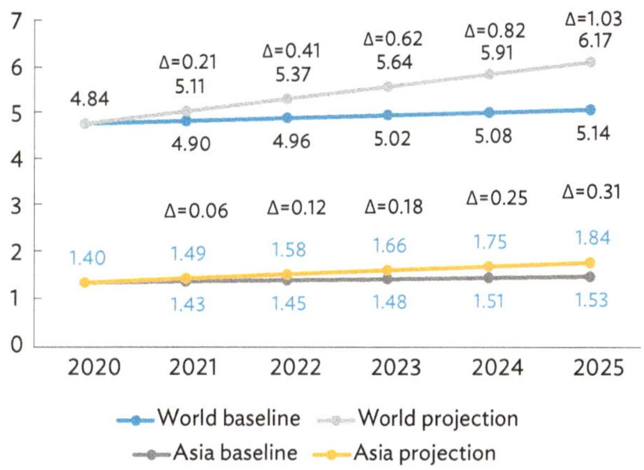

Notes: The calculations are based on the Global Trade Analysis Project (GTAP) database. Asia refers to Asia and the Pacific and, in this case, it includes economies that are not ADB members due to the aggregation of the Pacific subregion in GTAP. Numbers may not sum precisely because of rounding. The detailed table is in Annex 8c.

Source: Narayanan and Villafuerte (2020).

The simulation results show that increased digitalization will have tremendous impact on growth, export, and employment. Globally, if the digital sector expands such that its size is 20% higher than the baseline by 2025, global GDP will increase by about $4.3 trillion per year (5.4% of the baseline 2020 GDP), or by $21.4 trillion in 5 years. More than 40% of this increase in global output will be accounted for by Asia, where output will increase

Box 8.1: Simulating the Benefits of Digital Sector Expansion

For this exercise, a recursive-dynamic GDyn model developed by Ianchovichina and Walmsley (2012) was employed. This dynamic computable general equilibrium model combines aspects of capital accumulation, financial assets and associated income flows, and investment theory. The model also takes a disequilibrium approach to modeling capital mobility, allowing short- and medium-term variances in the rates of return across regions (implying imperfect capital mobility). In the long term, these different rates can be eliminated to achieve perfect capital mobility across regions. Financial assets (equity for physical capital) are treated in this model only to represent international capital mobility with no leaks in foreign accounts, rather than to show the real finance sector. Adaptive expectations in investment are assumed, and as the expected rates of return fall over time, the expected and actual net rates of return within and across regions converge in the long term.

The simulation draws from Global Trade Analysis Project (GTAP) 10A database with a reference year of 2014 (Carrico, Corong, and van der Mensbrugghe 2020), which are updated to 2019 using World Bank macro data sets and the Asian Development Bank (ADB) Multi-Region Input–Output (MRIO) database. The results from the long containment scenario of a previous ADB study on global economic impact of the coronavirus disease (COVID-19) were employed to capture this as part of the 2020 baseline. Moreover, many of the parameters used in the simulation are based on Golub and McDougall (2006).

Beyond 2020, the baseline is developed for macro variables, particularly gross domestic product (GDP) and population. This is based on projections by organizations such as the Organisation for Economic Co-operation and Development (OECD), the World Bank, the International Monetary Fund (IMF), and the United Nations (UN), which are further revised and collated in the Shared Socioeconomic Pathways data set by the International Institute for Applied Systems Analysis (Riahi et al. 2017). The exact details of the methods employed are documented in Moss et al. (2010); Arnell, van Vuuren, and Isaac (2011); van Vuuren et al. (2012); and Kriegler et al. (2012). In general, GDP projections come from IMF, the UN, and the World Bank, while the population and labor force growth projections come from the UN and the International Labour Organization. From a multitude of scenarios in the Shared Socioeconomic Pathways data set, capturing different levels of interactions between sustainability and growth, a balanced projection was chosen for this exercise. It represents the middle path based on OECD methodology.

After the baseline is developed, the policy simulation is defined, which is primarily the expansion of the digital sector in all countries by 20% from the baseline by 2025. In addition, it is assumed that the total factor productivity grows by 1% per year in all sectors, due to the use of digital platforms across all parts of the economy. Before doing this, the communication sector in GTAP is split into the digital platform sector and other communication sector, using several global and national datasets and literature.

Source: Narayanan and Villafuerte (2020).

by more than $1.7 trillion annually (6.1% of its 2020 baseline GDP), or more than $8.6 trillion over the 5 years (Table 8.8).

Broadly, the increase in GDP comes from the expansion of the digital sector and the corresponding improvement in productivity. Roughly about a third of the GDP increase accrues from the increased size of the digital sector while productivity enhancement accounts for the rest.

Similarly, global trade is projected to add close to $2.4 trillion per year to the baseline levels from 2021 to 2025 (5.5% of the baseline total trade in 2020) (Figure 8.8a). This translates to over $11.8 trillion in additional trade value in the 5-year period to 2025. About 43% of the increase in trade will be recorded in Asia, whose cross-border transactions are estimated to increase by more than $1 trillion annually (6.8% of their regional trade in 2020). With this, the region's total 5-year trade gains are set to breach $5 trillion.

Global employment will also rise by almost 140 million jobs every year (5.0% of the baseline global employment in 2020) (Figure 8.8b). With this rate of expansion, the cumulative job generation will reach roughly 698 million by the end of 2025. Employment in Asia is projected to increase by more than 65 million annually from the baseline levels (3.9% of the 2020 baseline employment). The increases sum to over 327 million jobs over 5 years.

The estimated impact of this digital expansion is not the same across all subregions. The most notable winner is the Pacific, where the increased size of the digital sector

Table 8.8: GDP Impact from Greater Usage of Digital Inputs, 2021–2025

Economy	Gains from Same Year Baselines ($ billion)						
	2021	2022	2023	2024	2025	Total	Average
World	**1,532.6**	**2,950.4**	**4,311.0**	**5,646.0**	**6,974.4**	**21,414.4**	**4,282.9**
Asia	**606.5**	**1,180.2**	**1,738.0**	**2,287.6**	**2,832.9**	**8,645.0**	**1,729.0**
Australia and New Zealand	35.1	62.9	86.7	108.1	127.9	420.7	84.1
Central Asia	13.0	27.8	44.3	62.6	82.5	230.3	46.1
East Asia ex-PRC and Japan	50.5	95.4	137.0	176.5	214.7	674.0	134.8
PRC	183.2	338.8	470.6	580.2	667.9	2,240.7	448.1
Japan	137.1	268.8	398.9	529.5	662.1	1,996.4	399.3
Southeast Asia	88.9	181.8	280.2	385.1	496.9	1,432.9	286.6
South Asia	91.4	192.9	304.8	427.1	559.4	1,575.6	315.1
Pacific	7.2	11.8	15.4	18.6	21.5	74.4	14.9
G2	**565.5**	**1,048.3**	**1,479.1**	**1,875.7**	**2,249.4**	**7,217.9**	**1,443.6**
United States	232.1	422.5	586.1	730.8	862.0	2,833.5	566.7
EU-28	333.4	625.8	893.0	1,144.8	1,387.4	4,384.4	876.9
Rest of the World	**360.6**	**721.9**	**1,094.0**	**1,482.7**	**1,892.2**	**5,551.4**	**1,110.3**
Economy	**Gains as Proportion of 2020 Baseline GDP (%)**						
	2021	2022	2023	2024	2025	Total	Average
World	**1.9**	**3.7**	**5.5**	**7.2**	**8.8**	**27.1**	**5.4**
Asia	**2.1**	**4.1**	**6.1**	**8.0**	**9.9**	**30.3**	**6.1**
Australia and New Zealand	2.5	4.4	6.1	7.6	8.9	29.4	5.9
Central Asia	3.2	6.9	11.1	15.7	20.6	57.6	11.5
East Asia ex-PRC and Japan	2.2	4.2	6.0	7.7	9.4	29.4	5.9
PRC	1.5	2.9	4.0	4.9	5.6	18.9	3.8
Japan	2.7	5.3	7.9	10.5	13.1	39.5	7.9
Southeast Asia	2.6	5.4	8.3	11.3	14.6	42.2	8.4
South Asia	2.2	4.7	7.5	10.5	13.8	38.7	7.7
Pacific	13.0	21.2	27.8	33.5	38.7	134.2	26.8
G2	**1.7**	**3.2**	**4.5**	**5.7**	**6.8**	**21.9**	**4.4**
United States	1.4	2.5	3.5	4.3	5.1	16.7	3.3
EU-28	2.1	3.9	5.6	7.1	8.6	27.3	5.5
Rest of the World	**2.1**	**4.2**	**6.3**	**8.5**	**10.9**	**31.9**	**6.4**

EU = European Union, GDP = gross domestic product, PRC = People's Republic of China.

Notes: The calculations are based on the Global Trade Analysis Project database. The Pacific subregion includes economies that are not ADB members. This is due to the aggregation of the Pacific subregion in project data.

Source: Narayanan and Villafuerte (2020).

Figure 8.8: Total Trade and Employment Impact from Greater Usage of Digital Inputs

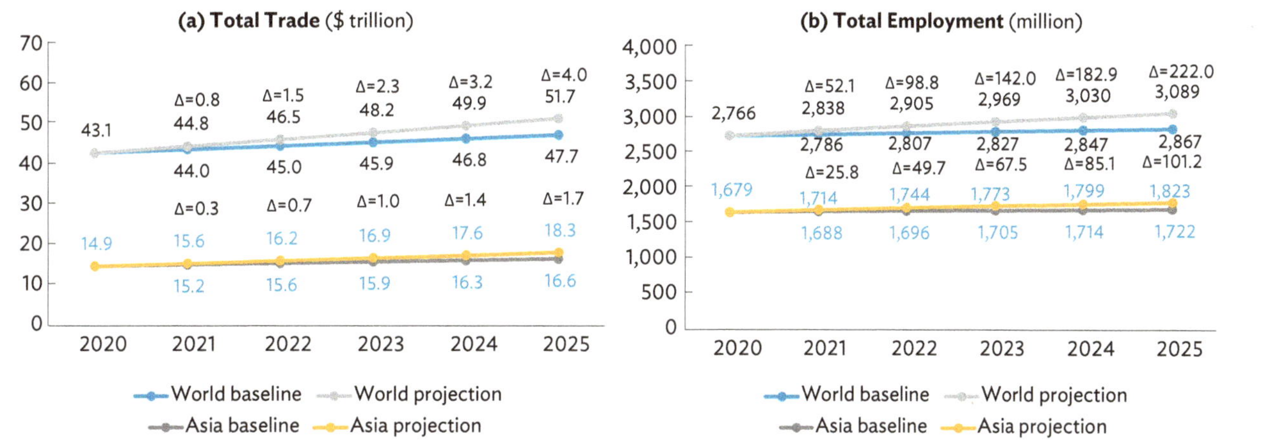

Notes: The calculations are based on the Global Trade Analysis Project (GTAP) database. Asia refers to Asia and the Pacific and, in this case, it includes economies that are not ADB members due to the aggregation of the Pacific subregion in GTAP. The numbers do not necessarily sum up because of rounding. The detailed tables are in Annex 8c.

Source: Narayanan and Villafuerte (2020).

will contribute to an average annual gain of 26.8% in GDP, 15.6% in trade, and 26.1% in employment from 2021 to 2025, compared with the respective 2020 baseline levels. Next is Central Asia, whose annual gains run to an average of 11.5% in GDP, 7.7% in trade, and 7.1% in employment relative to the 2020 baseline levels during the same period. Southeast Asia follows with average annual gains of 8.4% in GDP, 8.0% in trade, and 6.2% in employment relative to the 2020 baselines, also for the same period. The stronger output, trade, and employment responses in these subregions reflect the important role that digital connectivity plays in handling geographic challenges. It also shows the stronger productivity boost and larger return on investment in the digital sector for economies with nil or nascent digital presence. Another reason behind the stronger impact is the increased importance of digital-enabled trade in services as well as the heightened role of services in the internal and external flow of goods.

Figure 8.9: Investment Requirement, 2021–2025 ($ trillion)

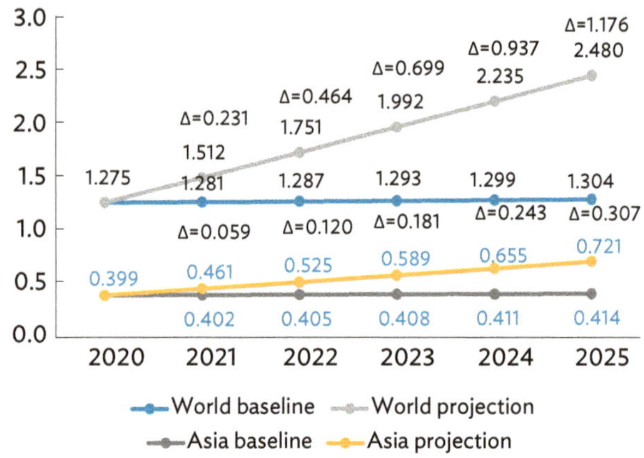

Notes: The calculations are based on the Global Trade Analysis Project (GTAP) database. Asia refers to Asia and the Pacific and, in this case, it includes economies that are non-ADB members due to the aggregation of the Pacific subregion in GTAP. Numbers may not sum precisely because of rounding. The detailed tables are in Annex 8c.

Source: Narayanan and Villafuerte (2020).

Key Policy Support to Realize Potential Gains

To realize potential gains from the digital economy, however, critical policy support and reforms are needed on multiple fronts. First, investments in the digital sector will have to increase dramatically to carry out this projected expansion in the digital sector output. Globally, investment in the digital sector in the next 5 years to 2025 needs to increase by an average of $701 billion annually or by $3.5 trillion in total over the 5-year period (Figure 8.9). For Asia, additional investment equivalent to around $182 billion yearly or $910 billion will be needed over the 5-year span. These additional investments are needed to deliver affordable mobile and broadband services and expand internet access and coverage.

Another key reform area is to improve trade and logistics processes and infrastructure to address existing barriers to the delivery of goods. Presently, the gap in the Logistics Performance Index between the best and worst-connected countries remains wide. Enhancing the application of digital technology to automate customs clearance and border procedures is important along with broadening the access to a safe and secure digital financial services and payment systems and options. Investing in training for digital skills and literacy by providing access to ICT devices and online teaching platforms is critical. It is important to create a smart, robust, and transparent regulatory system to protect personal data, prevent illegal activities, and strengthen cybersecurity.

Usage of Digital Platforms during the COVID-19 Pandemic

The COVID-19 pandemic has accelerated the adoption and usage of digital technologies while also highlighting the need to bridge the digital divide and enhance cybersecurity. The shift is most evident in activities that used to rely on human-to-human contact such as entertainment, shopping, dining, social interaction, and work. With the pandemic, many companies and consumers have shifted their businesses and services from offline to online (Figure 8.10).

E-commerce has expanded. E-commerce platforms have emerged with the closure of enterprises, such as grocery stores, owing to regulations and general consumer aversion to close contact. In a survey by Rakuten Insight Surveys (Rakuten Insight 2020), more respondents indicated higher online purchases during the pandemic (Figure 8.10a). Online retail dipped in the PRC (Figure 8.10b) at the start of the pandemic in January 2020, but picked up by February when the quarantine restrictions were put in place.

Figure 8.10: COVID-19-Related Changes in Asian Consumer Behavior and Retail Sales in the PRC

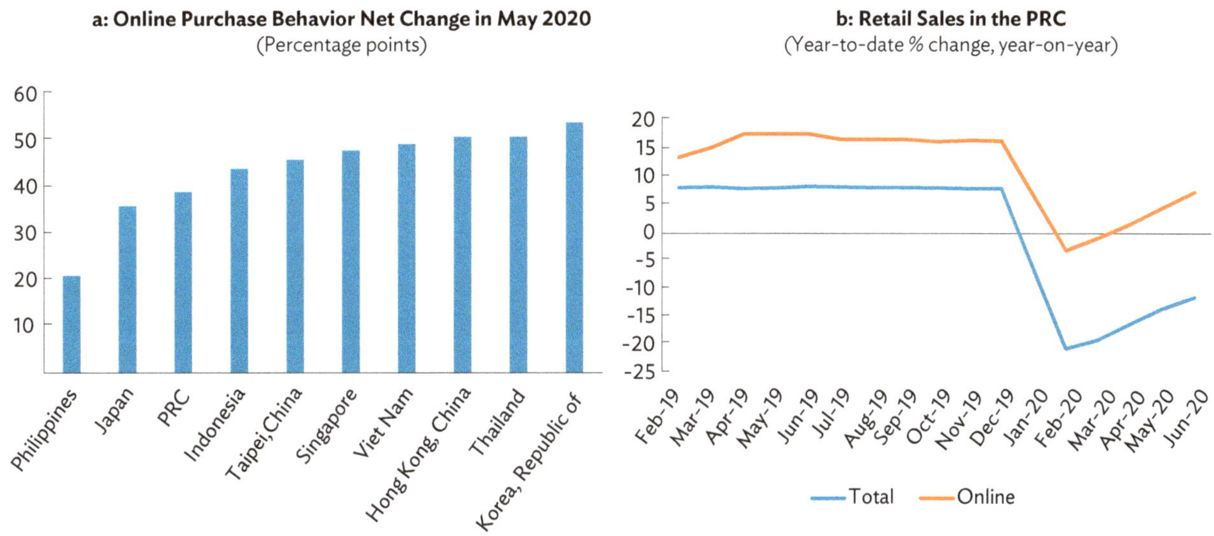

COVID-19 = coronavirus disease, PRC = People's Republic of China.

Note: The online purchase behavior net change data refer to the difference in the proportion of survey respondents that indicated they increased online purchases and those that say that online purchase has decreased.

Sources: ADB calculations using data from the Government of the People's Republic of China, National Bureau of Statistics. https://data.stats.gov.cn/english/?cn=A01 (accessed July 2020); and Rakuten Insight (2020). In Statista—The Statistics Portal. http://statista.com (accessed August 2020).

Accordingly, those in the business-to-business (B2B) segment implemented a shift from in-person interactions to remote sales (Figure 8.11). The Indonesian government teamed up with e-commerce platform Lazada to assist in transitioning 2 million MSMEs to the digital economy in order to provide small firms alternative streams of income to cope with the ongoing stress (Government of Indonesia, Ministry of Cooperatives and Small and Medium Enterprises 2020). Indonesia has over 60 million MSMEs, but only 13% of these businesses have online presence.

Figure 8.11: Adjustments of B2B Companies during COVID-19 (% of respondents)

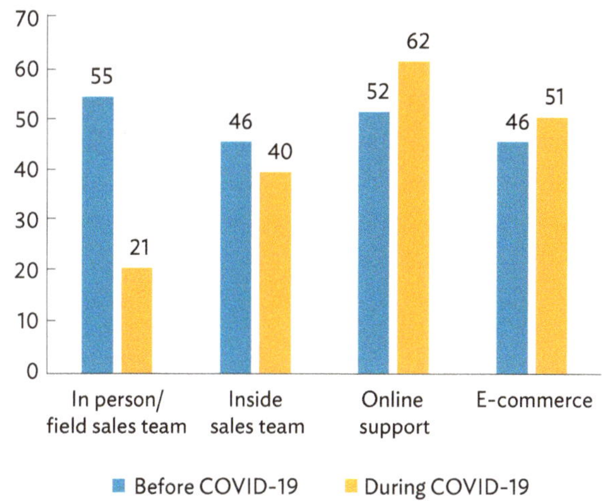

B2B = business-to-business, COVID-19 = coronavirus disease.

Notes: The questions were "In what ways were your company's product or service sold before COVID-19?" and "Now today, in what ways are your company's product or service sold during COVID-19?." The survey period is from 20 to 28 April 2020.

Source: Ray et al. (2020) using McKinsey. 2020. McKinsey B2B Decision-Maker Pulse Survey No. 2. April.

Telecommuting has spread while digital health and education gained traction. The disruption in traditional work arrangements has increased the usage of platforms for telecommuting, videoconferencing, and instant messaging. For instance, Zoom, a videoconferencing platform, has posted extraordinary growth in usage during the pandemic, with daily meeting participants surpassing 300 million in April 2020, up from 10 million in December 2019 (Zoom 2020).

The adoption of digital health services also accelerated in the region with governments and other agencies capitalizing on increased mobile phone penetration to improve their COVID-19 responses through increased health sector meetings, more efficient contact tracing apps (e.g., TracerTogether and Go.Data), and tele-consultations with medical professionals (e.g., PingAn Good Doctor and MyDoc).

On the education front, online (or at least blended) learning through platforms has become the common strategy to mitigate the impact of school closures on more than 1.5 billion affected learners globally based on estimates in late April 2020, which comprise over 90% of the world's student population (UNESCO 2020a , UNICEF 2020). Countries have partnered with telecommunications companies to increase bandwidth, with television and radio channels serving as alternatives to reach those without mobile phones and computers and with limited access to the internet. While promising, digital platform-enabled education poses problems for the vulnerable and disadvantaged communities, who have limited access to digital education modalities.

Patronage of recreation and digital payments services has risen markedly. The lockdown orders have driven digital media consumption as well. As reported by Media Partners Asia (2020), online video streaming weekly consumption in four Southeast Asian countries reached 58 billion minutes in the second quarter, compared with 36.4 billion minutes in first quarter of 2020. Netflix registered a 38.6% increase in paid subscribers in Asia from the end of 2019 based on the data obtained from the company's June 2020 quarterly report filed at the US Securities and Exchange Commission (Netflix 2020).

The establishment of digital payment platforms early on encouraged the transition from offline to online transactions, and their use will continue to rise. In the Philippines, the leading mobile wallet company GCash, reportedly saw a 700% year-on-year increase in transaction volume for the month of May (Globe Telecom, Inc. 2020) and its registered users doubled in number during the first half of 2020 (based on interview with Ron Testa, Vice President of Strategy, GCash in July 2020). The adoption of digital payments by the public sector has also been beneficial in delivering aid and related services in times of health crisis like COVID-19 as elaborated in the subsequent subsection on this topic.

Benefits and Opportunities from Digital Platforms

Sustainable Development Goal Agenda: Digital Platforms Can Help Leave No One Behind

Digital platforms can contribute to the achievement of the 2030 Agenda for Sustainable Development which builds on the principle of "leaving no one behind." Inclusive credit and finance programs, agriculture extension initiatives, educational opportunities, health projects, and efforts to grow MSMEs are now enabled by digital platforms creating vast opportunities for the promotion of sustainable and inclusive growth within the region. Digital platforms can support development efforts by helping remove market frictions caused by insufficient information, weak institutions, and poor infrastructure (Koskinen, Bonina, and Eaton 2019). For instance, the convenience afforded by digital platforms in ease of use and speed of scaling up have allowed governments to extend the reach of economic support more quickly to the unbanked, the women and children, and the poor especially in the rural and geographically isolated and disadvantaged areas. By 2020, over a billion people will be served by platforms in Asia alone, suggesting, as elaborated in Box 8.2, that they can be powerful tools in the fight to end poverty and promote social inclusion (The Asia Foundation 2017).

While more local small businesses are able to participate in e-commerce, they need better digital infrastructure, marketing support, skilled labor, and protection from unfair competition from digital market giant platforms. Moreover, as more women are empowered to join the digital economy due to the flexibility it offers, there is a need to assure them social protection like health insurance and old-age pension, skills training, and security from unscrupulous contractual work terms. Likewise, as more young people are engaged in short-term, intermittent, or nonstandard work arrangements, job and income security become pressing concerns, including the erosion of social insurance contribution base that may weaken existing social protection schemes, endangering future entitlements,

Box 8.2: How Platforms Help Achieve Sustainable Development Goals

Platforms can help local entrepreneurs launch their ideas on the global stage. Online platforms give small and medium-sized enterprises global reach, enabling access to customers at a fraction of the cost, effort, and difficulties of traditional sales and marketing channels. As a result, platforms help small businesses become global faster; diversifying sales to a broader customer base.

Platforms can help where the state may face a range of obstacles. Online platforms have the potential to quickly fill the gap and provide services and solutions when state mechanisms are unavailable. For example:

- In unserved rural areas, conduct online consults with professional physicians.
- Giving unbanked populations the ability to open a payments account and store value securely through a mobile payments bank.
- Where there is a lack of local educational institutions, a mobile device can be used to access the curriculum, coursework, and lectures from other sources.

Platforms can help overcome the "last mile" challenge. Underserved communities in the developing world are typically isolated geographically, are unbanked, or lack access to information. These "last mile" challenges reduce the impact of even the smartest, most well-funded development initiatives. Using online platforms, new mechanisms for delivering products and services to vulnerable communities at a low cost and at scale can be made available.

Platforms can help development assistance go further. Platforms can augment traditional development initiatives with new capabilities that offset shrinking aid allocations through the use of technologies. For example, cloud computing has made it much easier and cheaper for platform business to quickly expand capacity and meet demand for services. This helps keep operating costs low relative to their capacity to reach customers.

Source: The Asia Foundation (2017).

and increasing public finance strain because of social assistance especially during times of crises. Developing economies in Asia must harness resources to provide requisite digital infrastructure, responsive education and health systems, to prepare their populations to participate in and reap the benefits from the expansion of the digital market in the region. Regional cooperation should be pursued to tackle cross-border issues related to trade, e-commerce, labor regulations, and data use and privacy.

Digital Payments Enabling Financial Inclusion

State of Play

In 2019, digital payments accounted for 77% of the global fintech transaction value. This number is even higher in Asia at 86%. Up to 92% of the fintech users in Asia are in digital payments (Statista 2020a). Fintech presents a unique opportunity to leapfrog for emerging economies, where traditional financial systems are rather underdeveloped.

Digital payment systems emerged with debit cards, credit cards and electronic fund transfers, and mobile wallets and e-money, among other mechanisms. Since higher volumes of payments of smaller value can now be implemented electronically, recordkeeping is facilitated and reliance on cash for smaller payments is reduced, increasing transparency and lowering transaction and carrying costs.

The rise of mobile money and fintech payment systems, in general, fosters financial inclusion of previously unbanked or underbanked individuals. For example, in Association of Southeast Asian Nations (ASEAN) economies, 41% of the users of fintech payments in 2018 are unbanked or underbanked. Unlike debit or credit cards which typically require access to a financial account, e-money only necessitates a regular mobile phone and a SIM card in some cases—even without internet connections or a smartphone (Nachappa and Lathesh 2018). Moreover, fintech payments can create virtuous cycles with activities such as e-commerce, other fintech usage, and MSMEs.

Digital Payment Adoption and Use

The relative importance of card and e-money payments is significant and rising in emerging economies. Card and e-money are the dominant and rising cashless payment instruments in both emerging and developed economies, taking up around 70% and 60% of the total cashless payment volume based on data from 2014 to 2018 (Figure 8.12).

Global mobile money transactions have increased substantially in volume and value in recent years. The rise in mobile money service that is not linked to a formal financial institution account is particularly evident in sub-Saharan Africa and South Asia as well as in East Asia and the Pacific (Figure 8.13). Disaggregation by use shows that airtime top-up comprised most of the activity in both East Asia and the Pacific, followed by peer-to-peer transfers and cash-in/cash-out services. Mobile money is also revealed to be useful in facilitating remittances and bills payment. Indeed, the increasing provision of financial services to the population segments excluded by the traditional channels is vital in significantly advancing the agenda of financial inclusion in the coming years.

Public sector use of mobile payment has increased rapidly, especially in the distribution of cash assistance via digital systems during the COVID-19 pandemic. Prominent examples include the distribution of consumption coupons via Alipay and WeChat Pay in the PRC (Agur, Martinez Peria, and Rochon 2020), the PromptPay system in Thailand (Rutkowski et al. 2020), the "JAM (Jan Dhan-Aadhaar-Mobile) Trinity" system in India and "Bono COVID-19" in Chile (Prady 2020).

Digital G2P (government-to-person)/G2B (government-to-business) payments have the advantage of being more transparent, more timely, less costly, better at identifying intended beneficiaries through digital ID, and more accurate in targeting the most deserving recipients, particularly those who are unbanked or in the informal sector (Agur, Martinez Peria, and Rochon 2020; Una et al. 2020). The potential cost reduction in digital G2P transfer can be huge.

Figure 8.12: Relative Importance by Noncash Payment Instrument (average share in total cashless payments volume, %)

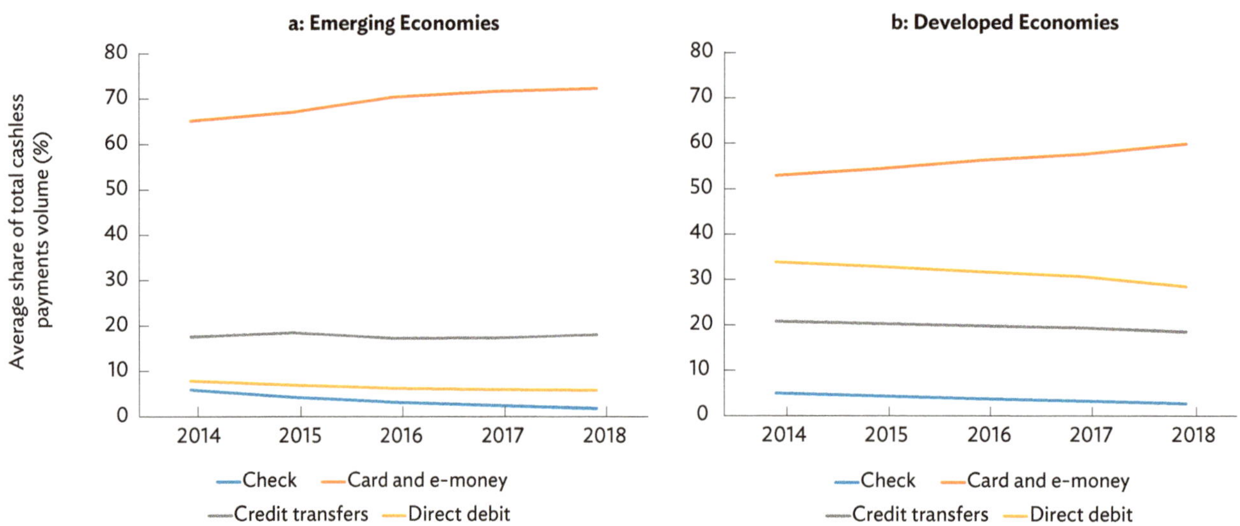

Source: Huang (2020) using Bank for International Settlements. The Red Book Statistics for CPMI Countries. https://www.bis.org/statistics/payment_stats.htm (accessed June 2020).

Figure 8.13: Trends in Mobile Money Transaction Volume and Value

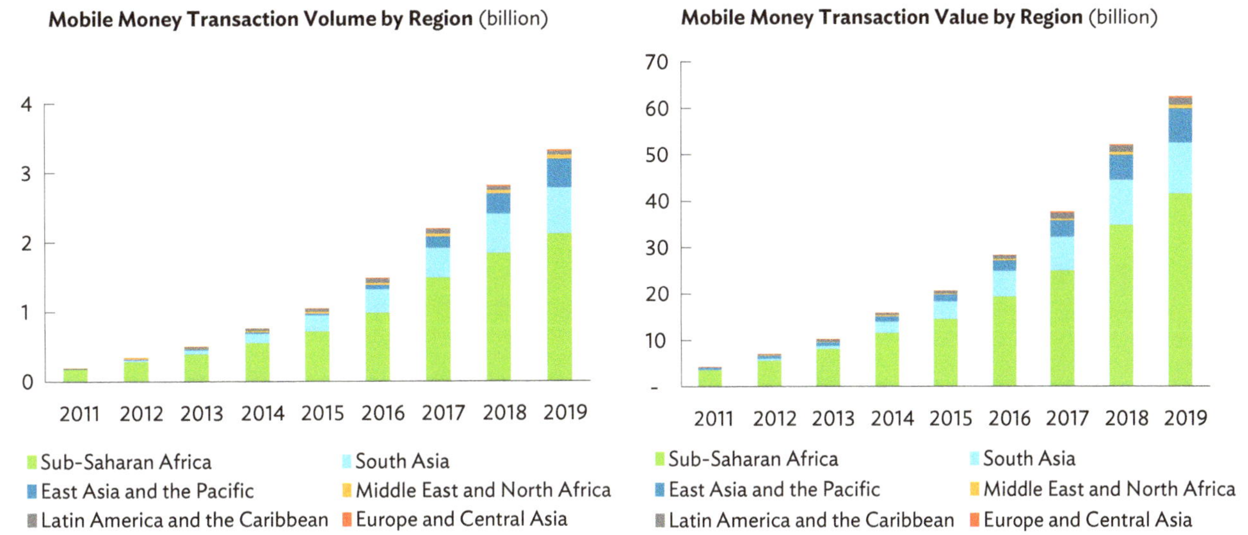

Notes: The Global System for Mobile Communications Association (GSMA) database only considers mobile money services that are "available to the unbanked, e.g., people who do not have access to a formal account at a financial institution." Therefore, fintech payment systems that need to be linked to a financial account or credit card (e.g., Alipay, Wechat Pay, Apple Pay, Google Pay) do not qualify as mobile money. The regional groups are defined by GSMA.

Source: GSMA Mobile Money Metrics Database. https://www.gsma.com/mobilemoneymetrics/#global?y=2019?v=overview?g=global (accessed June 2020).

For instance, during the Ebola crisis, Sierra Leone's shift to mobile wallets to distribute payments to frontline workers is estimated to have resulted in savings of more than $10 million (Bangura 2016).

Impact of FinTech Payments on E-commerce

Separately, a number of studies have posited that digital payment solutions tend to significantly bolster consumer spending—even for offline businesses. The introduction of the quick response (QR) code mobile wallet payment system in Singapore positively impacted sales of offline enterprises (Agarwal et al. 2019) due to its convenience of use.[82] In India (Agarwal et al. 2020), digital payment options spurred consumer "overspending" when demonetization happened in November 2016.[83] Xu, Ghose, and Xiao (2019) observed the same phenomenon in the PRC, where the adoption of the Alipay payment facility was associated with a significant increase in transaction frequency and value.[84]

These key observations reinforce findings of studies on the consumption effect of innovation in payment options (Soman 2001). Two policy issues arise from these findings. First, as pointed out by Agarwal et al. (2020), policy makers should consider the way digital tools shape consumer saving and spending behavior as economies pursue the agenda of going cashless in the coming years.[85] Second, the results emphasize the importance of access to reliable digital payment solutions in facilitating enterprise growth, even those in traditional brick-and-mortar setup.

82 The database has information on consumers' location, amount, time, and manner of spending as well as the nature of the receiving merchant. The analysis also focused on the sales of offline businesses that are charged on credit and debit cards of the consumers. Difference-in-difference estimation was employed to quantify the impact of the shock. It was also shown that the use of mobile payment in the country has surpassed ATMs in both amount and count of transactions before the end of 2017 despite the stable trend of the latter.

83 Difference-in-difference estimation was employed to quantify the impact of the shock.

84 The study also employed difference-in-difference estimation to quantify the impact of the shock.

85 Agarwal et al. (2020) noted that producing cash entails costs related to manufacturing, safeguarding, collecting, and circulating the instruments as well as costs to contain illegal activity and tax evasion.

Huang (2020) has likewise established the beneficial impact of fintech payments on e-commerce activity (Box 8.3). The results are an affirmation of the importance of reliable digital infrastructure, especially in financial intermediation, in order to foster growth in the platform economy.

FinTech Solutions for Remittances, Taxation, and the Informal Economy

Apart from e-commerce, remittance transfer is another service that benefits from the developments in payment mechanisms. Domestic remittance by mobile phone

Box 8.3: Exploring the Link between FinTech and E-commerce

The key results of Huang (2020) validate the strength of association between e-commerce and fintech payments. The study capitalized on the Alipay data in the PKU Digital Financial Inclusion Index of the People's Republic of China (PKU-DFIIC) data set covering 31 provinces from 2011 to 2018 (Institute of Digital Finance-Peking University 2019). Alipay, which was launched in 2004, is currently the dominant player in the payments space in the People's Republic of China. It has over 1.2 billion users (Klein 2020) and has a market share of about 55.4% in the first quarter of 2020 according to iResearch (2020).

Following the box table, the results of the empirical exercise show that a 1% increase in the payment index in the previous period is associated with at least 0.67% increase in e-commerce sales. The payment index is a composite of three elements—the number of payments per capita, amount of payments per capita, and proportion of the number of high frequency active users (that is defined as 50 times or more each year) to number of users with at least one frequency each year. Moreover, the estimates are derived after controlling for income, urbanization, age segmentation, and broadband users as well as for time and location fixed effects. As can be gleaned from the results, income and urbanization (i.e., a lower share of rural population), and broadband subscription are also significantly positively associated with e-commerce development.

FinTech Payment and E-commerce: Case of the PRC

Dependent Variable: Log of E-commerce Sales	(1)	(2)	(3)
Log of payment index	1.756*** (0.300)	0.316** (0.141)	0.900* (0.522)
Log of GDP per capita	0.350 (0.265)	0.336 (0.251)	0.560** (0.279)
Share of rural population	-2.489*** (0.746)	-3.464*** (0.695)	-2.901*** (0.798)
Share of population aged 65+	0.883 (2.396)	-2.511 (2.885)	-2.404 (3.297)
Log of broadband subscribers	0.799*** (0.0558)	0.738*** (0.0647)	0.781*** (0.0749)
Constant	-5.189 (3.055)	3.598 (2.658)	-2.393 (3.580)
Time fixed effects	Yes	No	No
Region fixed effects	No	Yes	No
Region-time fixed effects	No	No	Yes
Observations	186	186	186
R-squared	0.848	0.878	0.893

GDP = gross domestic product, PRC = People's Republic of China.

Notes: *** $p<0.01$, ** $p<0.05$, * $p<0.1$. Robust standard errors in parentheses.

Source: Huang (2020).

Source: Huang (2020).

has risen considerably between 2014 and 2017 (Figure 8.14). In contrast, cash/in-person transfers dropped from a cross-country average of 50% in 2014 to 30% in 2017. The convenience brought by digital transfers of income increases the welfare of migrant workers and their families. This is particularly crucial in developing countries with a considerable number of nationals working overseas, and in increasing opportunities in rural areas.

Figure 8.14: Payment Methods for Domestic Remittances Transfers (%)

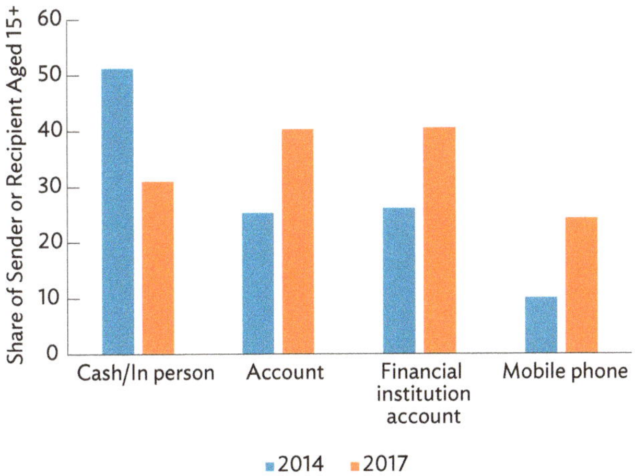

Notes: The data refer to the proportion of population aged 15+ who have sent or received domestic remittances by type of modality. The total number of countries with data is 110 in 2014 and 109 in 2017.

Source: Huang (2020) using World Bank. Global Findex Database. https://globalfindex.worldbank.org/ (accessed July 2020).

Furthermore, fintech payments can play a role in curbing tax avoidance and in reducing informality. Digital payment promotes electronic recordkeeping, which reduces tax evasion, fraud, and money laundering. Digital payment also helps with tax collection and refunds, which incentivizes tax filing. Digital payment reaches the recipient directly, which can curb unauthorized deductions in the distribution of wages or government transfers. More importantly, mobile money services have the capacity to serve the unbanked. The absence of associated fees for merchants, as noted by Klein (2020), likewise encourages smaller merchants to accept fintech payments in place of cash. However, safeguards must be established to prevent potential money laundering and tax avoidance due to underreporting and noncapture of fintech transactions.

Challenges and Risks

As payment systems embrace new digital technologies to deliver more efficient and socially beneficial solutions, there are also risks and challenges that need to be addressed.

The divide in access to digital payments is a crucial policy challenge. With fintech payments, carrying and transaction costs fall, and real-time settlement raises efficiency, particularly for liquidity-constrained firms and households. While these benefits extend to many unbanked individuals, the less tech-savvy and those who lack access to the relevant device or digital infrastructure may be excluded from taking advantage of the efficiency and convenience brought by fintech payments. Lack of financial literacy may also put consumers and businesses at risk due to the unfamiliarity to new fintech payment systems. Since most of these groups are also more socially deprived, this "payment divide" can exacerbate existing social disparities.

Transparency is equally essential. Digitalized payment options can help enhance electronic recordkeeping, contributing to efficient tax collection, reduction of the informal economy, as well as the detection of illegal activities such as fraud, money laundering, and corruption if properly designed. With the advent of blockchain technologies, the irrevocability of electronic records can be further strengthened.

The use of digitalized payment options generates huge amount of data which can be analyzed to predict customer behaviors to enhance business growth. Governments can leverage these data to better identify cash assistance beneficiaries and assist in crime detection. Unbanked individuals can have access to credits as their transaction and credit histories are now verifiable. However, unrestricted use of personal data could imperil consumer privacy and rights.

Security is key to building trust. Electronic recordkeeping protects consumers and fosters trust. While advanced technology for privacy and security in digital payment options provides additional layers of safety, they face other vulnerabilities such as network disruptions. A diversified set of payment methods promotes resilience as they can back up each other in case of temporary disruption. New forms of illegal activities may arise as the digital economy pervades—criminals can steal devices, identity, information, and assets in e-wallets. Although greater transparency improves the detection of fraud, money laundering, and corruption, cross-border transactions may also open the way for cross-border crimes and money laundering.

Network effects can dampen competition. Digital payment platforms can leverage their customer data, broad user base, multipurpose nature (BIS 2020), and associated networks to encourage the adoption of other fintech services such as e-saving, credit payment, credit scoring, peer-to-peer lending, and wealth management, thereby expanding their businesses. These unique characteristics could create excessive market power for digital platform companies.

Policy Recommendations

Policies can be broadly categorized to fulfill the following goals: (i) close existing loopholes of the regulatory system to reflect key changes of digitalization; (ii) expand access, particularly to the more socially disadvantaged groups; and (iii) promote regional cooperation. Governments and central banks are also encouraged to utilize digital technology in their own business practices.

Digital payments and the rise of the digital economy introduce unprecedented types of risks, including but not limited to data privacy breach, violation of consumer rights, cybersecurity, identity theft, and anticompetitive practices. Regulatory systems should keep up with developments in the fintech industry and bridge the existing gaps.

Encourage interoperability among platforms. Since technology can be widely applicable, many fintech payment providers mix a variety of services such as e-saving, wealth management, peer-to-peer lending, online shopping, ride hailing, social networks and food delivery. These "super apps" greatly increase convenience, but without regulation they may induce excessive market power and eventually harm consumer welfare and innovation. Encouraging interoperability among platforms is a way to reduce switching costs and maintain sufficient competition.

Provide relevant devices and connectivity, promote digital ID/digital KYC (Know-Your-Customers) mechanisms, and foster technological/financial literacy, especially to the more socially disadvantaged groups. To mitigate the "payment divide," governments should address obstacles to participation and provide relevant devices and connectivity to those who cannot afford/reside remotely; promote digital ID/digital KYC mechanisms to expand access, particularly those without an official ID; and improve technological and financial literacy through education programs for those who lack knowledge, especially for the elderly and the less literate. However, the more traditional payment options, especially cash and mobile money cash-in/cash-out services, should continue to be made available to serve those who cannot yet cross the "payment divide."

Promote regional cooperation to standardize industry practices, address cross-border cybercrimes, and integrate payment systems. Digital payment platforms and fintech payment options can enable cross-border transactions through lower transaction costs, faster settlement, and greater convenience. Governments should collaborate at the regional level and promote payment systems integration as this can also help in dealing with cross-border cybercrimes. Standardization of industry practices is a crucial first step in payment systems integration. In February 2020, the G20 recognized the importance of enhancing cross-border payments and planned a three-stage process to address this pressing need.

Introduce digital G2P/G2B/P2G/B2G payments and central bank digital currencies to promote the use of digital tools and fintech innovations in their own business models. The digitalization of government-related payments improves resilience and financial inclusion, especially in crisis times. Agur, Martinez Peria, and Rochon (2020) point out that central bank digital currencies can be used to track transactions and consumption behaviors to achieve a more efficient distribution of emergency funds. They can also fill the lack of scrutiny in cryptocurrencies and excessive market power of Big Tech (Sender 2020). Moreover, as a form of public digital currency, it is far easier to coordinate cross-border payments using central bank digital currencies than private platforms. Nevertheless, the risk of disintermediation, extended role of the central bank in the financial system, changing implications for monetary policies, counterfeiting, accessibility of the less tech-savvy individuals should all be taken into consideration.

Expanding Cross-Border Trade through E-commerce

State of Play

E-commerce continues to expand globally, modifying business models and amplifying the service industries. Enterprise participation in digital platforms is arguably underpinned by the positive externalities through network effects (Kinda 2019). Global e-commerce sales to businesses and consumers are estimated to have breached $25 trillion in 2018, or about 30% of GDP of the countries included in the assessment (UNCTAD 2020a). The B2B segment accounts for about 83% of the sales, according to the report, and the rest by B2C sales.[86]

The deepening penetration of e-commerce is particularly important in Asia and the Pacific. The data of UNCTAD show that Japan, the PRC, and the Republic of Korea land in the top five economies by total e-commerce sales, led by the United States. The presence of Asian economies is strong in both B2B and B2C segments. In a separate report, Asia and the Pacific was estimated to account for the largest share—about 44%—in the global B2C e-commerce turnover in 2019 (Ecommerce Foundation 2019).

The role of digital platforms in e-commerce, particularly in moving goods across national borders cannot be overlooked. E-commerce transforms trade in at least three ways: (i) making the flow of information and products across borders more cost-efficient, (ii) faster flow of funds through e-payment systems with built-in validation mechanisms, and (iii) increasing the traffic of parcelized cross-border shipments (Figure 8.15).

Figure 8.15: E-commerce and Cross-Border Trade Linkages

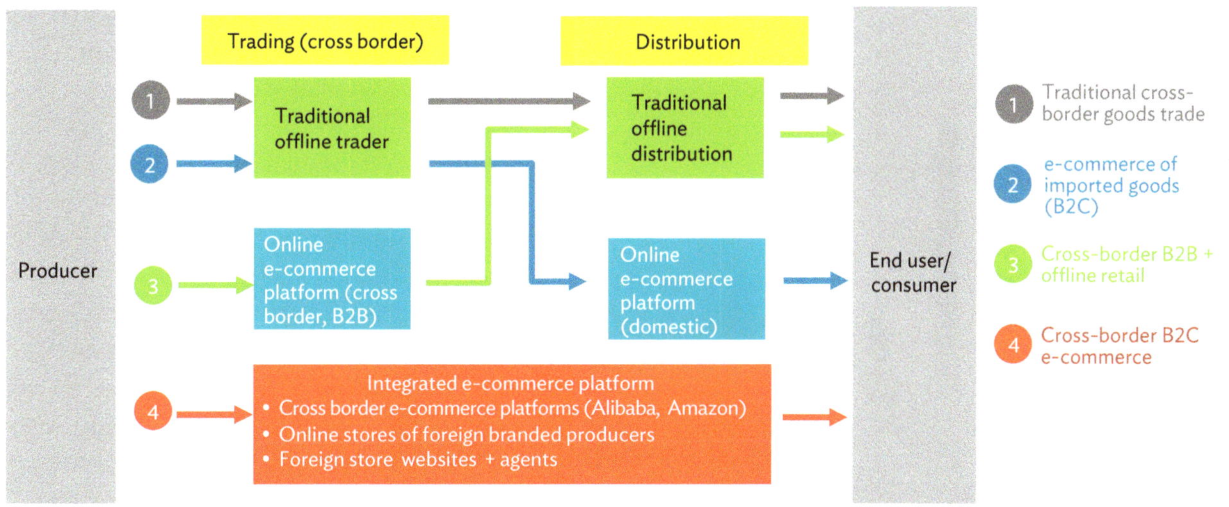

B2B = business-to-business, B2C = business-to-customer, C2C = customer-to-customer.

Source: Ali Research and Accenture (2016).

86 There is no mention of the business-to-government segment in UNCTAD (2020a).

E-commerce Trends and Patterns

Growth in internet retailing has been robust across Asian economies. Growth has accelerated in recent years in a number of Asian countries. Notably, the share of foreign retailing sales has grown at a faster pace across geographic clusters in the past few years. Compounded annualized growth is highest in Pakistan, while the share of foreign internet retailing in Uzbekistan tops the region. The range of internet retailing sales-to-GDP ratios in 2018 remains wide, i.e., between 20% and less than 0.02%.

Digital e-commerce platforms are important as conduits of digital retailing, and internet retailing is positively influencing cross-border consumer goods trade. The total e-commerce platform revenue in Asia is about 3% of GDP in 2017 and 2018 (Figure 8.16), with East Asia showing the highest ratio at close to 4%. The ratios are highly dispersed across countries, i.e., between 5% and less than 0.04% in Turkmenistan. Empirical estimation further shows that the progress in e-commerce is significantly positively associated with consumer goods trade between trading economies—a relationship that appears to strengthen in recent years (Box 8.4).

Figure 8.16: E-commerce Platform Revenues, 2017–2018
(% of GDP)

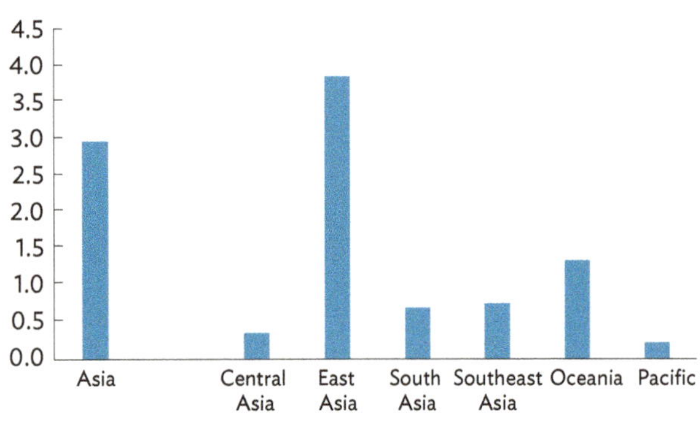

GDP = gross domestic product.

Note: Asia includes Armenia; Australia; Azerbaijan; Bhutan; Brunei Darussalam; Cambodia; Fiji; Georgia; Hong Kong, China; India; Indonesia; Japan; Kazakhstan; the Kyrgyz Republic; the Lao People's Democratic Republic; Malaysia; Mongolia; Myanmar; Nepal; New Zealand; Pakistan; Papua New Guinea; the People's Republic of China; the Philippines; the Republic of Korea; Singapore; Sri Lanka; Tajikistan; Thailand; Timor-Leste; Turkmenistan; Uzbekistan; and Viet Nam.

Sources: ADB calculations using data from Statista (2020a, 2020b) and World Bank. World Development Indicators. https://databank.worldbank.org/source/worlddevelopment-indicators (accessed July 2020).

Policy Implications and Recommendations

The Asian Development Bank (ADB) and United Nations Economic and Social Commission for Asia and the Pacific (UNESCAP) (2018) have highlighted a number of crucial policy issues, such as digitalization and e-commerce-induced trade, which need to be studied to help economies foster e-commerce. The report emphasized the need to roll out official statistics for monitoring and analysis, harmonize pertinent laws and standards including income taxation, improve quality and access to ICT infrastructure including e-payments systems, attract foreign players looking to benefit from technology transfer, and promote development of locals' ICT skills. It also pointed to needs to enact requisite regulations on intellectual property, consumer protection, data protection, and cybersecurity, among others.

Cross-border e-commerce transactions highlight three important policy areas: (i) trade taxation, competition, and customs administration issues; (ii) the role of multilateral initiatives and trade agreements in ironing out policy disconnects; and (iii) the responsiveness of free trade zone (FTZ) or economic processing zone (EPZ) strategies given the increasing role of platforms and other digital media in trade.

Addressing trade taxation, competitiveness, and customs administration issues is a fundamental concern for many economies in the region. Parcelization of orders has allowed overseas e-commerce suppliers to benefit from customs duties exemptions subject to countries' de minimis rules. The principle of de minimis is to avoid spending more on tax collection than what can be collected. In a meeting of the Asia-Pacific Economic Cooperation (APEC) in 2011, a de minimis threshold of $100 was endorsed but has not gained much traction. After the World Trade Organization (WTO) formally adopted its Work Programme on Electronic Commerce in 1998, members have extended a moratorium on imposing customs duties on electronic transmissions, and discussions on further extensions have intensified as some WTO members are concerned about its implications for government revenue (WTO 1998a, 1998b).

Box 8.4: E-commerce and Bilateral Consumer Goods Trade

Poisson pseudo maximum likelihood estimations of gravity-model equations reveal that combined internet retailing activity of trading economies is positively and significantly associated with their bilateral consumer goods trade (box table, column 1). Subsample inspection (2012–2016) suggests that the influence of internet retailing e-commerce sales on cross-border trade of consumer goods has risen in recent years (box table, column 2), i.e., the parameter value rises from 0.148 to 0.165. These estimates are aligned with the results using Heckman, gamma Poisson maximum likelihood and ordinary least squares.

Estimation using the bilateral e-commerce platform revenues yields the same story (box table, column 3). This finding holds across subregions in Asia, though the sensitivity of consumer goods trade to e-commerce platforms is marginally higher in East Asia and Southeast Asia. Estimates using regional subsets show that trade with regional partners is more sensitive to e-commerce platform development than trade with partners outside Asia (box table, column 4). This is indicative of the maturity of intraregional e-commerce ties relative to outside the region. It is seemingly not the case in Europe, Africa, and the Americas.

The exercise made use of the internet retailing data compiled by Euromonitor International (Retailing Industry Edition 2019) from 2006 to 2018, which cover 19 economies in Asia. E-commerce platform revenues data, on the other hand, cover 150 economies, of which 34 are from the region, from 2017 to 2018.

Bilateral E-commerce Indicators and Consumer Goods Trade—Asia

Dependent Variable: Bilateral Consumer Goods Exports				
	(1)	(2)	(3)	(4)
Period:	2006–2018	2012–2018	2017–2018	2017–2018
Partner:	Asian economies	Asian economies	All economies	Asian economies
Distance	-0.659 *** (0.1046)	-0.632 *** (0.1169)	-0.737 *** (0.1084)	-0.639 *** (0.0849)
Common colonial ties	-0.042 (0.1879)	-0.011 (0.1935)	0.543 *** (0.1806)	0.369 ** (0.1786)
Common language	0.604 *** (0.1492)	0.594 *** (0.1541)	-0.073 (0.1353)	0.194 (0.1568)
Contiguity	0.508 *** (0.142)	0.466 *** (0.1545)	0.162 (0.1492)	0.381 *** (0.1395)
E-commerce[a]	0.148 ** (0.0575)	0.165 ** (0.0644)		
E-commerce platform			0.147 *** (0.0513)	0.224 *** (0.0669)
Constant	24.759	24.215	24.972	21.323
Fixed effects:				
Exporter-Year	Yes	Yes	Yes	Yes
Importer-Year	Yes	Yes	Yes	Yes
Cluster exporter-importer	Yes	Yes	Yes	Yes
Total Observations	1,977	1,239	6,453	1,552
Pseudo R-squared	0.9612	0.9586	0.954	0.9477

[a] Refers to internet retailing.

Notes: The numbers in parentheses are the standard errors. *** $p < 0.01$, ** $p < 0.05$, * $p < 0.10$.

Source: Jacildo (2020) using data from Centre d'Etudes Prospectives et d'Informations Internationales (the French Research Center in International Economics). Geography Database. http://www.cepii.fr/CEPII/en/cepii/cepii.asp (accessed April 2020); Euromonitor International. Retailing Industry Edition 2019; and Statista (2020a, 2020b).

Table 8.9: Customs Administration Challenges Related to Cross-Border E-commerce

Trade Facilitation and Security	Fair and Efficient Collection of Duties and Taxes	Protection of Society–Criminal Exploitation of E-commerce
Ensuring speed and efficiency in the clearance process for an increasing volume of transactions	Identifying abuse or misuse of de minimis for illicit trade purposes (splitting of consignments and/or undervaluation)	Setting up a specialized unit to trawl the web for information which might be of use in preventing, detecting, investigating, and prosecuting a customs-related offense (drug trafficking/counterfeited and pirated goods/ illicit financial flows/money laundering)
Managing change from a few large/bulk shipments into a large number of low-value and small shipments	Ensuring compliance with classification and origin rules	Enhancing international cooperation and ensuring that agreements on mutual legal assistance are in place to allow for investigations or prosecutions when websites are hosted outside a national territory
Managing risks posed by limited knowledge on importers and the e-commerce supply chain (new class of sellers and buyers/ occasional shippers and buyers)	Integration of e-commerce versus traditional trade	Making the most of existing technologies, especially those related to data analysis
Ensuring data quality (accuracy and adequacy of the data received)		
Defining the role and responsibility (liability) of e-commerce operators to assist governments (e-vendors/ intermediaries)		

Source: World Customs Organization. http://www.wcoomd.org/en/topics/facilitation/activities-and-programmes/ecommerce.aspx?p=1 (accessed August 2020).

Terzi (2011) noted that digital innovations, like the internet, open markets that were previously closed, which is construed as another form of trade liberalization. It is argued that keeping the de minimis thresholds lessens trade friction, facilitates trade flows, and generates substantial net economic benefits (Holloway and Rae 2012, International Chamber of Commerce 2015). On the other hand, the thresholds have become the regulatory gateway for the influx of relatively cheaper products that compete with domestic firms. In this sense, e-commerce also tends to magnify comparative advantages in international trade for certain goods. To this end, Indonesia lowered its threshold to $3 from $75 effective in January 2020 (Indonesia Ministry of Finance 2019) with the intent of creating a fair tax treatment and protect domestic small and medium-sized industries, amid clamor from local business associations.

In the absence of appropriate policies, economies unable to produce goods competitive in the e-commerce market may render local players largely confined to the distribution segment of the cross-border supply chain. Thus, interventions should go beyond supporting local players and providing digital infrastructure. It is necessary for countries to have a clear road map on the kind of enterprises that they intend to nurture in the e-commerce space and the manner in which they will be supported.

The World Customs Organization (WCO) compartmentalized the cross-border e-commerce customs administration into three clusters: trade facilitation and security, fairness and efficiency in tax collection, and protection against criminal exploitation of e-commerce (Table 8.9). The first cluster covers policy adjustments to the cross-border trade landscape to promote an efficient trading process and to ensure that information is transmitted timely, and the data are credible. The second cluster is about spotting mechanisms that abuse the systems' rules on parcelized goods and ensuring compliance with other rules (e.g., rules of origin classification and valuation rules). The third cluster concerns the possible ways to prevent, detect, and prosecute customs-related legal offenses in the digital space.

It is crucial to leverage multilateral initiatives and trade agreements in promoting regulatory catch-up. One area that can be addressed by these trade initiatives and agreements is the easing up of information exchange among all parties involved in e-commerce transactions. This mainly involves still underdeveloped linkages between customs offices (WCO 2017), as well as linkages between producers or sellers, postal authorities, customs offices, and buyers.

At the global level, the WTO is leading the policy dialogues and the framing of multilateral accords which are essential in harmonizing the policy actions of different countries. The WTO Work Programme on Electronic Commerce sets to "to examine all trade-related issues relating to global electronic commerce" (WTO 1998a). Notably, a number of WTO members have signed the Joint Statement Initiative (JSI) on e-commerce in 2017 and started negotiating trade-related aspects of e-commerce thereafter (Ismael 2020). The issuance of the JSI is in line with the view of forging a plurilateral agreement based on existing WTO agreements and frameworks.

The WCO created a Working Group on E-Commerce to lay out the framework of standards on cross-border e-commerce and their implementation (WCO 2018a) to establish a robust and transparently governed e-commerce global supply chain covering primarily B2C and customer-to-customer (C2C) transactions but could include business-to-business transactions as well. It specifically targets to harmonize risk assessment procedures, revenue collection, and border cooperation. The WCO also published in 2018 a set of guidelines to update specific rules in both customs and trade on expediting the clearance of low-value and small e-commerce shipments and parcels (WCO 2018b). What these frameworks need are rules and regulations covering the supply chain in every jurisdiction to strengthen cross-border governance. The deepening of automation in customs procedures through national single windows and the progress in creating integrated national single windows (e.g., ASEAN single window) can be leveraged to pursue the objectives in these frameworks.

Lopez-Gonzalez and Ferencz (2018) likewise highlighted the increasing importance and usage of regional trade agreements. E-commerce-related provisions in regional trade agreements typically cover promotion of the e-commerce activity, cooperation activities and the moratorium on customs duties, and the domestic legal framework, including electronic authentication, consumer protection, personal information protection, and paperless trading (Monteiro and Teh 2017). One key challenge is to ensure that overlapping regional trade agreements do not exacerbate the "spaghetti or noodle bowl effect" resulting in unintended implementation frictions such as many rules of origin that affect the cost of trading.

The rapid developments in the digital space call for a timely review of FTZ and EPZ strategies. The FTZ or EPZ strategies are valuable in facilitating compliance to trade rules and in helping customs authorities address the challenges they face. The PRC has taken a lead in this area by establishing in 2015 the first cross-border e-commerce comprehensive pilot zones; there are now 105 zones spread over four regions in the country (Zhang 2020). The objectives of these zones include building brands, propagating a comprehensive cross-border e-commerce development, stabilizing capital flows related to trade, raising the quality of digitally-enabled trade, and holistically addressing pertinent security concerns. Likewise, preferential tax treatments like value-added tax exemption, consumption tax on retail exports exemption, and corporate income tax reduction are offered in the pilot zones.

Malaysia is another early mover in the region and it could serve as a good benchmark case for other countries. The government launched a digital free trade zone (DFTZ) in 2017 that was designed to strengthen the participation of local enterprises in cross-border e-commerce activities (Malaysia External Trade Development Corporation n.d.). One notable recent initiative of the zone is to take part in the Alibaba Group-led electronic World Trade Platform (eWTP) (Yean 2018). Malaysia's hub is the first eWTP pilot project outside of the PRC (eWTP n.d.). eWTP is deemed to be a step toward establishing the digital version of the Silk Road, designed to complement the Belt and Road Initiative.[87]

Promoting Sustainable Tourism through Online Travel

State of Play

Digital platforms operate and facilitate travel and tourism through two segments, eight subcategories, and two primary ways of servicing. The first segment is through "direct bookings" where consumers purchase travel products directly from the supplier, website, or mobile application. The second segment is through indirect channels known as online travel agencies (OTAs), which are web-based marketplaces that give consumers the ability to research, compare, review, and book travel products and services from multiple suppliers simultaneously (Expedia Group 2019).[88] Another segment uses third-party travel metasearch engines and travel review sites which can also display the various travel products across multiple suppliers, including OTAs, offering consumers a wide scope for comparing numerous attributes (Little Hotelier 2020). Table 8.10 lists some of the OTAs and the more popular global travel metasearch engines.

Table 8.10: Major Global OTAs and Travel Metasearch Companies

Major Global OTAs	Major Global Travel Metasearch Companies
Airbnb	Google Hotel Ads
Agoda	HotelCombined
Booking	Kayak
Expedia	SkyScanner
Orbitz	Tripadvisor
Priceline	Trivago
Hotels	Wego
HRS	
Travelocity	
Trip.com (formerly Ctrip)	

HRS = Hotel Reservation System, OTA = online travel agency.

Source: ADB and United Nations World Tourism Organization (forthcoming).

The history of online travel started in 1985 when American Airlines launched the first consumer-facing booking platform, called eAAsySabre, to book airline tickets (Schaal 2016). In 1996, Microsoft launched Expedia Travel Services in the United States, followed by European counterpart Priceline in 1997 (Barthel and Perret 2015). Since then, online travel has grown substantially. The total global revenue is estimated to be about $570.3 billion in 2017 and is projected to almost double to $1,134.6 billion by 2023, suggesting a compounded annual growth rate (CAGR) of 13.2% (Market Research Future 2019). Already, online travel accounts for nearly 50% of total global bookings, and is expected to continue growing at a rate faster than the overall travel market (Businesswire 2019). The impact of online travel on local business and employment is huge. For example, the Tripadvisor site and app are used to browse around 8.8 million accommodations, restaurants, experiences, airlines and cruises" (Tripadvisor 2020). The Expedia Group states that it has a supply of 1 million hotel properties, 500 airlines, 35,000 activities, 175 rental car companies, dozens of cruise lines, and 1.8 million listings on HomeAway (Expedia Group 2019).

The Asian Market

Asia is now the world's largest regional travel market. In 2018, the total gross travel market in the region was valued at $418.1 billion (Phocuswright 2019). About 44% of this, equivalent to roughly $182.2 billion, is accounted for by online travel. The share is forecast to grow beyond 50% by 2021 at an impressive CAGR of 15.9% to 2023 (Market Research Future 2019).

In addition to the major global players, numerous local and regional domestic booking platforms and players have captured traveler demand. In the PRC, the Trip.com Group Limited generated approximately $105 billion in gross merchandise value in 2018 for Chinese consumers

87 As of this writing, the eWTP has at least six partner countries in at least three continents (eWTP n.d.).

88 The travel and tourism subcategories are holiday packages, flights, hotels, vacation rentals, tours, activities, ride-hailing, trains and buses, and car rentals.

alone. The company has, among other assets, more than 1.4 million hotel and hostel properties and 1.2 million vacation rental properties around the world; more than 2 million global air routes; and vacation packages, guided tours, and in-destination services including insurance, visa services, attraction tickets, and local activities, covering over 3,000 destinations in more than 160 countries and territories (Trip.com Group n.d.).

The importance of tourism for many economies in developing Asia cannot be overstated. Combined international and domestic tourism totals exceed 10% of GDP in most destinations across the region, while in some developing destinations such as Palau and Maldives, international receipts alone account for upwards of 40% of GDP (Abiad et al. 2020).

The success of digital travel platforms in Asia is tied both to tourism's healthy global growth generally pre-COVID-19 pandemic, as well as a strong enabling environment in the region. Globally, the UN World Tourism Organisation (UNWTO) reports 1.5 billion international tourist arrivals were recorded in 2019, a 4% increase on the previous year, while also forecasting 4% growth for 2020 pre-COVID-19 (UNWTO 2020).

The World Travel and Tourism Council (WTTC) reports that Asia is the top-performing market worldwide, with an impressive growth rate of 5.5% for 5 consecutive years. Regional travel and tourism generated $2,971 billion, or 9.8% of the region's GDP, with international visitor spending reaching $548 billion, or 6.6% of the region's total exports (WTTC 2020a).

Impact of COVID-19 on Travel and Tourism

The COVID-19 pandemic has also put the global travel industry into a "fight for survival" mode due to the widespread and continued application of border control and quarantine measures.

Wong (2020), using the data of travel industry insights company ForwardKeys, reported that the international travel net bookings (i.e. bookings net of cancellations) on flights departing from Asia have declined sharply between February and August 2020. While the rate of decline has eased in recent months, the latest available data show a dip of over 104%. Meanwhile, hotel analytics company, STR, in a year-on-year comparison between July 2020 and July 2019, reported hotel occupancy down 36.5% to 46.3% (STR, Inc. 2020).

In light of the circumstances, it is reported that online travel companies stand to lose at least $11.5 billion in 2020 in missed bookings, potentially reaching $20 billion given a prolonged containment period (Borko 2020). This has resulted in many online travel players laying off and furloughing thousands of staff in the region and around the world, as they try to withstand the economic impacts.

Globally, over 100 million tourism jobs are at risk with projected revenue losses of $2.9 trillion in 2020, with Asia to be the most heavily affected (Table 8.11). The baseline scenario for the region is currently 69.3 million jobs at risk and a loss of nearly $1.14 trillion in revenues, while the worst case scenario stands at 115 million jobs at risk and a loss of approximately $1.89 trillion (WTTC 2020b). Thus, the online travel industry is severely impacted by COVID-19, with no clear end in sight yet.

Table 8.11: Impact Scenarios of COVID-19 on Asian Tourism

Scenario	Jobs (million)	GDP ($ billion)	Arrivals	
			Domestic	International
Best case	-59.7	-980	-40%	-23%
Baseline	-69.3	-1,137	-48%	-27%
Worst case	-115.0	1,888	67%	-55%

COVID-19 = coronavirus disease, GDP = gross domestic product.

Source: WTTC (2020b).

Challenges and Priorities of the Online Travel and Tourism Industry

The online travel market has features that pose several challenges in advancing online travel and tourism industry in the region as highlighted by the ADB and UNWTO (forthcoming). The first one is the intense competition among online travel platforms for market share. This has caused many closures for small local players not able to compete. However, this has also given rise to a strong trend of innovation in the services offered. For example in 2018 and 2019, the industry saw several prominent OTAs and travel metasearch sites begin to diversify their product bases and brand positioning away from hotel and accommodations bookings to include more food, activities, and rides—all three forecast to play a significant role in how such companies deepen their competitive advantage into the future (Schaal 2019).

The second challenge is the competition threats posed by super apps to local players. For example, Google and Amazon are forecast to continue deepening their move into the online travel space. Given their enormous consumer data and insights, reputations for innovation, cash reserves, efficient consumer technology systems, and upstream booking funnel ownership (in the case of Google), both represent a major disruptive threat to online travel providers of all types. The regional super apps, such as WeChat, Line, Gojek, Grab, Meituan Dianping, are already well-entrenched in their markets and can potentially compete with the other global brands. But, unless they can increase their partnerships and not compete with local players, superapps will disrupt local business and fragmentize the local supply chains for travel and tourism.

There is also rising concern within the industry in terms of policy changes related to digital taxation and data localization. For individual countries, the problem is how and when to capture taxes from the revenues being made by offshore online travel providers. Another concern is how to effectively combat the monopoly advantage of technology giants who collect, process, and control data giving them unfair advantage over local business players and governments.

While managing the impact of COVID-19 remains the utmost priority for the industry, there are several strategies that can help the industry survive and hasten the prospects for a safe reopening. Government could work with the industry to deliver integrated technical innovations such as digital health passports, digitized testing certifications, and contact tracing, among others. The travel industry and platforms have existing technical hardware and software, and technical expertise at their disposal for this purpose.

Another strategy to stimulate the local travel and tourism market is to support domestic travel, while international border closures remain in effect. Online travel platforms are well-placed to help drive domestic tourism and also promote key local destinations. In this regard, Thailand is a great early example. The Tourism Authority of Thailand partnered with Agoda beginning in 2018 on a multifaceted campaign to drive more domestic travelers to key destinations (Agoda 2018). More importantly, governments can also encourage individuals and MSMEs to go online and partner with OTAs to provide their services and goods domestically.

As Asia is an emerging global leader in both digitalization trends and travel industry growth, the outlook for online travel platforms in the region remains strong. However, this is contingent on the timely reopening of travel post COVID-19. Until then, regional governments should support online travel platforms to bolster their domestic tourism efforts while border closures remain in place, and further continue to address the general underlying policy and regulatory issues related to online travel that existed before the pandemic, such as taxation and data control.

Broadening Opportunities for Decent Work through Labor Platforms

State of Play

Platforms have created new jobs, such as crowdworkers, drivers of ride-hailing apps, and riders of food delivery services. While some of these jobs are not new, the modalities of matching workers to jobs through platforms is new, including payment schemes and value accumulation in platforms.

Digital technologies have helped offshore outsourcing evolve into a work arrangement mediated by digital platforms. These platforms bring together markets in the fastest, most efficient, and most convenient ways. Firms now have access to a pool of diverse and geographically dispersed human resources while individuals now face economic opportunities that are not available in the local labor market.

One of the defining features of online work (used interchangeably with platform work hereafter) is the flexibility in the labor markets. Firms can choose from a number of workers to finish short-term tasks at a relatively low cost (firm-driven flexibility) and at the same time, allow workers to achieve work-life balance (worker-driven flexibility) (Hunt and Samman 2019). This flexibility is an important selling pitch to most women due to the realities of care economy and housework, and these labor platforms can help achieve Sustainable Development Goal (SDG) targets on women empowerment and gender equality (targets 5.b, 5.c, 5.5), and on the eradication of poverty (target 1.1).

There are concerns on skills development, job security, and safety nets. Online workers do not have security benefits and protection entitlements because they are classified as contractors or self-employed (Forde et al. 2017; Hunt, Samman and Mansour-Ille 2017). As the young population may be naturally drawn to platform work, there could be erosion of contribution base, leading to problematic gaps in social protection coverage. Critical issues such as the lack of collective representation (Berg 2018; Graham, Hjorth and Lehdonvirta 2017), duration of employment (Barnes, Green, and de Hoyos 2015; Graham et al. 2017), and the types of skills developed in platform engagements (Barnes, Green, and de Hoyos 2015; Forde et al. 2017) are relevant to young and productive workers. The lack of social protection is likely to exacerbate gender inequalities since women, who are responsible for care economy and housework, are more likely to engage in online work.

These serious concerns can outweigh the flexibility and monetary gains, raising the question of sustainability. Platforms are not mere facilitators that minimize job search costs but are legitimate avenues that broaden knowledge and improve workers' opportunity sets. However, in the absence of employer–employee relationships, contracting firms cannot be compelled to provide training and security benefits to workers. Workers learn skills on their own and contribute to social security fund on a voluntary basis if they want coverage. Given these, the overarching policy questions should focus on online work/platform work sustainability, skills development, income, and social protection. Addressing these issues will help countries be on track in SDG targets on social protection (1.3, 1.a and 10.4), skills (4.4), and care economy (5.4).

Definition and Typologies

There is an apparent lack of consensus on taxonomy that classifies the broad range of economic activities mediated by platforms due to the complex dimensions that pertain to differences in skills, market structure and clients, and employment status. The typologies are based mostly on whether the worker output is delivered online and across borders or in the same location (Figure 8.17). For example, taxi services and food delivery are work that is highly controlled by platforms and serve the local market, while creative projects serve either the local or global market and give workers a higher degree of autonomy (Forde et al. 2017). Other studies like Hunt, Samman, and Mansour-Ille (2017) and Graham et al. (2017) classify these activities into either *crowdwork* that is transacted and delivered online or *on-demand* work that requires a close interaction between workers and demanders (e.g., food delivery, ride hailing services, and so on).

At least four popular terms are used in the literature to describe the platform economy: gig economy, platform economy, collaborative economy, and sharing economy. In the *gig economy*, workers take on sometimes low-paying precarious work as independent contractors without any guarantee of further employment. Graham et al. (2017) and Hunt, Samman and Mansour-Ille (2017) refer to the gig economy as the commodification of labor and the sharing/collaborative/platform economy as the commodification of assets. Used interchangeably with the *sharing economy*, the *collaborative economy* refers to the monetization of assets or the sharing of idle resources such as in Airbnb, Uber, and Lyft (PwC 2015), or the *on-demand economy* (Vaughan and Davario 2016). The *platform economy* is viewed in the context of platform-mediated jobs that can be delivered online or offline, a typology consistent with the crowdwork and on-demand work classifications.

Figure 8.17: Economic Activities and Terminology in Labor Platforms

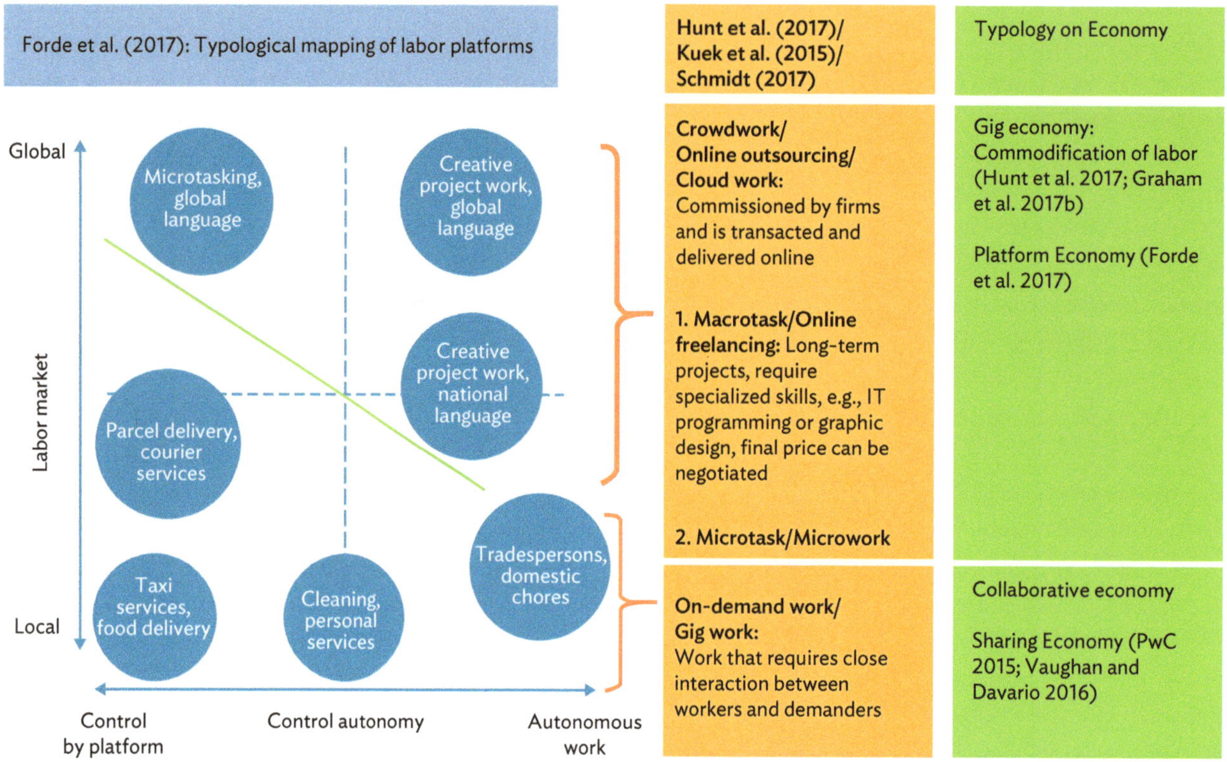

Note: The diagram is based on Forde et al. (2017); Graham et al. (2017); Hunt, Samman, and Mansour-Ille (2017); Kuek et al. (2015); PwC (2015); Schmidt (2017); and Vaughan and Davario (2016).

Source: Bayudan-Dacuycuy et al. (2020a).

These distinctions are important as they determine how the platform operates, the situation of the independent contractor, the legal framework that applies, and potential regulatory measures (Schmidt 2017).

Online Work in Asia

Online work is gaining traction globally and in Asia. Data on nonstandard work arrangement are scarce, although national statistics offices in the United States and the United Kingdom have started to develop methodologies that integrate this work arrangement into their labor force surveys (Hunt and Samman 2019). Based on the Online Labor Index (OLI) of Kässi and Lehdonvirta (2018), projects or tasks in online work have increased by 72% since it started compiling data in September 2016.[89] Data in 2019 show that projects were concentrated in North America (47%), followed by Europe (24%) and Asia (19%). Among the top 15 economies where projects are located, the US dominates the market with 40% share (Figure 8.18a). Five Asian economies—India; Singapore; Pakistan; Hong Kong, China; and the PRC—are included in the top 15 although their shares are way below that of the US (Figure 8.18b).

89 The index measures the utilization of online labor platforms or those through which buyers and sellers of labor or services are delivered digitally, excluding platforms for local services such as Airbnb and Uber. The samples are limited to the largest English language platforms accounting for at least 70% of all traffic to online labor platforms (Kässi and Lehdonvirta 2018, and Oxford Internet Institute). OLI database is maintained by the Oxford Internet Institute and the University of Oxford.

Figure 8.18: Distribution of Online Work by Employer, Location, and Occupation (% of total)

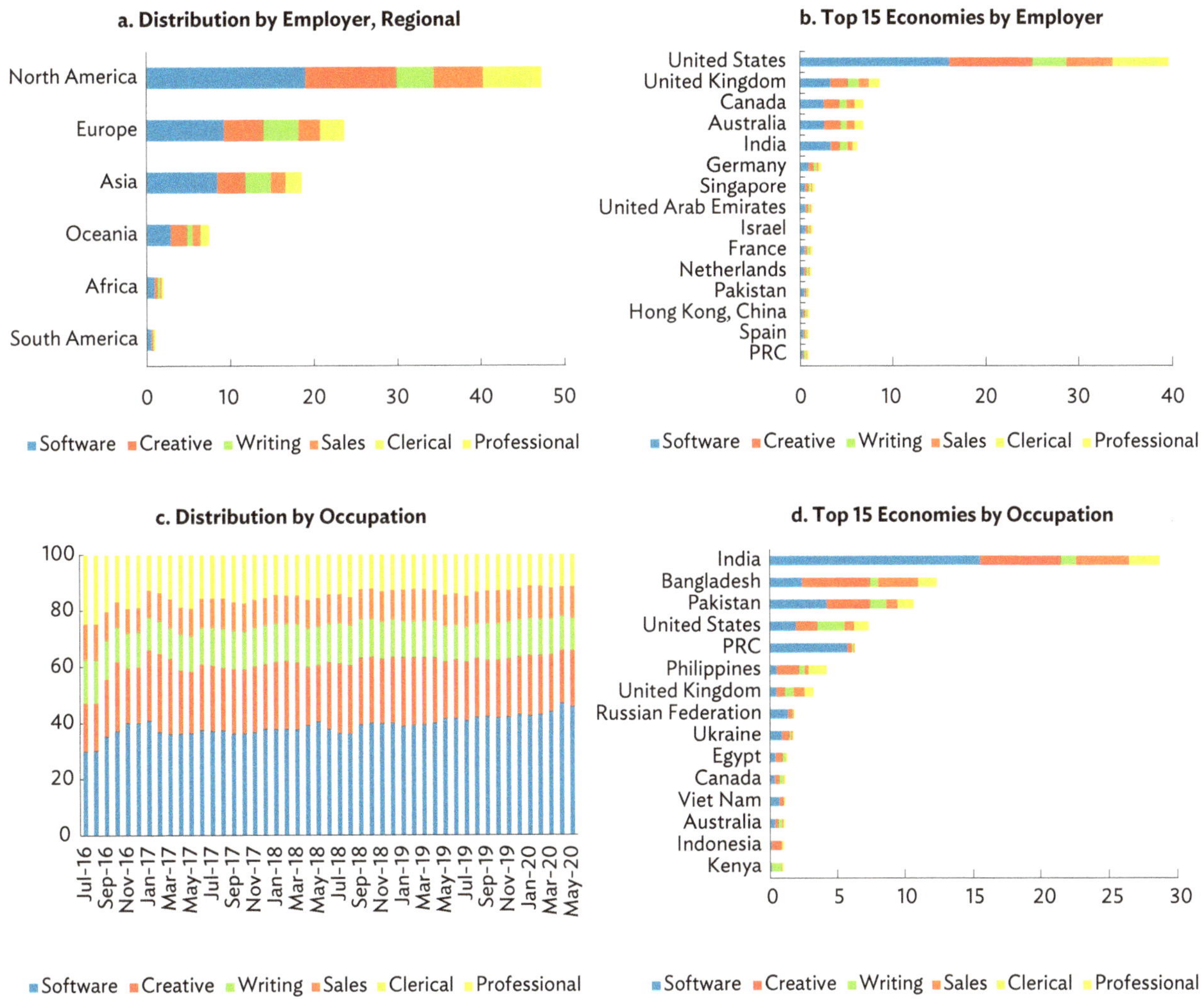

PRC = People's Republic of China.

Sources: Kässi and Lehdonvirta (2018); and Oxford Internet Institute. The Online Labour Index Database. https://ilabour.oii.ox.ac.uk/online-labour-index (accessed May 2020).

The share of software development/technology has been rising to almost 50% of the global online work in 2020 while around 20% is in creative and multimedia (Figure 8.18). Initial evidence indicates that jobs related to software development/technology appear resilient while those related to creative and multimedia and sales/marketing support have decreased during the COVID-19 pandemic (see for example, Stephany et al. 2020).

The top three Asian countries that provide online workers—India, Bangladesh, and Pakistan (Figure 8.18)—combine for 52% of the global online workforce. The Philippines is a distant sixth. Majority of online work are tasks related to software development/technology (led by the PRC and India) and creative/multimedia. This is consistent with the earlier models of offshore outsourcing that took advantage of the large pool of low-cost talents in Asian countries.

From 2017 to 2020, the share of workers in creative and multimedia has increased by 34% in Bangladesh and by 40% in Indonesia. To date, it accounts for around 59% of Bangladesh's online workforce and 74% in Indonesia's. In the Philippines, creative and multimedia online workers share the bulk of online employment (47%) while its share is 31% in Pakistan. At the global stage, the world exports of creative goods[90] has grown in value from $208 billion in 2002 to $509 billion in 2015 while the trade in creative services[91] in developed economies as a share of total export services has increased from 17.3% in 2011 to 18.9% in 2015 (UNCTAD 2018). In Asia, the creative industry is likely to flourish, as countries boast of a big pool of young, creative, and technology-savvy people.

Cross-country differences reflect comparative advantage and workers' bargaining power differs across economies. There is a disparity in the distribution of online work reflecting how a country's comparative advantage is viewed by the global market. A large percentage of online workers in India, Pakistan, the PRC, the Russian Federation, Ukraine, and Viet Nam are in software development/technology, while a large fraction of workers in Bangladesh, Indonesia, and the Philippines perform creative and multimedia tasks. In the United Kingdom and the US, large portions of online workers are engaged in professional services or tasks that have high value added.

Although the Philippines has a large share of online workers in creative and multimedia, many are in jobs that have low value-added. Around 25% of online workers in the Philippines are into clerical and data services while such workers account for fewer than 10% in Bangladesh, India, Indonesia, and Pakistan. Only around 14% of Filipino online workers do tasks that are related to software development and technology, much lower compared with the proportion of such workers in India (59%), Pakistan (45%) and even Viet Nam (52%).

Initial evidence shows that crowdworkers in Northern America, Europe, and Central Asia earn more than those in Africa and Asia (see Berg et al. 2018) and that workers outside high-income industrialized nations could be poorly rewarded in online work (Beerepoot and Lambregts 2014). Compensation and bargaining power may also be driven downward by the number of people seeking jobs. In one platform, evidence shows that the Philippines accounts for 12% of the global labor oversupply (Table 8.12).

Table 8.12: Labor Oversupply in One Major Platform
(number of workers)

Country	Potential Workforce	Successful Workers	Oversupply
Global	1,775,500	198,900	1,576,600
Philippines	221,100	32,800	188,300
Malaysia	11,900	500	11,400
Viet Nam	7,700	1,000	6,700
Kenya	21,700	1,500	20,200
Nigeria	7,000	200	6,800
South Africa	10,200	800	9,400

Source: Graham et al. (2017).

Lack of social protection in the platform economy is a growing concern. Based on the 2015 International Labour Organization (ILO) Survey of Crowdworkers, around 60% were covered by health insurance but only around 35% had a pension plan (Berg et al. 2018). In a survey of five major platforms in 2017, Forde et al. (2017) found that only around 36% are subscribed into a personal pension plan while 70% could not access protections such as maternity, childcare, and housing benefits.

Despite this reality in platform work, there are certain segments of the population, e.g., the young and women, which may be naturally drawn to online work. Workers in developing countries are much younger (28 years) than those in developed economies (35 years). The young age composition of platform workers can impact the sustainability of existing social protection schemes jeopardizing the financing of future

[90] This consists of art crafts, audiovisuals, design, digital fabrication, new media, performing arts, publishing, and visual arts (UNCTAD 2018).

[91] This consists of advertising, market research, and public opinion services; architectural, engineering, and other technical services; research and development services; personal, cultural, and recreational services; audiovisual and related services; and other personal, cultural, and recreational services (UNCTAD 2018).

entitlements especially in societies with an increasing elderly population.

In addition, more women will likely engage in platform work since it promises flexibility in performing nonmarket work or care work alongside gainful economic opportunities (see example of the Philippines in Box 8.5). This state of affairs can exacerbate gender gaps in social protection.

There are work practices in the online work market that are difficult to monitor and regulate. Price or rate underbidding could help individual workers land a job but could be disadvantageous to online workers as a group (Forde et al. 2017; Graham, Hjorth, and Lehdonvirta 2017). Likewise, re-intermediation—where successful online workers take on work that they farm out to other less visible and less experienced online workers—can lead to exploitation. On the positive side, workers are able to perform "skills arbitrage," in which workers are no longer confined to the local labor market and are able to get more for their talents (Graham, Hjorth, and Lehdonvirta 2017).

Local On-Demand Work

The most familiar forms of employment created through the platform economy are classified as gig work or local on-demand work. For example, in recent years, ride-

Box 8.5: Platform Work in the Philippines

Bayudan-Dacuycuy et al. (2020b) provide a closer look on the nature of platform work from the perspective of the workers. The Philippine Institute for Development Studies (PIDS) with the assistance of the Department of Information and Communications Technology conducted the "Online Survey of Market and Non-Market Work" from April to May 2020. The survey yielded 639 respondents with the following distribution: 35% of the respondents have neither platform nor non-platform work, 14% have platform work only, 42% have non-platform work only, and 9% have both platform and non-platform work. Platform work had been done by 40% of respondents during the survey month and/or the past 12 months, and about 65% of them are women. While the survey is based on nonrandom sampling and results hold true only for the sample, findings are consistent with the results of studies abroad that used representative surveys.

- There are segments of the population that may be naturally drawn to online work. Platform workers in the Philippines are young, which has implications on skill formation and human capital development since a quarter of Filipino online workers perform tasks that are at the lower end of the value chain.
- Work experience is essential in securing a job in platform work. Those who have no work experience have practically zero chance of securing online work. On the demand side, this suggests that firms use experience as a signal of worker's ability and output quality. On the supply side, this suggests that the accumulation of experience depends on the requisite hard skills such as information and communication technology skills, numeracy, and literacy, and soft skills such as negotiation, communication, and networking.
- Workers take advantage of economies of scope as they leverage skills and resources common across platform work and other economic activities. There are risks, however, of potential tradeoffs between output quality and work intensification which may result in physical and mental strain. Thus, it is vital to develop organizational, planning, and time management skills, as workers exploit the flexibility and autonomy in the platform.
- Women are more likely to engage in platform work than men, due to the flexibility that allows them to perform nonmarket work as well. This highlights the need for crafting policies to enhance the social protection of platform workers, without which will likely exacerbate gender inequalities.
- Factors associated with lower wage/hour include engagement in microtasks and the lack of investment in training courses. Constraints in investments in human capital and connectivity are also proximate factors of lower wage/hour.

Source: Bayudan-Dacuycuy et al. (2020b).

hailing digital platforms[92] have provided an increasing driver-partner employment[93] to individuals who had no prior paid work.[94] In 2019, ride-hailing digital platform Grab had 2.8 million active drivers in all countries of operation, while Gojek in Indonesia and Ola Cabs in India each employed 1 million drivers (Table 8.13). However, the type of jobs created by such digital platforms can be categorized as informal work.

Over 9 million micro-entrepreneurs in the region have earned income using the Grab platform (Grab 2019). Small merchant partners experienced a 21% increase in revenues. In the Philippines, the company partnered with the Department of Agriculture to support farmers and agripreneurs by utilizing GrabExpress in delivering fresh produce and meats from the department's eKadiwa website. Grab, through GrabMart and GrabFood, also started a program in Malaysia with the Ministry of Rural Development to assist in marketing and increase revenues for rural entrepreneurs (Grab 2020).

A study in 2018 found that Gojek contributed about $3 billion to the Indonesian economy, mostly from the partnership of GoFood and MSMEs which generated about $1.57 billion revenues (Walandouw et al. 2019). While 86% of Go-ride, 71% of Go-car, and 91.5% of Go-Life partners have only high school diploma or lower, they earn higher than the average income in the nine areas surveyed. Go-Life consists of 70% female workers, 93% of MSME partners went on e-commerce because of partnership with Gojek, 93% had increased transaction volume, and 55% reported increased revenues.

In South Asia, Pathao in Bangladesh now has 50,000 motorbikes and a group of 500 workers in three urban communities and has added to its services bike sharing, and delivery of parcel and food (Ahmed et al. 2018). This kind of platform has opened the door for businesses and improved logistics and helped e-commerce in the country to grow (Chun, Kumar, Rahman 2019). Cheetay in Pakistan has over 300 partner restaurants and offers a digital tool for home-based food businesses' e-commerce to create employment opportunities (ProPakistani 2019).

Table 8.13: Delivery and Transport Services Online Platforms

Platform	Monthly Visits	Users (million)	Economies	Funding ($ million)	Number of Employees	Drivers (million)
Uber	50,047,522	91 (2018)	63 economies including Bangladesh; Hong Kong, China; India; Japan; the Republic of Korea; Sri Lanka; Taipei,China	24,700	10,001+	3.9 (2018)
Grab	8,841,950	163 (2019)	Indonesia, Malaysia, the Philippines, Singapore, Thailand, Viet Nam	10,100	1,001—5,000	2.8 (2019)
Didi	642,717	550	Hong Kong, China; India; PRC; Taipei,China	21,200	5,001-10,000	31
Gojek	144,430	-	Indonesia, Singapore, Thailand, Viet Nam	4,800	5,001-10,000	1
Pathao	190,586	-	Bangladesh	12.8	1,001-5,000	-
Cheetay	58,381	-	Pakistan	9.8	501-1,000	-

PRC = People's Republic of China.

Sources: Crunchbase Database. https://www.crunchbase.com; DBS Group Research. 2019. Number of Active Drivers of Asia Pacific Ride-Sharing Companies as of 2019 (in millions). 27 May. In Statista—The Statistics Portal. https://www.statista.com/statistics/1034777/apac-number-of-active-drivers-of-ride-sharing-companies/; Didi. About Us—More Than a Journey: The World's Leading Transportation Platform. https://www.didiglobal.com/about-didi/about-us; and Uber. Company Info: Facts and Figures as of December 2018. https://www.uber.com/en-PH/newsroom/cUberompany-info/ (all accessed August 2020).

92 Grab in Southeast Asia, Gojek in Indonesia, and Ola in India are some examples.

93 Since its launch in 2012, Grab has diversified its services and recently integrated all its solutions in one mobile application. It has expanded to supplying other services such as food and express package deliveries, thereby tapping more idle labor.

94 Reportedly, 21% of its total driver-partners in 2018–2019 had no prior employment (Grab 2019).

Policy Implications and Recommendations

Digital platforms offer new opportunities and channels to participate in the labor market and earn supplemental income. Nonetheless, the arrangements employed have raised some welfare concerns. For one, work contracts with limited social and employment protection are common in the platform setting. Younger and female members of the labor force are particularly susceptible to such arrangements since they are more inclined to participate in the flexible platform job market. Workers are likewise exposed to race-to-the-bottom wage determination while some of the jobs generated can be considered as informal.

Designing a social protection system that covers all workers is a necessity and a challenge. As more young people are engaged in short-term, intermittent, or nonstandard work arrangements, the erosion of a social insurance contribution base may exacerbate coverage gaps, weakening existing social protection schemes, endangering future entitlements, and increasing public finance strain because of social assistance to the unemployed and elderly, especially during times of crises. In addition, women are more likely to work in the platform for flexibility, which can exacerbate gendered inequalities in the current patterns of employment-based social protections. In the context of the future of work, there have been calls for social protection to be decoupled from employment or be replaced by a universal basic income.

However, decoupling social protection from employment will likely result in inadequate coverage and limited benefits since some workers may not be able to accumulate sufficient entitlements due to the nature of their work and income patterns, and in the weakening of the employers' responsibility toward their workers (Behrendt and Nguyen 2018). Other issues include the inadequate benefit levels to cover a decent standard of living and the potential crowding-out of other public services (Browne and Immervoll 2017).

While the exact types of social protection are being debated, there appears to be a consensus on the desirable characteristics of a social protection system, such as the following:

- **Universal and equal access** (ILO and OECD 2018; WEF 2018) and **flexibly designed** (Johal 2018): This will involve flexible eligibility definitions that will cover workers in any work arrangements and can be customized to accommodate the needs and preferences of workers.

- **Portable** (WEF 2018), **agile** (WEF 2017b), or **transferable** (ILO and OECD 2018): Following the general principle that the facility follows the worker rather than being bound to a specific employment, the system should seamlessly support workers' mobility and recognize that workers will move in response to local and global opportunities. One way of doing this is to explore a central entity that manages contribution and benefits of workers and provides a range of benefits even if they move from employer to employer or job to job (WEF 2017b). However, it should guard against delegating greater roles to private entities that may exacerbate the gaps in the provision of social protection (Behrendt and Nguyen 2018).

- **Integrated with allied services and programs** (Johal 2018): Social protection systems should have links with allied services and programs covering related risks. An example of a potential linkage is an unemployment insurance that not only provides minimum income while unemployed but also covers reskilling/upskilling and training cost to make it easier to move in between jobs.

- **Facilitated by technology:** The system should leverage on technology not only in facilitating enrollment and payments of contributions and benefits but also providing nudges through information campaigns that can reshape behavior and mindsets.

Creating skills and training systems is vital in fostering a suitable ecosystem. Just like other jobs, online work may be affected by adverse shocks. Online creatives and multimedia workers in Bangladesh, Indonesia, and the Philippines have experienced substantial downturn due to the ongoing COVID-19 pandemic. On one hand, these countries may want to invest in ICT skills and focus on training and education systems in science, technology, engineering, and mathematics programs to capture some jobs in software development and technology. On the other hand, they can enhance their niche on the creative and multimedia sector. Thus, at the country level, there is a need to assess and match the skills of the workforce with the requisite skills of the target occupation and industries and create enabling environments for workers to prosper in platform work. For example, women should be provided skills training support that will allow them to continue to perform both platform and non-platform work. In this way, platform work can be an effective way to achieve Sustainable Development Goal 5 of women empowerment.

However, a much better emphasis of training would be on the creation of a sustainable ecosystem encompassing skills development programs and training support initiatives that are useful in any type of work setting, affording workers the ability to transition quickly between jobs or tasks. As a starting point, countries need to craft a competency framework and a national strategy for skills and human capital development.

Strengthening the underlying infrastructure is key to support the creative industry and the creative process outsourcing. At the national level, countries are aware that creative services will grow with the expansion of the ICT frontiers. Some Asian countries have shown big strides in innovation, an important ingredient for the creative economy to prosper. Among the Asian countries in the top 15 economies where platform work is outsourced, India and the Philippines belong to economies with innovation performance that exceeds expectations commensurate to their level of development. In terms of creative outputs, the Philippines ranks 63rd out of the 130 countries surveyed in the 2019 Global Innovation Index, and is 40th in the creative goods and services subindex. Meanwhile, Indonesia ranks 76th, Pakistan 104th, and Bangladesh 115th in the same index. Indonesia established the Creative Economy Agency to oversee development of the creative sectors, with the view of integrating these into Indonesia's economy. In 2017, the sector employed 15.9 million people and generated more than 7% of Indonesia's GDP (Jewell 2019).

Although the improvement in innovations in creative goods and services bodes well for Asian online workers, there are challenges that need to be addressed. These include slow connectivity, which hampers the efficient production of creative outputs in audiovisual arts and causes inefficient production of visual graphics. While this is a problem for all online work, this is more pronounced for the creative industry due to the bandwidth requirement necessary to execute the creative production.

Improving data collection and measurement is needed for proper regulation. As platform work becomes increasingly integrated into the spectrum of various work arrangements, crucial issues on regulation and taxation arise. While developed economies have started to develop methodologies to integrate this work arrangement in their labor force surveys, there are still outstanding challenges on data collection that need to be addressed. For instance, including a module on platform work as a rider to standard labor surveys may not be adequate to capture the scope and complexity of existing work arrangements in the platform (Abraham et al. 2019). Moreover, tracking down platform workers and enticing them to participate and truthfully disclose information are problems that need to be highlighted on their own but more so on the heels of the potential taxation of the online economy.

Including the platform economy as an area of cooperation and policy coordination among Asian economies has ample merits. Mounting a call to action or organizing a labor rights group can be a challenge to a geographically dispersed and anonymous pool of platform workers who likely view each other as competitors. Thus, the platform economy can be an area of cooperation among Asian nations to collectively address critical issues, to influence the narrative from competition to collaboration, and to influence workers' unfavorable practices such as underbidding and "race to the bottom" mentality, among other things. Currently, the power is skewed in favor of firms while most risks and costs are borne by workers. A starting point would be to include the platform economy in the national and regional agenda so that issues and challenges can be mapped to potential solutions. Agreeing to a wage floor, for example, can help address the "race to the bottom" mentality. While putting a united front in the digital space is a challenge, sending a cohesive message has the potential to balance the fulcrum of power.

EdTech and Quality Education for All

State of Play

The global online education market has witnessed a rapid growth, powered by the onset of disruptive digital technologies. The technological revolution has brought viable virtual means of education and training as an alternative to traditional education delivery within the walls of institutions. The growth of the global EdTech industry has further fueled the expansion of online learning. Moving forward, as suggested by Jagannathan and Li (2020), a number of factors are expected to drive the adoption of online or digital learning:

- **The need to scale up affordable access to tertiary education.** As developing countries look to significantly scale up access to education, particularly for tertiary and adult learning, online education provides a viable alternative to the conventional brick and mortar universities.
- **The demand for flexible learning opportunities in new domains.** Traditional institutions are also increasingly embracing digital and blended learning as a way to offer more flexible and tailored education to students. Digital platforms play a critical role in offering knowledge and skills for trends such as the Fourth Industrial Revolution and to serve emerging industries for which mainstream institutions are not yet well equipped to offer courses.
- **The call to match the learning styles of millennials and next generation learners.** Digital platforms have become essential for the education of the millennials who are also termed "digital natives," with a vastly different style of learning.
- **The ability to offer personalized and individualized learning.** Digital solutions help to personalize learning to suit individual needs while at the same time accommodating more students within the learning platform. Student progress is tracked in real time, making adjustments in teaching methods and materials more efficient and appropriate.

Online Learning at the Time of COVID-19

The COVID-19 pandemic has also provided an impetus for online learning. The nationwide and localized closures of educational institutions implemented in more than 190 countries have affected over 1.5 billion learners at its peak (UNESCO 2020a, UNICEF 2020). Such unprecedented and sudden closure of educational institutions caused a dramatic shift to online learning, which became the main response to the widespread disruptions in schooling caused by the pandemic.

Moreover, post-pandemic, it is expected that digital platforms will redefine the balance between physical and virtual education; the role of private players will increase; and workforce styles will show greater reliance on digital and remote working as revealed by the results of the McKinsey Global Institute surveys (Lund et al. 2020). Indeed, the COVID-19 pandemic has created the opportunity for education to undergo a massive transformative shift to online learning. Students have turned to private EdTech platforms to support distance learning during the COVID-19 crisis (see Annex 8d).

EdTech can be at the center of strategies that aim to turn this health crisis into an opportunity to improve the quality and delivery of education. However, the switch to online strategies has also revealed major barriers and issues of inequity in access to devices and connectivity for students in poor and rural-based communities that must be addressed quickly.

While countries are preoccupied with responding to the crisis in the short term, it is important to consider strategies and solutions that not only provide immediate relief but also incorporate a vision for medium- to longer-term support to enable the recovery, revival, and improvement of education systems. ADB recommends that dealing with COVID-19 should go beyond the immediate crisis. Governments must initiate far-reaching reforms to strengthen the resilience of education and training systems, and frame the actions to be taken in the form of three Rs—response, recovery, and rejuvenation (ADB 2021).

Barriers and Issues

The first barrier is an obvious one and well known—access to connectivity. Table 8.14 shows how poor connectivity limits the ability to roll out digital strategies that benefit all population groups. Within developing countries there is also disparity in access between urban and rural areas, between rich and the poor, and between men and women. Meanwhile, Table 8.15 draws attention to the need to consider home environment, including presence of digital devices and connectivity, in designing digital strategies for home education. And Figure 8.19 highlights the imperative to first improve information technology (IT) infrastructure and connectivity required in schools to roll out digital strategies in education.

With the onset of COVID-19, governments have tried to negotiate with telecom providers to extend connectivity free or heavily discounted for education purposes. While many private platforms offered their courses free during the COVID-19 pandemic, connectivity has been an issue. There are a number of collaborative efforts in the region. For instance, Azerbaijan implemented the Virtual School with Microsoft (CEE Multi-Country News Center 2020), while Georgia's Ministry of Education and the

Table 8.15: Connectivity for Home Learning

	Proportion of Households with Computer (%)	Proportion of Households with Internet Access at Home (%)	Year
Singapore	88.7	97.7	2018
United States	90.8	83.8	2018
Indonesia	20.1	66.2	2018
Georgia	62.1	69.5	2018
Azerbaijan	64.1	78.2	2018
Cambodia	15.0	40.0	2018
Viet Nam	32.9	47.1	2018
Philippines	23.4	39.1	2016
Bangladesh	5.6	37.6	2019
India	16.6	25.4	2018

Sources: International Telecommunication Unit (ITU). Country ICT Data. https://www.itu.int/en/ITU-D/Statistics/Pages/stat/default.aspx; and ITU. ICT Eye Database. https://www.itu.int/net4/ITU-D/icteye/#/ (both accessed June 2020).

Table 8.14: Access to Connectivity

Economy	Percentage of Individuals Using the Internet, 2017	Mobile-Broadband Subscriptions per 100 Inhabitants, 2016	Fixed-Broadband Subscriptions per 100 Inhabitants, 2018
Singapore	84.4	147.6	25.9
United States	87.3	126.7	35.6
Indonesia	32.3	33.9	3.3
PRC	54.3	68.8	28.5
Georgia	59.7	61.8	21.0
Azerbaijan	79.0	56.2	18.2
Cambodia	32.4	50.7	1.0
Viet Nam	58.1	46.9	13.6
Philippines	60.1	54.6	3.2
Sri Lanka	34.1	41.8	7.2
Bangladesh	15.0	27.9	6.3
India	34.5	16.4	1.3

PRC = People's Republic of China.

Sources: International Telecommunication Unit (ITU). Country ICT Data. https://www.itu.int/en/ITU-D/Statistics/Pages/stat/default.aspx; and ITU. ICT Eye Database. https://www.itu.int/net4/ITU-D/icteye/#/ (both accessed June 2020).

Figure 8.19: Internet Access in Schools

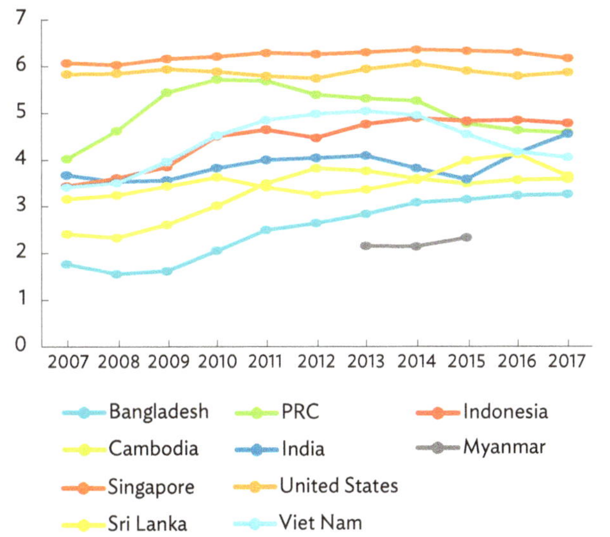

PRC = People's Republic of China.

Notes: The data refer to weighted average scores across survey respondents in each economy. The survey question is: In your country, to what extent is the internet used in schools for learning purposes (1 = not at all, 7 = to a great extent)?

Source: World Economic Forum. The Global Competitiveness Index 2017–2018 Database. https://reports.weforum.org/global-competitiveness-index-2017-2018/downloads/ (accessed August 2020).

First Channel of Georgia collaborated in creating a TV School (Government of Georgia, Ministry of Education and Science 2020).[95] Similarly in India, one of many examples is the partnership between the Zoho company and the government to provide a learning app where students and teachers could connect online—that is free to government schools (BusinessLine 2020).

Learning issues are a critical challenge. Technology alone cannot transform education unless it is targeted at redressing critical gaps that include lack of adequate teacher preparation, and inadequate use of student learning assessment data to improve teaching and learning. While governments were initially focused on providing computers and technology in schools, it has become apparent that students need access to connectivity, a conducive learning environment at home, and instructional support to effectively use technology to improve learning levels. This calls for schools to rethink curriculum design for digital skills. As a result of growing options for digital learning, universities will redefine cost parameters of face-to-face and online education, acquiring license and capacities to offer fully online courses.

Special efforts to serve disadvantaged students need to be bolstered. Strategies for ensuring uninterrupted education during the COVID-19 crisis rely on using a variety of media not limited to the provision of technology and/or devices to close the digital divide. Azerbaijan, for example, employed a multimedia strategy to reach families with different technologies—most households have televisions, so lessons are streamed on national television channels (Dreesen et al. 2020). The PRC adopted flexible methods based on local e-readiness to encourage learning. Programming on satellite TV was used to accommodate regions without internet access while Guangdong province equipped 9,262 students with tablets (Zhang et al. 2020). In Viet Nam, a variety of media were used to reach students including digital website or apps, TV programs, radio programs, and paper-based take-home packages (Dreesen et al. 2020). To serve children without technological resources, teachers and volunteers walked or drove long distances to deliver paper material and assignments to the village heads who then distributed them to students (Flowers 2020). UNICEF likewise distributed "Pad and Puck" packages, i.e., tablets and Wi-Fi in the country (Dreesen et al. 2020).

Despite massive efforts of governments to extend digital learning, some students continue to face learning barriers that disproportionately affect rural and low-income students and minority groups. In the PRC, for example, 2% of students still have no access to online live teaching and some children have to walk for hours to find stable network signals (Zhang et al. 2020). There is also a need for multilingual content for ethnic minorities, curriculum designed for children with disabilities, and development of teacher skills in rural areas (UNESCO 2020b). In Indonesia, issues include poor network streaming, mobile data quota limits, network reception where students live, and bandwidth and server capacity (Yamin 2020).

95 The Government of Georgia, Ministry of Education and Science (2020) also noted that Georgia is considered one of the best examples of distance learning according to the OECD report (Reimers and Schleicher 2020).

EdTech: Conclusions and Recommendations

It is clear from trends that digital platforms have great promise, and that technology will influence all aspects of education and training, career coaching, job matching, and employment services. The implication is that adequate investments in EdTech must be made in a way that equalizes opportunities. Unless access to connectivity and devices is equalized, EdTech cannot live out its potential. However, while technology is necessary, it is not a sufficient condition for success in ensuring achievement of learning objectives.

There is a need to develop instructional designs and approaches that are better suited for digital platforms. Appropriate digital solutions for K-12, technical and vocational education and training (TVET), and higher education need to be nuanced to the specific curriculum goals. Digital platforms for skills need to consider how hands-on-training will be handled. Support will also be needed for the development of basic and foundational digital skills covering all sections of the population. Developing member countries (DMCs) need to develop cost-effective solutions to move to the advanced EdTech frontier to embrace technologies such as augmented reality, virtual reality, and machine learning, given budget constraints.

Governments would need to keep up with the rapidly changing nature of new technologies. To take advantage of and foster growth in private enterprises, arrangements for "technology as a service" can be made where governments need not invest in production but rather buy the services—like the kind of services offered by Amazon Web Services, or by Khan Academy to US school districts.

In adopting and scaling up EdTech, governments must not neglect addressing low levels of learning outcomes. While gains have been made in universalizing access to elementary education and other levels of education as well, the pace of improvement in learning outcomes has been very slow. In order to convert the impressive gains in access and enrollment into long-term gains, there is a critical need to address the lags and deficits in learning outcomes.

The following are six overarching priorities for addressing learning outcomes through digital strategies:

(1) Sustain uninterrupted learning through multiple channels depending on the country context (no tech, low tech, mid tech, and high tech). As evidenced by the COVID-19 pandemic, education systems need to deal with and adapt to disasters, climate events, conflict, and other causes that may occur. Hence, bounce-back strategies need to ensure that quality learning is sustained and education systems are resilient in all settings.

(2) Revamp training of teachers and trainers to transform learning experiences beyond the traditional cascade approach is needed in recognition of increasingly blended approaches to learning. Digital tools can help link improved teaching practices with enhanced student learning while also offering new pathways for teacher professional development.

(3) Develop high quality digital content reflecting 21st century skills in partnership with national and global institutions. To gradually ensure high quality and relevant content aligned with regional and global standards, it is important to partner with selected national and international institutions to draw on innovative good practices from selected benchmark countries and adapt to local contexts.

(4) Ensure equal attention to equity in quality of learning and in access requires attention to how girls and other disadvantaged groups are learning. Breaking the digital divide is a fundamental instrument to equalize access to high quality and relevant education. Technology needs to help universalize and scale up equity in learning for all by making available high quality learning materials to all students.

(5) Reform high-stake examinations and assessments for higher order learning. Personalized and adaptive learning powered through technology can go a long way in bringing new metrics to assess soft skills and higher order learning like creative thinking, collaboration, problem solving, and applying

skills to a context. Building on the COVID-19 experience, this requires articulating clear policies toward assessments and examinations, and targeting lagging students that include both digital and non-digital solutions.

(6) Ensure social protection measures for continued learning in key disciplines. In addition to scholarships to ensure enrollments and participation of vulnerable groups, there is a need to consider the support needed to bridge learning gaps that include poor language, and digital and science-based attainments. Here, too, tech tools can help to diagnose the gaps, identify student cohorts that need specific attention, and put in motion teaching and learning that can help to bring such students on par. Subventions for connectivity and devices can be an important equalizer for online learning.

Leveraging Digital Technologies for Good Health and Well-Being

State of Play

Digital health is a generic term describing the application of information and communication technology (ICT) to drive better health outcomes. In the next 3 years to 2023, it is projected that the digital health market in Asia will grow at a compounded annual rate of 5.7% (Deloitte 2019). In 2018, around 4,500 start-ups in Asia were granted regulatory approval to deploy digital health solutions (Timmers et al. 2020). For example, Halodoc, a start-up based in Indonesia has raised almost $100 million in 2018. However, countries in the region are at different levels of digital maturity and health literacy, as well as in the development or implementation of their national health and digital health strategies. As a consequence, much investment is being wasted in proprietary unsustainable and ad hoc implementations.

Universal health coverage is seen as one of the major reasons why countries in the region are starting to use digital health. It requires everyone to have access to quality health care anytime, anywhere without experiencing financial hardship. Patient centric, precise, and personalized universal coverage should be delivered in the community; reducing the focus on hospital-based treatments (Koh 2019). In order to achieve this, countries need to increase investment in primary health-care models by 1% of GDP (Roth, Parry, and Landry 2015).

Properly designed digital health offerings can make it easier to deliver patient-centric health care. Current generation personal health records (PHRs), cloud-based health databases (subject to security, privacy, and confidentiality measures); mobile solutions for clinicians; and access through browsers, phones and tablets for patients are important. Wearable and even implantable technologies are already empowering patient-centric health-care service delivery. Indeed, digital platform solutions carry substantial promise in making health service delivery more efficient and inclusive (Box 8.6).

High quality data capture and analysis ensure that proper financing models can be utilized to achieve universal health coverage. Accurate population databases of actual and potential service users allow better planning and procurement. But, measures must be in place to avoid claim fraud. There is good evidence that where patient records produce better claiming, health facilities and providers are incentivized to use digital health systems at the point of care and avoid double data entry.

Barriers to Implementing Digital Health

Successful digital health implementation increases access to health care, drives better quality of provision, and more comprehensive health services, and generates higher user satisfaction. In order to achieve these successes, strong technical, analytical, and organizational foundations need to be in place. However, barriers exist, such as the following:

- **Inadequate digital infrastructure.** Without a reliable and appropriate digital infrastructure, the health system (a) cannot benefit from online medical consultations that can address access constraints in underserved areas; (b) faces a limited market for service delivery

Box 8.6: The Benefits of Digital Health to Health Service Delivery Networks

The World Health Organization (WHO) identifies the following key characteristics for efficient health service delivery (Webb, Small, and Gregor 2019): **comprehensiveness, accessibility, coverage, continuity, quality, person centeredness, coordination, and accountability and efficiency.** Digital health drives health care along these WHO delivery lines by:

- **Reducing geographic barriers.** Applications like TeleDoctor (in Pakistan) and eHealthPoint (India) have demonstrated reductions in geographic barriers as doctors are able to connect with patients in areas that are hard to reach.
- **Improving access to health care.** Studies in rural areas in the People's Republic of China (PRC) and India (WHO 2017; Lewis et al. 2012; Haenssgen and Ariana 2017) show that patients using mHealth have a higher chance of reporting symptoms and accessing primary care centers compared with those who are not using mHealth.
- **Improving the quality of health care received.** Symptom checkers, like Fullerton Health (Singapore), allow patients to check the symptoms they experience using the application on their phone. If the app suggests that the patients stay at home and self-care then the patient need not go to an actual health facility to see a clinician. This gives more convenience for the patient and allows health facilities to focus on the patients that are in the facilities.
- **Improving the coverage of health services.** In Indonesia, an increasing number of digital services across the region enable citizens to access doctors, anytime and anywhere.
- **Enabling comprehensive health service delivery.** Health service delivery should be comprehensive enough to provide preventive, wellness, and personalized health care. Personalized health information applications like Tangtang Quan allows diabetic patients in the PRC to receive preventive information and provides a social network among diabetics so that they can share their health regimen with one another.

Source: Bainbridge et al. (2020).

networks that require good communication channels; (c) will not be able to implement real-time referrals and consults during emergencies, especially in far flung areas; and (d) is denied the advantages derived from comprehensive data that drives good policy formulation. There is good evidence that successful electronic health records (EHR) adoption requires a good communications infrastructure (Haenssgen 2015). Figure 8.20 shows a strong relationship between in-country internet penetration and EHR adoption. Emerging markets with lower internet penetration have lower EHR adoption.

- **Missing regulatory framework.** Adopting digital health platforms requires regulations that ensure security and privacy of patients and providers, efficiently capture online transactions for taxation and revenue accounting purposes, and provide parameters within which platform providers operate.

Figure 8.20: Electronic Health Records Adoption versus Internet Penetration

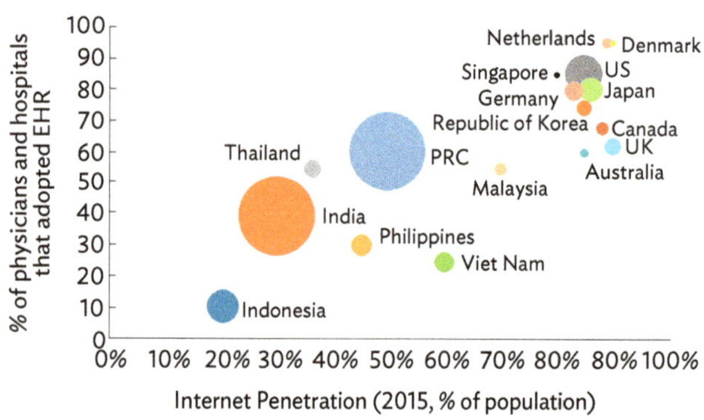

EHR = electronic health records, PRC = People's Republic of China, UK = United Kingdom, US = United States.

Notes: The bubble size corresponds to the population size. EHR Adoption includes usage of medical records, health records, and other digital solutions by hospitals and physicians to deliver healthcare service.

Source: McKeering, Norton, and Gulati (2017) as cited in Bainbridge et al. (2020).

- **Limited data sharing.** One of the key benefits that should be achieved in implementation of digital health is the ability to share data between different information systems (according to safety, privacy, and consent). Fragmented and proprietary systems limit this ability on technical and safety grounds.

- **Scant funding.** Most digital health programs are still structured as pilots and mostly government-funded technical assistance programs or implemented with loans from development partners. Sustainable financing that can support scaling is necessary. It is estimated that 77% of digital health programs around the world receive government funding, while 66% receive donor funding. Private funding (either via public–private partnership [PPP] or purely commercial endeavors) is present in only 40% of digital health programs (Greene 2013).

- **Poor skills training and stewardship in the health sector.** Digital health is still regarded as separate from the mainstream of health-care delivery. Clinical informatics is still not available as a career option in most countries in the region.

Digital Health: Policy Implications and Recommendations

There are three foundational frameworks that can be used by countries as they set up their digital health infrastructure: WHO-ITU eHealth strategy toolkit, Broadband Commission Digital Health Building Blocks, and Asia eHealth Information Network—Mind the Gaps, Fill the Gaps. These frameworks all include common themes which are needed for successful implementation:

Continuous effort to foster strong governance and regulation is vital. Digital health is frequently driven top-down by governments often with little consultation with clinical and ancillary workforce leadership. A strong governance structure must be in place to help drive digital health solutions with clear and agreed goals with clinical buy-in and clinical governance. There are three common digital health governance models in use across the world—government-led, multisector, or independent (Box 8.7).

A digital health strategy must be aligned with a country's overall health, education, and ICT strategies to reap the benefits from coordinated investments and complementary infrastructure. Governance is also responsible for implementing legislation, policies, and regulations needed to govern digital health, including data management policies, privacy and security laws,

Box 8.7: Digital Health Governance Models

Ministry of Health-led governance. The Ministry of Health leads in the development of the digital health strategy and is tasked to handle digital health operations. This model is used in Viet Nam where the eHealth Administration, under the Ministry of Health, is responsible for the development and adoption of a digital health strategy for the whole country.

Multisector governance structure. An interagency group is tasked to develop and implement the digital health strategy, drawing on the strengths of the various government units to ensure a robust and sustainable strategy. This is the governance structure used in the Philippines, led by the National e-Health Steering Committee, with the Departments of Health, Science and Technology, Information and Communications Technology, and the PhilHealth as members. A secretariat group under the Department of Health supports the e-Health Working group.

Stand-alone agency. An entity independent of the existing government agencies is established to drive the digital health strategy. This ensures that the unique needs of setting up a digital health infrastructure can be addressed. Examples of this model include the Australian Digital Health Agency and the Canadian Health Infoway.

Source: Bainbridge et al. (2020).

clinical use regulations, software compliance regulations, and telehealth regulations, among others.

There is a strong case to build common infrastructure. Common infrastructure is a system that is shared both by government and private sector entities and can also be used across sectors. Examples are mobile/telco towers or fiber optic cables for internet connectivity, or even electricity in remote areas. They can also be soft infrastructure like citizen identifiers, common government platforms, e-Government systems, and health-related shared systems like health information exchanges or electronic health records. By investing in these common types of infrastructures, governments are able to provide a baseline infrastructure that health sector related systems can use, enable more innovations to occur as systems can share infrastructure resources, level the playing field as it allows small players to deploy innovative solutions on the shared platforms, improve technology adoption, reduce the barriers of entry in digital health, and test technologies before they are used in digital health use cases.

Promoting and adopting standards and interoperability measures are necessary. Interoperability is the capability of a software system to safely share patient data and meaning with other systems. Interoperability enables health facilities and health providers to provide better care and expands the options for patients. It would be important to establish an overarching health system architecture that can encompass and integrate internationally known health data standards that will be utilized by the various components of the ecosystem. An interoperable structure also opens up the marketplace to a wide range of vendors and reduces the risk of proprietary lock-in that can lead to high switching costs for patients and monopolistic behavior of providers.

Health standards are also important in attaining interoperability. Standards like the Digital Imaging and Communications in Medicine (DICOM) for images (NEMA 2020), the Health Level Seven-Fast Health Interoperability Resources (HL7 FHIR) (HL7 International 2019) and the Information Systems Interoperability Maturity Model (ISIMM) (van Staden and Mbale 2012) are widely used allowing any system using them to easily integrate. Standards for terminology and classification are equally important—with the Systematized Nomenclature of Medicine (SNOMED) (Bhattacharyya 2016) and the International Classification of Diseases (ICD) being in frequent use for these purposes (Benson and Grieve 2016).

Currently, in Asia, ADB has led the establishment of a regional reference interoperability lab, the Standards and Interoperability Lab (SIL)—Asia (Bhattacharyya 2016). They have already helped in the development, conceptualization, and capacity development of several in-country interoperability labs in Indonesia, the Philippines, Thailand and Viet Nam.

The real challenge for digital health implementation is on scaling up as this requires sustained funding. To reduce the cost of developing health platforms to a minimum, it is important to share methodologies and even software components, particularly those for use in public health. Governments can use several business models to ensure sustained financing and implementation of digital health platforms:

(1) **Software Development Deployment.** The health facility pays for the whole cost of software development, including installation and system maintenance. Future enhancements are done either by the facility or by the original software developer.

(2) **Software License Procurement.** Health facilities procure licenses to use digital health solutions developed by software companies. The cost of development and maintenance of the software is shared among the various health facilities that use the same software. Customization can be done but this will entail additional costs to the facilities.

For options 1 and 2, health facilities still need to invest in infrastructure to host the digital health solutions, such as devices and other hardware, and to train technical staff to operate and manage the systems.

(3) **Software as a Service Model.** Health facilities procure a license to use existing digital health solutions. However, the digital health solutions will not be deployed to the respective facilities but on the cloud, and the original software company maintains and operates the software.

Challenges and Risks from Digital Platforms

Even as there are many benefits gained from digital platforms, it is important to recognize that there are attendant risks that have to be effectively managed. For one, the winner-takes-all dynamics typical in platform-based economies leads to significant market concentration. Appropriate policy responses will need to be designed to address possible negative impacts from the abuse of dominant position. Likewise, concerns about security, privacy, and movement and ownership of data have to be considered when formulating policies especially since the growth of the digital economy is fueled by the generation, storage, and processing and transfer of data, both within and across borders.

That online labor platforms have created new income-generating opportunities and transformed labor markets is well recognized. These new arrangements, however, have implications on income security, health-care benefits, and pensions as well as the provision of relevant education and training. Another major concern is that many of the key features of the growing digital economy heighten base erosion and profit shifting (BEPS) risks, which will impact on the availability of domestic resources for development.

As documented in section on benefits and opportunities, the economic gains from digital platforms are aplenty, and these benefits also help economies achieve their SDGs. However, the impact of digital platforms on the environment, on social cohesion, and the individuals' psychological well-being cannot be overlooked. These also have economic costs that could eventually negate the benefits if not managed properly. For instance, digital e-commerce platforms are fostering the movement toward paperless transactions and are helping reduce the need to operate physical stores which free up spaces for other uses (Tiwari and Singh 2011). On the downside, the parcelization of cross-border shipments has intensified the use of packaging materials, particularly plastic-based materials that are causing environmental damage.

The impact of the expanding internet retailing and parcelization of products on the environment has to be recognized and addressed properly. While most of the benefits are privately gained, the environmental problems become the concerns of governments, which in Asia are hard pressed for resources. There are ongoing pocket efforts to reduce wasteful packaging of parcels, but there is a need for more vigorous regulations and widespread implementation (Box 8.8).

The overarching challenge is to foster a regulatory climate that would optimize digital platforms' market and economic and social outcomes. This section examines the cross-sector policy issues that can help countries manage the risks to sustainable and inclusive development from digital platforms.

Competition

How Successful Digital Platforms Grow

High concentration and the presence of dominant digital platforms are common features across the globe. The Big Four (Amazon, Apple, Facebook, and Google) have already become household names and their market presence continues to expand. Of interest to competition policy is the trend of market leaders expanding their businesses by leveraging their position in one market to establish themselves in adjacent markets, sometimes to the detriment of its competitors. For example, Amazon is not just an e-commerce platform operator, it also competes with its own merchants by directly selling its own products in the platform, and is also one of the leading providers of cloud services through Amazon Web Services.

Regional markets such as Southeast Asia also exhibit the same pattern of high concentration. A 2019 end-of-year report on Southeast Asia's map of e-commerce covering Indonesia, Malaysia, the Philippines, Singapore, and Viet Nam identified Lazada and Shopee as the two leading firms, accounting for more than 55% of visits to the top 10 e-commerce websites (Iprice Group, App Annie, and SimilarWeb 2020). In the Philippines, Lazada

Box 8.8: E-commerce and the Environment

A typical e-commerce parcel will involve multiple packaging materials including cardboard boxes, plastic bags, adhesive tapes, and buffer materials (e.g., bubble wraps, expanded polystyrene, packing peanuts). Plastic packaging is usually the first choice for e-commerce sellers due to the material's relative durability, light weight, flexibility, and lower cost. Mordor Intelligence (2020) reports that the global e-commerce plastic packaging market was worth $10.26 billion in 2019, and it is expected to reach $21.78 billion by 2025 (a compound annual growth rate of 13.6% for 2020–2025). While this is a huge growth opportunity for packaging and plastics producers, the long-term potential damaging impact on the environment must be considered in the overall development equation. Management of plastic waste is particularly important in Asia, where a study by Jambeck et al. (2015) found the biggest contributors of plastic pollution in marine ecosystems were Indonesia, the People's Republic of China, the Philippines, Sri Lanka, and Viet Nam, accounting for 54.5% of the world's total mismanaged plastic waste.

While recycling technologies can potentially mitigate the problem, this route has been historically inadequate. For example, the United States (US) Environmental Protection Agency (2020), citing data from the American Chemistry Council, noted that the US produced 35.7 million tons of plastic in 2018, of which only 3 million tons (8.5%) were recycled. A study by Geyer, Jambeck, and Law (2017) on the product life cycle of plastics estimates that 8.3 billion metric tons of virgin plastic have been produced in the world, of which only 9% have been recycled. Limits to effective recycling efforts include unsustainable packaging production and design, lack of waste management infrastructure, and limited waste tracking solutions.

A potential framework for tackling this issue is the adoption of circular economy models which promote sustainable production and consumption patterns, maximize the value of materials that circulate in the economy, minimize waste generation, and reduce hazardous components in products and their packaging. Governments play a crucial role in enacting policies and developing infrastructure that support a circular economy—such as discouraging single-use plastics through regulation, and ensuring adequate facilities for proper waste collection and management.

Manufacturers can augment these efforts by developing and using more sustainable products and packaging, exploring other materials such as bio-based or biodegradable packaging. A circular economy may also open up new markets and opportunities for businesses to offer products and services that reuse or recycle plastic products. For instance, start-ups have provided employment and income opportunities for women and out-of-school youth in poor areas to produce, for example, handicrafts, bags, footwear, reusing discarded plastics, cloth, and paper.

Source: Asian Development Bank.

and Shopee account for more than 90% of the visits. Likewise, Grab has been enjoying a virtual monopoly in car-hailing, while Angkas is just as dominant in motorcycle-hailing services. Grab is also able to leverage its market leadership in car-hailing to gain a foothold in other markets such as digital payments (GrabPay), food delivery (GrabFood), and point-to-point parcel delivery (GrabExpress).

Evans and Schmalensee (2007) posit that there are five determinants which influence market concentration in digital platform markets: network effects, scale economies, congestion, platform differentiation, and multi-homing. The first two, indirect network effects and scale economies, tend to lead to higher concentration while the other three have the opposite influence on market concentration.

Network effects further entrenches first-movers who are able to reach critical mass, making it more difficult for newer players to gain market share and introduce more competition in markets. First-mover digital platforms have the additional advantage of having the market space to scale up operations due partly to the amount of data they are able to collect and process. Ezrachi and Stucke (2018) identify negative market distortions from the emergence of what they call "data-opolies." They argue that dominant incumbents use their advantageous positions in data ownership which can lead to the degradation of product quality and increasing information asymmetry. Dominant platform operators also have the ability to engage in exclusionary behavior, steering users and advertisers to its own products and services away from rival providers.

In Asia, some digital platform leaders, like Alibaba, are also first movers in their home countries and in the region. Alibaba has been successful in keeping at bay marketplace competitors from the region, and can compete with older global players, such as Amazon. Similarly, Grab controls considerable market power in 8 of the 10 economies in Southeast Asia. High barriers to entry induced by regulations magnify these advantages, paving the way for larger concentration of market power among few players.

Mergers and acquisitions are employed by larger and typically global players to penetrate or increase their presence in local markets (Box 8.9). As such, it is crucial for regulators to be well-equipped in terms of technical capacity in crafting responsive and unambiguous regulations.

Tirole (2020) argues that in situations where competition in the market is not feasible, it is important to preserve contestability by ensuring that there is competition for the market or what he calls "dynamic competition." Instead of compelling the entry or creation of multiple competitors, an alternative is to incentivize incumbents to act competitively with the threat of entry.

A means to preserve contestability is through multi-homing or by limiting the ability of platforms to enforce exclusivity arrangements, such as drivers in ride-hailing apps. Multi-homing refers to the ability of users to join and use multiple platforms with minimal switching costs.

Box 8.9: Mergers and Acquisitions—Some Examples

Grab's acquisition of Uber's operations in Southeast Asia significantly increased its market share in the platform-based transportation sector. This particular merger was subject to heavy regulatory scrutiny among the competition authorities in the region. The Competition and Consumer Commission of Singapore (CCCS) found that the transaction violated Section 54 of their Competition Act, and imposed $9.5 million in penalties on the parties.[a] Similarly, the Philippine Competition Commission found the transaction to be anticompetitive, and also imposed a fine. In contrast, the Indonesia Competition Commission viewed the transaction not as a merger but an asset acquisition without any transfer of control from Uber Indonesia to Grab Indonesia.

Incidentally, Yandex.Taxi also merged with Uber in Armenia, Azerbaijan, Belarus, Georgia, Kazakhstan, and the Russian Federation in 2018 (Yandex.Taxi n.d.) creating a private company called MLU B.V., incorporated in the Netherlands. In 2019, the Federal Antimonopoly Service of the Russian Federation ordered Yandex, Uber, and their joint venture "*... not to impose a ban on partners, drivers and passengers to work with other taxis aggregators*" (Government of the Russian Federation, FAS 2019) to improve competition in the market for taxi aggregators.

Walmart India's acquisition of more than three-quarters of Flipkart's shares in 2018 likewise posed certain competition concerns. While the deal received approval from India's Competition Commission, it induced calls for the creation of an exclusive e-commerce policy and regulator (Saraswathy 2019).

Alibaba's acquisition of a controlling stake in Lazada in 2016 highlights a different aspect of increasing the platform's market power. The deal not only neutralized one strong regional competitor for Alibaba, but, through Aliexpress, it also gained additional access channels for online retail in six of the largest economies in the Association of Southeast Asian Nations. This acquisition gave Alibaba a distinct competitive advantage in countries where operations of the two affiliates overlap despite it not raising any red flags among competition authorities when the merger was notified.

[a] As of April 2019, the $6.58 million fine for Uber has been suspended because Uber decided to appeal the CCCS decision.

Source: Villafuerte et al. (2020).

Chisholm and Jung (2015) warn against long-standing dominance in a market and barriers that prevent users from moving across platforms, in part, due to their exclusivity and data capture (Box 8.10).

The Role of Big Data in (Stifling) Competition

The economies of scale and scope, data-driven network effects, and control of data pose a high barrier to potential entrants effectively rendering the platform a non-neutral intermediary. In a case initiated by the European Commission and the Federal Cartel Office in Germany, for instance, Amazon is being scrutinized on the grounds of "abusing its market position to the detriment of sellers active on its marketplace" following complaints received by the German competition agency (Government of Germany, Federal Cartel Office 2018). Google was also fined by the European Commission in 2017 for giving its shopping service illegal advantage in search results (European Commission 2017).

In Asia, Müller (2020) noted that the Japan Free Trade Commission is investigating issues on data collection and digital cartels, and carrying out sector-wide inspections of large digital, globally operating platforms. The competition authority in the Republic of Korea has similarly signified intent to launch a probe into practices of big players like Google, Naver, Facebook, and Apple that lead to data monopolies (Kim 2019).

Big data collected and utilized by platforms matter in switching cost. For example, when the historical data (e.g., health, financial, or tax records) stored in platforms are important to the users, the switching cost can deter user movement between platforms (Tucker 2019a). Switching costs are also an issue when advertisers face high cost of leaving behind their data or converting it to a new format (Tucker 2019b). Network effects play a role in switching cost, as do the tailored content and ancillary services that in turn are produced using the extensive user data that platforms collect.

Box 8.10: Barriers to Multi-Homing

- **Contractual restrictions.** Contractual restrictions are commonly embodied in wide-scoping most favored nation (MFN) clauses and exclusivity and tying provisions.[a] European competition authorities consider wide MFN clauses as those which "require suppliers and retailers to publish on a price comparison tool of online marketplace the same or better price and conditions as those published on any other sales channel," while narrow ones necessitate publication directly on personal websites (Chappatte, O'Connell, and de Morant 2019).
- **Lack of capacity of customers to transfer existing profiles to a different competing platform.** This inability unduly locks-in a user and creates greater investments both to stay and to exit. Aside from large network effects, an inability to multi-home may likewise be attributed to high transaction costs as a disincentive to switch.
- **Dominant players' exclusive access to proprietary data.** A platform's access to personal data, such as commonly searched items and historical transactions, enable an incumbent to better understand an individual's consumer behavior. This allows dominant firms to provide better suggestions and insights to a user, as in the shape of targeted advertisements and promotions, which competitors are not able to do.

[a] A popular citation of the use of a wide MFN clause is in the hotel booking market, particularly the Bundeskartellamt (Government of Germany, Federal Cartel Office) case against Booking.com in December 2015, which was dismissed because of mixed views of the narrowness of an MFN provision. In Booking.com's clause, hotels were prohibited to offer favorable prices and conditions, namely, better booking and cancellation conditions or terms of availability on their own websites or through distribution channels offline. However, these would be permissible on portals such as Booking.com. A similar case was filed in Sweden. The Düsseldorf Higher Regional Court later quashed the initial decision by the Federal Cartel Office in June 2019 because narrow MFN clauses were found to be well-matched with competition law as they would permit a "fair and balanced contractual exchange of services between the portal and the hotels." As such, Booking.com's provision was required to subvert a "disloyal rechanneling" of portal customer bookings if the hotel were to establish more desirable prices and terms on their own online and offline media (BCLP 2019; Chappatte, O'Connell, and de Morant 2019).

Source: Villafuerte et al. (2020).

Advancing Competition Regulations Should Consider Multiple Dimensions of Transactions

The responsiveness and precision of the regulatory framework are crucial in enabling a competitive landscape. OECD (2018b) has up-to-date competition policy and robust regional cooperation framework as well as clear and actionable consumer protection and data privacy. The quality and coverage of digital infrastructure is likewise crucial, along with rules on taxation, intellectual property, and labor protection.

Competition authorities should consider both monetary transactions and data flows in defining a multisided market (UNCTAD 2019b). For example, Germany revised its competition law in 2017 to recognize products or services provided free by platforms as a market. There is also a need to thoroughly reexamine the tools used in reviewing cases, such as the effectiveness of traditional ex-post competition instruments in dealing with digital markets that thrive in highly concentrated market structures dominated by very few big players. Perhaps utilizing well-timed and carefully targeted measures where anticompetitive behavior emerges can help tackle competition issues.

International cooperation cannot be overemphasized. Considering the prominent cross-border dimension of digital platforms, efforts to strengthen competition laws, policy-setting, and regulatory agencies could benefit from multilateral cooperation, especially in standards regulation, data privacy rules, protectionist trade and industrial policies, and taxation, among others. Additionally, by working closely with various countries, authorities can harness synergies and respond faster and more effectively to emerging challenges by adapting key features of best practices.

The ASEAN Competition Action Plan 2025 sought to advance competition regulations in Southeast Asian economies and the implementation capacities of the designated agencies in a collective fashion (ASEAN 2016). In line with the ASEAN Economic Community Blueprint 2025, the action plan and other regional mechanisms (such as the ASEAN Competition Conference and the ASEAN Competition Enforcers' Network) can be leveraged to advance digital economy-specific regulations in the economic bloc.

Due consideration ought to be given to consumer protection and data privacy. The extent of the collection and usage of data is critical to digital platforms. As it can be a mechanism to preserve and increase market power while exposing clients to privacy risks, this presents a strong case to integrate competition law and implementation with consumer protection and data privacy. In 2011, the Asia-Pacific Economic Cooperation (APEC) rolled out the Cross-Border Privacy Rules (CBPR) in an attempt to set the guidelines for transfer of personal information across participating economies (APEC 2019). The CBPR is a follow-up initiative to the APEC Privacy Framework launched in 2005. As of April 2019, 8 out of the 21 APEC member economies have formally joined the CBPR system.

Having strong and consumer-centric data privacy rules can foster a market ecosystem where consumers can trust businesses and authorities with their data. Secure and portable data will lower switching costs for consumers while also easing entry barriers for new businesses that can now access, with consumer consent, the data being held by dominant incumbents. Asian economies are following the lead of the European Union in this respect. Blackmore (2019) observed that there is a "consistent strengthening of data protection laws throughout the region" which are in line with the EU's General Data Protection Regulation standards. However, the tightening of consumer protection and data privacy rules raises the operations cost of firms, which could deter competition. For example, as cited by Barker (2020), estimates of compliance cost to the regulation standards ranges from just under £1 million to £2.3 million per business in the United Kingdom, depending on the size of the company based on Calligo (2017); while most US firms surveyed indicated that they intend to allocate between $1 million and $10 million for compliance following PwC (2017).

Barker (2020) emphasized the importance of data rules in mergers arguing that this could reduce the quality of data protection and privacy and increase the barriers to entry or rivals' costs. A relevant case is the Google–DoubleClick merger in 2008, where the European Commission deferred privacy considerations to the data protection law, given the precedent set by the Asnef-Equifax case.[96] The merger was eventually approved, but the European Commission pressed the new entity to respect the fundamental rights of all parties involved to privacy and data protection.

Taxation and intellectual property rules matter in enhancing competition. Specific features of the digital economy, such as the lack of clarity in classifying digital activities and absence of harmonized cross-border tax rules, pose critical challenges to tax systems. In e-commerce, for example, the de minimis rules come into play in competition between digital platforms and traditional enterprises. Collection of value-added tax (VAT) or goods and services tax (GST) from digital platforms is a related concern. Indeed, plugging the gaps in consumption tax collection is one of the key objectives of the OECD-G20 BEPS Initiative.

The extent of protection of intellectual property likewise has implications on competition in the digital platform space. A standard tool in competition policy and intellectual property law is the requirement for a fair, reasonable, and nondiscriminatory access to certain assets, like software applications, hardware technology, or even digital content, that are necessary for entry and operation in the market.

Income Security and Social Protection

Persistent Work Informality and Lack of Social Protection

The emergence of the platform economy has exacerbated work informality in Asia. Work informality is highly present among the self-employed or own-account workers—86.2% of the region's self-employed are informal workers (ILO 2018)—where digital platform workers who self-enlist are found.

Informal workers usually lack coverage from social insurance or contributory schemes due to exclusion from legal coverage, low and inconsistent earnings, and complicated administrative processes. They also tend to be excluded from social assistance or noncontributory schemes that are typically targeted to the poor. In the process, informal workers are often left without any social protection coverage, hence, the case of the "missing middle" exists (ILO 2017, 2019; Ulrichs 2016).

Likewise, the adverse impact of digital technology on the health outcomes of users and workers is a growing concern. For example, constant use of digital devices could lead to physical illness, while exposure to unfiltered information and potentially exploitative methods may contribute to mental health issues (Box 8.11).

Among the informal workers vulnerable during the COVID-19 crisis are digital platform workers who lost jobs and experienced income shocks. For instance, it is estimated that around 90% of those working in the informal sector in India (400 million workers including rural–urban migrants) can be pushed deeper into poverty amid the government's lockdown measures (ILO 2020a). Location-based gig workers involved in household services would have seen a decline in income opportunities given the lockdown measures. On the other hand, transport and delivery gig workers have ongoing demand as most people who self-isolate rely on digital platforms to access goods and services.[97] They have been on the forefront during the pandemic, despite their lack of proper social protection coverage.[98] These impacts have stirred global discussions on health insurance, sick pay, and other work-related benefits, and underscore the need for the extension of social protection (PYMNTS 2020).

96 The case of Asnef-Equifax in 2006 was eventually cleared. However, issues about the sensitivity of personal data regarding the applicable competition laws were noted.

97 Digital platforms offering delivery services like Grab, Lalamove, and Foodpanda have supported demand of households during the crisis. Other digital platforms like Didi have disabled their transport services and converted to delivery and grocery shopping services (Abacus 2020; Hung 2020; Sukumaran 2020).

98 Grab announced measures such as contactless delivery to safeguard drivers from contracting the disease. Also, amid the ongoing discussions on the need for social protection, Grab has rolled out initiatives such as providing a one-time payment to cover loss of income for driver-partners who must undergo quarantine or medical treatment for COVID-19. It has also offered medical subsidies for affected driver-partners in some its countries of operation (Grab 2020).

Box 8.11: Digital Platforms and Mental Health

A growing body of evidence suggests a nexus between the ubiquity of digital platforms and trends in mental health outcomes. Indeed, the nature of social interactions through digital technologies could lead to mental health conditions including anxiety, depression, bipolar disorder, and lower self-esteem among users (Blachnio et al. 2016). Frequent internet use triggers neurological processes similar to other addictive substances and activities and these effects are more prevalent at younger ages. Some evidence also indicates that digital technologies can have negative impacts on physical health by crowding out healthy activities and deteriorating the quality of sleep (OECD 2019b). From a social perspective, research suggests children and teenagers can be vulnerable to cyberbullying and online harassment through social media platforms (Lindert 2017, Mirsky and Omar 2015).

While findings have been documented, the causal effects of digital access on psychological and physical outcomes needs to be further explored. At present, most countries lack a proper indicator framework to monitor mental health outcomes and their link to digital technologies. National Statistical Offices have included questions and modules on self-reported health and subjective well-being in surveys on information and communication technology. However, more longitudinal data are needed to establish causal linkages between the use of digital technologies and people's well-being.

Source: Asian Development Bank.

Properly functioning social security systems can help address persisting challenges such as work informality poverty, population aging, and gender inequality. Recently, governments have adopted a long-term perspective on social protection—seeing it as an investment that would yield social, economic, and political dividends. In fact, developing Asian countries have explored implementing, oftentimes concurrently, various social assistance programs such as social support services, noncontributory health insurance, food subsidies, training, fuel and electricity subsidies, unconditional in-kind transfers, school feeding programs, educational fee waiver, and conditional and unconditional cash transfers (IPC-IG and UNICEF 2019). However, due to limited fiscal space, some countries continue to make tradeoffs among different social protection investments depending on their priorities. For instance, a study shows that India, Indonesia, Kazakhstan, Nepal, and the Philippines would need to open new fiscal space to improve social protection up to the level required to achieve the SDGs, while, the PRC would have to increase its tax rates (Handayani, Cichon, and Carraro 2018).

The Appeal of Universal Basic Income

In this context, countries like India and the PRC have been examining the feasibility of a universal and unconditional cash-based social assistance scheme known as universal basic income (UBI).[99] UBI is a form of social assistance that involves regular unconditional transfer of uniform amounts of cash to all individuals of a given country. Although critics argue that UBI can create disincentives to work, inflationary effects, and fiscal pressure, it has potential to eliminate huge administrative costs and inclusion/exclusion errors associated with targeted social assistance schemes. The core features of a UBI can be defined along three dimensions (Box 8.12).

UBI benefits informal workers such as digital workers by providing them a guaranteed income not only during times of unemployment but also when they are employed yet still outside social protection systems. With UBI, transfers can act as top-up income during periods of employment, which they can utilize for any lifecycle shocks that may occur. UBI may also improve

[99] In India, a wide range of proposals have emerged following decades of debate and concerns over fragmentation (Banerjee 2016; Bardhan 2017; Ghatak 2016; Joshi 2017; Ray 2016). UBI proposals from politicians were also part of electoral campaigns in 2019. In the PRC, recent studies—mainly by UNDP China—were conducted to stir debate on UBI in the country and assess compatibility with the PRC social and economic system (UNDP China 2020a, 2020b; Zheng et al. 2017). A UBI scheme is also ongoing in Macau, China.

Box 8.12: Key Features of Universal Basic Income

Universality means that there is guaranteed coverage for everyone. Unlike targeted schemes that involve some types of means testing, universal basic income avoids the intrinsic risk of exclusion and inclusion errors associated with needs-based targeting and the transaction costs incurred to access benefits (e.g., time spent in applying for the program or verification of recipients' eligibility). From a political economy perspective, the universality of UBI "makes the public expenditure system more transparent and prevents problems of benefit fraud and not reporting income, which are typical disadvantages of means-tested benefit policies" (Fitzpatrick 1999; Zheng et al. 2017).

Another key feature of UBI rests on the provision of assistance ***without conditions***. Conditionality is used to influence recipients' behaviors, typically toward nutrition, health and education—aspects where a gap commonly exists between an individual's perceived and expected returns. Implementation of a conditional social assistance requires institutional and administrative capacity (Gentilini et al. 2020), and proper coordination across the whole government system is critical to monitor compliance to conditionalities.[a] In most developing countries where complex government systems often lack coherence, public development programs need a robust design so they could perform well despite weak institutional environment. In this regard, given its unconditional nature, UBI may prove compatible with the existing institutional and governance scenario in developing countries in Asia.

UBI is a ***cash-based*** social assistance. Compared with public transfers of in-kind goods, cash transfers provide flexibility and power of choice to individuals, and are much easier for governments to move to recipients. The use of electronic payments to disburse cash transfers also reduces security risks. Cash transfers also entail a shorter process that does not require procurement, storage, and physical distribution making the scheme less prone to issues of red tape and corruption. Moreover, cash transfers like UBI can also promote greater transparency in fiscal accounting than other types of social security programs (Gentilini et al. 2020).

[a] For example, the conditional cash transfers in the Philippines need to be coordinated to regional government offices, local government units, and so on.

Source: Arbo and Takenaka (2020).

overall work conditions as it gives workers the option to quit unsatisfying jobs, assured by the guaranteed cash income.

The most identifiable tradeoffs on whether to choose UBI over other social protection programs include "generosity vs. work disincentives, effective coverage of poor households vs. leakages to richer individuals, alternative use of available resources vs. fiscal cost, and implementation challenges vs. objectives" (Francese and Prady 2018). Macroeconomic implications of UBI should also be considered including inflationary effects of disbursing huge amounts of cash. The gravity of these tradeoffs may differ for each developing Asian country, but, there is some indication that UBI may offer solutions to some of the existing problems surrounding targeted and in-kind social protection programs, such as large transaction costs associated with in-kind support, mis-targeting and uneven coverage of programs due to a paucity of human resources to administer programs and corruption. The appeal of broad or universal targeting will increase further as the per-person costs of delivering transfers is greatly reduced through the convenience and efficiency in digital payment infrastructures (Banerjee, Niehaus, and Suri 2019).

During the COVID-19 pandemic, cash transfers served as income support to the population, especially those with low income, while stimulating the macro-economy by encouraging consumption. As of 27 March 2020, there were 99 cash transfer programs adopted worldwide in response to the pandemic, with two of them (Hong Kong, China; Singapore) considered as quasi-UBI (Box 8.13).

Social Protection: Policy Implications and Recommendations

Digitalization has altered business models and created new types of jobs in developing Asia. However, a large

Box 8.13: Cash Transfer Measures Related to COVID-19 Pandemic

Some of the announced COVID-19-related cash transfer schemes in developing Asia are the following:

- **Hong Kong, China:** One-time universal cash transfer of HK$1,280 ($165) for 7 million adult residents in its effort to boost economic growth by 1% in 2020.
- **Singapore:** One-time payment of S$300 ($205), S$200 ($137) or S$100 ($61), based on income, to all Singaporeans aged 21 years and above.
- **People's Republic of China:** Increase in coverage and benefits of *dibao* assistance to people on low incomes, with differences in specificities at the local level. For example, temporary assistance of CNY3,000 ($423) was provided to quarantine migrant population in Wuhan as well as CNY500 ($70) for urban *dibao* recipients and CNY300 ($42) for rural *dibao* recipients throughout Hubei province.
- **India:** Cash payment of ₹1,000 ($13) each to all beneficiaries of the National Social Assistance Programme (NSAP) for elderly, widows, and disabled receiving social pensions; a monthly cash transfer of ₹500 ($7) to all female Jan Dhan accounts for 3 months; and top-up of ₹2,000 ($26) for farmers of the Pradhan Mantri Kisan Samman Nidhi (PM-KISAN) for 3 months.
- **Indonesia:** Monthly cash transfer of RP200,000 ($14) to low-income households for 6 months.
- **Kazakhstan:** Monthly payment equal to the minimum wage, T45,000 ($110) to those who have lost income during the crisis.
- **Malaysia:** Cash transfer of RM200 to household beneficiaries as part of the Bantuan Sara Hidup (BSH) program with BSH 2020 households receiving additional RM100 ($24) and RM50 ($12) as e-cash; one-off payment of RM600 ($144) to taxi, tourist, and trishaw drivers and tourist guides; and special monthly critical worker allowance of RM400 ($96) for medical doctors and other medical personnel and RM200 ($48) for immigration and related frontline staff until end of outbreak.
- **Philippines:** Cash transfer of ₱5,000 ($99) to ₱8,000 ($158) monthly for 2 months to low-income households working in the informal economy (considering current conditional cash transfer grants and rice subsidy in the computation of emergency aid) as part of the Emergency Subsidy Program; launch of five new cash transfer programs: (i) compensation of ₱1,000 ($20) to public and private health workers who contract the disease while on duty and ₱1 million to their families in case of their death, (ii) financial assistance for urgent medical and burial needs, (iii) payment of ₱5,000 ($99) to workers in private establishments affected by the lockdown regardless of employment status, (iv) cash aid to overseas Filipino workers affected by the travel ban due to COVID-19, and (v) cash assistance of ₱10,000 ($200) to stranded workers who are members of the Overseas Workers Welfare Administration Trust Fund.
- **Republic of Korea:** Reintroduction of jobseekers' allowance amounting to W500,000 ($406) for up to 3 months; a new cash transfer scheme to roll out W200 billion to low-income households getting unemployed and to those under COVID-19 treatment.
- **Thailand:** Cash transfer of B5,000 ($153) for 3 months, especially for people not covered by the Social Security Fund.

Sources: Gentilini, Almenfi, and Orton (2020); ILO (2020b); and IMF (2020).

share of the population is still not covered by any form of social protection, such as social assistance and social insurance. Providing these, and also achieving the SDGs and the social protection agenda, entails fiscal requirements beyond the limited resources in developing Asian countries.

Governments must learn to respond to the informality and fast-changing nature of the digital platform labor market with appropriate labor policies and social protection programs. The convenience offered by digital cash transfers can make it easier to distribute social amelioration funds; while accurate capture of digital platform workers in the labor force data enables the crafting of polices to address job security and mitigate abuses arising from contractual dominance of platform owners over digital workers.

Efficient fiscal management is needed to find space to extend social protection. Although resources are limited, some governments in developing Asia likely have not yet maximized their fiscal and revenue capacity to close the social protection gap. In 2015, public spending on social assistance or noncontributory cash transfers in Asia was only 1.1% of GDP, while expenditure on social insurance or contributory programs including pensions was 4.2% of GDP (Figure 8.21). On average, total spending for the broad categories of social protection was 5.3% of GDP in Asian countries (ADB 2019a). For lower-middle-income countries in the region, the figures are even smaller than the regional average: 0.9% of GDP for social assistance and 3.0% for social insurance (ADB 2019a).

Figure 8.21: Expenditure on Social Protection in 24 Asian Economies, 2015 (% of GDP)

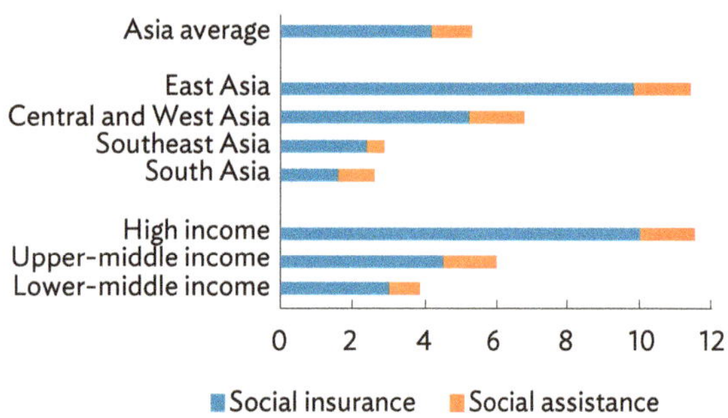

GDP = gross domestic product.

Note: The economies included are Armenia, Azerbaijan, Bangladesh, Bhutan, Cambodia, Georgia, Indonesia, Japan, the Kyrgyz Republic, the Lao People's Democratic Republic, Malaysia, Maldives, Mongolia, Nepal, Pakistan, the People's Republic of China, the Philippines, the Republic of Korea, Singapore, Sri Lanka, Tajikistan, Thailand, Uzbekistan, and Viet Nam.

Source: ADB (2019a).

This means that there may be a manageable fiscal space to extend social protection in some developing countries in the region. To take advantage of this fiscal space, governments should focus on prioritizing social protection investments that cover informal workers, and improving the design and management of social protection schemes, such as UBI, to take advantage of the convenience offered by digital payment schemes.

Regulating Data Access, and Ensuring Privacy and Security

Learning and Contextualizing Policies from Advanced Economies

The globalized data flows present legal implications on the ability of states and data subjects to control and protect data, especially since digital platforms can conclude transactions beyond national borders (Serzo 2020). Data may be monetized by processing the same for targeted advertising and marketing communications, and other data science and machine learning applications such as credit scoring and market research.

The COVID-19 pandemic and the subsequent mobility restrictions set in place by government authorities sped up the adoption of technology and digital platforms. The pandemic also exposed ways that data may be exploited: identities of suspected patients are leaked in social media; employers require personnel to disclose travel and medical history; and local government units publish the names and addresses of individuals entitled to financial assistance. Academic and policy debates also abound relating to the implementation of GPS tracking technology to implement better contact tracing tools, and artificial-intelligence-enabled technologies that assist doctors identify COVID-19-infected patients through X-ray.

Challenges of Regulating Data Protection and Processing

The absence of enforceable intergovernmental data protection policies ought to be addressed by the governments in the region. The borderless nature of digital platform transactions will necessarily involve cross-border sharing and/or transfers of data. A transaction may therefore trigger the regulations of several jurisdictions. Except for the General Data Protection Regulation of the European Union, there is no enforceable and legally binding international standard for data regulation. Asian economies are not subjected to any overarching, international data protection regulation. This is in spite of intergovernmental initiatives meant to encourage alignment of data protection policies.

The exponential developments in technologies are a big regulatory challenge that requires a fresh approach. Effective implementation of data protection measures is complicated by the fast-moving nature of technology development impacting operations of entities that process data. As such, existing regulations may not be sufficient to consider novel structures and processes. Due to lack of information and expertise, regulators may be tempted to immediately regulate a new business model, possibly discouraging further experimentation and innovation.

The normative challenges cannot be overlooked. Data protection is normatively and culturally challenging to enforce. Data protection legislation necessitates the regulation of the behavior of different actors with regard to data. Unlike other prohibitive regulations, the benefits of restricting the processing of data may not be clearly apparent. Moreover, the expanding capacities of digital platforms to utilize data for various purposes, including manipulation of perceptions and distortion of information, have led to some erosion of trust in social and political institutions (Box 8.14).

Rules on Data Localization in Selected Countries in ASEAN

The importance of regional data protection structures cannot be overstated. There are a number of international and regional frameworks for data protection, but not all countries have data protection legislation or regulation. According to data from

Box 8.14: Digital Platforms and Trust

Together with their effect on individuals, digital platforms have also altered basic features of the social tissue, in particular the notion of trust, both among individuals (*interpersonal* trust) and toward institutions (*institutional* trust). Institutional trust is the basis upon which the legitimacy of governments is built, and trust in public institutions originates from their capacity to deliver public services, engage with citizens, and use public resources ethically.

Some concerns have surged among policy makers regarding the role of digital platforms to advance private or partisan interests and undermine institutional credibility. Evidence suggests that technology platforms played a pivotal role in the results of recent elections, making policy makers aware of the way social media undermines the democratic process. The mechanisms are diverse, from decentralized fundraising of parties, to targeted advertising of political information without accountability, to using algorithms to amplify content undermining trust in institutions. Digital platforms could have been instrumental in the political polarization and erosion of democracy in several countries as measured, for example, by the Democracy Index (EIU 2020).

To what extent the perils of digital platforms in political processes can be contained is still to be seen. As of 2019, more than 40 governments had introduced laws against disinformation and regulation of digital platforms to tackle some of the issues posing challenges to democratic political systems (Marsden, Meyer, and Brown 2020). Some of the measures include co-regulation (i.e., platforms self-regulate once measures are approved by state legislators), using artificial intelligence technologies to regulate online content, building trust indicators for media, improving transparency on platforms' data and algorithms, and promoting news literacy.

Despite this grim picture, digital technologies can also offer a platform for citizen participation. A telling example is Taipei,China, where increased participation on political debates—with nearly 90% of the population having access to social media—can also result in more trust in government. Decentralized technologies can provide an opportunity to capturing citizens' perspective on more complex issues and creating engagement in decision-making processes (OECD 2020a). Through a bottom-up approach, digital platforms could also contribute to improve transparency and accountability of public processes, including budgeting, nomination of civil servants, and public procurement.

Source: Asian Development Bank.

UNCTAD and based on UNCTAD's grouping, 34 economies in Asia have some form of data protection legislation, 6 have draft legislations, 16 have no data protection legislation, and no available information is available for 4 of them. Brunei Darussalam, Cambodia, and Timor-Leste have no data protection legislation, while Myanmar's draft data protection legislation has yet to be enacted (UNCTAD 2020b).

The foregoing situation is interesting especially since these countries are parties to several existing international frameworks. For instance, in 2013, the United Nations General Assembly adopted a resolution on privacy rights in the digital age (UNGA 2013). The OECD has issued its Privacy Guidelines as early as 1980 (updated in 2013) which uphold certain principles with regard to data protection such as limits to the collection of personal data, safeguards on use and processing, among others, as well as the adoption of certain measures to foster international cooperation among regulators, including enforceability of country data protection laws and redress in all jurisdictions for relevant violations.

Additionally, the APEC Privacy Framework encourages improvement of the interoperability of privacy frameworks to enable information flows. APEC leaders then endorsed the APEC CBPR system which is "a voluntary accountability-based scheme to facilitate privacy-respecting data flows among APEC economies." Nonetheless, only a handful of countries agreed to join the APEC CBPR System.[100] Among ASEAN countries, only the Philippines and Singapore have thus far joined the CBPR. There is also the WTO General Agreement on Trade in Services (GATS) that could function to limit the ability of states to implement arbitrary and unreasonable data protection policies that hinder data transfers and data sharing (GATS 1994).

Harmonizing data protection policies across borders remains a key issue. Despite these international agreements and frameworks, data protection policies vary, driven by different country motivations: some treat data as a data sovereignty, national security, big-data driven economy issue (the "Chinese Model"); some recognize privacy as a fundamental human right (the "European Model"); and some treat data protection regulation through liberal and market-driven approach (the "American Model"). The three models may be concurrently applied in one region, thus making it difficult to achieve a supranational method of regulating data (Girot 2018).

Inconsistencies in cross-border data transfer regulations are another important concern. The legal standards for data transfers vary among jurisdictions. Some require consent before the data of a subject is exported to another jurisdiction; while some jurisdictions require that the receiving country is on a whitelist drafted by the regulator before data may be exported. The standards for what constitutes valid consent also vary from state to state.

In Asia, a working document published by the Asia Business Law Institute (ABLI) in May 2020 compiled the standards required under each country's regulation for data transfers to other jurisdictions. An abridged version quoting portions of the ABLI's comparative table and findings are compiled in Annex 8e. The table will show how standards for data transfer are implemented differently in each country (ABLI 2020).

Gaps and Challenges in Existing Regulations

Uncertainty and divergence in regulations are a key business concern. Despite the existing frameworks in place to regulate digital data collection and use, there is no binding international framework which provides a single standard for legal data transfers among different jurisdictions in Asia. Personal information is regulated by each state individually.

Business representatives across Asia mentioned compliance and adapting to new regulations as the biggest challenge facing Asian businesses

[100] As of 9 March 2020, the economies that have joined are Australia; Canada; Japan; Mexico; the Philippines; the Republic of Korea; Singapore; Taipei,China; and the United States.

(Baker McKenzie 2017) as cited in Girot (2018). An UNCTAD publication cited some concerns from businesses such as too stringent protection could stifle innovation and limit investments on emerging technologies reducing potential accompanying societal benefits (UNCTAD 2016). The compliance process is multijurisdictional, making it resource-intensive and costly to adopt, assess risk, and operate regionally.

The digital platform needs to ensure that its mechanism for procuring consent is recognized and enforceable in all jurisdictions that require these prior to data transfers. For a platform, additional steps for opt-ins could dampen user experience and limit transactions. The divergence in data protection legislation may also lead to tedious compliance measures from the digital platforms such as blanket consent forms that are all-encompassing, lengthy, and oftentimes, full of legalese.

Privacy regulations ought to take into account the likelihood of regulatory arbitrage and business climate competitiveness. Data protection legislation and regulations may act as nontariff trade barriers that can push platforms toward jurisdictions with less stringent data protection regulations. For example, due to the cost of compliance and the amount of risk they face when processing data in the Philippines, digital platforms may choose not to provide services to Philippine citizens and locate elsewhere. Some platforms try to avoid being subject to the Data Privacy Act (DPA) but still target the lucrative Philippine market by locating offshore. Despite the extraterritorial provisions of the DPA, its applicability and actual enforceability will be difficult for Philippine law enforcement agencies to enforce on offshore entities, without the cooperation of other concerned jurisdictions.

Broad protection for personal information empowers individuals. Most of the data protection regulations of Asian economies provide a blanket coverage for all personal information and for all persons processing personal information. This regime may provide greater privacy protection as it will be difficult for entities to try and circumvent the law in order to escape coverage.

For data subjects and the public, the explicit grant of certain rights under data protection legislation gives data subjects more control over how their personal information is being processed. The greater transparency and autonomy operationalize the constitutional protection to one's privacy. At the same time, this may lead to greater trust for businesses that are compliant with such regulations.

Weakness in mechanisms on self-management of privacy rights leads to legal exploitation of data. Self-management of privacy rights can be time-consuming and confusing, especially for those using and accessing numerous online services. One study estimated it would cost $781 billion in lost productivity if everyone were to read every privacy policy at websites they visited over 1 year (McDonald and Cranor 2008). Lessig (2006) explains that "cluttering the web with incomprehensible words ... drives consumers away from even attempting to understand what rights they give away as they move from site to site." The weakness, therefore, of a consent-based regime is that it may enable the legal exploitation of personal data.

Data Protection: Policy Implications and Recommendations

Stronger intergovernmental and multilateral data protection frameworks are needed. A more viable approach in the short to medium term may be to focus on intergovernmental mechanisms that will assist in the cross-border transfer of data, instead of lobbying for a general and comprehensive international data protection regime. This may include promoting cooperation among enforcement authorities; instituting mechanisms that will allow data subjects to enforce data protection rights in all relevant jurisdictions; and pushing for uniform certification standards for controllers, similar to the existing mechanism provided under the APEC CBPR to make data transfer standards more objective and predictable. Efforts should also be made in eliminating data transfer restrictions for data categories necessary for digital platform transactions, with due regard to each particular country's national security considerations.

More light-touch or flexible regulatory regime is worth considering. Regulators must balance public protection and the need to ensure that legislation and regulation do not have a chilling effect on innovation. The details of data protection rules may be ironed out in other instruments such as light-touch regulatory approaches and tools that provide oversight such as best practices guidelines, issuing warnings and advisories, providing official speeches, interpretations, and meetings with regulated parties. This allows the government to supervise developments in certain industries while observing how the technology will develop and affect consumers. Intergovernmental organizations may also consider issuing uniform guidelines and best practices suggestions.

The regulators may also consider adopting and issuing rules for regulatory sandboxes which are limited frameworks that allow certain, prequalified entities to soft-launch their products in controlled environments.

Taxation

The emerging digital economy is characterized by new features that have implications for tax systems. These include (i) the mobility of intangibles and platform players; (ii) the increasing reliance on data and other intangible assets; (iii) the networks effects; (iv) the spread of multisided business models; (v) the tendency toward monopoly or oligopoly in a digital economy; and (vi) the volatility that accompanies the low barriers to entry owing to technological advances (OECD 2015).

It is essential to balance the granting of incentives to attract foreign investment and the need to enhance international taxation for domestic resource mobilization in Asian economies. Asia's appeal as a destination for foreign direct investment (FDI) has grown considerably, underlining the need for reinforcing mechanisms against tax avoidance. Despite declining global trends, Asia's inward FDI attracted 33% of the global total (estimated at $1.5 trillion) in 2019. Inward FDI in services in Asia, often with a strong digital component, has increased steadily to reach $243.2 billion in business, communications, financial, software, IT, and transportation services (ADB 2019b).

Asian governments have to balance their policy mix to offer a competitive tax environment to international investors with the need to ensure that an appropriate share of domestic tax is collected from multinationals. Cross-border flow analyses suggest that, on average, FDI decreases by 3.7% following a 1 percentage-point increase in the tax rate on FDI (OECD 2008). This sensitivity has risen over time as capital has become increasingly mobile. Southeast Asian economies like Thailand and Indonesia, for example, have introduced aggressive cuts in statutory tax rates and offered tax holiday incentives to attract FDI.

Policy makers in the region need to consider how international tax cooperation can help mobilize domestic tax revenues and address development gaps. With large variations among countries, domestic tax collection in Asia remains low relative to the OECD average (Figure 8.22). In 15 Asian economies for which comparable data are available, the average tax revenue as a share of GDP was lower than the 34.2% OECD average in 2018 (OECD 2020b). Value-added taxes still account for a large share of tax revenues, while shares from corporate income taxes vary across countries, ranging from 11% (Samoa) to 47% (Malaysia). The uneven composition highlights the different priorities of governments in regard to the digital economy. These figures also highlight the importance of broadening the tax base and enhancing tax compliance. Strengthening international taxation to increase domestic tax revenues should be an important long-term objective for Asian economies to help achieve the Sustainable Development Goals.

Challenges of Digitalization on Taxation and International Tax Cooperation

The ongoing evolution of the digital economy presents challenges for tax systems, broadly in terms of the reduced need for physical presence (nexus), the growing utilization of data, and uncertainties surrounding the adequate capturing of business income. The digital economy poses three main challenges: (i) the ability of digital businesses to operate in an area without a physical presence entails a review of the rules on physical presence (nexus rules),

Figure 8.22: Tax-to-GDP Ratios in Asian Economies, 2018 (%)

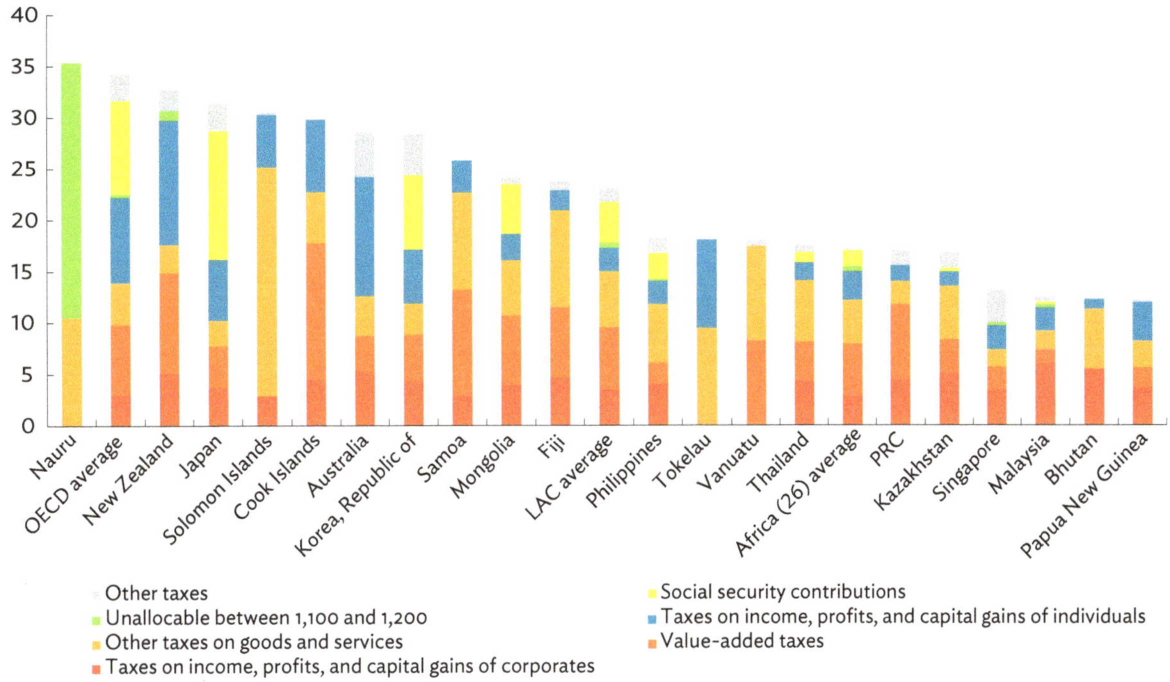

GDP = gross domestic product, LAC = Latin America and the Caribbean, OECD = Organisation for Economic Co-operation and Development, PRC = People's Republic of China.

Notes: The figures do not include subnational tax revenue for the Cook Islands, Fiji, Malaysia, Papua New Guinea, Samoa, and Solomon Islands. The averages for Africa (26 economies), for LAC (25 economies), and the OECD (36 economies) are unweighted. Australia, Japan, New Zealand, and the Republic of Korea are part of the OECD group. 2017 data are used for the Africa (26) average, Australia, Japan, and the OECD average. The tax-to-GDP ratio for the PRC does not include revenue from social security contributions as detailed data were not available.

Sources: OECD (2019c, 2020b).

(ii) the extensive use and monetization of data requires examination of the economic value this generates and whether it is appropriately captured for tax purposes, and (iii) new business models such as cloud computing present difficulties in properly characterizing income for tax purposes (OECD 2015).

The current COVID-19 pandemic has accelerated the adaptation and use of technology, triggered rapid growth in the digital economy, and changed the corporate landscape. Survey data suggest that consumers expect to continue to participate in the digital economy even beyond the pandemic, with more than 50% of the respondents from India and the PRC stating that they will shop online more extensively after the COVID-19 outbreak is over (Figure 8.23). Against the backdrop of rapid digitalization and adoption of digital platforms triggered by the COVID-19 crisis, issues on the applicability of existing tax regimes, including

Figure 8.23: Share of Respondents Who Expect to Shop Online More Frequently Post-COVID-19 (%)

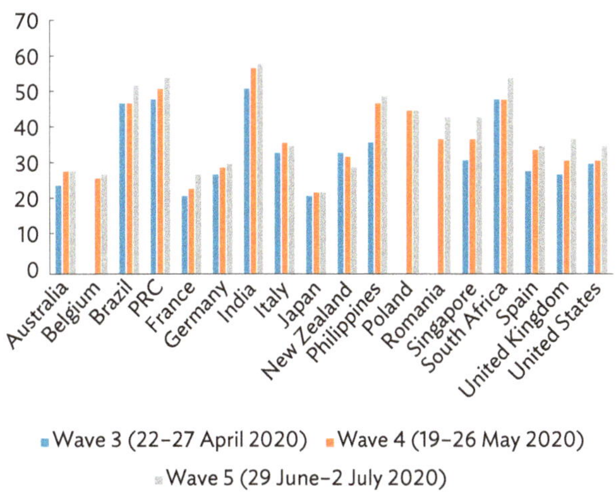

COVID-19 = coronavirus disease, PRC = People's Republic of China.

Note: The survey question was stated as the following: "After the outbreak is over, do you think you'll do any of the following: shop online more frequently?"

Source: GlobalWebIndex (2020).

cross-border components of taxing rights under tax treaty rules have come to the fore. As companies face major disruptions in business practices and the allocation of the working force, national tax regimes are starting to be redesigned. This in turn poses challenges to prevent BEPS, as large multinational corporates are the ones primarily engaging in these practices.

But progress in tackling tax and digitalization issues in the OECD/G20 Inclusive Framework has been considerable. As of June 2020, 19 developing member countries (DMCs) and all 21 non-DMCs of ADB's 68 member countries had joined the G20/OECD inclusive framework. Concrete proposals were made in 2019 on two complementary pillars: one revisiting the allocation of profit and nexus rules, and another on a global anti base-erosion mechanism, including the consideration of a global minimum tax (Box 8.15 lays out the negative impact of BEPS on tax revenues). Together with these initiatives, international guidelines on making digital platforms fully and solely liable for assessing, collecting, and remitting the VAT/GST due on the online sales they enable are being developed (OECD 2019d). The experiences of the three largest digital platforms in the PRC illustrate this issue (Box 8.16).

Asia has made progress in committing to the international exchange of information (EOI), which is critical for tackling tax evasion. To date, 27 DMCs have joined the Global Forum on Transparency and Exchange of Information for Tax Purposes. Asia's rapid growth and global integration in recent years has prompted tax authorities to work together toward establishing better mechanisms for information exchange, and EOI agreements are an effective tool for tax administrations to track and assess cross-border transactions. DMCs have made progress in some areas relating to the Exchange of Information on Request and the Automatic Exchange of Information (Figure 8.24). At the same time, the region has continued to strengthen the rules on tax agreements, double taxation treaties, and other mechanisms for exchanging tax information.

Proposed measures for a country to counter BEPS practices include active participation in international forums, the adoption of domestic tax measures in the interim, the collection of value-added tax for C2C transactions, and improvement in tax administration capacity. Absent specific guidance on digital economy taxation, measures that countries can take include active participation in international forums for tax matters and the adoption of domestic

Box 8.15: Negative Impact of Base Erosion and Profit Shifting on Tax Revenues

There are significant negative effects of base erosion and profit shifting (BEPS) activities on tax revenues—which could be amplified by digitalization. Utilizing foreign direct investment (FDI) data of 79 countries, Jansky and Palansky (2019) estimated annual tax revenue losses of $125 billion owing to profit-shifting activities, and that low-income and lower-middle-income economies incur the highest losses in corporate tax revenue, both as a percentage of gross domestic product and of total tax revenue. Johansson et al. (2017) estimated that annual revenue losses range from $100 to $240 billion per year or 4% to 10% of global corporate tax revenues.[a] In estimating the fiscal effects of FDI-related BEPS, Bradbury, Hanappi, and Moore (2018) found that figures ranged widely from $80 billion to $647 billion annually. In contrast, preliminary estimates of the combined effects of Pillars 1 and 2 of the BEPS Action Plan found a potential annual global net revenue gain of up to $100 billion or 4% of global corporate income tax revenues.[b] Such revenue gains are projected to be largely similar across high-, middle-, and low-income countries and the reforms are expected to significantly decrease profit shifting (OECD 2020d).

[a] This estimate takes into account the effects of these reforms and the United States' Global Intangible Low Taxed Income (US GILTI) Regime. Excluding the US GILTI regime, the potential annual net revenue gain would reach about $80 billion or 3.2% of global corporate income tax revenues (OECD 2020c).

[b] Pillar 1 involves the reallocation of taxing rights and Pillar 2 concerns the global anti-base erosion mechanism. In particular, change the allocation of taxing rights through a coherent and concurrent review of the profit allocation and nexus rules (Pillar 1); and remaining BEPS issues and minimum taxation (Pillar 2).

Source: Avendaño and Rosenkranz (2020).

Box 8.16: Issues and Challenges Relating to Big Tech

The digital economy, led by the Baidu, Alibaba, and Tencent (or the BAT) companies, has grown at an unprecedented scale in the People's Republic of China. In 2019, e-commerce constituted 35.3% of retail sales—compared with a 10.9% share in the United States—accounting for an estimated 56% of the global total in 2019 and expected to be over 60% in 2022 (Turley and Leung 2019). The country's Big Tech platform giants figure heavily in this trend, with Alibaba and Tencent featuring in the 10 biggest global companies by market capitalization as of March 2019 (PwC 2019).

There are 10 million active sellers on the Alibaba e-commerce platform—which constitutes 60% of the domestic e-commerce market. The superapps embedded within the Tencent and Alibaba ecosystems encompass a wide range of economic activities, spanning entertainment and social media, payments and finance, shopping and dining, to health and education. The volume of data at the disposal of the BAT companies places them in a position to help potential partner firms optimize their offerings or targeting, streamline supply chains, or determine the distribution of store placements (Turley, Ho, and Leung 2018). The reach of the BAT firms has expanded to South Asian and Southeast Asian markets, where Alibaba, Tencent, and others have invested substantially in regional e-commerce platforms (Turley and Leung 2019).

The challenges such giant companies operating cross-borders pose to tax systems span regulatory issues, classifying digital platforms, tax collection difficulties, as well as cross-border issues. Regulatory constraints have emerged such as (i) mismatches between the regulatory and taxation classifications (e.g., ride sharing or transport services); (ii) ambiguity in the treatment of platforms as brokers or as principals affecting requirements to meet tax obligations and compounding upon already low tax compliance levels among vendors; (iii) limited categorization of outbound payments within foreign exchange rules; (iv) defining when imported digital services can be said to be fully consumed outside the country; and (v) limited guidance on a definition of a permanent establishment, such as those pertaining to mirror servers or user interfaces (Turley and Leung 2019).

Source: Avendaño and Rosenkranz (2020).

Figure 8.24: Compliance to Exchange of Information Standards in Developing Asia

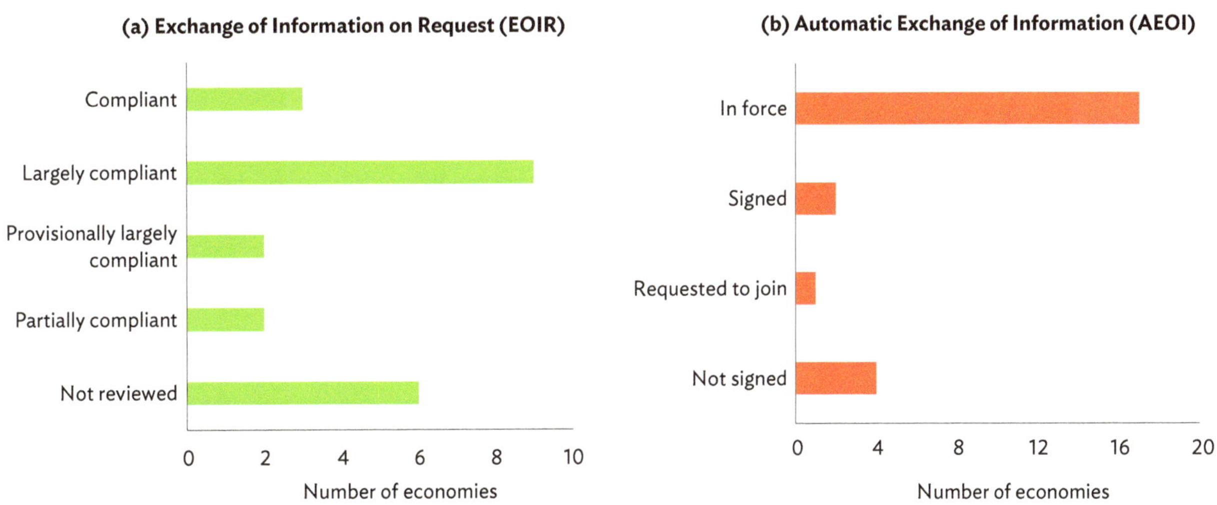

Notes: In panel (a), Compliance refers to Automatic Exchange of Information on Request, which includes relevant information for the administration or enforcement of the domestic tax laws of a requesting party. In panel (b), Compliance refers to the Common Reporting Standard regarding financial accounts on a global level between tax authorities.

Source: Avendaño and Rosenkranz (2020) using OECD. International Tax Co-operation: Key Indicators and Outcomes Database. https://www.oecd.org/tax/international-tax-co-operation-map.htm (accessed July 2020).

measures that comply with the country's international obligations in the interim.

As it stands, some economies in Asia have undertaken measures to improve taxation of digital transactions in the last few years (Avendaño and Rosenkranz 2020). In 2019, India introduced an expanded definition of nexus for corporate income tax purposes by accounting for significant economic presence, based on income and number of users thresholds, and allowing for the taxation of profits of a nonresident corporation regardless of the level of physical presence of that company in the taxing jurisdiction (OECD 2018c).

In Australia, the Multinational Anti-Avoidance Law seeks to deter nonresident enterprises belonging to large multinational enterprises from avoiding establishing local permanence and evading taxes. Trade structures falling under this law are subject to a re-allocation of income in line with traditional permanent establishment terms and an additional penalty of a percentage of the tax avoided. It was estimated that an additional $77 million in annual corporate tax revenue will be collected, translating to an annual $5.4 billion in tax base recovered owing to this measure (OECD 2018c).

In Malaysia, Singapore, and other countries, electronic systems are used to enhance tax compliance, such as issuance of pre-filled returns for some or all sources of personal income. In Malaysia and the Philippines, measures have been taken to expand royalties by including payments for the right to use software, visual images, or sound transmissions under the scope of royalties. In India, a 6% charge is levied on gross consideration for online advertisement services offered by nonresidents (Terada-Hagiwara, Gonzales, and Wang 2019). As digital economy gains more traction during COVID-19, the Philippines has proposed a tax on digital platforms in the form of value-added tax and income tax.

Indeed, a value-added tax imposed on customer-to-customer transactions can be considered. Yet, while domestic measures can be effective to some extent, a proliferation of unilateral approaches, such as the introduction of a digital services tax, might not be a sustainable approach for domestic resource mobilization in the long term. Providing conditions for equal treatment among national tax systems in the region is therefore necessary in reducing tax competition and potential loopholes. Importantly, improvements in tax administration capacity for both cross-border and domestic e-commerce transactions can be adopted, including digitizing tax invoices, the creation of a centralized and uniform tax administration system, and the introduction of risk-based management, self-assessment and tax audits to help collect tax information and reduce compliance costs for taxpayers (Terada-Hagiwara, Gonzales, and Wang 2019). Several economies in the region have crafted VAT or GST guidelines (Table 8.16) pursuant to the aforementioned objective and following the international standards.

Taxation: Policy Implications and Recommendations

The fast-changing nature and rapid expansion of the digital economy have posed challenges for tax systems. Countries have had to find ways to respond quickly to define aspects of digital transactions—such as valuing data as commodity, nexus requirements for multinationals that engage in cross-border transactions—in order to capture revenues and, at the same time, attract investments. While regional cooperation structures have been put in place, countries need to continue to coordinate to mitigate network effects, plug tax leaks, and foster cooperation.

Many of the key features of the growing digital economy heighten BEPS risks, necessitating careful examination by policy makers. Countries need to ensure that multinational firms do not gain inappropriately from exceptions from permanent establishment status. The presence of intangibles, growing pervasiveness of data in digital business, and the spread of global value chains across different locations have allowed firms to benefit from BEPS activities. Moreover, the ability of firms to operate from remote locations and to conduct business with minimal personnel, allow fragmentation of operations in order to evade taxes. In addition, measures to adapt controlled foreign company rules to advances in the

Table 8.16: Progress in Selected Asian Economies in Solving Challenges of the Digital Economy (BEPS Action 1)

	Cross-Border B2C Supplies of Services and Intangibles		Low Value Imports
Jurisdiction	Applies Principles of the International VAT/GST Guidelines On Cross-Border B2C Supplies of Services and Intangibles	Simplified Registration and Collection Mechanisms	Implementation of Mechanism for Collecting VAT/GST on Imports of Low-Value Goods from Online Trade
Hong Kong, China	N/A (no VAT/GST)	N/A (no VAT/GST)	N/A (no VAT/GST)
India	Yes [a]	Yes	No
Indonesia	Under consideration	N/A	No
Japan	Yes [b]	Yes	No
Kazakhstan	No	No	
Malaysia	Yes [c]	No	N/A
Philippines	Under consideration	No	No
PRC	Yes [d]	No	No
Republic of Korea	Yes [b]	Yes	No
Singapore	Yes	Yes	Under consideration
Sri Lanka	No	No	
Taipei,China	Yes	Yes	
Thailand	Under consideration	`	No
Viet Nam	Yes [e]	No	

B2C = business-to-costumer, BEPS = base erosion and profit shifting, GST = goods and services tax, N/A = not applicable, PRC = People's Republic of China, VAT = value-added tax.

[a] Adoption of actions based on guidelines in 2017.
[b] Adoption of actions based on guidelines in 2015.
[c] Services tax policy on digital services.
[d] Adoption of actions based on guidelines in 2009.
[e] Adoption of actions based on guidelines in 2020.

Note: Blank cells indicate no public information available.

Sources: ADB compilation using OECD (2017, 2018e, 2019e); and national tax offices.

digital economy and to respond to tax planning by companies involved in VAT-exempt activities need to be considered (OECD 2015).

The predominance of digital transactions could also offer some opportunities to national tax authorities. In many cases, the increasing use of digital platforms for economic purposes could facilitate tracing of taxable transactions. Digital transactions can be traced and information shared among concerned tax authorities, whereas cash transactions cannot be traced. Tax authorities in some countries have introduced tax credits and other incentives to promote electronic payments. Current discussions on the implementation of VAT/GST guidelines for online sales illustrate the importance of information sharing among platforms and tax authorities. There are, however, significant gaps in the technological and operational capacities of tax administrations to implement these practices. Communication with digital platforms and businesses on their fiscal obligations will also be important if a cooperative compliance model is to be implemented.

As regional trade agreements gradually incorporate provisions on digital trade and data flows, coordination with the implementation of BEPS measures is important. About 27% of the 275 existent regional trade agreements in the WTO explicitly address e-commerce issues, ranging from customs duties and consumer protection to data privacy (Monteiro and Teh 2017). From this group, about one-third specify a right to impose an internal tax or charge on digital products. As these agreements include further measures against BEPS practices, Asian economies will need to incorporate these in their tax schemes.

Large-scale policy responses to COVID-19 will likely increase sovereign debt levels, underpinning the need for efficient tax systems and tackling BEPS to assure public debt sustainability in the longer term. It is expected that the sovereign debt-to-GDP ratio in Asian DMCs will increase by 7 percentage points in 2020 compared with 2019.[101] With the prospect of a significant economic downturn, high debt levels—potentially further increased by accommodative monetary and fiscal policies to mitigate the COVID-19 economic impact—not only pose considerable risks to Asian economies and financial markets, but will also weigh on governments' future fiscal space. Consequently, in order to assure public debt sustainability and maintain needed public spending post-COVID-19, tackling BEPS becomes even more important for domestic resource mobilization.

Regional and international cooperation and coordination are necessary elements underlying effective response to BEPS. Such cooperation should expand beyond OECD and G20 member economies to encompass developing economies. This encapsulates knowledge sharing on the best practices in tax administration and the monitoring of new developments. The OECD Inclusive Framework can facilitate and monitor the implementation of BEPS mitigation efforts. Critically, BEPS Action 1 on the Digital Economy may become a minimum standard, and countries will be assessed on their progress regardless of their membership in the Inclusive Framework. Meanwhile, the region should continue to strengthen the rules on tax agreements, double taxation treaties, and other mechanisms for exchanging tax information. Another promising area for cooperation in the region is the promotion of a unique legal entity identifier (LEI) to allow for cross-border data exchange on taxation. Regional policy forums (such as ASEAN/+3 and APEC) and multilateral development banks (such as ADB) can also help advance these efforts.

As part of these efforts, ADB recently announced the establishment of a Regional Hub on Domestic Resource Mobilization and International Tax Cooperation in Asia. The regional hub will provide an open and inclusive platform for (i) strategic policy dialogue, institutional and capacity development, and exchange of information and ideas through a dialogue among DMCs; (ii) knowledge sharing across knowledge partners, international financial institutions, other bilateral revenue organizations, and DMCs in Asia; and (iii) collaboration and development coordination across development partners (Asakawa 2020). Through policy dialogue, research, capacity development and knowledge-sharing activities, the hub will assist each DMC to define differentiated domestic resource mobilization and international tax cooperation goals that will be appropriate for their circumstances and level of development.

Preparing for Greater Digital Inclusion in Asia

Digital Readiness

Digital connectivity has generally improved in Asia since the turn of the century. Between 2002 and 2018, the proportion of population that has accessed the internet has risen by 31 to 50 percentage points across subregions in Asia (Figure 8.25), translating to about 1.7 billion more people in the region having gained access to the digital space during the period. The increase in usage is bolstered by lower costs, better connection quality, increased adoption of online services, and the proliferation of smart phones.

Digital readiness is crucial to leave no one behind in the digital economy. The extent of penetration of online marketplaces still varies substantially across Asian economies. The digital platform penetration indexes (see Annex 8f) show that digital platform use and activity are generally more established in developed

[101] This is based on the simple average of the difference in the 2020 and 2019 general government gross debt as percentage of GDP for ADB's developing member countries, using data from the International Monetary Fund. World Economic Outlook October 2020 Database. The calculation does not include Mongolia and Palau as data are unavailable.

Figure 8.25: Share of Population Using the Internet (%)

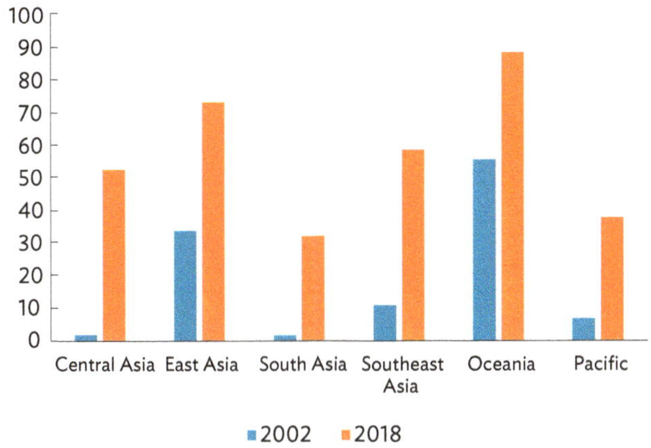

Notes: The data are simple averages of country-level shares. Subregional groupings follow ADB's convention. The Pacific does not include Palau due to absence of data since 2010. For Niue, the most recent data point is as of 2016.

Source: ADB calculations using data from International Telecommunication Union. ICT Eye Database. https://www.itu.int/net4/ITU-D/icteye/#/ (accessed April 2020).

economies in the region (Table 8.17). Incidentally, with the exception of East Asia, where all but Mongolia are in the top group, economies in the other subregions do not appear to cluster together in terms of digital platform penetration. This means there is a large potential for subregional forums to promote learning between neighboring countries and extract synergy gains.

A structural assessment of drivers of digital platform penetration shows that apart from digital connectivity, factors such as urbanization, working age population, the expansion of the services sector, and governance quality exert a positive influence on digital platform penetration (Box 8.17).

The Digital Divide

The performance of the digital economy is tempered by the digital divide and the deeper issue of inequality. The benefits of the platform economy are not equitably distributed within and across countries, and gaps can exist based on levels of income, education, gender, and geographic location. There are four kinds of barriers to access (called divides) corresponding to each of the four types of access: motivational or mental, material, skills, and usage (van Dijk 2006).

The *motivational or mental access divide* is driven by the lack of basic digital experience, presence of technology anxiety, and a perceived intimidation from new technology. Other factors include low levels of income and education, and lack of time to learn new things (Ghobadi and Ghobadi 2013). The *material access divide* includes barriers that limit physical access to devices and network connection. Low levels of income and education, and the absence of occupation also contribute to this barrier.

There are three types of skills that define the *skills access divide*: (i) *operational skills* or the ability to work with hardware and software; (ii) *information skills* or the proficiency in searching, selecting, and processing information using computer and network sources; and (iii) *strategic skills* or the competence to use a computer and related network sources (van Deursen, van Dijk, and Peters 2011; Ghobadi and Ghobadi 2013). Skills access can be limited by insufficient digital skills caused by a lack of user-friendliness in technologies, inadequate education, or social support. Ghobadi and Ghobadi (2013) point out that education is a critical factor on all three types of skills.

The *usage access divide* is about the various ways ICT applications are used and is generally associated with demographic characteristics and technical connections. Those who contribute to the internet (e.g., publishing a personal website, creating a web blog, and so on) are called active or creative users, while the passive users merely consume information available online.

The skills needed to participate in the platform economy are conditional on having the motivation to learn and the physical access to the basic technology on which one can practice and apply the skills. A person can participate in the platform economy or gain usage access only when the necessary skills have been acquired.

Trust and perceived security of the internet affects usage. One of the main barriers for accessing the internet is lack of knowledge about it. In a survey conducted by

Table 8.17: Digital Platform Penetration Index, 2019

Economy	DPP Index	Digital Platform Penetration Subcomponents			
		Revenue-to-GDP Ratio	Per User Spending, Proportion of per Capita Income	User accounts-to-Population Ratio	Revenue-to-Population Ratio (PPP Adjusted)
PRC	2.5847				
Korea, Republic of	2.5283				
Australia	2.1010				
Hong Kong, China	2.0323				
New Zealand	1.8795				
Japan	1.7794				
Singapore	1.7644				
Malaysia	1.1008				
India	1.0220				
Viet Nam	0.9429				
Indonesia	0.9190				
Brunei Darussalam	0.8322				
Philippines	0.8221				
Armenia	0.8077				
Pakistan	0.7960				
Kazakhstan	0.7929				
Thailand	0.7902				
Azerbaijan	0.7833				
Sri Lanka	0.6501				
Georgia	0.5751				
Kyrgyz Republic	0.5018				
Uzbekistan	0.4840				
Nepal	0.4619				
Fiji	0.4579				
Cambodia	0.4416				
Tajikistan	0.4155				
Bangladesh	0.3928				
Myanmar	0.3909				
Bhutan	0.3119				
Mongolia	0.2824				
Lao PDR	0.2523				
Timor-Leste	0.2486				
Papua New Guinea	0.2111				
Turkmenistan	0.1565				

DPP = digital platform penetration, Lao PDR = Lao People's Democratic Republic, PCA = principal components analysis, PPP = purchasing power parity, PRC = People's Republic of China.

Notes: The subcomponents were normalized. Low- to high-value spectrum:

The PCA was estimated using data from 2017 to 2019. The divisions represent the groups above and below the 33rd and 66th percentiles. Users in the second column refer to AdTech-exposed Internet users.

Source: ADB calculations using data from Statista (2020a, 2020b).

Box 8.17: Drivers of Digital Platform Penetration

The analysis of the underlying drivers of digital platform penetration follows the technology-organization-environment (TOE) framework of DePietro, Wiarda, and Fleisher (1990)[a] which provides a taxonomy for classifying adoption factors depending on the context (Tweneboah-Koduah, Endicott-Popovsky, and Tsetse 2014). In this exercise, the revenue per population (purchasing power parity-adjusted) and digital platform accounts per population serve as the measures of digital platform adoption and diffusion. In line with the nodes of the TOE framework, the independent variables include internet penetration, education index, services sector's share, urbanization, work age population, and government integrity—all lagged by one period.[b]

Results using panel estimation with country group and time fixed effects covering 34 Asian economies with data from 2017 to 2019 indicate that apart from internet penetration, there is a positive association between digital platform diffusion on one hand, and urbanization, working age population, the expansion of the services sector and governance quality, on the other hand (box table). Unsurprisingly, the coefficients of the group dummies suggest that pace of adoption is faster in economies where platform activity is already well-established. In a separate estimation, income per capita, which tends to be collinear with education and urbanization, is also found to be significantly positively associated with digital platform penetration.

Factors Anchoring Diffusion of Digital Platform Participation—Asia

	Accounts per 100 Persons		LN (Revenue per Person)	
Dependent Variable	(1)	(2)	(3)	(4)
Proportion of internet users_lag1	0.780**	0.596*	0.009**	0.008**
	(0.296)	(0.293)	(0.003)	(0.003)
Education index_lag1	-58.54	-33.30	0.138	0.292
	(33.67)	(31.65)	(0.393)	(0.416)
Urban population share_lag1	1.336***	0.711**	0.007*	0.004
	(0.315)	(0.250)	(0.003)	(0.003)
Working age population share_lag1	0.563	1.179	0.036***	0.041***
	(1.011)	(0.933)	(0.009)	(0.009)
Services share in GVA_lag1	1.933***	1.233***	0.013***	0.009**
	(0.257)	(0.280)	(0.003)	(0.003)
Government integrity index_lag1		1.291***		0.008*
		(0.315)		(0.003)
Constant	-81.99	-112.0	5.132	4.897
	(64.71)	(61.94)	(0.609)	(0.643)
Year fixed effects	Yes	Yes	Yes	Yes
Country-group fixed effects	Yes	Yes	Yes	Yes
Group dummies: Base is the lowest group				
Mid group	21.09*	21.95*	0.690***	0.688***
	(9.789)	(9.541)	(0.109)	(0.105)
Top group	101.8***	98.05***	1.566***	1.514***
	(22.46)	(22.06)	(0.200)	(0.199)
Observations	102	102	102	102
R-squared	0.909	0.923	0.932	0.936

GVA = gross value added.

Notes: Standard errors in parentheses. * p<0.05; ** p<0.01; *** p<0.001. Economies are divided into three groups based on the dependent variables (digital platform penetration metrics). The low-tier group consists of economies from 33rd percentile and below. The mid-tier group comprises economies higher than the 33rd percentile to the 67th percentile. Meanwhile, the top-tier comprises economies above the 67th percentile. The idea is to take into account changing dynamics in the stage of platform penetration an economy has reached relative to others.

Sources: ADB calculations using data from The Heritage Foundation. Index of Economic Freedom Database. https://www.heritage.org/index/explore (accessed October 2020); International Telecom Union. ICT Eye Database. https://www.itu.net/net4/ITU-D/icteye/#/ (accessed April 2020); Statista (2020a, 2020b); United Nations Development Programme. Human Development Report Database. http://hdr.undp.org/en/data; United Nations Statistics Division. National Accounts Main Aggregates Database. https://unstats.un.org/unsd/snaama/ (both accessed October 2020); and World Bank. World Development Indicators. https://databank.worldbank.org/source/worlddevelopment-indicators (accessed July 2020).

[a] In a number of papers, the development of the TOE framework is associated with Tornatzky and Fleischer, editors of the book, *The Processes of Technological Innovation*, that contains the chapter on TOE by DePietro, Wiarda, and Fleisher (1990).

[b] The network readiness index data set components were not used as independent variables because data have been available for only 1 year as of this writing, and economy coverage in Asia is limited.

Source: Asian Development Bank.

Wu et al. (2016) in 11 countries from 2014 to 2015, only 13% of respondents in Thailand, 11% in Indonesia, and 5% in India knew what the internet is (Figure 8.26). When trust is low and corruption is perceived in the policy environment, this affects the use of digital technology to undertake e-commerce transactions.

Figure 8.26: Awareness and Understanding of the Internet among Nonusers (2014–2015, % of non-internet users)

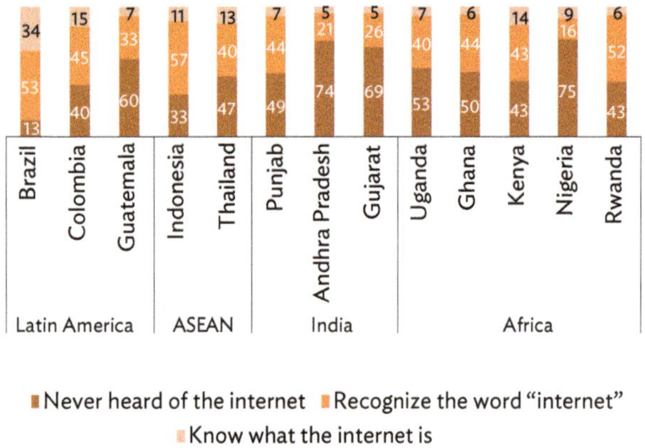

ASEAN = Association of Southeast Asian Nations.

Source: Wu et al. (2016).

Trusting and comfortably using ICT does not translate to trusting digital platforms. This is especially true for e-learning, digital health, and even mobile banking. For example, teachers and students in Viet Nam perceive that e-learning is inferior to face-to-face learning (CUTS International 2018, MacCallum and Jeffrey 2009). Privacy concerns (Binsaleh and Binsaleh 2013; Cummings, Merrill, and Borrelli 2010; Popescu and Ghita 2013), and distractions (Handal, MacNish, and Petocz 2013; Morales 2013) also impact the use of e-learning methods.

Similarly, e-clinic services in India face issues of trust and confidence in the efficacy of services obtained through digital platforms (CUTS International 2019). The presence of alternatives also reduces the use of e-clinic services as clients prefer face-to-face interaction with specialist doctors.

The gender divide persists but is narrowing. The difference between male and female internet user penetration rates is on average about 22.8% in developing countries and 2.3% in developed countries. The more significant gaps are observed in least developed countries at 42.8% and Africa at 33.0%. The gap has widened from 11% in 2013 to 17.0 % in 2019—an increase of 6 percentage points in 6 years (Figure 8.27). Data for a number of countries[102] also show that ICT access is commonly better for males than females (Figure 8.28). Only data for the Philippines show females having better access to the internet.

Figure 8.27: Internet User Gender Gap (%)

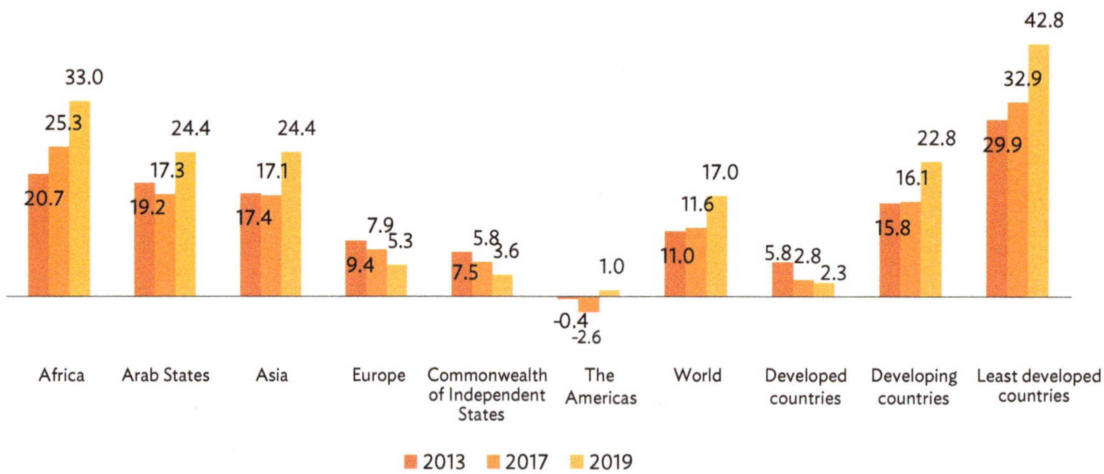

Sources: International Telecommunication Union (2017, 2019).

[102] These economies are India; the People's Republic of China; the Philippines; Sri Lanka; Taipei,China; and Viet Nam.

Figure 8.28: Indicators of ICT Access in Selected Asian Economies, by Gender

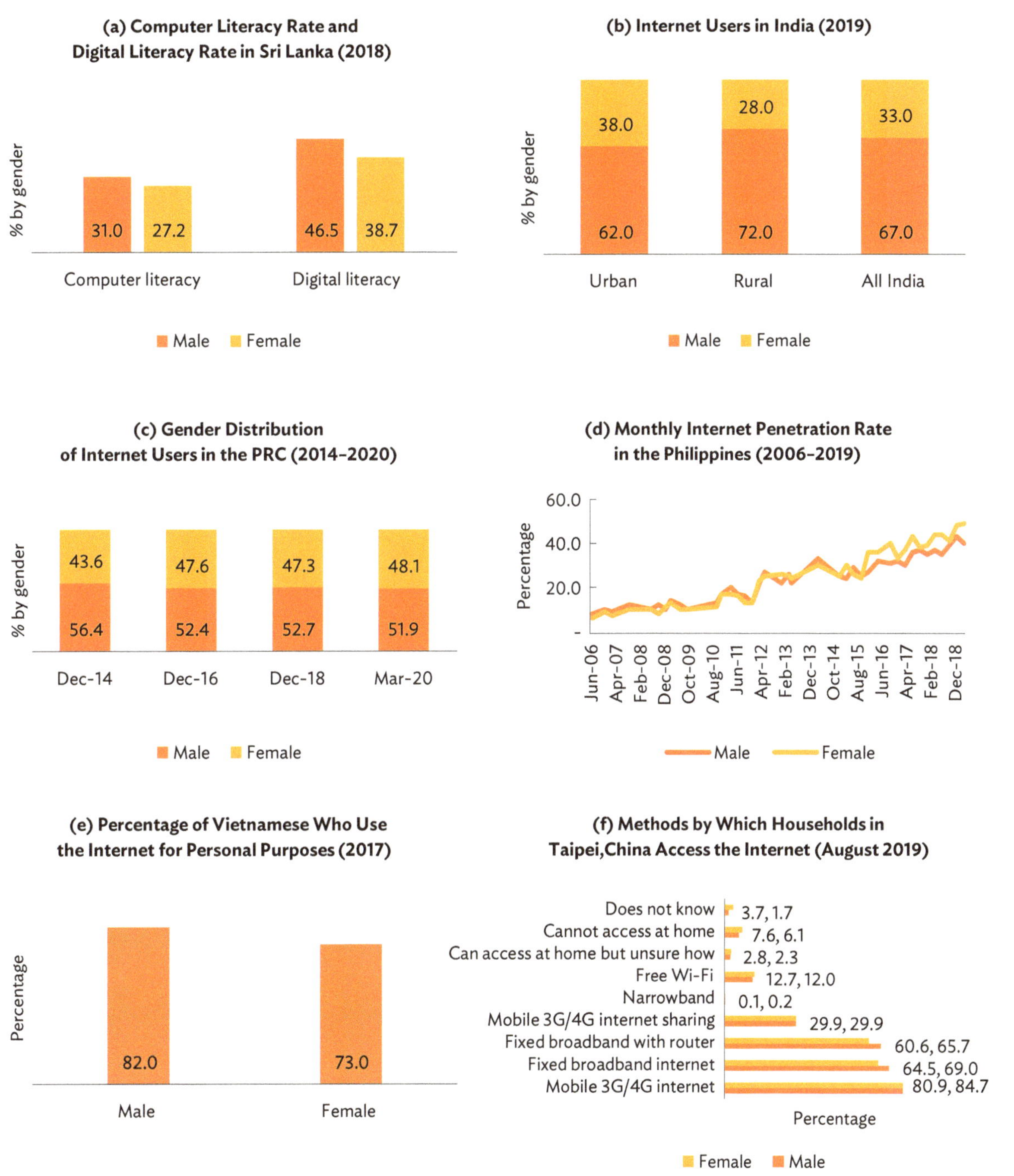

ICT = information and communication technology, PRC = People's Republic of China.

Sources: China Internet Network Information Center (2020). In Statista—The Statistics Portal. https://www.statista.com/statistics/265148/percentage-of-internet-users-in-china-by-gender/ (accessed May 2020); Ecomobi (2017); Government of Taipei,China, National Development Council (2019). In Statista—The Statistics Portal. http://statista.com (accessed May 2020); Government of Sri Lanka, Department of Census and Statistics (2018); IAMAI and Nielsen (2010); and SWS (2019). In Statista—The Statistics Portal. https://statista.com/statistics/1104737/philippines-monthly-internet-user-penetration-rate-by-gender/ (accessed May 2020).

Beyond ICT, Junio (2019) found that while there is a gender divide in digital financial services, more women have become increasingly active in e-commerce, mobile payments, and e-learning. Indeed, country-level data reveal that more women are using online banking and mobile payments than men in Taipei,China; e-commerce activity is higher for women than men in the PRC; and access to e-learning is higher for women than men in the Philippines and Viet Nam (Quimba, Rosellon, and Calizo Jr. 2020).

Material access in Asia is increasing but still lags behind developed countries. The number of internet users as a percentage of total population is an indicator of the availability of the internet to the population. In late 2019, it is estimated that more than 85% of the population in developed countries accessed the internet, while it was only around 54% in developing countries and 16% in least developed economies (Figure 8.29).

At the regional level, Asia has the second-lowest proportion of people having used the internet in a 3-month period of 2019, while the Commonwealth of Independent States (CIS)[103] shows usage increased

Figure 8.29: Selected Material Access Indicators, by Income Groups

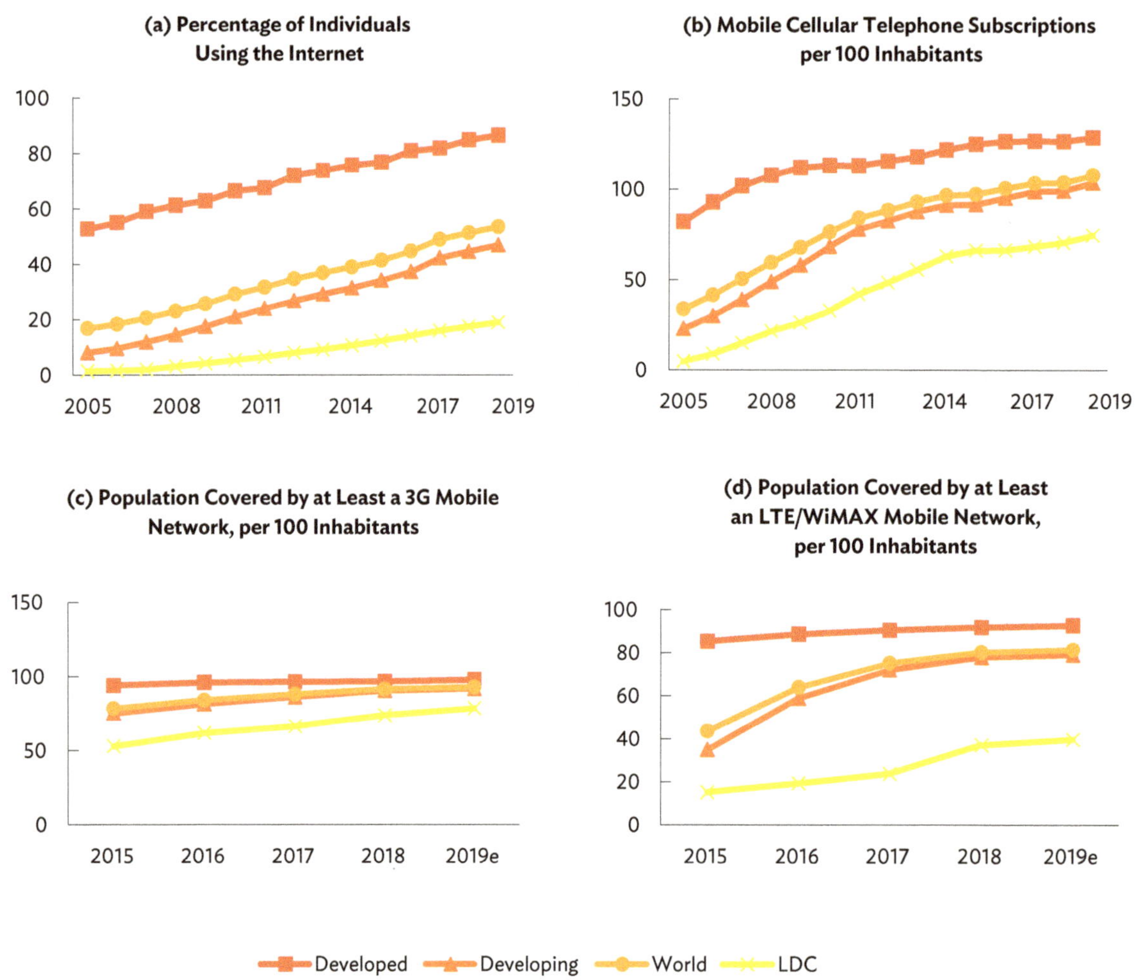

e = estimate, LDC = least developed country.

Source: Quimba, Rosellon, and Calizo Jr. (2020) using data from International Telecommunication Union. World Telecommunication/ICT Indicators 2020 Database. https://www.itu.int/en/ITU-D/Statistics/Pages/publications/wtid.aspx (accessed July 2020).

[103] The Commonwealth of Independent States (CIS) was founded in 1991 after the dissolution of the Soviet Union. The CIS refers to 12 countries: Armenia, Azerbaijan, Belarus, Georgia, Kazakhstan, the Kyrgyz Republic, Moldova, the Russian Federation, Tajikistan, Turkmenistan, Ukraine, and Uzbekistan.

significantly from 2009 (Figure 8.30), fueled by mobile phone subscriptions that outpaced even Europe. The Asian region has nonetheless steadily increased mobile phone subscriptions, in line with the trend in Asia's performance in the digital economy (Google, Temasek, and Bain and Company 2019).

Notably, reducing the material access divide does not necessarily translate to a more equitable distribution of benefits from the digital platform economy. According to UNCTAD (2019a), gaps exist within countries based on levels of income, education, gender, and even geographic location, regardless of the country's level

Figure 8.30: Selected Material Access Indicators, by Region

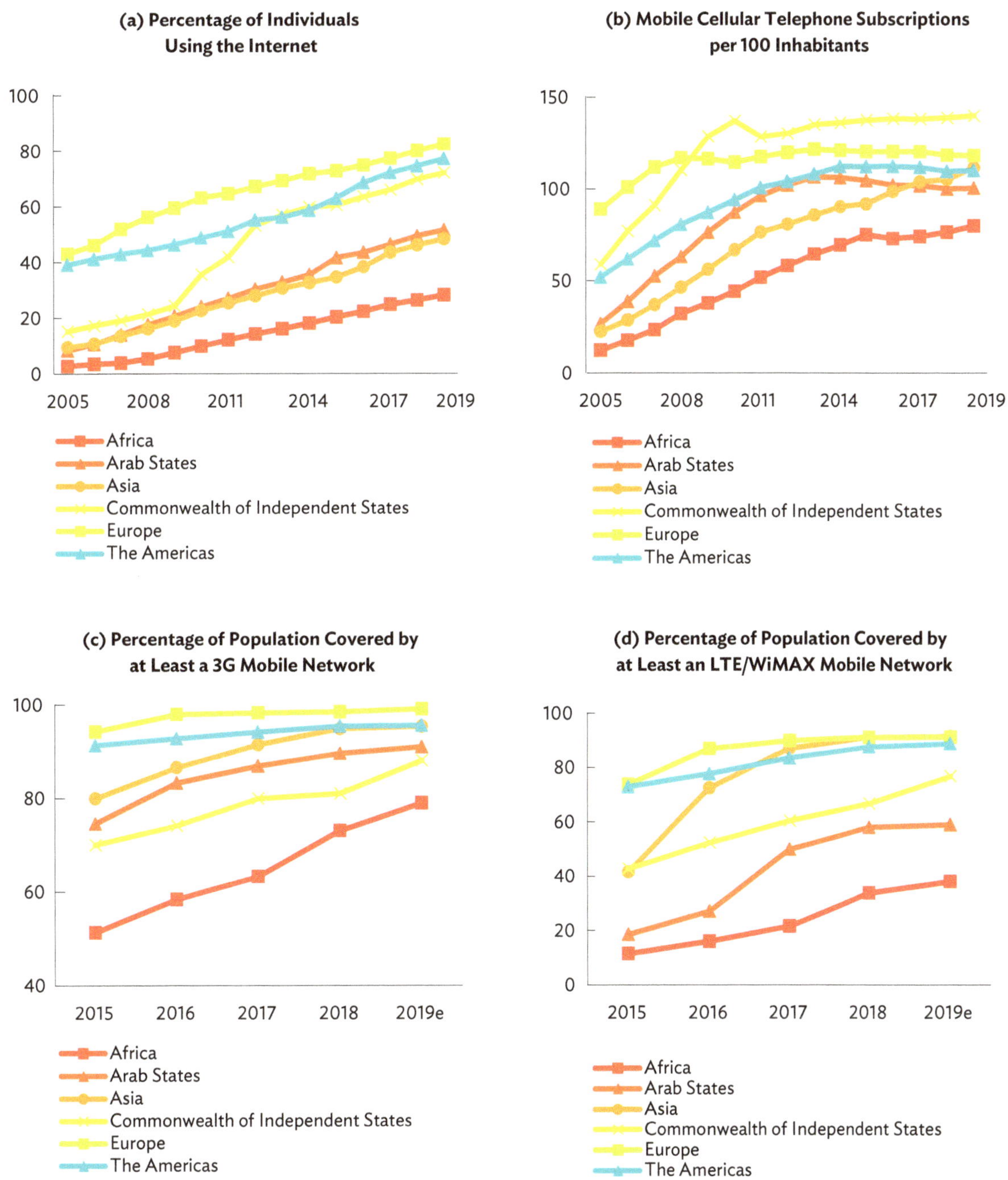

e = estimate.

Source: Quimba, Rosellon, and Calizo Jr. (2020) using data from International Telecommunication Union. World Telecommunication/ICT Indicators 2020 Database. https://www.itu.int/en/ITU-D/Statistics/Pages/publications/wtid.aspx (accessed July 2020).

of development. Hence, on top of the infrastructure and hardware, the policy strategy ought to give due consideration to the social, demographic, and location dimensions in an effort to bridge the gaps in digital access and participation.

The skills access divide exacerbates inequality. In general, the population of higher income countries tends to have more digital skills. It is noteworthy that the upper- and upper-middle-income groups in East Asia and the Pacific exhibit more digital skills than their counterparts in Europe and Central Asia (Table 8.18). However, as the benefits of the digital economy accrue more to the richer and more digitally skilled countries, this exacerbates the digital divide, causing the poorer countries to lag farther behind.

Platforms may disproportionately benefit those who are already better off. For example, the concentration of the Airbnb platform in central districts and busy areas may exacerbate the highly unequal distribution of income and development between urban and rural areas, resulting in an observable gap in development. Similarly, crowdworkers are well-educated (Figure 8.31). Additionally, a study by Farrel and Greig (2016) shows that those with assets that can be rented out can earn supplemental income from digital platforms (Figure 8.32), unlike those who participate only in labor platforms.

Table 8.18: Digital Skills by Region and Income Group

Region and Income Group	2017	2019
East Asia and the Pacific	4.7	4.6
High income	5.1	5.0
Upper-middle income	4.8	4.8
Lower-middle income	4.1	4.1
Europe and Central Asia	4.7	4.6
High income	4.9	4.9
Upper-middle income	4.3	4.3
Lower-middle income	4.4	4.3
Low income	no data	4.4
South Asia	3.8	4.0
Upper-middle income	3.9	4.2
Lower-middle income	3.9	4.0
Low income	3.7	3.7

Notes: The extent to which the population possesses sufficient digital skills (e.g., computer skills, basic coding, and digital reading); [1 = not all; 7 = to a great extent]. The data used for this table are based on the World Economic Forum (WEF) Global Competitiveness Index 4.0: Digital Skills Among Population indicator. A change in methodology occurred in 2018 and 2017 data have been backcasted. WEF published a technical note on how they backcasted data, which can be read in full here: https://reports.weforum.org/global-competitiveness-report-2018/appendix-c-the-global-competitiveness-index-4-0-methodology-and-technical-notes/.

Source: Quimba, Rosellon, and Calizo Jr. (2020) using data from the World Bank. TCdata360. https://tcdata360.worldbank.org/ (accessed May 2020).

Figure 8.31: Educational Level of Crowdworkers, by Platform (%)

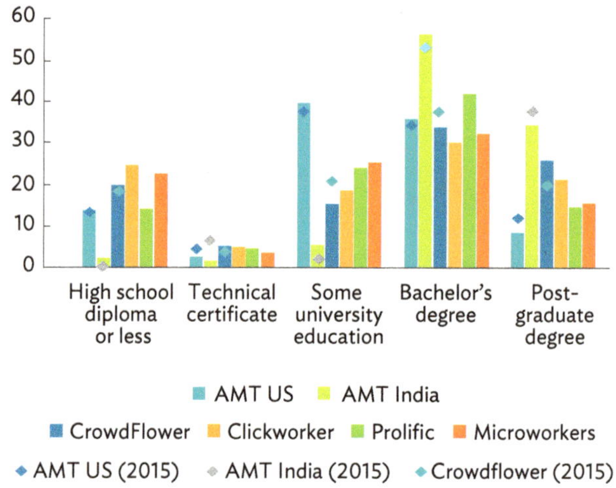

AMT = Amazon Mechanical Turk, ILO = International Labour Organization, US = United States.

Notes: The ILO conducted two surveys of crowdworkers: one in 2015 (diamonds) and another in 2017 (bars). The 2015 survey's sample consisted of workers who were based in either the US or India, had completed at least 500 tasks, and had achieved a 95.0% or greater task acceptance rate from the platform AMT. Apart from AMT, the 2015 survey also included quality workers from CrowdFlower. In 2017, the survey's sample was expanded to include other quality workers from other crowdsourcing platforms, such as Clickworker, Microworkers, and Prolific.

Source: Berg et al. (2018).

Figure 8.32: Earnings in Months with and without Platform Earnings in the United States (%)

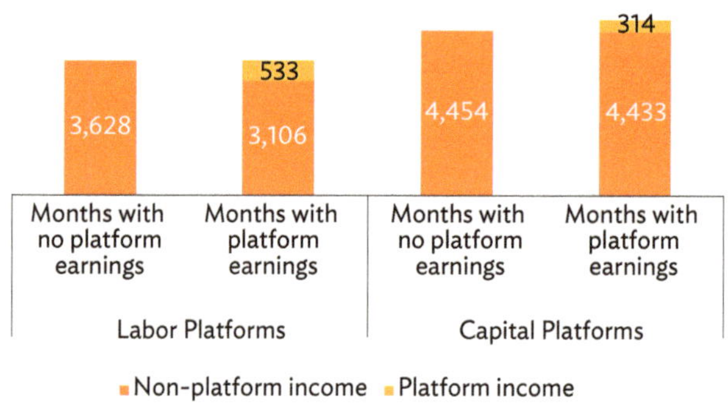

Source: Farrel and Greig (2016).

The challenge of bridging digital divides requires a multidimensional approach. The digital divide is manifested in different forms and varies across gender, age, and income groups as well as geographic areas. This has implications on who gets to benefit from the platform economy. Addressing the digital divide will involve, among others:

(1) Coordination among member countries to define and measure various indicators in the four areas of access and participation in digital platforms. For example, this assessment suffers from the limited examples from Oceania and other Pacific island countries. Moreover, the cross-border cooperation should ensure convergence among Asian economies in the degree of ICT access and participation in the platform economy.

(2) Simultaneously removing the barriers for each type of access divide to maximize benefits gained from participation in the digital economy. Providing material access and the requisite infrastructure to support internet access are necessary conditions for digital platform participation, but are not sufficient alone. Cultural and skills barriers also need to be lowered.

(3) Support from international and regional organizations to provide material access to ICT in least-developed countries. Without the basic ICT infrastructure on which people can begin to practice and learn using ICT, it would be hard for them to reach the level of developed economies.

(4) Formulation of plans for utilizing digitization, facilitating innovation, and supporting start-ups. Governments should address the income inequality that may worsen because of the digital divide.

(5) Greater skills development for the youth and retraining of adults. There is also a need to change the mindset on using technology to increase participation in the digital economy and reap the benefits it affords in terms in convenience, increased income, and access to more products and services including health and education.

Conclusions and Recommendations

As digital platform markets expand in Asia, there will be expected disruptions in trade, finance, and investment, among other areas. However, while technology could be disruptive, it also ushers in positive and inclusive development impacts. For instance, the diffusion and application of existing digital platforms have the tremendous potential to substantially raise rural and agricultural productivity, increase access to health and education, and greatly improve living standards. These new emerging technology platforms could also enable economies to pursue a different innovation pathway and develop more appropriate systems for their particular needs. How Asian economies manage this digital transformation will determine their economic fortune, dividing the winners from losers.

Governments should help shape how platforms lead to better outcomes. They need to lead collective efforts to understand this new market behavior and identify policy and regulatory needs based on sound fundamental principles. Governments should formulate plans for utilizing digitization, facilitating innovation, and developing a digital business start-up ecosystem. They should also focus on dissemination of digitization plans, upscaling the value chain, and facilitating agglomeration economies. As software, apps, and data are core to digital platforms, government should invest in basic internet or broadband technology to encourage app accumulation and the flow of data. Governments also have a role in acquiring essential technology by forging partnership with the private sector through smart policies and effective but light touch regulations.

Adopting a harmonized and clear definition and measurement of indicators in the digital market is an important first step. Presently, obtaining information from digital platforms is a big challenge because of their complexity, cross-sector and cross-border activities, and rapid growth amid vastly changing goods and services. Improving the visibility of digital platform through a well-thought-out taxonomy of indicators and data collection method is crucial to understanding their socioeconomic impact, tax implications, and link to growth and development. It is essential that national statistical agencies work with platform companies to obtain key information by using and expanding on traditional and alternative data sources.

Planning and coordination among key institutions are critical. Innovation and digital platforms require new forms of public policy and public–private partnerships. It demands multisector support and coordination especially in areas of regulation, taxation and accounting, investment in materials and infrastructure, dissemination of knowledge, and training and education.

A flexible policy and regulatory environment can nurture growth and innovation. Regulating technologies that are quickly developing and continuously changing is difficult. It may be more effective to use policies to enhance an ecosystem that supports innovation-driven entrepreneurship to bolster the competitiveness of domestic enterprises in the digital space. This requires governments to improve access to entrepreneur finance, enact competition policies to mitigate rent-seeking behavior, and improve education systems to incorporate entrepreneurship besides technical skills. Policies to protect intellectual property, consumers, and the privacy of personal data are crucial, as are those promoting effective cybersecurity.

Regulators must protect public interests while ensuring that legislation or regulations do not have a chilling effect on innovation. Implementing light-touch regulatory approaches on technologies that involve the processing of data, alongside more general data protection legislation is helpful. Likewise, policies that encourage innovation to manage the harmful impact of digital technology and the digital economy (e.g., devices and the packaging materials used in e-commerce) on the environment and those that deal with the adverse health outcomes of users (e.g., physical and mental health issues) must be considered as well. These could take the form of best practices guidelines, issuing warnings and advisories, providing official speeches, interpretations, and meetings with regulated parties.

Upgrading of education and labor market policies will help spread the benefits of digital platforms more widely. Digital platforms hold great promise to solve critical problems in education and learning, especially as the COVID-19 pandemic has eased more than 1.5 billion students out of face-to-face learning at one point when the countries closed their educational institutions. Governments should improve technology service in public education by addressing obsolescence in hardware and software. Creating an ecosystem for skills development and training to prepare workers for the digital future by improving access to connectivity, devices, and learning environments is crucial. This way, workers can easily access education and training materials to allow them to reenter the labor market at different levels. Developing arrangements for online quality assurance and online credentials such as micro-credentials, digital badges, among others will be helpful. To support start-ups, experiential entrepreneurship education among students and faculty may also be relevant as digital platforms create a pool of human resources with skills and expertise that are useful in many work settings. Governments may also use social media for citizen education and engagement. Strengthening of the social protection system and making it portable and flexible to be applicable to a wide range of work arrangements is important to protect digital workers' welfare.

Software and data management, and competition are crucial. Within the realm of digital platforms, competition has become indispensable and essential to ensure its continued development and accessibility on all fronts. The quickly evolving nature of this sector and consequent tendency to entrench incumbents underscore the need to lower barriers to entry to simultaneously promote consumer welfare and safeguard a level playing field among players of all sizes.

Certain tools such as intellectual property rights implemented on fair, reasonable, and nondiscriminatory terms can serve as incentives for businesses to innovate and preclude the exclusive ownership of dominant players' assets, such as interfaces or software. From a competition lens, open ecosystems serve to benefit all sides of a platform because of increased component compatibility, network effects, economies of scale, ease in entry, and intra-ecosystem competition. In closed structures or highly concentrated systems, interoperability and multi-homing create access points and integration and combat abuses of market power. However, the former requires careful and timely intervention to avoid distortions and to protect user privacy, particularly with regard to data-sharing policies.

The same circumspection is integral to the harmonization of universal criteria of transferability and translatability policies for a trustworthy data ecosystem. The best practices in other jurisdictions on pro-competitive data access policy include securing consumers' control of personal and machine-generated data, setting standards for data portability, accountability, and accuracy, and prioritizing consumer-centric policies.

Despite advances in technology and digital platforms, a large segment of the population is still left behind. Many in Asia still lack access to power, clean water, or infrastructure that supports communication and information sharing, creating a digital and economic divide. To narrow these divides, the key ingredients are the provision of material access; infrastructure investments; and education and training to remove barriers pertaining to location, age, gender, culture, skills, and trust.

Some key infrastructure, trade, and logistics reforms are needed to reap the benefits from the digital economy. The first is to improve infrastructure connectivity and services which would deliver affordable mobile communications, access to broadband and the internet, and set the foundation for interoperable systems. It is also important to improve trade and logistics systems, and interoperability among land, sea, and air transport to expedite the movement of goods and services. Reforms to speed customs clearance and border procedures are also important. There is a need to broaden e-payment availability options and to harmonize different national norms and standards while reducing risk of fraud and establishing consumer protection. Attracting FDI, venture capital and equity, and working with established businesses could supply the needed financing for technology and innovation start-ups.

Funding for investment to support technology adoption in the region is important. With limited fiscal and financial resources in the region, a comprehensive approach to raise finance for technology is important. Generally, three key factors could help close the technology funding gap: (i) increasing the pipeline of technology projects; (ii) crowding in private capital; and (iii) mitigating the risks and costs of technology projects.

International tax cooperation, including the development of digital tax policies and options, is important. Large-scale policy responses to COVID-19 will inevitably result in increased levels of sovereign debt, underpinning the need for efficient tax systems and addressing of BEPS to assure public debt sustainability in the longer term. Thus, strengthening international cooperation for effective response to BEPS and better taxation is important. Policy makers in the region need to consider how enhanced international taxation can help mobilize domestic tax revenues, including tax issues that are tied to cross-border transactions, such as the de minimis rule.

Regional cooperation is also critical to address cross-border issues and challenges. Cooperation could be initiated through sharing of country lessons and experience, conducting regional dialogue, and working together to collect data and produce knowledge products that will help understand how digital platforms could either accelerate or derail progress toward inclusive and sustainable development. Cooperation could further focus on forging an intergovernmental mechanism to discuss a regionally consistent framework, strategy, and regulations—especially on cross-border data transfers. Although a unified cross-border data-sharing regime and protection framework may not be feasible at this point, the regional mechanism could help deliver a general and comprehensive international data protection regime. It may also help eliminate data transfer restrictions for data categories essential for the region's growth and development, without any prejudice to each country's national security.

Development organizations can play an important role in supporting a more sustainable and equitable transition to the digital economy. Development organizations can support investments in technologies that will help bring the benefits of digital platforms to more people, and they can support creation of national and regional policies in many important areas like competition, security, privacy, social protection, and education. Development organizations can also support knowledge creation and capacity building to help developing countries build up their institutions and human capital to better understand and take advantage of emerging technologies.

Background Papers

Abell, T. E. 2020. Key Technologies Critical to Growth of Digital Platforms and the Digital Economy. Background Paper for the *Asian Economic Integration Report 2021* Theme Chapter on "Making Digital Platforms Work for Asia and the Pacific." Manuscript.

Albert, J. R. 2020. Towards Measuring the Platform Economy: Concepts, Indicators, and Issues. *PIDS Discussion Paper Series.* No. 2020-28. Manila: Philippine Institute for Development Studies (PIDS). https://www.pids.gov.ph/publications/7153.

Arbo, M. D. G., and A. K. Takenaka. 2020. Digitalization of Work and the Role of Universal Basic Income in Developing Asia. Background Paper for the *Asian Economic Integration Report 2021* Theme Chapter on "Making Digital Platforms Work for Asia and the Pacific." Manuscript.

Asian Development Bank and United Nations World Tourism Organization (ADB and UNWTO). Forthcoming. *Big Data for Better Tourism Policy, Management, and the Sustainable Recovery from COVID-19.* Manila.

Avendaño, R. and P. Rosenkranz. 2020. Digital Platforms and International Taxation in Asia. Background Paper for the *Asian Economic Integration Report 2021* Theme Chapter on "Making Digital Platforms Work for Asia and the Pacific." Manuscript.

Bainbridge, M., P. C. Zuniga, R. F. Sarmiento, and E. Banzon. 2020. Leveraging Digital Technologies and Platforms for the Delivery of Health Services in Asia and the Pacific. Background Paper for the *Asian Economic Integration Report 2021* Theme Chapter on "Making Digital Platforms Work for Asia and the Pacific." Manuscript.

Bayudan-Dacuycuy, C., A. Orbeta Jr., R. Serafica, and L. K. Baje. 2020a. Online Work in the Philippines: Some Lessons in the Asian Context. *PIDS Discussion Paper Series No. 2020-29.* Manila: Philippine Institute for Development Studies. https://www.pids.gov.ph/publications/7154.

———. 2020b. Towards a Sustainable Online Work in the Philippines: Learnings from the Online Survey of Market and Nonmarket Work during the Enhanced Community Quarantine. *PIDS Discussion Paper Series No. 2020-27.* Manila: Philippine Institute for Development Studies. https://www.pids.gov.ph/publications/7152.

Huang, Y. 2020. Advancing Asia's Payment Systems Through Financial Technology. Background Paper for the *Asian Economic Integration Report 2021* Theme Chapter on "Making Digital Platforms Work for Asia and the Pacific." Manuscript.

Jacildo, R. 2020. Trade and E-commerce in Asia: Empirics and Policy Considerations. Background Paper for the *Asian Economic Integration Report 2021* Theme Chapter on "Making Digital Platforms Work for Asia and the Pacific." Manuscript.

Jagannathan, S. , and Y. Li. 2020. Digital Platforms for Education and Skills: Tipping the Balance. Background Paper for the *Asian Economic Integration Report 2021* Theme Chapter on "Making Digital Platforms Work for Asia and the Pacific." Manuscript.

Narayanan B., and J. Villafuerte. 2020. Macroeconomic Impact of Digitalization in Asia. Background Paper for the *Asian Economic Integration Report 2021* Theme Chapter on "Making Digital Platforms Work for Asia and the Pacific." Manuscript.

Quimba, F. M., M. A. Rosellon, and S. Calizo Jr. 2020. Digital Divide and the Platform Economy: Looking for the Connection from the Asian Experience. *PIDS Discussion Paper Series No. 2020-30.* Manila: Philippine Institute for Development Studies. https://www.pids.gov.ph/publications/7155.

Serzo, A. L. 2020. Cross-Border Issues for Digital Platforms: A Review of Regulations Applicable to Philippine Digital Platforms. *PIDS Discussion Paper Series No. 2020-47.* Manila: Philippine Institute for Development Studies. https://www.pids.gov.ph/publications/7176.

Villafuerte, J., P. Libre, R. Jacildo, K. Diet, and J. Elvina. 2020. Promoting Competition in the Digital Platform Economy. Background Paper for the *Asian Economic Integration Report 2021* Theme Chapter on "Making Digital Platforms Work for Asia and the Pacific." Manuscript.

References

Abacus. 2020. Drivers for Ride-hailing Giant Didi Will Now Go Grocery Shopping for You. 11 March. https://www.scmp.com/tech/article/3074709/drivers-ride-hailing-giant-didi-will-now-go-grocery-shopping-you.

Abiad, A., M. Arao, S. Dagli, B. Ferrarini, I. Noy, P. Osewe, J. Pagaduan, D. Park, and R. Platitas. 2020. The Economic Impact of the COVID-19 Outbreak on Developing Asia. *ADB Briefs*. No. 128. Manila: Asian Development Bank.

Abraham, K., J. Haltiwanger, K. Sandusky, and J. Spletzer. 2019. The Rise of the Gig Economy: Fact or Fiction. *American Economic Association (AEA) Papers and Proceedings*. 109. pp. 357–361.

Agarwal, S., P. Ghosh, J. Li, and T. Ruan. 2020. *Digital Payments and Consumption: Evidence from the 2016 Demonetization in India*. http://dx.doi.org/10.2139/ssrn.3641508.

Agarwal, S., W. Qian, B. Yeung, and X. Zou. 2019. Mobile Wallet and Entrepreneurial Growth. *AEA Papers and Proceedings* 109: pp. 48–53.

Agoda. 2018. Agoda and Tourism Authority of Thailand Team up to Promote Domestic Travel. 18 July. https://www.agoda.com/press/agoda-tourism-authority-thailand-team-promote-domestic-travel?cid=1844104.

Agur, I., S. Martinez Peria, and C. Rochon. 2020. Digital Financial Services and the Pandemic: Opportunities and Risks for Emerging and Developing Economies. *IMF Fiscal Affairs: Special Series on COVID-19*. Washington, DC: International Monetary Fund (IMF).

Ahmed, S. P., G. M. Ullah, F. Mahtab, and S. Uddin. 2018. Valuation of Startup Firms: A Case Study on Pathao. *Independent Business Review*. 11 (1-2). pp. 1–51. Special Issue.

Albert, J. R., A. Martinez, Jr., K. Miradora, J. A. Lapuz, M. Martillan, C. de Dios and I. Sebastian-Samaniego. 2019. Readiness of National Statistical Systems in Asia and the Pacific for Leveraging Big Data to Monitor the SDGs. *ADB Briefs*. No. 106. Manila: ADB.

Ali Research and Accenture. 2016. *Global Cross Border B2C e-Commerce Market 2020: Report Highlights and Methodology Sharing*. Presented at the United Nations Conference on Trade and Development (UNCTAD). Geneva. 18–22 April. https://unctad.org/meetings/en/Presentation/dtl_eweek2016_AlibabaResearch_en.pdf.

Ardolino, M., N. Saccani, and M. Perona. 2016. *The Rise of Platform Economy: A Framework to Describe Multisided Platforms*. Presented at the XXI Summer School "Francesco Turco"—Industrial Systems Engineering. Naples. 13–15 September. http://www.summerschool-aidi.it/edition-2016/cms/extra/papers/final_42.pdf.

Arnell, N., D. van Vuuren, and M. Isaac. 2011. The Implications of Climate Policy for the Impacts of Climate Change on Global Water Resources. *Global Environmental Change*. 21 (2). pp. 592–603.

Asakawa, M. 2020. *Achieving the Sustainable Development Goals by Strengthening Domestic Resource Mobilization and International Tax Cooperation*. Speech delivered at ADB 53rd Annual Meeting of the Board of Governors. Virtual. 17–18 September. https://www.adb.org/news/speeches/achieving-sdgs-strengthening-domestic-resource-mobilization-masatsugu-asakawa.

The Asia Foundation. 2017. *Six Stories, Six Paths to Development Online Platforms as Drivers of Inclusive Growth*. https://asiafoundation.org/publication/six-stories-six-paths-to-development/.

Asia-Pacific Economic Cooperation (APEC). 2011. *Annex A-Pathfinder to Enhance Supply Chain Connectivity by Establishing a Baseline De Minimis Value.* 2011 APEC Ministerial Meeting. Honolulu. https://www.apec.org/Meeting-Papers/Annual-Ministerial-Meetings/2011/2011_amm/annex-a.

———. 2019. *APEC Cross-border Privacy Rules System Policies, Rules and Guidelines—Updated as of November 2019.* Singapore. http://cbprs.org/wp-content/uploads/2019/11/4.-CBPR-Policies-Rules-and-Guidelines-Revised-For-Posting-3-16-updated-1709-2019.pdf.

Asian Business Law Institute (ABLI). 2020. *Comparative Table of Laws and Regulations on Cross-Border Personal Data Flows in Asia.* Singapore.

Asian Development Bank (ADB). 2019a. *The Social Protection Indicator for Asia: Assessing Progress.* Manila.

———. 2019b. *Asian Economic Integration Report 2019–2020: Demographic Change, Productivity, and the Role of Technology.* Manila.

———. 2021. *COVID-19 and Education in Asia and the Pacific: Guidance Note.* Manila.

Asian Development Bank and United Nations Economic and Social Commission for Asia and the Pacific (ADB and UNESCAP). 2018. *Embracing the E-commerce Revolution in Asia and the Pacific.* Manila.

Association of Southeast Asian Nations (ASEAN). 2016. *ASEAN Competition Action Plan (ACAP) 2016–2025.* Jakarta. https://asean.org/storage/2012/05/ACAP-Website-23-December-2016.pdf.

Baker McKenzie. 2017. *Asia Pacific Business Complexities Survey 2017: Simplifying Business in a Complex World.* Chicago. In Girot, C. ed. 2018. Regulation of Cross-Border Transfers of Personal Data in Asia. *ABLI Legal Convergence Series.* Singapore: ABLI.

Banerjee, A. 2016. The Best Way to Welfare. *The Indian Express.* 18 June. https://indianexpress.com/article/opinion/columns/swiss-voted-against-the-idea-of-a-universal-basic-income-but-the-debate-continues-2859528/.

Banerjee, A., P. Niehaus, and T. Suri. 2019. Universal Basic Income in the Developing World. *Annual Review of Economics.* 11. pp. 959–983.

Bangura, J. A. 2016. *Saving Money, Saving Lives: A Case Study on the Benefits of Digitizing Payments to Ebola Response to Workers in Sierra Leone.* New York: Better Than Cash Alliance. https://btca-prod-1.s3.amazonaws.com/documents/186/english_attachments/BTCA-Ebola-Case-Study.pdf?1502739794.

Bank for International Settlements (BIS). 2020. *BIS Annual Economic Report 2020.* Basel.

———. The Red Book Statistics in CPMI Countries. https://www.bis.org/statistics/payment_stats.htm (accessed June 2020).

Bardhan, P. 2017. Universal Basic Income–Its Special Case for India. *Indian Journal of Human Development* 11(2). pp. 141–143.

Barker, A. 2020. *Consumer Data Rights and Competition—Background Note.* Paris: Organisation for Economic Co-operation and Development (OECD).

Barnes, S., A. Green, and M. de Hoyos. 2015. Crowdsourcing and Work: Individual Factors and Circumstances Influencing Employability. *New Technology, Work and Employment.* 30 (1). pp. 16–31.

Barthel, J., and S. Perret. 2015. *OTAs—A Hotel's Friend or Foe? How Reliant are Hotels on OTAs?* London: HVS London. https://www.hospitalitynet.org/file/152005663.pdf.

Beerepoot, N. and B. Lambregts. 2014. Competition in Online Job Marketplaces: Towards a Global Labour Market for Outsourcing Services? *Global Networks: A Journal of Transnational Affairs.* 15 (2). pp. 236–255.

Behrendt, C., and Q. Nguyen. 2018. Innovative Approaches for Ensuring Universal Social Protection for the Future of Work. *ILO Future of Work Research Paper Series.* Geneva: International Labour Organization (ILO).

Benson, T., and G. Grieve. 2016. *Principles of Health Interoperability: SNOMED CT, HL7 and FHIR. Third Edition.* Health Information Technology Standards Book Series. London: Springer-Verlag London.

Berg, J., M. Furrer, E. Harmon, U. Rani, and M. S. Silberman. 2018. *Inter Digital Labour Platforms and the Future of Work: Towards Decent Work in the Online World.* Geneva: ILO.

Bhattacharyya, S.B. 2016. *Introduction to SNOMED CT.* Singapore: Springer Science+Business Media.

Bindra, V. 2020. With COVID 19 Providing a Major Disruption, The Future of EdTech Platforms Looks Promising. *Express Computer.* 2 July. https://www.expresscomputer.in/industries/education/with-covid-19-providing-a-major-disruption-the-future-of-edtech-platforms-looks-promising/59609/.

Binsaleh, S., and M. Binsaleh. 2013. Mobile Learning: What Guidelines Should We Produce in the Context of Mobile Learning Implementation in the Conflict Area of the Four Southernmost Provinces of Thailand. *Asian Social Science.* 9 (13). pp. 270–281.

Blachnio, A., A. Przepiorka, M. Benvenuti, D. Cannata, A. Ciobanu, E. Senol-Durak, M. Durak, M. Giannakos, E. Mazzoni, I. Pappas, C. Popa, G. Seidman, S. Yu, A. M. S. Wu, and M. Ben-Ezra. 2016. Cultural and Personality Predictors of Facebook Intrusion: A Cross-cultural Study. *Frontiers in Psychology.* 7. https://doi.org/10.3389/fpsyg.2016.01895.

Blackmore, N. 2019. Moving Towards Europe: Recent Trends in Asia-Pacific Data Protection Law. https://www.kennedyslaw.com/thought-leadership/article/moving-towards-europe-recent-trends-in-asia-pacific-data-protection-law.

Borko, S. 2020. *The Impact of COVID-19 on the Online Travel Industry*. https://research.skift.com/report/the-impact-of-covid-19-on-the-online-travel-industry/.

Botsman, R., and R. Rogers. 2010. *What's Mine Is Yours: The Rise of Collaborative Consumption.* New York: Harper Collins.

Bradbury, D., T. Hanappi, and A. Moore. 2018. Estimating the Fiscal Effects of Base Erosion and Profit Shifting: Data Availability and Analytical Issues. *Transnational Corporations.* 25(2). pp. 91–106.

Browne, J., and H. Immervoll. 2017. Mechanics of Replacing Benefit Systems with a Basic Income. *Journal of Economic Inequality*. 15(4). pp. 325-344.

Bryan Cave Leighton Paisner LLP (BCLP). 2019. Price Parity Clauses and Booking.com–A More Unified Approach or a Reminder of Diverging Opinions? 10 June. https://www.bclplaw.com/en-US/insights/price-parity-clauses-and-booking-com-a-more-unified-approach-or.html

Bukht R., and R. Heeks. 2017. Defining, Conceptualising and Measuring the Digital Economy. *Development Informatics. Working Papers Series.* No. 68. Manchester: University of Manchester.

BusinessLine. 2020. Zoho Launches Swadeshi Sankalp Initiative to Help Ease Covid Impact. 29 April. https://www.thehindubusinessline.com/info-tech/zoho-launches-swadeshi-sankalp-initiative-to-help-ease-covid-impact/article31461302.ece.

BusinessWire. 2019. Online Travel World-Markets 2019–2022. 4 December. https://www.businesswire.com/news/home/20191204005603/en/Online-Travel-World-Markets-2019-2022---Leading.

Calligo. 2017. *The Clock is Ticking: The Truth About GDPR Compliance*. Jersey.

Carrico, C., E. Corong, and D. van der Mensbrugghe. 2020. The Global Trade Analysis Project (GTAP) Version 10A Multi-Region Input Output (MRIO) Data Base. *GTAP Research Memorandum*. No. 34. https://www.gtap.agecon.purdue.edu/resources/res_display.asp?RecordID=6164.

CEE Multi-Country News Center. 2020. Azerbaijan: How One Ministry Found the Right Strategy, Resources, and Technology to Quickly Create Online Classrooms. *Microsoft*. 9 July. https://news.microsoft.com/en-cee/2020/07/09/azerbaijan-how-one-ministry-found-the-right-strategy-resources-and-technology-to-quickly-create-online-classrooms/.

Centre d'Etudes Prospectives et d'Informations Internationales (the French Research Center in International Economics). Geography Database. http://www.cepii.fr/CEPII/en/bdd_modele/bdd_modele.asp (accessed April 2020).

Chappatte, P., K. O'Connell, and S. de Morant. 2019. European Union–E-commerce: Most Favoured Nation Clauses. In C. Jeffs, ed. *Global Competition Review (GCR) Insight: Guide E-Commerce Competition Enforcement Guide*, London: Law Business Research Ltd.

Cheng, X., S. Fu, and G. J. de Vreede. 2018. A Mixed Method Investigation of Sharing Economy Driven Car-Hailing Services: Online and Offline Perspectives. *International Journal of Information Management*. 41. pp. 57–64.

China Internet Network Information Center (CNNIC). 2020. Distribution of Internet Users in China from December 2014 to March 2020, By Gender. 28 April. In *Statista—The Statistics Portal*. https://www.statista.com/statistics/265148/percentage-of-internet-users-in-china-by-gender/ (accessed May 2020).

Chisholm, A. and N. Jung. 2016. Platform Regulation–Ex-ante Versus Ex-post Intervention: Evolving Our Antitrust Tools and Practices to Meet the Challenges. Competition Policy International. https://www.competitionpolicyinternational.com/platform-regulation-ex-ante-versus-ex-post-intervention-evolving-our-antitrust-tools-and-practices-to-meet-the-challenges/.

Chun, Y., R. Kumar, and A. Rahman. 2019. The Impacts of Ride-Sharing on Traditional Transportation Sectors: A Case Study of Dhaka, Bangladesh. *IOSR Journal of Business and Management (IOSR-JBM)*. 21 (5). pp. 16–25.

Consumer Unity and Trust Society (CUTS) International. 2018. *Going Digital: From Innovation to Inclusive Growth in Vietnam*. Jaipur.

———. 2019. *E-clinic Services in Rajasthan, India: A Case Study*. Jaipur.

Crunchbase Inc. https://www.crunchbase.com (accessed August 2020).

Cummings, J., A. Merrill, and S. Borrelli. 2010. The Use of Handheld Mobile Devices: Their Impact and Implications for Library Services. *Library Hi Tech*. 28 (1). pp. 22–40.

DBS Group Research. 2019. Number of Active Drivers of Asia Pacific Ride-Sharing Companies as of 2019 (in millions). 27 May. In *Statista—The Statistics Portal*. https://www.statista.com/statistics/1034777/apac-number-of-active-drivers-of-ride-sharing-companies/ (accessed August 2020).

Deloitte. 2019. *The Future of Life Sciences and Health Care in Asia Pacific: Embrace, Build and Grow*. Singapore.

DePietro, R., E. Wiarda, and M. Fleisher. 1990. The Context for Change: Organization, Technology and Environment. In L. G. Tornatzky and M. Fleischer, eds. *The Processes of Technological Innovation*. Lexington: Lexington Books.

Didi. About Us—More Than a Journey: The World's Leading Transportation Platform. https://www.didiglobal.com/about-didi/about-us (accessed August 2020).

Dreesen, T., M. Brossard, S. Akseer, P. Dewan, J. Giraldo, A. Kamei, S. Mizunoya, and J. Santiago Ortiz Correa. 2020. *Promising Practices for Equitable Remote Learning: Emerging Lessons from COVID-19 Education Responses in 127 Countries*. Florence: United Nations International Children's Fund (UNICEF). https://www.unicef-irc.org/publications/1090-promising-practices-for-equitable-remote-learning-emerging-lessons-from-covid.html.

Dutta, S., and B. Lanvin, eds. 2020. *Network Readiness Index 2020: Benchmarking the Future of the Network Economy*. Washington, DC: Portulans Institute.

Ecommerce Foundation. 2019. *Global B2C E-commerce Report: Global*. Light Report Edition. Amsterdam.

Ecomobi. 2017. *Vietnam Digital Landscape 2017*. Ha Noi. https://www.vietnambusiness.tv/market-research/marketing-media/628/vietnam-digital-landscape-2017.

The Economist Intelligence Unit (EIU). 2020. Global Democracy Has Another Bad Year. 22 January. https://www.economist.com/graphic-detail/2020/01/22/global-democracy-has-another-bad-year.

Euromonitor International. Retailing Industry Edition 2019.

European Commission. 2017. Antitrust: Commission fines Google €2.42 billion for Abusing Dominance as Search Engine by Giving Illegal Advantage to Own Comparison Shopping Service. 27 June. https://ec.europa.eu/commission/presscorner/detail/en/MEMO_17_1785.

European Commission, International Monetary Fund, Organisation for Economic Co-operation and Development, United Nations, and World Bank (European Commission et al.). 2009. *System of National Accounts 2008*. New York: United Nations.

Eurostat. 2018. Measuring the Digital Collaborative Economy. Luxembourg: European Commission.

Evans, D. 2018. *Essential Principles for the Design of Antitrust Analysis for Multisided Platforms*. Boston and London: Global Economics Group and University College London.

Evans, D., and R. Schmalensee. 2007. The Industrial Organization of Markets with Two-Sided Platforms. *Competition Policy International*. 3 (1). pp. 151–79.

Evans, P. 2016. The Rise of Asian Platforms: A Regional Survey. *The Emerging Platform Economy Series*. 3. New York: The Center for Global Enterprise.

Evans, P., and A. Gawer. 2016. The Rise of the Platform Enterprise: A Global Survey. *The Emerging Platform Economy Series*. 1. New York: The Center for Global Enterprise. https://www.thecge.net/app/uploads/2016/01/PDF-WEB-Platform-Survey_01_12.pdf.

Electronic World Trade Platform (eWTP). n.d. Milestones. https://www.ewtp.org/milestones.html.

———. n.d. Public Service Platform. https://www.ewtp.org/psp.html.

Expedia Group. 2019. Expedia Group Overview. https://www.expediagroup.com/about/.

Express Computer. 2020. EdTech Startup WhiteHat Jr. Ramps Up Hiring to Meet Massive Surge in Student Enrollment. 8 May. https://www.expresscomputer.in/news/edtech-startup-whitehat-jr-ramps-up-hiring-to-meet-massive-surge-in-student-enrolment/55276/.

Ezrachi, A. and M. Stucke. 2018. eDistortions: How Data-Opolies are Dissipating the Internet's Potential. *Digital Platforms and Concentration*. Chicago: ProMarket.

Farrell, D., and F. Greig. 2016. *Paychecks, Paydays, and the Online Platform Economy: Big Data on Income Volatility*. New York: JPMorgan Chase Institute.

Fitzpatrick, T. 1999. *Freedom and Security: An Introduction to the Basic Income Debate*. London: Macmillan Press Ltd.

Flowers, R. 2020. *Ethnic Minority education in Viet Nam: Challenges and Opportunities During COVID-19 Outbreak*. Ho Chi Minh: UNICEF.

Forde, C., M. Stuart, S. Joyce, L. Oliver, D. Valizade, G. Alberti, K. Hardy, V. Trappman, C. Umney, and C. Carson. 2017. *The Social Protection of Workers in the Platform Economy: Study for the European Parliament Committee on Employment and Social Affairs (EMPL)*. Brussels: European Parliament.

Fortanier, F., and S. Matei. 2017. *Measuring Digital Trade: Results of the OECD-IMF Stocktaking Survey*. Presented at 30th Meeting of the IMF Committee on Balance of Payments Statistics. Paris. 24–26 October. www.imf.org/external/pubs/ft/bop/2017/pdf/17-07.pdf .

Francese, M., and D. Prady. 2018. Universal Basic Income: Debate and Impact Assessment. *IMF Working Paper*. No. 18/273. Washington, DC: International Monetary Fund (IMF).

Friedman, G. 2014. Workers Without Employers: Shadow Corporations and the Rise of the Gig Economy. *Review of Keynesian Economics*. 2 (2). pp. 171–88.

Gentilini, U., M. Almenfi, and I Orton. 2020. *Social Protection and Jobs Responses to COVID-19: A Real-Time Review of Country Measures*. A "living paper", version 2. http://www.ugogentilini.net/wp-content/uploads/2020/03/Social-protection-responses-to-COVID19_March27.pdf.

Gentilini, U., M.E. Grosh, I. Rigolini, and R. Yemtsov. 2020. *Exploring Universal Basic Income: A Guide to Navigating Concepts, Evidence, and Practices*. Washington, DC: World Bank.

Geyer, R., J. Jambeck, and K. Law. 2017. Production, Use, and Fate of All Plastics Ever Made. American Association for the Advancement of Science. *Science Advances*. 3 (7). e1700782.

Ghatak, M. 2016. The Price of Basic Income. *The Indian Express*. 1 July. https://indianexpress.com/article/opinion/columns/basic-income-in-india-brexit-referendum-switzerland-basic-income-jan-dhan-yojana-guarantee-employment-programme-mgnrega-2879930/.

Ghobadi, S., and Z. Ghobadi. 2013. How Access Gaps Interact and Shape Digital Divide: A Cognitive Investigation. *Journal of Behaviour and Information Technology*. 34 (4). pp. 330–40.

Girot, C., ed. 2018. Regulation of Cross-Border Transfers of Personal Data in Asia. *ABLI Legal Convergence Series*. Singapore: ABLI.

Global System for Mobile Communications Association (GSMA). Mobile Money Metrics Database. https://www.gsma.com/mobilemoneymetrics/#global?y=2019?v=overview?g=global (accessed June 2020).

GlobalWebIndex. 2020. *Commerce: GlobalWebIndex's Flagship Report on the Latest Trends in Commerce*. London.

Globe Telecom, Inc. 2020. *Filipinos More Inclined to Use Digital Finance: GCash Transactions Balloon by 700% YoY in May*. Globe Newsroom, Manila. 22 June. https://www.globe.com.ph/about-us/newsroom/917ventures/gcash-transactions-700percent-yoy-May.html#gref.

Golub, A., and R. McDougall. 2006. *New Household Saving Behavior in the Dynamic GTAP Model*. Presented at the 9th Annual Conference on Global Economic Analysis. Addis Ababa. 15–17 June. https://www.gtap.agecon.purdue.edu/resources/res_display.asp?RecordID=2129.

Google, Temasek, and Bain. 2019. e-Conomy SEA 2019. https://www.temasek.com.sg/en/news-and-views/subscribe/google-temasek-e-conomy-sea-2019

Government of Georgia, Ministry of Education and Science. 2020. Georgia is Considered One of the Best Examples of Distance Learning According to the OECD report. *News*. 6 April. http://www.mes.gov.ge/content.php?t=srch&search=covid&id=10284&lang=eng.

Government of Germany, Federal Cartel Office. 2018. Bundeskartellamt Initiates Abuse Proceeding Against Amazon. Press Release. 29 November. https://www.bundeskartellamt.de/SharedDocs/Meldung/EN/Pressemitteilungen/2018/29_11_2018_Verfahrenseinleitung_Amazon.html;jsessionid=11C05880250D8CE386B865348EB44E98.2_cid378?nn=3591568.

Government of Indonesia, Ministry of Cooperatives and Small and Medium Enterprises. 2020. Kemenkop UKM Luncurkan Kau Untuk Percepat UMKM Go Marketplace. Kementerian Koperasi dan Usaha Kecil dan Menengah Republik Indonesia, Jakarta. 15 June. http://www.depkop.go.id/read/kemenkop-ukm-luncurkan-kau-untuk-percepat-umkm-go-marketplace.

Government of Indonesia, Ministry of Finance. 2019. Ciptakan Perlakuan Perpajakan Yang Adil Dan Lindungi Industri Kecil Dan Menengah Dalam Negeri, Pemerintah Ubah Ketentuan Impor Barang Kiriman (E-Commerce). *Siaran Pers*. Kementerian Keuangan Republik Indonesia, Jakarta. 23 December. https://www.kemenkeu.go.id/publikasi/siaran-pers/siaran-pers-ciptakan-perlakuan-perpajakan-yang-adil-dan-lindungi-industri-kecil-dan-menengah-dalam-negeri-pemerintah-ubah-ketentuan-impor-barang-kiriman-e-commerce/.

Government of Malaysia, External Trade Development Corporation. n.d. Digital Free Trade Zone (DFTZ). http://www.matrade.gov.my/en/digital-free-trade-zone-dftz.

Government of the People's Republic of China, National Bureau of Statistics. Statistical Database. https://data.stats.gov.cn/english/?cn=A01 (accessed July 2020).

Government of the Philippines, Philippine Statistics Authority (PSA). n.d. Philippine Standard Industrial Classification. https://psa.gov.ph/classification/psic/.

Government of the Russian Federation, Federal Antimonopoly Service (FAS). 2019. On Consideration of the Merger Between Uber and Yandex. Taxi. Moscow. http://en.fas.gov.ru/documents/documentdetails.html?id=15350.

Government of Sri Lanka, Department of Census and Statistics. 2018. *Computer Literacy Statistics 2018 (Annual)*. http://www.statistics.gov.lk/ComputerLiteracy/StaticalInformation/Bulletins/2018-Annual (accessed May 2020).

Government of Taipei,China, National Development Council (NDC). 2019. In Statista—*The Statistics Portal*. https://www.statista.com.

Government of the United States, Environmental Protection Agency (EPA). 2020. Facts and Figures about Materials, Waste and Recycling. 10 September. https://www.epa.gov/facts-and-figures-about-materials-waste-and-recycling/plastics-material-specific-data

Government of Viet Nam, Ministry of Information and Communications. 2020. Online Applications Blooming in Vietnam during Covid-19 Outbreak. News. 18 March. https://english.mic.gov.vn/Pages/TinTuc/140855/Online-applications-blooming-in-Vietnam-during-Covid-19-outbreak.html.

Grab. 2019. *Social Impact Report 2018–2019*. https://assets.grab.com/wp-content/uploads/media/Grab-Social-Impact-Report-2018-2019.pdf.

———. 2020. Grab Announces Additional COVID-19 Support Measures. Press Centre, Singapore. 30 March. https://www.grab.com/sg/press/others/grab-announces-additional-covid-19-support-measures/.

Graham, M., I. Hjorth, and V. Lehdonvirta. 2017. Digital Labour and Development: Impacts of Global Digital Labour Platforms and the Gig Economy on Worker Livelihoods. *Transfer: European Review of Labour and Research.* 23 (2). pp. 135–62.

Graham, M., V. Lehdonvirta, A. Wood, H. Barnard, I. Hjorth, and D. Simon. 2017. *The Risks and Rewards of Online Gig Work at the Global Margins*. Oxford: Oxford Internet Institute.

Greene, A. 2013. Tom Ferguson's Triangles in the 21st Century: An Initial Proposal. *Journal of Participatory Medicine.* https://participatorymedicine.org/journal/opinion/editorials/2013/11/27/tom-fergusons-triangles-in-the-21st-century-an-initial-proposal/.

Haenssgen, M. 2015. Exploring the Mismatch Between Mobile Phone Adoption and Use Through Survey Data from Rural India and China. Dublin: IEEE International Symposium on Technology and Society (ISTAS). https://doi.org/10.1109/istas.2015.7439402.

Haenssgen, M., and P. Ariana. 2017. The Social Implications of Technology Diffusion: Uncovering the Unintended Consequences of People's Health-Related Mobile Phone Use in Rural India and China. *World Development.* 94. pp. 286–304.

Handal, B., J. MacNish, and P. Petocz. 2013. Adopting Mobile Learning in Tertiary Environments: Instructional, Curricular and Organizational Matters. *Education Sciences.* 3 (4). pp. 359–74.

Handayani, S. W., M. Cichon, and L. Carraro. 2018. *Asia's Fiscal Challenge: Financing the Social Protection Agenda of the Sustainable Development Goals.* Manila: ADB.

Health Level Seven (HL7) International. 2019. *Fast Healthcare Interoperability Resources Version 4.0.1.* https://www.hl7.org/fhir/overview.html.

Heerschap, N., N. Pouw, and C. Atmé. 2018. *Measuring Online Platforms in the Context of the Sharing Economy*. The Hague: Statistics Netherlands.

The Heritage Foundation. Index of Economic Freedom Database. https://www.heritage.org/index/explore (accessed October 2020).

Holloway, S., and J. Rae. 2012. De Minimis Thresholds in APEC. *World Customs Journal.* 6 (1). pp. 31–62.

Hung, J. 2020. Delivery People Are Risking Their Lives to Keep Asia Running—Here's What People Are Doing to Say Thank You. *The Diplomat.* 1 April. https://thediplomat.com/2020/04/delivery-people-are-risking-their-lives-to-keep-asia-running-heres-what-people-are-doing-to-say-thank-you/.

Hunt, A., and E. Samman. 2019. Gender and the Gig Economy: Critical Steps for Evidence-based Policy. *ODI Working Paper 456*. London: Overseas Development Institute (ODI).

Hunt, A., E. Samman, and D. Mansour-Ille. 2017. Syrian Women Refugees: Opportunity in the Gig Economy? *ODI Report*. London: ODI.

Ianchovichina, E., and T. Walmsley, eds. 2012. *Dynamic Modeling and Applications for Global Economic Analysis*. Cambridge: Cambridge University Press.

Institute of Digital Finance-Peking University. 2019. *The Peking University Digital Financial Inclusion Index of China (2011–2018)*. In Collaboration with the Ant Financial Services Group. Beijing.

International Chamber of Commerce (ICC). 2015. ICC Policy Statement on Global Baseline De Minimis Value Thresholds. February. https://iccwbo.org/publication/icc-policy-statement-on-global-baseline-de-minimis-value-thresholds-2015/.

International Labour Organization (ILO). 2017. *World Social Protection Report 2017–19: Universal Social Protection to Achieve the Sustainable Development Goals*. Geneva.

———. 2018. *Women and Men in the Informal Economy: A Statistical Picture*. Third Edition. Geneva.

———. 2019. *Extending Social Security to Workers in the Informal Economy: Lessons from International Experience*. Geneva.

———. 2020a. *ILO Monitor: COVID-19 and the World of Work. Second Edition: Updated Estimates and Analysis*. Geneva.

———. 2020b. *Social Protection Responses to the COVID-19 Crisis: Country Responses in Asia and the Pacific*. Geneva.

International Labour Organization (ILO) and OECD. 2018. *Promoting Adequate Social Protection and Social Security Coverage for All Workers, Including Those in Non-standard Forms of Employment*. Paper presented at the 1st Meeting of the G20 Employment Working Group. Buenos Aires. 20–22 February. https://www.ilo.org/wcmsp5/groups/public/---dgreports/---inst/documents/publication/wcms_646044.pdf.

International Monetary Fund (IMF). 2018. *Measuring the Digital Economy*. Washington, DC..

———. 2020. *Policy Responses to COVID-19*. https://www.imf.org/en/Topics/imf-and-covid19/Policy-Responses-to-COVID-19.

———. World Economic Outlook October 2020 Database. https://www.imf.org/en/Publications/WEO/weo-database/2020/October (accessed November 2020).

International Policy Centre for Inclusive Growth and United Nations International Children's Fund. (IPC-IG and UNICEF). 2019. *Social Protection in Asia and the Pacific: Inventory of Non-contributory Programmes*. https://socialprotection.org/discover/publications/social-protection-asia-and-pacific-inventory-non-contributory-programmes.

International Telecommunication Union (ITU). 2017. *ICT Facts and Figures 2017*. Geneva.

———. 2019. *Measuring Digital Development: Facts and Figures 2019*. Geneva.

———. Country ICT Data. https://www.itu.int/en/ITU-D/Statistics/Pages/stat/default.aspx (accessed June 2020).

———. ITU ICT Eye Database. https://www.itu.int/net4/ITU-D/icteye/#/ (accessed April and June 2020).

———. World Telecommunication/ICT Indicators Database 2020. https://www.itu.int/en/ITU-D/Statistics/Pages/publications/wtid.aspx (accessed July 2020).

Internet and Mobile Association of India and Nielsen Holdings plc (IAMAI and Nielsen). 2019. *Internet in India 2019*. https://cms.iamai.in/Content/ResearchPapers/d3654bcc-002f-4fc7-ab39-e1fbeb00005d.pdf.

Iprice Group, App Annie and SimilarWeb. 2020. Year-End Report on Southeast Asia's Map of E-Commerce 2019. https://marketinginasia.com/wp-content/uploads/2020/03/2019-Year-End-Report-of-Map-of-E-commerce-iPrice-Group.pdf.

iResearch. 2020. 2020 Q1 Chinese Third-Party Mobile Payments Market Report. https://www.iresearch.com.cn/Detail/report?id=3601&isfree=0.

Ismael, Y. 2020. *E-commerce in the World Trade Organization: History and latest developments in the negotiations under the Joint Statement*. Geneva: International Institute for Sustainable Development and CUTS International. https://www.iisd.org/system/files/publications/e-commerce-world-trade-organization-.pdf.

Jambeck J., R. Geyer, C. Wilcox, T. Siegler, M. Perryman, A. Andrady, R. Narayan, and K. Lavender Law. 2015. Plastic Waste Inputs from Land into the Ocean. *Science*. 347 (6223). pp. 768–771.

Jansky, P., and M. Palansky. 2019. Estimating the Scale of Profit Shifting and Tax Revenue Losses Related to Foreign Direct Investment. *International Tax and Public Finance.* 26. pp. 1048–1103.

Jena, P. K. 2020. Impact of COVID-19 on Education in India. *International Journal of Current Research.* 12(7). pp. 12582–12586.

Jewell, C. 2019. Leveraging Indonesia's creative economy. *WIPO Magazine*. Madrid: World Intellectual Property Organization (WIPO). October. https://www.wipo.int/wipo_magazine/en/2019/05/article_0003.html.

Johal, S. 2018. Getting Ahead of the Future of Work: Focus on the Systems not the Skills. In *The Future of Work in the Global South*. Ottawa: International Development Research Centre.

Johansson, A., O.B. Skeie, S. Sorbe, and C. Menon. 2017. Tax Planning by Multinational Firms: Firm-level Evidence from a Cross-Country Database. *OECD Economics Department Working Papers* 1355. Paris: OECD.

Joshi, V. 2017. Universal Basic Income Supplement for India: A Proposal. *Indian Journal of Human Development.* 11 (2). pp. 144–149.

Junio, D. 2019. Gender Equality in ICT Access. In *Taking Stock: Data and Evidence on Gender Equality in Digital Access, Skills, and Leadership. United Nations University and EQUALS*. Macau, China: United Nations University Institute on Computing and Society/International Telecommunications Union (ITU). https://i.unu.edu/media/cs.unu.edu/attachment/4040/EQUALS-Research-Report-2019.pdf.

Kässi, O., and V. Lehdonvirta. 2018. Online Labour Index: Measuring the Online Gig Economy for Policy and Research. *Technological Forecasting and Social Change.* 137. pp. 241–48.

Kenney, M., and J. Zysman. 2016. The Rise of the Platform Economy. *Issues in Science and Technology.* 32 (3).

Kim, J. 2019. Tech Giants Brace Against Korea's New Antitrust Enforcer. *Asia Nikkei Review.* 5 September. https://asia.nikkei.com/Business/Technology/Tech-giants-brace-against-Korea-s-new-antitrust-enforcer.

Kinda, T. 2019. E-commerce as a Potential New Engine for Growth in Asia. *IMF Working Paper* WP/19/135. Washington, DC: IMF.

Klein, A. 2020. China's Digital Payments Revolution. In *Global China: Assessing China's Growing Role in the World*. Washington, DC: Brookings Institution.

Kobrata, D. 2018. Jurisdictional Report: Indonesia. In Girot, C., ed. *Regulation of Cross-Border Transfers of Personal Data in Asia.* Singapore: ABLI.

Koh, D. 2019. The Rise of Digital Health in Asia. *Mobile Health News—Asia Pacific.* 13 November. https://www.mobihealthnews.com/news/asia-pacific/rise-digital-health-asia.

Koh, T. K., and M. Fichman. 2014. Multi-Homing Users' Preferences for Two-Sided Exchange Networks. *MIS Quarterly* 38 (4). pp. 977–96..

Koskinen, K., C. Bonina, and B. Eaton. 2019. Digital Platforms in the Global South: Foundations and Research Agenda. In P. Nielsen and H. Kimaro, eds. *Information and Communication Technologies for Development: Strengthening Southern-Driven Cooperation as a Catalyst for ICT4D*. ICT4D 2019. IFIP Advances in Information and Communication Technology 551. New York: Springer.

Kriegler, E., B. O'Neill, S. Hallegatte, T. Kram, R. Lempert, R. Moss, and T. Wilbanks. 2012. The Need For and Use of Socio-economic Scenarios for Climate Change Analysis: A New Approach Based on Shared Socio-economic Pathways. *Global Environmental Change.* 22 (4). pp. 807–822.

Kuek, S., C. Paradi-Guilfor, T. Fayomi, S. Imaizumi, and P. Ipeirotis. 2015. *The Global Opportunity in Online Outsourcing*. Washington, DC: International Bank for Reconstruction and Development/World Bank. https://openknowledge.worldbank.org/bitstream/handle/10986/22284/The0global0opp0n0online0outsourcing.pdf?sequence=1&isAllowed=y.

Langley, P., and A. Leyshon. 2017. Platform Capitalism: The Intermediation and Capitalisation of Digital Economic Circulation. *Finance and Society*. 3 (1).

Lessig, L. 2006. *Code: And Other Laws of Cyberspace, Version 2.0*. New York: Basic Books.

Lewis T., C. Synowiec, G. Lagomarsino, and J. Schweitzer. 2012. E-health in Low- and Middle-income Countries: Findings from the Center for Health Market Innovations. *Bulletin of the World Health Organization*. 90 (5). pp. 332–40.

Lindert, J. 2017. Cyber-bullying and Its Impact on Mental Health. *The European Journal of Public Health*. 27 (3).

Little Hotelier. 2020. Metasearch Engines and OTAs: What's the Difference? https://www.littlehotelier.com/r/distribution/metasearch-engines-otas-whats-difference/.

Lopez-Gonzalez, J., and J. Ferencz. 2018. Digital Trade and Market Openness. *OECD Trade Policy Papers* No. 217. Paris: OECD.

Lund, S. W. L. Cheng, A. Dua, A. De Smet, O. Robinson, and S. Sanghvi. 2020. What 800 Executives Envision for the Postpandemic Workforce. https://www.mckinsey.com/featured-insights/future-of-work/what-800-executives-envision-for-the-postpandemic-workforce.

MacCallum, K., and L. Jeffrey. 2009. Identifying Discriminating Variables that Determine Mobile Learning Adoption by Educators: An Initial Study. *Same Places, Different Spaces*. Proceedings. Auckland: Ascilite.

Market Research Future. 2019. *Global Online Travel Market*. https://www.marketresearchfuture.com/reports/online-travel-market-5182.

Marsden, C., T. Meyer, and I. Brown. 2020. Platform Values and Democratic Elections: How Can the Law Regulate Digital Disinformation? *Computer Law & Security Review*. 36.

Martinez, A., and J. R. Albert. 2018. Big Data Can Transform SDG Performance: Here's How. *Asian Development Blog*. https://blogs.adb.org/blog/big-data-can-transform-sdg-performance-here-s-how

McDonald, A., and L.F. Cranor. 2008. The Cost of Reading Privacy Policies. *I/S: A Journal of Law and Policy for the Information Society*. 4 (3). pp. 543–568.

McKeering, D., C. Norton, and A. Gulati. 2017. *The Digital Healthcare Leap: Digital Health in Emerging Markets*. London: PricewaterhouseCoopers (PwC).

Medhi, T. 2020. Meet The 6 Edtech Startups That Have Seen Record Growth Amid COVID-19 Lockdown. *YourStory*. 16 June. https://yourstory.com/2020/06/edtech-startups-growth-coronavirus-byjus-unacademy-toppr-startups.

Media Partners Asia. 2020. Online Video Streaming Minutes in Southeast Asia Skyrocket after COVID-19 Impact According to New MPA Study. *MPA Views*. https://www.media-partners-asia.com/article.php?id=2325.

Mirsky, E.L., and H.A. Omar. 2015. Cyberbullying in Adolescents: The Prevalence of Mental Disorders and Suicidal Behavior. *Pediatrics Faculty Publications*. 170. Lexington: University of Kentucky.

Monteiro, J.A., and R. Teh. 2017. Provisions on Electronic Commerce in Regional Trade Agreements. *WTO Working Paper*. ERSD-2017-11. Geneva: WTO.

Morales, L. 2013. What is mLearning and How Can it be Used to Support Learning and Teaching in Econometrics? *Higher Learning Research Communications.* 3 (1). pp. 18–37.

Mordor Intelligence. 2020. *E-Commerce Plastic Packaging Market—Growth, Trends, Forecasts (2020–2025).* Hyderabad. https://www.mordorintelligence.com/industry-reports/e-commerce-plastic-packaging-market (accessed November 2020).

Moss, R.H., J. A. Edmonds, K. A. Hibbard, M. R. Manning, S. K. Rose, D. P. van Vuuren, T. R. Carter, S. Emori, M. Kainuma, T. Kram, G. A. Meehl, J. F. B. Mitchell, N. Nakicenovic, K. Riahi, S. J. Smith, R. J. Stouffer, A. M. Thomson, J. P. Weyant, and T. J. Wilbanks. 2010. The Next Generation of Scenarios for Climate Change Research and Assessment. *Nature.* 463 (7282). pp. 747–756.

Müller, M. 2020. Antitrust Regulation in Japan and South Korea—What Influence Does Chicago School of Antitrust Exercise on Competition Policy and Digital Economy? *SSRN Electronic Journal.*

Nachappa, M. N., and C. K. Lathesh. 2018. Optimized e-Transaction to Have a Secure Safe: E-Wallet. *International Journal of Innovative Science, Engineering and Technology.* 5 (9). pp. 15–24.

National Electrical Manufacturers Association (NEMA). 2020. Digital Imaging and Communications in Medicine (DICOM) Standard. https://www.dicomstandard.org/current.

Netflix Inc. 2020. *Quarterly Report Pursuant to Section 13 or 15(d) of the Securities Exchange Act of 1934, For the Quarterly Period Ended June 30, 2020.* Delaware. http://d18rn0p25nwr6d.cloudfront.net/CIK-0001065280/bcff7d52-7a7d-4e0c-8265-4b6860929fb1.pdf (accessed August 2020).

Organisation for Economic Co-operation and Development (OECD). 2008. Tax Effects on Foreign Direct Investment. *Policy Brief.* Paris: OECD.

———. 2011. *OECD Guide to Measuring the Information Society*. https://doi.org/10.1787/9789264113541-en.

———. 2015. Addressing the Tax Challenges of the Digital Economy, Action 1–2015 Final Report. *OECD/G20 Base Erosion and Profit Shifting Project.* https://doi.org/10.1787/9789264241046-en.

———. 2017. *International VAT/GST Guidelines.* https://doi.org/10.1787/9789264271401-en.

———. 2018a. *Online Platforms: A Practical Approach to Their Economic and Social Impacts.* Paris. As cited in Heerschap, N., N. Pouw, and C. Atmé. 2018. *Measuring Online Platforms in the Context of the Sharing Economy*. The Hague: Statistics Netherlands.

———. 2018b. *Rethinking Antitrust Tools for Multi-Sided Platforms.* Paris.

———. 2018c. Tax Challenges Arising from Digitalisation—Interim Report 2018: Inclusive Framework on BEPS. *OECD/G20 Base Erosion and Profit Shifting Project.* Paris.

———. 2019a. *An Introduction to Online Platforms and Their Role in the Digital Transformation.* Paris.

———. 2019b. *How's Life in the Digital Age?: Opportunities and Risks of the Digital Transformation for People's Well-being.* Paris.

———. 2019c. *Revenue Statistics 2019.* Paris.

———. 2019d. *The Role of Digital Platforms in the Collection of VAT/GST on Online Sales.* Paris.

———. 2019e. *OECD/G20 Inclusive Framework on BEPS Progress Report July 2018—May 2019.* Paris.

———. 2020a. *How's Life? 2020: Measuring Well-being.* Paris.

———. 2020b. *Revenue Statistics in Asian and Pacific Economies 2020.* Paris.

———. 2020c. *OECD Secretary-General Tax Report to G20 Finance Ministers and Central Bank Governors—October 2020*. Paris.

———. 2020d. Tax Challenges Arising from Digitalisation—Economic Impact Assessment: Inclusive Framework on BEPS. *OECD/G20 Base Erosion and Profit Shifting Project*. Paris.

———. International Tax Co-operation: Key Indicators and Outcomes Database. https://www.oecd.org/tax/international-tax-co-operation-map.htm (accessed July 2020).

Organisation for Economic Co-operation and Development, World Trade Organization, and International Monetary Fund (OECD, WTO, and IMF). 2019. *Handbook on Measuring Digital Trade*, Version 1. Paris, Geneva, and Washington, DC.

Oxford Internet Institute. The Online Labour Index Database. https://ilabour.oii.ox.ac.uk/online-labour-index/ (accessed May 2020).

Pagani, M. 2013. Digital Business Strategy and Value Creation: Framing the Dynamic Cycle of Control Points. *MIS Quarterly*. 37 (2). pp. 617–32.

Phocuswright. 2019. APAC: Big and getting bigger. *Research Insights*. https://www.phocuswright.com/Travel-Research/Research-Updates/2019/APAC-big-and-getting-bigger.

Popescu, E., and D. Ghita. 2013. Using Social Networking Services to Support Learning. In J.F. Wang and R. Lau, eds. *Advances in Web-Based Learning—ICWL (Lecture Notes in Computer Science)* 8167. Berlin and Heidelberg: Springer.

Prady, D. 2020. Reaching Households in Emerging and Developing Economies: Citizen ID, Socioeconomic Data, and Digital Delivery. *IMF Fiscal Affairs: Special Series on COVID-19*. Washington, DC: IMF.

ProPakistani. 2019. Cheetay News: Cheetay and IRA Committed to Grow and Improve the Restaurant Industry in Islamabad. 27 November. https://propakistani.pk/2019/11/27/cheetay-ira-committed-to-grow-improve-the-restaurant-industry-in-islamabad/.

PricewaterhouseCoopers (PwC). 2015. The Sharing Economy. *Consumer Intelligence Series*. https://www.pwc.fr/fr/assets/files/pdf/2015/05/pwc_etude_sharing_economy.pdf

———. 2017. GDPR Compliance Top Data Protection Priority for 92% of US Organizations in 2017. Press Release. https://www.pwc.com/us/en/press-releases/2017/pwc-gdpr-compliance-press-release.html.

———. 2019. *Global Top 100 Companies by Market Capitalisation*. https://www.pwc.com/gx/en/audit-services/publications/assets/global-top-100-companies-2019.pdf.

PYMNTS. 2020. *Gig Economy Tracker April 2020*. https://www.pymnts.com/tracker/gig-economy-tracker-april-2020/.

Rakuten Insight. 2020. Share of Respondents Who Changed their Online Purchase Behavior During the Coronavirus (COVID-19) Pandemic. 30 May. In *Statista—The Statistics Portal*. https://www.statista.com (accessed August 2020).

Ray, D. 2016. The Universal Basic Share. Ideas For India: For More Evidence-based Policy. September 29. http://www.ideasforindia.in/topics/poverty-inequality/the-universal-basic-share.html.

Ray, M., S. Redaelli, D. Rudich, and A. Wong. 2020. A Post–COVID-19 Commercial-Recovery Strategy for B2B Companies. https://www.mckinsey.com/industries/advanced-electronics/our-insights/a-post-covid-19-commercial-recovery-strategy-for-b2b-companies#.

Reimers, F., and A. Schleicher. 2020. *A Framework to Guide an Education Response to the COVID-19 Pandemic of 2020*. Paris: OECD

Riahi, K., D. P. van Vuuren, E. Kriegler, J. Edmonds B. C. O'Neill, S. Fujimori, N. Bauer, K. Calvin, R. Dellink, O. Fricko. W. Lutz A. Popp, J. C. Cuaresma, S. Kc, M. Leimbach, L. Jiang, T. Kram, S. Rao, J. Emmerling, K. Ebi, T. Hasegawa, P. Havlik, F. Humpenöder, L. A. Da Silva, S. Smith, E. Stehfest, V. Bosettii, J. Eom, D. Gernaat, T. Masui, J. Rogelj, J. Strefler, L. Drouet, V. Krey, G. Luderer, M. Harmsen, K. Takahashi, L. Baumstark, J. C. Doelman, M. Kainuma. Z. Klimont, G. Marangoni, H. Lotze-Campen, M. Obersteiner, A. Tabeau and M. Tavoniijo. 2017. The Shared Socioeconomic Pathways and their Energy, Land Use, and Greenhouse Gas Emissions Implications: An Overview. *Global Environmental Change*. 42. pp. 153–168.

Roth S., J. Parry, and M. Landry. 2015. Universal Health Coverage by Design: ICT-enabled Solutions are the Future of Equitable, Quality Health Care and Resilient Health Systems. *ADB Briefs No. 36*. Manila: ADB.

Rutkowski, M., A. Garcia Mora, G. Bull, B. Guermazi, and C. Grown. 2020. Responding to Crisis with Digital Payments for Social Protection: Short-Term Measures with Long-Term Benefits. *World Bank Blogs*. https://blogs.worldbank.org/voices/responding-crisis-digital-payments-social-protection-short-term-measures-long-term-benefits.

Samantaray, P.K. 2020. COVID Challenges to India Education System. *Article*. Uttar Pradesh: Digital Learning. https://digitallearning.eletsonline.com/2020/06/covid-challenges-to-india-education-system/.

Saraswathy, B. 2019. The Flipkart-Walmart Deal in India: A Look into Competition and Other Related Issues. *The Antitrust Bulletin*. 64 (1).

Scassa, T. 2017. Sharing Data in the Platform Economy: A Public Interest Argument for Access to Platform Data. *UBC Law Review*. 50 (4).

Schaal, D. 2016. Definitive Oral History of Online Travel. https://skift.com/history-of-online-travel/.

———. 2019. Travel Megatrends 2019: Online Travel Agencies Scurry for Salvation Beyond Hotels. https://skift.com/2019/02/11/travel-megatrends-2019-online-travel-agencies-scurry-for-salvation-beyond-hotels/.

Schmidt, F. 2017. *Digital Labour Markets in the Platform Economy: Mapping the Political Challenges of Crowd Work and Gig Work*. Bonn: Friedrich-Ebert Stiftung.

Sender, H. 2020. China's New Digital Currency Takes Aim at Alibaba and Tencent. *Financial Times*. 4 August. https://www.ft.com/content/fec06de9-ac43-4ab8-81f3-577638bd3c16.

Social Weather Stations (SWS). 2019. Monthly Internet User Penetration Rate in the Philippines from June 2006 to March 2019, By Gender. 4 June. In *Statista—The Statistics Portal*. https://www.statista.com/statistics/1104737/philippines-monthly-internet-user-penetration-rate-by-gender/ (accessed May 2020).

Soman, D. 2001. Effects of Payment Mechanism on Spending Behavior: The Role of Rehearsal and Immediacy of Payments. *Journal of Consumer Research*. 27. pp. 460-474.

Statista. 2020a. *Statista Digital Market Outlook*. https://www.statista.com/outlook/digital-markets.

———. 2020b. *Mobility Market Outlook*. https://www.statista.com/outlook/digital-markets.

Stephany, F., M. Dunn, S. Sawyer, and V. Lehdonvirta. 2020. Distancing Bonus or Downscaling Loss? The Changing Livelihood of US Online Workers in Times of COVID-19. *Journal of Economic and Social Geography—Tijdschrift voor economische en sociale geografie*. 111 (3) pp. 561–573.

STR, Inc. 2020. STR: Asia Pacific Hotel Performance for July 2020. https://str.com/press-release/str-asia-pacific-hotel-performance-july-2020.

Sukumaran, T. 2020. Food Delivery Workers Keep Malaysia Connected Amid Virus Lockdown. 31 March. https://www.scmp.com/week-asia/health-environment/article/3077719/coronavirus-delivery-workers-keep-malaysia-connected.

Sundararajan, A. 2016. *The Sharing Economy: The End of Employment and the Rise of Crowd-Based Capitalism*. Cambridge: MIT Press.

Tan, B., S.L. Pan., X. Lu, and L. Huang. 2015. The Role of IS Capabilities in the Development of Multi-Sided Platforms: The Digital Ecosystem Strategy of Alibaba.com. *Journal of the Association for Information Systems* 16. (4). pp. 248–280.

Terada-Hagiwara, A., K. Gonzales, and J. Wang. 2019. Taxation Challenges in a Digital Economy—The Case of the People's Republic of China. *ADB Briefs*. 108. Manila: ADB.

Terzi, N. 2011. The Impact of E-commerce on International Trade and Employment. *Procedia—Social and Behavioral Sciences*. 24. pp. 745-753.

Timmers, T., L. Janssen, J. Stohr, J. Murk, and M. Berrevoets. 2020. Using eHealth to Support COVID-19 Education, Self-Assessment, and Symptom Monitoring in the Netherlands: Observational Study. *JMIR Mhealth Uhealth*. 8 (6). e19822.

Tirole, J. 2020. Competition and the Industrial Challenge for the Digital Age. Background paper for the *IFS Deaton Review* on "Inequalities in the Twenty-First Century." https://www.tse-fr.eu/sites/default/files/TSE/documents/doc/by/tirole/competition_and_the_industrial_challenge_april_3_2020.pdf.

Tiwari, S., and P. Singh. 2011. Environmental Impacts of E-Commerce. *International Conference on Environment Science and Engineering (IPCBEE)*. 8. Singapore: IACSIT Press.

Trip.com Group. n.d. Corporate Profile. https://investors.trip.com/homeprofile.

Tripadvisor. 2020. About Tripadvisor. https://tripadvisor.mediaroom.com/US-about-us.

Tucker, C. 2019a. Digital Data, Platforms and the Usual [Antitrust] Suspects: Network Effects, Switching Costs, Essential Facility. *Review of Industrial Organization*. 54. pp. 683–694.

———. 2019b. Online Advertising and Antitrust: Network Effects, Switching Costs, and Data as an Essential Facility. *CPI Antitrust Chronicle, April*. https://www.analysisgroup.com/globalassets/content/news_and_events/news/2019-tucker-online-advertising-and-antitrust.pdf.

Turley, C., and S. Leung. 2019. We Need to Talk About Platforms: Ongoing Tax Challenges in China. *International Tax Review*. 3 December. https://www.internationaltaxreview.com/article/b1j8y77w953x5t/we-need-to-talk-about-platforms-ongoing-tax-challenges-in-china.

Turley, C., K. Ho, and S. Leung. 2018. A Sisyphean Task?—Tax Plays Catch Up with China's Rapid Digitalisation. *International Tax Review*. 10 December. https://www.internationaltaxreview.com/article/b1f7n29dkqsyz8/a-sisyphean-task-tax-plays-catch-up-with-chinas-rapid-digitalisation.

Tweneboah-Koduah, S., B. Endicott-Popovsky and A. Tsetse. 2014. Barriers to Government Cloud Adoption. *International Journal of Managing Information Technology*. 6 (3).

Uber. Company Info: Facts and Figures as of December 2018. https://www.uber.com/en-PH/newsroom/cUberompany-info/ (accessed August 2020).

Ulrichs, M. 2016. Informality, Women and Social Protection: Identifying Barriers to Provide Effective Coverage. *ODI Working Paper*. No. 435. London: ODI.

Una, G., R. Allen, S. Pattanayak, and G. Suc. 2020. Digital Solutions for Direct Cash Transfers in Emergencies. *IMF Fiscal Affairs: Special Series on COVID-19.* Washington, DC: IMF.

United Nations Conference on Trade and Development (UNCTAD). 2016. FDI Recovery is Unexpectedly Strong, But Lacks Productivity Impact. *Global Investment Trends Monitor.* No. 22. Geneva.

———. 2018. *Creative Economy Outlook: Trends in International Trade in Creative Industries Services.* Geneva.

———. 2019a. *Digital Economy Report 2019: Value Creation and Capture: Implications for Developing Countries.* New York: United Nations Publications.

———. 2019b. Competition Issues in the Digital Economy: Note by the UNCTAD Secretariat. Trade and Development Board Trade and Development Commission. Intergovernmental Group of Experts on Competition Law and Policy. Geneva.

———. 2020a. UNCTAD Estimates of Global E-commerce in 2018. *UNCTAD Technical Notes on ICT for Development.* No. 15. Geneva.

———. 2020b. Data Protection and Privacy Legislation Worldwide Database. Geneva. https://unctad.org/en/Pages/DTL/STI_and_ICTs/ICT4D-Legislation/eCom-Data-Protection-Laws.aspx (accessed July 2020).

United Nations Development Programme (UNDP). Human Development Report Database. http://hdr.undp.org/en/data (accessed October 2020).

United Nations Development Programme (UNDP) China. 2020a. *Universal Basic Income in China.* https://www.cn.undp.org/content/china/en/home/library/innovation-/universal-basic-income-in-china.html.

———. 2020b. Universal Basic Income–Findings from China and Implications for Responses in COVID-19. *Issue Brief.* Beijing.

United Nations Educational, Scientific and Cultural Organization (UNESCO). 2020a. UN Secretary-General Warns of Education Catastrophe, Pointing to UNESCO Estimate of 24 million Learners at Risk of Dropping Out. 6 August. Paris. https://en.unesco.org/news/secretary-general-warns-education-catastrophe-pointing-unesco-estimate-24-million-learners-0.

———. 2020b. How is China Ensuring Learning when Classes are Disrupted by Coronavirus? 19 February. Paris. https://en.unesco.org/news/how-china-ensuring-learning-when-classes-are-disrupted-coronavirus.

———. 2020c. *National Learning Platforms and Tools.* https://en.unesco.org/covid19/educationresponse/nationalresponses.

United Nations General Assembly (UNGA). 2013. *The Right to Privacy in the Digital Age.* Resolution Adopted by the General Assembly on 18 December 2013. Sixty-eighth Session, Agenda Item 69 (b). A/RES/68/167. https://undocs.org/pdf?symbol=en/a/res/68/167.

United Nations International Children's Fund (UNICEF). 2020. *What Have We Learnt? Findings from a Survey of Ministries of Education on National Responses to COVID-19.* https://data.unicef.org/resources/national-education-responses-to-covid19

United Nations International Children's Fund (UNICEF) Azerbaijan Country Office. 2020. *COVID-19 Situation Report* No. 9. Baku.

United Nations Statistics Division (UNSD). National Accounts Main Aggregates Database. https://unstats.un.org/unsd/snaama/ (accessed October 2020).

United Nations World Tourism Organisation (UNWTO). 2020. International Tourism Growth Continues to Outpace the Global Economy. 20 January. https://www.unwto.org/international-tourism-growth-continues-to-outpace-the-economy.

van Deursen, A., J. van Dijk, and O. Peters. 2011. Rethinking Internet Skills: The Contribution of Gender, Age, Education, Internet Experience, and Hours Online to Medium- and Content-related Internet skills. *Poetics*. 39 (2). pp. 125–144.

van Dijck, J., T. Poell and M. de Waal. 2016. *De Platform Samenleving: Strijd om Publieke Waarden in een Online Wereld. (The Platform Society: A Struggle for Public Values in an Online World)*. Amsterdam: Amsterdam University Press.

van Dijk, J. 2006. Digital Divide Research, Achievements and Shortcomings. *Poetics*. 34 (4-5). pp. 221–235.

van Gorp, N., and O. Batura. 2015. Challenges for Competition Policy in a Digitalised Economy. *Study for the European Parliament's Committee on Economic and Monetary Affairs*. IP/A/ECON/2014-12. PE 542.235.

van Staden, S., and J. Mbale. 2012. The Information Systems Interoperability Maturity Model (ISIMM): Towards Standardizing Technical Interoperability and Assessment within Government. *International Journal of Information Engineering and Electronic Business*. 4 (5). pp. 36–41.

van Vuuren, D., M. Kok, B. Girod, P. Lucas, and B. de Vries. 2012. Scenarios in Global Environmental Assessments: Key Characteristics and Lessons for Future Use. *Global Environmental Change*. 22 (4). pp. 884–895.

Vaughan, R., and R. Davario. 2016. *Assessing the Size and Presence of the Collaborative Economy in Europe*. European Commission. Luxembourg: Publications Office of the European Union.

Walandouw, P., A. Primaldhi, D. G. K. Wisana, and A. H. Nugroho. 2019. *GOJEK's Impact on the Indonesian Economy in 2018*. Lembaga Demografi Faculty of Economics and Business Universitas Indonesia in collaboration with GOJEK Indonesia. 21 March. https://ldfebui.org/wp-content/uploads/2019/11/Lembaga-Demografi-University-of-Indonesia-GOJEK%E2%80%99s-Impact-on-the-Indonesian-Economy-ENG-Nov-2019.pdf

Wang, C., and T. Quin. 2020. *How COVID-19 is Transforming Chinese Education*. New York: Oliver Wyman. https://www.oliverwyman.com/content/dam/oliver-wyman/v2/publications/2020/March/how-covid-19-is-transforming-chinese-education.pdf.

Webb D., R. Small, and E. Gregor. 2019. Universal Health Coverage for Sustainable Development. *Issue Brief*. New York: UNDP.

Wong J. 2020. Impact of COVID-19 Crisis on Inbound Air Travel to APAC. *Presentation*. Valencia: ForwardKeys.

World Bank. 2019. *World Development Report 2019: The Changing Nature of Work*. Washington, DC. http://documents1.worldbank.org/curated/en/816281518818814423/pdf/2019-WDR-Report.pdf.

———. 2020. *EdTech in Indonesia—Ready for Take-off?* Washington, DC.

———. The Global Findex Database. https://globalfindex.worldbank.org/ (accessed July 2020).

———. TCdata360. https://tcdata360.worldbank.org (accessed May 2020).

———. World Bank Education and COVID-19. https://www.worldbank.org/en/data/interactive/2020/03/24/world-bank-education-and-covid-19. (accessed July 2020).

——. World Development Indicators. https://databank.worldbank.org/source/worlddevelopment-indicators (accessed July 2020).

World Customs Organization (WCO). 2017. *WCO Study Report on Cross-Border E-Commerce*. Brussels.

——. 2018a. *Cross-Border E-Commerce Framework of Standards*. Brussels.

——. 2018b. *Immediate Release Guidelines (Guidelines for the Immediate Release of Consignments by Customs)*. Brussels.

——. n.d. Cross-Border e-Commerce. http://www.wcoomd.org/en/topics/facilitation/activities-and-programmes/ecommerce.aspx?p=1.

World Economic Forum (WEF). 2017a. *Digital Transformation Initiative: Unlocking B2B Platform Value*. White Paper. In collaboration with Accenture. Geneva.

——. 2017b. *Realizing Human Potential in the Fourth Industrial Revolution: An Agenda for Leaders to Shape the Future of Education, Gender and Work*. White Paper. Geneva.

——. 2018. *Eight Futures of Work: Scenarios and their Implications*. White Paper. In collaboration with The Boston Consulting Group. Geneva.

——. The Global Competitiveness Report 2017–2018 Database. https://reports.weforum.org/global-competitiveness-index-2017-2018/downloads/ (accessed August 2020).

World Health Organization (WHO). 2017. Reforming Health Service Delivery for UHC. Geneva.

World Trade Organization (WTO). 1994. Uruguay Round Agreement: General Agreement on Trade in Services. https://www.wto.org/english/docs_e/legal_e/26-gats_01_e.htm.

——. 1998a. *Work Programme on Electronic Commerce*. https://www.wto.org/english/tratop_e/ecom_e/wkprog_e.htm.

——. 1998b. *Declaration on Global Electronic Commerce*. Geneva.

World Travel and Tourism Council (WTTC). 2020a. Travel & Tourism will be Critical to Asia Pacific's Economic Recovery, says WTTC. *News Article*. 9 April. London. https://wttc.org/News-Article/Travel-and-Tourism-will-be-critical-to-Asia-Pacifics-economic-recovery-says-WTTC.

——. 2020b. *Asia Pacific Recovery Scenarios 2020 & Economic Impact from COVID-19*. London.

Wu, J. 2020. *Infographic: Coronavirus-Impacted Economy Brings New Opportunities to These Tech Sectors. KR Asia*. https://kr-asia.com/infographic-coronavirus-impacted-economy-brings-new-opportunities-to-these-tech-sectors.

Wu, P., M. Jackman, D. Abecassis, R. Morgan, H. de Villiers, and D. Clancy. 2016. *State of Connectivity 2015: A Report on Global Internet Access*. New Delhi: Internet.org.

Xu, Y., A. Ghose, and B. Xiao. 2019. *The Impact of Mobile Payment Channel on Consumer Consumption: Evidence from Alipay*. http://dx.doi.org/10.2139/ssrn.3270523.

Yamin, K. 2020. Mixed Response But Online Classes to Stay Post COVID-19. *University World News*. May 14. https://www.universityworldnews.com/post.php?story=20200514121749886.

Yandex.Taxi. n.d. About Company. https://taxi.yandex.com/company/.

Yean, T.S. 2018. The Digital Free Trade Zone (DFTZ): Putting Malaysia's SMEs onto the Digital Silk Road. *Perspective*. Issue 2018, No.17. Singapore: Institute of Southeast Asian Studies.

Yoshino, N. and F. Taghizadeh-Hesary. 2018. The Role of SMEs in Asia and Their Difficulties in Accessing Finance. *ADBI Working Paper*. No 911. Tokyo: Asian Development Bank Institute.

Zhang, W., Y. Wang, L. Yang, and C. Wang. 2020. Suspending Classes Without Stopping Learning: China's Education Emergency Management Policy in the COVID-19 Outbreak. *Journal of Risk and Financial Management.* 13 (3). pp. 55.

Zhang, Z. 2020. 46 New Cross-Border E-Commerce Zones Unveiled by China. *China Briefing.* 15 May. Dezan, Shira and Associates, Hong Kong [,China]. https://www.china-briefing.com/news/china-unveils-46-new-cross-border-e-commerce-zones-incentives-foreign-investors-faqs/.

Zheng, Y., M. Guerriero, E. V. Lopez, and P. Haverman. 2017. *Universal Basic Income: A Working Paper A Policy Option for China Beyond 2020?* Beijing: UNDP China.

Zoom. 2020. Zoom Q1FY21 Earnings—Prepared Remarks. https://investors.zoom.us/static-files/cb76de11-5579-4d09-94b0-a61344d410d6.

Annex 8a: Data and Indicators Needed for Measuring Platform Economy

To get an accurate, robust, and meaningful profile of platforms in a country, data have to be collected from the various actors of the platform ecosystem: the providers, users, and platforms themselves. That means three different groups should be respondents for surveys to measure the platform economy.

Dimension	Data	Indicators
General Information on Platforms	Business name, registered name, and address of owner of platform (including headquarters/main office and parent company, if any) URL(s) of the platform(s) Birth date or year that the platform(s) started operations Geographic reach of the platform's operations (i.e., local, national, global) Type of platform: (based on either general or specific functional base, or other typology) Whether platform is part of C2C economy (yes/no) Whether platform is part of sharing economy (broad and narrow definition) (yes/no) Product/s and service/s exchanged between providers and users: asset and service mix (economic activity group) Breakdown of providers by type (professional or nonprofessional) Advertisement parties involved	Number of platforms by region Proportion of platforms by age Number of platforms by geographic reach Proportion of platforms by type of platform Number of platforms in the C2C economy, in the sharing economy Number (and size) of platforms by economic activity group Number (and size) of platforms by type of provider Number (and size) of platforms by advertisement parties involved
Economic Information on Platforms	Business model: profit-orientation (profit, nonprofit, commission-based, advertisement-based or a combination); other sources of income from other services or add-ons; or more general: how the platform makes money Employment: number of persons directly employed by platform (employers + employees, e.g., those maintaining tech infrastructure, administration and marketing); Characteristics of employed: breakdown by sex, breakdown by educational attainment, hours worked Type of investors and investments made in the platform Tax payment (and type, i.e., income tax, VAT, etc.) Type of network effects: what drives the growth of the online platform (e.g., more participants, more transactions, more content, etc.) Who sets the prices and circumstances of logistics (e.g., delivery of good or service) Turnover, including source/s of the turnover Value added: i.e., turnover minus costs for intermediate goods and services Investments made in the platform, including the type of partners Type of providers: noncommercial and commercial	Number (and size) of platforms by business model Number of employed (by sex) by type of platform (or economic group) Number of employed by educational attainment and by type of platform (or economic group) Hours worked by type of platform (or economic group) Number of platforms by type of investors (or investments made) Percentage of platforms that paid taxes Number of platforms by type of network effects Number of platforms by mechanism for setting prices and logistics Average turnover, by source and by type of platform Average value added, by type of platform (or economic activity group) Average investments in platform, by type of platform (or economic activity group) Number of platforms by type of providers

continued on next page

Appendix 8a continued

Dimension	Data	Indicators
Social Information on Platforms	Verifying providers and their offers and checking for illegal content Verifying clients Advertisement parties involved Collection of data of providers and clients and the uses of these data (e.g., algorithms and selling of data)	Number of platforms by type of verification process for providers Percentage of platforms with verification process for clients by type of platform (or economic activity group) Percentage of platforms with advertisement parties involved by type of platform (or economic activity group) Number of platforms by type of platform and by type of data collection activities on platform users Number of platforms by type of platform and by data collection use
Basic Information on Platform Providers	Name of individual/household respondent or business Background characteristics: location; year that the provider(s) started offering good or service in platform/s; individual/household or business Reasons to use a platform Type of goods or services offered (relative to some classification system); part of sharing economy (i.e., offering use of idle asset, or not) Number of transactions per year (including turnover)	Total number of unique providers by type (individual/household vs. business) Total number of unique individual providers (active or passive) by location (urban/rural, or region) Growth rates in number of unique providers (active or passive) Total number of providers by reasons to use a platform Total number of providers by type of goods or services offered Percentage of providers in sharing economy, by location
Economic Information on Platform Providers	Number of transactions per year in past 2 years Average prices per transaction Average transaction costs made to use the platform (commission and/or access) Investments and value added Tax payment International trade/cross-border transactions (percentage compared with all transactions) Main source or supplementary source of income	Total number of transactions per year by location Growth/decline of transactions per year, including total turnover; estimate of total turnover: average price x number of transactions per year (minus transaction costs) Total investments and value added Percentage of providers paying tax Share of international trade/cross-border transactions (in percentage) to total transactions Percentage of providers whose income from platforms is main source (or supplementary source) of income
Social Information on Platform Providers	If provider has working relationship to the platform (relates mostly to indirect employment): hours worked and earnings (does this constitute the main income?). Account should be taken of the fact that people can work for or be associated to more than one online platform Total income Social security Legal contracts Training possibilities	Percentage of providers with working relationship to the platform Average hours worked, by sex and location Average earnings, by sex and location (for those with platform incomes constituting the main source of income, and for others) Average income by sex and location Percentage of providers with social security Percentage of providers with legal contract Percentage of providers with training possibilities

continued on next page

Appendix 8a continued

Dimension	Data	Indicators
Basic Information on Platform Clients	Name of platform client Background characteristics: location; year that the client(s) started purchasing good or service in platform/s; individual-household or business; number of visits to a platform per year; type of goods or services bought or shared, including prices; reasons to use platform(s) Number of visits to an online platform per year (or month or week) Number of transactions per year (money spent, including the commission to the platform) Type of goods or services bought or shared Reasons to use online platform(s) Trust in platforms (e.g., role of reviews and rating systems) International trade/cross-border transactions (percentage compared with all transactions)	Total number of unique clients by type (individual/ household vs. businesses) Total number of unique clients by sex and location (and growth or decline) Average number of visits to a platform per year (or month or week) Total number of clients by type of goods or services bought or shared Average prices for major good or service bought or shared Total number of clients by reason for using platform(s) Average share of cross-border transactions to total transactions
Economic Information on Platform Clients	Average number of transactions per year (or month or week) Average expenditures on platforms, including the commission to the platform) International trade/cross-border transactions (to total transactions) in platform	Number of transactions per year Growth/decline of transactions per year Average expenditures on platforms by type of platforms (including the commission to the platform) Share of cross-border transactions to total transactions in platform
Social Information on Platform Clients	Trust in platforms (e.g., role of reviews and rating systems) Number of complaints in platform (and of which, how much got sufficiently resolved)	Average trust rating of platforms by type of platform Average number of complaints in platform(s) by type of platform

C2C = customer-to-customer, ICT = information and communication technology, VAT = value-added tax.

The data for the indicators mentioned above can be collected in different ways. An important first step is to have a target population or list frame of platforms. Such a frame is likely not available in many countries except perhaps those attempting to measure the platform economy, specifically the sharing economy. National statistical offices (NSOs) could start with the most "important" platforms, in terms of public visibility, and so limit the coverage of examination.

Some data collection methods are better for particular actors of the platform ecosystem. When it concerns cross-border digital trade, international cooperation is necessary. Possible options of data collection are as follows:

1. Setting up a new dedicated survey for measuring the platform economy. Survey questionnaires can be sent to providers and users, but especially to the platforms. Households are no longer just consumers, but also producers; the nature and extent of their productive activities including direct imports of goods and services need to be properly recorded in national accounts. NSOs need to work with platforms to obtain aggregate information on productive activities of households, and cross-border flows. It is likely, however, that most platforms will not be very willing to share information, thus it could be considered to legally mandate data sharing to NSOs, even when the headquarters of a platform company is outside the country (Scassa 2017).
2. Alternatively, NSOs could add a module of questions for measuring the platform economy to existing surveys, such as the Labor Force Survey, household and business surveys of ICT usage. These surveys can target the providers and users of platforms (but not the platforms themselves).
3. The available digital footprints on platforms could be web-scraped. NSOs can use web scraping and application programming interfaces to collect some desired information from the websites of platforms (such as site visits of users, and possibly financial accounts). If the list of platforms in not available, an initial list could be created on the basis of a web search of the whole internet (focusing on a country domain) with a bot. The bot, with the aid of machine learning, should be able to distinguish "normal" websites from websites with platforms on the basis of available data from the web search.

Source: Adopted from Heerschap, Pouw, and Atmé (2018).

Annex 8b: Key Technologies Critical to Growth of Digital Platforms and the Digital Economy

Technology	Description
Semiconductor Technologies	**Integrated Circuits** represent the fundamental basis of most technology improvements, as they are the main technology underpinning microprocessors, memory, communications, sensors, and imaging.
Infrastructure Technologies	**Connectivity:** In 2019, internet connectivity reached 54% of the global population. Universal connectivity is a key requirement for continued growth of the digital economy.
	Devices: Currently the smartphone is the dominant device globally, and wearables (smartwatches, glasses, headphones, etc.) are positioned to be the next trend.
	Imaging: Imaging technologies, like smartphone cameras, are a key technology that is enabling rapid advances in the use of photography and video.
	Cloud Computing: Cloud technology represents on-demand computing infrastructure that is more scalable and cost-effective than traditional computing infrastructure, enabling new services and tech start-ups.
Transactional Technologies	**Digital Payments:** Secure, low-cost digital payment technologies are critical in enabling digital commerce. Digital payments via mobile money accounts, online banking or smartphone app-based platforms offer a more secure payment model with the ability to enable participation in the digital economy.
	Digital Identity: Secure, low-cost identity services are critical in enabling access to services, like health, education, and bank accounts, and citizenship rights like the ability to vote or receive social benefits. Digital technologies, leveraging biometrics like fingerprinting, facial recognition, and iris scanning, are providing an opportunity to build dependable and low-cost ID systems that can scale to national levels.
	Cybersecurity and Privacy: Cybersecurity is crucial for keeping company and customer data safe, enabling secure transactions and management of devices. Cybersecurity concepts are used to protect against unauthorized access to data centers and other computerized systems.
Integrating Technologies	**Artificial Intelligence (AI):** Artificial intelligence is a set of algorithms that aim to imitate the human's cognitive functions to tackle complex real-world problems. As a subfield of AI, machine learning algorithms automatically improve in solving a problem through experience, also called training. Recent advances in AI are due to advances in computational power and the availability of big data. Examples include image recognition, language translation, medical diagnosis, etc.
	Robotics/Drones: The combination of AI, communications, processing and sensor technologies enable autonomous operations of robots, vehicles and drones, leading to new services. Robotic technology has been used extensively in manufacturing for several decades, and the recent advances in computing have enabled new, low-cost applications of robotics into new areas. Self-driving cars employ a range of technologies from machine vision systems powered by digital cameras, radar, and lidar to advanced computing platforms for navigation running AI solutions. Drones offer low-cost flight platforms for mapping and monitoring of physical infrastructure. Drones can also be powered by autonomous navigation systems to perform more complex tasks like package delivery or search and rescue missions.
	Internet of Things (IoT): IoT involves connecting devices or sensors directly to the internet over wireless networks without the need to connect through a computer or mobile phone; they can be remotely monitored and controlled. In commercial settings, IoT devices are typically sensors that monitor conditions like temperature and humidity, or devices that track movement or may even include cameras to track imagery. In household settings, IoT devices are often used for "smart home" solutions to control lighting, thermostats, cameras, and security systems.
	Earth Observation: Satellite technology, combined with communications and sensors, enable low-cost imagery covering the entire globe for services such as for land management, agriculture, environment, etc.
	Geospatial Information Services (GIS): GIS systems play a critical role in the platform economy due to their ability to accurately map and measure physical locations, allowing more sophisticated tracking and analysis of land, infrastructure, resources, and human activity. This has opened up new opportunities for designing and managing transportation systems.
Future Technologies	**Genetics:** Genetic technologies, including gene sequencing and gene editing, are among of the most promising future technologies. Gene sequencing has enabled the study of genetic origins associated with many human diseases as well as the study of evolution. Gene editing, using the recently discovered CRISPR system, is rapidly developing into new solutions for disease treatment and agricultural improvement.
	Quantum Computing: Quantum technologies have the potential to outpace digital computing and to enable unbreakable encryption systems. Although current technologies are mainly limited to research laboratories, quantum is positioned as a breakthrough disruptive technology.

continued on next page

Appendix 8b continued

Technology	Description
	Artificial General Intelligence (AGI): Although highly controversial, there is a potential for the emergence of general intelligence that could perform traditional human activities like writing, research, art, etc. as AI becomes more powerful, driven by larger data sets, more computing resources, and new models.
	Human-Computer Interfaces: Current digital technologies are limited by the ability of people to speak or type into their devices. New interface technologies are being envisioned that would enable humans to interact with digital solutions more directly. Direct neural interfaces, for example, are being developed for people with disabilities who are unable to move their hands or speak.

AGI = Artificial General Intelligence, AI = Artificial Intelligence, GIS = Geospatial Information Services, IoT = Internet of Things.

Source: Abell (2020).

Annex 8c: Trade and Employment Impact from Greater Usage of Digital Inputs, 2021–2025

Trade Impact from Greater Usage of Digital Inputs, 2021–2025

Economy	Gains from Same Year Baselines ($ billion)						
	2021	2022	2023	2024	2025	Total	Average
World	**771.8**	**1,546.4**	**2,341.4**	**3,166.0**	**4,025.1**	**11,850.7**	**2,370.1**
Asia	**342.9**	**678.3**	**1,013.7**	**1,352.8**	**1,697.2**	**5,084.9**	**1,017.0**
Australia and New Zealand	10.5	19.1	26.9	34.1	41.0	131.5	26.3
Central Asia	7.1	14.7	23.0	31.8	41.2	117.7	23.5
East Asia ex-PRC and Japan	41.0	81.4	122.1	163.8	206.7	614.9	123.0
PRC	104.4	188.9	256.0	307.1	343.1	1,199.5	239.9
Japan	61.1	131.6	212.4	304.4	408.3	1,117.8	223.6
Southeast Asia	76.7	157.6	243.4	334.4	430.8	1,242.9	248.6
South Asia	35.2	74.2	116.4	161.3	208.5	595.5	119.1
Pacific	7.0	10.8	13.6	15.9	17.8	65.1	13.0
G2	**269.8**	**524.6**	**773.9**	**1,023.1**	**1,275.4**	**3,866.8**	**773.4**
United States	37.3	71.8	105.0	138.0	171.0	523.1	104.6
EU-28	232.5	452.8	668.9	885.1	1,104.4	3,343.7	668.7
Rest of the World	**159.1**	**343.6**	**553.8**	**790.1**	**1,052.5**	**2,899.0**	**579.8**
	Gains as Proportion of 2020 Baseline Trade (%)						
Economy	**2021**	**2022**	**2023**	**2024**	**2025**	**Total**	**Average**
World	**1.8**	**3.6**	**5.4**	**7.3**	**9.3**	**27.5**	**5.5**
Asia	**2.3**	**4.6**	**6.8**	**9.1**	**11.4**	**34.2**	**6.8**
Australia and New Zealand	1.6	2.9	4.1	5.2	6.2	20.0	4.0
Central Asia	2.3	4.8	7.5	10.4	13.5	38.6	7.7
East Asia ex-PRC and Japan	1.7	3.3	5.0	6.7	8.5	25.1	5.0
PRC	2.0	3.6	4.9	5.8	6.5	22.8	4.6
Japan	3.8	8.1	13.1	18.7	25.1	68.8	13.8
Southeast Asia	2.5	5.1	7.9	10.8	13.9	40.2	8.0
South Asia	2.5	5.4	8.4	11.7	15.1	43.1	8.6
Pacific	8.3	12.9	16.3	19.0	21.3	77.8	15.6
G2	**1.5**	**2.9**	**4.3**	**5.6**	**7.0**	**21.2**	**4.2**
United States	0.8	1.5	2.2	2.9	3.5	10.8	2.2
EU-28	1.7	3.4	5.0	6.6	8.3	25.0	5.0
Rest of the World	**1.6**	**3.4**	**5.5**	**7.9**	**10.5**	**28.8**	**5.8**

EU = European Union, G2 = Group of 2, PRC = People's Republic of China.

Notes: The calculations are based on the Global Trade Analysis Project (GTAP) database. The Pacific subregion includes non-ADB member economies. Asia and the Pacific includes economies that are non-ADB members due to the aggregation of the Pacific subregion in GTAP.

Source: Narayanan and Villafuerte (2020).

Employment Impact from Greater Usage of Digital Inputs, 2021–2025

Economy	2021	2022	2023	2024	2025	Total	Average
	Gains from Same Year Baselines (million)						
World	**52.1**	**98.8**	**142.0**	**182.9**	**222.0**	**697.8**	**139.6**
Asia	**25.8**	**47.9**	**67.5**	**85.1**	**101.2**	**327.5**	**65.5**
Australia and New Zealand	0.2	0.4	0.6	0.8	0.9	2.9	0.6
Central Asia	0.8	1.6	2.4	3.1	3.8	11.7	2.3
East Asia ex-PRC and Japan	0.6	1.1	1.5	1.9	2.3	7.4	1.5
PRC	7.5	12.6	15.8	17.6	18.2	71.7	14.3
Japan	1.3	2.5	3.7	4.8	6.0	18.3	3.7
Southeast Asia	6.5	12.5	18.2	23.7	29.0	89.9	18.0
South Asia	8.3	16.4	24.3	32.1	39.8	120.9	24.2
Pacific	0.5	0.8	1.0	1.1	1.2	4.7	0.9
G2	**4.7**	**8.5**	**11.9**	**14.9**	**17.7**	**57.8**	**11.6**
United States	1.1	1.9	2.7	3.3	3.8	12.8	2.6
EU-28	3.6	6.6	9.3	11.7	13.9	45.0	9.0
Rest of the World	**21.6**	**42.3**	**62.6**	**82.8**	**103.2**	**312.5**	**62.5**
	Gains as Proportion of 2020 Baseline Employment, %						
Economy	2021	2022	2023	2024	2025	Total	Average
World	**1.9**	**3.6**	**5.1**	**6.6**	**8.0**	**25.2**	**5.0**
Asia	**1.5**	**2.9**	**4.0**	**5.1**	**6.0**	**19.5**	**3.9**
Australia and New Zealand	3.0	5.3	7.2	8.9	10.5	34.9	7.0
Central Asia	2.5	4.9	7.2	9.4	11.5	35.5	7.1
East Asia ex-PRC and Japan	2.2	4.0	5.7	7.1	8.4	27.5	5.5
PRC	1.1	1.9	2.4	2.7	2.7	10.8	2.2
Japan	2.9	5.6	8.2	10.7	13.2	40.5	8.1
Southeast Asia	2.2	4.3	6.3	8.1	10.0	30.9	6.2
South Asia	1.4	2.7	4.0	5.3	6.5	19.9	4.0
Pacific	14.4	22.3	27.7	31.6	34.6	130.6	26.1
G2	**2.0**	**3.7**	**5.1**	**6.4**	**7.6**	**24.9**	**5.0**
United States	1.2	2.2	3.0	3.7	4.4	14.6	2.9
EU-28	2.5	4.6	6.4	8.0	9.6	31.1	6.2
Rest of the World	**2.5**	**5.0**	**7.3**	**9.7**	**12.1**	**36.6**	**7.3**

EU = European Union, G2 = Group of 2, PRC = People's Republic of China.

Notes: The calculations are based on the Global Trade Analysis Project (GTAP) database. The Pacific subregion includes non-ADB member economies. Asia and the Pacific includes economies that are non-ADB members due to the aggregation of the Pacific subregion in GTAP.

Source: Narayanan and Villafuerte (2020).

Change in Digital Sector Size, 2021–2025

Economy	Gains from Same Year Baselines ($ billion) 2021	2022	2023	2024	2025	Total	Average
World	**205.8**	**411.5**	**617.3**	**823.1**	**1,028.9**	**3,086.6**	**617.3**
Asia	**61.3**	**122.6**	**183.8**	**245.1**	**306.4**	**919.1**	**183.8**
Australia and New Zealand	4.6	9.2	13.8	18.4	23.0	69.1	13.8
Central Asia	0.6	1.1	1.7	2.2	2.8	8.3	1.7
East Asia ex-PRC and Japan	5.2	10.3	15.5	20.7	25.9	77.6	15.5
PRC	21.2	42.4	63.5	84.7	105.9	317.6	63.5
Japan	17.3	34.6	51.9	69.2	86.5	259.5	51.9
Southeast Asia	6.7	13.4	20.1	26.8	33.5	100.4	20.1
South Asia	4.8	9.7	14.5	19.3	24.2	72.5	14.5
Pacific	0.9	1.9	2.8	3.8	4.7	14.1	2.8
G2	**104.2**	**208.5**	**312.7**	**417.0**	**521.2**	**1,563.7**	**312.7**
United States	39.8	79.6	119.3	159.1	198.9	596.7	119.3
EU-28	64.5	128.9	193.4	257.9	322.3	967.0	193.4
Rest of the World	**40.3**	**80.5**	**120.8**	**161.0**	**201.3**	**603.8**	**120.8**
Economy	**Gains as Proportion of 2020 Baseline Trade (%) 2021**	**2022**	**2023**	**2024**	**2025**	**Total**	**Average**
World	**4.3**	**8.5**	**12.8**	**17.0**	**21.3**	**63.8**	**12.8**
Asia	**4.4**	**8.8**	**13.1**	**17.5**	**21.9**	**65.7**	**13.1**
Australia and New Zealand	4.1	8.1	12.2	16.3	20.4	61.1	12.2
Central Asia	5.3	10.5	15.8	21.0	26.3	78.8	15.8
East Asia ex-PRC and Japan	3.9	7.7	11.6	15.5	19.3	57.9	11.6
PRC	5.2	10.5	15.7	21.0	26.2	78.6	15.7
Japan	3.6	7.1	10.7	14.3	17.8	53.5	10.7
Southeast Asia	4.7	9.3	14.0	18.6	23.3	69.9	14.0
South Asia	5.3	10.5	15.8	21.1	26.3	79.0	15.8
Pacific	5.5	11.1	16.6	22.1	27.7	83.0	16.6
G2	**4.1**	**8.2**	**12.2**	**16.3**	**20.4**	**61.2**	**12.2**
United States	4.3	8.6	12.8	17.1	21.4	64.2	12.8
EU-28	4.0	7.9	11.9	15.9	19.8	59.4	11.9
Rest of the World	**4.5**	**9.1**	**13.6**	**18.2**	**22.7**	**68.2**	**13.6**

EU = European Union, G2 = Group of 2, PRC = People's Republic of China.

Notes: The calculations are based on the Global Trade Analysis Project (GTAP) database. The Pacific subregion includes non-ADB member economies. Asia and the Pacific includes economies that are non-ADB members due to the aggregation of the Pacific subregion in GTAP.

Source: Narayanan and Villafuerte (2020).

Investment Requirement, 2021–2025

Economy	2021	2022	2023	2024	2025	Total	Average
	Markup from Same Year Baselines ($ billion)						
World	**231.1**	**464.2**	**699.3**	**936.6**	**1,175.8**	**3,507.0**	**701.4**
Asia	**59.3**	**119.7**	**181.0**	**243.4**	**306.7**	**910.2**	**182.0**
Australia and New Zealand	3.0	6.1	9.3	12.5	15.7	46.6	9.3
Central Asia	0.5	1.1	1.7	2.3	2.9	8.5	1.7
East Asia ex-PRC and Japan	4.1	8.3	12.5	16.8	21.1	63.0	12.6
PRC	6.6	13.2	19.9	26.7	33.5	99.9	20.0
Japan	36.1	72.8	110.1	148.0	186.5	553.4	110.7
Southeast Asia	5.3	10.8	16.4	22.2	28.0	82.8	16.6
South Asia	2.9	5.9	9.0	12.2	15.4	45.4	9.1
Pacific	0.7	1.4	2.1	2.8	3.5	10.6	2.1
G2	**119.5**	**239.2**	**359.2**	**479.4**	**599.8**	**1,797.0**	**359.4**
United States	5.0	10.0	15.1	20.1	25.2	75.5	15.1
EU-28	114.5	229.2	344.1	459.2	574.6	1,721.6	344.3
Rest of the World	**52.2**	**105.3**	**159.1**	**213.8**	**269.4**	**799.8**	**160.0**
	Markup as Proportion of 2020 Baseline Investment (%)						
Economy	2021	2022	2023	2024	2025	Total	Average
World	**18.1**	**36.4**	**54.8**	**73.4**	**92.2**	**275.0**	**55.0**
Asia	**14.9**	**30.0**	**45.4**	**61.0**	**76.9**	**228.2**	**45.6**
Australia and New Zealand	14.7	29.7	44.9	60.3	75.9	225.6	45.1
Central Asia	14.3	29.2	44.7	60.7	77.5	226.3	45.3
East Asia ex-PRC and Japan	12.9	26.0	39.2	52.5	66.0	196.6	39.3
PRC	6.0	12.0	18.1	24.2	30.4	90.8	18.2
Japan	23.9	48.2	72.9	98.0	123.4	366.4	73.3
Southeast Asia	10.2	20.7	31.5	42.5	53.8	158.7	31.7
South Asia	10.6	21.5	32.7	44.3	56.1	165.3	33.1
Pacific	44.1	88.5	133.2	178.2	223.5	667.5	133.5
G2	**20.8**	**41.6**	**62.4**	**83.3**	**104.3**	**312.4**	**62.5**
United States	4.7	9.4	14.1	18.8	23.5	70.4	14.1
EU-28	24.5	49.0	73.5	98.1	122.8	367.9	73.6
Rest of the World	**17.3**	**34.9**	**52.8**	**71.0**	**89.4**	**265.5**	**53.1**

EU-28 = European Union, G2 = Group of 2, PRC = People's Republic of China.

Note: The calculations are based on the Global Trade Analysis Project (GTAP) database. Southeast Asia includes Timor-Leste. The Pacific subregion includes non-ADB member economies. Asia and the Pacific includes economies that are non-ADB members due to the aggregation of the Pacific subregion in GTAP.

Source: Narayanan and Villafuerte (2020).

Annex 8d: Public and Private Platforms for e-Learning

	National Platforms	Private Platforms
Azerbaijan	• E-resurs – free learning resources • Elektron Dərslik Portalı – Electronic Textbook Portal • Video.edu.az – Video lessons • Virtual School http://mesafedenmekteb.edu.az[a] • Over 1 million students registered for virtual school[b] (out of 2 million total students)[c] • Three-fourths (75%) of schoolchildren supported by distance learning[d]	
People's Republic of China	• National Cloud-Platform for Educational Resources and Public Service • EduCloud • Empower Learning[e]	• ClassIn – Daily active users, 10 times higher than previous year • Zhiboyun – customer numbers have increased 8–10 times • Baijiayun – customer leads have increased by a factor of 15–20 times[f] • Xueersi users have increased 2680%[g]
Georgia	• EL.GE – resources based on national curriculum • Email.mes – instructive site on COVID-19 • Feedc Edu – national online learning platform • Teleskola – TV program[h]	
India	• MHRD – collection of platforms by the Ministry of Human Resource Development • National Digital Library of India[i] • Dishka – e-learning content • e-Pathshala – app by the National Council of Educational Research and Training in multiple languages • National Repository of Open Educational Resources • Swayam – platform for higher education • Swayam Prabha – TV channels broadcasting educational programming • e-PG Pathshala – platform for postgraduate students[j]	• "Ed-tech firms have witnessed 10-fold rise in registration for trial or free coaching"[k] • BYJUs have witnessed a 200% increase in students using its "Think and Learn app"[l] • BYJU – 7.5 million new users since the company started offering free content. Time spent on the app increased from 70 minutes pre-lockdown to 91 minutes during lockdown. Despite offering free content, April was the company's most profitable month to date. • "Toppr has seen a 100 percent growth in paid users' on a monthly basis, with free user engagement witnessing a 100 percent spike."[m] • White Hat Jr. – "The company has been growing at 40% MoM growth over the past 12 months and with the current lockdown, MoM growth has accelerated to 100 percent."[n]
Indonesia	• Rumah Belajar – distance learning resources • SPADA – e-learning for tertiary[o]	• More than 200% growth in EdTech platforms' active users and downloads in March 2020[p]
Viet Nam	• Elearning – Ministry of Education distance learning • National and local TV channels • Taphuan – additional resources from Ministry of Education[q]	• VNPT E-Learning users increased by 4 times • ViettelStudy gained 41 million visits in a month[r]

COVID-19 = coronavirus disease.

[a] UNESCO. 2020c. *National Learning Platforms and Tools.* 7 July. https://en.unesco.org/covid19/educationresponse/nationalresponses.

[b] CEE Multi-Country News Center. 2020. Azerbaijan: How One Ministry Found the Right Strategy, Resources, and Technology to Quickly Create Online Classrooms. *Microsoft.* 9 July. https://news.microsoft.com/en-cee/2020/07/09/azerbaijan-how-one-ministry-found-the-right-strategy-resources-and-technology-to-quickly-create-onlineclassrooms/.

[c] World Bank. World Bank Education and COVID-19. https://www.worldbank.org/en/data/interactive/2020/03/24/world-bank-education-and-covid-19 (accessed July 2020).

[d] UNICEF Azerbaijan Country Office. 2020. *COVID-19 Situation Report* No. 9. Baku.

[e] UNESCO. 2020c. *National Learning Platforms and Tools.* 7 July. https://en.unesco.org/covid19/educationresponse/nationalresponses.

[f] Wang, C., and T. Quin. 2020. *How COVID-19 is Transforming Chinese Education.* New York: Oliver Wyman. https://www.oliverwyman.com/content/dam/oliver-wyman/v2/publications/2020/March/how-covid-19-is-transforming-chinese-education.pdf.

[g] Wu, J. 2020. *Infographic: Coronavirus-Impacted Economy Brings New Opportunities to These Tech Sectors. KR Asia.* https://kr-asia.com/infographic-coronavirus-impacted-economy-brings-new-opportunities-to-these-tech-sectors.

[h] UNESCO. 2020c. *National Learning Platforms and Tools.* 7 July. https://en.unesco.org/covid19/educationresponse/nationalresponses.

[i] Ibid.

[j] Jena, P. K. 2020. Impact of COVID-19 on Education in India. *International Journal of Current Research.* 12(7). pp. 12582–12586.

[k] Samantaray, P. K. 2020. COVID Challenges to India Education System. *Article.* Uttar Pradesh: Digital Learning. https://digitallearning.eletsonline.com/2020/06/covid-challenges-to-india-education-system/.

[l] Bindra, V. 2020. With COVID 19 Providing a Major Disruption, The Future of EdTech Platforms Looks Promising. *Express Computer.* 2 July. https://www.expresscomputer.in/industries/education/with-covid-19-providing-a-major-disruption-the-future-of-edtech-platforms-looks-promising/59609/.

[m] Medhi, T. 2020. Meet The 6 Edtech Startups That Have Seen Record Growth Amid COVID-19 Lockdown. *YourStory.* 16 June. https://yourstory.com/2020/06/edtech-startups-growth-coronavirus-byjus-unacademy-toppr-startups.

[n] *Express Computer.* 2020. EdTech Startup WhiteHat Jr. Ramps Up Hiring to Meet Massive Surge in Student Enrollment. 8 May. https://www.expresscomputer.in/news/edtech-startup-whitehat-jr-ramps-up-hiring-to-meet-massive-surge-in-student-enrolment/55276/.

[o] UNESCO. 2020c. *National Learning Platforms and Tools.* 7 July. https://en.unesco.org/covid19/educationresponse/nationalresponses

[p] World Bank 2020. *EdTech in Indonesia—Ready for Take-off?* Washington, DC.

[q] UNESCO. 2020c. *National Learning Platforms and Tools.* 7 July. https://en.unesco.org/covid19/educationresponse/nationalresponses.

[r] Ministry of Information and Communications of the Socialist Republic of Vietnam. 2020. Online Applications Blooming in Vietnam during Covid-19 Outbreak. 18 March. https://english.mic.gov.vn/Pages/TinTuc/140855/Online-applications-blooming-in-Vietnam-during-Covid-19-outbreak.html.

Annex 8e: Data Protection Measures, Select Asian Countries

Jurisdiction and Data Protection Regulation	Consent	White Lists, Adequacy Findings
Australia Privacy Act (1988), Australian Privacy Principle (APP) 8.1 Accountability Principle: Before an entity discloses personal information to an overseas recipient, the entity must "take such steps as are reasonable in the circumstances to ensure that the overseas recipient does not breach the APPs (other than APP 1) in relation to that information." S16C: If an entity discloses personal information about an individual to an overseas recipient and APP 8.1 applies to the disclosure of the information, the entity is accountable for any acts or practices of the overseas recipient that would breach the APPs in relation to the information.	Yes (optional) The accountability principle in APP 8.1 does not apply where the individual consents to the cross-border disclosure after the entity informs the individual that APP 8.1 will no longer apply (APP Guidelines at para. 8.27 ff.). Consent means "express consent or implied consent" (Privacy Act s 6[1]).	No.
Indonesia Law No. 11 of 2008 on Electronic Information and Transactions (EIT Law), Art 26 Regulation No. 20 of 2016 of the Ministry of Communication and Information (MCI 20/2016), Arts 21 and 22 Principle: Electronic System Providers (ESPs) may transfer data only with the individual's consent; and following "coordination with the Ministry" (in the current case the Ministry of Communication and Information, or "Kominfo"). The coordination requirement seems closer to a notification requirement than to a prior authorization but sometimes regulatory scrutiny is applied.[a]	Yes (required): The written consent of the "data owner" is required unless specific regulations apply (MCI 20/2016, Art 21[1]). Express opt-in is not explicitly required by Art 21(1) but is derived from MCI 20/2016, Art 1(4).	Uncertain: It is not known if the ministry would assess the level of protection in certain countries (e.g., countries with data protection laws) in the context of the coordination provided in MCI 20/2016 Art 22.
Malaysia Personal Data Protection Act (PDPA) 2010: Data transfers outside Malaysia may in principle take place only to places specified by the Minister where there is in force any law which is substantially similar to, or that serves the same purposes as the PDPA or which ensures an adequate level of protection which is at least equivalent to the level of protection afforded by PDPA.	Yes (optional): Consent may operate as an exception to the requirement that transfers may take place only to places specified by the Minister (s 129[2][a]).	Yes: The minister, upon the recommendation of the commissioner, may specify any place outside Malaysia to where data may freely flow.
New Zealand Privacy Act 1993: International transfers are permitted, as long as the legal requirements in the privacy principles and appropriate conditions for privacy protection are observed. However, in exceptional circumstances the Privacy Commissioner may prohibit a transfer to another State when: - The personal information has been received from another State and will be transferred to a third State where it will not be subject to a law providing comparable safeguards to the Privacy Act; and - The transfer would be likely to breach the basic principles of national application set out in the OECD Guidelines.	No: Consent is neither optional nor required, and would not currently appear to waive the requirements of existing privacy safeguards in the country of destination.	No: The Privacy Act does not provide for the possibility to adopt "white lists." However, the commissioner may prohibit a transfer "if the information has been, or will be, received in New Zealand from another State and is likely to be transferred to a third State where it will not be subject to a law providing comparable safeguards to this Act" and the transfer would be likely to lead to a contravention of the basic principles of national application.

continued on next page

Appendix 8e continued

Jurisdiction and Data Protection Regulation	Consent	White Lists, Adequacy Findings
Philippines Data Privacy Act (DPA) of 2012 and its Implementing Rules and Regulations (IRRs)	Yes (optional): Data may only be processed (includes transfer) if there is a lawful criteria for doing so. Consent is one lawful criterion. The IRR provides that data sharing shall be allowed in the private sector if the data subject consents to the data sharing.	No: The DPA does not recognize or consider the data protection regulations in the country of destination.
Singapore Personal Data Protection Act (PDPA), 2012: s. 26: An organization shall not transfer any personal data to a country or territory outside Singapore except in accordance with requirements prescribed under the PDPA to ensure that organizations provide a standard of protection to personal data so transferred that is comparable to the protection under PDPA.	Yes (optional): The requirements of s 26 may be satisfied if the transferring organization obtains the individual's consent to the effect of transferring the data (Reg 9[3][a]). Consent cannot be used to waive the requirement of existing privacy safeguards in the country of destination.	Conceivable: The exporting organization must have taken "appropriate steps to ascertain whether, and to ensure that, the recipient of the personal data in that country or territory outside Singapore (if any) is bound by legally enforceable obligations to provide to the transferred personal data a standard of protection that is at least comparable to the protection under the Act."
Thailand Personal Data Protection Act 2019: s. 28: Data transfers may freely take place to a foreign country or international organization that have adequate data protection standards, and in accordance with the data protection rules prescribed by the Data Protection Committee. -- Exceptions to the "adequacy" requirement apply in four series of circumstances: the data subject's consent has been obtained; specific statutory exemptions apply; the receiving organization provides suitable protection measures which enable the enforcement of the data subject's rights; or the receiving organization has put in place a "Personal Data Protection Policy" app.	Yes (optional): Obtaining the data subject's consent will be one of the circumstances in which the data controller may derogate to the rule that transfers may take place only to a destination country or international organization that has adequate data protection standards under PDPA. Where consent is obtained, data subject must be informed of the inadequate data protection standards of the destination country or international organization. The conditions for obtaining valid consent are defined in the PDPA.	Conceivable: When PDPA Chapter 3 enters into force, in the event that the data controller sends or transfers the personal data to a foreign country, unless an exemption applies, the destination country or international organization that receives such personal data must have an "adequate data protection standard," and the transfer must be carried out in accordance with the rules for the protection of personal data as prescribed by the Committee (s 28).

[a] Kobrata (2018) as cited in ABLI (2020).

Source: Asia Business Law Institute (2020).

Annex 8f: Construction of the Digital Platform Penetration Index and Insights from the Network Readiness Index

The digital platform index is constructed using the data compiled from Statista (2020a, 2020b) and national sources. The full data set comprises seven sectors: AdTech, Digital Media, E-Commerce, E-Services, Online Travel, and Transportation. This exercise covers 34 Asian economies and data from 2017 to 2019.

To construct the index, principal components analysis (PCA) was employed. PCA is a common method used to reduce the number of dimensions of large data sets with the intent of explaining the variations. The specific variables used in the index construction are revenue-to-GDP ratio, per user spending as proportion of GDP per capita, active user accounts-to-population ratio and revenue-to-population ratio (PPP adjusted). Revenue-to-GDP and revenue-to-population ratios are straightforward self-explanatory metrics in terms of the extent of digital platform penetration. Per user spending as proportion of GDP per capita captures the relative size of spending of every internet user to income. In the absence of data on unique digital platform users, internet users derived from the AdTech data set is used. Notably, users refer to AdTech-exposed internet users in the AdTech source file while it refers to active user accounts in the other sectors. This is understandable considering that AdTech from a consumer perspective is more of a rider in other platforms as opposed to a stand-alone platform itself. Finally, active and paying user accounts-to-population ratio captures another dimension of the willingness of the population to participate in various digital platforms. These accounts cover the data of the six sectors excluding AdTech and can be more than one per actual person user within sector and across sectors.

The variables were normalized before the estimation and the resulting index is essentially a linear combination of them. The subsequent equation summarizes the construction of the index, whereby the normalized right-hand side variables are weighted by the principal component (PC) 1 loadings. Two notes regarding the results. Firstly, the component 1 turns out to account for about 64% of the observed variance given the data set. Second, the PC loadings are eigenvectors normalized by the square root of the eigenvalue.

Equation: DPP Index = 0.8955(revenue-to-GDP ratio) + 0.4793*(per user spending as a proportion of per capita income) + 0.8990*(user accounts-to-population ratio) + 0.8990*(revenue to population, PPP)*

Cybersecurity, integrity, and privacy of systems are crucial to the overall credibility of the ecosystem. While physical infrastructure, education, and skills remain an integral component in line with the Sustainable Development Goals, mitigating the risks of fraud, data privacy breach, intellectual property infringement, and consumer rights violations are equally crucial in ICT policy making.

One of the metrics that captures this multidimensionality is the network readiness index (NRI). The NRI incorporates quality and access to ICT infrastructure; readiness of the people, businesses, and governments; responsiveness of regulations and trust in authorities; and the impact of technology on the economy, quality of life, and the Sustainable Development Goals.

Plotting the DPP index against the NRI indicates that digital platform penetration is high in countries where digital readiness is also high, which is intuitive (Annex 8f Figure). Indeed, it is no coincidence that large digital platforms operating in the region have established headquarters in countries where the infrastructure base is robust and absorptive capacities are large, such as Singapore, Japan, and the People's Republic of China. This suggests that in order to sustainably develop the domestic digital platform economy, governments cannot slacken in upgrading the underlying infrastructure and regulatory foundations.

Digital Platform Penetration and Network Readiness—Asia, 2019

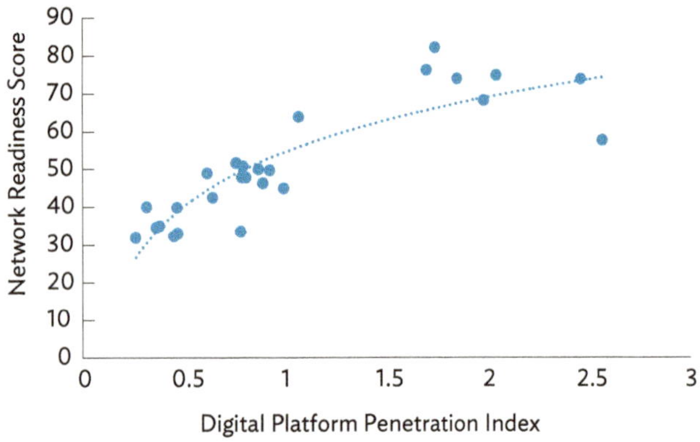

Source: ADB estimates and Dutta and Lanvin (2020).

For countries in the lowest group, there is a great need to catch up in all four aspects of network readiness (Annex 8f Table). Drawing specific lessons from neighboring countries can be a viable strategy to improve the competitiveness of and access to technology infrastructure as well as regulatory foresight.

Digital platforms have the potential to promote economic inclusion in various dimensions with the right mix of policies. Empowering MSMEs, which account for over 90% of the total number of firms in many economies in the region (Yoshino and Taghizadeh-Hesary 2018) is one policy area where digital platforms can contribute significantly. Increasing the flow of funds to population segments not served by traditional financial institutions is another target, considering that around 1.5 billion people in developing Asia are assessed to be still unbanked (Mylenko and Park 2015). The platforms' potential to broaden health and education services also appears promising where the infrastructure and requisite skills are already well established.

Digital Platform Penetration Index and Network Readiness Subindexes

		Network Readiness Main Subindexes			
Economy	DPP Index	Technology	People	Governance	Impact
PRC	2.5847				
Korea, Rep. of	2.5283				
Australia	2.1010				
Hong Kong, China	2.0323				
New Zealand	1.8795				
Japan	1.7794				
Singapore	1.7644				
Malaysia	1.1008				
India	1.0220				
Viet Nam	0.9429				
Indonesia	0.9190				
Brunei Darussalam	0.8322	n.d.			
Philippines	0.8221				
Armenia	0.8077				
Pakistan	0.7960				
Kazakhstan	0.7929				
Thailand	0.7902				
Azerbaijan	0.7833				
Sri Lanka	0.6501				
Georgia	0.5751				

continued on next page

Appendix 8f continued

Economy	DPP Index	Network Readiness Main Subindexes			
		Technology	People	Governance	Impact
Kyrgyz Republic	0.5018				
Uzbekistan	0.4840	n.d.			
Nepal	0.4619				
Fiji	0.4579	n.d.			
Cambodia	0.4416				
Tajikistan	0.4155				
Bangladesh	0.3928				
Myanmar	0.3909	n.d.			
Bhutan	0.3119	n.d.			
Mongolia	0.2824				
Lao PDR	0.2523				
Timor-Leste	0.2486	n.d.			
Papua New Guinea	0.2111	n.d.			
Turkmenistan	0.1565	n.d.			

Lao PDR = Lao Democratic People's Republic, n.d. = no available data, PRC = People's Republic of China.

Notes:

(i) Maximum and minimum values are set at 0 and 100, following the scale in Dutta and Lanvin (2020).

(ii) Low to high value spectrum: .

(iii) The Technology sub-index captures access, content, and future technologies.

(iv) The People sub-index captures the readiness and aptitude of individuals, businesses, and governments.

(v) The Governance sub-index captures trust, regulation, and inclusion.

(vi) The Impact sub-index captures economic value, quality of life, and contribution to sustainable development goals.

(vii) The specific indicators used and the methodology are laid out in Appendixes 1 to 3 of Dutta and Lanvin (2020), https://networkreadinessindex.org/wp-content/uploads/2020/11/NRI-2020-V8_28-11-2020.pdf.

Source: ADB estimates and Dutta and Lanvin (2020).

9 Statistical Appendix

The statistical appendix comprises 12 tables of selected indicators on economic integration for the 49 Asia and Pacific members of the Asian Development Bank (ADB). The succeeding notes describe the country groupings and the calculation procedures undertaken.

Regional Groupings

- Asia refers to the 49 regional members of ADB.
- Developing Asia refers to Asia excluding Australia, Japan, and New Zealand.
- European Union-28 (EU-28) consists of Austria, Belgium, Bulgaria, Croatia, Cyprus, Czechia, Denmark, Estonia, Finland, France, Germany, Greece, Hungary, Ireland, Italy, Latvia, Lithuania, Luxembourg, Malta, the Netherlands, Poland, Portugal, Romania, Slovakia, Slovenia, Spain, Sweden, and the United Kingdom.

Table Descriptions

Table A1: Asia-Pacific Regional Cooperation and Integration Index

The Asia-Pacific Regional Cooperation and Integration Index (ARCII) is a composite index that measures the degree of regional cooperation and integration in Asia and the Pacific. It comprises six dimensional indexes based on 26 indicators to capture the contributions of six different aspects of regional integration: (i) trade and investment, (ii) money and finance, (iii) regional value chains, (iv) infrastructure and connectivity, (v) free movement of people, and (vi) institutional and social integration.

The construction of ARCII follows two steps: first, the 26 indicators have been weight-averaged in each of the six dimensions to produce six composite dimensional indexes; second, these six dimensional indexes are weight-averaged to generate an overall index of regional integration. In each step, the weights are determined based on principal component analysis. For more details on the methodology and to download the data, please see Asia-Pacific Regional Cooperation and Integration Index Database. https://aric.adb.org/database/arcii.

Table A2: Regional Integration Indicators—Asia (% of total)

The table provides a summary of regional integration indicators for three areas: movement in trade and investment, movement in capital, and people movement (migration, remittances, and visitors); for Asian subregions, including Association of Southeast Asian Nations (ASEAN) plus 3 (including Hong Kong, China). Cross-border flows within and across subregions are shown as well as total flows with Asia and the rest of the world. Table descriptions of Tables A3 and A9 (movement in trade and investment), Tables A7 and A8 (movement in capital), and Tables A10, A11, and A12 (people movement), provide additional description for each indicator.

Table A3: Trade Share—Asia (% of total trade)

It is calculated as $(T_{ij}/T_{iw})*100$, where T_{ij} is the total trade of economy "i" with economy "j" and T_{iw} is the total trade of economy "i" with the world. A higher share indicates a higher degree of regional trade integration.

Table A4: Free Trade Agreement Status—Asia

It is the number and status of bilateral and plurilateral free trade agreements (FTAs) with at least one of the Asian economies as signatory. FTAs only proposed are excluded. It covers FTAs with the following status: Framework agreement signed—the parties initially negotiate the contents of a framework agreement, which serves as a framework for future negotiations; Negotiations launched—the parties, through the relevant ministries, declare the official launch of negotiations or set the date for such, or start the first round of negotiations; Signed but not yet in effect—parties sign the agreement after negotiations have been completed, however, the agreement has yet to be implemented; and Signed and in effect—provisions of the FTA come into force, after legislative or executive ratification.

Table A5: Time to Export and Import—Asia (number of hours)

Time to export (import) data measures the number of hours required to export (import) by ocean transport, including the processing of documents required to complete the transaction. It covers time used for documentation requirements and procedures at customs and other regulatory agencies as well as the time of inland transport between the largest business city and the main port used by traders. Regional aggregates are weighted averages based on total exports (imports).

Table A6: Logistics Performance Index—Asia (% to EU)

Logistics Performance Index scores are based on the following dimensions: (i) efficiency of border control and customs process; (ii) transport and trade-related infrastructure; (iii) competitively priced shipments; (iv) ability to track and trace consignments; and (v) timeliness of shipments. Regional aggregates are computed using total trade as weights. A score above (below) 100 means that it is easier (more difficult) to export or import from that economy compared with the EU.

Table A7: Cross-Border Portfolio Equity Holdings Share—Asia (% of total cross-border equity holdings)

It is calculated as (E_{ij}/E_{iw})*100 where E_{ij} is the holding of economy "i" of the equity securities issued by economy "j" and E_{iw} is economy i's total holdings of cross-border equity securities. Calculations are based solely on available data in the Coordinated Portfolio Investment Survey (CPIS) database of the International Monetary Fund (IMF). Rest of the world (ROW) includes equity securities issued by international organizations defined in the CPIS database and "not specified (including confidential) category." A higher share indicates a higher degree of regional integration.

Table A8: Cross-Border Portfolio Debt Holdings Share—Asia (% of total cross-border debt holdings)

It is calculated as (D_{ij}/D_{iw})*100 where D_{ij} is the holding of economy "i" of the debt securities issued by economy "j" and D_{iw} is economy i's total holdings of cross-border debt securities. Calculations are based solely on available data in the CPIS database of the IMF. ROW includes debt securities issued by international organizations defined in the CPIS database and "not specified (including confidential) category." A higher share indicates a higher degree of regional integration.

Table A9: Foreign Direct Investment Inflow Share—Asia (% of total FDI inflows)

It is calculated as (F_{ij}/F_{iw})*100 where F_{ij} is the foreign direct investment (FDI) received by economy "i" from economy "j" and F_{iw} is the FDI received by economy "i" from the world. Figures are based on net FDI inflow data. A higher share indicates a higher degree of regional integration. The bilateral FDI database was constructed using data from the United Nations Conference on Trade and Development, ASEAN Secretariat, Eurostat, and national sources. For missing data from 2018 to 2019, bilateral FDI estimates derived from a gravity model are used. All bilateral data available from 2001–

2019 from the data sources were utilized to estimate the following gravity equation: $\ln FDI_{ijt} = \alpha + \beta_1 \ln GDP_{it} + \beta_2 \ln GDP_{jt} + \gamma \cdot X_{ijt} + \delta_i \cdot F_i + \delta_j \cdot F_j + \delta_t \cdot F_t + \nu_{ijt}$, where FDI_{ijt} is the FDI from economy "j" (home) to economy "i" (host) in year t, GDP_{it} is the gross domestic product (GDP) of economy "i" in year t, GDP_{jt} is the GDP of economy "j" at year t, X_{ijt} are the usual gravity variables (distance, contiguity, common language, colonial relationship) between economies "i" and "j", and F_j, F_i, F_t, are home, host, and year fixed effects, and ν_{ijt} is the error term. Data on distance, contiguity, common language, colonial relationship are from the Centre d'Études Prospectives et d'Informations Internationales (the French Research Center in International Economics) and data on GDP are from the World Development Indicators of the World Bank. For more details on methodology and data sources, please see *Asian Economic Integration Report 2018* online Annex 1: http://aric.adb.org/pdf/aeir2018_onlineannex1.pdf.

Table A10: Remittance Inflows Share—Asia (% of total remittance inflows)

It is calculated as (R_{ij}/R_{iw})*100 where R_{ij} is the remittance received by economy "i" from partner "j" and R_{iw} is the remittance received by economy "i" from the world. Remittances refer to the sum of the following: (i) workers' remittances which are recorded as current transfers under the current account of the IMF's Balance of Payments (BOP); (ii) compensation of employees which includes wages, salaries, and other benefits of border, seasonal, and other nonresident workers and which are recorded under the "income" subcategory of the current account; and (iii) migrants' transfers which are reported under capital transfers in the BOP's capital account. Transfers through informal channels are excluded.

Table A11: Outbound Migration Share—Asia (% of total outbound migrants)

It is calculated as (M_{ij}/M_{iw})*100 where M_{ij} is the number of migrants of economy "i" residing in economy "j" and M_{iw} is the number of all migrants of economy "i" residing overseas. This definition excludes those traveling abroad on a temporary basis. A higher share indicates a higher degree of regional integration.

Table A12a: Inbound Visitor Share—Asia (% of total inbound visitors)

It is calculated as (TR_{ij}/TR_{iw})*100 where TR_{ij} is the number of nationals of economy "i" that have arrived as visitors in destination "j" and TR_{iw} is the total number of nationals of economy "i" that have arrived as visitors in all international destinations. A higher share indicates a higher degree of regional integration.

Table A12b: Outbound Visitor Share—Asia (% of total outbound visitors)

It is calculated as (TR_{ij}/TR_{iw})*100 where TR_{ij} is the number of nationals of economy "i" that have traveled as visitors in destination "j" and TR_{iw} is the total number of nationals of economy "i" that have traveled as visitors abroad. A higher share indicates a higher degree of regional integration.

Table A1a: Overall Asia-Pacific Regional Cooperation and Integration Index and Dimensional Subindexes—Asia

	Overall Index	Dimensional Subindexes					
		Trade and Investment	Money and Finance	Regional Value Chain	Infrastructure and Connectivity	Movement of People	Institutional and Social Integration
2006	0.526	0.525	0.520	0.528	0.486	0.564	0.312
2007	0.514	0.475	0.543	0.535	0.487	0.566	0.314
2008	0.515	0.503	0.471	0.517	0.482	0.568	0.321
2009	0.513	0.525	0.459	0.519	0.482	0.569	0.330
2010	0.530	0.532	0.506	0.519	0.484	0.564	0.332
2011	0.530	0.562	0.501	0.504	0.489	0.563	0.333
2012	0.525	0.522	0.464	0.508	0.493	0.572	0.334
2013	0.523	0.514	0.467	0.508	0.490	0.580	0.337
2014	0.530	0.515	0.453	0.509	0.490	0.579	0.339
2015	0.527	0.574	0.455	0.497	0.492	0.580	0.339
2016	0.539	0.542	0.470	0.498	0.495	0.582	0.339
2017	0.517	0.541	0.362	0.500	0.507	0.587	0.342
2018	0.535	0.569	0.471	0.490	0.505	0.623	0.342

Table A1b: Asia-Pacific Regional Cooperation and Integration Index—Asia Subregions and Subregional Initiatives

	Central	East	Southeast	South	Oceania	ASEAN	CAREC	GMS	SASEC
2006	0.382	0.584	0.589	0.448	0.568	0.589	0.423	0.575	0.462
2007	0.366	0.555	0.597	0.463	0.543	0.597	0.433	0.583	0.466
2008	0.370	0.560	0.584	0.461	0.546	0.584	0.427	0.574	0.473
2009	0.381	0.558	0.587	0.454	0.549	0.587	0.430	0.573	0.465
2010	0.356	0.566	0.588	0.478	0.567	0.588	0.439	0.578	0.487
2011	0.384	0.562	0.596	0.482	0.550	0.596	0.437	0.581	0.498
2012	0.375	0.567	0.589	0.462	0.547	0.589	0.447	0.578	0.464
2013	0.387	0.572	0.589	0.452	0.551	0.589	0.452	0.582	0.457
2014	0.399	0.582	0.594	0.458	0.550	0.594	0.468	0.588	0.457
2015	0.396	0.564	0.595	0.470	0.531	0.595	0.457	0.586	0.476
2016	0.379	0.594	0.591	0.492	0.544	0.591	0.460	0.587	0.508
2017	0.398	0.569	0.574	0.465	0.530	0.574	0.463	0.561	0.469
2018	0.432	0.559	0.605	0.492	0.518	0.605	0.471	0.593	0.501

ASEAN = Association of Southeast Asian Nations, CAREC = Central Asia Regional Economic Cooperation, GMS = Greater Mekong Subregion, SASEC = South Asia Subregional Economic Cooperation.

Notes:

(i) The Asia-Pacific Regional Cooperation and Integration Index (ARCII) for each subregion (subregional initiative) for each year is calculated by averaging the ARCII scores for all the economies in each subregion (member economies in each subregional initiative).

(ii) The economy coverage for subregions and subregional initiatives includes: Central Asia (Georgia, Kazakhstan, and the Kyrgyz Republic); East Asia (the People's Republic of China [PRC]; Hong Kong, China; Japan; the Republic of Korea; and Mongolia); Southeast Asia (Cambodia, Indonesia, the Lao People's Democratic Republic [Lao PDR], Malaysia, the Philippines, Singapore, Thailand, and Viet Nam); South Asia (Bangladesh India, Nepal, Pakistan, and Sri Lanka); Oceania (Australia and New Zealand); ASEAN (Cambodia, Indonesia, the Lao PDR, Malaysia, the Philippines, Singapore, Thailand, and Viet Nam); CAREC (the PRC, Georgia, Kazakhstan, the Kyrgyz Republic, Mongolia, and Pakistan); GMS (Cambodia, the PRC, the Lao PDR, Thailand, and Viet Nam); SASEC (Bangladesh, India, Nepal, and Sri Lanka).

Sources: ADB. Asia Regional Integration Center. Asia-Pacific Regional Cooperation and Integration Index Database. https://aric.adb.org/database/arcii (accessed October 2019); and methodology from C. Y. Park and R. Claveria. 2018. Constructing the Asia-Pacific Regional Integration Index: A Panel Approach. *ADB Economics Working Papers*. No. 544. Manila: Asian Development Bank (ADB); H. Huh and C. Y. Park. 2018. Asia-Pacific Regional Integration Index: Construction, Interpretation, and Comparison. *Journal of Asian Economics*. 54. pp. 22–38; and H. Huh and C. Y. Park. 2017. Asia-Pacific Regional Integration Index: Construction, Interpretation, and Comparison. *ADB Economics Working Papers*. No. 511. Manila: ADB.

Table A1c: Regional Integration Index—Asia versus Other Regions

	Asia	European Union	Latin America	Africa
2006	0.444	0.561	0.374	0.385
2007	0.433	0.562	0.354	0.371
2008	0.439	0.559	0.362	0.386
2009	0.433	0.564	0.362	0.400
2010	0.447	0.553	0.362	0.384
2011	0.446	0.551	0.358	0.386
2012	0.445	0.553	0.368	0.393
2013	0.443	0.542	0.368	0.400
2014	0.451	0.549	0.359	0.396
2015	0.448	0.541	0.370	0.378
2016	0.459	0.550	0.380	0.388
2017	0.447	0.539	0.373	0.376
2018	0.453	0.546	0.380	0.379

Notes:

(iii) The regional integration index for each region (Table A1c) is calculated using the same method as ARCII but is based on worldwide normalization, i.e., normalizing raw indicator values using global minimum and maximum values.

(iv) In the Money and Finance dimension, there was a substantial decrease in the weight of Indicator II-d (Pair-wise correlation of equity returns averaged regionally minus that averaged globally).

(v) Remittance data used in Indicator V-c (Proportion of intra-regional remittances to total remittances) was changed to outward remittances.

Sources: ADB. Asia Regional Integration Center. Asia-Pacific Regional Cooperation and Integration Index Database. https://aric.adb.org/database/arcii (accessed October 2019); and methodology from C. Y. Park and R. Claveria. 2018. Constructing the Asia-Pacific Regional Integration Index: A Panel Approach. *ADB Economics Working Papers*. No. 544. Manila: Asian Development Bank (ADB); H. Huh and C. Y. Park. 2018. Asia-Pacific Regional Integration Index: Construction, Interpretation, and Comparison. *Journal of Asian Economics*. 54. pp. 22–38; and H. Huh and C. Y. Park. 2017. Asia-Pacific Regional Integration Index: Construction, Interpretation, and Comparison. *ADB Economics Working Papers*. No. 511. Manila: ADB.

Table A2: Regional Integration Indicators — Asia (% of total)

	Movement in Trade and Investment		Movement in Capital		People Movement		
	Trade (%)	FDI (%)	Equity Holdings (%)	Bond Holdings (%)	Migration (%)	Tourism (%)	Remittances (%)
	2019	2019	2019	2019	2019	2018	2019
Within Subregions							
ASEAN+3 (including HKG)[a]	46.3 ▼	54.0 ▼	17.2 ▲	12.2 ▲	37.4 ▼	72.8 ▼	30.2 ▼
Central Asia	7.8 ▲	1.1 ▼	0.0 ▼	0.0 ▼	9.0 ▼	60.7 ▲	6.2 ▼
East Asia	34.7 ▼	65.2 ▲	13.2 ▲	8.8 ▲	31.7 ▼	54.9 ▼	32.5 ▼
South Asia	5.6 ▼	0.4 ▼	0.4 ▼	0.0 ▼	21.6 ▼	13.5 ▼	7.1 ▼
Southeast Asia	22.4 ▼	11.7 ▼	6.0 ▼	6.3 ▼	31.3 ▼	51.8 ▼	12.7 ▼
The Pacific and Oceania	5.8 ▼	(2.2) ▼	4.3 ▼	3.8 ▲	47.9 ▼	19.8 ▼	36.6 ▲
Across Subregions							
ASEAN+3 (including HKG)[a]	11.6 ▲	2.3 ▼	3.2 ▼	5.4 ▼	11.3 ▲	5.1 ▼	8.7 ▲
Central Asia	27.9 ▲	31.0 ▼	9.7 ▼	17.6 ▲	0.4 ▼	1.9 ▼	0.2 ▼
East Asia	21.0 ▲	3.1 ▼	2.9 ▼	7.2 ▼	14.9 ▼	18.8 ▲	14.7 ▼
South Asia	33.3 ▼	40.1 ▼	34.4 ▼	0.7 ▼	7.3 ▲	28.3 ▼	8.0 ▲
Southeast Asia	46.1 ▼	24.4 ▼	32.3 ▼	19.3 ▲	18.8 ▲	40.0 ▲	17.5 ▲
The Pacific and Oceania	66.0 ▲	34.9 ▲	12.5 ▲	17.8 ▲	4.1 ▼	38.4 ▼	7.2 ▼
TOTAL (within and across subregions)							
Asia	**57.5** ▼	**51.7** ▲	**19.9** ▲	**17.9** ▲	**35.2** ▼	**73.9** ▼	**26.9** ▼
ASEAN+3 (including HKG)[a]	57.9 ▼	56.3 ▼	20.3 ▲	17.6 ▲	48.7 ▼	77.9 ▼	38.9 ▼
Central Asia	35.7 ▲	32.0 ▼	9.7 ▼	17.6 ▼	9.4 ▼	62.7 ▲	6.5 ▼
East Asia	55.7 ▲	68.2 ▲	16.1 ▲	16.0 ▲	46.6 ▼	73.8 ▼	47.2 ▼
South Asia	38.9 ▼	40.5 ▼	34.8 ▼	0.7 ▼	28.9 ▼	41.9 ▼	15.1 ▲
Southeast Asia	68.4 ▼	36.1 ▼	38.2 ▼	25.5 ▲	50.1 ▲	91.7 ▼	30.2 ▼
The Pacific and Oceania	71.8 ▲	32.7 ▲	16.7 ▲	21.6 ▲	52.0 ▼	58.1 ▼	43.8 ▲
With the rest of the world							
Asia	**42.5** ▲	**48.3** ▼	**80.1** ▼	**82.1** ▼	**64.8** ▲	**26.1** ▲	**73.1** ▲
ASEAN+3 (including HKG)[a]	42.1 ▲	43.7 ▲	79.7 ▼	82.4 ▼	51.3 ▲	22.1 ▲	61.1 ▲
Central Asia	64.3 ▼	68.0 ▲	90.3 ▲	82.4 ▲	90.6 ▲	37.3 ▼	93.5 ▲
East Asia	44.3 ▼	31.8 ▼	83.9 ▼	84.0 ▼	53.4 ▲	26.2 ▲	52.8 ▲
South Asia	61.1 ▲	59.5 ▲	65.2 ▲	99.3 ▲	71.1 ▲	58.1 ▲	84.9 ▼
Southeast Asia	31.6 ▲	63.9 ▲	61.8 ▲	74.5 ▼	49.9 ▼	8.3 ▲	69.8 ▲
The Pacific and Oceania	28.2 ▼	67.3 ▼	83.3 ▼	78.4 ▼	48.0 ▲	41.9 ▲	56.2 ▼

▲ = increase from previous period; ▼ = decrease from previous period.

( ) = negative; ASEAN = Association of Southeast Asian Nations; FDI = foreign direct investment; HKG = Hong Kong, China.

[a] Includes ASEAN (Brunei Darussalam, Cambodia, Indonesia, the Lao People's Democratic Republic, Malaysia, Myanmar, the Philippines, Singapore, Thailand, and Viet Nam) plus the People's Republic of China; Hong Kong, China; Japan; and the Republic of Korea.

Trade—no data available on the Cook Islands and Niue.

Equity and bond holdings—based on investment from Australia; Bangladesh; Hong Kong, China; India; Indonesia; Japan; Kazakhstan; Malaysia; Mongolia; New Zealand; Pakistan; Palau; the People's Republic of China; the Philippines; the Republic of Korea; Singapore; and Thailand.

Migration—share of migrant stock to total migrants in 2019 (compared with 2015).

Tourism—share of outbound international visitors to total international visitors in 2018 (compared with 2017).

Remittances—share of inward remittances to total remittances in 2017 (compared with 2016).

Sources: ADB calculations using data from Association of Southeast Asian Nations Secretariat. ASEANstats Database. https://www.aseanstats.org (accessed July 2020); CEIC; Eurostat. Balance of Payments. http://ec.europa.eu/eurostat/web/balance-of-payments/data/database (accessed June 2020); International Monetary Fund (IMF). Coordinated Portfolio Investment Survey. http://cpis.imf.org (accessed September 2020); IMF. Direction of Trade Statistics. http://data.imf.org/dot (accessed December 2020); United Nations. Department of Economic and Social Affairs, Population Division. International Migrant Stock 2019. http://www.un.org/en/development/desa/population/migration/data/index.shtml (accessed May 2020); United Nations Conference on Trade and Development. World Investment Report 2020 Statistical Annex Tables. http://unctad.org/en/Pages/DIAE/World%20Investment%20Report/Annex-Tables.aspx (accessed June 2020); United Nations World Tourism Organization. Tourism Satellite Accounts. http://statistics.unwto.org (accessed October 2020); and World Bank. Global Knowledge Partnership for Migration and Development. Bilateral Remittance Estimates May 2020.

Table A3: Trade Shares—Asia, 2019 (% of total trade)

Reporter	Partner					
		of which				
	Asia	PRC	Japan	EU-28	US	ROW
Central Asia	**35.7**	**17.5**	**1.3**	**26.1**	**2.3**	**35.9**
Armenia	20.9	11.6	2.5	21.3	4.1	53.8
Azerbaijan	19.5	6.6	0.9	38.7	2.4	39.5
Georgia	30.0	8.1	2.0	24.2	6.1	39.7
Kazakhstan	32.9	15.0	1.5	32.6	2.3	32.1
Kyrgyz Republic	48.6	26.4	0.4	17.4	1.3	32.6
Tajikistan	36.7	13.4	0.7	6.5	0.4	56.4
Turkmenistan	76.2	64.8	0.1	8.0	0.3	15.4
Uzbekistan	45.8	20.2	1.1	10.1	1.4	42.7
East Asia	**55.7**	**15.1**	**5.7**	**12.8**	**11.8**	**19.7**
China, People's Republic of	47.0		6.9	15.4	11.9	25.7
Hong Kong, China	78.7	50.3	4.4	7.9	6.0	7.4
Japan	55.6	21.3		12.0	15.5	16.8
Korea, Republic of	57.7	23.3	7.3	10.4	13.0	18.9
Mongolia	75.0	64.0	4.4	6.9	2.3	15.8
Taipei,China	71.9	31.3	9.6	8.7	11.7	7.7
South Asia	**38.9**	**11.8**	**2.3**	**14.3**	**10.3**	**36.4**
Afghanistan	72.9	15.5	2.6	2.0	0.7	24.4
Bangladesh	42.3	15.2	3.0	23.5	7.2	27.0
Bhutan	95.8	1.0	0.6	2.6	0.2	1.3
India	36.6	10.6	2.2	13.2	11.1	39.1
Maldives	62.9	15.4	1.2	11.7	2.3	23.1
Nepal	82.8	13.2	0.5	2.9	1.9	12.5
Pakistan	38.9	19.6	2.1	18.2	9.0	33.9
Sri Lanka	54.8	13.5	5.6	16.5	11.4	17.4
Southeast Asia	**68.4**	**18.0**	**8.0**	**10.0**	**10.5**	**11.1**
Brunei Darussalam	83.1	8.9	21.3	5.6	2.9	8.4
Cambodia	64.0	23.9	5.6	15.8	13.2	7.0
Indonesia	71.8	21.3	9.3	7.9	7.9	12.4
Lao People's Democratic Republic	93.2	30.0	1.9	3.5	1.2	2.2
Malaysia	72.3	17.2	7.0	9.5	9.0	9.2
Myanmar	81.3	33.2	5.3	11.5	3.2	4.1
Philippines	71.0	19.1	11.4	9.5	10.5	9.0
Singapore	67.1	13.4	4.9	11.0	10.4	11.5
Thailand	66.0	16.5	12.0	9.2	10.1	14.7
Timor-Leste	93.2	14.1	1.8	2.7	1.4	2.6
Viet Nam	64.5	22.7	7.8	11.0	14.7	9.8
The Pacific	**84.4**	**17.7**	**9.0**	**9.6**	**2.9**	**3.2**
Fiji	73.7	10.6	3.6	13.8	8.5	4.1
Kiribati	91.6	3.6	1.5	1.1	1.4	5.9
Marshall Islands	84.2	19.6	10.7	12.2	0.9	2.7
Micronesia, Federated States of	46.7	5.8	7.2	0.3	19.0	34.0
Nauru	69.8	1.2	2.4	1.0	4.5	24.7
Niue	–	–	–	–	–	–
Palau	44.9	10.7	12.4	0.6	27.0	27.5
Papua New Guinea	90.1	18.3	10.0	7.3	1.3	1.2
Samoa	84.2	11.0	3.9	0.9	9.3	5.6
Solomon Islands	87.3	41.1	1.7	8.6	2.7	1.4
Tonga	81.6	5.0	8.1	1.5	15.2	1.6
Tuvalu	82.1	1.4	5.7	1.4	3.6	12.9
Vanuatu	86.3	10.4	1.9	4.7	3.5	5.5
Oceania	**71.1**	**31.3**	**10.5**	**12.2**	**7.7**	**8.9**
Australia	72.4	32.5	11.2	12.0	7.4	8.1
New Zealand	62.8	24.0	6.2	13.5	9.7	14.0
Asia	**57.5**	**16.2**	**6.1**	**12.5**	**11.1**	**18.9**
Developing Asia	**57.0**	**14.8**	**6.6**	**12.6**	**10.7**	**19.7**

– = unavailable, EU = European Union, PRC = People's Republic of China, ROW = rest of the world, US = United States.

Source: ADB calculations using data from International Monetary Fund. Direction of Trade Statistics. http://data.imf.org/dot (accessed December 2020).

Table A4: Free Trade Agreement Status—Asia

Economy	Under Negotiation		Signed but not yet In Effect	Signed and In Effect	Total
	Framework Agreement Signed	Negotiations Launched			
Afghanistan	0	0	0	2	2
Armenia	0	3	3	12	18
Australia	0	6	1	16	25
Azerbaijan	0	1	0	9	10
Bangladesh	0	3	1	3	7
Bhutan	0	2	0	2	4
Brunei Darussalam	0	1	0	10	12
Cambodia	0	2	1	7	10
China, People's Republic of	0	10	4	18	32
Cook Islands	0	0	1	3	4
Fiji	0	0	1	4	5
Georgia	0	0	1	13	14
Hong Kong, China	0	1	0	8	9
India	1	16	0	13	30
Indonesia	0	7	3	12	22
Japan	0	8	0	18	27
Kazakhstan	0	5	3	12	20
Kiribati	0	0	1	3	4
Korea, Republic of	0	14	1	17	32
Kyrgyz Republic	0	3	3	12	18
Lao People's Democratic Republic	0	1	0	9	10
Malaysia	1	6	1	16	25
Maldives	0	1	2	1	4
Marshall Islands	0	0	1	4	5
Micronesia, Federated States of	0	0	1	4	5
Mongolia	0	0	0	2	2
Myanmar	1	2	0	7	10
Nauru	0	0	1	3	4
Nepal	0	1	0	2	3
New Zealand	0	7	1	12	21
Niue	0	0	1	3	4
Pakistan	1	6	1	9	17
Palau	0	0	1	3	4
Papua New Guinea	0	0	1	5	6
Philippines	0	3	0	9	12
Samoa	0	0	1	3	4
Singapore	0	7	1	25	36
Solomon Islands	0	0	1	4	5
Sri Lanka	0	3	0	6	9
Taipei,China	0	1	0	8	9
Tajikistan	0	0	0	8	8
Thailand	1	9	0	14	24
Tonga	0	0	1	3	4
Turkmenistan	0	0	0	5	5
Tuvalu	0	0	1	3	4
Uzbekistan	0	0	0	9	9
Vanuatu	0	0	1	4	5
Viet Nam	0	3	1	12	17

Notes:

(i) Framework agreement signed: The parties initially negotiate the contents of a framework agreement, which serves as a framework for future negotiations.

(ii) Negotiations launched: The parties, through the relevant ministries, declare the official launch of negotiations or set the date for such, or start the first round of negotiations.

(iii) Signed but not yet In Effect: Parties sign the agreement after negotiations have been completed. However, the agreement has yet to be implemented.

(iv) Signed and In Effect: Provisions of free trade agreement come into force, after legislative or executive ratification.

Source: ADB. Asia Regional Integration Center FTA Database. https://aric.adb.org/database/fta (accessed October 2020).

Table A5: Time to Export or Import—Asia (hours)

	Time to Export		Time to Import	
	2018	2019	2018	2019
Central Asia	**178**	**164**	**87**	**86**
Armenia	41	29	4	4
Azerbaijan	50	50	33	47
Georgia	8	8	17	17
Kazakhstan	233	233	8	8
Kyrgyz Republic	77	77	153	153
Tajikistan	117	93	233	233
Turkmenistan	–	–	–	–
Uzbekistan	208	128	285	261
East Asia	**26**	**24**	**50**	**39**
China, People's Republic of	35	29	72	48
Hong Kong, China	2	2	20	20
Japan	25	29	43	43
Korea, Republic of	14	14	7	7
Mongolia	302	302	163	163
Taipei,China	22	22	51	51
South Asia	**104**	**90**	**156**	**124**
Afghanistan	276	276	420	420
Bangladesh	315	315	360	360
Bhutan	14	14	13	13
India	81	64	126	85
Maldives	90	90	161	161
Nepal	73	54	106	59
Pakistan	130	113	216	216
Sri Lanka	91	91	120	120
Southeast Asia	**63**	**64**	**90**	**98**
Brunei Darussalam	272	272	180	180
Cambodia	180	180	140	140
Indonesia	124	118	206	206
Lao People's Democratic Republic	69	69	71	71
Malaysia	38	38	43	43
Myanmar	286	286	278	278
Philippines	78	78	216	216
Singapore	12	12	3	36
Thailand	55	55	54	54
Timor-Leste	129	129	144	144
Viet Nam	105	105	132	132
The Pacific	**133**	**97**	**145**	**126**
Cook Islands	–	–	–	–
Fiji	112	112	76	69
Kiribati	96	96	144	144
Marshall Islands	84	84	144	144
Micronesia, Federated States of	62	62	91	91
Nauru	–	–	–	–
Niue	–	–	–	–
Palau	174	174	180	180
Papua New Guinea	138	90	192	120
Samoa	75	75	109	109
Solomon Islands	170	170	145	145
Tonga	160	160	98	98
Tuvalu	–	–	–	–
Vanuatu	110	110	174	174
Oceania	**42**	**42**	**40**	**40**
Australia	43	43	43	43
New Zealand	40	40	26	26
Asia	**41**	**39**	**69**	**61**
Developing Asia	**41**	**39**	**71**	**62**

– = unavailable.

Note: Time to export (import) data measures the number of hours required to export (import) by ocean transport, including the processing of documents required to complete the transaction. It covers time used up for documentation requirements and procedures at customs and other regulatory agencies as well as the time of inland transport between the largest business city and the main port used by traders. Regional aggregates are weighted averages based on total exports (imports).

Source: ADB calculations using data from World Bank. Doing Business Database. https://doingbusiness.org (accessed June 2020).

Table A6: Logistics Performance Index (LPI) Scores—Asia (% EU-28)

	2014	2016	2018
Central Asia	**66.5**	**64.1**	**68.9**
Armenia	69.2	55.9	67.0
Azerbaijan	63.4	–	–
Georgia	64.9	59.7	62.8
Kazakhstan	69.8	69.8	72.2
Kyrgyz Republic	57.2	54.7	65.5
Tajikistan	65.4	52.3	60.1
Turkmenistan	59.6	56.1	61.9
Uzbekistan	62.0	61.0	66.3
East Asia	**94.8**	**95.8**	**95.5**
China, People's Republic of	91.4	92.9	92.7
Hong Kong, China	99.0	103.2	100.8
Japan	101.3	100.7	103.5
Korea, Republic of	94.9	94.3	92.9
Mongolia	61.0	63.6	61.0
Taipei,China	96.2	93.8	92.5
South Asia	**77.5**	**83.1**	**77.8**
Afghanistan	53.5	54.3	50.1
Bangladesh	65.9	67.6	66.2
Bhutan	59.3	58.9	55.8
India	79.7	86.7	81.7
Maldives	71.1	63.7	68.5
Nepal	67.0	60.3	64.6
Pakistan	73.1	74.1	62.2
Sri Lanka	69.7	–	66.8
Southeast Asia	**90.8**	**86.0**	**87.7**
Brunei Darussalam	–	72.8	69.6
Cambodia	70.9	71.0	66.3
Indonesia	79.7	75.7	81.0
Lao People's Democratic Republic	61.8	52.4	69.4
Malaysia	92.9	86.9	82.8
Myanmar	58.2	62.4	59.1
Philippines	77.7	72.4	74.6
Singapore	103.6	105.1	102.7
Thailand	88.7	82.6	87.7
Timor-Leste	–	–	–
Viet Nam	81.6	75.5	84.2
The Pacific	**63.8**	**62.5**	**57.5**
Cook Islands	–	–	–
Fiji	65.9	58.7	60.5
Kiribati	–	–	–
Marshall Islands	–	–	–
Micronesia, Federated States of	–	–	–
Nauru	–	–	–
Niue	–	–	–
Palau	–	–	–
Papua New Guinea	62.9	63.7	55.9
Samoa	–	–	–
Solomon Islands	67.0	61.3	66.1
Tonga	–	–	–
Tuvalu	–	–	–
Vanuatu	–	–	–
Oceania	**98.0**	**94.7**	**96.9**
Australia	98.6	96.2	96.4
New Zealand	94.3	85.9	99.6
Asia	**92.3**	**92.5**	**92.2**
Developing Asia	**90.8**	**91.3**	**90.5**

– = unavailable, EU = European Union.

Source: ADB calculations using data from World Bank. Logistics Performance Index. https://lpi.worldbank.org (accessed June 2020).

Table A7: Cross-Border Equity Holdings—Asia, 2019 (% of total cross-border equity holdings)

	Partner					
		of which				
Reporter	Asia	PRC	Japan	EU-28	US	ROW
Central Asia	**9.7**	**0.0**	**7.1**	**22.9**	**59.1**	**8.4**
Armenia	–	–	–	–	–	–
Azerbaijan	–	–	–	–	–	–
Georgia	–	–	–	–	–	–
Kazakhstan	9.7	0.0	7.1	22.9	59.1	8.4
Kyrgyz Republic	–	–	–	–	–	–
Tajikistan	–	–	–	–	–	–
Turkmenistan	–	–	–	–	–	–
Uzbekistan	–	–	–	–	–	–
East Asia	**16.1**	**6.2**	**1.1**	**14.9**	**24.4**	**44.6**
China, People's Republic of	49.2		2.2	11.0	25.1	14.6
Hong Kong, China	22.2	17.7	1.3	11.1	4.1	62.6
Japan	5.7	0.7		16.3	32.6	45.4
Korea, Republic of	17.0	3.7	5.6	24.8	46.9	11.4
Mongolia	56.6	1.1	0.2	17.0	11.6	14.8
Taipei,China	–	–	–	–	–	–
South Asia	**34.8**	**25.3**	**1.0**	**21.0**	**29.9**	**14.4**
Afghanistan	–	–	–	–	–	–
Bangladesh	100.0	0.0	0.0	0.0	0.0	0.0
Bhutan	–	–	–	–	–	–
India	37.3	27.4	1.1	22.2	31.8	8.7
Maldives	–	–	–	–	–	–
Nepal	–	–	–	–	–	–
Pakistan	0.0	0.0	0.0	6.4	6.4	87.2
Sri Lanka	–	–	–	–	–	–
Southeast Asia	**38.2**	**11.3**	**6.5**	**12.6**	**22.0**	**27.2**
Brunei Darussalam	–	–	–	–	–	–
Cambodia	–	–	–	–	–	–
Indonesia	56.6	13.0	0.2	0.5	38.4	4.4
Lao People's Democratic Republic	–	–	–	–	–	–
Malaysia	54.3	6.1	5.2	17.7	20.4	7.6
Myanmar	–	–	–	–	–	–
Philippines	18.0	0.1	0.2	50.8	25.9	5.3
Singapore	37.2	12.4	7.0	10.8	22.2	29.8
Thailand	21.4	0.8	1.4	37.2	18.6	22.9
Timor-Leste	–	–	–	–	–	–
Viet Nam	–	–	–	–	–	–
The Pacific	**–**	**–**	**–**	**–**	**–**	**–**
Cook Islands	–	–	–	–	–	–
Fiji	–	–	–	–	–	–
Kiribati	–	–	–	–	–	–
Marshall Islands	–	–	–	–	–	–
Micronesia, Federated States of	–	–	–	–	–	–
Nauru	–	–	–	–	–	–
Niue	–	–	–	–	–	–
Palau	–	–	–	–	–	–
Papua New Guinea	–	–	–	–	–	–
Solomon Islands	–	–	–	–	–	–
Timor-Leste	–	–	–	–	–	–
Tonga	–	–	–	–	–	–
Tuvalu	–	–	–	–	–	–
Vanuatu	–	–	–	–	–	–
Oceania	**16.7**	**2.1**	**4.8**	**17.9**	**47.1**	**18.2**
Australia	14.5	2.2	4.9	18.8	48.0	18.6
New Zealand	34.3	1.0	4.2	10.7	40.0	15.0
Asia	**19.9**	**6.5**	**2.5**	**14.9**	**27.0**	**38.2**
Developing Asia	**23.4**	**8.2**	**2.9**	**14.4**	**24.0**	**38.2**

– = unavailable, EU = European Union, PRC = People's Republic of China, ROW = rest of the world, US = United States.

Source: ADB calculations using data from International Monetary Fund. Coordinated Portfolio Investment Survey. http://data.imf.org/cpis (accessed September 2020).

Table A8: Cross-Border Debt Holdings—Asia, 2019 (% of total cross-border debt holdings)

	Partner					
		of which				
Reporter	Asia	PRC	Japan	EU-28	US	ROW
Central Asia	**17.6**	**1.5**	**5.1**	**17.6**	**49.7**	**15.2**
Armenia	–	–	–	–	–	–
Azerbaijan	–	–	–	–	–	–
Georgia	–	–	–	–	–	–
Kazakhstan	17.6	1.5	5.1	17.6	49.7	15.2
Kyrgyz Republic	–	–	–	–	–	–
Tajikistan	–	–	–	–	–	–
Turkmenistan	–	–	–	–	–	–
Uzbekistan	–	–	–	–	–	–
East Asia	**16.0**	**4.2**	**1.7**	**27.8**	**38.9**	**17.4**
China, People's Republic of	31.3		2.1	12.3	25.3	31.1
Hong Kong, China	43.9	22.0	7.8	15.8	23.6	16.7
Japan	7.7	0.5		32.4	43.8	16.0
Korea, Republic of	14.5	1.9	3.3	25.4	40.7	19.4
Mongolia	61.8	19.1	0.0	3.6	12.1	22.4
Taipei,China	–	–	–	–	–	–
South Asia	**0.7**	**0.0**	**0.0**	**0.5**	**92.3**	**6.5**
Afghanistan	–	–	–	–	–	–
Bangladesh	0.0	0.0	0.0	0.0	0.0	0.0
Bhutan	–	–	–	–	–	–
India	0.1	0.0	0.0	0.5	96.9	2.5
Maldives	–	–	–	–	–	–
Nepal	–	–	–	–	–	–
Pakistan	12.7	0.0	0.0	0.0	0.0	87.3
Sri Lanka	–	–	–	–	–	–
Southeast Asia	**25.5**	**7.2**	**0.5**	**7.2**	**31.1**	**36.2**
Brunei Darussalam	–	–	–	–	–	–
Cambodia	–	–	–	–	–	–
Indonesia	8.0	1.8	0.1	62.9	7.2	21.9
Lao People's Democratic Republic	–	–	–	–	–	–
Malaysia	38.9	3.1	2.6	11.8	18.2	31.1
Myanmar	–	–	–	–	–	–
Philippines	31.4	2.7	0.8	5.8	39.5	23.2
Singapore	24.0	7.3	0.0	5.9	32.8	37.2
Thailand	55.4	12.9	11.8	8.3	6.5	29.8
Timor-Leste	–	–	–	–	–	–
Viet Nam	–	–	–	–	–	–
The Pacific	**–**	**–**	**–**	**–**	**–**	**–**
Cook Islands	–	–	–	–	–	–
Fiji	–	–	–	–	–	–
Kiribati	–	–	–	–	–	–
Marshall Islands	–	–	–	–	–	–
Micronesia, Federated States of	–	–	–	–	–	–
Nauru	–	–	–	–	–	–
Niue	–	–	–	–	–	–
Palau	–	–	–	–	–	–
Papua New Guinea	–	–	–	–	–	–
Samoa	–	–	–	–	–	–
Solomon Islands	–	–	–	–	–	–
Tonga	–	–	–	–	–	–
Tuvalu	–	–	–	–	–	–
Vanuatu	–	–	–	–	–	–
Oceania	**21.6**	**1.8**	**6.6**	**28.1**	**30.8**	**19.5**
Australia	21.2	2.0	6.6	30.7	29.7	18.5
New Zealand	24.6	0.0	6.7	8.2	39.9	27.4
Asia	**17.9**	**4.5**	**1.9**	**24.3**	**37.3**	**20.5**
Developing Asia	**30.8**	**10.3**	**3.5**	**12.9**	**29.6**	**26.7**

– = unavailable, EU = European Union, PRC = People's Republic of China, ROW = rest of the world, US = United States.

Source: ADB calculations using data from International Monetary Fund. Coordinated Portfolio Investment Survey. http://data.imf.org/cpis (accessed September 2020).

Table A9: Foreign Direct Investment Inflow Share—Asia, 2019 (% of total FDI inflows)

	Partner					
		of which				
Reporter	Asia	PRC	Japan	EU-28	US	ROW
Central Asia	**32.0**	**19.5**	**4.1**	**111.4**	**51.7**	**(95.1)**
Armenia	0.6	0.0	0.0	48.6	(0.8)	51.5
Azerbaijan	3.3	0.7	0.5	8.9	1.6	86.2
Georgia	16.2	3.5	3.1	51.1	8.8	23.9
Kazakhstan	90.2	54.3	12.9	348.0	178.0	(516.2)
Kyrgyz Republic	185.9	162.0	2.8	83.0	3.2	(172.0)
Tajikistan	0.0	0.0	0.0	5.4	0.0	94.6
Turkmenistan	(1.5)	(1.8)	0.0	12.0	(0.2)	89.8
Uzbekistan	4.7	4.3	0.0	3.4	0.2	91.7
East Asia	**68.2**	**16.6**	**4.1**	**10.1**	**8.7**	**13.0**
China, People's Republic of	82.7		2.6	5.2	1.9	10.2
Hong Kong, China	61.3	55.3	4.6	14.9	3.6	20.2
Japan	12.4	13.1		42.1	99.1	(53.6)
Korea, Republic of	29.3	0.0	23.1	4.3	13.4	53.0
Mongolia	27.9	13.4	3.8	11.8	5.7	54.6
Taipei,China	37.7	9.2	8.0	3.9	2.1	56.3
South Asia	**40.5**	**1.9**	**6.6**	**18.8**	**6.9**	**33.8**
Afghanistan	0.0	0.0	0.0	3.4	0.0	96.6
Bangladesh	67.4	5.6	1.9	34.1	10.4	(11.9)
Bhutan	(3.8)	0.0	0.0	(165.6)	126.5	142.8
India	40.2	0.3	7.0	18.0	7.1	34.7
Maldives	1.5	0.0	1.5	0.7	0.0	97.8
Nepal	29.6	27.7	0.8	22.2	1.6	46.6
Pakistan	52.2	33.9	5.1	30.2	5.2	12.4
Sri Lanka	(0.9)	1.0	(3.9)	19.7	1.1	80.1
Southeast Asia	**36.1**	**5.0**	**11.7**	**10.9**	**4.1**	**48.9**
Brunei Darussalam	32.6	0.0	9.0	2.8	0.0	64.6
Cambodia	0.0	0.0	0.0	0.2	0.0	99.8
Indonesia	86.0	9.0	20.6	(5.2)	5.2	14.0
Lao People's Democratic Republic	270.3	223.9	0.0	1.9	0.0	(172.2)
Malaysia	1.2	0.0	0.0	1.3	0.0	97.6
Myanmar	0.8	0.0	0.0	1.0	0.0	98.2
Philippines	37.1	4.0	1.7	5.3	3.7	53.9
Singapore	20.9	4.1	5.4	17.2	4.7	57.2
Thailand	257.1	12.9	137.7	43.7	14.8	(215.6)
Timor-Leste	(13.7)	(13.8)	0.1	(15.8)	0.0	129.6
Viet Nam	16.8	0.0	15.6	0.7	0.0	82.5
The Pacific	**(354.2)**	**(7.0)**	**(256.6)**	**32.5**	**12.0**	**409.7**
Cook Islands	352.5	0.0	0.0	4.6	0.0	(257.1)
Fiji	(2.9)	0.0	(2.9)	0.4	0.0	102.5
Kiribati	3,156.3	0.0	0.0	0.0	0.0	(3,056.3)
Marshall Islands	–	–	–	–	–	–
Micronesia, Federated States of	–	–	–	–	–	–
Nauru	–	–	–	–	–	–
Niue	–	–	–	–	–	–
Palau	0.0	0.0	0.0	0.0	0.0	100.0
Papua New Guinea	(263.3)	(23.7)	0.1	47.5	23.9	291.9
Samoa	(263.3)	(23.7)	0.1	47.5	23.9	291.9
Solomon Islands	37.1	0.0	0.0	(66.6)	0.0	129.5
Tonga	47.4	0.4	0.0	5.7	0.0	47.0
Tuvalu	220.0	0.0	0.0	0.0	0.0	(120.0)
Vanuatu	0.8	0.0	0.8	8.0	0.0	91.2
Oceania	**39.9**	**7.3**	**0.0**	**10.8**	**5.9**	**43.3**
Australia	42.7	8.3	0.0	14.0	7.5	35.8
New Zealand	21.3	0.4	0.0	(10.1)	(4.3)	93.2
Asia	**51.7**	**10.8**	**5.9**	**13.6**	**7.8**	**27.0**
Developing Asia	**54.0**	**11.0**	**6.7**	**12.9**	**5.0**	**28.1**

() = negative, – = unavailable, EU = European Union, FDI = foreign direct investment, PRC = People's Republic of China, ROW = rest of the world, US = United States.

Source: ADB calculations using data from Association of Southeast Asian Nations Secretariat. ASEANstats Database. https://www.aseanstats.org (accessed July 2020); CEIC; Eurostat. Balance of Payments.https://ec.europa.eu/eurostat/data/database; and United Nations Conference on Trade and Development. World Investment Report 2020 Statistical Annex Tables. http://unctad.org/en/Pages/DIAE/World%20Investment%20Report/Annex-Tables.aspx (both accessed June 2020).

Table A10: Remittance Inflows Share—Asia, 2019 (% of total remittance inflows)

	Partner				
Reporter	Asia	Middle East	EU-28	US	ROW
Central Asia	**6.5**	**0.9**	**9.0**	**2.5**	**81.1**
Armenia	17.6	0.4	9.9	12.2	60.0
Azerbaijan	14.1	4.2	4.3	2.3	75.1
Georgia	12.8	2.1	20.2	3.9	61.0
Kazakhstan	1.5	0.5	26.8	0.8	70.3
Kyrgyz Republic	3.4	0.7	14.2	1.2	80.4
Tajikistan	5.4	0.4	6.4	1.2	86.7
Turkmenistan	–	–	–	–	100.0
Uzbekistan	–	–	–	–	100.0
East Asia	**47.2**	**0.2**	**9.8**	**30.2**	**12.5**
China, People's Republic of	49.5	0.2	9.7	27.5	13.1
Hong Kong, China	40.4	0.0	13.1	23.9	22.6
Japan	22.9	0.3	17.4	42.9	16.6
Korea, Republic of	41.1	0.0	5.3	50.6	3.1
Mongolia	42.0	0.3	24.6	–	33.1
Taipei,China	–	–	–	–	–
South Asia	**15.1**	**59.1**	**9.5**	**12.6**	**3.7**
Afghanistan	21.8	59.2	13.7	2.6	2.7
Bangladesh	38.3	51.0	5.9	3.7	1.1
Bhutan	83.4	0.0	4.6	–	12.0
India	8.7	60.7	8.1	17.3	5.3
Maldives	69.4	0.5	18.2	–	11.8
Nepal	43.8	44.6	4.8	6.0	0.9
Pakistan	7.6	67.2	15.8	8.2	1.1
Sri Lanka	19.7	52.9	20.5	3.4	3.4
Southeast Asia	**30.2**	**22.6**	**10.7**	**33.3**	**3.2**
Brunei Darussalam	–	–	–	–	–
Cambodia	65.6	0.0	8.3	23.1	3.0
Indonesia	41.1	51.2	4.1	2.6	1.0
Lao People's Democratic Republic	72.7	0.0	4.5	21.3	1.5
Malaysia	87.9	0.0	4.8	4.6	2.6
Myanmar	84.6	8.9	0.8	5.2	0.5
Philippines	17.8	31.5	9.2	38.8	2.6
Singapore	–	–	–	–	–
Timor-Leste	32.4	2.1	25.3	29.3	10.9
Thailand	84.7	0.0	14.9	–	0.4
Viet Nam	28.5	0.0	14.9	53.5	3.2
The Pacific	**55.6**	**0.0**	**3.2**	**26.1**	**15.1**
Cook Islands	–	–	–	–	–
Fiji	60.6	0.0	3.3	24.2	11.9
Kiribati	89.4	–	7.6	–	3.0
Marshall Islands	1.8	0.0	0.2	95.8	2.2
Micronesia, Federated States of	2.8	–	0.8	55.2	41.1
Nauru	–	–	–	–	–
Niue	–	–	–	–	–
Palau	20.3	–	7.0	–	72.7
Papua New Guinea	14.5	0.0	0.8	–	84.8
Samoa	70.9	0.0	0.8	18.6	9.7
Solomon Islands	83.4	0.0	13.3	–	3.3
Tonga	49.8	–	0.7	31.4	18.1
Tuvalu	55.9	0.0	1.6	–	42.4
Vanuatu	34.5	0.1	21.9	–	43.5
Oceania	**39.9**	**1.0**	**36.9**	**14.0**	**8.2**
Australia	25.4	1.3	45.9	17.0	10.5
New Zealand	82.8	0.1	10.6	5.0	1.5
Asia	**26.9**	**31.8**	**10.0**	**21.8**	**9.4**
Developing Asia	**26.9**	**32.5**	**9.7**	**21.6**	**9.3**

– = unavailable, EU = European Union, ROW = rest of the world, US = United States.

Source: ADB calculations using data from World Bank. Global Knowledge Partnership for Migration and Development. Bilateral Remittance Estimates May 2020.

Table A11: Outbound Migration Share—Asia, 2019 (% of total outbound migrants)

Reporter	Partner					
		of which				
	Asia	PRC	Japan	EU-28	US	ROW
Central Asia	**9.4**	**–**	**–**	**14.4**	**2.5**	**73.7**
Armenia	18.9	–	–	9.3	10.5	61.3
Azerbaijan	14.6	–	–	4.0	2.1	79.4
Georgia	11.1	–	–	19.7	3.4	65.7
Kazakhstan	1.5	–	–	25.4	0.8	72.4
Kyrgyz Republic	3.8	–	–	11.6	0.9	83.8
Tajikistan	6.2	–	–	5.1	0.9	87.9
Turkmenistan	2.3	–	–	3.6	1.0	93.1
Uzbekistan	21.4	–	–	3.5	3.3	71.8
East Asia	**46.6**	**3.3**	**8.4**	**10.2**	**30.8**	**12.4**
China, People's Republic of	50.0		7.3	10.3	27.0	12.7
Hong Kong, China	40.6	25.7	–	12.4	24.2	22.8
Japan	23.0	0.9		18.2	41.9	16.9
Korea, Republic of	41.9	9.0	21.8	5.2	49.8	3.1
Mongolia	40.1	–	–	26.7	–	33.2
Taipei,China	–	–	–	–	–	–
South Asia	**28.9**	**0.1**	**0.2**	**9.2**	**8.7**	**53.3**
Afghanistan	32.8	–	–	8.7	1.6	56.9
Bangladesh	47.5	0.1	0.2	5.5	3.1	44.0
Bhutan	85.8	–	–	4.0	–	10.2
India	18.1	0.1	0.2	8.2	15.2	58.4
Maldives	73.6	–	–	16.5	–	9.9
Nepal	55.8	–	–	3.3	5.0	35.9
Pakistan	24.2	0.1	0.2	15.2	6.4	54.1
Sri Lanka	21.4	0.3	1.0	22.3	3.2	53.1
Southeast Asia	**50.1**	**0.8**	**2.6**	**7.9**	**20.6**	**21.3**
Brunei Darussalam	75.0	–	–	13.9	–	11.0
Cambodia	72.2	–	0.3	7.3	17.9	2.6
Indonesia	42.9	0.9	1.0	4.0	2.5	50.6
Lao People's Democratic Republic	77.5	–	–	4.0	17.1	1.4
Malaysia	86.3	0.4	0.6	6.4	4.6	2.7
Myanmar	88.0	–	–	0.7	3.9	7.4
Philippines	18.8	1.4	4.8	9.8	38.1	33.3
Singapore	64.7	–	0.8	21.4	11.5	2.5
Timor-Leste	33.7	1.6	4.9	25.1	28.4	12.9
Thailand	86.8	–	–	13.0	–	0.2
Viet Nam	31.2	1.1	7.8	15.5	51.0	2.4
The Pacific	**42.8**	**–**	**–**	**1.8**	**15.0**	**40.4**
Cook Islands	99.9	–	–	0.0	–	0.1
Fiji	61.9	–	–	3.3	22.7	12.0
Kiribati	91.3	–	–	6.1	–	2.7
Marshall Islands	1.8	–	–	0.0	94.6	3.6
Micronesia, Federated States of	3.1	–	–	0.6	39.9	56.4
Nauru	95.4	–	–	1.3	–	3.3
Niue	99.1	–	–	–	–	0.9
Palau	12.1	–	–	7.5	–	80.4
Papua New Guinea	1.0	–	–	0.9	–	98.1
Samoa	69.8	–	–	0.8	16.2	13.1
Solomon Islands	87.9	–	–	11.8	–	0.3
Tonga	51.7	–	–	0.7	28.5	19.1
Tuvalu	78.7	–	–	2.0	–	19.3
Vanuatu	26.2	–	–	15.5	–	58.3
Oceania	**57.0**	**0.4**	**1.1**	**27.5**	**9.8**	**5.7**
Australia	25.6	1.0	1.9	46.5	16.7	11.2
New Zealand	80.3	–	0.4	13.4	4.7	1.5
Asia	**35.2**	**0.8**	**2.1**	**9.9**	**14.6**	**40.3**
Developing Asia	**35.0**	**0.8**	**2.2**	**9.5**	**14.4**	**41.1**

– = unavailable, EU = European Union, PRC = People's Republic of China, ROW = rest of the world, US = United States.

Source: ADB calculations using data from United Nations. Department of Economic and Social Affairs, Population Division. International Migrant Stock 2019. http://www.un.org/en/development/desa/population/migration/data/index.shtml (accessed May 2020).

Table A12a: Inbound Tourism Share—Asia, 2018 (% of total inbound visitors)

	Origin				
		of which			
Destination	Asia	PRC	EU-28	US	ROW
Central Asia	**68.9**	**0.6**	**3.2**	**0.7**	**27.2**
Armenia	14.1	1.6	27.6	15.7	42.6
Azerbaijan	29.2	0.6	4.0	0.6	66.2
Georgia	43.6	0.5	5.7	0.6	50.0
Kazakhstan	73.9	0.6	2.5	0.4	23.3
Kyrgyz Republic	90.3	0.4	0.9	0.2	8.6
Tajikistan	81.7	0.8	0.9	0.3	17.0
Turkmenistan	–	–	–	–	–
Uzbekistan	89.6	0.6	1.5	0.2	8.6
East Asia	**80.7**	**14.6**	**2.8**	**2.6**	**13.8**
China, People's Republic of	77.1		2.0	1.6	19.3
Hong Kong, China	88.6	67.6	4.2	3.2	4.0
Japan	87.2	26.9	4.9	4.9	3.0
Korea, Republic of	83.8	31.7	4.2	6.4	5.6
Mongolia	59.7	31.0	8.7	3.4	28.2
Taipei,China	90.6	24.7	2.5	5.3	1.5
South Asia	**49.1**	**6.4**	**25.2**	**10.9**	**14.8**
Afghanistan	–	–	–	–	–
Bangladesh	–	–	–	–	–
Bhutan	47.6	10.9	25.4	16.7	10.4
India	49.0	2.7	21.4	13.8	15.7
Maldives	42.2	19.1	38.6	2.9	16.3
Nepal	65.3	15.1	21.1	9.0	4.6
Pakistan	–	–	–	–	–
Sri Lanka	46.8	11.4	35.7	3.2	14.3
Southeast Asia	**83.2**	**22.2**	**8.5**	**3.4**	**4.9**
Brunei Darussalam	89.4	23.2	7.0	1.5	2.1
Cambodia	80.7	32.7	11.1	4.1	4.2
Indonesia	80.5	14.2	11.6	2.6	5.4
Lao People's Democratic Republic	94.9	19.4	3.1	1.2	0.9
Malaysia	92.1	11.4	4.0	1.0	2.9
Myanmar	92.7	27.6	4.7	1.9	0.8
Philippines	69.5	17.9	8.7	14.8	7.0
Singapore	84.6	19.1	8.7	3.6	3.0
Thailand	78.5	28.9	11.0	3.0	7.5
Timor-Leste	78.7	12.2	16.4	3.8	1.2
Viet Nam	82.1	33.4	7.8	4.6	5.5
The Pacific	**83.0**	**7.2**	**4.6**	**8.6**	**3.8**
Cook Islands	85.7	0.4	6.4	4.8	3.1
Fiji	81.3	6.3	5.5	10.9	2.2
Kiribati	55.1	–	8.7	32.6	3.5
Marshall Islands	–	–	–	–	–
Micronesia, Federated States of	–	–	–	–	–
Nauru	–	–	–	–	–
Niue	–	–	–	–	–
Palau	88.2	39.2	3.1	7.6	1.2
Papua New Guinea	88.5	7.0	4.7	5.2	1.6
Samoa	79.3	1.8	1.7	8.7	10.2
Solomon Islands	86.4	5.9	5.3	7.4	0.9
Tonga	81.1	2.3	3.7	14.4	0.7
Tuvalu	–	–	–	–	–
Vanuatu	84.0	4.3	–	–	–
Oceania	**67.5**	**14.4**	**15.9**	**8.8**	**7.8**
Australia	66.6	15.5	16.7	8.5	8.1
New Zealand	69.5	11.8	14.0	9.3	7.3
Asia	**79.1**	**15.5**	**5.7**	**3.2**	**11.9**
Developing Asia	**78.9**	**14.7**	**5.5**	**2.9**	**12.8**

– = unavailable, EU = European Union, PRC = People's Republic of China, ROW = rest of the world, US = United States.

Source: ADB calculations using data from United Nations World Tourism Organization. Tourism Satellite Accounts. http://statistics.unwto.org (accessed October 2020).

Table A12b: Outbound Tourism Share—Asia, 2018 (% of total outbound visitors)

Origin	Destination				
		of which			
	Asia	PRC	EU-28	US	ROW
Central Asia	**62.7**	**1.0**	**0.9**	**0.2**	**36.2**
Armenia	59.1	0.4	1.1	0.6	39.2
Azerbaijan	30.6	0.3	0.8	0.1	68.5
Georgia	21.7	0.4	3.8	0.0	74.5
Kazakhstan	55.4	2.0	1.1	0.3	43.3
Kyrgyz Republic	80.7	1.2	0.1	0.1	19.1
Tajikistan	84.2	1.3	0.1	0.1	15.7
Turkmenistan	40.8	2.1	0.3	0.1	58.7
Uzbekistan	93.5	0.4	0.3	0.1	6.0
East Asia	**73.8**	**33.0**	**6.2**	**3.3**	**16.7**
China, People's Republic of	60.0		8.4	2.6	29.0
Hong Kong, China	92.1	84.9	0.5	0.2	7.2
Japan	59.9	10.9	15.8	14.2	10.0
Korea, Republic	72.8	12.8	9.2	6.8	11.2
Mongolia	82.9	74.7	0.1	0.5	16.5
Taipei,China	84.0	32.3	4.9	2.5	8.6
South Asia	**41.9**	**4.0**	**7.2**	**5.3**	**45.7**
Afghanistan	16.4	1.1	0.7	0.2	82.8
Bangladesh	81.0	2.8	0.4	1.0	17.7
Bhutan	87.1	2.7	1.8	2.0	9.0
India	39.3	3.9	10.7	7.6	42.4
Maldives	90.6	2.6	3.5	0.1	5.7
Nepal	77.3	22.1	0.6	4.5	17.7
Pakistan	11.8	3.0	3.1	2.2	83.0
Sri Lanka	78.2	5.8	1.3	1.9	18.5
Southeast Asia	**91.7**	**25.9**	**1.3**	**0.9**	**6.0**
Brunei Darussalam	99.6	0.6	0.0	0.1	0.3
Cambodia	96.7	6.6	0.0	0.4	2.9
Indonesia	80.7	6.1	1.3	0.9	17.1
Lao People's Democratic Republic	99.8	11.8	0.0	0.1	0.1
Malaysia	90.9	9.2	2.2	0.6	6.3
Myanmar	99.7	93.3	0.0	0.1	0.2
Philippines	72.1	15.0	2.5	3.9	21.5
Singapore	94.8	5.3	2.0	0.9	2.3
Thailand	91.7	7.1	2.2	0.9	5.2
Timor-Leste	99.9	0.0	0.0	0.0	0.0
Viet Nam	97.8	57.0	0.2	0.9	1.1
The Pacific	**89.2**	**2.7**	**0.5**	**2.6**	**7.8**
Cook Islands	96.0	–	0.1	0.5	3.4
Fiji	87.2	4.0	1.4	6.5	4.9
Kiribati	90.5	28.2	0.2	2.3	7.0
Marshall Islands	45.8	9.3	0.7	2.7	50.8
Micronesia, Federated States of	11.2	1.2	0.4	3.5	84.9
Nauru	92.1	3.1	1.6	1.5	4.7
Niue	93.9	–	0.2	1.3	4.7
Palau	18.4	1.3	0.2	2.5	78.9
Papua New Guinea	99.1	0.9	0.1	0.4	0.5
Samoa	97.8	4.2	0.1	–	–
Solomon Islands	91.0	6.3	1.1	1.7	6.3
Tonga	92.0	3.5	0.2	6.8	1.0
Tuvalu	78.7	8.5	1.6	2.7	16.9
Vanuatu	79.1	2.5	0.2	0.7	20.0
Oceania	**57.3**	**4.3**	**22.8**	**8.0**	**11.9**
Australia	53.8	4.4	25.3	8.0	12.9
New Zealand	73.1	3.8	11.5	8.0	7.4
Asia	**73.9**	**26.0**	**5.6**	**2.9**	**17.6**
Developing Asia	**75.6**	**27.9**	**4.2**	**2.0**	**18.3**

– = unavailable, EU = European Union, PRC = People's Republic of China, ROW = rest of the world, US = United States.

Source: ADB calculations using data from United Nations World Tourism Organization. Tourism Satellite Accounts. http://statistics.unwto.org (accessed October 2020).

www.ingramcontent.com/pod-product-compliance
Ingram Content Group UK Ltd.
Pitfield, Milton Keynes, MK11 3LW, UK
UKHW062013041026
15591UKWH00017B/1305

9 789292 627157